Blackstone's
Counter-Terrorism
Handbook

Third Edition

Police National Legal Database
Dr Andrew Staniforth

PNLD Contributors:
Marnie Ratcliffe and Christiane Rabenstein

Consultant Editors:
Clive Walker and Stuart Osborne QPM

OXFORD
UNIVERSITY PRESS

OXFORD
UNIVERSITY PRESS

Great Clarendon Street, Oxford, OX2 6DP,
United Kingdom

Oxford University Press is a department of the University of Oxford.
It furthers the University's objective of excellence in research, scholarship,
and education by publishing worldwide. Oxford is a registered trade mark of
Oxford University Press in the UK and in certain other countries

British Library Cataloguing in Publication Data
Data available

ISBN 978–0–19–965809–1

Printed in Great Britain by
Ashford Colour Press Ltd, Gosport, Hampshire

Links to third party websites are provided by Oxford in good faith and
for information only. Oxford disclaims any responsibility for the materials
contained in any third party website referenced in this work.

Foreword

It is a real privilege to be invited to write the Foreword to the third edition of *Blackstone's Counter-Terrorism Handbook*. When the first edition appeared I was confident that it would be used and useful. The second edition confirmed its importance. The arrival of the third edition, founded on sales and demand, demonstrates the indispensability of this excellent book.

Originally it was designed for practitioners at the sharp end of counter-terrorism, especially police officers, UK Border Agency staff, and others with a practical involvement in counter-terrorism. As the former independent reviewer of counter-terrorism legislation, and as a legal practitioner and Parliamentarian, I now observe it on the desks of barristers, solicitors, MPs, members of the House of Lords, and elsewhere. Its full information, and succinct and descriptive commentary, make it at the very least the starting point of many researches.

The new edition takes into account changes made by the Coalition Government elected in 2010. These include the replacement of Control Orders by Terrorism Prevention and Investigation Measures (TPIMs). This is surely a piece of legislative tinkering motivated by political considerations rather than the merits of the argument. Fortunately, however, most of the characteristics of Control Orders have been retained in TPIMs. The one major difference is the removal of the power of compulsory relocation, a power which certainly enabled the removal from associates and familiar places of an individual found to be a terrorist.

Counter-terrorism legislation and practice continue to offer some of the most energetic and contentious arguments in British politics.

As I write, controversy rages in Parliament as to how evidence related to terrorism and other aspects of national security should be treated in civil cases in the courts of the UK. This is of real concern to all involved in counter-terrorism, as the potential for civil proceedings looms larger as a possible outcome of activity carried out for the protection of national security and of the citizens of our country. Those engaged in criminal and intelligence-based enquiries must be increasingly conscious, and sometimes wary, of the possible subsequent examination of their work through civil legal actions. The Security Service (MI5) and the Secret Intelligence Service (MI6) have already had to face up to these problems and to connected investigations.

Another contentious item has been the retention or otherwise of biometric data and samples from past events. By the time of publication of this book we should know the identity of the first biometrics commissioner, who will have the difficult task of determining how potentially valuable material should be dealt with. This is another responsible reviewing role, involving the ever difficult task of balancing the national interest and the liberties of individuals.

I mention these subjects because they demonstrate that the law about and around counter-terrorism continues to develop and change. I am confident that, as a consequence, we shall see the fourth and fifth editions of this valuable Handbook. Blackstone's as well as the authors are to be congratulated on its success.

A hobby horse of mine and of some others is the regrettably large number of Acts of Parliament in which counter-terrorism legislation is to be found. Whilst it might reduce the length of the Handbook, surely the time has come for a Consolidation Act, a single Statute into which all counter-terrorism legislation can be placed and codified. It would be for the benefit of all if counter-terrorism law set the example for the codification of UK criminal and regulatory law. No area of the law, no set of legislative provisions, is of greater interest to an audience stretching far beyond lawyers, academics, and the police. I receive puzzled contacts from postgraduate students from all over the world, many struggling even to find all the material provisions. Counter-terrorism law has an inherent international flavour and importance. Other countries look to the UK for illustration and even guidance. I often refer them to this Handbook for accessible reference, but consolidation would make sense.

The hope we all share is that exceptional powers (of which almost all counter-terrorism laws provide examples) will cease to be necessary. The London 2012 Olympic and Paralympic Games were of sufficient security concern for there to be caution rather than relaxation of the law. That this great festival of sport passed without major incident confirms that the UK authorities, working closely with similar services in other countries, are continuing to succeed in attrition and detection against a still significant number of determined terrorists.

In Northern Ireland too, despite the existence of some determined dissident groups, the control authorities are well informed, penetrative, and achieving commendable protection of the vast majority who turn their faces against all forms of political violence.

I hope that the next edition of this Handbook will reflect that success. I hope and anticipate that at least some aspects of the exceptional counter-terrorism legislation will cease to be necessary, and that something closer to normal criminal law will be applied. This will depend on a shared public mood against terrorism, and on eternal vigilance. If we drop measures, we should not drop our guard. The experience of the past 15 years, and especially since 9/11, has demonstrated the importance of correctly funded, superbly trained, and professionally excellent counter-terrorism activity. This book is part of the toolkit of that work.

Lord Carlile of Berriew CBE QC
Independent Reviewer of National Security Policy
in Northern Ireland

Notes from the Editors

Since I became the Senior National Coordinator for Counter Terrorism in 2009, a key priority was the delivery of a safe and secure London 2012 Olympic Games in which terrorism was assessed as presenting the gravest of threats. Preparing to tackle such security challenges, while maintaining the continued delivery of safety to the public from a sustained terrorist threat, was a demanding undertaking. It was, however, due in no small part to the commitment of colleagues across the UK Police Counter Terrorism Network and all our partners and the public that the London Olympics passed free from terrorist incident.

While we have learned valuable lessons from the extensive planning and preparation of our Olympic counter-terrorism policing response, I hold the view that complacency based upon the absence of a major terrorist event remains both misplaced and unwise. To keep our communities safe from the ambitions of terrorists we must remain alert. To protect the public from the excesses of extremist violence in all its forms continues to require a determined response. The police service has a vital role to ensure that not only are the public protected so that members of our communities can go about their lives freely and with confidence, but in doing so we deliver a professional service of the highest standards ensuring that our use of special terrorism powers are necessary, justified, and proportionate in all circumstances.

To provide a professional service the police and our partners are required to develop their knowledge and understanding of this complex area of policing. I am therefore delighted that the *Blackstone's Counter-Terrorism Handbook* continues to offer a unique guide to meeting these challenges in this new third edition. The authors have, again, compiled an excellent operational reference for countering terrorism, the very first of its kind, bringing it up to date with changes in legislation. This volume remains a trusted companion for all police officers and our partners engaged in counter-terrorism, the reading of which will serve to develop our collective knowledge and understanding of terrorism and the law so that we are better prepared today to meet the challenges of tomorrow.

Stuart Osborne QPM
Deputy Assistant Commissioner
Head of Counter Terrorism Command, Metropolitan Police
Service, and Senior National Coordinator of Counter Terrorism

Preface

The purpose of the *Blackstone's Counter-Terrorism Handbook* is to provide all professional practitioners with an authoritative guide to countering terrorism and the law. There are a number of unique challenges that confront those in authority when attempting to increase their awareness of terrorism and counter-terrorism issues. The perceived complexity of the subject, the sensitivity of operational information, and the nature of specialist roles are just some of the contributory factors. In recognizing these challenges, this third edition is specifically designed to meet the needs of all professionals who wish to broaden their knowledge and understanding of this critical subject.

The Handbook is formulated and written by operational practitioners and anti-terrorism legal advisers. It clearly explains the concept of terrorism, including its key characteristics and core motivations providing the essential information required by those charged with the responsibility of making operational decisions. The Handbook also explains in great detail the increasing complexities of counter-terrorism policy, procedure, and powers, providing the wording of offences, points to prove, meanings, explanatory notes, relevant cases, and practical considerations. While not disclosing secret or sensitive techniques, this book, for the very first time, provides details of counter-terrorism investigations, profiles of proscribed terrorist groups, and practical guidance and advice to assist in the interpretation and application of anti-terrorism legislation.

The first edition of the Handbook was used by counter-terrorism operational practitioners, as well as lawyers and civil servants, who found it to be of significant value as a reliable reference and resource. The first edition was also used by academics and their students proving to be a unique text offering an insight into the practical and operational reality of countering terrorism today. The second edition built upon the first in which the authors reflected upon the lessons we must all learn from previous terrorist events while signposting future security challenges, including those resulting in the successful delivery of a safe and secure Olympic Games in London during 2012. This third edition has been informed by senior professionals, practitioners, and leading academics in the UK, throughout Europe, and beyond. Their expertise has served to shape this third edition, which has been thoroughly revised and brought up to date, reflecting the pace of the evolving threats from terrorism and the measures employed to counter them.

Throughout my professional practice I have continued to maintain that preventing terrorism is a responsibility for all members of the police family. We must be alert but not alarmed. That being said, when compared against other types of serious crime, terrorism, thankfully, remains a relatively rare occurrence but the cost is high when attacks succeed. Terrorism therefore continues to demand a determined response. Our history of terrorism in the UK reveals with alarming regularity that terrorist plotters achieve their intended objectives, defeating all of the state's security measures put in place at the time. Unfortunately, this pattern is not set to change, we will prevent further terrorist atrocities, but there is a very strong likelihood that we will not stop them all. In light of that conclusion we must dedicate ourselves to increasing our knowledge and understanding of counter-terrorism and the laws passed by Parliament to protect the public we serve. Our recent history also informs us that the introduction of new anti-terror powers are very often poorly applied. If we are to build the public's confidence in our use of specialist powers and retain the integrity and credibility of the legal instruments put in place to protect them, this must not be repeated. Terrorism law should be used only for terrorism purposes. Every step outside those purposes provides terrorists with an argument. All in authority are required never to forget that such laws are a step outside the norms of criminal justice legislation: the right to stop and search in the street in a way different from, and more extensive than, a non-terrorism intervention is a power to be exercised with caution. The obtaining of an authority to cordon an area is a potentially serious interference with the private and economic lives of law-abiding citizens. This new third edition shall therefore serve as an integral part of the practitioner's counter-terrorism toolkit. It is an accessible reference and resource to ensure that all counter-terrorism practitioners have the confidence and support they require operationally to interpret and professionally apply a growing body of complex anti-terror law.

Dr Andrew Staniforth
Detective Inspector
North East Counter Terrorism Unit,
and Senior Research Fellow, Centre of Excellence for Terrorism,
Resilience, Intelligence and Organised Crime Research (CENTRIC)

Acknowledgements

The third edition of *Blackstone's Counter-Terrorism Handbook* would not have been created without the foresight of Detective Inspector Dr Andrew Staniforth (North East Counter Terrorism Unit and Senior Research Fellow, Centre of Excellence for Terrorism, Resilience, Intelligence and Organised Crime Research (CENTRIC)) and the commitment and dedication of Christiane Rabenstein and Marnie Ratcliffe (PNLD Legal Advisors).

Dr Andrew Staniforth would like to thank Lord Carlile of Berriew CBE QC (Independent Reviewer of National Security Policy in Northern Ireland and former Independent Reviewer of Terrorism Legislation 2001–2011) for his continued support, as well as the valuable contributions provided by the Consultant Editors: Clive Walker (Professor of Criminal Justice Studies, School of Law, University of Leeds) and Deputy Assistant Commissioner Stuart Osborne QPM (Head of Counter Terrorism Command, Metropolitan Police Service and Senior National Coordinator for Counter Terrorism).

Thanks are also extended to the team at Oxford University Press, especially Commissioning Editor Peter Daniell and Assistant Commissioning Editor Lucy Alexander for sharing their expertise, together with the support provided by Nigel Hughes, Head of PNLD.

And finally, Dr Andrew Staniforth would like to acknowledge the contribution provided by Sue Hemming OBE, the Head of the Counter Terrorism Division, Crown Prosecution Service, and the research support provided by Professor Simeon Yates and Professor Babak Akhgar at the Centre of Excellence for Terrorism, Resilience, Intelligence and Organised Crime Reserach (CENTRIC), a multi-disciplinary and end-user centric research body located within Cultural, Communication and Computing Research Institute (C3RI) at Sheffield Hallam University which provides a platform for researchers, practitioners, policymakers, and the public to focus on applied research in the security domain.

Acknowledgements

Contents

Contents

Contents

Contents

Table of Legislation

Table of Legislation

European Union

International

Table of Secondary Legislation, Codes of Practice, and Home Office Circulars

Secondary Legislation

Secondary Legislation—European Union

Codes of Practice

Home Office Circulars

List of Abbreviations

ACPO	Association of Chief Police Officers
ACPOS	Association of Chief Police Officers for Scotland
AG	Attorney General
AQ-AP	Al Qa'ida in the Arabian Peninsula
AQ-I	Al Qa-ida in Iraq
AQ-KB	Al Qa'ida Kurdish battalions
AQ-M	Al Qa'ida in the Maghreb
BPC	Border Policing Command
CBRN	chemical, biological, radiological, and nuclear
CBRNE	chemical, biological, radiological, nuclear, and explosive
CEOP	Child Exploitation and Online Protection Centre
CO	Cabinet Office
COBR	Cabinet Office Briefing Room
CONTEST	Her Majesty's Government's Counter-Terrorism Strategy
CPS	Crown Prosecution Service
CSOC	Cyber Security Operations Centre
CTA	Common Travel Area
CTIRU	Counter Terrorism Internet Referral Unit
CTIU	Counter Terrorism Intelligence Unit
CTLP	Counter Terrorism Local Profile
CTU	Counter Terrorism Unit
DIS	Defence Intelligence Staff
DPP	Director of Public Prosecutions
ECC	Economic Crime Command
FATA	Federally Administered Tribal Areas
FATF	Financial Action Task Force
GCHQ	Government Communications Headquarters
GLO	Government Liaison Officer
GPMS	Government Protective Marking Scheme
HMIC	Her Majesty's Inspectorate of Constabulary
IED	improvised explosive device
ISAF	International Security Assistance Force
JIC	Joint Intelligence Committee
JTAC	Joint Terrorism Analysis Centre
LGD	Lead Government Department
LT	Lashkar e Tayyaba
MI5	Military Intelligence 5 (Security Service)
MI6	Military Intelligence 6 (Secret Intelligence Service)

List of Abbreviations

NCA	National Crime Agency
NCTT	National Community Tension Team
NIRT	Northern Ireland Related Terrorism
NJU	National Joint Unit
NSC	National Security Council
NSRA	National Security Risk Assessment
OCC	Organised Crime Command
OCSIA	Office of Cyber Security & Information Assurance
OSCT	Office for Security and Counter-Terrorism (Home Office)
PACE	Police and Criminal Evidence Act 1984
PCSO	Police Community Support Officer
PVE	preventing violent extremism
RIRA	Real Irish Republican Army
SCCTD	Special Crime and Counter Terrorism Division
SIS	Secret Intelligence Service (MI6)
SPR	Strategic Policing Requirement
TACT	Terrorism Act 2000/Terrorism Act 2006
TAM	Terrorism & Allied Matters (ACPO)
TCMJ	Terrorism Case Management Judge
TPIMs	Terrorism Prevention and Investigation Measures
TTP	Tehrik-e Taliban Pakistan

Icons List

AG✓ **Attorney General's consent required**
Proceedings may only be started by or with the consent of the Attorney General.

DPP✓ **Director of Public Prosecutions' consent required**
Proceedings may only be started with the consent of the Director of Public Prosecutions.

🕐 **Time limit for prosecution**
The time limit allowed for submission of the file (laying of information).

♿ **Mode of trial: summary**
To be tried in the magistrates' court.

🏛 **Mode of trial: indictable**
To be tried in the Crown Court.

Part 1

An Introduction to Counter-Terrorism

Chapter 1

Terrorist Threat to the UK

1.1 **An Island Under Siege**

For several generations, terrorist groups pursuing their political, religious, and ideological beliefs have planned and executed attacks on the free and democratic communities of the Western world. The UK, in particular, has a long history of tackling terrorists and extremists who have had cause to challenge and violently oppose British values of tolerance, human rights, and the rule of law. In a world of startling change, the first duty of our government remains the security of our country. Today, we are both more secure and more vulnerable than in our long history: more secure in the sense that we do not currently face, as we have so often in our past, a conventional threat of attack on our territory by a hostile power; but more vulnerable because we are one of the most open societies in a world that is more networked than ever before.

In the long history of preserving the UK's security, previous governments have grappled with the brutal certainties of the Cold War—with an existential danger that was clear and present, with Soviet armies arrayed across half of Europe and the constant threat of nuclear confrontation between the superpowers. Contemporary Britain faces a different and more complex range of threats from a myriad of sources. Terrorism, cyber attack, unconventional attacks using chemical, nuclear, or biological weapons, as well as large-scale accidents or natural hazards—any one of which could cause grave damage to British citizens and our interests at home and overseas.

1.2 **Al Qa'ida**

In 2009, there were approximately 11,000 terrorist attacks around the world causing nearly 15,000 casualties. Attacks took place primarily in Pakistan, Afghanistan, and Iraq with the victims being mainly Muslim and the perpetrators primarily al Qa'ida-linked terrorist groups. In 2010, over 11,500 terrorist attacks caused more than 13,000 fatalities; with the vast majority of attacks still carried out by al Qa'ida and associated terrorist groups. Most attacks continue to take place in Afghanistan, Pakistan, Somalia, and Iraq and the majority of victims are Muslims. The UK assesses that the primary threat from terrorism comes from al Qa'ida: primarily from four sources which include the leadership of al-Qa'ida, terrorist groups affiliated to al-Qa'ida, self-starting networks and lone actors, and terrorist groups following the al Qa'ida ideology (see Figure 1.1).

Al Qa'ida leadership

and their immediate associates, located mainly on the Pakistan and Afghanistan border

Terrorists groups affiliated to al Qa'ida

particularly those based in North Africa, the Arabian Peninsula, Iraq, and Yemen

The threat to the UK from al Qa'ida

Terrorists Groups following the al Qa'ida ideology;

but which have their own identity and regional agenda

'Self-starting' networks;

or even lone individuals, motivated by an ideology similar to that of al Qa'ida but with no connection to the organization

Figure 1.1 Al Qa'ida threat to the UK

1.2.1 Al Qa'ida leadership

In recent years, the leadership and core of al Qa'ida (based primarily in the Federally Administered Tribal Areas—FATA—of Pakistan) have been severely weakened by the operations of the Pakistani military and security agencies, the US, and the International Security Assistance Force (ISAF) in Afghanistan. The operational capability of al Qa'ida's leadership is now less than at any time since 11 September 2001. Many of the terrorists have been killed, captured, or dispersed and communications, training, and planning have been significantly disrupted. Al Qa'ida's senior leadership has been forced to rely more on other terrorist groups for operational support and has increasingly called for extremists to conduct independent attacks without further guidance or instruction.

The death of Usama bin Laden on 2 May 2011 was a significant blow against al Qa'ida and has further disrupted al Qa'ida operations and decision making, leaving a gap which it will not be possible for the al Qa'ida leadership to fill effectively. Al Qa'ida has long sought to overturn what it regards as un-Islamic governments across the Muslim majority world, claiming that the only way to do so is through indiscriminate violence against these regimes and those who support them. The 'Arab Spring' in 2011 again demonstrated that al Qa'ida is wrong: change followed popular and largely non-violent protests with terrorism in general and al Qa'ida in particular having been irrelevant. Conscious of its marginal role, al Qa'ida has made a number of attempts to broaden its popular appeal: there is no evidence it has succeeded.

Throughout the two-year period since May 2011, al Qa'ida's senior leadership has continued to plan and attempt terrorist attacks both in the West and in other countries. Hundreds of people from Europe (including the UK) have joined al Qa'ida in Pakistan and the organization has continued to try to send operatives back into Western countries. Plots have been disrupted in the UK and elsewhere in Europe. But, above all, al Qa'ida has continued to try to attack the US and its interests.

1.2.2 Al Qa'ida affiliates

An unintended consequence of the disruption of the al Qa'ida leadership in Pakistan was an increase in threat from al Qa'ida affiliates. This small number of groups use the al Qa'ida name but often operate without reference to the al Qa'ida leadership. These groups include:

- Al Qa'ida in the Arabian Peninsula (AQ-AP);
- Al Qa'ida in the Maghreb (AQ-M);
- Al Qa'ida in Iraq (AQ-I);
- Al Qa'ida Kurdish battalions (AQ-KB).

The most significant of these groups has proved to be al Qa'ida in the Arabian Peninsula, formed in January 2009 when members of al Qa'ida fled Saudi Arabia and joined an al Qa'ida network based in

Yemen. Nine tourists were kidnapped in Yemen by AQ-AP in June 2009, seven of whom were killed, including a British citizen. AQ-AP also attempted to assassinate the deputy interior minister in Saudi Arabia in August 2009 and, since then, has conducted further attacks in Yemen. But their most ambitious attack was over the US city of Detroit.

Case Study—Al Qa'ida in the Arabian Peninsula

On 25 December 2009, 23-year-old Nigerian-born Umar Farouk Abdulmutallab boarded Northwest Airlines Flight 253 at Amsterdam's Schipol airport. Identified as suspicious for only being in possession of hand luggage for a transatlantic flight, and for having no coat, Abdulmutallab nevertheless evaded all the sophisticated security screening in place at one of Europe's premier international aviation hubs as he is alleged to have successfully boarded the flight having concealed an improvised explosive device (IED) in his clothing. Abdulmutallab took his reserved seat, 19A (located directly over the wings and fuel tanks of the aircraft), as it taxied away from the gate and took off towards Detroit. As the aircraft made its descent, Abdulmutallab is believed to have attempted to detonate the IED, which consisted of a primary and secondary explosive sealed in a plastic package in the crotch of his underwear. Although the device ignited, it failed to detonate but it alerted the passengers and crew who extinguished the flames coming from Abdulmutallab who was hiding beneath a travel blanket in an attempt to conceal his actions—after explaining to fellow passengers that he was suffering from a stomach upset. Abdulmutallab was restrained on board the flight and was later arrested by US authorities upon arrival in Detroit. On 2 January, US President Barrack Obama addressed the world's media stating that Abdulmutallab 'joined an affiliate of Al-Qaeda, and that this group, Al-Qaeda in the Arabian Peninsula, trained him, equipped him with those explosives and directed him to attack the plane headed for America.'

Yet again, this failed attack serves to demonstrate the intention of al Qa'ida to use commercial passenger jets to deliver death and destruction on an unimaginable scale. It also provides potential further evidence of their continued desire to mount spectacular terrorist attacks and serves as a reminder of the threat we face from violent Jihadists all over the world who are operating in networks affiliated to al Qa'ida.

AQ-AP was formed in January 2009 by a merger between two regional offshoots of the international Islamist militant network

---

in neighbouring Yemen and Saudi Arabia. AQ-AP has vowed to attack oil facilities, foreigners, and security forces as it seeks to topple the Saudi monarchy and Yemeni Government in order to establish an Islamic caliphate. It has claimed responsibility for a number of attacks in Saudi Arabia and Yemen, including the murder, kidnapping, and beheading of Westerners.

After news of the failed attempt to destroy the Northwest Airlines Airbus A330 emerged, AQ-AP released a statement saying it had sought to avenge recent raids by Yemeni security forces which they suspected of being supported by US intelligence. 'We tell the American people that since you support the leaders who kill our women and children we have come to slaughter you and will strike you with no warning, our vengeance is near', going on to state that, 'We call on all Muslims to throw out all unbelievers from the Arabian Peninsula by killing crusaders who work in embassies or elsewhere in a total war on all crusaders in the Peninsula of Muhammad.'

The failed attack over Detroit did not kerb the ambitions of AQ-AP. On 31 October 2010, they attempted two further attacks on commercial cargo aircraft en route to the US and narrowly failed. The two devices were discovered before they detonated, one during a search at East Midlands Airport. AQ-AP continues to conduct operations against both internal and Western diplomatic targets in Yemen, with terrorist attacks against all targets increasing very significantly (more than 250 per cent) over 2009 and 2010, including 11 UK diplomats attacked in April and October 2010. The situation was exacerbated by the breakdown of law and order in parts of Yemen and the departure to Saudi Arabia of President Saleh on 4 June 2011, which enabled AQ-AP to seize territory and weapons from the Yemeni armed forces. The death of Usama bin Laden made no difference to AQ-AP's operational capability since its internal and external operations have not been closely coordinated with the al Qa'ida leadership.

Operational activity by al Qa'ida in the Maghreb (AQ-M) has been confined to the Maghreb and sub-Saharan Africa and has not extended to Europe or the US. But AQ-M has repeatedly taken Western hostages, including many from Europe, and in June 2009 it seized and subsequently murdered a British national. In some cases, these operations have been coordinated with the al Qa'ida leadership. Funds raised from ransom payments have significantly enhanced AQ-M's operational capability (National Centre for Counter Terrorism (2011), worldwide incidents tracking system: data obtained by searching for incidents in Yemen in 2009 (56) and 2010 (196)) and have enabled it to operate more widely through Mali and Niger. Recent instability in Libya has also enabled AQ-M to seize weapons from military sources. Further south, AQ-M has established contact with the Nigerian terrorist group, Boko Haram, and extended its reach into the volatile region of northern Nigeria, an area which has long been of interest to the leadership of al Qa'ida.

Since 2009, terrorist attacks in Iraq have decreased but casualties from terrorism remain very high. Although it no longer receives significant external support and appears to have little contact with the al Qa'ida leadership, Al Qa'ida in Iraq (AQ-I) has conducted more attacks and caused more fatalities than any other affiliate. AQ-I targets are primarily internal and sectarian.

Since its formation in March 2007, a separate al Qa'ida affiliate based in Iran and Iraq, the Al Qa'ida Kurdish battalions (AQ-KB), has established a foothold in some Kurdish areas. We judge that both AQ-I and AQ-KB aspire to conduct terrorist attacks in the West and will be prepared to conduct these attacks independently.

KEY POINT—PROSCRIBED TERRORIST ORGANIZATIONS

There are a number of terrorist organizations currently proscribed under UK legislation, and which are therefore outlawed in the UK. A list of proscribed organizations is given in **Appendix 1**, accompanied by a profile of each proscribed organization in **Appendix 2**.

There are 47 international terrorist organizations proscribed under the provisions of Schedule 2 to the Terrorism Act 2000 as glorifying terrorism, of these two organizations are proscribed under powers introduced in the Terrorism Act 2006. There are also 14 organizations in Northern Ireland proscribed under previous anti-terror legislation.

The list of proscribed organizations and the names of terrorist groups may change, therefore to keep updated on the current list of outlawed organizations in the UK, consult the Home Office website following the links at: <http://www.homeoffice.gov.uk>.

1.2.3 **Al Qa'ida followers**

There are a small number of terrorist groups which follow the ideology of al Qa'ida but which have their own identity and regional agenda. Such groups include the Pakistan Taliban (Tehrik-e Taliban

Pakistan (TTP) meaning 'student movement of Pakistan'), which has grown significantly in recent years (at one point seizing control not only of significant areas of the FATA but also areas closer to Islamabad) and collaborates on occasion with al Qa'ida and other local militant groups. In May 2010, TTP claimed responsibility for the attempted detonation of an explosive device in Times Square, New York. In September 2010, the group made explicit threats against both the US and European member states and, following the death of Usama bin Laden, led a wave of retaliatory attacks in Pakistan.

Many other terrorist groups remain active in the FATA and more widely in Pakistan. Some have a purely sectarian agenda; others regard the West, India, and Indian-administered Kashmir as priority targets. We judge that Lashkar e Tayyaba (LT, meaning 'Army of the Pure or Righteous') is the most capable. Although in theory banned since 2002, LT has a front organization (Jamaatud- Dawa) in Pakistan which engages in relief work, social welfare, and education pro-grammes. It conducts attacks in Afghanistan and, in the West, it recruits, raises funds, and has also planned operations. LT has been responsible for planning and conducting major terrorist attacks, including a major armed assault in Mumbai.

Case Study—Massacre in Mumbai

The terrorist attack in Mumbai during 2008 was an armed assault operation incorporating a series of coordinated shootings and bombings conducted inside India's largest city and financial capi-tal. The attacks, which began on 26 November and lasted until 29 November, killed 175 people and wounded at least 308, and drew widespread condemnation from across the world. Eight separate attacks occurred in South Mumbai at Chhatrapati Shivaji Termi-nus, the Oberoi Trident, the Taj Mahal Palace, Leopold Cafe, Cama Hospital, the Orthodox Jewish-owned Nariman House, the Metro Cinema, and a lane behind the Times of India building and St Xavier's College. There was also an explosion at the Mazagaon docks in Mumbai's port area and in a taxi at Vile Parle. By the early morning of 28 November, all sites except for the Taj Mahal Palace had been secured by Mumbai police and security forces. An opera-tion conducted by India's National Security Guards on 29 Novem-ber resulted in the death of the remaining suspected terrorists at the Palace, ending all fighting. One suspected terrorist, Moham-med Ajmal Amir Kasab, was captured alive.

Investigations by Indian authorities revealed that ten terrorists had arrived in Mumbai from Pakistan, via a stolen boat, before dis-

---

persing into the city in five separate pairs. The terrorists, armed with grenades and semi-automatic weapons, used modern communication satellite technology which allowed terrorists in Pakistan to command and control their activities. A dossier of evidence compiled by the Indian investigators revealed that the terrorists in Pakistan who had commanded the operation, had monitored news coverage and relayed information to the attackers on the ground in Mumbai. As they monitored the media coverage, one terrorist in Pakistan told an attacker inside the Taj Mahal Hotel, 'There are three ministers and one secretary of the cabinet in your hotel. Find those three or four persons and get whatever you want from India.' He then said, 'Throw one or two grenades on the navy and police teams which are outside.' It remains unclear from the investigators' dossier if any specific media report contributed in any way to the deaths of civilians or security forces personnel but the constant encouragement and guidance provided by the commanders in Pakistan assisted in sustaining the operation. In addition to receiving information from media reports, the terrorists in Mumbai also took direction from their commanders in Pakistan. A terrorist in the Oberoi Hotel said, 'We have five hostages', to which a commander replied, 'Kill all hostages, except the two Muslims. Keep the phone switched on so that we can hear the gunfire.' The terrorists in Mumbai were following direct orders and throughout the armed assault appeared to make few operational decisions themselves.

Following the attack, the Indian Government announced what many security commentators described as a 'major overhaul' of the country's internal security, which included measures to establish a federal investigation agency, strengthening of coastal security, training of additional commandos, increasing anti-terror laws, and recruiting to fill vacancies in the depleted intelligence agencies.

Other groups following the ideology of al Qa'ida include the clan-based militia, al Shabaab (meaning 'the Youth') in Somalia which continues to control significant parts of the south and centre of the country, conducting regular attacks against the African peacekeeping force (AMISOM). Parts of al Shabaab have adopted the global jihadist ideology associated with al Qa'ida and have attracted hundreds of foreign fighters, including people from the UK. They have links to al Qa'ida and to AQ-AP and operate more widely in East Africa. In June 2010, al Shabaab carried out its first terrorist attack outside Somalia, killing 74 people in suicide bombings in Kampala, Uganda. The British Government believes that further operations are likely and al Shabaab may formally affiliate to al Qa'ida.

KEY POINT—CONFLICT IN AFGHANISTAN

The UK faces a real and pressing threat from international terrorism, particularly that inspired by al Qa'ida and its affiliates. British Armed Forces are fighting in Afghanistan because of this threat, with the UK and its allies supporting the Government of Afghanistan to prevent Afghan territory from again being used by al Qa'ida as a secure base from which to plan attacks on the UK or its allies. Terrorists can also exploit instability in countries like Somalia or Yemen, with instability spreading from one country to another and lawless regions providing a haven for terrorist groups and organized criminal networks alike.

Following the 11 September attacks, the international community played a critical role in driving al Qa'ida from Afghanistan and now they must be kept out. The British Government wants an Afghanistan that is not a threat to the UK or the wider international community and, to achieve this, it is supporting an Afghan-led process to develop the Afghan security forces and build a more effective Afghan state that can control its own security and, ultimately, achieve a lasting political settlement. While there has been significant cost, the British Government believes that we are making progress, identifying that the Afghan security forces are now 260,000 strong and increasingly showing the capability of providing their own security. The transition of security responsibility to the Afghans has begun and joint Afghan and international operations across the country are putting pressure on the insurgency. The Afghan economy is growing rapidly and the Afghan Government's ability to deliver key services, such as health and education, has significantly improved. The British Government will continue to work with the Afghans to secure further progress on corruption, regional engagement, and political and economic reform but it must not be complacent. The insurgency remains strong and adaptable and our continued resolve and commitment is required to ensure success and the consequent withdrawal of British combat troops by 2014.

1.2.4 Lone al Qa'ida terrorists

Al Qa'ida and some al Qa'ida affiliates have increasingly encouraged acts of terrorism by individuals or small groups independent of the al Qa'ida chain of command and without reference to, or guidance and instruction from, the leadership. The internet has enabled this type of terrorism by providing material which encourages and guides radicalization and gives instructions on how to plan and conduct operations. In practice, some attacks have been conducted or attempted by groups or sole individuals seemingly on their own initiative; in other cases, they have had some contact with other terrorist networks.

Since 2009, one lone terrorist attack has been conducted in the UK but there have been others elsewhere, notably the killing of 13 people by a US army officer at Fort Hood in November 2009. In both these cases the assailants had read propaganda on the internet from an al Qa'ida affiliate and (at Fort Hood) corresponded with an al Qa'ida member; but the attacks seem to have been planned and conducted without guidance or instruction.

There are many potential factors which may influence an individual towards adopting an extremist perspective. These include not only politics, religion, race, and ideology—the very core motivations of terrorism—but may also include elements of a sense of grievance or injustice. Terrorists will recruit and radicalize new members to their cause by providing their version of history or recent events which is negative towards the actions of government. The process of globalization also acts as a potential driver for radicalization, not simply in economic terms but also in social and cultural aspects where local ways of life, traditions, and cultures are being modernized. Many people may be suspicious of the West, which is portrayed as deliberately attempting to replace traditional structures with a Western model way of life, and extremists recruiting terrorists to al Qa'ida will encourage an often simplistic but virulent anti-Westernism. Despite the legitimate presence of Western interests and sometimes military forces in Muslim countries, this is seen by some as an affront and a source of shame. In addition, recruiters have cited the inconstancy of Western standards in its international behaviour. Conflicts such as Bosnia and Chechnya are highlighted, where Muslims have been the victims of violence and where recruiters argue that the Western nations failed to act quickly or effectively enough to protect them, whilst ignoring many of the West's positive interventions. In particular, this applies to perceptions of the West's relations with Israel and its approach to the Middle East Peace Process, where the UK is actively committed to a two-state solution with a viable Palestinian state alongside a secure Israel.

The UK Government and its Security Service also believe that another potential factor for radicalization is a sense of personal alienation or community disadvantage, arising from socio-economic factors such as discrimination, social exclusion, and lack of opportunity. While an individual may not be relatively disadvantaged, he or she may identify with others seen as less privileged; also different generations within the same family may have significantly different views about these issues. The Security Service also specifically identifies an important factor in radicalization as exposure to radical ideas, stating that it may 'come from reading radical literature on Islamic and other subjects or surfing the Internet where many types of radical views are strongly promoted, but more often radicalization seems to arise from local contacts and from peers.' They also believe that, 'Exposure to a forceful and inspiring figure, already committed to extremism, can be important here. This person may be associated with a particular place or can be a national or international figure, seen on video or heard on tapes.' It is also vital to understand that inspiration from a distance is important and the rise of the internet, with its ability to connect people, to pass ideas between them, and then pass those ideas on to others, has had a significant impact on the accessibility and flow of radical ideas.

Figure 1.2 shows some of the factors which may potentially push or pull an individual towards an extremist perspective. This is not an absolute list, there are many smaller factors that are important to an individual on the road to radicalization that are specific to their experience. Nor are any of these factors conclusive; they are best viewed as considerations which may influence radicalization in any given individual. They do, however, show the diverse range of potential radicalization factors influencing members of our communities towards adopting extremist perspectives, but it is important for all in authority to understand that no single factor predominates. The catalyst for any given individual to become a terrorist will more probably be a combination of different factors, which makes prediction with any certainty a challenging task.

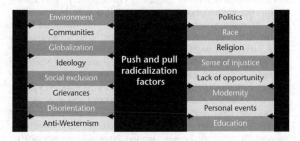

Figure 1.2 Radicalization factors

POINT TO NOTE—RADICALIZATION

Identifying the factors which may lead to radicalization, and some of the arguments used to justify it, are important so that we can focus our responses in order to reduce the risk of terrorism. Setting out these factors does not in any way imply that we accept their validity or that resorting to terrorist violence could ever be justified. Nor does it imply that an alienated individual who has become highly radicalized is a terrorist. Only a small minority of radicalized individuals actually cross over to become terrorists. All in authority, and especially police officers who have direct contact with the communities they serve, must continue to distinguish between extremism and terrorism; one does not necessarily lead to the other, and simply to hold extremist views is not an offence and is not terrorism. To be terrorism, there must be elements of violence or intimidation or the planning of it.

It is also important to acknowledge that the treatment of individuals at the hands of government agencies, including discriminatory and abusive treatment by authorities such as the police, can also give rise to extremist behaviour. Where individuals in authority fail to live up to the professional standards and expectations we have set ourselves in the application of authority and the interpretation of anti-terrorism powers, may also be used to convince others vulnerable to those who recruit and radicalize that we are the aggressor.

1.3 Northern Ireland-Related Terrorism

The UK has a long experience of Northern Ireland-Related Terrorism (NIRT). Following the Good Friday Agreement in 1998, many Northern Ireland terrorist groups agreed a ceasefire and subsequently decommissioned their weapons. But, despite the significant and continuing progress in stabilizing the political situation in Northern Ireland, some republican terrorist groups continue to carry out terrorist attacks. Support for NIRT remains low and dissident groups do not represent mainstream opinion across Northern Ireland but the frequency of attacks has increased significantly, from 22 in 2009 to 40 in 2010, which includes the murder of Police Constable Stephen Caroll during March 2009. There were also 16 attacks from January to June 2011, including the murder of Police Constable Ronan Kerr in April 2011. Many more attacks have been successfully disrupted: between January 2009 and December 2010, there were 316 arrests in connection with terrorism-related activity in Northern Ireland. Over the same period, there were 97 charges for terrorist offences and nine people were convicted for terrorist activity. But not all paramilitary operations have been disrupted by the combined efforts of the security forces in Northern Ireland.

Case Study—Murder at Massereene Barracks

At 9.20 pm on Saturday 7 March 2009, soldiers of the 38 Engineer Regiment at the Massereene Barracks in County Antrim in Northern Ireland ordered pizzas from a local take-away restaurant. The soldiers were due to depart the following morning for a tour in Afghanistan to play a vital role maintaining the living and working conditions of British soldiers. When the pizza delivery arrived at the main barracks gates, four soldiers came out to collect them. As they did so, two gunmen opened fire from a nearby car. From the 60 shots they fired, two soldiers were killed—Sapper Mark Quinsey, aged 23 from Birmingham, and Sapper Patrick Azimkar, aged 21 from Wood Green, London. Four other people were also injured in the shooting, including one pizza delivery man.

In a statement claiming responsibility for the attack, the South Antrim Brigade of the Real Irish Republican Army (RIRA), said that it made no apology for shooting the delivery man, accusing the pizza delivery men of 'collaborating' with the British Army by delivering food to the base. Politicians and communities from across the political divide were united in their condemnation of the attack and, in an historic moment for Northern Ireland, Sinn Féin's Gerry Adams and Martin McGuinness backed the police manhunt to catch the killers and denounced the terrorists. McGuinness, the deputy first minister, said: 'I was a member of the IRA, but that war is over now. The people responsible for last night's incident are clearly signalling that they want to resume or restart that war. Well, I deny their right to do that.' Adams said: 'Sinn Féin has a responsibility to be consistent. The logic of this is that we support the police in the apprehension of those involved in last night's attack.'

Lieutenant Colonel Roger Lewis, the regiment's commanding officer, said of Azimkar that he was 'shocked and stunned by the death of this very promising young soldier' and described Quinsey, a soldier for four years, as a 'mature, reliable and hugely capable young soldier with a bright future ahead of him'.

POINT TO NOTE—RESURGENCE

Following the terrorist attack, the then Northern Ireland First Minister and Democratic Unionist Party leader, Peter Robinson, spoke to the Irish Assembly stating, 'The events of Saturday evening were a throwback to a previous era. We must never return to such terrible days. The police need the support and cooperation of the entire community. Let the answer be loud and clear: We are not turning back.' The show of solidarity amongst all in authority served to reject the violence that was brought to bear on the unarmed soldiers. However, despite the passionate words of the First Minister, they failed to prevent a further incidence of terrorist violence two days later that again brought back vivid memories of the death, destruction, and damage caused by this political struggle.

The resurgence of political violence on the streets of Northern Ireland during March 2009 must serve as a reminder to all those in authority of the devastating impact of Irish-related terrorism. For those unfamiliar with the modern history of Ireland, 'The Troubles', the threats, and the efforts required on all sides to bring peace, there is a need to dedicate time to raise awareness and understanding of the counter-terrorism challenges this threat may present in future as a new generation of terrorists in Ireland may have to be tackled.

In May 2011, a number of coded warnings were received which suggested that a bomb had been left in a central London location. These were the first coded warnings relating to Great Britain from Northern Ireland terrorist groups for ten years.

1.4 Extreme Right-Wing Terrorism

Violent right-wing political extremism leading to terrorism can take various forms. Some individuals and groups seek strong centralized government and the preservation of their national domestic culture; others, such as militia in the US, believe in the preservation of personal rights, including strong forms of personal property and privacy rights and the right to bear arms, with a subsequent weakening of central government. Extreme right-wing views are often associated with fascism and racism. They are individuals and groups who advocate severe, stringent, and immoderate measures using violence and intimidation to promote their beliefs and their priority over other cultures and communities and present a clear and present danger to UK national security.

Case Study—Right-Wing Terrorism

During November 2007, police officers searching premises for child pornography at Martin Gilleard's East Yorkshire flat, uncovered ammunition, weapons, home-made bombs, and a large amount of white extremist literature. The officers seized a diary belonging to Gilleard where he recorded his intentions, stating that: 'I'm so sick and tired of hearing Nationalists talk of killing Muslims, of blowing up Mosques, of fighting back, only to see these acts of resistance fail to appear. The time has come to stop the talk and start to act.'

It appeared that Gilleard was preparing for an ethnic war; his aim being to protect the purity of the white race. Frustrated by a perceived lack of action, Gilleard had started to collect dozens of weapons and had made four nail bombs which he hid under his bed—bizarrely, he would make his young son sleep on the bed whenever he came to visit. At the time his premises were searched Gilleard was not at home, thus prompting a large 'man hunt'. Police officers successfully located Gilleard three days later in Dundee where he was arrested for terrorism offences.

This case revealed that Counter Terrorism Units, together with their local force Special Branch counterparts, are increasingly having to investigate far right groups, with Gilleard being one of the first right-wing extremists to be prosecuted under counter-terrorism legislation. Then Head of the North East Counter Terrorism Unit, Temporary Chief Constable John Parkinson OBE stated that:

> Martin Gilleard is a very dangerous individual and not only did he express his intentions to carry out acts of terrorism, he had the capacity to do so. Terrorism in its rawest form is someone who possesses those extreme views who then moves on to violence or threats of violence for an ideological or political cause and that is equally applicable to right-wing extremism or to an Islamist cause.

A judge at Leeds Crown Court stated that he believed that Martin Gilleard intended to cause havoc with the devices found by police under his bed. Gilleard was found guilty of terrorist offences and possessing child pornography and was sentenced to 16 years' imprisonment.

POINT TO NOTE—DISTINGUISH BETWEEN EXTREMISM AND TERRORISM

In a liberal, pluralist, and democratic society, a wide range of political views are acceptable and desirable, even views which are highly unpopular or may offend others are aggressively pursued. A sophisticated democracy allows space for these views as all should tolerate and respect each other's position learning to live in peace, side by side and accepting one another's differences. It is this tolerance and acceptance that is not only essential in a democracy but also to a successful and progressive multi-cultural society. It is, however, important to understand that political views that are at the extreme ends of the political spectrum can cause serious issues within society as people who hold such views often cannot tolerate others. That said, all in authority, and especially police officers who have direct contact with the communities they serve, must continue to distinguish between extremism and terrorism; as stated earlier, one does not necessarily lead to the other, and simply to hold extremist views is not an offence and is not terrorism. To be terrorism, there must be elements of violence or intimidation or the planning of it.

1.5 Cyber-Terrorism

The growing role of cyberspace in society has opened up new threats as well as new opportunities. A growing number of adversaries are looking to use cyberspace to steal, compromise, or destroy critical data—the national security machinery of governments have no choice but to find ways to confront and overcome these threats if they are to flourish in an increasingly competitive and globalized world. As citizens put more of their lives online, this matters more and more. People want to be confident that the networks that support our national security, our prosperity, and our own private lives as individuals are safe and resilient. The scale of our dependence now means that our economic well-being, our key infrastructure, our places of work, and our homes can all be directly affected.

It is now clear to Western national security intelligence practitioners that al Qa'ida and its global network of affiliated groups is resilient, becoming increasingly independent, mobile, and unpredictable. Of critical concern for the security of the Western world remains the way in which individuals from our own communities are being influenced by the single narrative and extreme version of religious ideology promoted by al Qa'ida. This narrative, when combined with a complex array of social, political, and economic factors set within the specific environment of each nation, has served to manipulate individuals towards extremist perspectives cultivating a home-grown terrorist threat which presents security concerns to the free and democratic way of life enjoyed in the West. The way in which the recruiters and radicalizers of al Qa'ida have influenced and indoctrinated the young and vulnerable across the world has alarmed national security professionals. The direct impact they have made upon impressionable members of our communities, who require safeguarding from this terrorist tactic, continues to damage the confidence of our communities in the ability of the state security apparatus to police the internet and protect their online experience. Al Qa'ida have also preyed upon individuals of school age which reveals the extent to which they are prepared to go to progress their cause. During June 2006, Hammad Munshi, a 16-year-old school boy from Dewsbury in West Yorkshire, was arrested and charged on suspicion of committing terrorism-related offences. Following his arrest, searches were conducted at his family home where his wallet was recovered from his bedroom. It was found to contain handwritten dimensions of a sub-machine gun, taken from a book entitled *Expedient Homemade Firearm*. At the time, Munshi had excellent IT skills and had registered and ran his own website on which he sold knives and other extremist material, passing on information on how to make Napalm as well on how to make detonators for IEDs. Although the online rhetoric of al Qa'ida cyber recruiters reached the computer in the bedroom of Hammad Munshi, authorities on this occasion were able to intervene before any critical security risks to citizens were realized. That said, not all individuals recruited online will be prevented from carrying out attack-planning by UK security forces.

Case Study—Cyber Suicide Bomber

On 22 May 2008, Nicky Reilly, aged 22, left his home in Plymouth with a rucksack containing six bottles full of nails and home-made explosives (HME). His target was the Giraffe restaurant in Exeter, a popular place for shoppers to lunch. Reilly, who has Asperger's syndrome and a mental age of 10, was a suicide bomber recruited online in local internet cafes by extremists in chat rooms who had fuelled a hatred of the West. The extremists had moulded a home-grown terrorist and had directed him to bomb-making websites discussing what his target should be. As Reilly sat in the restaurant, 44 customers also sat down to dine. One of the 11 members of staff working that day brought Reilly a drink and he sat for ten minutes

---

before making his way to the lavatory taking his rucksack with him. Once inside a cubicle, the device detonated prematurely causing injury to Reilly and damage to the restaurant. No other person was injured in the blast.

A note left at Reilly's home revealed the motivation for his actions, paid tribute to Usama bin Laden, and called on the British and US Governments to leave Muslim countries. The note declared that Western states must withdraw their support of Israel and that violence would continue until 'the wrongs have been righted'. Reilly, appearing at court as Mohammed Abdulaziz Rashid Saeed, pleaded guilty to offences of attempted murder and preparing for acts of terrorism and, at the Old Bailey on 30 January 2009, he was sentenced to life imprisonment. Mr Justice Calvert-Smith said that: 'I am quite satisfied that these offences are so serious that only a life sentence is appropriate. This defendant currently represents a significant risk of serious harm to the public.' He went on to state: 'The offence of attempted murder is aggravated by the fact that it was long planned, that it had multiple intended victims and was intended to terrorize the population of this country. It was sheer luck or chance that it did not succeed.' Defence counsel, Kerim Fraud, representing Reilly stated that: 'He may comfortably be deemed to be the least cunning person ever to have come before this court for this type of offence.'

The use of the internet by terrorist recruiters and radicalizers was a matter of concern to national security professionals but violent extremists had also harnessed the power of the internet to conduct remote hostile reconnaissance and other terrorist attack-planning activities.

Case Study—Cyber Terrorist 007

When Metropolitan Police officers raided a flat in West London during October 2005, they arrested a young man, Younes Tsouli. The significance of this arrest was not immediately clear but investigations soon revealed that Moroccan-born Tsouli was the world's most wanted 'cyber terrorist'. In his activities, Tsouli adopted the user name 'Irhabi 007' (Irhabi meaning 'terrorist' in Arabic), and his activities grew from posting advice on the internet on how to hack into mainframe computer systems to assisting those in planning terrorist attacks. Tsouli trawled the internet searching for home movies made by US soldiers in the theatres of conflict in Iraq and Afghanistan that would reveal the inside layout of US military bases. Over time, these small pieces of information were collated and passed to those planning attacks against armed forces bases. This virtual hostile reconnaissance provided insider data illustrating how it was no longer necessary for terrorists to conduct physical reconnaissance if relevant information could be captured and meticulously pieced together from the internet.

Police investigations subsequently revealed that Tsouli had €2.5 million worth of fraudulent transactions passing through his bank accounts which he used to support and finance terrorist activity. Pleading guilty to charges of incitement to commit acts of terrorism, Tsouli received a 16-year custodial sentence to be served at Belmarsh High Security Prison in London where, perhaps unsurprisingly, he has been denied access to the internet. The then National Coordinator of Terrorist Investigations, Deputy Assistant Commissioner Peter Clarke, said that Tsouli: 'provided a link to core al Qa'ida, to the heart of al Qa'ida and the wider network that he was linking into through the internet', going on to say: 'what it did show us was the extent to which they could conduct operational planning on the internet. It was the first virtual conspiracy to murder that we had seen.'

The case against Tsouli was the first of its kind in the UK which quickly brought about the realization that cyber-terrorism presented a real and present danger to the national security of the UK. Law enforcement practitioners understood that the internet clearly provided positive opportunities for global information exchange, communication, networking, and education, and could be used as a major tool in the fight against crime, but a new and emerging contemporary threat had appeared within the communities they sought to protect. The internet had being hijacked and exploited by terrorists not only to progress attack-planning but to radicalize and recruit new operatives to their cause. It was also the core and affiliated networks of al Qa'ida which were quick to realize the full potential of the global platform provided by the internet.

KEY POINT—CYBER THREATS

Criminals from all corners of the globe are already exploiting the internet to target Western democracies in a variety of ways. There are crimes that only exist in the digital world, in particular those that target the integrity of computer networks and online services.

But cyberspace is also being used as a platform for committing crimes such as fraud, and on an industrial scale, with online identity theft and fraud now dwarfing their offline equivalents. The internet has provided new opportunities for those who seek to exploit children and the vulnerable and, additionally, cyberspace allows criminals to target countries in other jurisdictions thus making it harder to enforce the law. As businesses and government services move more of their operations online, the scope of potential targets will continue to grow. Some of the most sophisticated threats to cyberspace come from other states which seek to conduct espionage with the aim of spying on or compromising government, military, industrial, and economic assets, as well as monitoring opponents of their own regimes. 'Patriotic' hackers can act on a state's behalf to spread disinformation, disrupt critical services, or seek an advantage during times of increased tension. In times of conflict, vulnerabilities in cyberspace could be exploited by an enemy to reduce a nation's technological military advantage or to reach past it to attack critical domestic infrastructures.

Cyberspace has now grown to become a domain where strategic advantage—industrial or military—can be won or lost due to the internet underpinning the complex systems used by commerce and the military. The growing use of cyberspace means that its disruption can affect a nation's ability to function effectively in a crisis; this is emphasized by nearly two-thirds of critical infrastructure companies reporting regularly the discovery of software designed to sabotage their systems. Some states also regard cyberspace as providing a way to commit hostile acts 'deniably'. Alongside existing defence and security capabilities, nations must be capable of protecting their national interests in cyberspace. Iain Lobban, Director of the Government Communications Headquarters (GCHQ), has stated that: 'There are over 20,000 malicious emails on UK government networks each month, 1,000 of which are deliberately targeting them.' These kinds of attack are increasing; the number of emails with malicious content detected by government networks during 2010 was double the number seen in 2009 and law enforcement agencies are themselves being targeted.

1.6 **European Threat**

Over 200 terrorist attacks were reported in eight EU member states during 2010, compared to more than 300 in 2009, with a key factor in the lower number of attacks being the ceasefire in Spain by ETA. In 14 other EU member states, 566 people were arrested for terrorist-related offences in 2010 and 587 arrests were reported by 13 member states in 2009. In 2009, nine states reported 307 convictions for terrorist-related offences and, in 2010, nine states reported 227 convictions. Most terrorist attacks in Europe in 2010 and 2009 were conducted or attempted by separatist groups and since 2007 the majority of those arrested for terrorist offences in reporting countries have been from separatist organizations. But the vast majority of the attacks and the arrests were in Spain and France (and many of the attacks in France may have been related to criminal extortion). During 2010, 179 people were arrested for offences linked to Islamist terrorism (as defined by Europol) in 14 reporting states, a significant increase on 2009 when nine states reported 72 convictions. Al Qa'ida-affiliated terrorist groups carried out only one successful attack in Europe in 2009 (in Italy) and three in 2010 (two in Denmark and one in Sweden).

Significantly, more people were arrested in France and the UK for Islamist terrorist offences than in any other country. The data suggests that of the total arrested for Islamist offences in Europe, about 20 per cent had links to Islamist groups, including AQ-AP, AQ-M, and al Shabaab. The remainder appear to have been unaffiliated. Across eight states, some 45 attacks were conducted by left-wing or anarchist groups in 2010 (mainly in Greece and Spain), an increase of 12 per cent over 2009. Six people were killed. There were no right-wing terrorist attacks in Europe in 2010 and in 14 countries only one reported arrest; there were four right-wing terrorist attacks in 2009 (all in Hungary). Although not comprehensive these statistics indicate:

- More people were arrested for all terrorism-related activities in the UK than in any other European country between January 2009 and December 2010. In France and Spain more people were convicted.

- A range of terrorist groups continues to pose a significant threat to the security of countries in Europe; states face threats from separatist, anarchist, left-wing, and Islamist organizations.

- Although a significant number of people are engaged in Islamist terrorist-related activity, there continue to be very few successful attacks.

- There appears to be a significant threat from people unaffiliated to any Islamist group.

1.7 **An Age of Uncertainty**

To coordinate the UK's security response, during 2010 the British Government published *A Strong Britain in an Age of Uncertainty: The National Security Strategy*. This new strategy, designed to span the full extent of this parliamentary term until 2015, provides a cohesive, pan-governmental response to the variety of threats we face. The strategy reveals that new threats can emanate from states, but also from non-state actors: terrorists (home-grown or overseas), insurgents, or criminals, as well as highlighting that the security of our energy supplies increasingly depends on fossil fuels located in some of the most unstable parts of the planet. Nuclear proliferation is also identified as a growing danger as well as our security vulnerability to the effects of climate change and its impact on food and water supplies. The concept of national security today is very different to ten or twenty, let alone fifty or a hundred, years ago and an essential ingredient running through the fabric of our nation's security is the protection of our ports and borders.

KEY POINT—OPPORTUNITIES AND VULNERABILITIES

Geographically Britain is an island, but economically and politically it is a vital link in the global network. That openness brings great opportunities, but also vulnerabilities. We know, for example, that terrorist groups like al Qa'ida are determined to exploit our openness to attack us and to plot to kill as many of our citizens as possible or to inflict a crushing blow to our economy. This specific threat is the most pressing threat we face today and all in authority stationed at ports must work together to secure our borders if we are to protect the UK from individuals who wish to destroy our free and democratic way of life.

Any strategy to build a strong Britain and to protect our national security must begin with the role we want Britain to play in the modern world. In a world that is changing at an astonishing pace, Britain's interests remain surprisingly constant. We are an open, outward-facing nation that depends on trade and has people living all over the world—in fact, one in ten British citizens now lives permanently overseas. We are a country whose political, economic, and cultural authority far exceeds our size. The global force of our language, the ingenuity of our people, the intercontinental reach of our time zone—allowing us to trade with Asia in the morning and with the Americas in the evening—mean we have huge advantages. To build a strong Britain, the Coalition Government believes that a radical transformation is required in relation to the way we think about national security, as well as how we organize ourselves to protect it. This is particularly important as we enter an age of uncertainty, especially economic uncertainty where an effective strategy can weigh up all of the threats we face, and prepare the government to deal with them.

KEY POINT—ECONOMIC SECURITY

The UK's ability to meet current and future threats depends crucially on tackling the budget deficit: our national security depends on our economic security and vice versa. An economic deficit is also a security deficit. So, at the heart of protecting our nation's security are some tough choices to bring the defence and security apparatus budget back to balance. These choices are informed by the risks, analysis, and prioritization set out in the *National Security Strategy*. The Coalition Government believes that our financial position in the world is the largest single challenge facing the Government which affects both national security and all other areas of public policy. The most urgent task of government is to return our nation's finances to a sustainable footing as it believes that we cannot have effective foreign policy or strong defence without a sound economy and a sound fiscal position to support them.

All government departments, including those contributing to national security, will be required to play their part and programmes of austerity are already impacting upon those government agencies which supply port and border security. Finding

> new and efficient ways of working and maximizing the potential of current assets while seeking innovative collaborative approaches to an increasingly integrated border security system, are all key components to protect our nation's security while rebuilding our finances in these times of economic uncertainty.

1.8 **Impact of Globalization**

We live in an age of unparalleled opportunity. Globalization has opened up possibilities which previous generations could not have dreamed of and is lifting billions out of poverty. More open markets mean more open societies, and more open societies mean more people living in freedom. These developments are unambiguously in Britain's national interest and the Government believes we should seize the opportunities they present, not fear for our future.

In order to protect our interests at home, we must project our influence abroad but, as the global balance of power shifts, it will become harder for us to do so. However, we should be under no illusion that our national interest requires our continued full and active engagement in world affairs. It requires our economy to compete with the strongest and the best and our entire government effort overseas must be geared to promoting our trade, which is the lifeblood of our economy.

1.9 **British Values**

The *National Security Strategy* reveals that the preservation of our national interest requires the UK to stand up for our shared values which include the rule of law, democracy, freedom of speech, tolerance, and respect for human rights. It also suggests that these are the very attributes for which Britain is admired throughout the world, stating that we must continue to advance those attributes because Britain will be safer if our values are upheld and respected around the world.

1.10 **Delivering Security to the Nation**

The British Government believes that the UK is well placed to benefit from the world of the future but in its *National Security Strategy* it sets out three key steps for a secure and prosperous Britain. These steps include using all our national capabilities to build Britain's prosperity, to extend our nation's influence in the world, and to strengthen our security (Figure 1.3).

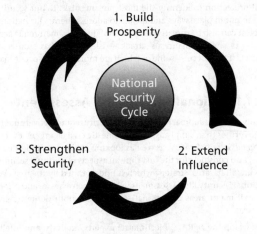

Figure 1.3 The national security cycle

KEY POINT—NATIONAL SECURITY COUNCIL

The British Government has given national security the highest priority. One of the Coalition Government's first acts in leading the country in 2010 was to create a National Security Council (NSC). This development, which marked a key change in the security machinery of government, brought together all the senior ministers concerned under the chairmanship of the Prime Minister. The NSC ensures a strategic and tightly coordinated approach across the whole of government to the risks and opportunities the country faces. The NSC is an essential part of the national security cycle ensuring that key decisions from across the full landscape of government are made to strengthen the UK.

1.11 Risks to UK National Security

The *National Security Strategy* requires all agencies of government engaged in law enforcement, security, intelligence collection, and civil protection to identify the most pressing risks to our security, and to put in place ways and means to address them. Our national interest can also be threatened by natural disasters, man-made accidents, as well as malicious attacks—risks which have different impacts if they occur—some of which are more likely to occur than others.

1.11.1 National Security Risk Assessment

A truly strategic approach to national security requires governments to go further than simply assessing domestic civil emergencies. The *National Security Strategy*, as well as looking at short-term domestic risks, also considers for the first time all aspects of national security. It is an 'all hazards' strategy which is underpinned by the first ever National Security Risk Assessment (NSRA) which assesses and prioritizes all major areas of national security risk, both domestic and overseas.

To develop the NSRA, subject-matter experts, analysts, and intelligence specialists were asked to identify the full range of existing and potential risks to our national security which might materialize over a 5- and 20-year horizon. All potential risks of sufficient scale or impact to require action from government and/or which had an ideological, international, or political dimension were assessed based on their relative likelihood and relative impact. The impact was assessed based on the potential direct harm a risk would cause to the UK's people, territories, economy, key institutions, and infrastructure.

From the rigorous risk analysis process, the results of the first NSRA suggest that, over the next 20 years, the UK could face risks from an increasing range of sources, and that the means available to our adversaries are increasing in number, variety, and reach. Our increasingly networked world, which creates great opportunities but also new vulnerabilities, means that we must, in particular, protect the virtual assets and networks on which our economy and way of life now depend. This has quickly become just as important as directly protecting physical assets and presents a seismic shift in national security planning.

The NSRA serves to inform strategic judgements—it is not a forecast. The British Government cannot predict with total accuracy the nature or source of the next major national security incident we will face but the NSRA can help to make informed choices. In particular, it assists the British Government to prioritize the risks which represent the most pressing security concerns in order to identify the actions and resources needed to deliver our responses to those risks.

The NSRA was presented to the NSC which then identified 15 generic priority risk types and allocated them into three tiers in which terrorism and cyber-terrorism were highlighted as being primary tier one threats shown as follows.

National Security Strategy: Tier One Priority Risks

Tier One: the National Security Council considered the following groups of risks to be those of highest priority for UK national security looking ahead, taking account of both likelihood and impact.

- *International terrorism* affecting the UK or its interests, including a chemical, biological, radiological, or nuclear attack by terrorists; and/or a significant increase in the levels of terrorism relating to Northern Ireland.

- *Hostile attacks upon UK cyberspace* by other states and large-scale cyber crime.

1.12 **Threat Level System**

On 1 August 2006, the Government made information available to the public on the terrorism threat level system in the UK. The then Home Secretary, Dr John Reid, stated that:

Previously, the Government has not made public the way in which this system works or the national threat level that emerges from it. Following a review, we have decided to inform the general public about the process and the national threat level, which applies to the UK as a whole.

This decision now recognizes the important role the public plays in countering terrorism when confronted with such a sustained and heightened threat. The Government has a duty of care to protect the UK which is a key component of its national strategy to counter international terrorism and it continues to maintain a state of readiness in response to the threats. It remains the Government's policy to issue warnings or advice if ever it became necessary to protect the public in the event of a specific and credible terrorist threat. However, there is a delicate balance to maintain between keeping the public informed of current threats whilst ensuring the secrecy and security of covert operations. Information which is made available to the public is also available to terrorists and the challenge is to keep the public updated whilst not providing an unnecessary advantage to terrorist cells: disclosing too much information to the public may alert terrorists to police or intelligence agency activities. There is a need to share information with the public so that we can all adjust our security measures according to specific threats, but this has to be communicated sensitively and has to be put into a broader context.

POINT TO NOTE—THE PUBLIC

It is important that the public is informed about terrorist activity but in doing so their perceived fear of terrorism should not be increased as this may become disproportionate to the actual threat, thereby potentially provoking an over-reaction which may be neither necessary nor justified. The Government encourages the public at all times to be alert to, but not alarmed by, terrorist threats.

1.12.1 National threat level system

The terrorist threats to the UK are diverse which requires a dedicated response to assessing such threats effectively. The Joint Terrorism Analysis Centre (JTAC) provides analysis and assessment of information relating to the threats from international terrorism. A new system has been created to keep the public informed and is designed to give a broad indication of the likelihood of a terrorist attack. The threat levels are shown in Figure 1.4.

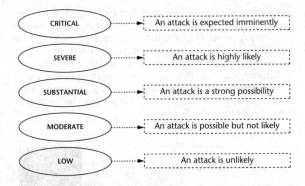

Figure 1.4 National threat level system

POINT TO NOTE—THREAT LEVEL

The UK threat level may change. To keep updated on the current threat to the UK from international terrorism, access the Home Office website at <http://www.homeoffice.gov.uk/counter-terrorism/current-threat-level>.

1.12.2 Assessing the threat

It is rare that a single source of reliable information relating to an event is available. More often, judgements about the threat will be based on a wide range of information which is often fragmented, with small pieces of information being required to be put together, including analysis of previous attacks and similar events in other countries. Intelligence is not an exact science and it will never reveal the whole picture which is why information supplied by police partners and members of the public is important no matter how insignificant it may appear to be at the time—it just might provide corroboration and strengthen analytical judgements.

Assessing the threat includes the gathering and analysis of information around four core areas: the terrorist's intention, capabilities, timescales, and the vulnerability of the chosen target. Intelligence gathered concerning the intentions of terrorist activities and an assessment of whether the aims are achievable or realistic given the terrorist's capabilities are key to this process. Timescales are also a crucial element of assessing threat levels as knowing when a terrorist group is to strike may provide a higher degree of urgency to respond to unfolding events. Once this data is captured, an analysis of the potential vulnerability to such an attack can be conducted. Compiling a picture to make an accurate assessment of the actual threat is a real challenge and one that requires a thorough understanding of terrorism-related activity. The formula in Figure 1.5, which is used in other areas of business to identify **'threat'** and **'risk'**, is used to assess specific terrorist-related threats.

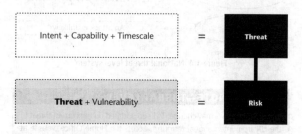

Figure 1.5 Threat and risk formula

KEY POINT—THREAT FROM TERRORISM

The threat the UK faces is changing. Although al Qa'ida is still capable of terrorist attacks in the UK it is weaker now than it has been since 9/11. It has failed to achieve its objectives and has been marginalized by events in the Middle East and North Africa. This presents the UK with an opportunity which it and our international allies will wish to seize. But persistent longer term factors—fragile and failed states, technology, radicalization—will continue to sustain terrorist groups. New violent jihadist Fronts opening in Mali and Algeria during January 2013 provide new security concerns. In addition, the UK must not underestimate the resilience of al Qa'ida and of other groups—some affiliated to al Qa'ida—which now pose a high threat to UK security. The threat from lone terrorism is also significant, as is terrorism in Northern Ireland which has increased in recent years. Although the UK now has significant opportunities to reduce the threat, it will continue to face challenges and the priority of UK counter-terrorism practice remains as high as it has ever been.

Chapter 2

Counter-Terrorism Strategy

2.1 The UK Counter-Terrorism Strategy

At the time of the catastrophic terrorist attack in the US on 11 September 2001, the UK Government, like the US and many other countries in the developed world, had no sophisticated or coherent cross-departmental strategy to counter international terrorism. In short, the UK had no plan to institute of any rigour that would have been able to respond effectively to a major indiscriminate attack by al Qa'ida. However, the UK security apparatus had memories of the long counter-terrorist campaign in Northern Ireland to draw on, and the foundations that had been laid down in terms of a corpus of emergency terrorism legislation on the statute book. Throughout the history of counter-terrorism practice in the UK, collaboration between government departments had been key to the success of many operations and the intelligence community had learned the value of close cooperation with the police service. Nevertheless, the characteristics of violent jihadist terrorism with its vaulting ambitions, strident ideology, and disregard for civilian casualties— indeed, for all human life, with adherents prepared to give their lives in the attacks—represented very new challenges for Parliament and public, government and law enforcement, alike.

In the immediate aftermath of 9/11, Sir David Omand GCB was appointed in the new position of UK Security and Intelligence Coordinator in the Cabinet Office in London and initiated work on the development of a comprehensive national counter-terrorism strategy. The threat from Islamist terrorism had been assessed as severe and numerous plots affecting British interests overseas and at home were of great concern to the security authorities. Sir David Omand recalls that: 'I launched work in November 2002 on a UK counter-terrorism strategy (that I called CONTEST: CouNter-TErrorism STrategy).' The strategy was later presented to Cabinet and adopted in 2003 but the details remained confidential and were not published by the government until 2006. An updated version, CONTEST 2, was published in 2009, and a third generation, CONTEST 3, was published in 2011 by the Coalition Government.

KEY POINT—CONTEST STRATEGIC AIM

The CONTEST strategy that emerged from the work of the Cabinet Office led by Sir David Omand GCB had a clear strategic aim:

> to make it possible for society to maintain conditions of normality so that people could go about their normal business, freely and with confidence.

The conditions, freely and with confidence, were an important reminder to seek security in ways that uphold British values such as liberty, tolerance, respect for human rights, and freedom under the law.

2.2 CONTEST Strategy Structure

The CONTEST strategy is divided into four key pillars which provide the scope to counter terrorism effectively. The four pillars are commonly known as the four Ps which are:

- **Prevent**: to stop people becoming terrorists or supporting violent extremism.
- **Pursue**: to stop terrorists.
- **Protect**: to strengthen our protection against terrorist attack.
- **Prepare**: where an attack cannot be stopped, to mitigate its impact.

The structure of CONTEST enables Prevent and Pursue to focus upon the actual human threat from terrorists designed to reduce the risk by stopping them while Protect and Prepare focus on the capacity and capability of the UK to reduce vulnerability of attacks when they occur. By simultaneously tackling areas to reduce the risk and to minimize vulnerability will collectively serve to reduce the threat as Figure 2.1 demonstrates.

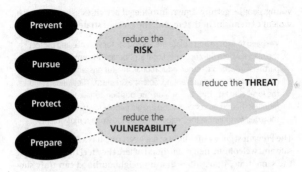

Figure 2.1 Mechanics of the CONTEST strategy

2.3 Prevent

The Prevent strand of CONTEST is concerned with tackling the radicalization of individuals. It aims to do this by addressing structural problems in the UK and overseas that may contribute to radicalization, such as inequalities and discrimination. To prevent terrorism and its underlying causes requires a long-term approach and the strategy intends to deter those who facilitate terrorism and deter those who encourage others to become terrorists. This requires a change in the environment where extremists and those who radicalize others operate. The Prevent strand also aims to engage in the battle of ideas, to win hearts and minds by challenging the ideologies that extremists believe can justify the use of violence.

Preventing violent extremism, often referred to as the 'PVE' agenda, is a key area of CONTEST; preventing terrorism and extremism is the proactive element of the strategy.

The Government believes that the UK, like many other countries, faces a challenge from terrorism and violent extremism where a very small minority seek to harm innocent people in the name of an ideology which causes division, hatred, and violence. The role of the Government is to take tough security measures needed to keep people safe but a security response alone is not enough—a response led and driven by local communities is vital. The very essence of the Prevent strategy seeks to engage partners to work together to challenge and expose the ideology that sanctions and encourages indiscriminate violence. There is a pressing need to stop people, especially young people, getting drawn into illegal activities associated with violent extremism. In that regard, the Prevent strategy states that:

> We need to expose and isolate the apologists for violence and protect the places where they operate. Local authorities, the police, and their partners in schools, other educational institutions and elsewhere, have a critical role in preventing violent extremism. They understand the local context. They are in a unique position to talk to local communities, hear their concerns and enable people to stand shoulder to shoulder, confident in their rejection and condemnation of violence.

The Prevent strategy highlights that everyone has a right to live in a safe and welcoming neighbourhood where they feel they belong. At the same time, it identifies that no neighbourhood can truly succeed unless local people define their future by working together to tackle the challenges they face. The Government firmly believes that when people have a say in the design and delivery of public services, those services better meet their needs. Places where local people have the opportunities, skills, and confidence to come together and address the problems they face are more likely to resolve them. Preventing terrorism at its source requires a cycle of sustained effort (see Figure 2.2) to:

Figure 2.2 The Prevent cycle

- challenge the violent extremist ideology and supporting mainstream voice;
- increase the resilience of communities to violent extremism;
- address the grievances that ideologies are exploiting;
- disrupt individuals who are being targeted and recruited to the cause of violent extremism;
- support those who reject violent extremism and who reject support of the institutions where extremists are active.

2.3.1 A fresh focus

In June 2011, the Government published a review of Prevent-related work and a new strategy for the next four years. This review concluded, first, that the UK Government does not believe that it is possible to resolve the threats we face simply by arresting and prosecuting more people and, secondly, it expressed the need to make Prevent more effective and, in particular, set out its intention to change both its scope and its focus. The new version of Prevent now addresses radicalization to all forms of terrorism. Having widened the scope of Prevent, the UK Government has progressed its intention to narrow the strategy's focus and placed greater emphasis on the delivery of a successful integration strategy which seeks to establish a stronger sense of common ground and shared values, thus enabling the participation and the empowerment of all communities which, in turn, provides social mobility. The key objectives of Prevent are to:

- respond to the ideological challenge of terrorism and the threat we face from those who promote it;
- prevent people from being drawn into terrorism and ensure that they are given appropriate advice and support; and
- work with a wide range of sectors (including education, criminal justice, faith, charities, the internet, and health) where there are risks of radicalization which we need to address.

The Government believes that success in delivering Prevent will mean that:

- there is a reduction in support for terrorism of all kinds in this country and in states overseas whose security most impacts on our own;
- there is a more effective challenge to those extremists whose views are shared by terrorist organizations and used by terrorists to legitimize violence; and

- there is more challenge to and isolation of extremists and terrorists operating on the internet.

The strategic aim of Prevent, its key objectives, and critical success factors are shown in Figure 2.3 which demonstrates their contribution towards the overall aim of CONTEST to the risk to the UK and its interests overseas from terrorism, so that people can go about their lives freely and with confidence.

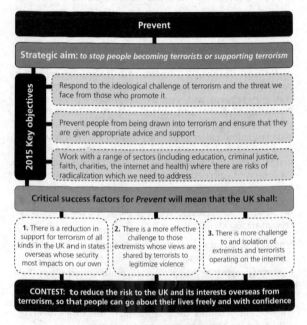

Prevent

Strategic aim: *to stop people becoming terrorists or supporting terrorism*

2015 key objectives

Respond to the ideological challenge of terrorism and the threat we face from those who promote it

Prevent people from being drawn into terrorism and ensure that they are given appropriate advice and support

Work with a range of sectors (including education, criminal justice, faith, charities, the internet and health) where there are risks of radicalization which we need to address

Critical success factors for *Prevent* will mean that the UK shall:

1. There is a reduction in support for terrorism of all kinds in the UK and in states overseas whose security most impacts on our own

2. There is a more effective challenge to those extremists whose views are shared by terrorists to legitimize violence

3. There is more challenge to and isolation of extremists and terrorists operating on the internet

CONTEST: to reduce the risk to the UK and its interests overseas from terrorism, so that people can go about their lives freely and with confidence

Figure 2.3 Prevent key objectives

2.3.2 **Prevent in communities**

Counter-terrorism research over recent years has focused upon answering questions concerning the challenge of radicalization, defined as 'the process by which people adopt an interpretation of religious, political or ideological belief that may lead to them legitimising the use of violence.' It is important for all in authority, and not just those working in counter-terrorism departments, to be aware of the findings of this research as it contributes to the Government's understanding of the precursors, processes, and operational characteristics of radicalization. Among the nodes of radicalization, academics and research institutes have identified what they view as the three primary physical venues of concern: radicalized religious premises, educational establishments, and prisons. It is in these areas that Prevent activity has been focused.

2.3.2.1 Prevent in schools

Schools have an important role to play in preventing violent extremism. We must first, however, face an uncomfortable truth: some terrorist organizations operating today have recruited children to their cause. All in authority must now recognize that terrorists operating in the UK are intentionally and systematically targeting young people, and individuals as young as 15 and 16 have already been implicated in terrorist-related activity. When compared against other types of crime, terrorist offences are relatively few in number, yet analysis of perpetrators indicates that the average age at the time of their arrest is 25. More notably, most of the individuals concerned have been educated in British schools and several have exhibited degrees of vulnerability while of school age prior to being radicalized as teenagers.

The purpose of Prevent in schools is simply to offer opportunities to help young people to understand the risks associated with violent extremism and to develop knowledge and skills to be able to challenge extremist arguments. Preventing violent extremism from emerging within young people in schools supports the Prevent cycle by:

- using teaching and learning to help young people to develop the knowledge and skills to challenge extremist narratives;
- identifying how to prevent harm to pupils by individuals, groups, or others who promote violent extremism;
- providing programmes to support pupils who are vulnerable;
- increasing the resilience of pupils and school communities through the curriculum, other learning opportunities, or activities;
- using teaching styles and curriculum opportunities which allow grievances to be aired.

POINT TO NOTE—A SHARED RESPONSIBILITY

Accepting that the potential radicalization of people of school age is an issue to be addressed, it is the first and most important step in countering this threat. It cannot, and must not, be ignored, yet preventative measures in schools require a sensitive, delicate, and morally justified response—but it does require a response. It is widely acknowledged across government, in particular departments responsible for schools, education, children, and families, that preventing violent extremism in schools is a challenging issue which needs to be a shared endeavour across local partners and communities, with activities tailored to meet local needs. Young people are our future and as society protects and educates them to identify a variety of risks such as alcohol, tobacco, and drugs, it is also important to support the welfare of pupils who may be particularly vulnerable to recruitment and radicalization. Prevent in schools serves to highlight the complexity of the threat of today's terrorism and the reach required of countermeasures to protect the public now and in the future.

2.3.2.2 Prevent in prison

The radicalization of prison inmates has become an issue of high priority for public policymakers in the UK, Europe, and beyond. Radicalization in prison is not a new phenomenon in the UK, it is something that has occurred throughout our penal history, especially during the detention of Irish dissidents at the height of 'The Troubles'. There are many lessons we have learned from our previous experiences that remain valid in countering the contemporary threats from al Qa'ida-inspired terrorist prisoners. However, there are unique challenges that arise from the extreme Islamist genre of today's terrorism and none more so than the immediacy of the threat, the way in which self-starting groups and individuals are recruited, and its total disregard of human rights in its embrace of suicide martyrdom missions.

Over recent years, individuals have emerged from our communities as 'home-grown' terrorists. The prison environment is now regarded as a 'community' itself and the Government is keen to prevent individuals within the prison community from emerging as 'prison-grown' terrorists on their release. However, prisons are unlike other communities in that they maintain a barrier to social intercourse with the outside world and their deliberate and stated purpose is to punish the inmates on behalf of the wider society. Therefore, radicalization within prison is unique when compared to other locations where radicalization is taking place. In the UK, we have learned already that prison is a location which is vulnerable to extremists who propagate their ideas and draw individuals down a path of willingness to condone or even participate in violence for political ends. Extremists are able to exploit the psychological and emotional shock that individuals experience on entering the prison system, as well as the difficulties individuals experience in coming to terms with daily life and the confined social interaction within the prison environment.

POINT TO NOTE—UNINTENDED CONSEQUENCES

As the UK has responded to the contemporary terrorist threat over the last decade, an unintended consequence of its relative success in disrupting major attacks and bringing terrorists to justice has resulted in the detention of approximately 130 convicted terrorists in prison, which includes a number of suspected terrorists remanded in prison while awaiting trial. As the terrorist prison population grows so, too, does the challenge of countering the threat it poses. The UK Government, police, and partner agencies are well aware of the risks this threat presents to the safety of the public and the Government has sought to improve the intelligence infrastructure across the prison system, developing intervention approaches for extremists in prison and putting in place post-prison supervision procedures. The challenge of tackling radicalization in prison is not simply confined to the UK, many EU member states, such as Germany and Italy, are also experiencing similar issues. This pan-EU challenge has also drawn research funding from the European Commission Director General of Justice for Freedom and Security in order to explore the risk of jihadist radicalization in European prisons with a view to constructing methods and models not only to prevent radicalization in the first instance, but also to counter radicalization where it is found to be taking place and to de-radicalize those inmates who are already adopting an extremist perspective.

What is clear from all research conducted to date concerning radicalization in UK and EU prisons, is that the challenge we face—as with countering the broader threat from al Qa'ida terrorism outside the prison walls—will not be defeated by a simple, single, momentary remedy but instead requires both a complex and concerted sustained effort by all in authority. Prisons must not be an incubator for terrorism as it simply defeats the wider efforts of those engaged in pursuing terrorists, potentially putting the public at risk from further attacks.

2.3.3 **Policing Prevent**

The long-term solution to preventing terrorism is to stop people becoming terrorists or becoming involved in violent extremism. Through the Government's Prevent strategy, the police service and its partners have an integral role to play in working with local communities to support people who are vulnerable to being drawn into criminal activity and to challenge those who support violent extremism.

In April 2008, the Association of Chief Police Officers (ACPO) published a wide-ranging Prevent strategy and delivery plan, 'The Policing Response to the Prevention of Terrorism and Violent Extremism' which set out the national police service contribution to the Government's Prevent strategy.

The main themes of the ACPO Prevent strategy are:

- to mainstream Prevent into day-to-day policing, through neighbourhood policing, community engagement, and related activity;
- to work in partnership to support vulnerable individuals and institutions;
- ensure a joined-up approach to all police counter-terrorism activity;
- develop Prevent capability at local, regional, and national level.

2.3.3.1 **The role of the ACPO Prevent Delivery Unit**

To take the police service's Prevent agenda forward, ACPO has established a Prevent Delivery Unit which sits within its Terrorism & Allied Matters (TAM) business area. The unit is made up of seconded police officers and staff from across the police service and supports Prevent activity, providing national coordination for the policing response to the prevention of violent extremism. The team is also responsible for driving forward the national projects set out in the ACPO Prevent strategy. These range from community engagement with women and young people, supporting educational institutions, through to the establishment of national information-sharing protocols for police and their partners.

A network of regional police Prevent coordinators and managers are in place across police forces, supported by ACPO Prevent leads, Community Engagement Officers, Counter Terrorism Intelligence Officers, and local neighbourhood policing teams. But Prevent is not just the responsibility of these particular teams: it lies at the heart of the work of local neighbourhood policing teams whose direct contact with the public and local organizations makes them ideally placed to support communities against the threat of violent extremism.

2.3.3.2 The National Community Tension Team

The ACPO Prevent Delivery Unit also incorporates the National Community Tension Team (NCTT) which has the policing lead for monitoring and encompasses a wide range of issues. To this end, the NCTT works closely with a number of internal and external partners including police forces, national policing units, national government department, and local government officers.

In relation to counter-terrorism and the Prevent agenda specifically, community intelligence derived from tension monitoring can provide an early indication of the vulnerability of groups or individuals to violent extremism. It also helps to build a picture of 'mood' and 'temperature' issues within communities in order to make policing more responsive to the needs of communities.

The NCTT receives tension updates from UK police forces on hate crime, critical incidents, community intelligence, and national/international incidents which may impact on community cohesion in the UK. The NCTT team also produce Community Impact Assessments in response to national and international critical incidents which document specific risks to communities and policing and ways of mitigating those risks.

Case Study—Prevent in Practice: Channel

Supporting those who may be vulnerable to being drawn into violent extremism is a key strand of the Prevent strategy. All areas of the country are required to have local action plans in place to support vulnerable individuals; in some areas this support is provided by a process known as Channel.

Channel provides a mechanism for supporting those who may be vulnerable to violent extremism by assessing the nature and the extent of the potential risk and, where necessary, providing an appropriate support package tailored to an individual's needs. A multi-agency panel decides on the most appropriate action to support individuals taking their circumstances into account.

The partnership-focused structure is similar to existing, successful partnership initiatives which aim to support individuals and protect them from harm, such as those in relation to drugs or involvement in knife and gun crime. Supporting those most at risk of being drawn into violent extremism is about diverting people

---

away from potential risk at an early stage thus preventing them from being drawn into criminal activity.

Partnership involvement ensures that those at risk have access to a wide range of support, ranging from diversionary activities through to providing access to specific services such as education, housing, and employment.

Partners may, depending on local circumstances, include:

- statutory partners such as those concerning education, health, probation, prisons, police, and others;
- social services;
- children's and youth services;
- the Youth Justice Board through offending teams;
- the UK Border Agency;
- voluntary services;
- credible and reliable communities, that demonstrate a commitment to shared values as defined in CONTEST—the Government's strategy for tackling international terrorism.

Channel is not about reporting or informing on individuals in order to prosecute them, it is about communities working together to support vulnerable people at an early stage, preventing them from being drawn into violent extremism.

There are currently 28 local coordinators across more than 70 local authorities and those in communities who have concerns about individuals who may be vulnerable are advised to contact their local authority, the police, or other trusted local organization for further advice.

2.3.3.3 Counter Terrorism Local Profile

The Counter Terrorism Local Profile (CTLP) is a product which drives the sharing of two-way information and enables police and partners to understand and identify at local level the threat from all forms of violent extremism in our communities. The CTLP aims to identify where violent extremism activity is or has the greatest potential of occurring and to provide suggested recommendations to address any risk.

The Prevent strategy aims to help build stronger, safer communities which feel empowered to reject extremism in all forms. However, the nature of the threat can vary greatly from place to place which means that the Prevent response should be community-based, specific, and relevant to local needs and circumstances. Local authorities, in conjunction with police, are taking the lead, working closely with other voluntary and statutory sector partners to help to strengthen communities to deliver the Prevent agenda. Effective information sharing, with a strict protocol, is key to the success of local partnerships, to ensure that our response is risk-based and proportionate to local needs.

Sharing information between police and local partner agencies is not a new concept; since the introduction of Crime Disorder Reduction Partnerships (CDRPs), the sharing of information on criminal activity has taken place for over a decade, with the introduction of CTLPs building on and replicating this two-way information-sharing process. This allows police and partners to identify the threat from violent extremism so that, together, appropriate action can be taken. This is an evolving process based on the 'need to share' information at a local level which is driving forward police and partnership engagement activity. Increasingly, this should involve a wider range of partners, including local councillors and MPs where appropriate.

The CTLP forms an integral part of Prevent policing in the UK which complements the expanding tool-kit of ways in which to tackle extremism within communities which may lead to violence and terrorist activity.

Case Study—The Conviction Project

Andrew Ibrahim was arrested in April 2008 after members of the Muslim community in Bristol alerted the police. In his flat, the police found two homemade suicide vests, homemade explosives, a quantity of ball bearings, and air gun pellets. On 17 July 2009 he was given an indeterminate life sentence with a minimum of ten years for terrorist offences.

The Conviction project is a 20-minute DVD with supportive learning materials and was produced in 2011 as a direct result of the Ibrahim case. Conviction aims to highlight the importance of early intervention work, illustrate how quickly a vulnerable person can be adversely influenced by extremist rhetoric, and raise awareness of the issues around violent extremism and radicalization. Access to the Conviction film can be found at <http://www.convictionfilm.co.uk>. The work of this project has been supported by Andrew Ibrahim and his mother, Vicky Ibrahim, who stated that: 'I feel there is a need to help individuals at risk of radicalisation and guide them. Views should be challenged to prevent incidents like the one that affected Andy happening again. If only others who had become aware of his increasing radicalisation had taken action earlier, then Andy might not have been allowed to continue along his route as far as he did.'

POINT TO NOTE—LEADING AND DELIVERING PREVENT

Our country, like many others, faces a real and sustained threat from terrorism and violent extremism and tough security measures are needed to keep communities safe. But a preventative response led and driven by local partners is also vital and Prevent has been established as a response to this longer term challenge.

Violent extremists are constantly seeking to exploit new tactics and technologies in both attack-planning and recruitment. The Prevent strategy enables the police service to adapt and strengthen its response to deter people from joining the recruitment line. Although it is difficult to measure success at such an early stage in the journey of policing Prevent, extensive feedback from communities and police partners shows that the police service is moving in the right direction and beginning to make a difference. The police service is gaining a better understanding of the communities they serve and is engaging more actively with hitherto hard-to-reach communities and working more closely with key partners—all of which are key to building an atmosphere of trust rather than grievance and resentment.

Prevent is, without doubt, a challenging and complex arena that requires a whole community approach to empower communities, challenge those who espouse violence, and support those who are vulnerable to being drawn into violent extremism. It will only have effect if the police service continues to build trust and confidence through renewed and consistent engagement activity.

The police service responsibility to deliver Prevent is not a short-term priority to be discontinued as the threat level recedes. The threat from terrorism remains high and it is vital that the policing response remains dynamic in response to violent extremism from wherever it emerges. Prevent is something that the police service is doing with its partners and all our communities with a longer term objective. It is a shared objective that, most importantly, brings the police service closer to the communities they serve and protect.

2.4 **Pursue**

The purpose of Pursue is to stop terrorist attacks in the UK and against UK interests overseas. This means detecting and investigating threats at the earliest possible stage, disrupting terrorist activity before it can endanger the public, and, wherever possible, prosecuting those responsible. The key objectives of Pursue are to:

- continue to assess our counter-terrorism powers and ensure that they are both effective and proportionate;
- improve our ability to prosecute and deport people for terrorist-related offences;
- increase our capabilities to detect, investigate, and disrupt terrorist threats;
- ensure that judicial proceedings in the UK can better handle sensitive and secret material to serve the interests of both justice and national security; and
- work with other countries and multilateral organizations to enable us better to tackle the threats we face at their source.

To achieve its objectives, Pursue focuses upon gathering intelligence and improving the ability to identify and understand the terrorist threat. It also aims to take action to frustrate terrorist attacks and to bring terrorists to justice through developing a legal framework. New anti-terrorism legislation has greatly assisted in the pursuit of terrorists but bringing them to justice also involves international cooperation and joint working with partners and allies overseas. Pursue also recognizes the dependence the UK intelligence agency and law enforcement departments have on international partners, many less experienced than the UK in countering terrorism. To support Pursue, the Government has provided significant assistance and capability building to over 20 countries in a range of counter-terrorism skills and techniques which has included advice on legal structures and human rights.

> **POINT TO NOTE—ACQUAINTANCE WITH ANTI-TERROR POWERS**
>
> It is important for counter-terrorism practitioners to understand that given the current level of threat from international terrorism there may be a need to stop terrorist activity prior to gathering sufficient evidence to secure a conviction at court. The Government is very much aware of this

issue and the Home Office is currently seeking to increase detection and investigation capability and capacity, increase the effectiveness of the prosecution process, from evidential collection to post-prison supervision, and develop more effective non-prosecution actions. All those in authority, and in particular operational police officers of all ranks, roles, and responsibilities, should acquaint themselves with these provisions. These are powers to be utilized by all police officers, not only those assigned to specialist counter-terrorism units. Taking time to study these laws will serve the efficiency of investigations where officers may be requested to carry out duties in support of achieving the objectives of a counter-terrorism operation.

While anti-terror provisions have helped counter-terrorism officers to disrupt terrorist activity at an early stage where required, it is not always possible to prosecute people who intelligence indicates are engaged in terrorist-related activity. For this reason the CONTEST strategy identifies that, 'the Government has developed a range of alternative non-prosecution actions to protect the public. They include T-PIMS [Terrorism Prevention and Investigation Measures] orders; the exclusion of foreign nationals from entering the UK; revocation of citizenship; and deportation.'

The Government believes that success in delivering Pursue will mean that:

- at home, we are able to disrupt terrorist-related activity and prosecute or deport more of those responsible;
- overseas, we have seized the opportunity we now have to reduce further the threat from al Qa'ida, its affiliates, and other terrorist organizations and we have disrupted attacks planned against this country; and
- our counter-terrorism work is effective, proportionate, and consistent with our commitment to human rights.

The strategic aim of Pursue, its key objectives, and critical success factors are shown in Figure 2.4 which demonstrates their contribution towards the overall aim of CONTEST to the risk to the UK and its interests overseas from terrorism, so that people can go about their lives freely and with confidence.

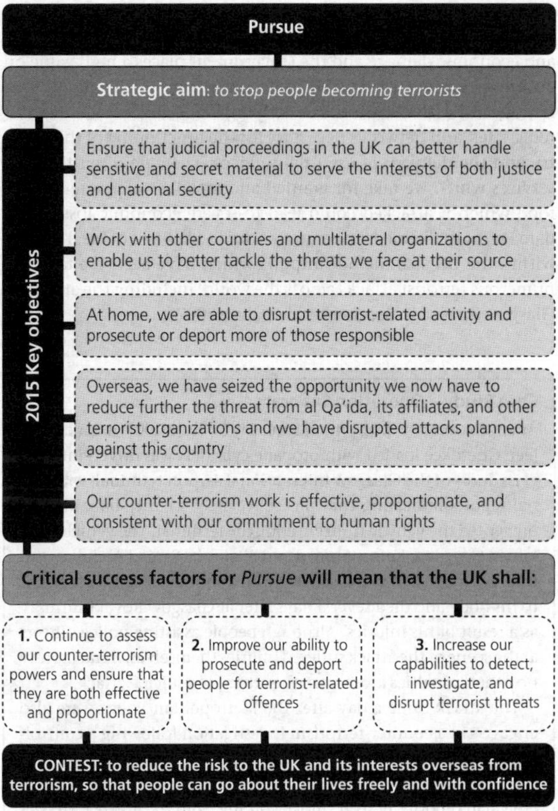

Figure 2.4 Pursue key objectives

2.5 **Protect**

Reducing the vulnerability of the UK and its interests overseas to a terrorist attack is the purpose of Protect. It aims to strengthen border security and to protect key utilities, transport infrastructures, and crowded places. Protecting the UK is a vital component of the strategy as target-hardening key and vulnerable sites will deter terrorist attacks from taking place. It will also help to reduce the risks to the public in the event of an attack. Terrorists and extremists may attack vital information or communications systems to cause disruption and economic damage and the Government places a high value on ensuring that the UK is well protected against such attacks. Our national infrastructure is the underlying framework of facilities, systems, sites, and networks necessary for the functioning of the country and the delivery of essential services. They are often the very services which we take for granted and include water, energy, and food which if attacked could lead to severe economic loss, social damage, or in the most extreme cases large-scale loss of life. Key sites within the UK also include airports which have been the target of numerous terrorist attacks across the world, including the attack on Glasgow Airport in Scotland during June 2007.

Case Study—Operation Seagram

At approximately 3.11 pm on Saturday 30 June 2007, a dark green Jeep Cherokee loaded with propane cylinders was driven into the glass doors of the Glasgow International Airport terminal, with initial reports indicating that protective steel security bollards had prevented the vehicle from entering the terminal. The vehicle contained two men, Kafeel Ahmed and Bilal Talal Samad Abdulla, who were both arrested at the scene. Ahmed suffered 90 per cent burns to his body and died several days later at Glasgow Royal Infirmary as a result of his injuries. Although people assisting police officers at the scene of the attack suffered injuries themselves, miraculously no other casualties arose from the attempted suicide attack.

The attack came a day after the Metropolitan Police were also engaged in a counter-terrorism investigation following a controlled explosion carried out on a car also packed with gas cylinders in the Haymarket area of London on 29 June 2007. An ambulance crew had reportedly seen smoke coming from the green Mercedes which had been parked near to a nightclub at 1.30 am.

Two major incidents within the space of 48 hours raised concerns that the UK was the target of a potential series of coordinated terrorist attacks. Alex Salmond, the First Minister of Scotland, stated that, 'The incident at Glasgow Airport today as well as recent events in London show that we face threats both north and south of the border, and both the Scottish and UK Governments are united in our determination to stand up to that threat and protect our communities.'

The attack was the first to specifically target Scotland, providing evidence that no community is immune from the global reach of international terrorism. Images of the unfolding events at Glasgow Airport were beamed around the world by 24-hour news channels within minutes of the attack. Airports in the UK were quick to respond by taking measures to increase their security, while other countries also implemented counter-terrorism contingency plans. The US Secretary of Homeland Security, Michael Chertoff, stated, 'We have been in close contact with our counterparts in the UK regarding today's incident at the Glasgow airport and yesterday's car bomb discoveries in London. Our law enforcement and intelligence officials are closely monitoring the ongoing investigations.'

POINT TO NOTE—REVIEW OF PROTECT

As a direct result of the failed terrorist attacks in London and Glasgow in June 2007, that same year Lord West, then Minister for Homeland Security and Counter-Terrorism, conducted a review of security within the UK. The review specifically focused upon the protection of our strategic infrastructure, stations, ports, and airports, and other crowded places. There were three key findings from the review which included:

- a need for a new 'risk-based' strategic framework to reduce the vulnerability of crowded places;
- a focused effort on reducing the vulnerability of the highest risk crowded places by working with private and public sector partners at a local level;
- new efforts to 'design in' counter-terrorism security measures, building on good practice from crime prevention.

These three key findings have been developed over recent years to further strengthen the protection from terrorism provided to the public.

The key objectives of Protect are to:

- strengthen UK border security;
- reduce the vulnerability of the transport network;
- increase the resilience of the UK's infrastructure; and
- improve protective security for crowded places.

The Government believes that success in delivering Protect will mean that:

- we know where and how we are vulnerable to terrorist attack and have reduced those vulnerabilities to an acceptable and a proportionate level;
- we share our priorities with the private sector and the international community and, wherever possible, we act together to address them; and

- the disruptive effect and costs of our protective security work are proportionate to the risks we face.

The strategic aims of Protect, its key objectives, and critical success factors are shown in Figure 2.5 which demonstrates their contribution towards the overall aim of CONTEST to the risk to the UK and its interests overseas from terrorism, so that people can go about their lives freely and with confidence.

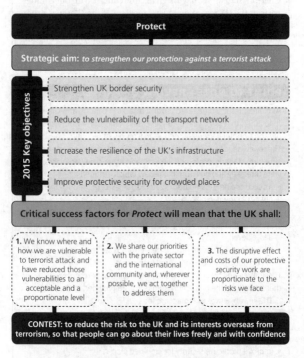

Protect

Strategic aim: *to strengthen our protection against a terrorist attack*

2015 Key objectives

Strengthen UK border security

Reduce the vulnerability of the transport network

Increase the resilience of the UK's infrastructure

Improve protective security for crowded places

Critical success factors for *Protect* will mean that the UK shall:

1. We know where and how we are vulnerable to terrorist attack and have reduced those vulnerabilities to an acceptable and a proportionate level

2. We share our priorities with the private sector and the international community and, wherever possible, we act together to address them

3. The disruptive effect and costs of our protective security work are proportionate to the risks we face

CONTEST: to reduce the risk to the UK and its interests overseas from terrorism, so that people can go about their lives freely and with confidence

Figure 2.5 Protect key objectives

2.6 **Prepare**

The purpose of our Prepare work is to mitigate the impact of a terrorist attack where that attack cannot be stopped. This includes work to bring a terrorist attack to an end and to increase our resilience so that we can recover from its aftermath. An effective and efficient response will save lives, reduce harm, and aid recovery and preparing for emergency incidents and planning for 'worst-case scenario' will reduce the impact of a terrorist attack. The primary government department responsible for delivering the national objectives of Prepare is the Home Office and its Office for Security and Counter-Terrorism (OSCT).

Case Study—The Role of the Office for Security and Counter-Terrorism

For over 30 years, the Office for Security and Counter-Terrorism (OSCT) has led the work on counter-terrorism in the UK engaging with the police and security services. The OSCT reports directly to the Home Secretary and the Minister of State for the Home Office. The OSCT currently has responsibility for:

- developing and coordinating the CONTEST strategy;
- exercising the UK's response to a terrorist incidents;
- developing security measures and protection packages for public figures;
- ensuring that the UK's critical national infrastructure is protected from attack (including electronic attack);
- ensuring that the UK is prepared to deal with a chemical, biological, or nuclear release;
- liaising with government and emergency services during terrorist incidents or counter-terrorism operations;
- overseeing the Regulation of Investigatory Powers Act 2000 (RIPA);
- overseeing the Security Service Acts 1989 and 1996; and
- overseeing Home Office-related elements of the Intelligence Services Act 1994.

POINT TO NOTE—NATIONAL COUNTER TERRORISM EXERCISE PROGRAMME

One of the primary functions of the OSCT is to exercise the UK's response to a terrorist incident. OSCT works with the police, security and intelligence agencies, other government departments, and the Armed Forces to devise, maintain, and regularly exercise capabilities and responses which would be used in the event of a terrorist incident. The National Counter Terrorism Exercise Programme reflects the changing nature of the terrorist threat we face, and aims to improve the ability of the police service and other key partners to prepare for, respond to, and manage terrorist investigations and incidents.

The National Counter Terrorism Exercise Programme delivers a mix of exercises, usually including three major national counter-terrorism exercises each year. In recent years, major exercises have been completed in most regions of the UK. Since 2009, major exercises have been conducted against scenarios which feature responses to aviation, CBRN (chemical, biological, radiological, and nuclear), marauding gunmen, maritime, and hostage-taking threats. Some exercises practise the ability to disrupt an imminent attack; others test the response to an attack in progress or to an attack that has occurred. A key element of exercising is periodically to test both the command chain (from the level of government down to the lowest level of police command) and coordination between emergency services during an incident. Ministers regularly participate in national counter-terrorism exercises and this ensures that the highest level strategic decision making is exercised through the government's crisis organization (Cabinet Office Briefing Room, COBR).

National counter-terrorism exercises are the culminating event in a structured series of smaller scale preparatory exercises, which may include live or simulated activity, and which are aimed at developing greater counter-terrorism preparedness. These exercises help to mitigate the risk that participants in a national counter-terrorism exercise may not have had recent training or experience in their counter-terrorism roles. Learning from exercises is taken forward either through existing or new programmes; progress is assessed through CONTEST structures and at the Police Counter Terrorism Board (including senior police officers and Home Office ministers).

2.6.1 **The Prepare cycle**

To stop terrorist attacks, and to recover effectively when attacks do succeed, requires a cycle of sustained effort as Figure 2.6 shows.

The key objectives of Prepare are to:

- continue to build generic capabilities to respond to and recover from a wide range of terrorist and other civil emergencies;
- improve preparedness for the highest impact risks in the National Risk Assessment;

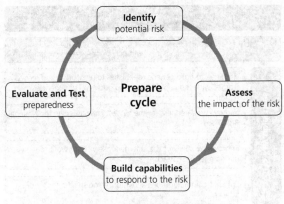

Figure 2.6 The Prepare cycle

- improve the ability of the emergency services to work together during a terrorist attack; and
- enhance communications and information sharing for terrorist attacks.

The Government believes that success in delivering Prepare will mean that:

- our planning for the consequences of all civil emergencies provides us with the capabilities to respond to and recover from the most likely kinds of terrorist attacks in this country;
- we have in place additional capabilities to manage ongoing terrorist attacks wherever required; and
- we have in place additional capabilities to respond to the highest impact risks.

The strategic aim of Prepare, its key objectives, and critical success factors are shown in Figure 2.7 which demonstrates their contribution towards the overall aim of CONTEST to the risk to the UK and its interests overseas from terrorism, so that people can go about their lives freely and with confidence.

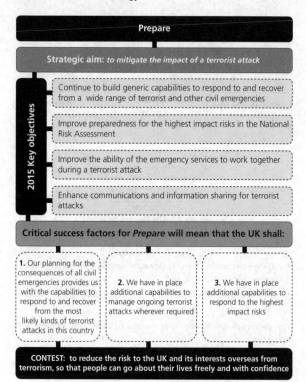

Prepare

Strategic aim: *to mitigate the impact of a terrorist attack*

2015 Key objectives

Continue to build generic capabilities to respond to and recover from a wide range of terrorist and other civil emergencies

Improve preparedness for the highest impact risks in the National Risk Assessment

Improve the ability of the emergency services to work together during a terrorist attack

Enhance communications and information sharing for terrorist attacks

Critical success factors for *Prepare* will mean that the UK shall:

1. Our planning for the consequences of all civil emergencies provides us with the capabilities to respond to and recover from the most likely kinds of terrorist attacks in this country

2. We have in place additional capabilities to manage ongoing terrorist attacks wherever required

3. We have in place additional capabilities to respond to the highest impact risks

CONTEST: to reduce the risk to the UK and its interests overseas from terrorism, so that people can go about their lives freely and with confidence

Figure 2.7 Prepare key objectives

2.7 **CONTEST Governance**

The National Security Council (NSC), chaired by the Prime Minister, will have oversight of CONTEST and take regular reports on its progress. The Home Secretary will continue to be the lead minister for domestic counter-terrorism and is a member of, and accountable to, the NSC. The Home Secretary also has oversight of the Security Service and is accountable for the activities of the police service in England and Wales. The NSC will regularly review progress of this strategy, consider specific risks, and agree the appropriate response and resources.

The CONTEST Board is responsible for developing and monitoring implementation of the strategy. The Board includes officials from key government departments, the police, security and intelligence agencies, and the Scottish and Welsh Governments to ensure that all those involved in countering terrorism are included in decision making. To ensure effective oversight of the strategy, sub-boards are responsible for Pursue, Prevent, Protect, and Prepare. There are also separate oversight boards for a range of cross-cutting issues, including the Overseas CONTEST Group (OCG), the Police Counter Terrorism Board, and the Internet Strategy Group.

2.8 **CONTEST Roles and Responsibilities**

Developing and delivering CONTEST involves numerous departments from across government which include the emergency services, voluntary organizations, the commercial sector, and partners from around the world. A full list of the government departments' roles and responsibilities to support and contribute towards achieving the strategic aim of CONTEST is given in **Appendix 3**. The primary contributors to CONTEST are the agencies of the government's intelligence machinery and the police counter-terrorism network.

2.8.1 **Intelligence machinery**

The National Intelligence Machinery is often referred to as the 'intelligence community' and is the name provided to the group of agencies which gather and assess secret intelligence to protect national security on behalf of the government. The intelligence community includes the Cabinet Office (CO), Secret Intelligence Service (SIS), Government Communications Headquarters (GCHQ), Security Service (MI5), Defence Intelligence Staff (DIS), and the Joint Terrorism Analysis Centre (JTAC) (see Figure 2.8). Each agency has a specific function to support and contribute towards the strategic aim of CONTEST and all act within the law with their operations conducted within a framework of legislation that defines their roles and activities.

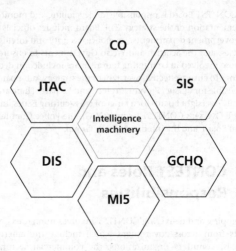

Figure 2.8 Intelligence machinery

POINT TO NOTE—COMMUNITY FOCUS

Countering international terrorism on a global scale requires a united and coordinated response but it also requires a local community focus. Many police officers and members of the public may not fully appreciate their role in countering terrorism but information passed on by members of the public and the police across the UK assists specialist police departments and partner agencies to counter terrorism. Also, police officers may not realize the value and importance of the information they provide. It is often for reasons of operational security that receipt of information may not be readily acknowledged although it does not mean that information is not acted upon, or that it is not significant; on the contrary, the data supplied may be of considerable value now or at some point in the future. This information may be used to provide background details, it may provide new lines of enquiry, and it could corroborate existing intelligence which independently corroborates other sources. It might also be the final piece of a much larger jigsaw that many colleagues have been searching for. Information provided by members of the public and police officers is a vital component in countering terrorism, information which feeds the 'UK intelligence machinery'.

2.8.1.1 Cabinet Office

The CO provides the central support and direction for the intelligence community. It represents the highest counter-terrorism authority in the UK which is led by the Permanent Secretary for Intelligence, Security and Resilience. The Permanent Secretary is directly responsible to the Prime Minister for advising on security, intelligence, and emergency-related matters with key responsibility for ensuring that the intelligence community has a clear strategy and system in place for prioritizing collection and analysis of information. This information supports the Government's national security policies which aim to protect the UK from a range of threats including terrorism. The Secretary also has the responsibility for chairing the Joint Intelligence Committee (JIC) which as part of the CO is responsible for providing ministers and senior officials with intelligence assessments. The JIC provides guidance on the collection, analysis, and assessment of secret intelligence, which each year establishes requirements and priorities for the agencies of the intelligence community. The assessments provided by the JIC are strategic assessments which direct the efforts of other agencies within the intelligence machinery.

2.8.1.2 Secret Intelligence Service

The SIS is commonly known as MI6 (Military Intelligence section 6) and is Britain's secret service, providing the Government with a global covert capability to promote and defend the national security and economic well-being of the UK. SIS operates throughout the world to collect secret foreign intelligence in accordance with the requirements and priorities established by the JIC. It collects intelligence through human and technical sources and liaises with a wide range of intelligence and security service agencies overseas.

SIS was established in 1909 in response to German espionage activity and the threat of Germany's military and naval expansion. The first tasks of SIS were to counter foreign espionage in the UK and to collect secret intelligence abroad. To meet these demands, SIS was divided into two sections: the Home Section, which later became MI5, and the Foreign Section, which later became SIS as we know it today. The role of SIS is now governed by the Intelligence Service Act 1994 which placed SIS on a statutory basis for the first time. The Act formalizes the Foreign Secretary's responsibility for the work of SIS as it protects national security with particular reference to government defence and foreign policies.

The role of SIS is fact and not fiction. It provides crucial high-grade intelligence from countries worldwide: international terrorism is global and SIS is in place to provide early warnings and is our first line of defence in identifying plots overseas which may target the UK or UK interests. In this regard, the development of air travel and communications technology, such as the internet, has made the world a much smaller place.

2.8.1.3 Security Service (MI5)

MI5 is responsible for protecting the UK against the threats to national security. The focus of this work is within the UK and MI5 is the lead domestic intelligence agency. The Security Service has a broad responsibility: it aims to frustrate terrorism, prevent damage to the UK from foreign espionage, and to frustrate the proliferation of materials, technologies, and expertise relating to the development of weapons of mass destruction. In addition, the Security Service detect new and re-emerging types of threat and offer security advice to a range of organizations and also protect government assets.

The role of the Security Service is defined by the Security Service Act 1989 which put the Service on a statutory footing for the first time. In collecting and assessing intelligence, the Service is guided by the requirements and priorities established by the JIC. Since the creation of the Serious Organised Crime Agency, the Service has suspended work on serious crime in order to concentrate more resources on countering terrorism through work which requires considerable secrecy. It is only in recent years, following the growth of international terrorism and subsequent threats to the UK, that the Service has embarked on an era of openness.

2.8.1.4 Government Communications Headquarters

The Government Communications Headquarters, commonly known as GCHQ, is an intelligence and security organization with two key missions: Signals Intelligence and Information Assurance. Signals Intelligence relates to the interception of communications and GCHQ is, therefore, often described as the UK's listening post. Signals Intelligence protects the vital interests of the UK by providing information to support Government decision-making processes in the fields of national security, military operations, and law enforcement. Information Assurance assists the Government communications and information systems and keeps them safe from hackers and other terrorist-related threats.

As a civil service department, GCHQ reports to the Foreign Secretary and, like SIS, it was also placed on a statutory basis by the Intelligence Services Act 1994 which defines the boundaries of GCHQ activities. Within these boundaries, the choice of what to intercept and report to the government and military commands is based on the intelligence requirements established by the JIC.

GCHQ provides a vital service to support national efforts to counter terrorism and the role of GCHQ is to keep the UK one step ahead of its adversaries.

2.8.1.5 Defence Intelligence Staff

The DIS is very different to the other agencies forming part of the intelligence community. It is a constituent part of the Ministry of Defence which brings together expertise from the Army, Air Force, and Navy and which conducts intelligence analysis from both overt and covert sources which provides intelligence assessments which are used by the military and the Government. The DIS collects intelligence in direct support of military operations as well as supporting operations by members of the intelligence community. The DIS is an integral part of the community and provides access to intelligence collected on the ground during military operations.

2.8.1.6 Joint Terrorism Analysis Centre

JTAC was established in 2003 to analyse and assess all intelligence relating to international terrorism, at home and overseas. The creation of JTAC brought together expertise from the police and key government departments and agencies. As a truly joint organization, it ensures that the sharing of information across separate organizations is successfully achieved—poor information sharing between agencies was an aspect highlighted by the 9/11 Commission as a deficiency of the US Government during the build-up to the terrorist attacks in 2001, a deficiency the UK Government was quick to identify and rectify in the UK with the creation of JTAC.

JTAC also sets the threat levels for the UK from international terrorism. It issues warnings of threats and other terrorist-related subjects for customers from a wide range of government departments and agencies. JTAC also produces more in-depth reports on trends, terrorist networks, and capabilities. It is an integral part of the intelligence machinery and is where information gathered by the police service is fed into the national picture for analysis.

2.8.2 Counter-terrorism policing

Counter-terrorism policing in England and Wales is delivered through the Police Counter Terrorism Network. The network, which consists of four Counter Terrorism Units (CTUs) and four smaller Counter Terrorism Intelligence Units (CTIUs), was established to complement the work of local force Special Branches and the

London-based Counter Terrorism Command—it links frontline police officers with regional counter-terrorism hubs and thereby national counter-terrorism policing. The Police Counter Terrorism Network and Special Branches have close and effective working relationships with the Security Service which is the result of joint working and joint intelligence assessments. In Scotland, the ACPOS Coordinator for Counter Terrorism coordinates all police counter-terrorism-related duties to ensure that the Scottish Police counter-terrorism capability is effective and remains an integral part of the UK Police Counter Terrorism Network. Coordination is delivered by CTIU (Scotland), which is broadly similar in capability to CTIUs in England and Wales. Counter-terrorism policing contributes to all four workstreams of the UK's counter-terrorism strategy CONTEST by:

- **pursue**: identifying and disrupting terrorist activity;
- **prevent**: working with communities and local authorities to identify and divert those involved in or vulnerable to radicalization;
- **protect**: policing the UK border, critical national infrastructure, civil nuclear sites, transport systems, and the public; and
- **prepare**: leading the immediate response after or during a terrorist attack, including responding to CBRNE (chemical, biological, radiological, nuclear, and explosive) incidents.

Counter-terrorism policing requires oversight due to the large budget and significant police powers. In this regard, the Home Secretary is accountable to Parliament for the provision and funding of counter-terrorism policing in England and Wales, and is responsible for setting strategic priorities.

2.8.2.1 Strategic policing requirements

From November 2012, the Strategic Policing Requirement (SPR) set by the Home Secretary empowers and enables Police and Crime Commissioners to deliver their important role of holding their Chief Constable to account for the totality of their policing—both local and national. They will be expected to drive collaboration between police forces and to ensure that forces can work effectively together and with their partners.

The SPR supports Chief Constables and Police and Crime Commissioners to ensure that they fulfil forces' national responsibilities. It:

- helps Police and Crime Commissioners, in consultation with their Chief Constable, to plan effectively for policing challenges that go beyond their force boundaries;
- guides Chief Constables in the exercise of these functions; and

- enables and empowers Police and Crime Commissioners to hold their Chief Constable to account for the delivery of these functions.

In doing so, Chief Constables and Police and Crime Commissioners must demonstrate that they have taken into account the need for appropriate capacity to contribute to the Government's counter-terrorism strategy (CONTEST) by:

- identifying, disrupting, and investigating terrorist activity, and prosecuting terrorist suspects;

- identifying and diverting those involved in or vulnerable to radicalization;

- protecting the UK border, the critical national infrastructure, civil nuclear sites, transport systems, and the public; and

- leading the immediate response after or during a terrorist attack, including responding to incidents involving chemical, biological, radiological, nuclear, firearms, and explosive material;

- having appropriate capacity to respond adequately to a major cyber incident through the maintenance of public order and supporting the overall incident.

2.8.2.2 Value for money

Given the unprecedented budget deficit, it is vital that all public resources are used as effectively and efficiently as possible. Following a Value for Money inspection of counter-terrorism policing in 2010 by Her Majesty's Inspectorate of Constabulary (HMIC), ACPO's TAM business area is working to maximize the effectiveness and efficiency of the Police Counter Terrorism Network to enable the best use of resources to meet current and future demands. The police are currently undertaking detailed work to drive value for money by sharing best practice across the Network.

2.8.2.3 National Crime Agency

The new National Crime Agency (NCA) established in 2013 will serve to strengthen the operational response to organized crime and better secure the border through more effective national tasking and enforcement action. The Government is clear that counter-terrorism policing already has effective national structures, and is considering how to ensure that these strengths are maintained and enhanced alongside its new approach to fighting crime. The creation of the NCA marks a significant shift in the UK's approach to tackling serious, organized, and complex crime, with an emphasis on greater collaboration across the whole law enforcement landscape. The NCA will build effective two-way relationships with police forces, law enforcement agencies, and other partners, and will be made up of four commands:

- the **Organised Crime Command (OCC)** will target organized crime groups operating across local, national, and international borders and will work with police forces and other agencies to ensure that prioritized and appropriate action is taken against every organized crime group identified;

- the **Border Policing Command (BPC)** will ensure that all law enforcement agencies operating in and around the border work to clear and mutually agreed priorities, ensuring illegal goods are seized, illegal immigrants are dealt with, and networks of organized criminals are targeted and disrupted, both overseas and at ports up and down the UK;

- the **Economic Crime Command (ECC)** will provide an innovative and improved capability to deal with fraud and economic crimes, including those carried out by organized criminals;

- the **Child Exploitation and Online Protection Centre (CEOP)** will work with industry, government, children's charities, and law enforcement to protect children from sexual abuse and to bring offenders to account.

All four commands will also benefit from:

- an intelligence hub, which will build and maintain a comprehensive picture of the threats to the UK from organized criminality;

- a national cyber crime centre, providing expertise, support, intelligence, and guidance to police forces and the commands of the NCA.

POINT TO NOTE—SOPHISTICATED STRATEGY

The CONTEST strategy provides a framework to coordinate, direct, and shape the Government's response to the threat from terrorism. A decade since its first presentation to the Cabinet in 2003, it continues to provide clear and focused direction. Over time, CONTEST has grown in size, scale, and scope and is now the world's most sophisticated counter-terrorism strategy. The latest version, published in July 2011 (CONTEST 3), is unprecedented in size and now stands at a total of 236 pages—some 62 pages longer than its 2009 iteration, and 203 pages longer than that of 2006. This expansion reflects the increasing breadth and depth of the UK's counter-terrorism policy but its expansion is only part of the story.

Whilst it is true that CONTEST 3 covers a greater diversity of threats and recommendations than its predecessors, the reason for this growth has been a calculated move by successive governments to bring counter-terrorism strategy out into the open. Whereas the first iteration of CONTEST, released in 2003, remained classified, its updated 2006 version did not, and the 2009 CONTEST took this transparency one stage further by offering an unparalleled insight into the UK's strategic approach to countering terrorism. CONTEST 3 has continued in this vein: it offers a candid assessment of the current threat landscape, situating UK counter-terrorism policy against a changing geopolitical backdrop in the Middle East and in light of shifting modes of terrorist attack.

The development of CONTEST reveals an important element of counter-terrorism practice in the UK, that the public, very often the victim of terrorist attacks, can help to prevent them, but in order to do so they need to be informed and kept updated in order that we can all work together towards our shared values. An important and implicit assumption that has been contained in CONTEST since its origins, is that there is no complete defence against the determination of contemporary terrorists, especially as they continued to develop new ways in which to deliver death and destruction on an inconceivable scale. Even during its early stages of development, CONTEST indicated that there were no frameworks that could guarantee peace, however, it does serve to augment the UK's response which is necessary to tackle all forms of contemporary terrorists' threats so that all communities can go about their lives freely and with confidence.

2.9 Cyber Security Strategy

The Office of Cyber Security & Information Assurance (OCSIA) was established with the task of driving forward a cross-government programme of work supporting the Minister for the Cabinet Office (the Rt Hon Francis Maude MP) and the NSC in determining priorities in relation to securing cyberspace. The unit provides strategic direction and coordinates action relating to enhancing cyber security and information assurance in the UK, while a new Cyber Security Operations Centre (CSOC) based at GCHQ in Cheltenham, provides the coordinated protection of the UK's critical information technology systems. The OCSIA, alongside the CSOC, work with lead government departments and agencies such as the Home Office, Ministry of Defence (MoD), GCHQ, Communications-Electronics Security Group (CESG), the Centre for the Protection of National

Infrastructure (CPNI), and the Department for Business, Innovation and Skills (BIS) in driving forward the cyber security programme for UK government which seeks to provide the UK with the balance of advantage in cyberspace.

Law enforcement agencies across the UK Government also have their part to play in providing safety and security online to UK citizens and business users. The police service, under the auspices of ACPO, developed a new E-Crime initiative to provide the strategic foundation and direction to ensure UK police services were alert to cyber crime and cyber-terrorism activities and that any suspected activity, no matter how small, was encouraged to be reported by the public and commerce and then to be recorded. This policing initiative was supported by others under the leadership of the OSCT at the Home Office. With primary responsibility for the cross-government strategy on tackling terrorist use of the internet, the Home Office has published guidance for those citizens who are responsible for vulnerable individuals and work within communities to help to ensure that the internet is an environment where terrorist and violent extremist messages are challenged. As part of their wider efforts to counter the threat of radicalization on the internet, a public-facing webpage was launched in February 2010 to encourage the public to take action against unacceptable violent extremist and hate websites and other online content. If individuals believe that material they have located is potentially unlawful, they are provided with the opportunity to complete a form on the webpage and refer it to the Counter Terrorism Internet Referral Unit (CTIRU), established by ACPO during 2010.

Case Study—Role of the Counter Terrorism Internet Referral Unit

The CTIRU provides a national coordinated response to referrals from the public as well as from government and industry. It also acts as a central, dedicated source of advice for the police service.

The CTIRU provides the UK police service with a unit of experts who can carry out an initial assessment of material located on the internet and is also responsible for alerting forces and the units of the UK Police Counter Terrorism Network to online terrorist offences that may fall within their jurisdiction. Powers under UK terrorism legislation provide for the CTIRU to take a national lead in serving notices on website administrators, web hosting companies, Internet Service Providers (ISPs), and other relevant parties within the UK, to modify or remove any unlawful content.

> The CTIRU also focuses on developing and maintaining relationships with the internet industry, an important part of ensuring the delivery of a safer and more secure online experience for citizens. A further challenge, given the global scope of cyberspace for UK law enforcement, is that the majority of terrorist content online is hosted in other countries outside the jurisdiction of the UK and to counter this challenge the CTIRU continues to forge links with law enforcement counterparts abroad to help to target those websites hosted overseas. UK Counter Terrorism and Extremism Liaison Officers (CTELOs) based in countries around the world have a key role in supporting this work. The ACPO national coordinator for Prevent, Assistant Chief Constable John Wright, describes the role of CTIRU as: 'providing the opportunity to effectively enforce, and control, access to material believed to be extreme. In addition, the CTIRU will help to develop a culture of collaboration between police, partners and service providers dedicated to making the internet a safer place, particularly for young people.'

To secure the vast economic and social opportunities that cyberspace has to offer, in 2010 the Coalition Government, under Prime Minister David Cameron, transformed its approach to cyber security, setting out a new vision towards 2015 in its cyber strategy—the UK Cyber Security Strategy: protecting and promoting the UK in a digital world. The new strategy revealed that the British Government believed that there was no such thing as 'absolute security' indicating that its strategy to counter cyber threats was to apply a risk-based approach to prioritizing its response. The new strategic vision for the strategy was for the UK in 2015 to derive huge economic and social value from a vibrant, resilient, and secure cyberspace, where its actions, guided by its core values of liberty, fairness, transparency, and the rule of law, enhance prosperity, national security, and a strong society. To counter all cyber challenges, the new strategy is divided into four strategic objectives shown in Figure 2.9.

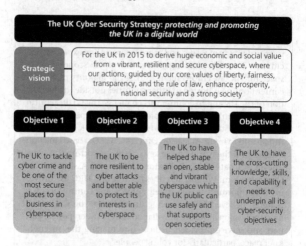

Figure 2.9 The UK Cyber Security Strategy

KEY POINT—CYBER SECURITY RESPONSIBILITIES

The British Government understands that achieving its vision for cyber security for 2015 within the framework of its guiding principles, will require everyone—the private sector, individuals, and government—to work together. Just as all citizens from all countries benefit from the use of cyberspace, all citizens have a responsibility to help to protect it. Therefore, ordinary citizens have an important role to play in keeping cyberspace a safe place to do business and live our lives. By 2015, the new approach by the British Government will seek to ensure that its citizens know how to get themselves a basic level of protection against online threats and that they have ready access to accurate and up-to-date information on the online threats that they face, together with the techniques and practices they can employ to guard against those threats. If citizens are careful about putting personal or sensitive information on the internet, are wary of email attachments or links from unrecognized senders, and are cautious about downloading files from websites they know little about, then they can significantly assist in countering the cyber-security challenge making cyberspace increasingly resilient to all manner of cyber threats posed to individual citizens. It is essential, therefore, that everyone in their homes, at their place of work, and on the move can help to identify threats in cyberspace and report possible offences which make cyberspace a hostile environment for those seeking unlawfully to exploit its potential.

2.10 **European Union Counter-Terrorism Strategy**

The European Union is an area of increasing openness in which the internal and external aspects of security are intimately linked. It is an area of increasing interdependence, allowing for free movement of people, ideas, technology, and resources and is the kind of environment which terrorists exploit to pursue their objectives. In this context, concerted and collective European action is vital in tackling terrorism that crosses the borders of its member states. The threat from contemporary terrorism is global and the EU has a major part to play in protecting all its citizens.

In December 2005, the Justice and Home Affairs Council adopted the EU Counter-Terrorism Strategy which was also welcomed by the heads of state and governments on 15 and 16 December 2005. The purpose of establishing a strategy was to progress the agenda of work set out during the March 2004 meeting of the European Council which was conducted in the wake of the Madrid bombings.

Case Study—Madrid, Spain, 2004

On the morning of Thursday 11 March 2004, terrorist cell members placed ten rucksack improvised explosive devices (IEDs) packed with nails on four separate commuter trains in Madrid. Within the space of three minutes, all the devices were detonated on busy carriages during the rush hour at El Pozo Station, Calle Tellez, Atocha Station, and Santa Eugenia Station.

The coordinated explosions claimed 191 lives and left more than 1,800 injured. The victims came from 17 countries including Spain, France, Bulgaria, and Poland, but they also came from as far afield as Brazil, Peru, Chile, and Cuba thus making this attack truly global in scale—an attack that so far remains Europe's worst terrorist incident this century.

> The attack was planned to coincide with the Spanish general election, occurring three days before voting commenced. The timing of the attack also had great significance, being committed exactly 911 days after the 9/11 terrorist attacks in the US. Was this just a coincidence of attack-planning by an al Qa'ida-inspired cell? Or part of the powerful delivery of their message?

The counter-terrorism strategy commits the EU to 'combat terrorism globally while respecting human rights, and to make Europe safer, allowing its citizens to live in an area of freedom, security and justice.' To reduce the threat from terrorism to the EU successfully, and to reduce the vulnerability of the EU to attack, the strategy is divided into four broad pillars of Prevent, Protect, Pursue, and Respond as Figure 2.10 shows.

2.10.1 **Prevent**

Under the pillar of Prevent, the EU aims to prevent people turning to terrorism by tackling the factors or root causes which can lead to radicalization and recruitment, both in Europe and internationally. The key priorities of Prevent are to:

- develop common approaches to identify and tackle problematic behaviour, in particular, misuse of the internet;
- address incitement and recruitment in key environments (eg, prisons and places of religious training or worship), notably by introducing new criminal offences covering such behaviour;
- develop a media and communication strategy to explain EU policies more effectively;
- promote good governance, democracy, education, and economic prosperity through EU and member state assistance programmes;
- develop inter-cultural dialogue within and outside the EU;
- develop a non-emotive lexicon for discussing the issues; and
- further develop our understanding of the issues and policy responses through continued research and the sharing of experience and analysis.

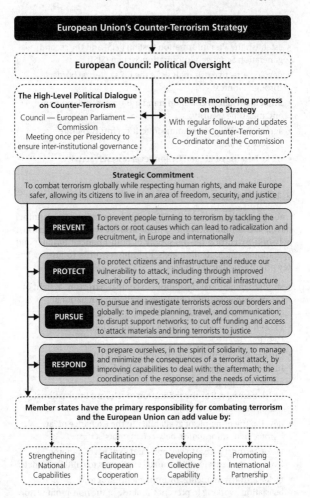

Figure 2.10 European Union Counter-Terrorism Strategy

2.10.2 **Protect**

Under the pillar of Protect, the EU seeks to reduce our vulnerability to attack through improved security of borders, transport, and critical infrastructure. The key priorities of Protect are to:

- improve the secure nature of EU passports through the introduction of biometrics;
- establish the Visa Information System (VIS) and the second-generation Schengen Information System (SISII);
- develop effective risk analysis of the EU's external borders through Frontex;
- implement agreed common standards on civil aviation, port, and maritime security;
- agree a European programme for critical infrastructure protection; and
- make best use of EU and Union-level research activity.

2.10.3 **Pursue**

Under the pillar of Pursue, the EU aims to impede terrorist planning, travel, and communications. Pursue also seeks to disrupt terrorist networks by cutting off the supply of both financial funding and operational materials ultimately to bring terrorists to justice. The key priorities of Pursue are to:

- strengthen national capabilities to combat terrorism, in light of the recommendations of the peer evaluation of national anti-terrorism arrangements;
- make full use of Europol, Eurojust, and the Joint Situation Centre;
- further develop mutual recognition of judicial decisions, including by adopting the European Evidence Warrant;
- ensure full implementation and evaluation of existing legislation as well as the ratification of relevant international treaties and conventions;
- develop the principle of availability in the exchange of law enforcement information between member states;
- tackle terrorist access to weapons and explosives, ranging from components for home-made explosives to CBRN materials;
- tackle terrorist financing, by implementing agreed legislation, working to prevent the abuse of the non-profit sector, and reviewing the EU's overall performance in this area; and
- provide technical assistance to priority countries in order to enhance their own counter-terrorism capabilities.

2.10.4 **Respond**

Under the pillar of Respond, the EU seeks to manage and minimize the consequences of a terrorist attack. This can be done by improving capabilities to deal with the aftermath, the coordination of response, and the needs of victims. The key priorities of Respond are to:

- agree EU Crisis Coordination Arrangements and support operational procedures;
- revise the legislation on the EU mechanism for civil protection;
- develop risk assessment as a tool to help to inform the building of capabilities to respond to an attack;
- improve coordination with international organizations on managing responses to terrorist attacks and other disasters; and
- share best practice and develop approaches for the provision of assistance to victims of terrorism and their families.

POINT TO NOTE—ADDED VALUE

The EU Counter-Terrorism Strategy makes clear that terrorism is a threat to all EU member states which is considered to be a criminal and unjustifiable act under any circumstances. Although the strategy suggests that member states themselves have the primary responsibility for combating terrorism, the EU can add significant value to the efforts of a single nation by:

- strengthening national capabilities;
- facilitating European cooperation;
- developing collective capability;
- promoting international partnership.

Acting through and in conjunction with the United Nations and other international or regional organizations, the EU works to build international consensus and promote efforts in the UN to develop a global strategy for combating terrorism. An essential element of the EU strategy is to work to resolve conflicts and promote good governance and democracy in which the dialogue and alliance between cultures, faiths, and civilizations is key in order to address the motivational and structural factors underpinning radicalization. The EU strategy for countering terrorism, shown in Figure 2.10, is essential to coordinate the responses of all member states so that Europe is united in the struggle against terrorism in whatever form it may threaten its citizens.

2.11 **United Nations Global Counter-Terrorism Strategy**

The United Nations Global Counter-Terrorism Strategy was adopted by member states on 8 September 2006 and reaffirmed at the 117th plenary meeting on 8 September 2010. The strategy, in the form of a resolution and an annexed Plan of Action, is a unique global instrument serving to enhance national, regional, and international efforts to counter terrorism as shown in Figure 2.11.

> ### KEY POINT—GLOBAL THREAT, GLOBAL RESPONSE
>
> The United Nations Global Counter-Terrorism Plan of Action is the first time that all member states have agreed to a common strategic approach to fight terrorism, not only sending a clear message that terrorism is unacceptable in all its forms and manifestation but also resolving to take practical steps individually and collectively to prevent and combat it. Those practical steps include a wide array of measures ranging from strengthening state capacity to counter terrorist threats, to better coordinating the UN system's counter-terrorism activities and ensuring that global threats from terrorism receive a global response.

United Nations Global Counter-Terrorism Plan of Action

Strategic statement

We, the States Members of the United Nations resolve:

1. To consistently, unequivocally and strongly condemn terrorism in all its forms and manifestations, committed by whomever, wherever and for whatever purposes, as it constitutes one of the most serious threats to international peace and security.

2. To take urgent action to prevent and combat terrorism in all its forms and manifestations and, in particular:
a). To consider becoming parties without delay to the existing international conventions and protocols against terrorism, and implementing them, and to make every effort to reach an agreement on and conclude a comprehensive convention on international terrorism;

b). To implement all General Assembly resolutions on measures to eliminate international terrorism, and relevant General Assembly resolutions on the protection of human rights and fundamental freedoms while countering terrorism;

c). To implement all Security Council resolutions related to international terrorism and to cooperate fully with the counter-terrorism subsidiary bodies of the Security Council in the fulfilment of their tasks, recognizing that many States continue to require assistance in implementing these resolutions.

3. To recognize that international cooperation and any measures that we undertake to prevent and combat terrorism must comply with our obligations under international law, including the Charter of the United Nations and relevant international conventions and protocols, in particular human rights law, refugee law, and international humanitarian law.

Measure1	Measure 2	Measure 3	Measure 4
Address the conditions conducive to the spread of terrorism	**Prevent** and combat terrorism	**Build** States' capacity to prevent and combat terrorism and to strengthen the role of the United Nations system in this regard	**Ensure** respect for human rights for all and the rule of law as the fundamental basis of the fight against terrorism

Figure 2.11 United Nations Global Counter-Terrorism Plan of Action

Chapter 3
Counter-Terrorism Practice

3.1 Responding to Terrorist Emergencies

Although police officers and other counter-terrorism practitioners on the front line may be aware of their local plans to respond to large-scale terrorist events and other similar emergencies, it is not often that they are afforded an opportunity to learn about the mechanisms at the highest levels of central government to coordinate a multi-agency response. An increased awareness of how central government manages to deliver its responses across all departments will serve to raise an understanding amongst police officers and other partner emergency service personnel to appreciate the challenges of coordinating national resources in times of crisis.

Following the tragic events of the 1972 Olympic Games in Munich where 11 members of the Israeli Olympic team were murdered by Black September terrorists, then Prime Minister Edward Heath directed his Government not only to re-evaluate its response to such incidents but also to provide a centralized mechanism which would be able to coordinate a full government response effectively. The Government created a series of measures that outlined its response to a range of emergencies which included at its very heart the Cabinet Office Briefing Room (COBR). COBR, invariably a room in a windowless office in the basement of Westminster, has served the nation well for nearly 40 years, managing a variety of civil emergencies. During March 2012, the Cabinet Office reviewed its central response to emergencies and published an updated strategy which set out its new arrangements for responding to and recovering from emergencies, irrespective of cause or location, requiring central government action which could include direction, coordination, expertise, or specialized equipment and financial support.

3.1.1 **Emergency definition**

The Government's concept of operations focuses primarily on the response to no-notice or short notice emergencies requiring UK central government engagement, although the principles, definitions, and roles underpin the more tailored approach that should also be adopted to manage rising tide emergencies that develop more slowly.

An emergency as defined by the Civil Contingencies Act 2004 is a situation or series of events that threatens or causes serious damage to human welfare, the environment, or security in the UK. This definition covers a wide range of scenarios which includes adverse weather conditions, severe flooding, animal diseases as well as terrorist incidents, all of which have the potential to impact or disrupt essential services and critical infrastructure.

The Government has categorized three levels of emergencies which include *significant*, *serious*, and *catastrophic* as shown in Figure 3.1.

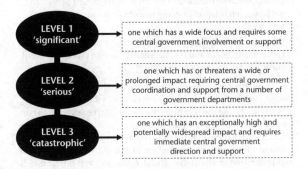

Figure 3.1 Levels of emergency

3.1.2 **Phases of an emergency**

The management of any emergency comprises three main phases as Figure 3.2 shows.

The response phase comprises two separate but closely related and often overlapping challenges: crisis management and consequence (or impact) management. These are both designed to control and minimize the immediate challenges arising from an incident:

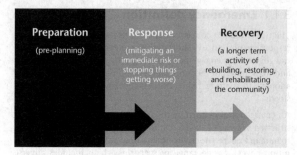

Figure 3.2 Phases of emergency

- **crisis management**: involves the phase of the response that attempts to prevent or avert an imminent emergency, along with protective or other measures to mitigate its effects, prevent further damage or disruption, and secure the scene. It also includes actions taken to address the immediate direct effects of an incident. The duration of the crisis management phase can vary from a few hours to many months depending on the scenario;

- **consequence management**: usually takes place in parallel with crisis management and is concerned with steps taken to prevent the impact of an incident escalating.

The recovery phase formally starts once the situation has been stabilized and can be defined as the process of rebuilding, restoring, and rehabilitating the community following an emergency. In contrast to the response phase, the recovery process can take a considerable amount of time (months or years), as it seeks to support affected communities in the reconstruction of the physical infrastructure and restoration of emotional, social, economic, and physical well-being.

3.1.3 Central government engagement in an emergency

The local responders are the basic building blocks of the response to any emergency in the UK. The police will normally take the lead in coordinating the local response where a crime has been committed, or if there is a threat to public safety. The local multi-agency response is coordinated through a Strategic Coordinating Group (SCG) located in the Strategic Coordination Centre (SCC). The chair of the group is known as the Strategic Coordinating Group Chair. The principle of subsidiarity emphasizes the importance of local decision making supported, where necessary, by coordination at a higher level.

3.1.4 **Emergency response principles**

There are eight guiding principles which have been developed by the Cabinet Office to capture the core characteristics of effective emergency response and they should be applied to the management of any emergency including terrorism. Table 3.1 shows the eight guiding principles.

Table 3.1 Emergency response guiding principles

Emergency response guiding principles	
Preparedness	All individuals and organizations that might have to respond to emergencies should be properly prepared, including having clarity of roles and responsibilities, specific and generic plans, and periodically rehearsing response arrangements
Continuity	The response to emergencies should be grounded within organizations' existing functions and their familiar ways of working—although, inevitably, actions will need to be carried out at greater speed, on a larger scale, and in more testing circumstances during the response to an incident
Subsidiarity	Decisions should be taken at the lowest appropriate level, with coordination at the highest necessary level. Local responders should be the building blocks of response for an emergency of any scale
Direction	Clarity of purpose should be delivered through an awareness of the strategic aims and supporting objectives for the response. These should be agreed and understood by all involved in managing the response to an incident in order to prioritize and focus the response effectively
Integration	Effective coordination should be exercised between and within organizations and local, regional, and national tiers of a response as well as having timely access to appropriate guidance and appropriate support for the local, regional, or national level

---

Emergency response guiding principles

Communication	Good two-way communications are critical to an effective response. Reliable information must be passed correctly and without delay between those who need to know, including the public
Cooperation	Positive engagement based on mutual trust and understanding will facilitate information sharing
Anticipation	In order to anticipate and manage the consequences of all kinds of emergencies, planners need to identify risks and develop an understanding of both the direct and indirect consequences in advance where possible

---

3.1.5 Lead responsibility within UK central government

For emergencies in England, or those involving reserved matters elsewhere in the UK, one UK central government department usually takes overall responsibility (the Lead Government Department (LGD)) for assessing the situation, ensuring that its ministers and other relevant ministers are briefed, handling media and parliamentary interests, and providing coordinated policy and other support as necessary to local responders. Other government departments will provide support to the LGD to ensure a coordinated response; however, individual departments remain responsible, including to Parliament, for their particular policy areas.

KEY POINT—CLARITY IN COORDINATION

Where the UK Government lead is unclear, it is the responsibility of the Cabinet Office to advise the Prime Minister's Office on where this should lie. A list of LGDs is maintained by the Cabinet Office and can be found at <http://www.cabinetoffice.gov.uk/ukresilience.aspx>.

The list sets out the broad expectation as to where the lead should lie in both the response and recovery phases for a wide range of emergencies, although in some areas this will need to be reaffirmed at the time in light of the precise nature of an event and the consequences arising.

In many cases, the LGD for the response phase is different from the recovery phase, reflecting the changing nature of the challenge, the different issues arising, and the expertise required. In some wide-area emergencies, it is possible that response and recovery activity will occur simultaneously in different parts of the country under the leadership of two different LGDs. In any event, careful consideration will be needed throughout the response phase to ensure the smooth transfer of responsibility and to ensure recovery issues are factored into planning.

Where an emergency occurs in Scotland, Wales, or Northern Ireland and falls within the competence of the relevant devolved administration, they will lead the response in their territory reporting through the relevant minister to the devolved legislature. In such circumstances, there will often be little if any involvement for UK government departments. The relevant UK central government territorial department (Scotland Office, Wales Office, and Northern Ireland Office) will usually be the first point of contact with the relevant devolved administration engaging other UK departments as necessary, unless the nature of the emergency raises specific issues that are best handled directly with the appropriate UK central government lead.

Where an emergency occurs in Scotland, Wales, or Northern Ireland but competence is reserved to Whitehall (and therefore the Westminster Parliament), the relevant UK government department will lead the response liaising closely with the relevant devolved administration(s) (as they will inevitably be affected and will usually lead on any issues arising for the local population) and UK territorial departments.

3.1.6 **The role of the Cabinet Office**

The Cabinet Office exists to make government work better. It does this through support to the Prime Minister and Cabinet, including its subcommittees, across the range of government activities, by managing the flow of business requiring collective ministerial consideration, brokering agreements between departments, and ensuring a common understanding of issues. As part of its ongoing work, the Cabinet Office engages with central, local, and regional partners to prepare for emergencies and to coordinate the central government response to major disruptive challenges.

3.1.7 **Organization of the Cabinet Office Briefing Rooms**

The UK central government response to a level 2 or 3 emergency is underpinned by COBR (the Cabinet Office Briefing Rooms), the physical location from which the central response is activated, monitored, and coordinated. COBR provides a focal point for the Government's response and an authoritative source of advice for local responders. Within COBR, a senior decision-making body oversees the Government's response supported as necessary by sub-groups and other sources of specialist advice.

In practice, the actual response to a specific emergency will need to take into account the nature of the challenge and other circumstances at the time. Where COBR is activated in response to a no-notice incident, its default strategic objectives are to:

- protect human life and, as far as possible, property and the environment;
- alleviate suffering;
- support the continuity of everyday activity;
- restore disrupted services at the earliest opportunity;
- uphold the rule of law and the democratic process.

These objectives are in no particular order of prominence and in reality they will evolve and their relative priority may shift as the emergency develops. In addition, not all the set objectives may be achievable at the outset of an emergency, however, ministers will advise on the appropriate balance to strike in light of the circumstances at the time. The interpretation of the objectives may also need to be refined and developed as the emergency progresses.

When COBR is activated, the early priorities will be to ensure that clear lines of communication are in place and to establish a common view of the issues, along with an understanding of immediate and emerging priorities and to identify or take any urgent decisions that are required. The pressure on the Government and local responders in the first few hours will be intense, and immediate action will be required on a variety of fronts, which will need careful consideration and coordination and, in some cases, prior preparation of information flows and plans.

When COBR is activated or in other situations where there is a significant central government role, a Government Liaison Officer (GLO) will normally be despatched immediately to act as the primary liaison channel between departments and local responders in the local Strategic Coordination Centre. The GLO will normally be from the relevant Government Office in England or the LGD.

POINT TO NOTE—A NATIONAL RESPONSE

COBR underpins the central government response from which the centre monitors, coordinates, and provides a focal point for local responders. Ministers and senior officials from relevant UK government departments and agencies along with representatives from other organizations as necessary are brought together in COBR to ensure a common appreciation of the situation to facilitate effective and timely decision making.

History has taught the police service and the wider government to expect the unexpected. Events can and do take place that, by their nature, cannot be entirely anticipated and while police officers engaged in countering terrorism continue to tackle a severe threat with the aim of pursuing terrorists and preventing their activities, it is right that our Government continues to develop a response should another attack break through our web of countermeasures.

3.2 **Tackling Domestic Extremism**

In recent years, the UK has seen increasing protest activity directed at a broad range of 'causes'. It is important for the police service to manage these potential threats: whilst they may not reach the threshold of terrorist activity or seriously threaten issues of national security, they can cause harm to communities and the economic well-being of the UK. It is important to keep the threat from 'domestic extremists' in perspective—the majority of protests in the UK are perfectly peaceful, lawful, and undertaken in pursuance of the right of assembly and freedom of speech that we all enjoy as part of living in a democratic society. There is, however, a more complex side to extremists who wish to further their cause by committing criminal acts, being involved in incidents of public disorder, and using violence and intimidation. It is these individuals who are of concern to the police service. It must be recognized that some extremists will, under certain circumstances, adopt a 'soft' style of protest, behaving in a perfectly law-abiding manner as part of a legitimate and peaceful protest. Their attendance at such events may, however, have different motives as they progress a more extreme agenda.

3.2.1 Categorization

There are a broad range of individual causes in which individuals can be engaged. These include anti-globalization, animal experimentation, medical research, the pharmaceutical industry, the food industry, hunting, sports involving animals, the financial industry, environmental issues, and many more which have been the subject of attention and protest. Protests have also been directed at commercial premises, city centres, as well as employees away from their place of work in addition to suppliers of those targeted companies, shareholders, and financial institutions providing funding. The key 'domestic extremist' groups are categorized in Table 3.2.

Table 3.2 Key 'domestic extremist' groups

Anarchism

Anarchism is the political belief that society should have no government, laws, police, or other authority, but should be a free association of all its members. Anarchism rests on the doctrine that no man has a right to control by force the action of any other man.

Animal rights

Animal rights, which is also referred to as animal liberation, is an ideology based upon the very basic interests of animals. There are a wide variety of individual belief structures within this movement but principally persons who support this cause believe that animals should be afforded the same consideration as humans in that they should not suffer harm, that they should not be considered as property, used as food, clothing, or the subject of experimental research or for entertainment. A widely accepted view amongst animal rights activists is that all animals should be regarded as legal persons and members of the moral community.

Capitalism

Capitalism is a term used to describe the economic system which promotes private ownership for profit operating within a free market. Those that oppose this system of economics are described as anti-capitalists who seek a fair central economic system based on the principles of safeguarding individual employees' rights.

Globalization

Globalization is the term used to describe the process or transformation of local or regional issues that rise into a global phenomena. Anti-globalization is the term used to describe those individuals with a political stance who oppose what is often an economic issue concerning the power, influence, and impact of large multinational corporations and the spread of migration, technology, and investment.

Anti-war

Anti-war protestors should be distinguished from 'peace' movements. Anti-war activists are engaged in more protest activities aiming to put an end to a nation's decision to begin or continue an armed conflict. There are a variety of belief strands within this category of domestic extremism as some anti-war protestors may believe that both sides of the conflict should discontinue their activities while others may only support the withdrawal of one side of the conflict which is often the more powerful body widely seen as the aggressor or invader.

Environmentalism

The protection of our planet has become a social movement centred upon a primary concern for the conservation and improvement of the natural environment. An extreme environmentalist is a person who would advocate unlawful activity to sustain the management of resources and stewardship of the natural environment through changes in policy or individuals or group direct action.

Fascism

Fascism is a political ideology that seeks to regenerate the social, economic, and cultural life of a country by basing it on a heightened sense of national belonging or ethnic identity. Fascists reject liberal ideas such as freedom and individual human rights and democracy. Fascism is often associated with right-wing fanaticism, racism, and violence. Nazism, the short name for national socialism, is considered to be a form of fascism focusing upon the belief in the superiority of an Aryan race. The term Neo-Nazism refers to post-Second World War activities and those who now seek to resurrect those social movements and ideologies in place during that time.

3.2.2 Tactics

Extremist groups use a wide variety of tactics and are creative in their approach to disrupting the activities of businesses and targeting employees. Police officers need to be aware of these tactics when deciding and developing responses. The targeting of protest activity is directed towards 'primary' and 'secondary' sites consisting of:

- **day-to-day activities**—protests by local group members at primary and sometimes secondary sites; and
- **regional and national days of action**—where substantially larger numbers of protesters gather together or in organized groups. They will target both primary and secondary sites. Often the majority of the protesters are not local people and there is more likelihood of more extremist involvement.

'Primary' and 'secondary' sites are defined as shown in Table 3.3.

Table 3.3 Primary and secondary sites

Primary	Primary sites consist of the main target premises or organizations where the activity of that business is the primary issue against which the protest is directed. It has to be recognized that protesters will sometimes deliberately target another site which is less prepared for such an eventuality. If a place is identifiable as being connected to or associated with a particular organization, protesters may regard it as a target.
Secondary	Secondary sites consist of all other sites, which are linked in any way whatsoever to the primary target site. For example, home addresses of directors, shareholders, employees of primary and secondary targets, suppliers or customers of primary and secondary targets, local authorities, solicitors, banks, shops, and public places. The list of potential secondary targets is extensive. A secondary target is generally any target that will have a direct impact on or assist in continuing and increasing pressure to bring about the closure of the primary target organization.

Table 3.4 provides examples of some of the wide variety of tactics that have been used by domestic extremist groups in the UK to progress their cause.

Table 3.4 Tactics used by extremist groups in the UK

Mass demonstrations	Organized and pre-planned mass demonstrations covering a large area, for example city centre May Day protests
Spontaneous demonstrations	Spontaneous or pre-planned demonstrations at specific locations, for example outside company addresses
Home address demonstrations	Pre-planned or spontaneous demonstrations at an individual's home address or immediate neighbourhood
Bomb telephone threats	Bomb or other malicious telephone threats to a third party, company premises, or an individual's home address
Improvised explosive devices (IEDs)	IEDs, for example in shops or on vehicles at distribution centres
Hoax devices	Real or hoax devices left at company premises or an individual's home address

Intrusions	Intrusions into company premises for 'sit ins', obtaining information, for example details of staff or supplying companies, or releasing or stealing animals
Malicious mail	Real, hoax, or malicious mail sent to company premises or an individual's home address
Harassment	Harassment of staff at or away from company premises
Intimidation	Intimidation of staff at or away from company premises
Unsolicited goods	Sending unsolicited goods to a company and/or individual employees' addresses
Assault	Physical assault on individuals
Switchboard jamming	Telephone switchboard-jamming campaigns
Fax machine blockades	Fax machine blockade—a continuous piece of black paper is faxed to the machine
Email saturation	Email saturation campaigns
Infiltration	Social engineering and infiltration, for example organizations unwittingly employing extremists or sympathizers

3.2.3 **Police response to domestic extremism**

Domestic extremism has become a concern to many organizations because it targets people and their homes as well as business premises. Domestic extremists move beyond the bounds of legitimate protest to intimidate individuals engaged in lawful activity and to impose economic costs on legal businesses. As such, it presents a criminal threat to the UK and its citizens that is national in scope and, in this regard, the UK police service is working hard to tackle domestic extremism and to respond effectively and appropriately to related criminal activities. The tactic of targeting suppliers, contractors, and financial service providers means that single, criminal domestic extremist incidents in local force areas are often part of a series of linked crimes. To tackle this, local police forces deal with domestic extremist crime and incidents locally and national police units ensure that the police service has a comprehensive picture of domestic-related extremist crime to provide a coordinated, effective, and consistent approach to policing and to maintain a strategic overview of domestic extremism-related public order issues.

POINT TO NOTE—WIDENING THE POLICE PORTFOLIO

The modern police service faces a widening mission. The increasing complexity of counter-terrorism operations and its efforts to protect the public and preserve the peace when tackling domestic extremism demands substantial specialist police skills and resources. In the malaise of modern police activity, the police service must not forget its primary role within the security forces infrastructure in the UK which is to protect the public from a law enforcement perspective and use its executive powers to bring terrorists to justice. The police service has increasingly acted as a bridge between what has been termed 'High Policing', the activity of the UK's intelligence machinery protecting national security, and 'Low Policing' carried out by police forces through their Basic Command Units and Neighbourhood Policing Teams across the country protecting local neighbourhood security. This bridge is vital to ensure a 'golden thread' of intelligence is woven throughout the security forces architecture. As a direct result of maintaining this 'golden thread', and to protect the public from al Qa'ida-inspired terrorism and the 'home-grown' terrorist threat, the police service gathers intelligence and evidence simultaneously, but it could not prosecute terrorists without specialist guidance and support from one of its key counter-terrorism partners, the Crown Prosecution Service.

3.3 Prosecuting Terrorists

The threat from al Qa'ida-inspired terrorism has served to shape how governments respond to protect their citizens. In the UK, we have constructed a new police counter-terrorism network and strengthened our intelligence machinery. Yet the severity of the terrorist threat we face today has also demanded an unprecedented period of change within the wider criminal justice system, not only through the introduction of a series of anti-terror powers necessary to pursue terrorists effectively, but also changes to the structures within the Crown Prosecution Service (CPS).

3.3.1 Crown Prosecution Service

In 2004, the CPS considered how it could best deliver its service in relation to its serious casework. During an internal review undertaken in 2005, the CPS recommended that three new casework divisions should be created. This new framework would concentrate expertise and resources to provide the best possible service to the public and CPS stakeholders. The new divisions were established in 2005 and included the Counter Terrorism Division (CTD), primarily established to deal with prosecuting terrorism cases which had been rapidly increasing in terms of size and complexity. During April 2011, the division merged with the Special Crime Division to create a new Special Crime and Counter Terrorism Division (SCCTD) at the CPS. Lawyers in the Counter Terrorism section of SCCTD now advise on and prosecute all cases involving allegations of terrorism, war crimes and crimes against humanity, racial and religious incitement and hatred because of sexual orientation, hijacking, piracy, and official secrets.

3.3.2 **Special Crime and Counter Terrorism Division**

The SCCTD is responsible for advising the police in all terrorism cases and is often consulted whilst the evidence is being gathered, with the SCCTD subsequently undertaking the prosecution of those terrorism offences. Terrorism-related cases continue to make up the majority of SCCTD work but it also deals with all allegations of incitement to racial and religious hatred, war crimes and crimes against humanity, official secrets cases and hijacking as similar legal skills are required to handle such work. The SCCTD has its main office in London with a smaller satellite office based in West Yorkshire. Terrorism and incitement cases are managed within both offices but war crimes, crimes against humanity, and official secrets cases are only dealt with in London.

> ## KEY POINT—LEADING THE SPECIAL CRIME AND COUNTER TERRORISM DIVISION, SUE HEMMING OBE
>
> The SCCTD is a vital element in protecting the public from terrorism. It is led by Sue Hemming OBE who states that:
>
> > Specialist prosecutors work closely with colleagues in the CJS [criminal justice system] to support tackling terrorism through due legal process and to continuously improve the management of terrorism cases both pre and post charge.
> >
> > Prosecutors begin from the perspective that terrorists are criminals and use the full remit of both criminal and terrorism

offences to prosecute fairly and proportionately according to the merits of each case. Prosecuting terrorism within a strict criminal framework is challenging but greatly enhanced by the strong tri lateral relationship that has been built up between police, prosecutors and the intelligence services and by developments in case management through the use of the Terrorism Case Management Protocol and the role of the Terrorism Case Management Judge (TCMJ). Additionally, the relationship with law enforcement abroad has been key to the success of recent prosecutions and the level of mutual support is unprecedented in any other area of work.

Prosecutors are independent but work collaboratively with police and others to build strong and sustainable cases from the outset. The need to arrest early for public safety reasons often means that a full evidential picture does not develop until shortly before or after arrest takes place. Such cases need to be investigated and built quickly as the evidence unfolds within the pre charge detention period.

Prosecutors give advice on the effects of proposed investigative action; ensure the developing case is complete, accurate and consistent by considering the intelligence picture and help identify evidentially weak cases to bring them to an early conclusion. Prosecutors prefer charges at the earliest opportunity using the Code for Crown Prosecutors and where further time is required, are involved in making some applications for warrants of further detention.

After charge, robust case management is essential to ensure the case moves efficiently through the criminal justice process and the prosecutor has a key role. Shortly after charge, the defence and the court are provided with an outline of the prosecution case and a proposed timetable. Following representations from both parties at an early preliminary hearing, the TCMJ gives directions for service of the evidence, disclosure of unused material, service of defence statements and an estimate for trial; thereafter he monitors progression of the timetable.

The joint protocols and systems which have been developed to complement the legal framework assist in successfully delivering justice through efficient but fair and transparent case management in this complex area of practice.

3.3.3 **Code for Crown Prosecutors**

Although cases against those suspected of terrorism may be specialist in nature, they are actually managed by the CPS in the same way as any other criminal case. All decisions are made in accordance with the Code for Crown Prosecutors which states that a prosecutor needs to have sufficient evidence to afford a realistic prospect of conviction before he or she can go on to consider the wider public interest. Commonly referred to as the 'evidential test', the CPS must be satisfied, first, that there is sufficient evidence to provide a realistic prospect of conviction against each defendant on each charge. This means that a jury or a bench of magistrates, properly directed in accordance with the law, is more likely than not to convict the defendant of the alleged charge. For there to be a conviction, the CPS have to prove the case so that the court is sure of the defendant's guilt. If the case does not pass the Evidential Test based on the strength of the evidence, it must not go ahead, no matter how important or serious the case may be.

If the case does pass the 'evidential test', the CPS must then decide if a prosecution is needed in the public interest. A prosecution will usually take place unless there are public interest factors tending against prosecution which clearly outweigh those tending in favour.

POINT TO NOTE—CRIMINAL JUSTICE

Terrorism is a crime and terrorists are criminals. In a free, democratic, and sophisticated society, a morally justified response to terrorism is to process criminals, no matter how abhorrent their actions may be, through a fair and transparent due legal process. Pursuing terrorists through a criminal justice system preserves and protects the democratic values of the prosecuting state while ensuring that the rights of all concerned are maintained. The role and responsibility of the SCCTD is essential to deliver justice to those who seek to destroy our way of life. Key to the success of the criminal justice system in pursuing terrorists effectively, is the degree of collaboration between all agencies and departments which share the common goal of protecting the public from terrorism. All in authority should be aware that the nature of the severe threat from today's terrorism demands that intelligence and evidence is gathered simultaneously, as potential attacks uncovered today may need to be disrupted tomorrow. Working together, sharing expertise, and seeking guidance and advice from one another at the earliest opportunity, provides all professional practitioners with the very best opportunity of preventing terror and protecting the public while securing justice.

When considering the public interest test, two of the factors the CPS should always take into account are the consequences for the victim of the decision whether or not to prosecute, and any views expressed by the victim or the victim's family.

3.4 Operational Security

The stark reality of the severe and sustained threat from terrorism in the UK is that right now some form of terrorist activity is taking place within our communities and those in authority should not believe that the area in which they work is immune from the terrorist threat. Thankfully, when compared against other types of crime, terrorism remains a very rare occurrence but its impact and far-reaching consequences demand a committed approach from all professional practitioners. Rural parts of the UK as well as densely populated towns and cities, make attractive locations for terrorists to operate. Simply hoping that the threat from terrorism will not result in activity in your communities or assuming that you will not be attacked again because you have recently sustained an attack, are the very complacencies that terrorists will exploit. Policing terrorism in the UK continues to develop in direct response to the threat we continue to endure and is being woven into the very fabric of policing. All police officers can contribute to countering terrorism and violent extremism but an understanding and awareness of operational security measures and key principles are fundamental for any practitioner engaged in this critical area of national security.

3.4.1 Protective marking

All professional practitioners working within counter-terrorism will, like many other public servants, have responsibility for viewing, handling, or disseminating sensitive material. Understanding the practice, policy, and procedures to maintain the confidentiality of this material is an essential professional practice. If the integrity of the information, intelligence, or evidence that is painstakingly collected and preserved is not correctly marked, handled, or treated with the respect it commands then devastating consequences may follow which could lead to the unintended disclosure of national secrets, an increased threat, or risk to fellow practitioners and the public or to the potential compromise of an ongoing operation.

Case Study—Operation Pathway

On Wednesday 8 April 2009, the North West Counter Terrorism Unit, working with Merseyside Police, Greater Manchester Police, Lancashire Constabulary, and the Metropolitan Police Service arrested 12 men under section 41 of the Terrorism Act 2000. The police operation, known as Operation Pathway, was believed to have disrupted a terrorist plot potentially to attack crowded places within the North West region. In his independent review of the operation published in October 2009, Lord Carlile, the Independent Reviewer of Terrorism Legislation, revealed that analysis of intelligence material on a wide front strongly suggested to the services concerned that this might be part of a very significant international plot. The initial priorities of the investigation were, first, the safe arrest and detention of the suspects and, secondly, to recover any materials that might be used in a terrorist attack. However, it was not originally intended for the arrests to take place as early as they did. The reason for this was that on Wednesday 8 April 2009 a briefing meeting had taken place at 10 Downing Street. Assistant Commissioner Quick, a very highly regarded officer and one of the most senior figures in the effort to counter terrorism, was seen and photographed by the media entering the front door of Number 10. He was carrying papers which were marked SECRET and were not contained in a briefcase, folder, or had a protective covering sheet— this was in breach of clear instructions to all public servants carrying highly confidential material. Some sensitive operational detail about the investigation was visible in press photographs and television footage taken of his arrival.

The actions of Assistant Commissioner Quick directly affected the arrests, causing them to be brought forward, and also materially affected the locations of the arrests, and thereby possibly increasing community tension and concern to the general public. Lord Carlile's review found no evidence that the change in arrest time led to the failure to find or the loss of any material evidence. Mr Quick tendered his resignation to Boris Johnson, the London mayor and chairman of the Metropolitan Police Authority, after admitting that he 'could have compromised a major counter terrorism operation'.

KEY POINT—SECURITY CULTURE

The security measures put in place by government are there to protect its assets and are vital to the success of countering terrorism. Developing a strong security culture and maintaining its effectiveness within the workplace is an important element in the professional practice of counter-terrorism operatives. If public servants cannot protect the information they hold then countering terrorism and extremism and protecting national security become increasingly difficult. All those in authority have an important part to play in adopting and enforcing security measures.

3.4.2 Government Protective Marking Scheme

The UK Government has strict guidance on the protective marking of its sensitive information. The Government Protective Marking Scheme (GPMS) is a common baseline for safeguarding information, particularly when it is shared with other organizations. A marking is applied to information to identify the standard procedures that are adopted in relation to their storage, security, distribution, handling, and destruction. The GPMS is a national policy and procedure for all government departments and partners and refers to all information assets such as papers, electronic documents, disks, storage devices, photographs, images, and drawings.

KEY POINT—BALANCING OPENNESS WITH SECURITY

The UK Government is committed to openness but recognizes that some information needs to be given special protection, for example to avoid breaching confidentiality, to assist in complying with the Data Protection Act and, in some cases, to protect national security. Under the Freedom of Information Act 2000, information is either proactively, or on request, made available to the public. Protectively marked information is not automatically exempt under the Freedom of Information Act. Where information is given a protective marking under this scheme, particular care must be taken when considering whether that information is disclosable under the Act. Disclosure will be judged on a case-by-case basis but all counter-terrorism practitioners must follow the

GPMS guidance and understand that any level of protective marking does not automatically make it exempt from public disclosure. In this new era of increased public accountability, professional responsibility, and integrity, all in authority are reminded of the need correctly to assess, mark, handle, distribute, and store sensitive information in accordance with the GPMS.

3.4.3 **Protective markings**

There are five protectively marked headings that may be used under the GPMS and they include:

- PROTECT;
- RESTRICTED;
- CONFIDENTIAL;
- SECRET;
- TOP SECRET.

With the exception of PROTECT, the classifications are also classed as national security markings. Material classified as PROTECT can be appropriately applied to sensitive information that needs to be protected (eg commercial or personal), which does not have a national security dimension and where the use of the RESTRICTED classification would be excessive. Table 3.5 provides information on the practical meanings of the protective markings.

Table 3.5 Government Protective Marking Scheme: meanings

PROTECT	The compromise of this information or material would likely:
	• Cause financial loss of earnings potential to, or facilitate improper gain or advantage for, individuals or companies.
	• Prejudice the investigation or facilitate the commission of crime.
	• Disadvantage government in commercial or policy negotiations with others.
	• Cause substantial distress to individuals.
	• Breach proper undertakings to maintain the confidence of information provided by third parties.
	• Breach statutory restrictions on the disclosure of information.

RESTRICTED	The compromise of this information or material would likely:

- Adversely affect diplomatic relations.
- Make it more difficult to maintain the operational effectiveness of the security of the UK or allied forces.
- Impede the effective development or operation of government policies.
- Undermine the proper management of the public sector and its operations.
- Cause financial loss of earnings potential to, or facilitate improper gain or advantage for, individuals or companies.
- Prejudice the investigation or facilitate the commission of crime.
- Disadvantage government in commercial or policy negotiations with others.

CONFIDENTIAL	The compromise of this information or material would likely:

- Damage diplomatic relations (ie cause formal protest or other sanction), to prejudice individual security or liberty.
- Cause damage to the operational effectiveness or security of the UK or allied forces, or the effectiveness of valuable security or intelligence operations.
- Work substantially against national finances or economic and commercial interests.
- Substantially undermine the financial viability of major organizations.
- Impede the investigation or facilitate the commission of serious crime.
- Impede seriously the development or operation of major government policies.
- Shut down or otherwise substantially disrupt significant national operations.

SECRET	The compromise of this information or material would likely:

- Raise international tension.
- Damage seriously relations with friendly governments.
- Threaten life directly, or seriously prejudice public order, individual security, or liberty.
- Cause serious damage to the operational effectiveness or security of the UK or allied forces, or to the continuing effectiveness of highly valuable security or intelligence operations.
- Cause substantial material damage to national finances or economic and commercial interests.

TOP SECRET   The compromise of this information or material would likely:

- Threaten directly the internal stability of the UK or friendly countries.
- Lead directly to widespread loss of life.
- Cause exceptionally grave damage to the effectiveness or security of the UK or allied forces or to the continuing effectiveness of extremely valuable security or intelligence operations.
- Cause exceptionally grave damage to relations with friendly governments.
- Cause severe long-term damage to the UK economy.

KEY POINT—PROTECTIVELY MARKING INFORMATION

It is the responsibility of the author of the material to apply the appropriate protective marking. The author must consider to what level the information must be protected: the higher the classification of the information, the greater administrative burden on the organization and the smaller the circulation of the information. The marking to be applied MUST be considered on a case-by-case basis—you should not apply 'blanket markings'. Once the author has marked the information, recipients will know from the marking what measures are required to be applied in protecting the information. If you are sharing information with an organization that does not use a protective marking scheme, then you should take extra precautions to make sure that the information is handled appropriately. This may entail setting out handling requirements to the recipient. If the information has some security classified information and other information less sensitive, the marking should relate to the most sensitive information.

3.5 Suspicious Sightings

One of the most important roles police officers and members of the public can carry out in support of countering terrorism is to report suspicious activity. This is vital not only for prevention of antisocial behaviour, public order, or the detection of serious and organized crime but also for terrorism and violent extremism. The police service believes that communities will defeat terrorism and they are now asking the public to trust their instincts and pass on information which could help to stop terrorists in their tracks. Members of the public may unknowingly have information which could be a crucial piece of the investigative jigsaw. To achieve this, however, police officers must be in a position to provide practical guidance and support to members of the public and to display a knowledge and understanding of terrorist-related activity. Police officers need to be aware of what the public should be alert to and what type of activity or incident should be reported. This will require officers to have an in-depth knowledge of their local force's intelligence requirements for countering terrorism and extremism which is outlined in local policing plans and force-level control strategies. Police officers also need to develop a sense of which information is a priority, and this requires an initial assessment of its potential importance and knowledge of what force protocols are in place to report such information.

Police officers need to encourage the public to be aware of what is happening around them and to think about anything or anyone that has struck them as unusual in their day-to-day lives. Police officers also need to ask members of the public to think carefully about anyone they know whose behaviour has suddenly changed. What has changed? Could it be significant? What about the people they associate with? Have they noticed activity where they live which is not the norm? The following checklist highlights key issues for practitioners to assess whether suspicious activity could be linked to terrorist activity.

Checklist—if you suspect it, report it

- Terrorists need transport—if you work in commercial vehicle hire or sales, has any rental made you suspicious?
- Terrorists use multiple identities—do you know someone with documents using different names for no obvious reason?
- Terrorists need communication—anonymous, pay-as-you-go and SIM card mobile phones are typical. Have you seen someone with large quantities of mobile phones which has made you suspicious?

- Terrorists need information—observation and surveillance help terrorist attacks. Have you seen anyone taking pictures of security arrangements?
- Terrorists use chemicals—do you know of someone buying large or unusual quantities of chemicals for no obvious reason?
- Terrorists use protective equipment—handling chemicals is dangerous. Maybe you have seen goggles or masks dumped somewhere?
- Terrorists need funding—cheque and credit card fraud are ways terrorists generate cash. Have you seen any suspicious transactions?
- Terrorists use computers—do you know someone who visits terrorist-related websites?
- Terrorists need to travel—meetings, training, and planning can take place anywhere. Do you know someone who travels but is vague about where they are going?
- Terrorists need storage—lock-ups, garages, and sheds can all be used to store equipment. Are you suspicious of anyone renting a commercial property?

POINT TO NOTE—TRUST YOUR INSTINCTS

If you suspect that any of the suspicious activity described in the checklist is taking place, or have received reports from members of the public about such activity, think about terrorist tactics, trust your instincts, and report it. In an emergency, which is believed as presenting an immediate threat such as a person observed acting suspiciously or a vehicle, unattended package, or bag which might pose an imminent danger, then the **999** emergency services telephone number should be used by members of the public at all times. There should be no delay in responding to such a perceived threat. The confidential anti-terrorism hotline number, **0800 789 321**, which is staffed around the clock by specialist counter-terrorism police officers and staff, provides an additional service and is waiting to receive information. As an alternative to speaking directly to police officers or staff, an online form is also available to complete which can be located at <https://secure.met.police.uk/athotline/>.

Police officers must be aware that the anti-terrorism hotline service is available for members of the public to report terrorism-related information confidentially. Members of the public may be concerned and have reservations about contacting the police, either because their friends or family may find out or their suspicions may prove to have innocent explanations but police officers must reassure the public that all calls and information received by the anti-terrorism hotline number are treated in the strictest of confidence. All information received is thoroughly researched and investigated before any police action is taken. Deputy Assistant Commissioner Stuart Osborne, the Senior National Co-ordinator for Counter Terrorism and Head of the Metropolitan Police Service Counter Terrorism Command states that 'We must not become complacent. We all have a responsibility to remain vigilant. I would urge anyone who has any concerns about possible terrorist-related activity to contact police through the Anti-Terrorist Hotline.'

3.6 **Stop and Search**

Stop and search powers provide police with an essential tool to detect and prevent terrorism, gather intelligence, and make communities safer. New stop and search powers under section 47A of the Terrorism Act 2000 now help police to protect the communities they serve from the risk of terrorism. This new power replaces the controversial provisions of section 44 of the Terrorism Act 2000, which Shami Chakrabarti, Director of the National Council for Civil Liberties (Liberty) described as: 'a good example of all that was wrong with counter terrorism legislation that trod all over our rights and freedoms', going on to state that:

> arming the police with a broadly worded, discretionary power to stop and search individuals without suspicion, not only was this crude and blunt instrument inappropriate, its negative impact on community relations made it entirely counterproductive. While the widespread use of power did nothing to enhance public safety, never leading to an arrest for a terror offence, it did cost us dearly by clamping down on peaceful protestors and disproportionately targeting young Black and Asian men.

Those in authority who have the responsibility under stop and search under terrorist legislation must understand the provisions it provides and be able to discharge their duties professionally and provide reassurance to the public. The following checklist provides essential guidance and advice for the practical application and interpretation of section 47A stop and search powers.

Checklist—stop and search, know your rights

What is section 47A stop and search?

Section 47A of the Terrorism Act 2000 gives police the power to search a person or vehicle within a defined geographical area if:

- they reasonably suspect that an act of terrorism will take place; and
- the power is necessary to prevent such an act.

Only senior police officers can issue the power. They must be at least the rank of Assistant Chief Constable and must inform the Secretary of State.

Once the authority has been issued, a police constable may then exercise the power, even if they do not have reasonable grounds to suspect an offence has been committed.

Who can stop you?

- a uniformed police officer;
- a uniformed Police Community Support Officer (PCSO).

Who can search you?

Under the legislation, a police officer in uniform may search:

- you;
- your clothes;
- your vehicle;
- anything you are carrying on your person;
- anything in or on your vehicle, including passengers.

A PCSO in uniform, **under the supervision of a police constable**, may search:

- anything you are carrying on your person;
- your vehicle;
- anything in or on your vehicle, including items carried by passengers;
- if your vehicle is unattended it may still be searched. A receipt will be left with your vehicle to notify you about the search.

Why is it done?

The purpose of a section 47A stop and search is to deter and detect terrorist activity.

Where can I be stopped and searched?

You can be stopped and searched under section 47A if you and/or your vehicle are within the geographical area defined by the authorization. If you are in a public place, the officer will only ask you to remove your coat or jacket and your gloves, unless the officer believes you are using your clothes to hide your identity.

If the officer asks you to take off any headgear, or anything you wear for religious reasons, they must take you somewhere out of public view.

What happens if I am stopped and searched?

Stop and search is for your safety. Being stopped and searched does not mean you are suspected of being a terrorist. Before you are searched the officer should tell you:

- the legislative power that allows the search;
- your rights;
- their identity;
- what they are looking for.

You must:

- stop when requested;
- stop your vehicle when requested;
- comply with the search.

If you fail to cooperate, or deliberately obstruct a search, you will have committed an offence and could be arrested.

What happens next?

If you are stopped and searched, the officer will complete an electronic form. They will then give you a receipt with a reference number. If you would like to see a copy of the form relating to your stop and search, you can take the reference number into any police station and request a copy of the form.

The officer will ask you questions and record:

- your name, address, and date of birth (you do not have to give this information if you do not want to, unless the officer says that they are reporting you for an offence which may or may not be related to terrorism. In this case, you could be arrested if you do not give them the information);
- a description of you and/or your vehicle;
- your ethnic background;
- when and where you were stopped and searched;
- the names and/or numbers of the officers involved in the search.

3.6.1 **Exercising stop and search powers**

When exercising powers authorized under section 47A, police officers **must** be in **uniform**. They do not need to form any reasonable grounds or suspect any suspicious behaviour to conduct the stop or search. Articles can be seized or retained if it is reasonably suspected they may be used in connection with terrorism but officers must note that there is **no** power to retain individuals for questioning. When stopping someone under section 47A, an officer must:

- identify themselves;
- explain why the person or vehicle has been stopped;
- reassure the individual that the stop is a routine part of counter-terrorist policing;
- complete a record and explain entitlement to a copy.

When applying the power the search officers should consider the following;

Authorization—what are the geographical limits?

Person—does the person fit any description provided by intelligence?

Location—is the place attractive to terrorists, for example critical transport routes?

Time—is it a significant period of the day, for example crowded or rush hour?

Behaviour—is the person acting in a concerning manner?

Clothing—could the clothing conceal a weapon or terrorist paraphernalia?

3.6.2 **Search guidelines**

The Home Office has provided detailed guidance for police officers in relation to the appropriate use of terrorism stop and search powers. The guidance specifically highlights that stop and search activity has raised concerns over the disproportionality of its use among black and ethnic minority groups and this is liable to be accentuated by its use in relation to terrorism, especially when countering the threat from international groups. It is not appropriate to stereotype people of a certain faith or ethnicity as terrorists but these factors may be significant when taken as part of a combination of other factors. It is known that some terrorists will adopt behaviours and appearances typical of local cultures to avoid identification and it is not, therefore, appropriate to use these factors as a preconceived basis for searches. It is important to remember that where profiles of suspects are available, they are subject to change and can become quickly outdated. All officers conducting stop and search powers under terrorism legislation should be aware of the cultural sensitivities surrounding the removal of clothing and especially headgear. In that respect, a thorough understanding of religious and cultural differences is an essential element of policing communities sensitively but effectively.

Prior to exercising stop and search powers under terrorism legislation, police officers should seek to 'PLAN' their action and be able to answer the following questions:

Proportionality—is the use of the power a proportionate response?

Legality—does the available information and intelligence establish appropriate legal grounds?

Accountability—are decision making and other processes documented and auditable?

Necessity—is the use of the power necessary in the circumstances?

POINT TO NOTE—EXERCISING CAUTION

Our recent history also informs us that the introduction of new anti-terror powers are very often poorly applied. If we are to build the public's confidence in our use of specialist powers, and retain the integrity and credibility of the legal instruments put in place to protect them, this must not be repeated. Terrorism law should be used only for terrorism purposes. Every step outside those purposes provides terrorists with an argument. All those in authority are required never to forget that such laws are a step outside the norms of criminal justice legislation: the right to stop and search in the street in a way different from, and more extensive than, a non-terrorism intervention is a power to be exercised with caution.

Part 2
Legislative and Procedural Content

Chapter 4

Terrorist Activities

4.1 Introduction—Definition of Terrorism/Terrorist

Section 1 of the Terrorism Act 2000 is central to the current anti-terrorism legislation. It defines the term 'terrorism'. This definition is used not only in the Terrorism Act 2000, but also in the Anti-terrorism, Crime and Security Act 2001, the Prevention of Terrorism Act 2005, the Terrorism Act 2006, and the Counter-Terrorism Act 2008. It has also been included in a number of different Acts, for example in the Civil Contingencies Act 2004.

Note that there is no general 'offence of terrorism' as such. The commission of an act of terrorism is not an offence, but the commission, preparation, or instigation of acts of terrorism is an element of a number of specific offences, for example training for terrorism (see **4.3.7**), possession of an article for a purpose connected with terrorism (see **4.3.10**), and collection of information (see **4.3.11**). 'Act of terrorism' is also referred to in legislation which provides police powers, such as the power of arrest in section 41 of the Terrorism Act 2000 (see **5.3.1**).

4.1.1 Terrorism

Terrorism means the use or threat of **actions** where:

1. the action:
   - involves serious violence against a person, *or*
   - involves serious damage to **property**, *or*
   - endangers a person's life, other than that of the person committing the action, *or*
   - creates a serious risk to the health or safety of the public or a section of the public, *or*

- is designed seriously to interfere with or seriously to disrupt an electronic system; *and*
2. the use or threat is designed to influence the government or an international governmental organization or to intimidate the public or a section of the public *or* involves the use of **firearms** or **explosives**; *and*
3. the use or threat is made for the purpose of advancing a political, religious, racial, or ideological cause.

Terrorism Act 2000, s 1(1) and (2)

Meanings

References to action, persons, property, the public, and the government are not restricted to the UK but include actions outside the UK and property or persons wherever situated as well as the public or the government of foreign countries (Terrorism Act 2000, s 1(4)).

Actions taken for the purpose of terrorism include actions taken for the benefit of a proscribed organization (Terrorism Act 2000, s 1(5) (see **4.2.1**)).

Action

Includes omission (Terrorism Act 2000, s 121).

Property

Includes property wherever situated and whether real or personal, heritable (ie inheritable) or moveable, and things in action (eg copyright, trademark, rights of repayment of loaned money), and other intangible (eg goodwill of business) or incorporeal property (eg mortgages, leases, etc) (Terrorism Act 2000, s 121).

Firearm

Includes an air gun or air pistol (Terrorism Act 2000, s 121).

Explosive

Means—
(a) an article or substance manufactured for the purpose of producing a practical effect by explosion,
(b) materials for making an article or substance within paragraph (a),
(c) anything used or intended to be used for causing or assisting in causing an explosion, and
(d) a part of anything within paragraph (a) or (c) (Terrorism Act 2000, s 121).

Notes

(a) The definition of terrorism is very wide. It basically includes any use or threat of violence for political, religious, racial, or ideological reasons. It also covers acts that are not in themselves violent, but which may nevertheless have a devastating impact, such as disrupting key computer systems or interfering with the supply of water or power where life, health, or safety may be put at risk. Some acts will also constitute criminal offences; other acts, such as those involving 'endangering another person's life' or 'creating a serious risk to the health or safety of the public or a section of the public', may involve conduct that would not itself be a criminal offence. The consent of the Director of Public Prosecutions (DPP) or the Attorney General (AG) is required for some offences which rely on the definition of terrorism, because it is so broad.

(b) The use or threat of action amounts to terrorism if it meets three elements. First, the action involves serious violence, damage, risk to the public, etc. Secondly, the use or threat of action has a certain purpose: to influence the government or intimidate the public (this does not have to be met if the action involves the use of firearms or explosives). And, thirdly, the purpose of the threat is to advance a political, religious, racial, or ideological cause.

(c) The definition of terrorism is not restricted to 'domestic' terrorism; it extends to terrorist activities in the UK and abroad. This reflects the international nature of terrorism, and perhaps also the fact that the UK wants to avoid becoming or appearing to be a safe haven for foreign terrorists wherever they want to or have committed their acts. Action against terrorism within a country's borders is also required by international law under UN Security Council Resolution 1373 of 2001. Many terrorism offences cover acts carried out abroad. There is no distinction made between those regimes which are seen as 'friendly' and those which, at least in the past, have been seen as a source of terrorism (see **R v F [2007]** in Related cases). See also **5.7.1**.

(d) Campaigns using firearms or explosives are deemed to be terrorism whether or not the action is designed to influence the government or intimidate the public.

Related cases

R v F [2007] EWCA Crim 243 The phrase 'government of a country other than the United Kingdom' in section 1(4) of the Terrorism Act 2000 is not restricted to representative or democratic governments.

The meaning of the phrase is plain enough: it applies to all countries, even those which are governed by tyrants and dictators, such as was the case with Libya under Muammar Gaddafi. There is no exemption from criminal liability for terrorist activities which are motivated or said to be morally justified by the alleged nobility of the terrorist cause. The terrorism legislation has an international dimension and citizens of certain countries governed by dictators are not excluded from legal protection from terrorist activities. In recognition of this wide reach, the prosecution of some offences based on foreign actions must have the consent of the Attorney General (Terrorism Act 2006, s 19) (see **5.7.4**).

R v Gul [2012] EWCA Crim 280 All governments are within the scope of this section (see **R v F**). There is no exemption for someone engaged in an internal armed insurrection or an armed struggle against a foreign government. Those who attack the military forces of a government or the coalition forces in Afghanistan or Iraq with the requisite intention set out in the Act are terrorists.

PNLD reference numbers

D8701, C1441, C2993

4.1.2 **Acts of terrorism**

Acts of terrorism include anything constituting an **action** taken for the purposes of terrorism, within the meaning of the Terrorism Act 2000 (Terrorism Act 2006, s 20(2)).

That means that it also includes actions taken for the purpose of a proscribed organization, Terrorism Act 2000, s 5(1) (see **4.2.1**).

Act/action

Includes omission (Terrorism Act 2000, s 121).

4.1.3 **Terrorist**

'Terrorist' means a person who is or has been concerned in the commission, preparation, or instigation of acts of **terrorism** or has committed an offence under any of the following sections of the Terrorism Act 2000:

Section 11 membership of a proscribed organization (see **4.2.2**)

Section 12 support of a proscribed organization (see **4.2.3**)

Section 15 invite, receive, provide funds (see **4.4.2**)

Section 16 use, possess money/property (see **4.4.3**)

Section 17 being concerned in the raising of funds (see **4.4.4**)

Section 18 money laundering (see **4.4.5**)

Section 54 weapons training (see **4.3.9**)

Section 56 directing terrorist organization (see **4.2.5**)

Section 57 possession for terrorism purposes (see **4.3.10**)

Section 58 collection of information (see **4.3.11**)

Section 59 inciting terrorism overseas (England and Wales) (see **4.3.5**)

Section 60 inciting terrorism overseas (Northern Ireland)

Section 61 inciting terrorism overseas (Scotland)

Section 62 terrorist bombing (see **5.7.1**)

Section 63 terrorist finance offences (see **5.7.1**)

(Terrorism Act 2000, s 40(1)).

Meanings

Terrorism (see **4.1.1**)

Note

This applies retrospectively and so applies to anyone who has been involved in the commission, instigation, or preparation of terrorism acts before the Terrorism Act 2000 came into force (Terrorism Act 2000, s 40(2)).

4.2 Proscribed Organizations

This section sets out the law relating to proscribed organizations, which can be found in sections 3 and 11–13 of the Terrorism Act 2000. Detailed information on proscribed organizations can be found in **Appendices 1 and 2**.

4.2.1 Proscription procedure

Section 3 of the Terrorism Act 2000 sets out the proscription of organizations. It states that any organization listed in Schedule 2 to the Terrorism Act 2000, or any organization that operates under the same name as one listed in Schedule 2, is proscribed and that the Secretary of State can add to, delete from, or amend the list at any time. A full list of proscribed organizations can be found in **Appendices 1 and 2**.

An **organization** may only be **proscribed** if the Secretary of State believes that the organization is concerned in **terrorism** (Terrorism Act 2000, s 3(4)).

(5) An organisation is concerned in terrorism if it—
   (a) commits or participates in acts of terrorism,
   (b) prepares for terrorism,
   (c) promotes or encourages terrorism, or
   (d) is otherwise concerned in terrorism.

(5A) The cases in which an organisation promotes or encourages terrorism for the purposes of subsection (5)(c) include any case in which activities of the organisation—
   (a) include the unlawful **glorification** of the commission or preparation (whether in the past, in the future or generally) of acts of terrorism; or
   (b) are carried out in a manner that ensures that the organisation is associated with **statements** containing any such glorification.

(5B) The glorification of any conduct is unlawful for the purposes of subsection (5A) if there are persons who may become aware of it who could reasonably be expected to infer that what is being glorified, is being glorified as—
   (a) conduct that should be emulated in existing circumstances, or
   (b) conduct that is illustrative of a type of conduct that should be so emulated.

Terrorism Act 2000, s 3(5), (5A), (5B)

Meanings

Organisation

Includes any association or combination of persons (Terrorism Act 2000, s 121). This is a very wide definition which could be used to describe anything from a large well-organized collection of people to a small gathering of two people.

Proscribed

Outlawed, prohibited.

Terrorism (see 4.1)

Glorification

Includes any form of praise or celebration.

Statement

Includes a communication without words consisting of sounds or images or both (ie includes videos, DVDs, and CDs).

PNLD reference number

D8702

4.2.2 **Membership of proscribed organizations**

Section 11 of the Terrorism Act 2000 creates the offence of being a member of a proscribed organization.

Offence

(1) A person commits an offence if he belongs to or professes to belong to a proscribed organisation.

Terrorism Act 2000, s 11(1)

Points to prove

✓ date and location
✓ belongs/professes to belong to
✓ a proscribed organization

Meanings

Proscribed organisation (see **4.2.1**)

Defence

(2) It is a defence for a person charged with an offence under subsection (1) to prove—

(a) that the organisation was not proscribed on the last (or only) occasion on which he became a member or professed to be a member, and

(b) that he has not taken part in the activities of the organisation at any time while it was proscribed.

Terrorism Act 2000, s 11(2)

The prosecution must prove in the first instance that the person was a member of the proscribed group. The defendant must then prove the defence on the balance of probabilities.

Police powers

Power of arrest under TACT (see **5.3.1**)

Power to stop and search under TACT (see **5.2.1**)

Related cases

Sheldrake v Director of Public Prosecutions; Attorney General's Reference (No 4 of 2002) [2004] UKHL 43 The burden in section 11(2) is an evidential one and not a legal one. In order to make it compliant with Article 6.2 of the European Convention on Human Rights, the burden had to be an evidential type which meant the defence only had to raise it in evidence as an issue as to the matter in question fit for consideration by the court.

R v Hundal and Dhaliwal [2004] EWCA Crim 389 If a person joins an organization in a country where the organization is not proscribed, he still commits an offence if he is a member of that organization when he travels to the UK.

Notes

(a) Section 11(4) lists a number of Acts for which the term 'proscribed' means any of those Acts. Most of those Acts have been or will be repealed, but this Act allows them to be the basis for a prosecution if evidence of membership of a proscribed organization relates to a pre-Act period.

(b) This offence applies to acts done outside the UK regardless of the nationality of the offender (Terrorism Act 2006, s 17) (see **5.7.1**).

(c) This offence can be tried in any place in the UK if it was committed in the UK (Counter-Terrorism Act 2008, s 28).

(d) Notification requirements apply (see **5.7.5**).

(e) See also support of proscribed organization (**4.2.3**) and wearing of uniform (**4.2.4**).

(f) There is a potential appeal under section 7 of the Terrorism Act 2000 which relates to the deproscription procedure therefore it is important to make a note of exact dates and times when the person was allegedly a member of a proscribed organization.

(g) *Post-charge questioning*—sections 22–27 of the Counter-Terrorism Act 2008 make provision for a Crown Court judge to authorize post-charge questioning of a person if the offence is a terrorism offence or the offence has a terrorist connection. This offence is a terrorism offence for the purposes of these provisions. Each authorization lasts for a maximum of 48 hours and runs continuously from the time questioning begins, irrespective of whether the questioning stops during that period. A Code of Practice has been issued for post-charge questioning—Counter-Terrorism Act 2008 (Code of Practice for the Video Recording with Sound of Post-Charge Questioning) Order 2012 and also amendments to PACE Codes of Practice (C, G, and H) (see **Appendices 4 and 7**).

PNLD reference numbers

H3551, D8703, D23729, C2003, C3025, S2048

 DPP/AG consent required: Terrorism Act 2000, s 117 (see **5.7.4**).

 Time limit for prosecution: None.

 Summary: Maximum six months' imprisonment and/or a fine not exceeding the statutory maximum.

 Indictment: Maximum ten years' imprisonment and/or a fine.

4.2.3 **Support of proscribed organizations**

Section 12 of the Terrorism Act 2000 provides for the offences of supporting a proscribed organization. There are three offences created by this section; invite support for a proscribed organization; arrange, manage, or assist in arranging or managing a meeting to support a proscribed organization; or address a meeting in support of a proscribed organization.

Offences

(1) A person commits an offence if—
   (a) he invites support for a **proscribed organisation**, and
   (b) the support is not, or is not restricted to, the provision of money or other property (within the meaning of section 15).
(2) A person commits an offence if he arranges, manages or assists in arranging or managing a **meeting** which he knows is—
   (a) to support a proscribed organisation,
   (b) to further the activities of a proscribed organisation, or
   (c) to be addressed by a person who belongs or professes to belong to a proscribed organisation.
(3) A person commits an offence if he addresses a meeting and the purpose of his address is to encourage support for a proscribed organisation or to further its activities.

Terrorism Act 2000, s 12(1)–(3)

Points to prove

Section 12(1)

- ✓ date and location
- ✓ invited support for
- ✓ proscribed organization
- ✓ other than support with money/other property

Section 12(2)

- ✓ date and location
- ✓ arranged/managed/assisted in arranging/managing a meeting
- ✓ which you knew
- ✓ was to support/further the activities of/be addressed by a person who belonged/professed to belong to
- ✓ a proscribed organization

Section 12(3)

- ✓ date and location
- ✓ addressed a meeting
- ✓ to encourage support for/further activities of
- ✓ a proscribed organization

Meanings

Proscribed organisation (see 4.2.1)

Meeting

Means a meeting of three or more persons, whether or not the public are admitted (Terrorism Act 2000, s 12(5)).

Defence

(4) Where a person is charged with an offence under subsection (2)(c) in respect of a private meeting it is a defence for him to prove that he had no reasonable cause to believe that the address mentioned in (2)(c) would support a proscribed organisation or its activities.

Terrorism Act 2000, s 12(4)

This defence would, for example, cover meetings between a government representative and a member of a proscribed organization.

A meeting is private if the public are not admitted (Terrorism Act 2000, s 12(5)).

Police powers

Power of arrest under TACT (see 5.3.1)

Power to stop and search under TACT (see 5.2.1)

Notes

(a) The offence in section 12(1) is concerned with support 'other than money or other property' as that kind of support is dealt with in section 15 (see **4.4.2**).

(b) The intention behind this offence is to prevent public address and debate which would support and/or further the activities of a proscribed organization.

(c) The provisions on post-charge questioning apply to this offence (see **4.2.2 note (g)**).

(d) This offence can be tried in any place in the UK if it was committed in the UK (Counter-Terrorism Act 2008, s 28).

(e) Notification requirements apply (see **5.7.5**).

(f) See also membership of proscribed organization (**4.2.2**) and wearing of a uniform (**4.2.4**).

PNLD reference numbers

H3552, H3553, H3555, D8704

 DPP✓ AG✓ **DPP/AG consent required:** Terrorism Act 2000, s 117 (see **5.7.4**).

 Time limit for prosecution: None.

Summary: Maximum six months' imprisonment and/or a fine not exceeding the statutory maximum.

 Indictment: Maximum ten years' imprisonment and/or a fine.

4.2.4 **Uniforms**

Section 13 of the Terrorism Act 2000 provides for the offence of wearing a uniform or insignia of a proscribed organization.

Offence

(1) A person in a **public place** commits an offence if he—
   (a) wears an item of clothing, or
   (b) wears, carries or displays an article, in such a way or in such circumstances as to arouse reasonable suspicion that he is a member or supporter of a **proscribed organisation**.

Terrorism Act 2000, s 13(1)

Points to prove

✓ date and location
✓ in a public place
✓ wore an item of clothing/wore/carried/displayed an article
✓ in such way/circumstances as to arouse
✓ reasonable suspicion
✓ that you were a member/supporter
✓ of a proscribed organization

Meanings

Public place

Means a place to which members of the public have or are permitted to have access, whether or not for payment.

Proscribed organisation (see **4.2.1**)

Police powers

Power of arrest under TACT (see **5.3.1**)

Power to stop and search under TACT (see **5.2.1**)

Notes

(a) This offence can only be committed in a public place.
(b) This offence is wider that the one contained in section 1 of the Public Order Act 1936 which covers only the wearing of a uniform. Items such as badges or caps can also be prohibited under section 13.
(c) This offence can be tried in any place in the UK if it was committed in the UK (Counter-Terrorism Act 2008, s 28).
(d) See also membership of proscribed organization (**4.2.2**) and support of proscribed organization (**4.2.3**).

(e) The provisions on post-charge questioning apply to this offence (see **4.2.2 note (g)**).

Related cases

Rankin v Murray (Procurator Fiscal, Ayr) 2004 SLT 1164, 2004 SCCR 422 (HC of Justiciary) (Sc) The wearing of jewellery which prominently bore the initials UVF (Ulster Volunteer Force, a proscribed organization) whilst in a ferry terminal travelling from Belfast to Troon was enough to commit an offence under section 13 of the Terrorism Act 2000 even though there was no evidence to suggest that the person was a member of the organization.

PNLD reference numbers

H3556, H3557, D8705

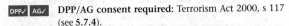 **DPP/AG consent required:** Terrorism Act 2000, s 117 (see **5.7.4**).

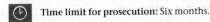 **Time limit for prosecution:** Six months.

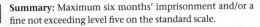 **Summary:** Maximum six months' imprisonment and/or a fine not exceeding level five on the standard scale.

4.2.5 **Directing a terrorist organization**

Section 56 of the Terrorism Act 2000 creates the offence of directing a terrorist organization.

Offence

(1) A person commits an offence if he **directs, at any level**, the activities of an **organisation** which is concerned in the commission of acts of terrorism.

Terrorism Act 2000, s 56(1)

Points to prove

✓ date and location
✓ directed the activities of
✓ an organization
✓ which was concerned in the commission
✓ of acts of terrorism

Meanings

Directs

Not defined in the Act but should be given its ordinary meaning. To give commands, directions, to take charge or control of, to manage, conduct the affairs of. It seems to embody the attributes of being able to order other people and of commanding some obedience from them.

At any level

Not defined in the Act but aims to encompass all those who direct, be it at a local, regional, or national level.

Organisation

Includes any association or combination of persons (Terrorism Act 2000, s 121). This is a very wide definition which could be used to describe anything from a large well-organized collection of people to a small gathering of two people. The offence is not confined to the direction of proscribed organizations.

Terrorism (see 4.1.1)

Police powers

Power of arrest under TACT (see 5.3.1)
Power to stop and search under TACT (see 5.2.1)

Notes

(a) The organization does not have to be proscribed for the commission of this offence.

(b) This offence is aimed at those who do not directly get involved in the commission of acts of terrorism but direct others to do so and who under previous legislation have escaped prosecution.

(c) The offence only relates to the commission (committing) of acts of terrorism and not to their instigation, preparation, or encouragement (see 4.1).

(d) It is the organization that must be involved in the commission of acts of terrorism and not the direction given. Therefore, this is a very wide-ranging offence that would cover orders that are unlawful (eg purchase of firearms) but also those that are lawful, such as directing someone to buy provisions for the terrorist organization.

(e) This offence can be tried in any place in the UK if it was committed in the UK (Counter-Terrorism Act 2008, s 28).

(f) Notification requirements apply (see **5.7.5**).

(g) The provisions on post-charge questioning apply to this offence (see **4.2.2 note (g)**).

(h) Consider confiscation of cash and property under the Proceeds of Crime Act 2002; this offence is specified in Schedule 2 to the Proceeds of Crime Act 2002 as a 'criminal lifestyle offence'.

PNLD reference numbers

H3788, D8742

 DPP/AG consent required: Terrorism Act 2000, s 117 (see **5.7.4**).

 Time limit for prosecution: None.

 Indictment: Life imprisonment.

4.3 Encouragement, Preparation, and Terrorist Training

The Terrorism Act 2006 created various offences that cover actions that may take place before the actual terrorist act is committed, such as encouragement, preparing terrorist acts, possessing certain items, or terrorist training. Further related offences, such as weapons training and incitement, and offences relating to articles and records are included in the Terrorism Act 2000.

4.3.1 Encouragement of terrorism

Section 1 of the Terrorism Act 2006 creates the offence of encouragement of terrorism which covers direct encouragement and indirect encouragement, including glorification of terrorism.

Offence

(1) This section applies to a **statement** that is likely to be understood by some or all of the members of **the public** to whom it is published as a direct or indirect encouragement or other inducement to them to the

commission, preparation or instigation of **acts of terrorism** or **Convention offences**.

(2) A person commits an offence if—

   (a) he **publishes a statement** to which this section applies or causes another to publish such a statement; and

   (b) at the time he publishes it or causes it to be published, he—

      (i) intends members of the public to be directly or indirectly encouraged or otherwise induced by the statement to commit, prepare or instigate acts of terrorism or Convention offences; or

      (ii) is reckless as to whether members of the public will be directly or indirectly encouraged or otherwise induced by the statement to commit, prepare or instigate such acts or offences.

Terrorism Act 2006, s 1(1) and (2)

Points to prove

- ✓ date and location
- ✓ publish/cause another to publish
- ✓ statement that is likely to be understood
- ✓ by some/all members of the public to whom it was published
- ✓ as direct/indirect encouragement/other inducement
- ✓ to commit/prepare/instigate acts of terrorism/Convention offences
- ✓ intending/being reckless as to
- ✓ direct/indirect encouragement/other inducement by the statement
- ✓ to commit/prepare/instigate acts of terrorism/Convention offences

---

Meanings

Statement

References to a statement are references to a communication of any description, including a communication without words consisting of sounds or images or both (Terrorism Act 2006, s 20(6)). This means it also includes images such as videos.

The public

References to the public—

(a) are references to the public of any part of the UK or of a country or territory outside the UK, or any section of the public; and

(b) also include references to a meeting or other group of persons which is open to the public (whether unconditionally or on the making of a payment or the satisfaction of other conditions) (Terrorism Act 2006, s 20(3)).

Publishing a statement

References to a person's publishing a statement are references to—

(a) his publishing it in any manner to the public;

(b) his providing electronically any service by means of which the public have access to the statement; or

(c) his using a service provided to him electronically by another so as to enable or to facilitate access by the public to the statement (Terrorism Act 2006, 20(4)).

The definition in section 20(4)(b) includes internet service providers, the definition in section 20(4)(c) includes those who run websites that contain message boards and those that post messages on such message boards.

Terrorism/act of terrorism (see **4.1**)

Convention offence

Means an offence listed in Schedule 1 to the Terrorism Act 2006 or an equivalent offence under the law of a country or territory outside the UK and includes offences such as causing explosions, hostage-taking, or terrorist fundraising (for a list see **5.7.3**).

Defence

(6) In proceedings for an offence under this section against a person in whose case it is not proved that he intended the statement directly or indirectly to encourage or otherwise induce the commission, preparation or instigation of acts of terrorism or Convention offences, it is a defence for him to show—

  (a) that the statement neither expressed his views nor had his endorsement (whether by virtue of section 3 or otherwise); and

  (b) that it was clear, in all the circumstances of the statement's publication, that it did not express his views and (apart from the possibility of his having been given and failed to comply with a notice under subsection (3) of that section) did not have his endorsement.

Terrorism Act 2006, s 1(6)

The defence applies only if the defendant is alleged to have acted recklessly. The defence is intended, for example, to cover television companies, news broadcasters, and publishers. It imposes an evidential burden on the defendant. The defendant only has to adduce sufficient evidence to raise this defence and it then remains for the prosecution to prove or disprove it. However, the defence does not apply if a person has received a notice under section 3 (eg internet service provider has been required to modify terrorism-related article) and has failed to comply with it, because this is regarded as endorsement of the statement (for details about notices under section 3 see **4.3.3**).

Police powers

Power of arrest under TACT (see 5.3.1)

Power to stop and search under TACT (see 5.2.1)

Notes

(a) This offence has three elements:
- the defendant must publish a statement or cause another to publish a statement (Terrorism Act 2006, s 1(2)(a)),
- the statement must be likely to be understood by some or all members of the public to whom it is published as a direct or indirect encouragement to them to commit or prepare or instigate acts of terrorism or Convention offences (Terrorism Act 2006, s 1(1)), and
- the defendant must have the necessary state of mind when publishing the statement/causing it to be published, he must act intentionally or recklessly (Terrorism Act 2006, s 1(2)(b)).

(b) The requirement of 'members of the public' means that statements made in private are not covered by this offence. However, if the statement is in writing, consider the offence of dissemination of terrorist publication (see **4.3.2**).

(c) *Indirect encouragement/glorification*—statements that are likely to be understood by members of the public as indirectly encouraging the commission or preparation of acts of terrorism or Convention offences include every statement which—
- **glorifies** the commission or preparation (whether in the past, in the future, or generally) of such acts or offences, and
- is a statement from which those members of the public could reasonably be expected to infer that what is being glorified is being glorified as **conduct** that should be emulated by them in existing circumstances (Terrorism Act 2006, s 1(3)).

Glorification, glorify, etc include any form of praise or celebration (Terrorism Act 2006, s 20(2)).

Conduct includes conduct that is illustrative of a type of conduct that should be so emulated (Terrorism Act 2006, s 20(7)).

Section 1(3) gives an example for statements that indirectly encourage terrorism and those that glorify acts of terrorism, but it does not restrict indirect encouragement to glorification. What else might be covered is nowhere explained, and there will, therefore, be a danger that too wide an interpretation will breach rights to free expression under Article 10 as not being 'in accordance with the law'. The offence can be committed by indirectly encouraging terrorism, either by glorifying terrorism, or by indirectly encouraging terrorism in any other way, even if the statement does not fall within section 1(3). In addition, section 1(3)(b) limits indirect encouragement to those statements from which the audience would conclude that they should do something that is similar to what has been glorified and, secondly, that it must be possible for them to carry out such conduct in this day and age ('in existing circumstances'). This means that not every statement that glorifies terrorism is automatically regarded as indirect encouragement. Glorification of distant historical events is therefore unlikely to be caught, although it can be committed by reference to past acts as long as they resonate with the present.

Example: Where it is reasonable to expect members of the public to infer from a statement glorifying the bomb attacks on the London Underground on 7 July 2005 that what should be emulated is action causing severe disruption to London's transport network, this will be caught. This example also shows that the conduct glorified and the conduct to be emulated does not have to be exactly the same, only of the same type.

The inclusion of the expression 'to glorify' was much criticized when the Act was made; it has been regarded as too wide and too vague and the offence as not being sufficiently clearly defined. Some argue that the offence might infringe the freedom of expression and therefore be incompatible with the Human Rights Act 1998.

(d) When determining how a statement is likely to be understood and what members of the public could reasonably be expected to infer from it, both the content of the statement as a whole and the circumstances and manner of its publication have to be considered (Terrorism Act 2006, s 1(4)). This is meant to ensure that the context of a statement is taken into account. It would, therefore, make a difference whether a specific issue is dealt with in an academic thesis or in an inflammatory pamphlet.

(e) It is irrelevant whether the encouragement relates to specific acts of terrorism or Convention offences or to such acts or offences generally and whether anyone is in fact encouraged or induced by the statement (Terrorism Act 2006, s 1(5)). This means that the statement, or how it is likely to be understood, need not relate to specific acts of terrorism or Convention offences and the offence is committed even if no such act or offence has actually taken place.

(f) The offence can be committed *intentionally or recklessly* (s 1(2)(b)). Intention requires that the defendant intends members of the public to be encouraged to commit, prepare, or instigate acts of terrorism or Convention offences. *Recklessness* requires that the defendant is reckless as to the possibility that the statement will have the effect of members of the public being encouraged. 'Reckless' should be interpreted in accordance with current case law on the meaning of recklessness. That means that in order to be reckless the defendant has to be shown to be aware of the risk that an effect of the statement would be to encourage terrorism or Convention offences, and in the circumstances known to him, it was unreasonable for him to take that risk (**R v G and R [2003] UKHL 50**).

(g) For the application of this section to internet activity, etc see **4.3.3**.

(h) The provisions on post-charge questioning apply to this offence (see **4.2.2 note (g)**).

(i) *Extra-territorial jurisdiction*—this offence applies to acts done outside the UK regardless of the nationality of the offender, insofar as the act is committed in relation to the commission, preparation, or instigation of one or more Convention offences, not in respect of acts of terrorism (Terrorism Act 2006, s 17) (see **5.7.1**).

Where an internet service provider established in the UK provides information society services in an EEA state (the EU states, plus Iceland, Lichtenstein, and Norway) other than the UK, refer to the Electronic Commerce Directive (Terrorism Act 2006) Regulations 2007 (SI 2007/1550) (see **4.3.3 note (g)**).

(j) This offence supplements the offences of encouraging or assisting an offender (see **5.8.5.1**). Also consider offences such as soliciting to commit murder (see **5.8.4.2**). The use of the terms 'terrorism' or 'Convention offences' and the use of the terms 'encouragement', 'inducement', and 'glorifies' all cover activity much wider than the incitement of a specific offence. There is an overlap with the offence of dissemination of terrorist publications in section 2 of the Terrorism Act 2006 (see **4.3.2 note (j)**).

(k) This offence can be tried in any place in the UK if it was committed in the UK (Counter-Terrorism Act 2008, s 28).

(l) Notification requirements apply (see **5.7.5**).

(m) *Corporate liability*—for the liability of company directors etc. see section 18 of the Terrorism Act 2006 (see **5.7.2.1**).

PNLD reference numbers

H8450, D18570, C1203

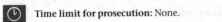 **DPP/AG consent required:** Terrorism Act 2006, s 19 (see **5.7.4**).

Time limit for prosecution: None.

Summary: Maximum six months' imprisonment and/or fine not exceeding the statutory maximum.

Indictment: Maximum seven years' imprisonment and/or fine.

4.3.2 **Dissemination of terrorist publication**

Section 2 of the Terrorism Act 2006 creates the offence of dissemination of terrorist publications.

Offences

(1) A person commits an offence if he engages in conduct falling within subsection (2) and, at the time he does so—

  (a) he intends an effect of his conduct to be a direct or indirect encouragement or other inducement to the commission, preparation or instigation **of acts of terrorism**;

  (b) he intends an effect of his conduct to be the provision of assistance in the commission or preparation of such acts; or

  (c) he is reckless as to whether his conduct has an effect mentioned in paragraph (a) or (b).

(2) For the purposes of this section a person engages in conduct falling within this subsection if he—

  (a) distributes or circulates a **terrorist publication**;

  (b) gives, sells or lends such a **publication**;

  (c) offers such a publication for sale or **loan**;

  (d) provides a service to others that enables them to obtain, read, listen to or look at such a publication, or to acquire it by means of a gift, sale or loan;

> (e) transmits the contents of such a publication electronically; or
> (f) has such a publication in his possession with a view to its becoming the subject of conduct falling within any of paragraphs (a) to (e).
>
> *Terrorism Act 2006, s 2(1) and (2)*

Points to prove

- ✓ date and location
- ✓ distributed/circulated *or*

  gave/sold/lent/offered for sale/loan *or*

  provided a service to others that enabled them to obtain/read/listen to/look at or to acquire by means of gift/sale/loan *or*

  transmitted electronically the contents of *or*

  possessed with a view to it being distributed/circulated/given/sold/lent/offered for sale/loan/being part of a service/being transmitted electronically a terrorist publication
- ✓ at the time of doing so intended/reckless as to
- ✓ effect of conduct being direct/indirect encouragement/other inducement to the commission/preparation/instigation of acts of terrorism *or*

  effect of conduct being the provision of assistance in the commission/preparation of acts of terrorism

---

Meanings

Acts of terrorism (see 4.1.2)

Publication

Means an **article** or **record** of any description that contains any of the following, or any combination of them—

(a) matter to be read;
(b) matter to be listened to;
(c) matter to be looked at or watched (Terrorism Act 2006, s 2(13)).

This means that as well as books this section also covers, amongst other things, films and videos (with or without sound), cassette tapes, electronic books, material contained on CDs and photographs. This definition of publication is different from that provided in section 20 of the Act which applies to section 1 (encouragement of terrorism, see **4.3.1**).

Article

Includes anything for storing data (Terrorism Act 2006, s 20(2)).

Record

Means a record so far as not comprised in an article, including a temporary record created electronically and existing solely in the course of, and for the purposes of, the transmission of the whole or a part of its contents (Terrorism Act 2006, s 20(2).

Terrorist publication

A publication is a terrorist publication, in relation to conduct falling within subsection (2), if matter contained in it is likely—

(a) to be understood, by some or all of the persons to whom it is or may become available as a consequence of that conduct, as a direct or indirect encouragement or other inducement to them to the commission, preparation, or instigation of acts of terrorism; or

(b) to be useful in the commission or preparation of such acts and to be understood, by some or all of those persons, as contained in the publication, or made available to them, wholly or mainly for the purpose of being so useful to them (Terrorism Act 2006, s 2(3)).

Matter that is likely to be understood by a person as indirectly encouraging the commission or preparation of acts of terrorism includes any matter which—

(a) **glorifies** the commission or preparation (whether in the past, in the future or generally) of such acts; and

(b) is matter from which that person could reasonably be expected to infer that what is being glorified is being glorified as conduct that should be emulated by him in existing circumstances (Terrorism Act 2006, s 2(4)).

Glorification, glorify etc

Includes any form of praise or celebration (Terrorism Act 2006, s 20(1)).

On indirect encouragement and glorification see also **4.3.1**.

Lend/loan

Lend includes let on hire, and loan is to be construed accordingly (Terrorism Act 2006, s 2(13)).

Defence

(9) In proceedings for an offence under this section against a person in respect of **conduct to which subsection (10) applies**, it is a defence for him to show—

   (a) that the matter by reference to which the publication in question was a terrorist publication neither expressed his views nor had his endorsement (whether by virtue of section 3 or otherwise); and

   (b) that it was clear, in all the circumstances of the conduct, that that matter did not express his views and (apart from the possibility of his having been given and failed to comply with a notice under subsection (3) of that section) did not have his endorsement.

Terrorism Act 2006, s 2(9)

Conduct to which subsection (10) applies

(10) This subsection applies to the conduct of a person to the extent that—

   (a) the publication to which his conduct related contained matter by reference to which it was a terrorist publication by virtue of subsection (3)(a) (ie matter contained in it was likely to be understood, by some or all of the persons to whom it is or may become available as a consequence of that conduct, as a direct or indirect encouragement or other inducement to them to the commission, preparation, or instigation of acts of terrorism); and

   (b) that person is not proved to have engaged in that conduct with the intention specified in subsection (1)(a) (ie he intends an effect of his conduct to be a direct or indirect encouragement or other inducement to the commission, preparation, or instigation of acts of terrorism).

This means that the defence does *not* apply to an offence committed *intentionally* under section 2(3)(a) (publication is likely to be understood as encouragement or inducement to prepare, instigate, or commit acts of terrorism) or to any offence under *section 2(3)(b)* (publication is likely to be useful for the commission or preparation of such acts).

In relation to the defence in section 2(9), the defendant need only show that the part of the publication which satisfies the test of terrorist publication in section 2(3) did not express his views or have endorsement in order to establish part (a) of the defence.

If a person has received a notice under section 3 (eg an internet service provider has been required to modify a terrorism-related article) and has failed to comply with it, it is regarded as endorsement of the publication, and the defence does not apply (for details about notices under section 3, see **4.3.3**).

Police powers

Power of arrest under TACT (see **5.3.1**)

Power to stop and search under TACT (see **5.2.1**)

Power of search, seizure, and forfeiture of terrorist publications—section 28 of the Terrorism Act 2006 (see **4.3.4**).

Notes

(a) The offence has three elements:
   - there must be a terrorist publication (s 2(3));
   - the person must engage in specific conduct (s 2(2)); and
   - the person must have the necessary state of mind; the offence can be committed recklessly or intentionally (s 2(1)).

(b) For the purposes of this section, the question whether a publication is a terrorist publication in relation to particular conduct must be determined as at the time of that conduct; and having regard both to the contents of the publication as a whole and to the circumstances in which that conduct occurs (s 2(5)). This means that account can be taken of the nature of the bookseller or other disseminator of the publication.

(c) In section 2(1), references to the effect of a person's conduct in relation to a terrorist publication include references to an effect of the publication on one or more persons to whom it is or may become available as a consequence of that conduct (s 2(6)). This means that the effect of a person holding a publication intending to disseminate it later, for example by way of sale, will include the effect on the audience to whom it is intended it will be made available by a later act of dissemination—that is, the sale itself. This is intended to cover the fact that if a person, for example, only holds a publication with the intention of disseminating it, the effect of that conduct is not to encourage terrorism or to be useful to terrorists, because only once the publication is disseminated can it have one of those effects.

(d) The offence covers not only bookshops but also those who sell books and publications over the internet, whether the publication is in hard copy or electronic. It also applies to libraries and the distribution of leaflets and flyers. It is sufficient to possess for distribution (s 2(2)(f)), therefore there is no need in that case to prove actual publication. The offence covers commercial and non-commercial transactions.

(e) The purpose mentioned in section 2(1) (encouragement or inducement to commit, prepare, or instigate acts of terrorism or provision of assistance to commit or prepare such acts) may be one of several. A person may, for example, say that his main purpose is to make money or to help his friend, but at the same time be reckless as to whether his conduct also encourages the commission of acts of terrorism. In that event, he still commits the offence. (Compare **R v Dooley [2005] EWCA Crim 3093** para 14: in this case, on the possession of indecent photographs of a child *with a view to their being distributed*, it was held to be sufficient that one of the purposes of the defendant's actions was the distribution of the photographs.)

(f) The offence is not committed where a person simply possesses a terrorist publication, but under certain circumstances he might commit an offence of 'possession of articles for terrorist purposes' (see **4.3.10**). The expression 'with a view' in section 2(2)(f) means less than a conditional intent, it might even cover a state of mind in which use is merely a contemplated possibility.

(g) It is irrelevant whether anything mentioned in subsections (1)–(4) is in relation to the commission, preparation, or instigation of one or more particular acts of terrorism, of acts of terrorism of a particular description, or of acts of terrorism generally (s 2(7)). Only a part of the publication needs to satisfy the test in section 2(3) for the publication to be a terrorist publication. The whole publication will then be considered a terrorist publication.

(h) It is also irrelevant, in relation to matter contained in any article, whether any person is in fact encouraged or induced by that matter to commit, prepare, or instigate acts of terrorism; or in fact makes use of it in the commission or preparation of such acts (s 2(8)).

(i) This offence can be committed *intentionally or recklessly* (s 1(2)(b)). 'Reckless' should be interpreted in accordance with current case law on the meaning of recklessness (**R v G and R [2003] UKHL 50**). That means in order to be reckless the defendant has to be shown to be aware of the risk that an effect of his conduct would be direct or indirect encouragement or inducement to commit, prepare, or instigate acts of terrorism or provision of assistance to commit or prepare such acts, and in the circumstances known to him, it was unreasonable for him to take that risk. Whether the offence is committed intentionally or recklessly is a matter of importance to sentence (see **Related cases**).

(j) Many cases of dissemination of terrorist publications will also fall under section 1 'encouragement of terrorism' ('publishing a statement' in section 1 includes 'publishing it in any manner to the public', see **4.3.1**). But the definition of 'publication' in section 2 is wider than that of 'statement' in section 1.

(k) For the application of this section to internet activity, etc see **4.3.3**.

(l) The provisions on post-charge questioning apply to this offence (see **4.2.2 note (g)**).

(m) The offence applies to conduct in the UK. It also applies where an internet service provider established in the UK provides information society services in an EEA state (the EU states, plus Iceland, Lichtenstein, and Norway) other than the UK; refer to the Electronic Commerce Directive (Terrorism Act 2006) Regulations 2007 (SI 2007/1550) (see **4.3.3 note (g)**).

(n) This offence can be tried in any place in the UK if it was committed in the UK (Counter-Terrorism Act 2008, s 28).

(o) Notification requirements apply (see **5.7.5**).

(p) *Forfeiture*—section 23A of the Terrorism Act 2000 provides that the court can order the forfeiture of money or other property, on conviction for this and other offences, if the money or property was in the possession or control of the person convicted and it had been used for terrorism purposes, was intended for that use, or the court believed it would be used for that purpose unless forfeited (see **4.4.12**).

(q) *Corporate liability*—for the liability of company directors, etc see section 18 of the Terrorism Act 2006 (see **5.7.2.1**).

Related cases

R v Rahman; R v Mohammed [2008] EWCA Crim 1465 The Court of Appeal recognized that the circumstances in which section 2 can be committed vary widely and that factors relevant to sentence include not only the quality and quantity of publications but also all other circumstances, whether the defendant had intended dissemination of terrorist publications to encourage the commission, preparation, or instigation of acts of terrorism or was merely reckless as to such consequences.

R v Iqbal (Abbas Niazi); R v Iqbal (Ilyas Niazi) [2010] EWCA Crim 3215 AI was arrested at Manchester Airport, intending to travel to Finland. He was found in possession of material in the UK with the relevant mens rea set out in section 2(1)—that the ultimate distribution may have taken place outside the UK is beside the point. The court noted that under section 2(8), it is irrelevant to subsection (2) whether or not anyone was actually encouraged by the material to commit, prepare, or instigate acts of terrorism. The prosecution did not have to prove actual distribution, but the possession of the material with the relevant intent. All of that activity occurred in the UK. (See also **4.3.6**.)

R v Brown [2011] EWCA Crim 2751 B was collecting material on bomb-making and poisoning from the internet and compiling CDs for sale. The CDs were called the 'Anarchist Cookbook' and contained the largest collection of its kind which had yet come to light—contained in two CDs, the printed form would have covered thousands of pages. It was not disputed that the information accumulated would be of practical assistance to a terrorist. Prosecution for the offence did not violate B's right to freedom of expression.

PNLD reference numbers

D18571, D18572, C3028, C3029, C3030, H8451, H8452, H8453, H8454, H8455

DPP✓ AG✓ **DPP/AG consent required:** Terrorism Act 2006, s 19 (see **5.7.4**).

🕐 **Time limit for prosecution:** None.

♿ **Summary:** Maximum six months' imprisonment and/or fine not exceeding the statutory maximum.

▦ **Indictment:** Maximum seven years' imprisonment and/or fine.

4.3.3 Use of the internet for encouragement of terrorism

Section 3 of the Terrorism Act 2006 contains additional provisions concerning the offences of encouragement of terrorism (see **4.3.1**) and dissemination of terrorist publications (see **4.3.2**) applying to the internet and other electronic services. It allows for the service of a notice by a constable, where he believes illegal terrorism-related material is available on a website. The person or persons responsible for that material may be required to secure that the material is not made available to the public or is modified. The effect of the notice is that if the person does not comply, he cannot use the statutory defence and claim that the publication did not have his endorsement (see **4.3.1** and **4.3.2**). But non-compliance is not as such an offence: this is because section 3 is intended as a quick enforcement measure rather than a longer term prosecution measure.

Police powers

(1) This section applies for the purposes of sections 1 and 2 in relation to cases where—

    (a) a **statement** is published or caused to be **published** in the course of, or in connection with, the provision or use of a service provided electronically (section 1); or

    (b) conduct falling within section 2(2) was in the course of, or in connection with, the provision or use of such a service (section 2).

(2) The cases in which the statement, or the **article** or **record** to which the conduct relates, is to be regarded as having the endorsement of a person ('the relevant person') at any time include a case in which:

    (a) a constable has given him a notice under subsection (3);

    (b) that time falls more than two **working days** after the day on which the notice was given; and

    (c) the relevant person has failed, without reasonable excuse, to comply with the notice.

(3) A notice under this subsection is a notice which—

    (a) declares that, in the opinion of the constable giving it, the statement or the article or record is **unlawfully terrorism-related**;

    (b) requires the relevant person to secure that the statement or the article or record, so far as it is so related, is not available to **the public** or is modified so as no longer to be so related;

    (c) warns the relevant person that a failure to comply with the notice within two working days will result in the statement, or the article or record, being regarded as having his endorsement; and

    (d) explains how, under subsection (4), he may become liable by virtue of the notice if the statement, or the article or record, becomes available to the public after he has complied with the notice.

Terrorism Act 2006, s 3(1)–(3)

Meanings

Statement (see **4.3.1**)

Publishing a statement (see **4.3.1**)

Article

Includes anything for storing data (Terrorism Act 2006, s 20(2)).

Record (see 4.3.2)

Working day

Means any day other than a Saturday or a Sunday; Christmas Day or Good Friday; or a day which is a bank holiday under the Banking and Financial Dealings Act 1971 in any part of the UK (Terrorism Act 2006, s 3(9)).

Unlawfully terrorism-related

A statement or an article or record is unlawfully terrorism-related if it constitutes, or if matter contained in the article or record constitutes:

(a) something that is likely to be understood, by any one or more of the persons to whom it has or may become available, as a direct or indirect encouragement or other inducement to the commission, preparation, or instigation of acts of terrorism or Convention offences; or

(b) information which—
   (i) is likely to be useful to any one or more of those persons in the commission or preparation of such acts; and
   (ii) is in a form or context in which it is likely to be understood by any one or more of those persons as being wholly or mainly for the purpose of being so useful (s 3(7)).

Something that is likely to be understood as an indirect encouragement to the commission or preparation of acts of terrorism or Convention offences includes anything which is likely to be understood as—

(a) the **glorification** of the commission or preparation (whether in the past, in the future, or generally) of such acts or such offences; and

(b) a suggestion that what is being glorified is being glorified as conduct that should be emulated in existing circumstances (s 3(8)).

Glorification, glorify etc

Includes any form of praise or celebration (Terrorism Act 2006, s 20(2)). For indirect encouragement and glorification see also 4.3.1.

The public (see 4.3.1)

Notes

(a) The purpose of serving a notice is to achieve the quick removal or modification of unlawful terrorism-related content from the internet. The consequence of non-compliance with the notice is that the person cannot use the statutory defence because the statement or publication is regarded as having his endorsement (see **4.3.1** and **4.3.2**). Non-compliance as such is not an offence in itself.

(b) The power to serve a notice is only available to police officers. It can be initiated by any constable, but in practice (pursuant to the 'Guidance on Notices Issued Under Section 3 of the Terrorism Act 2006', see **note (e)**) it will normally be an officer of the Metropolitan Police Service Counter Terrorist Command (SO15). The notice should be authorized by an officer of Superintendent rank or above after consultation with the ACPO Terrorism & Allied Matters (TAM) police lead, the National Co-ordinator of Special Branch, special branch of any force that might have a direct interest, and also the intelligence services.

(c) The notice must declare that the statement, article, or record in question is unlawfully terrorism-related (s 3(7)) in the view of the constable. This notice requires the relevant person, for example a webmaster, to ensure that the statement, article, or record is removed from public view or amended to ensure that it is no longer unlawfully terrorism-related. The notice must warn the person that he has two working days to comply with the notice, and that failure to do so will lead to that person being regarded as having endorsed the statement, article, or record. Such a notice will also explain how the relevant person may be liable if the statement, article, or record becomes available to the public again, following compliance with the notice. This final element relates to repeat statements (see **note (f)**).

(d) Notices can be served on any person who is involved in the provision or use of electronic services, such as a content provider, hosting internet service provider, webmaster, forum moderator, etc. The notices should mainly be used where material is not removed voluntarily. Where material might be removed voluntarily and there is no suspicion that the potential subject of the section 3 notice is involved in encouraging publication of the material, one should in the first place try to achieve voluntary removal, in particular where the material breaches the terms and conditions under which a service is provided (eg chat room rules, Acceptable Use Policy).

(e) The procedure for giving notices to persons, bodies corporate, firms, and unincorporated bodies or associations is set out in section 4 of the Terrorism Act 2006. Notices have to be given either in person or by recorded delivery. There is further 'Guidance on Notices Issued Under Section 3 of the Terrorism Act 2006' agreed between ACPO and the Internet Service Providers Association which is available on the Home Office Security website, including the question of when a notice should be issued, and the procedure for doing so. This guidance should be consulted before any notice is issued. (See <http://tna.europarchive.org/20100419081706/http://security.homeoffice.gov.uk/news-publications/publication-search/legislation/general/2007-05-24-s3-guidance.pdf?view=Binary>.)

(f) *Repeat statements*—where a notice has been served and the person has complied with it, but subsequently publishes or causes to be published a so-called 'repeat statement' which is (practically) the same or to the same effect as the statement to which the notice related, or to matter contained in the article or record to which it related, the repeat statement is deemed to have the person's endorsement (s 3(4)). It is not necessary to serve another notice on that person in respect of a repeat statement. However, a person is not deemed to have endorsed the statement under two conditions: first, the person has to show that, before the publication of the repeat statement, he had taken every step he reasonably could to prevent a repeat statement from becoming available to the public and to ascertain whether it did. And, secondly, if he was not aware of the publication of the repeat statement, or having become aware of its publication, had taken every step that he reasonably could to secure that it either ceased to be available to the public or was modified so as to be no longer unlawfully terrorism-related (Terrorism Act 2006, s 3(5)–(6)).

(g) Where a service provider established in the UK provides information society services in an EEA state (the EU states, plus Iceland, Lichtenstein, and Norway) other than the UK, refer to the Electronic Commerce Directive (Terrorism Act 2006) Regulations 2007 (SI 2007/1550) and to the Home Office Guidance (see **note (e)**). These Regulations ensure that UK law is compliant with EU law. They limit liability of intermediary internet service providers for offences under sections 1 and 2 (see **4.3.1** and **4.3.2**); they also implement the principle, that, within the EEA, internet services should be regulated by the country where the provider of the services is established.

(h) The Home Office has set up a website for the public to report terrorist-related materials, which may result in enforcement action: <https://www.reporting.direct.gov.uk/>.

PNLD reference numbers

D18573, D18574, D18575

4.3.4 **Search and seizure of terrorist publications**

Section 28 of the Terrorism Act 2006 provides powers for the search, seizure, and forfeiture of terrorist publications. These measures are directed against materials rather than persons, and so the objective is forfeiture rather than evidence-gathering.

Police powers

(1) If a justice of the peace is satisfied that there are reasonable grounds for suspecting that **articles** to which this section applies are likely to be found on any premises, he may issue a warrant authorising a constable—
   (a) to enter and search the **premises**; and
   (b) to seize anything found there which the constable has reason to believe is such an article.

(2) This section applies to an article if—
   (a) it is likely to be the subject of conduct falling within subsection (2)(a) to (e) of section 2 [*offence of dissemination of a terrorist publication, see 4.3.2*]; and
   (b) it would fall for the purposes of that section to be treated, in the context of the conduct to which it is likely to be subject, as a terrorist publication.

(4) An article seized under the authority of a warrant issued under this section—
   (a) may be removed by a constable to such place as he thinks fit; and
   (b) must be retained there in the custody of a constable until returned or otherwise disposed of in accordance with this Act.

Terrorism Act 2006, s 28(1), (2) and (4)

Meanings

Article

Includes anything for storing data (Terrorism Act 2006, s 20(2)).

Premises

Includes any place and in particular, includes—

(a) any vehicle, vessel, aircraft, or hovercraft;

(b) any offshore installation;

(ba) any renewable energy installation; and

(c) any tent or movable structure (Police and Criminal Evidence Act 1984, s 23).

Notes

(a) For the meaning of 'terrorist publication' and details on the offence of dissemination of terrorist publications, see **4.3.2**.

(b) Where an article is seized under this power under the authority of a warrant issued on an information laid by or on behalf of the Director of Public Prosecutions it is liable to forfeiture; and, if forfeited, may be destroyed or otherwise disposed of by a constable in whatever manner he thinks fit (Terrorism Act 2006, s 28(5)).

(c) For details regarding the procedure of seizure and forfeiture of articles refer to Schedule 2 to the Terrorism Act 2006 (not reproduced here).

(d) A person exercising the power conferred by a warrant may use such force as is reasonable in the circumstances for exercising the power (Terrorism Act 2006, s 28(3)).

(e) The power to seize articles attracts additional powers under sections 51 and 55 of the Criminal Justice and Police Act 2001. This enables a bulk of material to be taken away to be read, rather than being examined on the premises, to see if it should be seized. This is needed for cases where large numbers of publications are held at a set of premises. (For details see **5.1.2** (**note (g)**).)

(f) *Counter-Terrorism Act 2008*—sections 1–9 of the Act provide further powers to remove documents for examination etc. See PNLD reference number S1136 to check whether these sections are in force.

PNLD reference number

D18588

4.3.5 **Incite terrorism overseas**

Section 59 of the Terrorism Act 2000 creates the offence of inciting terrorism overseas.

Offences

(1) A person commits an offence if—

  (a) he **incites** another person to commit an act of **terrorism** wholly or partly outside the United Kingdom, and

  (b) the act would, if committed in England and Wales, constitute one of the **offences** listed in subsection **(2)**.

Terrorism Act 2000, s 59(1)

Points to prove

✓ date and location
✓ wholly/partly outside the UK
✓ incited
✓ another
✓ to commit an act of terrorism
✓ which if committed in the UK would constitute
✓ an offence of murder *or*
  an offence under section 18 of the Offences Against the Person Act 1861 *or*
  an offence under section 23 or 24 of the Offences Against the Person Act 1861 *or*
  an offence under section 28 or 29 of the Offences Against the Person Act 1861 *or*
  an offence under section 1(2) of the Criminal Damage Act 1971

Meanings

Incites

The *Oxford English Dictionary* defines it as 'encourage or stir up (violent or unlawful behaviour), urge or persuade to act in a violent or unlawful way'.

Terrorism (see **4.1.1**)

Offences listed in subsection (2)

Those offences are:

(a) murder (see **5.8.4.1**)

(b) an offence under section 18 of the Offences Against the Person Act 1861 (wounding with intent)

(c) an offence under section 23 or 24 of that Act (poisoning)

(d) an offence under section 28 or 29 of that Act (explosions); and

(e) an offence under section 1(2) of the Criminal Damage Act 1971 (endangering life by damaging property).

Police powers

Power of arrest under TACT (see **5.3.1**)

Power to stop and search under TACT (see **5.2.1**)

Notes

(a) It is irrelevant whether or not the person incited is in the UK when the incitement takes place (Terrorism Act 2000, s 59(4)).

(b) There is no criminal liability under this section for anyone acting on behalf of the Crown (Terrorism Act 2000, s 59(5)).

(c) The provisions on post-charge questioning apply to this offence (see **4.2.2 note (g)**).

(d) Section 59 does not really create a new offence but extends jurisdiction for existing offences if they are committed for the purposes of terrorism.

(e) *Forfeiture*—section 23A of the Terrorism Act 2000 provides that the court can order the forfeiture of money or other property, on conviction for this and other offences, if the money or property was in the possession or control of the person convicted and it had been used for terrorism purposes, was intended for that use, or the court believed it would be used for that purpose unless forfeited (see **4.4.12**).

PNLD reference numbers

H3789, D8745

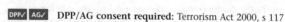 **DPP/AG consent required:** Terrorism Act 2000, s 117 (see **5.7.4**).

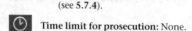 **Time limit for prosecution:** None.

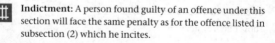 **Indictment:** A person found guilty of an offence under this section will face the same penalty as for the offence listed in subsection (2) which he incites.

4.3.6 **Preparation of terrorist acts**

Section 5 of the Terrorism Act 2006 creates the offence of preparation of terrorist acts. This is intended to cover the steps taken in preparation for the carrying out of a terrorist act, including planning or other forms of preparation, prior to an attempt being made.

Offence

(1) A person commits an offence if, with the intention of—
  (a) committing **acts of terrorism**, or
  (b) assisting another to commit such acts, he engages in any conduct in preparation for giving effect to his intention.

Terrorism Act 2006, s 5(1)

Points to prove

✓ date and location
✓ with the intention of committing/assisting another to commit acts of terrorism
✓ engaged in conduct in preparation for giving effect to your intention

Meanings

Acts of terrorism (see **4.1.2**)

Police powers

Power of arrest under TACT (see **5.3.1**)
Power to stop and search under TACT (see **5.2.1**)

Notes

(a) It is irrelevant whether the intention and preparations relate to one or more particular acts of terrorism, acts of terrorism of a particular description, or acts of terrorism generally (Terrorism Act 2006, s 5(2)). This makes the offence a very broad one.

(b) The offence consists of two elements: a person must have the necessary state of mind, which means he must have the intention to commit acts of terrorism or to assist another to do so, *and* he engages in any conduct in preparation for giving effect to his intentions.

(c) This is essentially an offence of facilitation and adds to existing common law offences of conspiracy to carry out terrorist acts (see **5.8.5.2**), and attempting to carry out such acts (see **5.8.5.5**). With the introduction of this offence more forms of preparatory acts are covered by the criminal law. This offence criminalizes acts at an earlier stage than the offence of attempt within the meaning of the Criminal Attempts Act 1981 which requires that the acts done are more than merely preparatory (see **5.8.5.5**). Conduct constitutes an offence at a stage before an attempted offence would be committed; this is similar to the offence of going equipped to steal (Theft Act 1968, s 25). The offence of conspiracy also requires more, namely that an agreement to commit an offence must have occurred (see **5.8.5.2**). In addition, both offences require that a specific offence is attempted or planned rather than just a general intention to carry out acts that amount to terrorism. The actus reus of this offence is not specific and should be very easy to prove, even if there is not sufficient evidence to prove other criminal offences. The offence emphasizes the intention and criminal thoughts of the offender rather than actions.

(d) Examples: this offence covers acts of preparation with the relevant intention, for example if a person possesses items that could be used for terrorism, even if not immediately, and that person has the necessary intention. It is intended to catch those who, knowing the connection with terrorism and an intention to commit terrorist acts, provide the facilities to do so. Another example of this offence would be if a person buys chemicals to make a poison in order to introduce it into the water supply with the intention to commit murder. He has at that stage not committed attempted murder because his actions would not be regarded as more than merely preparatory to the commission of the offence of murder. However, he intends to do an act that 'creates a serious risk to the health and safety of (a section of) the public'. If this is designed to intimidate the public and if the offender acts for the purpose of advancing a political, religious, racial, or ideological reason, he has committed the offence of preparation of terrorist acts merely by buying the chemicals. Another example might be the provision of accommodation for terrorists knowing they were such.

(e) This offence does not apply to acts done outside the UK; it is not included in section 17 of the Terrorism Act 2006. (See also **5.7.1.1.**)

(f) This offence can be tried in any place in the UK if it was committed in the UK (Counter-Terrorism Act 2008, s 28).

(g) The provisions on post-charge questioning apply to this offence (see **4.2.2 note (g)**).

(h) Notification requirements apply (see **5.7.5**).

(i) *Forfeiture*—section 23A of the Terrorism Act 2000 provides that the court can order the forfeiture of money or other property, on conviction for this and other offences, if the money or property was in the possession or control of the person convicted and it had been used for terrorism purposes, was intended for that use, or the court believed it would be used for that purpose unless forfeited (see **4.4.12**).

(j) Consider also other offences that cover preparatory acts, such as the common law offence of conspiracy to carry out terrorist acts which requires an agreement to commit an offence (see **5.8.5.2**); offences in relation to proscribed organizations (see **4.2.2** and **4.2.3**), in relation to articles (see **4.3.10**), and in relation to collection of information (see **4.3.11**). With regard to forms of assistance wider than these offences, it will often be more difficult to prove intention under section 5(1) since, by definition, there will be no tangible material and/or no tangible link to a proscribed group.

(k) *Corporate liability*—for the liability of company directors, etc see section 18 of the Terrorism Act 2006 (see **5.7.2.1**).

Related cases

R v A [2010] EWCA Crim 1958 Section 5 is expressed in ordinary English language which the jury will be able to apply with appropriate direction. The words of the statute are sufficiently clear to enable a person on proper legal advice and consideration of his own proposed actions to know what he can or cannot do.

R v Iqbal (Abbas Niazi), R v Iqbal (Ilyas Niazi) [2010] EWCA Crim 3215 Section 5 captures preparing in the UK for an act of terrorism to take place abroad.

PNLD reference numbers

H 8456, D18576, C3029, C3031

DPP✓	**DPP consent required:** Terrorism Act 2006, s 19 (see **5.7.4**).
🕐	**Time limit for prosecution:** None.
▥	**Indictment:** Maximum life imprisonment.

4.3.7 **Training for terrorist acts**

Section 6 of the Terrorism Act 2006 creates two offences of terrorist training: providing instruction or training for terrorist acts and receiving such instruction or training. These offences complement the offences of weapons training contained in section 54 of the Terrorism Act 2000 (see **4.3.9**) but allow for criminal prosecution of forms of training unrelated to weapons, such as surveillance or targeting techniques, or the handling of substances which might then be used in attacks.

Offences

(1) A person commits an offence if—

   (a) he provides instruction or training in any of the **skills mentioned in subsection (3)**; and

   (b) at the time he provides the instruction or training, he knows that a person receiving it intends to use the skills in which he is being instructed or trained—

     (i) for or in connection with the commission or preparation of **acts of terrorism** or **Convention offences**; or

     (ii) for assisting the commission or preparation by others of such acts or offences.

(2) A person commits an offence if—

   (a) he receives instruction or training in any of the skills mentioned in subsection (3); and

   (b) at the time of the instruction or training, he intends to use the skills in which he is being instructed or trained—

     (i) for or in connection with the commission or preparation of acts of terrorism or Convention offences; or

     (ii) for assisting the commission or preparation by others of such acts or offences.

Terrorism Act 2006, s 6(1) and (2)

Points to prove

Section 6(1)

✓ date and location

✓ provided training/instruction in a skill mentioned in section 6(3) of the Terrorism Act 2006

✓ knowing that a person receiving it intended to use the skills in which the person was instructed/trained

> ✓ for/in connection with the commission/preparation of acts
> of terrorism/Convention offences *or*
> for assisting the commission/preparation by others of such
> acts/offences
>
> ### Section 6(2)
>
> ✓ date and location
> ✓ received training/instruction in a skill mentioned in section
> 6(3) of the Terrorism Act 2006
> ✓ intending to use the skills in which you were instructed/trained
> ✓ for/in connection with the commission/preparation of acts
> of terrorism/Convention offence *or*
> for assisting the commission/preparation by others of such
> acts/offences

Meanings

Skills mentioned in subsection (3) are:

(a) the making, handling, or use of a **noxious substance**, or of
substances of a description of such substances;

(b) the use of any method or technique for doing anything else
that is capable of being done for the purposes of terrorism, in
connection with the commission or preparation of an act of
terrorism or Convention offence, or in connection with
assisting the commission or preparation by another of such an
act or offence; and

(c) the design or adaptation for the purposes of terrorism, or in
connection with the commission or preparation of an act of
terrorism or Convention offence, of any method or technique
for doing anything (Terrorism Act 2006, s 6(3)).

Noxious substance

Means—

(a) a dangerous **substance**, this is anything which consists or
includes a substance listed in Schedule 5 to the Anti-terrorism,
Crime and Security Act 2001 and anything which is infected
with or otherwise carries any such substance (substances listed
in the Schedule include numerous viruses, bacteria, fungi,
toxins, and animal pathogens); or

(b) any other substance which is hazardous or noxious or which
may be or become hazardous or noxious only in certain
circumstances (Terrorism Act 2006, s 6(7), and Anti-terrorism,
Crime and Security Act 2001, s 58(4)).

Substance

Includes any natural or artificial substance (whatever its origin or method of production and whether in solid or liquid form or in the form of a gas or vapour) and any mixture of substances (Terrorism Act 2006, s 6(7)).

Acts of terrorism (see **4.1.2**)

Convention offence (see **4.3.1**)

Police powers

Power of arrest under TACT (see **5.3.1**)

Power to stop and search under TACT (see **5.2.1**)

Notes

(a) It is irrelevant whether any instruction or training that is provided is provided to one or more particular persons or generally (which may arise through putting materials on a website); whether the acts or offences in relation to which a person intends to use skills in which he is instructed or trained consist of one or more particular acts of terrorism or Convention offences, acts of terrorism or Convention offences of a particular description, or acts of terrorism or Convention offences generally; and whether assistance that a person intends to provide to others is intended to be provided to one or more particular persons or to one or more persons whose identities are not yet known (Terrorism Act 2006, s 6(4)).

(b) Despite section 6(4), it will remain difficult to prove an offence committed by the internet since section 6(1) requires knowledge that the recipient intends to use the learned skills in terrorism. If one does not even know who is receiving the material (as in section 6(4) 'persons whose identities are not yet known'), it will be difficult to establish how they will be using the information for purposes of terrorism. In that case, it might be better to use the offences of encouragement of terrorism (Terrorism Act 2006, s 1) (see **4.3.1**), or dissemination of a terrorism publication (Terrorism Act 2006, s 2) (see **4.3.2**), in connection with section 3 which makes additional provisions relating to those two offences where they are committed by means of the internet (see **4.3.3**).

(c) The range of skills in subsection (3) is very wide, comprising legitimate skills such as flying a plane, and unlawful skills, such as making a bomb to disperse a virus. The latter is an example of the skills relating to the making, handling, or use of a noxious substance, or of substances of a description of such substances (but note that this could also be charged under the offence of weapons training, see **4.3.9**).

(d) An example of a skill relating to the use of any method or technique for doing anything else that is capable of being done for the purposes of terrorism would be a technique for causing a stampede in a crowd; or for the design or adaptation of a method or technique, such as giving instructions about places where a bomb would cause maximum disruption.

(e) The provisions on post-charge questioning apply to this offence (see **4.2.2 note (g)**).

(f) This offence applies to acts done outside the UK regardless of the nationality of the offender insofar as it is committed in relation to the commission, preparation, or instigation of one or more Convention offences (Terrorism Act 2006, s 17) (see **5.7.1.1**). This is important because the places at which terrorist training is taking place are likely to be located abroad rather than in the UK.

(g) This offence can be tried in any place in the UK if it was committed in the UK (Counter-Terrorism Act 2008, s 28).

(h) Notification requirements apply (see **5.7.5**).

(i) *Powers of forfeiture*—where a person is convicted of this offence the court before which the person was convicted may order the forfeiture of anything that has been in the convicted person's possession for purposes connected with this offence. This could, for example, include various noxious substances and equipment designed for the handling, and production, of such substances. Such an order can only come into force when there is no possibility of an appeal against the order which would vary it or set it aside. The court may also make other provisions which are necessary to give effect to the forfeiture, such as about the retention, handling, or destruction of what is forfeited (Terrorism Act 2006, s 7). Also, section 23A of the Terrorism Act 2000 provides that the court can order the forfeiture of money or other property, on conviction for this and other offences, if the money or property was in the possession or control of the person convicted and it had been used for terrorism purposes, was intended for that use, or the court believed it would be used for that purpose unless forfeited (see **4.4.12**). For forfeiture of terrorist cash in general see **4.4.17**.

(j) *Corporate liability*—for the liability of company directors, etc see section 18 of the Terrorism Act 2006 (see **5.7.2.1**).

(k) Also consider the offences of attendance at a place used for terrorist training (see **4.3.8**) and offences regarding weapons training (see **4.3.9**). Certain training may also be encouragement of terrorism (see **4.3.1**), and the provision of instruction could be dissemination of terrorism publications (see **4.3.2**).

PNLD reference numbers

H8457, H8458, D18577, D18578, D10396

 DPP/AG consent required: Terrorism Act 2006, s 19 (see **5.7.4**).

 Time limit for prosecution: None.

 Summary: Maximum six months' imprisonment and/or fine not exceeding the statutory maximum.

 Indictment: Maximum ten years' imprisonment and/or fine.

4.3.8 **Attendance at a place used for terrorist training**

Section 8 of the Terrorism Act 2006 makes it an offence to attend at a place used for terrorist training. This complements the offences of training for terrorist acts and weapons training.

Offence

(1) A person commits an offence if—

    (a) he **attends** at any place, whether in the United Kingdom or elsewhere;

    (b) while he is at that place, **instruction or training of the type mentioned in section 6(1) of this Act** (*training for terrorist acts*) or **section 54(1) of the Terrorism Act 2000** (*weapons training*) is provided there;

    (c) that instruction or training is provided there wholly or partly for purposes connected with the commission or preparation of **acts of terrorism or Convention offences**; and

    (d) the requirements of subsection (2) are satisfied in relation to that person.

(2) The requirements of this subsection are satisfied in relation to a person if—

    (a) he knows or believes that instruction or training is being provided there wholly or partly for purposes connected with the commission or preparation of acts of terrorism or Convention offences; or

(b) a person attending at that place throughout the period of that person's attendance could not reasonably have failed to understand that instruction or training was being provided there wholly or partly for such purposes.

Terrorism Act 2006, s 8(1) and (2)

Points to prove

✓ date and location

✓ attended at a place

✓ while instruction/training of the type mentioned in section 6(1) of the Terrorism Act 2006/section 54(1) of the Terrorism Act 2000 is provided there

✓ wholly or partly for purposes connected with the commission/preparation of

✓ acts of terrorism/Convention offences

✓ knowing/believing yourself *or*
a person attending at that place throughout the period of your attendance could not reasonably have failed to understand

✓ that instruction/training was being provided there

✓ wholly/partly for purposes connected with the commission/preparation of acts of terrorism/Convention offences

Meanings

Attendance

Implies voluntary participation, a purpose or intention of being there. The offence does not extend to a person who has been kidnapped or held against his own will.

Instruction or training of the type mentioned in section 6(1) of the Terrorism Act 2006 (see **4.3.7**)

Instruction or training of the type mentioned in section 54 of the Terrorism Act 2000 (see **4.3.9**)

Acts of terrorism (see **4.1.2**)

Convention offence (see **4.3.1**)

Defences

In order to avoid loopholes in the law, no specific defence to this offence has been included, such as informing the police or attendance for legitimate research purpose. A journalist attending at a camp or a member

151

of a non-governmental organization in a humanitarian capacity would therefore commit the offence. However, police informants and undercover police officers themselves, who would also be caught in the absence of any defence of lawful excuse, will be excused by operation of the refusal of the DPP to consent to a prosecution (see **5.7.4**).

Police powers

Power of arrest under TACT (see **5.3.1**)

Power to stop and search under TACT (see **5.2.1**)

Notes

(a) It is immaterial whether the person concerned receives the instruction or training himself; and whether the instruction or training is provided for purposes connected with one or more particular acts of terrorism or Convention offences, acts of terrorism or Convention offences of a particular description, or acts of terrorism or Convention offences generally (Terrorism Act 2006, s 8(3)).

(b) Instruction or training being provided also includes instruction or training being made available (Terrorism Act 2006, s 8(6)).

(c) Terrorist training for the purposes of this offence is defined by reference to training that may be given under other offences, namely training for terrorism (see **4.3.7**) and weapons training (see **4.3.9**). For an offence to have been committed, all or part of the training in such a place would need to have been provided for purposes connected with terrorism or Convention offences.

(d) The place used for terrorist training can be outside the UK (Terrorism Act 2006, s 8(1)(a)). Also, this offence applies to acts done outside the UK regardless of the nationality of the offender (Terrorism Act 2006, s 17) (see **5.7.1.1**). This is important because the places at which terrorist training is taking place are likely to be located abroad rather than in the UK.

(e) This offence can be tried in any place in the UK if it was committed in the UK (Counter-Terrorism Act 2008, s 28).

(f) Notification requirements apply (see **5.7.5**).

(g) The provisions on post-charge questioning apply to this offence (see **4.2.2 note (g)**).

(h) *Corporate liability*—for the liability of company directors etc see section 18 of the Terrorism Act 2006 (see **5.7.2.1**).

(i) Also consider the offences of training for terrorism (see **4.3.7**) and weapons training (see **4.3.9**).

PNLD reference numbers

H8459, D18579

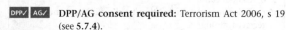 **DPP/AG consent required:** Terrorism Act 2006, s 19 (see **5.7.4**).

Time limit for prosecution: None.

Summary: Maximum six months' imprisonment and/or fine not exceeding the statutory maximum.

Indictment: Maximum ten years' imprisonment and/or fine.

4.3.9 **Weapons training**

Section 54 of the Terrorism Act 2000 deals with weapons training. It makes it an offence to instruct or train another in the making or using of firearms, explosives, or chemical, biological, or nuclear weapons and to receive such instruction or training. In addition to this, inviting another to receive such instruction or training is also an offence under this section.

Offences

(1) A person commits an offence if he **provides instruction** or training in the making or use of—

    (a) **firearms,**

    (aa) **radioactive material** or weapons designed or adapted for the discharge of any radioactive material,

    (b) **explosives,** or

    (c) **chemical, biological** or nuclear weapons.

(2) A person commits an offence if he receives instruction or training in the making or use of—

    (a) firearms,

    (aa) radioactive material or weapons designed or adapted for the discharge of any radioactive material,

    (b) explosives,

    (c) chemical, biological or nuclear weapons.

(3) A person commits an offence if he **invites another to receive instruction or training** and the receipt—

    (a) would constitute an offence under subsection (2), or

    (b) would constitute an offence under subsection (2) but for the fact that it is to take place outside the United Kingdom.

Terrorism Act 2000, s 54 (1)–(3)

Points to prove

✓ date and location
✓ provided/received instruction/training/invited another to receive training
✓ in use/making of
✓ firearms/radioactive material or weapons designed or adapted for the discharge of any radioactive material/explosives/chemical/biological/nuclear weapons

---

Meanings

Provision of instruction

Also includes making it available either generally or to one or more specific persons.

Invitation to receive instruction or training

May be either general or addressed to one or more specific persons (Terrorism Act 2000, s 54(4)).

Firearm

Includes an air gun or air pistol (Terrorism Act 2000, s 121).

Radioactive material

Means radioactive material capable of endangering life or causing harm to human health (Terrorism Act 2000, s 55).

Explosive

Means—

(a) an article or substance manufactured for the purpose of producing a practical effect by explosion,
(b) materials for making an article or substance within paragraph (a),
(c) anything used or intended to be used for causing or assisting in causing an explosion, and
(d) a part of anything within paragraph (a) or (c) (Terrorism Act 2000, s 121).

Chemical weapons are:

(a) **toxic chemicals** and their **precursors**;
(b) munitions and other devices designed to cause death or harm through the toxic properties of toxic chemicals released by them;
(c) equipment designed for use in connection with munitions and devices falling within paragraph (b).

An **object** is not a chemical weapon if the use or intended use is only for permitted purposes; and permitted purposes are—

(a) peaceful purposes;

(b) purposes related to protection against toxic chemicals;

(c) **legitimate military purposes**;

(d) purposes of enforcing the law (Chemical Weapons Act 1996, s 1(1) and (2)).

A toxic chemical

Is a chemical which through its chemical action on life processes can cause death, permanent harm, or temporary incapacity to humans or animals; and the origin, method of production, and place of production are immaterial (Chemical Weapons Act 1996, s 1(5)).

A precursor

Is a chemical reactant which takes part at any stage in the production (by whatever method) of a toxic chemical (Chemical Weapons Act 1996, s 1(6)).

Legitimate military purposes

Are all military purposes except those which depend on the use of the toxic properties of chemicals as a method of warfare in circumstances where the main object is to cause death, permanent harm, or temporary incapacity to humans or animals (Chemical Weapons Act 1996, s 1(4)).

References to an object include references to a substance (Chemical Weapons Act 1996, s 1(7)).

Biological weapon

Means a biological agent or toxin (within the meaning of the Biological Weapons Act 1974) in a form capable of use for hostile purposes or anything to which section 1(1)(b) of that Act applies (Terrorism Act 2000, s 55). Section 1 of the Biological Weapons Act 1974 provides that this means—

(a) any **biological agent** or **toxin** of a type and in a quantity that has no justification for prophylactic, protective, or other peaceful purposes; or

(b) any weapon, equipment, or means of delivery designed to use biological agents or toxins for hostile purposes or in armed conflict (Biological Weapons Act 1974, s 1(1)).

Biological agent

Means any microbial or other biological agent (Biological Weapons Act 1974, s 1(2)).

Toxin

Means any toxin, whatever its origin or method of production (Biological Weapons Act 1974, s 1(2)).

Defences

(5) It is a defence for a person charged with an offence under this section in relation to instruction or training to prove that his action or involvement was wholly for a purpose other than assisting, preparing for or participating in terrorism.

Terrorism Act 2000, s 54(5)

Terrorism (see **4.1**)

This defence covers activities, such as those of HM Armed Forces. The defence is fairly wide; the defendant does not have to prove a lawful purpose, it only needs to be a purpose other than terrorism.

Section 118 of the Terrorism Act 2000 shifts the burden of proof to the prosecution where the defendant adduces evidence that is sufficient to raise this defence (for details see **4.3.10**).

Police powers

Power of arrest under TACT (see **5.3.1**)

Power to stop and search under TACT (see **5.2.1**)

Notes

(a) The offence in section 54(1) does not require a recipient of the training or instruction. It could, therefore, cover someone who makes such information generally available, for example via the internet (see also the offences of encouragement of terrorism, **4.3.1**, and dissemination of terrorist publications, **4.3.2**).

(b) *Extra-territorial jurisdiction*—this offence applies to acts done outside the UK regardless of the nationality of the offender (Terrorism Act 2006, s 17) (see **5.7.1.1**). This is important because such training is likely to take place abroad rather than in the UK.

(c) This offence can be tried in any place in the UK if it was committed in the UK (Counter-Terrorism Act 2008, s 28).

(d) Notification requirements apply (see **5.7.5**).

(e) The provisions on post-charge questioning apply to this offence (see **4.2.2 note (g)**).

(f) *Forfeiture*—section 120A of the Terrorism Act 2000 makes provisions regarding forfeiture of anything that the court considers to have been in the possession of the person for purposes connected with the offence. Also, section 23A of the Terrorism Act 2000 provides that the court can order the forfeiture of money or other property, on conviction for this and other offences, if the money or property was in the possession or control of the person convicted and it had been used for terrorism purposes, was intended for that use, or the court believed it would be used for that purpose unless forfeited (see **4.4.12**). For forfeiture of terrorist cash in general see **4.4.17**.

(g) Also consider the offences of 'training for terrorism' (see **4.3.7**) and 'attendance at a place of terrorist training' (see **4.3.8**).

PNLD reference numbers

H 3785, H 3786, H 3787, D8741, D22143, D20357

DPP✓ AG✓ **DPP/AG consent required:** Terrorism Act 2000, s 117 (see **5.7.4**).

🕐 **Time limit for prosecution:** None.

♿ **Summary:** Maximum six months' imprisonment and/or fine not exceeding the statutory maximum.

▦ **Indictment:** Maximum ten years' imprisonment and/or fine.

4.3.10 **Possession of articles for terrorist purposes**

Section 57 of the Terrorism Act 2000 makes it an offence to possess articles connected with an act of terrorism.

Offence

(1) A person commits an offence if he possesses an **article** in circumstances which give rise to a reasonable suspicion that his possession is for a **purpose connected with** the commission, preparation or instigation of an **act of terrorism**.

Terrorism Act 2000, s 57(1)

Points to prove

✓ date and location
✓ possess article
✓ in suspicious circumstances
✓ purpose of the commission/preparation/instigation of act of terrorism

---

Meanings

Article

Includes substance and any other thing (Terrorism Act 2000, s 121).

For a purpose connected with terrorism

Requires a direct connection between the article and the act of terrorism. See **R v Zafar, Butt, Iqbal, Raja and Malik** (see **Related cases**).

Act of terrorism (see **4.1.2**)

Defence

(2) It is a defence for a person charged with an offence under this section to prove that his possession of the article was not for a purpose connected with the commission, preparation or instigation of an act of terrorism.

Terrorism Act 2000, s 57(2)

Section 118 of the Terrorism Act 2000 shifts the burden of proof to the prosecution where the defendant adduces evidence that is sufficient to raise this defence. It imposes an evidential burden on the accused.

If the person adduces evidence which is sufficient to raise an issue with respect to the matter, the court or jury shall assume that the defence is satisfied unless the prosecution proves beyond reasonable doubt that it is not (Terrorism Act 2000, s 118(2)).

The effect of this section is that, if a defendant adduces evidence to raise this defence, the burden of proof shifts to the prosecution of proving beyond reasonable doubt that the possession of the article was held for such purpose. That means that once the issue is raised by the accused, it remains for the prosecution to prove or disprove it.

Police powers

Power of arrest under TACT (see **5.3.1**)

Power to stop and search under TACT (see **5.2.1**)

Notes

(a) *Burden of proof*—there is a special provision regarding the burden of proof for some elements of this offence:

In proceedings for an offence under this section, if it is proved that an article—

   (a) was on any premises at the same time as the accused, or

   (b) was on premises of which the accused was the occupier or which he habitually used otherwise than as a member of the public, the court may assume that the accused possessed the article, unless he proves that he did not know of its presence on the premises or that he had no control over it (Terrorism Act 2000, s 57(3)).

Where the prosecution adduces evidence regarding the article being on premises, the court may make the assumption that the accused possessed the article unless the accused proves that he did not know of its presence or had no control over it. However, the accused then only has to adduce evidence which is sufficient to raise the issue whether he knew of the presence of the article or had control over it; it is then for the prosecution to disprove this beyond reasonable doubt (Terrorism Act 2000, s 118(4)). The issue remains for the prosecution to prove or disprove. This eases the evidential burden placed on the accused. He is simply required to raise the issue; this negates the presumption in the statute unless the prosecution can prove otherwise.

(b) *Extra-territorial jurisdiction*—this offence applies to acts done outside the UK if it is committed by a UK national or a UK resident (Terrorism Act 2000, s 63A(1)) (see also **5.7.1.4**).

(c) The possession of documentation may also fall within section 58 of the Terrorism Act 2000, to 'make/possess records or information useful to an act of terrorism' (see **R v Rowe** in Related cases and **4.3.11**). Actions that might have been prosecuted under this offence might now be prosecuted under the Terrorism Act 2006, for example 'publishing statements to encourage terrorism' (see **4.3.1**), 'preparation of terrorism acts' (see **4.3.6**), or 'training for terrorism' (see **4.3.7**). The courts accept that there is overlap between sections 57 and 58, although there are important differences in wording between them.

(d) This offence can be tried in any place in the UK if it was committed in the UK (Counter-Terrorism Act 2008, s 28).

(e) *Forfeiture*—section 120A of the Terrorism Act 2000 provides that the court may order the forfeiture of any article that is the subject matter of the offence. Also, section 23A of the Terrorism Act 2000 provides that the court can order the forfeiture of money or other property, on conviction for this and other offences, if the money or property was in the possession or control of the person convicted and it had been used for terrorism purposes, was intended for that use, or the court believed it would be used for that purpose unless forfeited (see **4.4.12**).

(f) Notification requirements apply (see **5.7.5**).

(g) The provisions on post-charge questioning apply to this offence (see **4.2.2 note (g)**).

Related cases

R v Zafar, Butt, Iqbal, Raja and Malik [2008] EWCA Crim 184 The connection between the article and the intended acts of terrorism is very important. The phrase 'for a purpose in connection with' is so imprecise that it could lead to uncertainty of the law, therefore, it has to be interpreted in a way that requires a direct connection between the article and the act of terrorism. Section 57(1) should be read: 'A person commits an offence if he possesses an article in circumstances which give rise to a reasonable suspicion that *he intends it to be used for the purpose of* the commission, preparation, or instigation of an act of terrorism.' An example where there is a direct and obvious connection is an article that is intended to be incorporated in a bomb or used as an ingredient of explosives designed for an act of terrorism.

Possessing a document for the purpose of inciting other persons to commit an act of terrorism is sufficient; an indirect connection between possession of the item and potential terrorist acts is not. Examples: possessing an airline ticket to fly to a foreign country to take part in terrorist training would not be an offence. It has to be proved that the purpose of possessing the article is to incite another person to commit acts of terrorism.

R v Rowe [2007] EWCA Crim 635 Documents and records, such as books and computer discs, can be 'articles' for the purpose of this offence. The court held that there is an overlap between this offence in section 57 and the offence in section 58 of the Terrorism Act 2000 but they deal with different characteristics of terrorist-related activities.

Section 57 deals with the possession of articles *for the purpose of terrorist acts* and section 58 with the collection or keeping of information *of a kind likely to be useful* to those involved in acts of terrorism. Only section 57 requires specific intent.

R v G, R v J [2009] UKHL 13 The House of Lords explained several issues regarding the offences in sections 57 and 58. For the offence in section 58(1), it must be proved that the defendant had control of a record which contained information which by its very nature was likely to provide practical assistance to a person committing or preparing an act of terrorism, knew that he had the record, and knew the kind of information which it contained. The offence in section 57(1) ('any article') covers far more items than section 58 ('a record'). It must be proved that the defendant possessed the article in question: that means he knew he had the article and that he had control of it. Section 57(3) allows assumptions to be made about the possession, unless the defendant adduces evidence to show that he did not know of the presence of the article or had no control over it. Further, it must be proved that the circumstances in which the defendant possessed the article gave rise to reasonable suspicion that his possession was for a purpose connected with the commission, preparation, or instigation of an act of terrorism. In contrast to section 58(1), the circumstances of the possession are a crucial element of the offence. The defendant is then given a defence under section 57(2). Most people will not have a lawful reason for possessing an explosive as such, but some may have a perfectly good reason for having a bag of fertilizer. There is an overlap between section 57(1) and section 58(1) and the difference lies in the scope of the offences (s 57—possession; s 58—collecting or making record) with section 57 applying to any 'article', widely defined, and section 58 to information of a certain kind contained in 'documents and records'. Because section 57 is so wide, it only applies to possession in certain circumstances; by contrast, section 58 covers information of a particular kind, therefore the nature of the information is the important element. The decision in **R v Rowe (2007)** is correct.

PNLD reference numbers

H3779, D8743, D8751, D8752, D20357, C1797, C1446, C2118

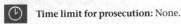 **DPP/AG consent required:** Terrorism Act 2000, s 117 (see **5.7.4**).

Time limit for prosecution: None.

Summary: Maximum six months' imprisonment and/or a fine not exceeding the statutory maximum.

Indictment: Maximum 15 years' imprisonment and/or fine.

For offences committed before 13 April 2006: maximum ten years' imprisonment and/or fine.

4.3.11 **Collection of information**

Section 58 of the Terrorism Act 2000 provides offences relating to the collection of information which may be useful to someone who commits or prepares acts of terrorism.

> ### Offence
>
> (1) A person commits an offence if—
>   (a) he collects or makes a **record** of information of a kind likely to be useful to a person committing or preparing an **act of terrorism**, or
>   (b) he possesses a document or record containing information of that kind.
>
> *Terrorism Act 2000, s 58(1)*

Points to prove

✓ date and location
✓ collect/make record of or possess document/record containing
✓ information likely to be useful to a person committing/preparing an act of terrorism

---

Meanings

Record

Includes a photographic or electronic record (Terrorism Act 2000, s 58(2)).

Act of terrorism (see 4.1.2)

> ### Defence
>
> (3) It is a defence for a person charged with an offence under this section to prove that he had a reasonable excuse for his action or possession.
>
> *Terrorism Act 2000, s 58(3)*

Section 118 of the Terrorism Act 2000 shifts the burden of proof to the prosecution where the defendant adduces evidence that is sufficient to raise this defence (for details see **4.3.10**). See also **R v F** in **Related cases**.

Police powers

Power of arrest under TACT (see **5.3.1**)

Power to stop and search under TACT (see **5.2.1**)

Notes

(a) *Extra-territorial jurisdiction*—this offence applies to acts done outside the UK if it is committed by a UK national or a UK resident (Terrorism Act 2000, s 63A(1)) (see also **5.7.1**).

(b) This offence can be tried in any place in the UK if it was committed in the UK (Counter-Terrorism Act 2008, s 28).

(c) Notification requirements apply (see **5.7.5**).

(d) The provisions on post-charge questioning apply to this offence (see **4.2.2 note (g)**).

(e) *Forfeiture*—section 120A of the Terrorism Act 2000 makes provision regarding forfeiture. It provides that the court may order the forfeiture of any document or record containing information of the kind mentioned in subsection (1)(a). Also, section 23A of the Terrorism Act 2000 provides that the court can order the forfeiture of money or other property, on conviction for this and other offences, if the money or property was in the possession or control of the person convicted and it had been used for terrorism purposes, was intended for that use, or the court believed it would be used for that purpose unless forfeited (see **4.4.12**).

(f) Consider also the offence of possessing articles in connection with an act of terrorism in section 57 of the Terrorism Act 2000 (see **4.3.10 note (c)** and **R v Rowe**). Where documents encourage the commission of acts of terrorism consider the offence of encouragement of terrorism (see **4.3.1**), and the offence of dissemination of terrorist publications (see **4.3.2**).

Related cases

R v K [2008] EWCA Crim 185 This case interpreted the meaning of 'information of a kind likely to be useful to persons committing or preparing acts of terrorism'. The literature must be, on the face of the document, wholly or mainly useful to terrorism. Section 58 could not catch, for example, the *A–Z of London* even if it might be used by suicide bombers. The literature must be intrinsically relevant to the commission or preparation of terrorism.

R v F [2007] EWCA Crim 243 It is not a reasonable excuse for the possession of documents for the purposes of section 58(3) that the documents originated as part of an effort to change an illegal or undemocratic regime. For more on this case and foreign government, see also **4.1**.

R v Rowe [2007] EWCA Crim 635 Guidance on prosecutions under sections 57 and 58 of the Terrorism Act 2000 (see **4.3.10**).

R v G, R v J [2009] UKHL 13 Interpretation of sections 57 and 58 of the Terrorism Act 2000 (see **4.3.10**).

R v Muhammed [2010] EWCA Crim 227 The submission that there should be a narrow interpretation of the words 'information of a kind likely to be useful to a person committing or preparing an act of terrorism' in section 58(1)(a) was rejected. Trying to draw distinctions between the various stages of preparation would bring an unnecessary and unjustified complication into cases under section 58. Nor did the fact that the document might be useful to persons other than terrorists mean that it fell outside section 58. The relevant information had to be such as to call for an explanation pursuant to section 58(3).

R v AY [2010] EWCA Crim 762 A defence of reasonable excuse advanced under section 58(3) had to be left to the jury unless it was quite plain that it was incapable of being held by any jury to be reasonable.

R v Brown [2011] EWCA Crim 2751 B was collecting material on bomb-making and poisoning from the internet and compiling CDs for sale. For details see **4.3.2**. The question whether B had a reasonable excuse on the basis of the exercise of the right to freedom of speech or freedom of expression, may be left to the jury.

PNLD reference numbers

H3780, H3781, H3793, D8744, D20357, C1818, C1441, C1446, C2118, C2397, C2459, C3030

| DPP✓ | AG✓ | **DPP/AG consent required:** Terrorism Act 2000, s 117 (see **5.7.4**). |

Time limit for prosecution: None.

Summary: Maximum six months' imprisonment and/or fine not exceeding the statutory maximum.

Indictment: Maximum ten years' imprisonment and/or fine.

4.3.12 **Eliciting, publishing, or communicating information about members of the armed forces, etc**

Section 58A of the Terrorism Act 2000 makes it an offence to elicit, publish, or communicate information about members of the armed forces or of the intelligence services or constables.

Offence

(1) A person commits an offence who—

    (a) elicits or attempts to elicit information about an individual who is or has been—

        (i) a member of Her Majesty's forces,

        (ii) a member of any of the **intelligence services**, or

        (iii) a constable,

which is of a kind likely to be useful to a person committing or preparing an **act of terrorism**, or

    (b) publishes or communicates any such information.

Terrorism Act 2000, s 58A(1)

Points to prove

✓ date and location

✓ elicited/attempted to elicit/published/communicated

✓ information about

✓ an individual who is/has been a member of Her Majesty's forces/member of any of the intelligence services/constable

✓ which was of a kind likely to be useful to a person committing/preparing an act of terrorism

Meanings

Intelligence services

Means the Security Service, the Secret Intelligence Service, and GCHQ (within the meaning of section 3 of the Intelligence Services Act 1994) (Terrorism Act 2000, s 58A(4)).

Act of terrorism (see 4.1.2)

> ### Defence
>
> (2) It is a defence for a person charged with an offence under this section to prove that they had a reasonable excuse for their action.
>
> *Terrorism Act 2000, s 58A(2)*

The defence in section 58A(2) must be read with section 118, the effect of which is to limit the burden on the accused to an evidential burden, so that if that person adduces evidence sufficient to raise an issue with respect to this defence, the prosecution must then prove beyond reasonable doubt that there is no such defence.

Police powers

Power of arrest under TACT (see 5.3.1)

Power to stop and search under TACT (see 5.2.1)

Notes

(a) The offence was not created to cover journalists, whistle-blowers, or plane spotters; they would normally be covered by the defence in section 58A(2). It is designed to catch those who are taking steps to target police and security officers, for example by gathering information about the person's house, car, routes to work, and other movements. One reason for introducing the offence was the Birmingham plots to kidnap and murder members of the armed forces.

(b) Home Office Circular 12/2009 'Photography and Counter-Terrorism legislation' provides additional information with regard to photography and using the powers under this section. It states that 'legitimate' journalistic activity (such as covering a demonstration for a newspaper) is likely to constitute such an excuse. Similarly, an innocent tourist or other sightseer taking a photograph of a police officer is likely to have a reasonable excuse.

(c) The phrase 'likely to be useful to a person committing or preparing an act of terrorism' should be interpreted in accordance with case law on sections 57 and 58 (**R v Zafar, Butt, Iqbal, Raja and Malik** and **R v Rowe**) (see **4.3.10** and **4.3.11**). There must be a reasonable suspicion that the information was intended to be used to assist in terrorism (Home Office Minister Tony McNulty, House of Commons Committee stage).

(d) The provisions on post-charge questioning apply to this offence (see **4.2.2 note (g)**).

(e) *Extra-territorial jurisdiction*—this offence applies to acts done outside the UK if they are committed by a UK national or a UK resident (Terrorism Act 2000, s 63A(1)) (see also **5.7.1**).

(f) This offence can be tried in any place in the UK if it was committed in the UK (Counter-Terrorism Act 2008, s 28).

(g) Notification requirements apply (see **5.7.5**).

(h) *Forfeiture*—section 120A of the Terrorism Act 2000 makes provision regarding forfeiture. It provides that the court may order the forfeiture of any document or record containing information of the kind mentioned in subsection (1)(a). Also, section 23A of the Terrorism Act 2000 provides that the court can order the forfeiture of money or other property, on conviction for this and other offences, if the money or property was in the possession or control of the person convicted and it had been used for terrorism purposes, was intended for that use, or the court believed it would be used for that purpose unless forfeited (see **4.4.12**).

PNLD reference numbers

H6742, H6743, D20367, D21572

 DPP/AG consent required: Terrorism Act 2000, s 117 (see **5.7.4**).

 Time limit for prosecution: None.

 Summary: Maximum six months' imprisonment and/or fine not exceeding the statutory maximum.

Indictment: Maximum ten years' imprisonment and/or fine.

4.4 **Terrorist Property and Finance**

Part III of the Terrorism Act 2000 and Parts I and II of and Schedules 1 and 3 to the Anti-terrorism, Crime and Security Act 2001 provide for terrorist property and finance. These provisions are in addition to the normal powers of seizure under the Proceeds of Crime Act

2002 and powers to freeze property pursuant to UN and European Union law.

4.4.1 Definition and interpretation of terrorist property

Section 14 of the Terrorism Act 2000 provides the definition of terrorist property.

(1) In this Act 'terrorist property' means—
    (a) money or other property which is likely to be used for the purposes of **terrorism** (including any resources of a **proscribed organisation**),
    (b) proceeds of the commission of acts of terrorism, and
    (c) proceeds of acts carried out for the purposes of terrorism.

(2) In subsection (1)—
    (a) a reference to proceeds of an act includes a reference to any property which wholly or partly, and directly or indirectly, represents the proceeds of the act (including payments or other rewards in connection with its commission), and
    (b) the reference to an organisation's resources includes a reference to any money or other property which is applied or made available, or is to be applied or made available, for use by the organisation.

Terrorism Act 2000, s 14

Meanings

Terrorism (see **4.1.2**)

Proscribed

Outlawed, prohibited.

Organisation

Includes any association or combination of persons (Terrorism Act 2000, s 121). This is a very wide definition which could be used to describe anything from a large well-organized collection of people to a small gathering of two people.

Proscribed organisation (see **4.2.1**)

Notes

(a) The definition in section 14(1) comes into play in section 18 (money laundering, see **4.4.5**) and the subsection makes it clear that terrorist property can include both property to be used for terrorism and the proceeds of acts of terrorism.

(b) This section clarifies that the proceeds of an act of terrorism cover not only the money stolen in, for example, a terrorist robbery but also any money paid in connection with the commission of terrorist acts.

(c) This section also states that not only any use of resources for bomb-making or arms purchase etc but also money set aside for other purposes, such as paying rent and supporting the families of prisoners, is included.

PNLD reference number

D8706

4.4.2 **Fundraising**

Section 15 of the Terrorism Act 2000 provides for the offences of fundraising.

Offences

(1) A person commits an offence if he—
   (a) invites another to **provide money or other property**, and
   (b) intends that it should be used, or has reasonable cause to suspect that it may be used, for the purposes of **terrorism**.
(2) A person commits an offence if he—
   (a) receives money or other **property**, and
   (b) intends that it should be used, or has reasonable cause to suspect that it may be used, for the purposes of terrorism.
(3) A person commits an offence if he—
   (a) provides money or other property, and
   (b) knows or has reasonable cause to suspect that it will or may be used for the purposes of terrorism.

Terrorism Act 2000, s 15(1)–(3)

Points to prove

Section 15(1) and (2)

✓ date and location
✓ invited another to provide/received/provided
✓ money/other property
✓ intending that it should be used *or*
  having reasonable cause to suspect that it might be used
✓ for the purposes of terrorism

Section 15(3)

✓ date and location
✓ provided
✓ money/property
✓ knowing/having reasonable cause to suspect
✓ it would/might be used
✓ for the purposes of terrorism

Meanings

Provision of money or other property

Is a reference to its being given, lent, or otherwise made available, whether or not for consideration (Terrorism Act 2000, s 15(4)).

Terrorism (see **4.1**)

Property

Includes property wherever situated and whether real or personal, heritable (inheritable), or moveable, and things in action (eg copyright, trademark, rights of repayment of loaned money) and other intangible (eg goodwill of business) or incorporeal property (eg mortgages, leases, etc) (Terrorism Act 2000, s 121).

Defences

There are four defences to the offences contained in sections 15–18 of the Terrorism Act 2000 (see **4.4.8**).

Police powers

Power of arrest under TACT (see **5.3.1**)

Power to stop and search under TACT (see **5.2.1**)

Notes

(a) A forfeiture order may also be made when sentencing for this offence (see **4.4.12**).

(b) When a disclosure is made to a constable under this section then they must inform a member of the Serious Organised Crime Agency as soon as practicable (s 21C).

(c) This offence applies to acts done outside the UK by any person (see **5.7.1**).

(d) This offence can be tried in any place in the UK if it was committed in the UK (Counter-Terrorism Act 2008, s 28).

(e) Notification requirements apply (see **5.7.5**).

(f) The provisions on post-charge questioning apply to this offence (see **4.2.2 note (g)**).

PNLD reference numbers

H3558, H3559, H3560, D8707

 DPP/AG consent required: Terrorism Act 2000, s 117 (see **5.7.4**).

 Time limit for prosecution: None.

 Summary: Maximum six months' imprisonment and/or fine not exceeding the statutory maximum.

 Indictment: Maximum 14 years' imprisonment and/or fine.

4.4.3 Using money and property for terrorism

Section 16 of the Terrorism Act 2000 creates the offence of using or possessing money or property for the purposes of terrorism.

Offences

(1) A person commits an offence if he uses money or other **property** for the purposes of **terrorism**.

(2) A person commits an offence if he—

    (a) possesses money or other property, and

    (b) intends that it should be used, or has reasonable cause to suspect that it may be used, for the purposes of terrorism.

Terrorism Act 2000, s 16

Points to prove

Section 16(1)

✓ date and location
✓ used
✓ money/property
✓ for the purposes of terrorism

Section 16(2)

✓ date and location
✓ possessed
✓ money/property
✓ intending/having reasonable cause to suspect that it might be used
✓ for the purposes of terrorism

Meanings

Property (see **4.4.2**)

Terrorism (see **4.1.2**)

Defences

There are four defences to the offences contained in sections 15–18 of the Terrorism Act 2000 (see **4.4.8**).

Police powers

Power of arrest under TACT (see **5.3.1**)

Power to stop and search under TACT (see **5.2.1**)

Notes

(a) This offence applies to acts done outside the UK by any person (see **5.7.1**).

(b) This offence can be tried in any place in the UK if it was committed in the UK (Counter-Terrorism Act 2008, s 28).

(c) Notification requirements apply (see **5.7.5**).

(d) A forfeiture order may also be made when sentencing for this offence (see **4.4.12**).

(e) When a disclosure is made to a constable under this section then they must inform a member of the Serious Organised Crime Agency as soon as practicable (s 21C).

(f) The provisions on post-charge questioning apply to this offence (see **4.2.2 note (g)**).

Related cases

R (on the application of O'Driscoll) v Secretary of State for the Home Department [2002] EWHC 2477 In order to prove an offence under section 16 of the Terrorism Act 2000, specific intent or state of mind must be proved. If the organization was properly proscribed under section 3 of the same Act, then section 16 is proportionate and compatible with human rights.

PNLD reference numbers

H3561, H3562, D8708, C3035

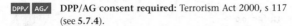 **DPP/AG consent required:** Terrorism Act 2000, s 117 (see **5.7.4**).

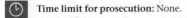 **Time limit for prosecution:** None.

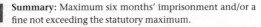 **Summary:** Maximum six months' imprisonment and/or a fine not exceeding the statutory maximum.

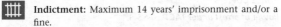 **Indictment:** Maximum 14 years' imprisonment and/or a fine.

4.4.4 Arranging availability of money and property for use in terrorism

Section 17 of the Terrorism Act 2000 details the offence of arranging funds or property for the purposes of terrorism.

Offence

(1) A person commits an offence if—
   (a) he enters into or becomes concerned in an arrangement as a result of which money or other **property** is made available or is to be made available to another, and
   (b) he knows or has reasonable cause to suspect that it will or may be used for the purposes of **terrorism**.

Terrorism Act 2000, s 17(1)

Points to prove

✓ date and location
✓ entered into/became concerned in arrangement
✓ whereby money/property was/was to be made available to
✓ another person knowing/having reasonable cause to suspect
  it would/might be used
✓ for the purposes of terrorism

Meanings

Property (see 4.4.2)

Terrorism (see 4.1.2)

Defences

There are four defences to the offences contained in sections 15–18 of the Terrorism Act 2000 (see **4.4.8**).

Police powers

Power of arrest under TACT (see 5.3.1)

Power to stop and search under TACT (see 5.2.1)

Notes

(a) This offence covers those who instigate an arrangement and also those who become involved in an existing arrangement.

(b) When a disclosure is made to a constable under this section then they must inform a member of the Serious Organised Crime Agency as soon as practicable (s 21C).

(c) A forfeiture order may also be made when sentencing for this offence (see **4.4.12**).

(d) Notification requirements apply (see **5.7.5**).

(e) This offence applies to acts done outside the UK by any person (see **5.7.1**).

(f) This offence can be tried in any place in the UK if it was committed in the UK (Counter-Terrorism Act 2008, s 28).

(g) The provisions on post-charge questioning apply to this offence (see **4.2.2 note (g)**).

PNLD reference numbers

H3563, D8709

DPP/AG consent required: Terrorism Act 2000, s 117 (see **5.7.4**).

 Time limit for prosecution: None.

 Summary: Maximum six months' imprisonment and/or a fine not exceeding the statutory maximum.

 Indictment: Maximum 14 years' imprisonment and/or a fine.

4.4.5 **Facilitate retention or control of terrorist property/money laundering**

Section 18 of the Terrorism Act 2000 creates the offence of laundering terrorist property for the purposes of terrorism.

Offence

(1) A person commits an offence if he enters into or becomes concerned in an arrangement which facilitates the retention or control by or on behalf of another person of **terrorist property**—

    (a) by concealment,

    (b) by removal from the jurisdiction,

    (c) by transfer to nominees, or

    (d) in any other way.

Terrorism Act 2000, s 18(1)

Points to prove

✓ date and location

✓ entered into/concerned in an arrangement

✓ for retention/control by/on behalf of another

✓ of terrorist property

✓ by concealment/removal from jurisdiction/transfer to nominee/other means

Meanings

Terrorist property (see **4.4.2**)

Defences

It is a defence for a person charged with an offence under subsection (1) to prove that he did not know and had no reasonable cause to suspect that the arrangement related to terrorist property.

Terrorism Act 2000, s 18(2)

The burden of proof is on the defendant to prove that he did not know or had no reasonable cause to suspect that the arrangement related to terrorist property.

There are four other defences to the offences contained in sections 15–18 of the Terrorism Act 2000 (see **4.4.8**).

Police powers

Power of arrest under TACT (see **5.3.1**)

Power to stop and search under TACT (see **5.2.1**)

Notes

(a) This offence covers funding used directly for terrorism purposes but also covers funding which is not directly linked to terrorism, such as payment to relatives of paramilitary/terrorist prisoners.

(b) When a disclosure is made to a constable under this section then they must inform a member of the Serious Organised Crime Agency as soon as practicable (s 21C).

(c) This offence applies to acts done outside the UK by any person (see **5.7.1**).

(d) This offence can be tried in any place in the UK if it was committed in the UK (Counter-Terrorism Act 2008, s 28).

(e) There are orders from the United Nations and European Union which create further offences of making funds available and dealing with funds of those who have been designated (suspected to be involved in terrorism).

(f) A forfeiture order may also be made when sentencing for this offence (see **4.4.12**).

(g) The provisions on post-charge questioning apply to this offence (see **4.2.2 note (g)**).

PNLD reference numbers

H3564, D8710

DPP/AG consent required: Terrorism Act 2000, s 117 (see **5.7.4**).

 Time limit for prosecution: None.

 Summary: Maximum six months' imprisonment and/or a fine not exceeding the statutory maximum.

 Indictment: Maximum 14 years' imprisonment and/or a fine.

4.4.6 Duty to disclose information relating to terrorism finance offences

Section 19 of the Terrorism Act 2000 creates a duty to disclose information relating to certain offences under this Act and an offence of failing to do so.

Offences

(1) This section applies where a person—
   (a) believes or suspects that another person has committed an offence under sections 15 to 18, and
   (b) bases his belief or suspicion on information which comes to his attention—
      (i) in the course of a trade, profession or business, or
      (ii) in the course of his **employment** (whether or not in the course of a trade, profession or business).
(2) The person commits an offence if he does not disclose to a **constable** as soon as is reasonably practicable—
   (a) his belief or suspicion, and
   (b) the information on which it is based.

Terrorism Act 2000, s 19(1) and (2)

Points to prove

✓ date and location
✓ failed to disclose to a constable
✓ as soon as reasonably practicable
✓ belief/suspicion and information on which knowledge/suspicion based
✓ that another person had committed an offence under sections 15–18 of the Terrorism Act 2000
✓ that belief/suspicion based on information

> ✓ which had come to his/her attention in the course of trade/
> profession/business/employment (whether or not in the
> course of a trade, profession, or business)

Meanings

Employment

Means any employment (whether paid or unpaid) and includes—

(i) work under a contract for services or as an office-holder,
(ii) work experience provided pursuant to a training course or
programme or in the course of training for employment, and
(iii) voluntary work (Terrorism Act 2000, s 22A).

This definition is wider than the usual definition of employment,
including contractors, office-holders (eg trustees of a charity), individuals on a formal work experience programme or training (eg
intern in a bank), and volunteers.

Constable

Includes a member of the Serious Organised Crime Agency authorized by its Director General for that purpose (Terrorism Act 2000,
s 19(7B)).

Defence

(3) It is a defence for a person charged with an offence under subsection (2)
to prove that he had a reasonable excuse for not making the disclosure.

(4) Where—

   (a) a person is in employment,

   (b) his employer has established a procedure for the making of
disclosures of the matters specified in subsection (2), and

   (c) he is charged with an offence under that subsection, it is a defence
for him to prove that he disclosed the matters specified in that
subsection in accordance with the procedure.

Terrorism Act 2000, s 19(3) and (4)

With reference to the defence provided by section 19(3), unlike
similar provisions in, for example, drug trafficking legislation, the
person handling the terrorist property must demonstrate not only
that he genuinely did not believe it necessary to make a disclosure
but also that it was reasonable not to do so. In this way, an objective
standard applies to those such as bankers, accountants, and charity

---

trustees in their recognition of circumstances which should be seen as being linked to terrorism.

Subsection (4) allows for the reporting of such suspicions to others where there is a set procedure for doing so, such as a money laundering reporting officer within the organization.

Police powers

Power of arrest under TACT (see 5.3.1)

Power to stop and search under TACT (see 5.2.1)

Notes

(a) Section 19(1) requires banks and other businesses to report any suspicion they may have that someone is laundering terrorist money or committing any of the other terrorist property offences (ss 15–18, see **4.4.2–4.4.5**).

(b) This is a very extensive duty as the suspicion is based on those raised by an individual during the course of their work and they must have a reasonable excuse not to disclose this information to the police or other intermediary (see the previous Defence box).

(c) Section 19 preserves the exemption in respect of a professional legal adviser's privileged material as long as the material came to him in privileged circumstances and the reason is not to further a criminal purpose.

(d) Privileged circumstances in this section mean that the information is obtained from a client or a client's representative, in connection with the provision of legal advice by the adviser to the client, from a person seeking legal advice from the adviser, or from the person's representative, or from any person, for the purpose of actual or contemplated legal proceedings (s 19(6)).

(e) This offence has a global element to it, if the person has been in possession of a thing or taken an action and where, if he had committed that offence he had been in the UK at the time he did so, he still commits the offence (s 19(7)).

(f) Although this duty is confined to business relationships, family members could commit this offence if they fail to disclose their suspicions about relatives if they are involved in a business relationship with those family members.

(g) When a disclosure is made to a constable under this section then he must inform a member of the Serious Organised Crime Agency as soon as practicable (s 21C).

PNLD reference numbers

H3778, D8711

| DPP✓ AG✓ | **DPP/AG consent required:** Terrorism Act 2000, s 117 (see **5.7.4**). |

🕐 **Time limit for prosecution:** None.

♿ **Summary:** Maximum six months' imprisonment and/or a fine not exceeding the statutory maximum.

▦ **Indictment:** Maximum five years' imprisonment and/or a fine.

4.4.7 Permission to disclose information relating to terrorism finance offences

Section 20 of the Terrorism Act 2000 provides permission for disclosures to be made under section 19 of the Act.

(1) A person may disclose to a **constable**—
   (a) a suspicion or belief that any money or other **property** is **terrorist property** or is derived from terrorist property
   (b) any matter on which the suspicion or belief is based.
(2) A person may make a disclosure to a constable in the circumstances mentioned in section 19(1) and (2).
(3) Subsections (1) and (2) shall have effect notwithstanding any restriction on the disclosure of information imposed by statute or otherwise.
(4) Where—
   (a) a person is in employment, and
   (b) his employer has established a procedure for the making of disclosures of the kinds mentioned in subsection (1) and section 19(2), subsections (1) and (2) shall have effect in relation to that person as if any reference to disclosure to a constable included a reference to disclosure in accordance with the procedure.

Terrorism Act 2000, s 20(1)–(4)

Meanings

Constable (see **4.4.6**)

Property (see **4.4.2**)

Terrorist property (see **4.4.2**)

Notes

(a) This section means that businesses etc can make disclosures without fear of breaching any other legal restrictions, such as the Official Secrets Act 1989, or any potential civil liability, such as an action for breach of confidence.

(b) When a disclosure is made to a constable under this section then he must inform a member of the Serious Organised Crime Agency as soon as practicable (s 21C).

(c) See **4.4.10** for a similar provision for those in the regulated sector.

PNLD reference number

D8712

4.4.8 **Exemptions of liability**

Sections 21, 21ZA, 21ZB, and 21ZC of the Terrorism Act 2000 provide specific exemptions from criminal liability in relation to acts done and transactions undertaken when dealing with terrorist property. Each defence has a similar premise in that they provide protection for those who make a disclosure before, during, or after becoming involved in a transaction.

(1) A person does not commit an offence under sections 15–18, if he is acting with the express consent of a **constable**.

(2) Subject to subsections (3) and (4), a person does not commit an offence under sections 15 to 18 by involvement in a **transaction or arrangement relating to money or other property** if he discloses to a constable—

(a) his suspicion or belief that the money or other **property** is **terrorist property**, and

(b) the information on which his suspicion or belief is based.

(3) Subsection (2) applies only where a person makes a disclosure—

(a) after he becomes concerned in the transaction concerned,

(b) on his own initiative, and

(c) as soon as is reasonably practicable.

(4) Subsection (2) does not apply to a person if—

(a) a constable forbids him to continue his involvement in the transaction or arrangement to which the disclosure relates, and

(b) he continues his involvement.

Terrorism Act 2000, s 21(1)–(4)

Meanings

Constable (see **4.4.6**)

Property (see **4.4.2**)

Terrorist property (see **4.4.2**)

Transaction or arrangement relating to money or other property

Includes a reference to use or possession (Terrorism Act, s 21(7)).

Defence

(5) It is a defence for a person charged with an offence under sections 15(2) and (3) and 16, 17 or 18, to prove that—

(a) he intended to make a disclosure of the kind mentioned in subsections (2) and (3), and

(b) there is reasonable excuse for his failure to do so.

(6) Where—

(a) a person is in employment, and

(b) his employer has established a procedure for the making of disclosures of the same kind as may be made to a constable under subsection (2), this section shall have effect in relation to that person as if any reference to disclosure to a constable included a reference to disclosure in accordance with the procedure.

Terrorism Act 2000, s 21(5) and (6)

Subsection (6) allows for the reporting of such suspicions to others where there is a set procedure for doing so, such as a money launder-ing reporting officer within the organization.

Notes

(a) Section 21(1) allows for the activities of informants who may have been involved with terrorist property if they are to conceal their identity.

(b) Section 21(2) to (4) makes it possible for someone involved with such property to avoid prosecution by telling the police as soon as is reasonably practical and to stop any involvement if asked to do so by the police.

(1) A person does not commit an offence under any of sections 15 to 18 by involvement in a transaction or an arrangement relating to money or other property if, before becoming involved, the person—

(a) discloses to an authorised officer the person's suspicion or belief that the money or other property is

---

terrorist property and the information on which the
suspicion or belief is based, and

- (b) has the authorised officer's consent to becoming
involved in the transaction or arrangement.

(2) A person is treated as having an authorised officer's
consent if before the end of the notice period the person
does not receive notice from an authorised officer that
consent is refused (s 21ZA).

(c) This covers the situation where the person has made a
disclosure to an authorized officer before the transaction has
been carried out and continues with the transaction with the
permission of that officer.

(d) An authorized officer in this section and the others in **note (e)**
is an appropriately authorized member of staff from the
Serious Organised Crime Agency.

(e) The notice period in this section is seven working days,
starting the day after the disclosure is made.

(1) A person does not commit an offence under any of
sections 15 to 18 by involvement in a transaction or an
arrangement relating to money or other property if, after
becoming involved, the person discloses to an authorised
officer—

- (a) the person's suspicion or belief that the money or
other property is terrorist property, and
- (b) the information on which the suspicion or belief is
based.

(2) This section applies only where—

- (a) there is a reasonable excuse for the person's failure to
make the disclosure before becoming involved in the
transaction or arrangement, and
- (b) the disclosure is made on the person's own initiative
and as soon as it is reasonably practicable for the
person to make it.

(3) This section does not apply to a person if—

- (a) an authorised officer forbids the person to continue
involvement in the transaction or arrangement to
which the disclosure relates, and
- (b) the person continues that involvement (s 21ZB).

(f) This section covers the situation where a person becomes
involved in a transaction and then discloses the fact to an
authorized officer, as long as the person has a reasonable
excuse for failing to make the disclosure before becoming
involved.

(g) If the person continues with the transaction after being told not to by an authorized officer then he cannot rely on this defence.

(h) This offence can be tried in any place in the UK if it was committed in the UK (Counter-Terrorism Act 2008, s 28).

(i) The provisions on post-charge questioning apply to this offence (see **4.2.2 note (g)**).

Defence

It is a defence for a person charged with an offence under any of sections 15 to 18 to prove that—

(a) the person intended to make a disclosure of the kind mentioned in section 21ZA or 21ZB, and

(b) there is a reasonable excuse for the person's failure to do so.

Terrorism Act 2000, s 21ZC

This section covers those who have failed to make a disclosure but have a reasonable excuse for failing to do so.

PNLD reference numbers

D8713, D21661, D21662, D21663

4.4.9 Disclosures and cooperation in the regulated sector

Section 21A of the Terrorism Act 2000 creates the offence of a person working in the regulated sector (ie banking) failing to disclose information.

Offence

(1) A person commits an offence if each of the following three conditions is satisfied.

(2) The first condition is that he—

(a) knows or suspects, or

(b) has reasonable grounds for knowing or suspecting, that another person has committeed, or attempted to commit, an offence under sections 15 to 18.

---

(3) The second condition is that the information or other matter—
   (a) on which his knowledge or suspicion is based, or
   (b) which gives reasonable grounds for such knowledge or suspicion,
      came to him in the course of a **business in the regulated sector**.
(4) The third condition is that he does not **disclose** the information or
   other matter to a constable or a **nominated officer** as soon as is
   practicable after it comes to him.

Terrorism Act 2000, s 21A(1)–(4)

Points to prove

✓ date and location
✓ in the course of a business in the regulated sector
✓ knowing or suspecting *or*
   having reasonable grounds for knowing or suspecting
✓ that another person has committed an offence under sections
   15–18 of the Terrorism Act 2000
✓ failed to disclose that information/other matter
✓ to a constable/nominated officer
✓ as soon as is practicable

Meanings

A business in the regulated sector

Simply put, is a business that carries on financial duties that are
regulated by the Financial Services Authority (ie banks, building
societies, bureaux de change, accountants, investment establishments). The full complex definition can be found in Schedule 3A to
the Terrorism Act 2000 (not reproduced here).

A disclosure to a nominated officer

Is a disclosure which—

(a) is made to a person nominated by the alleged offender's
   employer to receive disclosures under this section, and
(b) is made in the course of the alleged offender's employment
   and in accordance with the procedure established by the
   employer for the purpose (Terrorism Act 2000, s 21A(7)).

Defence

(5) But a person does not commit an offence under this section if—

    (a) he has a reasonable excuse for not disclosing the information or other matter;

    (b) he is a professional legal adviser, or relevant professional adviser, and the information or other matter came to him in privileged circumstances; or

    (c) subsection (5A) applies to him.

(5A) This subsection applies to a person if

    (a) the person is employed by, or is in partnership with, a professional legal adviser or relevant professional adviser to provide the adviser with assistance or support,

    (b) the information or other matter comes to the person in connection with the provision of such assistance or support, and

    (c) the information or other matter came to the adviser in privileged circumstances.

Terrorism Act 2000, s 21A(5) and (5A)

Police powers

Power of arrest under TACT (see 5.3.1)

Power to stop and search under TACT (see 5.2.1)

Notes

(a) The requirement to pass on information where there are reasonable grounds to know or suspect that someone has committed an offence lays down an objective test for criminal liability. In recognition of this, subsection (6) provides that the court must take any guidance issued by the supervisory authority or any other appropriate body into account when determining whether an offence has been committed. That guidance has to be approved by the Treasury and is published in a manner approved by the Treasury so as to bring it to the attention of persons likely to be affected by it. Guidance is issued via the Joint Money Laundering Steering Group (JMLSG). There is a long list of supervisory authorities contained in Schedule 3A. Examples are the Commissioners for Her Majesty's Revenue and Customs, the Financial Services Authority, the Gambling Commission, the Office of Fair Trading, and the Secretary of State.

(b) An appropriate body is any body which regulates or is representative of any trade, profession, business, or employment carried on by the alleged offender (s 21A(13)).

(c) Information is obtained in privileged circumstances if it is communicated or given—

- by (or by a representative of) a client of his in connection with the giving by the adviser of legal advice to the client,
- by (or by a representative of) a person seeking legal advice from the adviser, or
- by a person in connection with legal proceedings or contemplated legal proceedings.

But this does not apply to information or other matter which is communicated or given with a view to furthering a criminal purpose (s 21A(8) and (9)).

(d) This provision is only directed at persons who are carrying out activities in the regulated sector (see **4.4.9**) and reflects the fact that they should be expected to exercise a higher level of diligence in handling transactions than those engaged in other business. Where a business carries out some activities which are specified in Schedule 3A, Part 1 and some which are not, then it is only to the extent that information is obtained in the course of the specified activities that is covered by these provisions.

(e) This offence has a global element to it, if the person has been in possession of a thing or taken an action and where, if he had committed that offence he had been in the UK at the time when he did so, then he still commits the offence (s 21A(11)).

(f) When a disclosure is made to a constable under this section then he must inform a member of the Serious Organised Crime Agency as soon as practicable (s 21C).

(g) See **4.4.7** for those not in the regulated sector.

(h) The provisions on post-charge questioning apply to this offence (see **4.2.2 note (g)**).

PNLD reference numbers

H3573, D10407, D10409

| DPP✓ | AG✓ | **DPP/AG consent required:** Terrorism Act 2000, s 117 (see **5.7.4**). |

🕐 **Time limit for prosecution:** None.

♿ **Summary:** Maximum six months' imprisonment and/or a fine not exceeding the statutory maximum.

▥ **Indictment:** Maximum five years' imprisonment and/or a fine.

4.4.10 **Permission to disclose information relating to terrorism offences in the regulated sector**

Section 21B of the Terrorism Act 2000 provides that those in the regulated sector (ie banking, etc) can disclose information where disclosure would normally be restricted.

(1) A disclosure which satisfies the following three conditions is not to be taken to breach any restriction on the disclosure of information (however imposed).

(2) The first condition is that the information or other matter disclosed came to the person making the disclosure (the discloser) in the course of a **business in the regulated sector**.

(3) The second condition is that the information or other matter—

    (a) causes the discloser to know or suspect, or

    (b) gives him reasonable grounds for knowing or suspecting, that another person has committed or attempted to commit an offence under sections 15 to 18.

(4) The third condition is that the **disclosure** is made to a **constable** or a **nominated officer** as soon as is practicable after the information or other matter comes to the discloser.

Terrorism Act 2000, s 21B(1)–(4)

Meanings

Business in the regulated sector (see **4.4.9**)

A disclosure to a nominated officer

Is a disclosure which is made to a person nominated by the discloser's employer to receive disclosures under this section, and is made in the course of the discloser's employment and in accordance with the procedure established by the employer for the purpose (Terrorism Act 2000, s 21(B)(5)).

Constable

The reference to a constable includes a reference to a person authorized for the purposes of this section by the Director General of the Serious Organised Crime Agency (Terrorism Act 2000, s 21(B)(7)).

Note

This section means that banks, building societies, etc can make disclosures without fear of breaching any other legal restrictions, such as the Official Secrets Act 1989 or any potential civil actions. See **4.4.7** for those not in the regulated sector.

PNLD reference number

D10408

4.4.11 **Tipping off**

Section 21D of the Terrorism Act 2000 creates the offence of tipping off, for example a member of banking staff telling a customer that he had been reported for a suspected terrorist finance offence. Sections 21E–21G provide the exceptions to this offence.

Offences

(1) A person commits an offence if—
 (a) the person discloses any matter within subsection (2);
 (b) the disclosure is likely to prejudice any investigation that might be conducted following the disclosure referred to in that subsection; and
 (c) the information on which the disclosure is based came to the person in the course of a **business in the regulated sector**.

(2) The matters are that the person or another person has made a disclosure under a provision of this part—
 (a) to a constable,
 (b) in accordance with a procedure established by that person's employer for the making of disclosures under that provision,
 (c) to a nominated officer, or
 (d) to a member of staff of the Serious Organised Crime Agency authorised for the purposes of that provision by the Director General of that Agency, of information that came to that person in the course of a business in the regulated sector.

(3) A person commits an offence if—
 (a) the person discloses that an investigation into allegations that an offence under this part has been committed is being contemplated or is being carried out;
 (b) the disclosure is likely to prejudice that investigation; and
 (c) the information on which the disclosure is based came to the person in the course of a business in the regulated sector.

Terrorism Act 2000, s 21D(1)–(3)

Points to prove

✓ date and location
✓ made a disclosure
✓ that an investigation
✓ into allegations that an offence under Part III of the Terrorism Act 2000
✓ had been committed/was being contemplated/was being carried out
✓ knowing/suspecting the disclosure was likely to prejudice that investigation
✓ and the information on which the disclosure was based
✓ came to you in the course of a business in the regulated sector

Meanings

Business in the regulated sector (see **4.4.9**)

Defences

Sections 21E–21G of the Terrorism Act 2000 set out the exceptions to the tipping off offence under section 21D.

(1) An employee, officer or partner of an undertaking does not commit an offence under section 21D if the disclosure is to an employee, officer or partner of the same undertaking.

(2) A person does not commit an offence under section 21D in respect of a disclosure by a credit institution or a financial institution if—
   (a) the disclosure is to a credit institution or a financial institution,
   (b) the institution to whom the disclosure is made is situated in an EEA State or in a country or territory imposing equivalent money laundering requirements, and
   (c) both the institution making the disclosure and the institution to whom it is made belong to the same group.

(3) In subsection (2) 'group' has the same meaning as in Directive 2002/87/EC of the European Parliament and of the Council of 16th December 2002 on the supplementary supervision of credit institutions, insurance undertakings and investment firms in a financial conglomerate.

(4) A professional legal adviser or a relevant professional adviser does not commit an offence under section 21D if—
   (a) the disclosure is to a professional legal adviser or a relevant professional adviser,

(b) both the person making the disclosure and the person to whom it is made carry on business in an EEA state or in a country or territory imposing equivalent money laundering requirements, and

(c) those persons perform their professional activities within different undertakings that share common ownership, management or control.

Terrorism Act 2000, s 21E

This section covers those who disclose to other employees, partners, another financial institution, or other legal or professional adviser. Simplistically put, the disclosure must be to a person/organization which is part of the same overall company and which is in an EEA state or a country which has similar money laundering provisions.

(1) This section applies to a disclosure—
   (a) by a credit institution to another credit institution,
   (b) by a financial institution to another financial institution,
   (c) by a professional legal adviser to another professional legal adviser, or
   (d) by a relevant professional adviser of a particular kind to another relevant professional adviser of the same kind.

(2) A person does not commit an offence under section 21D in respect of a disclosure to which this section applies if—
   (a) the disclosure relates to—
      (i) a client or former client of the institution or adviser making the disclosure and the institution or adviser to whom it is made,
      (ii) a transaction involving them both, or
      (iii) the provision of a service involving them both;
   (b) the disclosure is for the purpose only of preventing an offence under this part of this Act;
   (c) the institution or adviser to whom the disclosure is made is situated in an EEA State or in a country or territory imposing equivalent money laundering requirements; and
   (d) the institution or adviser making the disclosure and the institution or adviser to whom it is made are subject to equivalent duties of professional confidentiality and the protection of personal data (within the meaning of section 1 of the Data Protection Act 1998).

Terrorism Act 2000, s 21F

This covers those mentioned in subsection (1) who make a disclosure to another and that disclosure involves a client or former client of either one of them and the service or transaction concerns them both. The disclosure must also only relate to preventing an offence under this part and they must both be under similar duties of confidentiality and also be in an EEA state or a country with similar money laundering provisions.

In this section, relevant professional adviser means an accountant, auditor, or tax adviser who is a member of a professional body which is established for accountants, auditors, or tax advisers (as the case may be) and which makes provision for—

(a) testing the competence of those seeking admission to membership of such a body as a condition for such admission; and

(b) imposing and maintaining professional and ethical standards for its members, as well as imposing sanctions for non-compliance with those standards (Terrorism Act 2000, s 21H).

Credit and financial institutions are organizations such as banks and building societies, a full definition can be found in Schedule 3A.

Defences

(1) A person does not commit an offence under section 21D if the disclosure is—
  (a) to the authority that is the supervisory authority for that person by virtue of the Money Laundering Regulations 2007 (S.I. 2007/2157); or
  (b) for the purpose of—
  (i) the detection, investigation or prosecution of a criminal offence (whether in the United Kingdom or elsewhere),
  (ii) an investigation under the Proceeds of Crime Act 2002, or
  (iii) the enforcement of any order of a court under that Act.

(2) A professional legal adviser or a relevant professional adviser does not commit an offence under section 21D if the disclosure—
  (a) is to the adviser's client, and
  (b) is made for the purpose of dissuading the client from engaging in conduct amounting to an offence.

(3) A person does not commit an offence under section 21D(1) if the person does not know or suspect that the disclosure is likely to have the effect mentioned in section 21D(1)(b).

(4) A person does not commit an offence under section 21D(3) if the person does not know or suspect that the disclosure is likely to have the effect mentioned in section 21D(3)(b).

Terrorism Act 2000, s 21G

Police powers

Power of arrest under TACT (see **5.3.1**)

Power to stop and search under TACT (see **5.2.1**)

Notes

(a) The section prohibits persons, in the course of business in the regulated sector (ie banking etc, see **4.4.9**), from disclosing to the customer concerned or to other third persons, the fact that information about known or suspected money laundering or terrorist financing has been transmitted and/or that a money laundering or terrorist financing investigation is being, or may be, carried out.

(b) This offence can be tried in any place in the UK if it was committed in the UK (Counter-Terrorism Act 2008, s 28).

(c) The provisions on post-charge questioning apply to this offence (see **4.2.2 note (g)**).

PNLD reference numbers

H9233, D21665, D21666, D21667, D21668

🕐 **Time limit for prosecution:** None.

♿ **Summary:** Maximum three months' imprisonment and/or a fine not exceeding the statutory maximum.

🏛 **Indictment:** Maximum two years' imprisonment and/or a fine.

4.4.12 Forfeiture of terrorist cash and property

Sections 23–23B of the Terrorism Act 2000 give details of the forfeiture orders available to the courts where a person has been convicted of certain terrorist offences. Section 23 is for terrorist finance offences (ss 15–18) and section 23A is for certain offences under the Terrorism Act 2000 and 2006.

(1) The court by or before which a person is convicted of an offence under any of sections 15 to 18 may make a forfeiture order in accordance with the provisions of this section.

(2) Where a person is convicted of an offence under sections 15(1) or (2) or 16, the court may order the forfeiture of any money or

other **property** which, at the time of the offence, the person had in their possession or under their control and which—

(a) had been used for the purposes of **terrorism**, or

(b) they intended should be used, or had reasonable cause to suspect might be used, for those purposes.

(3) Where a person is convicted of an offence under section 15(3) the court may order the forfeiture of any money or other property which, at the time of the offence, the person had in their possession or under their control and which—

(a) had been used for the purposes of terrorism, or

(b) which, at that time, they knew or had reasonable cause to suspect would or might be used for those purposes.

(4) Where a person is convicted of an offence under section 17 or 18 the court may order the forfeiture of any money or other property which, at the time of the offence, the person had in their possession or under their control and which—

(a) had been used for the purposes of terrorism, or

(b) was, at that time, intended by them to be used for those purposes.

(5) Where a person is convicted of an offence under section 17 the court may order the forfeiture of the money or other property to which the arrangement in question related, and which—

(a) had been used for the purposes of terrorism, or

(b) at the time of the offence, the person knew or had reasonable cause to suspect would or might be used for those purposes.

(6) Where a person is convicted of an offence under section 18 the court may order the forfeiture of the money or other property to which the arrangement in question related.

(7) Where a person is convicted of an offence under any of sections 15 to 18, the court may order the forfeiture of any money or other property which wholly or partly, and directly or indirectly, is received by any person as a payment or other reward in connection with the commission of the offence.

Terrorism Act 2000, s 23(1)–(7)

(1) The court by or before which a person is convicted of an offence to which this section applies may order the forfeiture of any money or other property in relation to which the following conditions are met—

(a) that it was, at the time of the offence, in the possession or control of the person convicted; and

(b) that—

(i) it had been used for the purposes of terrorism,

(ii) it was intended by that person that it should be used for the purposes of terrorism, or

        (iii) the court believes that it will be used for the purposes
           of terrorism unless forfeited.

(2) This section applies to an offence under—
  (a) any of the following provisions of this Act—
     section 54 (weapons training) (*see* **4.3.9**);
     section 57, 58 or 58A (possessing things and collecting
       information for the purposes of terrorism) (*see*
       4.3.10–4.3.12);
     section 59, 60 or 61 (inciting terrorism outside the United
       Kingdom) (*see* **4.3.5**);
  (b) any of the following provisions of part 1 of the Terrorism
     Act 2006—
     section 2 (dissemination of terrorist publications) (*see*
       4.3.2);
     section 5 (preparation of terrorist acts) (*see* **4.3.6**);
     section 6 (training for terrorism) (*see* **4.3.7**);
     sections 9 to 11 (offences involving radioactive devices or
       materials) (*see* **5.5.1–5.5.3**).

Terrorism Act 2000, s 23A(1)–(2)

(1) Before making an order under section 23 or 23A, a court must
give an opportunity to be heard to any person, other than the
convicted person, who claims to be the owner or otherwise
interested in anything which can be forfeited under that
section.

(2) In considering whether to make an order under section 23 or
23A in respect of any property, a court shall have regard to—
  (a) the value of the property, and
  (b) the likely financial and other effects on the convicted
    person of the making of the order (taken together with
    any other order that the court contemplates making).

Terrorism Act 2000, s 23B(1)–(2)

Meanings

Property (see **4.4.2**)

Terrorism (see **4.2.1**)

Police powers

Under Schedule 4, paragraph 7(1), a constable may seize any property subject to a restraint order for the purpose of preventing it from being removed from Great Britain (see **note (f)**).

Notes

(a) Subsection 23(7) closes a loophole by allowing the forfeiture of the proceeds of a terrorist property offence, for example if an accountant prepared accounts on behalf of a proscribed organization which facilitates the retention or control of the organization's money, the money he is paid for this task can be forfeited under this section. Previously the money could not be forfeited because it was not intended or suspected for use in terrorism nor could it be confiscated under the Criminal Justice Act 1988 because that confiscation regime does not include terrorist property offences.

(b) Section 23A allows the convicting court to order the forfeiture of money or other property in the possession or under the control of the convicted person at the time of the offence and which either had been used for the purposes of terrorism or was intended by that person to be used for those purposes, or which the court believes will be used for the purposes of terrorism unless forfeited. The offences to which this power is applicable are listed earlier.

(c) This is a 'criminal forfeiture'—that is, forfeiture following conviction for a criminal offence (for civil forfeiture see **4.4.17**).

(d) Where someone other than the convicted person claims to be the owner of or have an interest in anything to be forfeited under this section, they will have an opportunity to be heard by the court (s 23B).

(e) Schedule 4 to the Terrorism Act 2000 makes some further provisions about forfeiture orders. The court can order property (other than money or land) to be sold, require the forfeited property to be handed over to a proper officer (officer of the court) or a constable, appoint a receiver to deal with the property and order any part of the proceeds to a person with a valid claim under section 23B. It also allows victims to be compensated by the courts in certain circumstances.

(f) Schedule 4 also allows for the making of a restraint order by the High Court which prevents a person accused of an offence under sections 14–30 from selling/disposing of their property in order to avoid forfeiture. Applications for restraint orders may be made at an early stage of an investigation, even before proceedings have been formally instituted. Although a restraint order is formally made by the High Court, the prosecution can apply without notice to any other parties (ex parte) to a judge in chambers for the issue of such an order. This is because in some instances it is vital to act as quickly as possible.

PNLD reference numbers

D8714, D8755, D8756, D8757, D8758, D23685, D23686

4.4.13 **Freezing orders—contents**

Sections 4–15 of the Anti-terrorism, Crime and Security Act 2001 contain measures to allow the UK to take action to freeze the assets of overseas persons or governments which are threatening the economic interests of the UK or the life or property of UK residents. These provisions will allow the UK to impose sanctions in cases of urgency, where neither the United Nations nor the European Union has yet agreed a course of action, or in cases where it is appropriate for the UK to impose sanctions independently. Section 5 of and Schedule 3 to the Anti-terrorism, Crime and Security Act 2001 detail the contents of a freezing order.

(1) A freezing order is an order which prohibits persons from **making funds available to or for the benefit of a person** or persons specified in the order.
(2) The order must provide that these are the persons who are prohibited—
   (a) all persons in the United Kingdom, and
   (b) all persons elsewhere who are **nationals of the United Kingdom** or are bodies incorporated under the law of any part of the United Kingdom or are Scottish partnerships.
(3) The order may specify the following (and only the following) as the person or persons to whom or for whose benefit **funds** are not to be made available—
   (a) the person or persons reasonably believed by the Treasury to have taken or to be likely to take the action referred to in section 4;
   (b) any person the Treasury reasonably believes has provided or is likely to provide assistance (directly or indirectly) to that person or any of those persons.
(4) A person may be specified under subsection (3) by—
   (a) being named in the order, or
   (b) falling within a description of persons set out in the order.
(5) The description must be such that a reasonable person would know whether he fell within it.
(6) Funds are financial assets and economic benefits of any kind.

Anti-terrorism, Crime and Security Act 2001, s 5

Meanings

Making funds available to or for the benefit of a person

The freezing order must specify what this means in each case, but it can include—

(a) allowing a person to withdraw from an account;
(b) honouring a cheque payable to a person;
(c) crediting a person's account with interest;
(d) releasing documents of title (such as share certificates) held on a person's behalf;
(e) making available the proceeds of realization of a person's property;
(f) making a payment to or for a person's benefit (for instance, under a contract or as a gift or under any enactment such as the enactments relating to social security);
(g) such other acts as the order may specify (Anti-terrorism, Crime and Security Act 2001, Sch 3).

A national of the United Kingdom

Is an individual who is a British citizen, a British Overseas Territories citizen, a British National (Overseas) or a British Overseas citizen, a person who under the British Nationality Act 1981 is a British subject, or a British protected person within the meaning of that Act (Anti-terrorism, Crime and Security Act 2001, s 9).

Funds

Include gold, cash, deposits, securities (eg stocks, shares, and debentures), and such other matters as the order may specify (Anti-terrorism, Crime and Security Act 2001, Sch 3, para 2).

Notes

(a) Paragraph 4 of Schedule 3 to the Anti-terrorism, Crime and Security Act 2001 provides that a freezing order must include provisions for authorizing funds to be made available (eg for basic living expenses or legal costs) subject to conditions set out by the Treasury. The Treasury may charge fees to cover the administrative costs of granting such a licence.

(b) Paragraph 5 of Schedule 3 specifies that a freezing order may provide that a person must provide information or a document if it is reasonably needed in order to establish whether an offence under the order has been committed. The requirement to provide information or a document may be made by the Treasury or a person authorized by the Treasury. The requirement is to do so within a certain time and at a place set out in the order. The order may provide that the requirement to provide information is not to be taken to breach any restriction on the disclosure of information. However, the requirement does not apply to information or documents subject to legal privilege, except to the extent that the information or document is held with the intention of furthering a criminal purpose.

(c) Paragraph 6 of Schedule 3 provides that a freezing order may include a provision requiring a person to disclose information if three conditions apply. First, the person required to disclose must be specified in the order. Secondly, the person must know or suspect, or have grounds to know or suspect, that a person specified in a freezing order is a customer of his or has dealings with him. Thirdly, the information must have come to him in the course of a business in the regulated sector. The freezing order may include provisions: that the requirement to disclose information is not a breach of any restriction on the disclosure of information; on the use to which the information may be put and further disclosures; and that the obligation to disclose does not apply to privileged information except where the information is held with the intention of furthering a criminal purpose.

(d) Paragraph 10 of Schedule 3 provides that compensation may be paid in certain circumstances if the person has suffered loss. The entitlement to compensation may be made subject to a requirement that the claimant has behaved reasonably (eg by mitigating his loss).

(e) The Treasury can make a freezing order if two conditions are satisfied. First, the Treasury must reasonably believe that action threatening the UK's economy (or part of it) or the life or property of UK nationals or residents has taken place or is likely to take place. Secondly, the persons involved in the action must be resident outside the UK or be an overseas government (ie a foreign perpetrator) (Anti-terrorism, Crime and Security Act 2001, s 4).

(f) The Treasury is required to keep under review whether any freezing order should be kept in force or amended and a freezing order lapses after two years starting with the day on which it was made (Anti-terrorism, Crime and Security Act 2001, ss 7 and 8).

(g) Freezing orders are made by the government by statutory instrument. The freezing order must be approved by resolution of both Houses within 28 days of being made otherwise it will cease to have effect (Anti-terrorism, Crime and Security Act 2001, s 10).

(h) The scope of these measures is not confined to terrorism. As a result, they were invoked against Icelandic banks in 2008 when there was a threat by the Icelandic Government to leave British depositors at the back of the queue for compensation. The Landsbanki Freezing Order 2008 prevented the British branch of the bank from 'repatriating' assets back to Iceland.

(i) Procedures for challenging orders are set out in Part VI of the Counter-Terrorism Act 2008.

(j) There is another set of freezing powers under Part V of the Counter-Terrorism Act 2008. The rationale is the wish to provide a platform for the rapid translation into action of demands from the Financial Action Task Force (FATF). For example, an FATF statement on 16 October 2008 warned of the involvement of Iran in terrorism financing and of Uzbekistan in money laundering. An order has been issued against an Iranian bank which is accused of facilitating nuclear proliferation (see **Bank Mellat v HM Treasury [2010] EWCA Civ 483**). Procedures for challenging these orders are set out in Part VI of the Counter-Terrorism Act 2008.

PNLD reference numbers

D10304, D10305, D10307, D10384-94

4.4.14 Freezing orders—offences

Schedule 3 to the Anti-terrorism, Crime and Security Act 2001 creates the offences relating to freezing orders.

Offences

(1) A **freezing order** may include any of the provisions set out in this paragraph.

(2) A person commits an offence if he fails to comply with a prohibition imposed by the order.

(3) A person commits an offence if he engages in an activity knowing or intending that it will enable or facilitate the commission by another person of an offence under a provision included under sub-paragraph (2).

(4) A person commits an offence if—

(a) he fails without reasonable excuse to provide information, or to produce a document, in response to a requirement made under the order;

(b) he provides information, or produces a document, which he knows is false in a material particular in response to such a requirement or with a view to obtaining a **licence** under the order;

(c) he recklessly provides information, or produces a document, which is false in a material particular in response to such a requirement or with a view to obtaining a licence under the order;

(d) he fails without reasonable excuse to disclose information as required by a provision included under paragraph 6.

Anti-terrorism, Crime and Security Act 2001, Sch 3, para 7(1)–(4)

Points to prove

Paragraph 7(2) of Schedule 3

✓ failure
✓ to comply with a prohibition
✓ imposed by a freezing order

Paragraph 7(3) of Schedule 3

✓ engaged in an activity
✓ knowing/intending that it would
✓ enable/facilitate another person
✓ not to comply with a prohibition
✓ imposed by a freezing order

Paragraph 7(4)(a) of Schedule 3

✓ failed without reasonable excuse
✓ to provide information/produce a document
✓ in response to a requirement made
✓ by a freezing order

Paragraph 7(4)(b), (c) of Schedule 3

✓ provided information/produced a document/recklessly provided information/recklessly produced a document
✓ which you knew was false in a material particular
✓ in response to a requirement imposed by *or*
with a view to obtaining a licence under paragraph 4 of Schedule 3 to the Anti-terrorism, Crime and Security Act 2001
✓ in respect of a freezing order

Paragraph 7(4)(d) of Schedule 3

✓ failed without reasonable excuse

> ✓ to disclose information
> ✓ as required by a provision included in paragraph 6 of Schedule 3 to the Anti-terrorism, Crime and Security Act 2001

Meanings

Freezing order (see **4.4.13**)

Licence (see **4.4.13 note (a)**)

Defence

A person does not commit an offence under a provision included under sub-paragraph (2) or (3) if he proves that he did not know and had no reason to suppose that the person to whom or for whose benefit funds were made available, or were to be made available, was the person (or one of the persons) specified in the freezing order as a person to whom or for whose benefit funds are not to be made available.

Anti-terrorism, Crime and Security Act 2001, Sch 3, para 7(5)

Police powers

Power of arrest under TACT (see **5.3.1**)

Power to stop and search under TACT (see **5.2.1**)

Notes

(a) A freezing order *may* contain a provision that if an offence under this Schedule is committed by a body corporate and it can be proved the offence was committed with the knowledge or assistance of an officer of the company (manager, director, company secretary, etc) then they may also commit the offence and be proceeded against (Anti-terrorism, Crime and Security Act 2001, Sch 3) (see **5.7.2**).

(b) A freezing order *may* contain a provision that the consent of the DPP or the Treasury is required before proceedings can be instituted (Anti-terrorism, Crime and Security Act 2001, Sch 3, para 8(2)).

PNLD reference numbers

H4773, H4774, H4775, H4776, H4777, H4778, H4779, H4780, H4782, D10390, D10391

Offences in sub-paras (2) and (3)

 Time limit for prosecution: None.

 Summary: Maximum six months' imprisonment and/or a fine not exceeding the statutory maximum.

 Indictment: Maximum two years' imprisonment and/or a fine.

Offence in sub-para (4)

 Time limit for prosecution: A freezing order may contain a provision which states that an information relating to an offence under the order which is triable by a magistrates court in England and Wales may be tried if it is laid at any time in the period of one year starting with the date of the commission of the offence. Otherwise the time limit for prosecution would be six months.

 Summary: Maximum six months' imprisonment and/or a fine not exceeding level 5 on the standard scale.

4.4.15 Financial information

Section 38 of and Schedule 6 to the Terrorism Act 2000 provide a power to investigate terrorist finance. A police officer of at least the rank of Superintendent may apply for a disclosure order that requires a financial institution to provide customer information. The purpose of such an order is to enable a constable to identify accounts in relation to terrorist investigations. It is, therefore, intended to be used earlier in an investigation than production and explanation orders under Schedule 5 to the Act (see **5.1.4** and **5.1.6**).

Police powers

1(1) Where an order has been made under this paragraph in relation to a **terrorist investigation**, a constable named in the order may require a **financial institution** to which the order applies to provide **customer information** for the purposes of the investigation.

(1A) The order may provide that it applies to—
   (a) all financial institutions,
   (b) a particular description, or particular descriptions, of financial institutions, or

    (c) a particular financial institution or particular financial institutions.

(2) The information shall be provided—

    (a) in such manner and within such time as the constable may specify, and

    (b) notwithstanding any restriction on the disclosure of information imposed by statute or otherwise.

Criteria for making order

5   An order under paragraph 1 may be made only if the person making it is satisfied that—

    (a) the order is sought for the purposes of a terrorist investigation,

    (b) the tracing of **terrorist property** is desirable for the purposes of the investigation, and

    (c) the order will enhance the effectiveness of the investigation.

Terrorism Act 2000, Sch 6, para 1(1)–(2) and (5)

Meanings

Terrorist investigation (see **5.1**)

Financial institution

Means—

(a) a person who has permission under Part 4 of the Financial Services and Markets Act 2000 to accept deposits,

(b) *[Repealed.]*

(c) a credit union (within the meaning of the Credit Unions Act 1979 or the Credit Unions (Northern Ireland) Order 1985),

(d) a person carrying on a **relevant regulated activity**,

(e) the National Savings Bank,

(f) a person who carries out an activity for the purposes of raising money authorised to be raised under the National Loans Act 1968 under the auspices of the Director of National Savings,

(g) a European institution carrying on a home regulated activity (within the meaning of Directive 2006/48/EC of the European Parliament and of the Council of 14 June 2006 relating to the taking up and pursuit of the business of credit institutions as last amended by Directive 2009/111/EC),

(h) a person carrying out an activity specified in any of points 1 to 12, 14 and 15 of Annex 1 to that Directive, ...

(ha) an electronic money institution within the meaning of Directive 2009/110/EC of the European Parliament and of the Council of 16th September 2009 relating to the taking up, pursuit and prudential supervision of the business of electronic money institutions, and

(i) a person who carries on an insurance business in accordance with an authorization pursuant to Art 4 or 51 of Directive 2002/83/EC of the European Parliament and of the Council of 5th November 2002 concerning life assurance (Terrorism Act 2000, Sch 6, para 6(1)).

An institution which ceases to be a financial institution for the purposes of this Schedule (whether by virtue of sub-paragraph (2)(b) or otherwise) shall continue to be treated as a financial institution for the purposes of any requirement under paragraph 1 to provide customer information which relates to a time when the institution was a financial institution (Terrorism Act 2000, Sch 6, para 6(3)).

Relevant regulated activity

Means—

(a) dealing in investments as principal or as agent,
(b) arranging deals in investments,
(ba) operating a multilateral trading facility,
(c) managing investments,
(d) safeguarding and administering investments,
(e) sending dematerialized instructions,
(f) establishing etc collective investment schemes,
(g) advising on investments (Terrorism Act 2000, Sch 6, para 6(1A)).

Customer information

Means—

(a) information whether a **business relationship** exists or existed between a financial institution and a particular person ('a customer'),
(b) a customer's account number,
(c) a customer's full name,
(d) a customer's date of birth,
(e) a customer's address or former address,
(f) the date on which a business relationship between a financial institution and a customer begins or ends,
(g) any evidence of a customer's identity obtained by a financial institution in pursuance of or for the purposes of any legislation relating to money laundering, and
(h) the identity of a person sharing an account with a customer.

A business relationship exists between a financial institution and a person only if—

(a) there is an arrangement between them designed to facilitate the carrying out of frequent or regular transactions between them, and

(b) the total amount of payments to be made in the course of the arrangement is neither known nor capable of being ascertained when the arrangement is made (Terrorism Act 2000, Sch 6, para 7(1) and (2)).

There is also the possibility for the Secretary of State to make an order to provide for a class of information to be customer information for the purposes of this Schedule, or to cease to be customer information for the purposes of this Schedule (Terrorism Act 2000, Sch 6, para 7(3)).

Terrorist property

Means—

(a) money or other property which is likely to be used for the purposes of terrorism (including any resources of a proscribed organization),

(b) proceeds of the commission of acts of terrorism, and

(c) proceeds of acts carried out for the purposes of terrorism (Terrorism Act 2000, s 14(1) (for details see **4.4.1**)).

Notes

(a) This method of investigation is sometimes known as a 'general bank circular' investigation. It allows the police to find out whether a financial institution holds accounts in particular names. Where more detailed information is required, a production order under Schedule 5 will be necessary (see **5.1.4**), or an account monitoring order under Schedule 6A (see **4.4.16**).

(b) Only a police officer of at least the rank of Superintendent can apply for an order under this Schedule (Sch 6, para 2(a)).

(c) An order under paragraph 1 may be made only by a Circuit Judge or a District Judge (magistrates' courts) (Sch 6, para 3(a)).

(d) The investigation may include money or other property intended for use in terrorism as well as any proceeds of terrorist acts.

(e) *Offence—failure to comply* An institution which fails to comply with a requirement under paragraph 1 of Schedule 6 commits an offence. It is a defence to prove that the information required was not in the institution's possession, or that it was not reasonably practicable for the institution to comply with the requirement, for example where the amount of information required would be huge. The penalty on summary conviction is a fine not exceeding level 5 on the standard scale (Sch 6, para 1(3)–(5)).

(f) The provisions on post-charge questioning apply to this offence (see **4.2.2 note (g)**).

(g) Where the offence is committed by an institution and it is proved that the offence—

was committed with the consent or connivance of an officer of the institution, or

was attributable to neglect on the part of an officer of the institution, the officer, as well as the institution, shall be guilty of the offence. The penalty for an individual on summary conviction is a maximum six months' imprisonment and/or a fine not exceeding level 5 on the standard scale.

In the case of an institution which is a body corporate, 'officer' includes—

(a) a director, manager, or secretary,
(b) a person purporting to act as a director, manager, or secretary, and
(c) if the affairs of the body are managed by its members, a member.

In the case of an institution which is a partnership, 'officer' means a partner.

In the case of an institution which is an unincorporated association (other than a partnership), 'officer' means a person concerned in the management or control of the association (Sch 6, para 8).

(h) *Self-incrimination*—where a financial institution provides customer information under Schedule 8 this information is not admissible in evidence in criminal proceedings against the institution or any of its officers or employees. It may, however, be used in proceedings for an offence under paragraph 1(3) (including proceedings brought by virtue of paragraph 8, see **note (f)**) (Sch 6, para 9).

(i) This offence in paragraph 1 of Schedule 6 can be tried in any place in the UK if it was committed in the UK (Counter-Terrorism Act 2008, s 28).

PNLD reference numbers

D8772, D8773, D8774, D8775

4.4.16 **Account monitoring orders**

Section 38A of and Schedule 6A to the Terrorism Act 2000 provide for account monitoring orders. Such orders can be imposed on financial institutions. The financial institution then has to provide specified information in relation to an account (eg details of all transactions passing through the account) for a maximum of up to 90 days for the purpose of a terrorist investigation.

Police powers

(4) An account monitoring order is an order that the **financial institution** specified in the application for the order must—
   (a) for the period specified in the order,
   (b) in the manner so specified,
   (c) at or by the time or times so specified, and
   (d) at the place or places so specified,
   provide information of the description specified in the application to an appropriate officer.
(1) **A judge** may, on an application made to him by an **appropriate officer**, make an account monitoring order if he is satisfied that—
   (a) the order is sought for the purposes of a **terrorist investigation**,
   (b) the tracing of **terrorist property** is desirable for the purposes of the investigation, and
   (c) the order will enhance the effectiveness of the investigation.
(2) The application for an account monitoring order must state that the order is sought against the financial institution specified in the application in relation to information which—
   (a) relates to an account or accounts held at the institution by the person specified in the application (whether solely or jointly with another), and
   (b) is of the description so specified.
(3) The application for an account monitoring order may specify information relating to—
   (a) all accounts held by the person specified in the application for the order at the financial institution so specified,
   (b) a particular description, or particular descriptions, of accounts so held, or
   (c) a particular account, or particular accounts, so held.
   Terrorism Act 2000, Sch 6A, para 2(4), (1)–(3)

Meanings

Financial institution (see **5.1.7**)

A judge

Means a Circuit Judge (Terrorism Act 2000, Sch 6A, para 1(2)(a)).

Appropriate officer

Means a police officer (Terrorism Act 2000, Sch 6A, para 1(4)(a)).

Terrorist investigation (see **5.1**)

Terrorist property (see **4.4.15**)

Notes

(a) The information would normally be provided in the form of a bank statement.

(b) Orders under Schedule 6A to the Terrorism Act 2000 differ from those in Schedule 6. The main differences are that they relate to transactions, not to customer information; and they can allow for real-time disclosure rather than a single response to a request.

(c) *Applications*—an application for an account monitoring order may be made ex parte to a judge in chambers (ie without the financial institution being present). The description of information specified in an application for an account monitoring order may be varied by the person who made the application. This is necessary so that an application does not fail completely where the judge is prepared to make the order in relation to certain of the information specified but not all. This flexibility avoids the need for a further application to be made. If the application was made by a police officer, the description of information specified in it may be varied by a different police officer (Sch 6A, para 3).

(d) *Discharge or variation*—the person who applied for the account monitoring order and any person affected by the order may make an application to the Crown Court to discharge or vary the order. If the application was made by a police officer, a different officer may make such an application. The court may then discharge or vary the order (Sch 6A, paras 4 and 1(3)(a)).

(e) *Duration*—the period stated in an account monitoring order must not exceed the period of 90 days beginning with the day on which the order is made (Sch 6A, para 2(5)).

(f) *Effect*—paragraph 6(2) provides that the order must be complied with in spite of any restrictions on the disclosure of information (however imposed). This is necessary as the information which is described in the order will be held by the financial institution subject to various restrictions on its disclosure to third parties. This makes it clear that the order has effect, and must be complied with, despite the existence of such restrictions.

(g) *Evidence*—statements made by financial institutions in response to an account monitoring order may only exceptionally be used in evidence against it in criminal proceedings. The exceptions are proceedings for contempt of court; proceedings under section 23 of the Terrorism Act 2000 where the financial institution has been convicted of an offence under any of sections 15–18 (see **4.4.2–4.4.5**); and on a prosecution for an offence where, in giving evidence, the financial institution makes a statement inconsistent with a statement made in response to an account monitoring order (in the latter case, the statement may only be used if evidence relating to it is adduced, or a question relating to it is asked, by or on behalf of the financial institution in the proceedings arising out of the prosecution) (Sch 6A, para 7).

(h) *Breach of the order*—an account monitoring order is an order of the court (Sch 6A, para 6(1)). If a person breaches the order, he commits the offence of contempt of court.

PNLD reference number

D10406

4.4.17 **Forfeiture orders**

Section 1 of and Schedule 1 to the Anti-terrorism, Crime and Security Act 2001 provide for the forfeiture of terrorist cash. Cash which is intended to be used for the purposes of terrorism, consists of the resources of an organization which is a proscribed organization, or is, or represents, property obtained through terrorism, may be forfeited in civil proceedings before a magistrates' court. This is possible even where no criminal proceedings have been brought for an offence in connection with the cash.

Police powers

Seizure of cash

(1) An **authorised officer** may seize any **cash** if he has reasonable grounds for suspecting that it is **terrorist cash**.

(2) An authorised officer may also seize cash part of which he has reasonable grounds for suspecting to be terrorist cash if it is not reasonably practicable to seize only that part.

Anti-terrorism, Crime and Security Act 2001, Sch 1, para 2

Detention of seized cash

(1) While the authorised officer continues to have reasonable grounds for his suspicion, cash seized under this Schedule may be detained initially for a period of **48 hours**.

Anti-terrorism, Crime and Security Act 2001, Sch 1, para 3(1)

Meanings

Authorised officer

Means a constable, a **customs officer**, or an **immigration officer** (Anti-terrorism, Crime and Security Act 2001, Sch 1, para 19).

Customs officer

Means an officer of Customs and Revenue.

Immigration officer

Means a person appointed as an immigration officer under paragraph 1 of Schedule 2 to the Immigration Act 1971 (Anti-terrorism, Crime and Security Act 2001, Sch 1, para 19).

Note: the powers to seize and detain cash provided in Schedule 1 to the Anti-terrorism, Crime and Security Act 2001 are available to police officers, immigration officers, and customs officers.

However, according to the Code of Practice for authorized officers (see **4.4.18**) immigration and customs officers should only exceptionally exercise these powers. Where an officer, while exercising powers under other Acts, suspects that cash found is liable to be seized, he should alert a police officer as soon as possible to continue the investigation (see **Appendix 5, Code of Practice, para 6**).

Cash

Means—

(a) coins and notes in any currency,

(b) postal orders,

(c) cheques of any kind, including travellers' cheques,
(d) bankers drafts,
(e) bearer bonds and bearer shares, found at any place in the UK (Anti-terrorism, Crime and Security Act 2001, Sch 1, para 1(2)).

This does not include counterfeit cash, but see **note (f)**.

Terrorist cash

Means cash which—

(a) is intended to be used **for the purposes of terrorism**, or
(b) consists of resources of an organisation which is a **proscribed organisation**, or
(c) is property **earmarked as terrorist property** (Anti-terrorism, Crime and Security Act 2001, s 1 and Sch 1, para 1(2)).

The definition of cash is intended to cover the most readily realizable monetary instruments used by terrorists.

For the purposes of terrorism

Includes anything done or intended to be done for the benefit of a proscribed organization (Anti-terrorism, Crime and Security Act 2001, Sch 1, para 19(4)).

Proscribed organisation (see 4.2.1)

Property

(1) Property is all property wherever situated and includes—
    (a) money,
    (b) all forms of property, real or personal, heritable or moveable,
    (c) things in action and other intangible or incorporeal property.
(2) Any reference to a person's property (whether expressed as a reference to the property he holds or otherwise) is to be read as follows.
(3) In relation to land, it is a reference to any interest which he holds in the land.
(4) In relation to property other than land, it is a reference—
    (a) to the property (if it belongs to him), or
    (b) to any other interest which he holds in the property (Anti-terrorism, Crime and Security Act 2001, Sch 1, para 17).

Property earmarked as terrorist property

(1) **Property obtained through terrorism** is earmarked as terrorist property.

(2) But if property obtained through terrorism has been disposed of (since it was so obtained), it is earmarked as terrorist property only if it is held by a person into whose hands it may be followed.

(3) Earmarked property obtained through terrorism may be followed into the hands of a person obtaining it on a disposal by—
   (a) the person who obtained the property through terrorism, or
   (b) a person into whose hands it may (by virtue of this sub-paragraph) be followed (Anti-terrorism, Crime and Security Act 2001, Sch 1, para 12).

See **note (m)**.

Property obtained through terrorism

(1) A person obtains property through terrorism if he obtains property by or in return for **acts of terrorism**, or acts carried out for the purposes of terrorism.

(2) In deciding whether any property was obtained through terrorism—
   (a) it is immaterial whether or not any money, goods or services were provided in order to put the person in question in a position to carry out the acts,
   (b) it is not necessary to show that the act was of a particular kind if it is shown that the property was obtained through acts of one of a number of kinds, each of which would have been an act of terrorism, or an act carried out for the purposes of terrorism (Anti-terrorism, Crime and Security Act 2001, Sch 1, para 11).

Acts of terrorism (see **4.1**)

48 hours

In determining the period of 48 hours in sub-paragraph 3(1) any Saturday or Sunday, Christmas Day, Good Friday, and any bank holiday are to be disregarded (Anti-terrorism, Crime and Security Act 2001, Sch 1, para 3(1A)).

Notes

(a) These forfeiture powers may be exercised in relation to any cash whether or not any proceedings have been brought for an offence in connection with the cash (Anti-terrorism, Crime and Security Act 2001, s 1(2)).

(b) An authorized officer may use *reasonable force* when exercising these powers of seizure and detention (Terrorism Act 2000, Sch 14, para 3).

(c) An authorized officer may also *enter a vehicle*, aircraft, hovercraft, train, or vessel for the purpose of seizing and detaining cash (Terrorism Act 2000, Sch 14, para 2).

(d) There is a Code of Practice for authorized officers acting under Schedule 1. This gives more detailed guidance on the exercise of powers under this Schedule. See **4.4.18** and for the full text, see **Appendix 5**.

(e) There are no minimum or maximum limits on the amount of cash that may be seized.

(f) These provisions do not apply to counterfeit cash. Such cash could be seized under section 24 of the Forgery and Counterfeiting Act 1981.

(g) *Extension of detention of seized cash by court order*—a magistrates' court can make an order to extend the period for which cash or any part of it may be detained (Anti-terrorism, Crime and Security Act 2001, Sch 1, para 3(2)).

(h) The magistrates' court (or justice of the peace if first order, see **note (k)**) may make the order if satisfied, in relation to any cash to be further detained, that one of the following conditions is met.

First condition: reasonable grounds for suspecting that the cash is intended to be used for the purposes of terrorism and that either—

(a) its continued detention is justified while its intended use is further investigated or consideration is given to bringing (in the UK or elsewhere) proceedings against any person for an offence with which the cash is connected; or

(b) proceedings against any person for an offence with which the cash is connected have been started and have not been concluded.

Second condition: reasonable grounds for suspecting that the cash consists of resources of an organization which is a proscribed organization and that either—

(a) its continued detention is justified while investigation is made into whether or not it consists of such resources or consideration is given to bringing (in the UK or elsewhere) proceedings against any person for an offence with which the cash is connected; or

(b) proceedings against any person for an offence with which the cash is connected have been started and have not been concluded.

Third condition: reasonable grounds for suspecting that the cash is property earmarked as terrorist property and that either—

(a) its continued detention is justified while its derivation is further investigated or consideration is given to bringing (in the UK or elsewhere) proceedings against any person for an offence with which the cash is connected; or

(b) proceedings against any person for an offence with which the cash is connected have been started and have not been concluded (Anti-terrorism, Crime and Security Act 2001, Sch 1, para 3(5)–(8)).

(i) *Application*—the application for an order under sub-paragraph (2) may be made by the Commissioners of Customs and Excise or an authorized officer, that is, a constable, immigration, or customs officer (Anti-terrorism, Crime and Security Act 2001, Sch 1, para 3(5)).

(j) *Duration*—detention of cash may be authorized for up to three months from the date of the order and, in the case of any further orders, up to two years from the date of the first order (Anti-terrorism, Crime and Security Act 2001, Sch 1, para 3(2)).

(k) *First order*—a first order under sub-paragraph (2) to extend the period of detention of seized cash may be made by a justice of the peace. The application to a justice of the peace for such an order may be made and heard without notice of the application or hearing having been given to any of the persons affected by the application or to the legal representative of such a person, and may be heard and determined in private in the absence of persons so affected and of their legal representatives (Anti-terrorism, Crime and Security Act 2001, Sch 1, para 3(3A)). The person affected will have the opportunity to challenge the making of the order at a later date because he will be served with a copy (para 3(4)) and can apply for it to be discharged (para 5).

(l) *Notice*—an order under sub-paragraph (2) must provide for notice to be given to persons affected by it (Anti-terrorism, Crime and Security Act 2001, Sch 1, para 3(4)).

(m) *Terrorist property*—paragraphs 11–16 of Schedule 1 make detailed provisions about property earmarked as terrorist property. For tracing property, mixing property, accruing profits, and exceptions refer to Schedule 1 (not reproduced here).

(n) *Handling of detained cash*—paragraphs 4 and 5 of Schedule 1 make provision for the payment of detained cash into an interest-bearing account and for the release of such cash.

(o) *Forfeiture*—while cash is detained under Schedule 1, an application for its forfeiture may be made. Paragraphs 6–8 of Schedule 1 set out the procedure for doing this and how to appeal against the forfeiture. Note that these are civil proceedings and that this is a different procedure from the one provided for in section 23 of and Schedule 4 to the Terrorism Act 2000 which applies where a person had been convicted of a terrorist property or finance offence (see **4.4.12**).

(p) *Victims/compensation*—paragraphs 9 and 10 of Schedule 1 make provision for persons to apply to the magistrates' court for the release of their cash and for compensation.

PNLD reference numbers

D10303, D10367–D10383

4.4.18 **Code of Practice for authorized officers**

The Code of Practice for authorized officers acting under Schedule 1 to the Anti-terrorism, Crime and Security Act 2001 issued under Schedule 14 to the Terrorism Act 2000 applies to all authorizing officers, that is, constables, immigration officers, and customs officers, exercising functions under Schedule 1 (see **4.4.17**). It does not apply in the exercise of other powers of seizure, detention, or forfeiture under other Acts, for example under the Drug Trafficking Act 1994.

Notes

(a) The Code should be available at all police stations and at police offices at ports (for ports, see **5.4**) where the powers are, or are likely to be, used for consultation by the police and the public.

(b) Failure by an officer to observe a provision of a code does not of itself make him liable to criminal or civil proceedings (Terrorism Act 2000, Sch 14, para 6(2)).

(c) For the full text of the code, see **Appendix 5**.

Chapter 5

Terrorist Investigations

5.1 Meaning of Terrorist Investigation

Section 32 of the Terrorism Act 2000 defines the term 'terrorist investigation'. This definition applies, for example, to powers to use cordons, to obtain search warrants, production orders, and explanation orders; and to make financial information orders. There is also an offence in section 39 of 'tipping off' in relation to a terrorist investigation (see **5.1.8**).

Terrorist investigation means an investigation of—

(a) the commission, preparation, or instigation of **acts of terrorism**,
(b) an act which appears to have been done for the purposes of terrorism,
(c) the resources of a **proscribed organization**,
(d) the possibility of making an order under section 3(3), or
(e) the commission, preparation, or instigation of an offence under this Act or under Part 1 (*sections 1–20*) of the Terrorism Act 2006 other than an offence under section 1 (*encouragement of terrorism*) or 2 (*dissemination of terrorist publication*) of that Act.

Meanings

Acts of terrorism (see **4.1.2**)

Proscribed organization (see **4.2.1**)

Notes

(a) The terms used in the definition of 'terrorist investigation' will often cover not only investigations into possible criminal offences, but also other forms of preparatory work, such as in relation to proscription or transnational terrorism finances, and protective work.

(b) For details on the offences in sections 1 and 2 of the Terrorism Act 2006 see **4.3.1** and **4.3.2**.

PNLD reference number

D8722

5.1.1 **Obtaining of information—powers under Schedule 5**

Section 37 of and Schedule 5 to the Terrorism Act 2000 set out the procedure for obtaining information in terrorist investigations, either by warrant or order of the court or by the authority of a police officer. The powers differ from those under the Police and Criminal Evidence Act 1984 (PACE), but there are similarities. Essentially, searches under Schedule 5 require that the search is part of a terrorist investigation (see definition at **5.1**); it does not need to be connected to a specific offence as with PACE powers. The other notable extension of power is that it is possible to obtain excluded material and to conduct an 'area search' of non-residential premises. Schedule 5 also creates a number of offences, where searches are obstructed, false statements made, etc. When undertaking financial investigations the powers provided in Schedule 6 (see **4.4.15**) or account monitoring orders, Schedule 6A (see **4.4.16**), might be more appropriate.

Schedule 5 provides the following powers—

1. Search warrant under paragraph 1 (see **5.1.2**):
   - power to enter and search premises, search persons, seize and retain relevant material;
   - constable may apply to justice of the peace;
   - specific or all premises warrant, may include residential premises;
   - not excepted material;
   - urgency: written order by Superintendent (see **5.1.2 note (m)**).
2. Search warrant under paragraph 2 (see **5.1.3**):
   - power to enter and search premises, search persons, seize and retain relevant material;
   - Superintendent may apply to justice of the peace;

- justice need not be satisfied that warrant likely to be necessary;
- specific premises warrant, not residential premises;
- *not* excepted material.

3. Authority to search under paragraph 3—cordons (see **5.2.4**):
   - power to enter and search premises, search persons, seize and retain relevant material;
   - authority by Superintendent (urgency: constable);
   - in cordoned area;
   - *not* excepted material.

4. Production order under paragraph 5 (see **5.1.4**):
   - production of and access to excluded and special procedure material;
   - constable may apply to Circuit Judge.

5. Search warrant under paragraphs 11 and 12—excluded and special procedure material (see **5.1.5**):
   - power to enter and search premises, search persons, seize and retain relevant material, including excluded and special procedure material;
   - constable may apply to Circuit Judge;
   - specific or all premises warrant, may include residential premises;
   - urgency: written order by Superintendent (see **5.1.5 note (l)**).

6. Explanation orders under paragraph 13 (see **5.1.6**):
   - order to provide explanation of material seized under paragraph 1 or 11/produced under paragraph 5;
   - constable may apply to Circuit Judge;
   - different powers are appropriate depending on the different types of material that are the subject of the search, production order etc. Some do not apply to **excepted material**, some allow the search for **excluded material** or **special procedure material**. No power allows the search or seizure of **items subject to legal privilege**.

Meanings

Excepted material

Any of the following—

(a) 'excluded material',
(b) 'items subject to legal privilege', and
(c) 'special procedure material'

as defined in sections 11, 10, and 14 of the Police and Criminal Evidence Act 1984 (Terrorism Act 2000, Sch 5, para 4).

Excluded material

Means—

(a) personal records which a person has acquired or created in the course of any trade, business, profession, or other occupation or for the purposes of any paid or unpaid office and which he holds in confidence;
(b) human tissue or tissue fluid which has been taken for the purposes of diagnosis or medical treatment and which a person holds in confidence;
(c) journalistic material which a person holds in confidence and which consists of documents; or of records other than documents.

A person holds personal records and human tissue or fluid material in confidence if he holds it subject to an express or implied undertaking to hold it in confidence; or to a restriction on disclosure or an obligation of secrecy contained in any enactment, including an enactment contained in an Act passed after this Act.

A person holds journalistic material in confidence if he holds it subject to such an undertaking, restriction, or obligation; and it has been continuously held (by one or more persons) subject to such an undertaking, restriction, or obligation since it was first acquired or created for the purposes of journalism (Police and Criminal Evidence Act 1984, s 11).

Special procedure material

Means—

• journalistic material, other than excluded material; and
• material, other than items subject to legal privilege and excluded material, in the possession of a person who acquired or created it in the course of any trade, business, profession, or other occupation or for the purpose of any paid or unpaid office; and holds it subject—
  (i) to an express or implied undertaking to hold it in confidence; or
  (ii) to a restriction on disclosure or an obligation of secrecy contained in any enactment.

Where material is acquired by an employee from his employer and in the course of his employment, or by a company from an associated company, it is only special procedure material if it was special procedure material immediately before the acquisition.

Where material is created by an employee in the course of his employment, it is only special procedure material if it would have been special procedure material had his employer created it.

Where material is created by a company on behalf of an associated company, it is only special procedure material if it would have been special procedure material had the associated company created it (Police and Criminal Evidence Act 1984, s 14).

Items subject to legal privilege

Means—

(a) communications between a professional legal adviser and his client or any person representing his client made in connection with the giving of legal advice to the client;

(b) communications between a professional legal adviser and his client or any person representing his client or between such an adviser or his client or any such representative and any other person made in connection with or in contemplation of legal proceedings and for the purposes of such proceedings; and

(c) items enclosed with or referred to in such communications and made in connection with the giving of legal advice; or in connection with or in contemplation of legal proceedings and for the purposes of such proceedings, when they are in the possession of a person who is entitled to possession of them.

Items held with the intention of furthering a criminal purpose are not items subject to legal privilege (Police and Criminal Evidence Act 1984, s 10).

Related cases

R v Inner London Crown Court, ex p Baines and Baines (a firm) [1988] QB 579; R v Guildhall Magistrates' Court, ex p Primlaks Holdings Co (Panama) Inc [1990] 1 QB 261 'Legal privilege' relates to legal advice in connection with proceedings rather than legal documents in general.

R v R [1994] 1 WLR 758 A blood sample provided by the defendant to his doctor for a DNA test which his solicitors had requested was privileged.

Privilege does not apply to:

R v Leeds Magistrates' Court, ex p Dumbleton [1993] Crim LR 866, DC Forged documents.

R v Manchester Crown Court, ex p Rogers [1999] 1 WLR 832 Records of time spent with a client on attendance notes, time sheets, or fee records.

R v Central Criminal Court, ex p Francis and Francis (a firm) [1989] AC 346; R (on the application of Hallinan Blackburn-Gittings & Nott (a firm)) v Middlesex Guildhall Crown Court [2004] EWHC 2726 (Admin) Items held with the intention of either the holder or any other person of furthering a criminal purpose (including the perverting of justice) (Police and Criminal Evidence Act 1984, s 10(2)).

PNLD reference numbers

D8766, C99, C97, C283, C1176

5.1.2 **Search warrants**

Paragraph 1 of Schedule 5 to the Terrorism Act 2000 provides for warrants to enter and search premises, search persons, seize and retain relevant material.

(1) A constable may apply to a justice of the peace for the issue of a warrant under this paragraph for the purposes of a **terrorist investigation**.

(2) A warrant under this paragraph shall authorise any constable—

    (a) to enter **premises mentioned in sub-paragraph (2A)**,

    (b) to search the premises and any person found there, and

    (c) to seize and retain any **relevant material** which is found on a search under paragraph (b).

(5) Subject to paragraph 2, a justice may grant an application under this paragraph if satisfied—

    (a) that the warrant is sought for the purposes of a terrorist investigation,

    (b) that there are reasonable grounds for believing that there is material on premises to which the application relates which is likely to be of substantial value, whether by itself or together with other material, to a terrorist investigation and which does not consist of or include **excepted material** (within the meaning of paragraph 4 below),

    (c) that the issue of a warrant is likely to be necessary in the circumstances of the case, and

    (d) in the case of an application for an all premises warrant, that it is not reasonably practicable to specify in the application all the premises which the person so specified occupies or controls and which might need to be searched.

Terrorism Act 2000, Sch 5, para 1(1), (2) and (5)

Meanings

Terrorist investigation (see **5.1**)

Premises mentioned in sub-paragraph (2A)

These are:

(a) one or more sets of premises specified in the application (in which case the application is for a 'specific premises warrant'); or

(b) any premises occupied or controlled by a person specified in the application, including such sets of premises as are so specified (in which case the application is for an 'all premises warrant') (Terrorism Act 2000, Sch 5, para 1(2A)).

Material is relevant

If the constable has reasonable grounds for believing that—

(a) it is likely to be of substantial value, whether by itself or together with other material, to a terrorist investigation, and

(b) it must be seized in order to prevent it from being concealed, lost, damaged, altered or destroyed (Terrorism Act 2000, Sch 5, para 1(3)).

Excepted material (see **5.1.1**)

Notes

(a) The seizure and retention of *items subject to legal privilege* (see **5.1.1**) cannot be authorized by a warrant under this provision (Terrorism Act 2000, Sch 5, para 1(4)(a)).

(b) For access to excluded and special procedure material see **5.1.4** and **5.1.5**. This may include government material, see **5.1.4 note (f)** and paragraph 9 of Schedule 5.

(c) *Removal of clothing* under this provision: a constable may only require a person to remove headgear, footwear, an outer coat, a jacket, or gloves in public (Terrorism Act 2000, Sch 5, para 1(4)(b)).

(d) A constable may if necessary use *reasonable force* for the purpose of exercising a power of entry, search, or seizure (Terrorism Act 2000, s 114(2)).

(e) The power to search premises includes the power to search a container (Terrorism Act 2000, s 116(1)) and a vehicle (Terrorism Act 2000, s 121).

(f) If something is found during a search that is not relevant to the specific investigation but to a different terrorist investigation, the item may be seized and it is not necessary to return to court to get a further warrant; for example, a search is conducted as part of an investigation into the publication of material that is glorifying terrorism; during the search chemicals are found that might be used to build bombs.

(g) The power to seize and retain materials attracts additional powers under the Criminal Justice and Police Act 2001, sections 50, 51, and 55. Section 50 allows the seizure of bulk material in order to sift through it at another place where it is not reasonably practicable to sift through it at the place where it was found. Where only part of an item would be legally seizable, section 50 provides for the removal of the whole item where it is not reasonably practicable to separate the part that may otherwise lawfully be seized from the rest; for example, where material is on a computer. Section 51 provides similar powers where items are found on a person who is lawfully searched; for example, where a person carries a computer or a bag full of material that needs to be examined. Section 55 provides that any excluded or special procedure material must be returned as soon as practicable, unless it is not reasonably practicable to separate it from other lawfully seized material without prejudicing that material's use.

(h) Section 21 of the Police and Criminal Evidence Act 1984 provides a person, from whom material has been lawfully seized by the police, with certain rights to access to and/or copies of it.

(i) Section 22 of the Police and Criminal Evidence Act 1984 provides directions and powers in relation to items that have been seized by the police.

(j) As in the Police and Criminal Evidence Act 1984, the warrant may be a 'specific premises warrant' or an 'all premises warrant'. For a specific premises warrant, one or more sets of premises must be specified in the warrant (and in the application); the all premises warrant applies to any premises occupied or controlled by a person specified in the warrant, including those premises specified in the warrant.

(k) *Duration*—entry and search under a warrant must be within three months from the date of its issue (Police and Criminal Evidence Act 1984, s 16(3)).

(l) There is also a power to require a person to provide an explanation of the material seized in pursuance of a warrant under paragraph 1, see **5.1.6**.

(m) *Urgent cases*—the same authority that may be given by a search warrant under paragraph 1 may in urgent cases be given to a constable by a police officer of at least the rank of Superintendent by a written order signed by him. Such an order may only be made if the officer has reasonable grounds for believing that the case is one of great emergency, *and* that immediate action is necessary. Where such an order is made, particulars of the case must be notified as soon as is reasonably practicable to the Secretary of State. It is an offence to wilfully obstruct a search made under such an order (maximum penalty on summary conviction three months' imprisonment and/or a fine not exceeding level 4 on the standard scale) (Terrorism Act 2000, Sch 5, para 15).

(n) If a police officer of at least the rank of Superintendent has reasonable grounds for believing that the case is one of great emergency he may by a written notice signed by him require any person specified in the notice to provide an explanation of any material seized in pursuance of an order under paragraph 15 (Terrorism Act 2000, Sch 5, para 16(1)). Paragraphs 13(2)–(4) and 14 shall apply to a notice under this paragraph as they apply to an order under paragraph 13 (see **5.1.6**). It is an offence to fail to comply with a notice under paragraph 16. It is a defence to this offence if the person can show that he had a reasonable excuse for his failure. The maximum penalty on summary conviction is six months' imprisonment and/or a fine not exceeding level 5 on the standard scale (Terrorism Act 2000, Sch 5, para 16(3)–(5)).

PNLD reference numbers

D8764, D8771

5.1.3 **Search warrants—non-residential premises**

Paragraph 2 of Schedule 5 provides for a further power to enter and search premises. It is wider than the one in paragraph 1 (see **5.1.2**): a justice of the peace need not be satisfied that the issue of the warrant is likely to be necessary. Such an application must be made by a Superintendent and covers only non-residential premises.

(1) This paragraph applies where an application for a specific premises warrant is made under paragraph 1 and—

   (a) the application is made by a police officer of at least the rank of superintendent,

   (b) the application does not relate to **residential premises**, and

   (c) the justice to whom the application is made is not satisfied of the matter referred to in paragraph 1(5)(c) *[warrant likely to be necessary, see **5.1.2**]*.

(2) The justice may grant the application if satisfied of the matters referred to in paragraph 1(5)(a) and (b) *[terrorist investigation and reasonable grounds to believe material of substantial value is on premises, see 5.1.2]*.

Terrorism Act 2000, Sch 5, para 2

Meanings

Residential premises

Means any premises which the officer making the application has reasonable grounds for believing are used wholly or mainly as a dwelling (Terrorism Act 2000, Sch 5, para 2(4)).

Notes

(a) There is no equivalent power to this in the Police and Criminal Evidence Act 1984.

(b) This power may, for example, be used to search a number of premises in a specific area where it is suspected that terrorists are active, but where the exact location of the premises is not known. The power has been used, for example, to search rows of lock-up garages.

(c) *Duration*—the powers under paragraph 1(2)(a) and (2)(b) (to enter and search the premises and persons found therein) are only exercisable within 24 hours beginning with the time the warrant is issued (Terrorism Act 2000, Sch 5, para 2(3)). The power to seize and retain material found on such a search is exercisable within three months from the date of the issue of the warrant (Police and Criminal Evidence Act 1984, s 16(3)).

(d) Section 21 of the Police and Criminal Evidence Act 1984 provides a person, from whom material has been lawfully seized by the police, with certain rights of access to and/or copies of it.

(e) Section 22 of the Police and Criminal Evidence Act 1984 provides directions and powers in relation to items that have been seized by the police.

PNLD reference number

D8765

5.1.4 Production orders—excluded and special procedure material

Production of and access to excluded and special procedure material is provided for in paragraph 5 of Schedule 5 to the Terrorism Act

2000. There is also an option to search for such material; it applies where an order under paragraph 5 has not been complied with, if it is not practicable to communicate with the person concerned, or if immediate access is necessary (see **5.1.5**).

5(1) A constable may apply to a Circuit Judge for an order under this paragraph for the purposes of a **terrorist investigation**.

(2) An application for an order shall relate to particular material, or material of a particular description, which consists of or includes **excluded material** or **special procedure material**.

(3) An order under this paragraph may require a specified person—

    (a) to produce to a constable within a specified period for seizure and retention any material which he has in his possession, custody or power and to which the application relates;

    (b) to give a constable access to any material of the kind mentioned in paragraph (a) within a specified period;

    (c) to state to the best of his knowledge and belief the location of material to which the application relates if it is not in, and it will not come into, his possession, custody or power within the period specified under paragraph (a) or (b).

(4) For the purposes of this paragraph—

    (a) an order may specify a person only if he appears to the Circuit Judge to have in his possession, custody or power any of the material to which the application relates, and

    (b) a period specified in an order shall be the period of seven days beginning with the date of the order unless it appears to the judge that a different period would be appropriate in the particular circumstances of the application.

(5) Where a Circuit Judge makes an order under sub-paragraph (3)(b) in relation to material on any premises, he may, on the application of a constable, order any person who appears to the judge to be entitled to grant entry to the premises to allow any constable to enter the premises to obtain access to the material.

6(1) A Circuit Judge may grant an application under paragraph 5 if satisfied—

    (a) that the material to which the application relates consists of or includes excluded material or special procedure material,

    (b) that it does not include **items subject to legal privilege**, and

    (c) that the conditions in sub-paragraph (2) and (3) are satisfied in respect of that material.

(2) The first condition is that—
   (a) the order is sought for the purpose of a terrorist investigation, and
   (b) there are reasonable grounds for believing that the material is **likely to be of substantial value**, whether by itself or together with other material, to a terrorist investigation.

(3) The second condition is that there are reasonable grounds for believing that it is in the public interest that the material should be produced or that access to it should be given having regard—
   (a) to the benefit likely to accrue to a terrorist investigation if the material is obtained, and
   (b) to the circumstances under which the person concerned has any of the material in his possession, custody or power.

Terrorism Act 2000, Sch 5, paras 5 and 6

Meanings

Terrorist investigation (see **5.1**)

Excluded material (see **5.1.1**)

Special procedure material (see **5.1.1**)

Items subject to legal privilege (see **5.1.1**)

Likely to be of substantial value (see **Related case**)

Notes

(a) Special procedure material may be seized under any of the three powers set out in Schedule 5, paragraphs 1–3 (see **5.1.2**, **5.1.3**, and **5.2.4**); however, if it is intentionally sought, the power in paragraph 5 of Schedule 5 should be used.

(b) Paragraph 7 of Schedule 5 provides that an order may also extend to material that comes into existence within 28 days from the day of the date of the order and may be made in relation to a person who the Circuit Judge thinks is likely to have any of the material to which the application relates in his possession, custody, or power within that period (Terrorism Act 2000, Sch 5, para 7(1)).

(c) There is no requirement that the notice be given to the possessor of the materials or that the material must be potential 'evidence' for a court case.

(d) *Items subject to legal privilege* are exempt from any orders under Schedule 5, including paragraph 5 (Sch 5, para 8(1)(a)).

(e) Paragraph 5 has effect notwithstanding any restrictions on disclosure of information imposed by statute or otherwise (Sch 5, para 8(1)(b)).

(f) *Government material*—an order made under paragraph 5 may also cover material in the possession, custody, or power of a government department (for details see paragraph 9 of Schedule 5 which is not reproduced here).

(g) *Material on computer*—where the application under paragraph 5 relates to information contained in a computer, an order under paragraph 5(3)(a) to produce to a constable for seizure and retention any material has effect as an order to produce the material in a form in which it can be taken away and in which it is visible and legible; and an order under paragraph 5(3)(b) to give a constable access to material has effect as an order to give access to the material in a form in which it is visible and legible (Sch 5, para 8(2)).

(h) This power may be used to obtain journalistic material. However, the rights of journalists to protect their sources and the freedom of expression need to be balanced with the needs of the police investigation. See **Related case**.

(i) Where an order under paragraph 5 has not been complied with the police may apply for a warrant to search for excluded and special procedure material (see **5.1.5**).

(j) There is also a power to require a person to provide an explanation of the material produced or made available to a constable under paragraph 5 (see **5.1.6**).

Related case

Malik v Manchester Crown Court [2008] EWHC 1362 Where material that is relevant for a terrorist investigation is in the possession of a journalist, there is a potential conflict between the interests of the state in ensuring that the police are able to conduct terrorist investigations as effectively as possible and the rights of a journalist to protect his confidential sources. These rights of a journalist are important, but are not absolute. It is for the police to satisfy the court that the balance should be struck in favour of making a production order. When exercising discretion, the judge has to take into account Article 10 of the European Convention on Human Rights (freedom of expression). A production order cannot be made if and to the extent that it would violate a person's Convention rights.

Paragraph 6(2)(b) should be given its plain and ordinary meaning: 'likely' means 'probable'. A 'substantial value' is a value which is more than minimal: it must be significant. The judge has to be satisfied that there are reasonable grounds for believing that the material is likely to be of substantial value, mere suspicion will not suffice.

PNLD reference number

D8767

5.1.5 **Search warrants—excluded and special procedure material**

Paragraphs 11 and 12 of Schedule 5 to the Terrorism Act 2000 provide for warrants to enter and search premises, search persons, seize and retain relevant material including excluded and special procedure material. It applies where an order under paragraph 5 (see **5.1.4**) has not been complied with, if it is not practicable to communicate with the person concerned, or if immediate access is necessary.

11(1) A constable may apply to a Circuit Judge for the issue of a warrant under this paragraph for the purposes of a **terrorist investigation**.

(2) A warrant under this paragraph shall authorise any constable—

  (a) to enter **premises mentioned in sub-paragraph (3A)**,

  (b) to search the premises and any person found there, and

  (c) to seize and retain any **relevant material** which is found on a search under paragraph (b).

12(1) A Circuit Judge may grant an application for a specific premises warrant under paragraph 11 if satisfied that an order made under paragraph 5 in relation to material on the premises specified in the application has not been complied with.

(2) A Circuit Judge may also grant an application for a specific premises warrant under paragraph 11 if satisfied that there are reasonable grounds for believing that—

  (a) there is material on premises specified in the application which consists of or includes **excluded material** or **special procedure material** but does not include items subject to legal privilege, and

  (b) the conditions in sub-paragraphs (3) and (4) are satisfied.

(2A) A Circuit Judge or a District Judge (magistrates' courts) may grant an application for an all premises warrant under paragraph 11 if satisfied—

  (a) that an order made under paragraph 5 has not been complied with, and

  (b) that the person specified in the application is also specified in the order.

(2B) A Circuit Judge or a District Judge (magistrates' courts) may also grant an application for an all premises warrant under paragraph 11 if satisfied that there are reasonable grounds for believing—

(a) that there is material on premises to which the application relates which consists of or includes excluded material or special procedure material but does not include items subject to legal privilege, and

(b) that the conditions in sub-paragraphs (3) and (4) are met.

(3) The first condition is that—

(a) the warrant is sought for the purposes of a terrorist investigation, and

(b) the material is likely to be of substantial value, whether by itself or together with other material, to a terrorist investigation.

(4) The second condition is that it is not appropriate to make an order under paragraph 5 in relation to the material because—

(a) it is not practicable to communicate with any person entitled to produce the material,

(b) it is not practicable to communicate with any person entitled to grant access to the material or entitled to grant entry to premises to which the application for the warrant relates, or

(c) a terrorist investigation may be seriously prejudiced unless a constable can secure immediate access to the material.

Terrorism Act 2000, Sch 5, paras 11(1) and (2) and 12(1)–(4)

Meanings

Terrorist investigation (see **5.1**)

Premises mentioned in sub-paragraph (3A)

These are—

(a) one or more sets of premises specified in the application (in which case the application is for a 'specific premises warrant'); or

(b) any premises occupied or controlled by a person specified in the application, including such sets of premises as are so specified (in which case the application is for an 'all premises warrant') (Terrorism Act 2000, Sch 5, para 11(3A)).

Material is relevant

If the constable has reasonable grounds for believing that it is **likely to be of substantial value**, whether by itself or together with other material, to a terrorist investigation (Terrorism Act 2000, Sch 5, para 11(4)).

Likely to be of substantial value (see **Related case** in **5.1.4**)

Excluded material (see **5.1.1**)

Special procedure material (see **5.1.1**)

Notes

(a) *Items subject to legal privilege*—the seizure and retention of such items (see **5.1.1**) cannot be authorized by a warrant under this provision (see **5.1.1** , Terrorism Act 2000, Sch 5, para 11(3)(a)).

(b) *Removal of clothing*—under this provision a constable may only require a person to remove headgear, footwear, an outer coat, a jacket, or gloves in public (Terrorism Act 2000, Sch 5, para 11(3)(b)).

(c) The power to search premises includes the power to search a container (Terrorism Act 2000, s 116(1)) and a vehicle (Terrorism Act 2000, s 121).

(d) A constable may if necessary use *reasonable force* for the purpose of exercising a power of entry, search, or seizure (Terrorism Act 2000, s 114(2)).

(e) The power to seize and retain material attracts additional powers under the Criminal Justice and Police Act 2001, sections 50 and 51, namely additional powers of seizure from premises and additional powers of seizure from the person. For details see **5.1.2, note (g)**.

(f) Section 21 of the Police and Criminal Evidence Act 1984 provides a person, from whom material has been lawfully seized by the police, with certain rights of access to and/or copies of it.

(g) Section 22 of the Police and Criminal Evidence Act 1984 provides directions and powers in relation to items that have been seized by the police.

(h) The warrant may be a specific premises warrant or an all premises warrant, see **5.1.2, note (j)**.

(i) *Duration*—entry and search under a warrant must be within three months from the date of its issue (Police and Criminal Evidence Act 1984, s 16(3)).

(j) There is also a power to require a person to provide an explanation of the material seized in pursuance of a warrant under paragraph 11, see **5.1.6**.

(k) *Urgent cases*—the same authority that may be given by a search warrant under paragraph 11 may in urgent cases be given to a constable by a police officer of at least the rank of

Superintendent by a written order signed by him. Such an order may only be made if the officer has reasonable grounds for believing that the case is one of great emergency, and that immediate action is necessary. Where such an order is made, particulars of the case must be notified as soon as is reasonably practicable to the Secretary of State. It is an offence to wilfully obstruct a search made under such an order (maximum penalty on summary conviction three months' imprisonment and/or a fine not exceeding level 4 on the standard scale) (Terrorism Act 2000, Sch 5, para 15).

(l) If a police officer of at least the rank of Superintendent has reasonable grounds for believing that the case is one of great emergency, he may by a written notice signed by him require any person specified in the notice to provide an explanation of any material seized in pursuance of an order under paragraph 15 (Terrorism Act 2000, Sch 5, para 16(1)) (see also **5.1.2 note (n)**).

PNLD reference number

D8769

5.1.6 **Explanation orders**

Paragraph 13 of Schedule 5 to the Terrorism Act 2000 provides another investigatory power linked to the search powers in paragraph 1 (search of premises, see **5.1.2**) and paragraph 11 (search for excluded and special procedure material, see **5.1.5**) and the production order under paragraph 5 (excluded and special procedure material, see **5.1.4**). Where material has been seized or given to the police under these provisions a constable may apply for an order requiring a person to provide an explanation of that material.

Police power to require explanation of material

(1) A constable may apply to a Circuit Judge for an order under this paragraph requiring any person specified in the order to provide an explanation of any material—

(a) seized in pursuance of a warrant under paragraph 1 or 11, or

(b) produced or made available to a constable under paragraph 5.

Terrorism Act 2000, Sch 5, para 13(1)

Notes

(a) For search powers in paragraph 1 (search of premises) see **5.1.2**, and paragraph 11 (search for excluded and special procedure material) see **5.1.5**.

(b) For production orders under paragraph 5 (excluded and special procedure material) see **5.1.4**.

(c) There is no equivalent power to this in the Police and Criminal Evidence Act 1984.

(d) The order must not include legally privileged material (see **5.1.1**); it must not require a person to disclose information which he would be entitled to refuse to disclose on grounds of legal professional privilege in proceedings in the High Court. However, a lawyer may be required to provide the name and address of his client (Terrorism Act 2000, Sch 5, para 13(2) and (3)).

(e) It is an offence if a person, in purported compliance with an order under paragraph 13, makes a statement which he knows to be false or misleading in a material particular, or recklessly makes a statement which is false or misleading in a material particular. This is an either way offence, the maximum penalty on conviction on indictment is imprisonment up to two years and/or a fine, on summary conviction imprisonment up to six months and/or a fine not exceeding the statutory maximum (Terrorism Act 2000, Sch 5, para 14). The provisions on post-charge questioning apply to this offence, see **4.2.2 note (g)**.

(f) Where an order under paragraph 13 requires a person to explain material, he may make a statement orally or in writing (Terrorism Act 2000, Sch 5, para 13(4)(a)).

(g) Such a statement may only be used as evidence against the person on a prosecution for an offence under paragraph 14 (see **note (e)**, Terrorism Act 2000, Sch 5, para 13(4)(b)). The statement must not be used as evidence in any other case; this would contravene Article 6 of the European Convention of Human Rights (right against self-incrimination).

PNLD reference number

D8770

5.1.7 **Disclosure of information**

Part 3 (sections 17–20) of the Anti-terrorism, Crime and Security Act 2001 deals with the disclosure of information. Section 17 of the Act clarifies and extends a number of information disclosure provisions available to individuals working in public authorities.

(1) This section applies to the provisions listed in Schedule 4, so far as they authorise the disclosure of **information**.

(2) Each of the provisions to which this section applies shall have effect, in relation to the disclosure of information by or on behalf of a **public authority**, as if the purposes for which the disclosure of information is authorised by that provision included each of the following—

   (a) the purposes of any **criminal investigation** whatever which is being or may be carried out, whether in the United Kingdom or elsewhere;

   (b) the purposes of any criminal proceedings whatever which have been or may be initiated, whether in the United Kingdom or elsewhere;

   (c) the purposes of the initiation or bringing to an end of any such investigation or proceedings;

   (d) the purpose of facilitating a determination of whether any such investigation or proceedings should be initiated or brought to an end.

(5) No disclosure of information shall be made by virtue of this section unless the public authority by which the disclosure is made is satisfied that the making of the disclosure is proportionate to what is sought to be achieved by it.

(6) Nothing in this section shall be taken to prejudice any power to disclose information which exists apart from this section.

Anti-terrorism, Crime and Security Act 2001, s 17(1),(2),(5) and (6)

Meanings

Information

Includes—

(a) documents; and

(b) in relation to a disclosure authorized by a provision to which section 17 applies, anything that falls to be treated as information for the purposes of that provision (Anti-terrorism, Crime and Security Act 2001, s 20(1)).

Public authority

Includes—

(a) a court or tribunal, and

(b) any person certain of whose functions are functions of a public nature,

but does not include either House of Parliament or a person exercising functions in connection with proceedings in Parliament (Anti-terrorism, Crime and Security Act 2001, s 20(1), Human Rights Act 1998, s 6(3)).

Criminal investigation

Means an investigation of any **criminal conduct**, including an investigation of alleged or suspected criminal conduct and an investigation of whether criminal conduct has taken place (Anti-terrorism, Crime and Security Act 2001, s 20(1)). Note that these powers are not confined to terrorism investigations.

Conduct

Includes acts, omissions, and statements (Anti-terrorism, Crime and Security Act 2001, s 20(3)).

Criminal conduct

Means any conduct which—

(a) constitutes one or more criminal offences under the law of a part of the UK; or
(b) is, or corresponds to, conduct which, if it all took place in a particular part of the UK, would constitute one or more offences under the law of that part of the UK (Anti-terrorism, Crime and Security Act 2001, s 20(3)).

Proceedings outside the UK shall not be taken to be criminal proceedings unless the conduct with which the defendant in those proceedings is charged is criminal conduct or conduct which, to a substantial extent, consists of criminal conduct (Anti-terrorism, Crime and Security Act 2001, s 20(2)).

Notes

(a) The powers are listed in Schedule 4 and include, for example, section 28(7) of the Health and Safety at Work etc. Act 1974 (restriction on disclosure of information re investigations by Health and Safety Executive/inspectors of enforcing authorities), section 59(1) of the Data Protection Act 1998 (confidentiality of information obtained by Information Commissioner/staff/agent), and section 23(4) of the Civil Aviation Act 1982 (disclosure of information by Civil Aviation Authority).

(b) Section 17 of the Anti-terrorism, Crime and Security Act 2001 permits disclosure to assist any criminal investigation or criminal proceedings being carried out in the UK or abroad or to facilitate whether or not such investigations or proceedings should begin or end. The powers provided in this section do not limit any other powers to disclose that exists apart from this section.

(c) In determining whether they may disclose information, public authorities must ensure that their disclosure is proportionate to that which is intended by disclosing.

(d) *Overseas investigations/proceedings*—section 18 of the Anti-terrorism, Crime and Security Act 2001 enables the Secretary of State to prohibit the disclosure of information for the purposes of overseas criminal investigations or criminal proceedings that would otherwise be permitted by section 17 or, without section 17, by the provisions modified by that section.

Overseas proceedings are criminal proceedings which are taking place, or will or may take place, in a country or territory outside the UK; and criminal investigations which are, or will or may be, conducted by an authority of any such country or territory.

This power may be exercised where it appears that the overseas investigation or proceedings relates to a matter in respect of which it would be more appropriate for any jurisdiction or investigation to be exercised or carried out by the authorities of the UK or a third country. The implication is that it may not be in the UK's national security interests to entrust information to every foreign power that seeks it, or even to some friendly powers which are treading on the toes of British security operations. Any person who knowingly makes a disclosure prohibited by the Secretary of State pursuant to section 17 commits an offence.

(e) *HM Revenue and Customs*—section 19 of the Anti-terrorism, Crime and Security Act 2001 applies to information held by HM Commissioners for Revenue and Customs. It provides that no obligation of secrecy, with the exception of the Data Protection Act 1998 requirements, prevents the voluntary disclosure of information on the authority of the relevant Commissioners made for the following purposes: for the purpose of any criminal investigation or criminal proceedings in the UK or abroad or to begin or end such investigation or proceedings or to determine to do so (Anti-terrorism, Crime and Security Act 2001, s 19(2)).

Without the provision in section 19, staff of the HM Commissioners for Revenue and Customs would not be authorized to make such a disclosure. For further guidance refer to the 'Anti-terrorism, Crime and Security Act 2001: Code of Practice on the Disclosure of Information' (<http://www.hmrc.gov.uk/pdfs/cop_at.pdf>).

(f) *Proportionality*—the person who makes the disclosure has to be satisfied that the making of the disclosure is proportionate to what is sought to be achieved by it (Anti-terrorism, Crime and Security Act 2001, s 19(3)).

(g) *Further disclosure*—disclosed information cannot be further disclosed by the recipient except for the purposes permitted for original disclosures and with the consent of the relevant Commissioners (Anti-terrorism, Crime and Security Act 2001, s 19(5)).

(h) Much of the information falling within section 17 can have little relevance to terrorism—the Schedule 4 list includes, for example, the Merchant Shipping (Liner Conferences) Act 1982 and the Diseases of Fish Act 1983. Furthermore, the powers are not confined to terrorism investigations but relate to crimes in general. The definition of 'criminal investigation' in section 20 means not only an investigation of any criminal conduct, including an investigation of alleged or suspected criminal conduct, but also an investigation of whether criminal conduct has taken place.

(i) *Sharing of information*—there are some other statutory sharing arrangements (affecting the Customs under the Commissioners for Revenue and Customs Act 2005 and the Department of Social Security under the Social Security Administration (Fraud) Act 1997 and the Finance Act 1997), otherwise one official body has no authority to inform another of merely suspicious activity or simply on request and there may be offences if disclosure is made outside these bounds.

PNLD reference numbers

D10311, D10312, H4751, D10313, D10314

5.1.8 **Disclosure of information—offence**

Section 39 of the Terrorism Act 2000 creates two offences relating to the disclosure of certain material relevant to a terrorist investigation. These offences are sometimes called 'tipping off'.

Offence

(1) Subsection (2) applies where a person knows or has reasonable cause to suspect that a constable is conducting or proposes to **conduct a terrorist investigation**.

(2) The person commits an offence if he—
   (a) discloses to another anything which is likely to prejudice the investigation, or
   (b) **interferes with material** which is likely to be relevant to the investigation.

(3) Subsection (4) applies where a person knows or has reasonable cause to suspect that a disclosure has been or will be made under any of sections 19 to 21B or 38B.

(4) The person commits an offence if he—
   (a) discloses to another anything which is likely to prejudice an investigation resulting from the disclosure under that section, or
   (b) interferes with material which is likely to be relevant to an investigation resulting from the disclosure under that section.

Terrorism Act 2000, s 39(1)–(4)

Points to prove

Section 39(2)

✓ date and location
✓ knew/had reasonable cause to suspect that
✓ a constable
✓ was conducting/proposing to conduct
✓ a terrorist investigation
✓ disclosed to another
✓ something which was likely to prejudice the investigation *or*
✓ interfered with material
✓ which was likely to be relevant to the investigation

Section 39(4)

✓ date and location
✓ knew/had reasonable cause to suspect
✓ that a disclosure had been/was to be made
✓ under section 19/20/21/21A/21B/38B of the Terrorism Act 2000
✓ disclosed information/other matter
✓ likely to prejudice investigation conducted following disclosure *or*
✓ interfered with material
✓ likely to be relevant to an investigation
✓ resulting from the disclosure

Meanings

Terrorist investigation (see **5.1**)

Conducting a terrorist investigation

Includes a reference to taking part in the conduct of, or assisting, a terrorist investigation (Terrorism Act 2000, s 39(8)(a)).

A person interferes with material

If he falsifies it, conceals it, destroys it, or disposes of it, or if he causes or permits another to do any of those things (Terrorism Act 2000, s 39(8)(b)).

Defence

(5) It is a defence for a person charged with an offence under subsection (2) or (4) to prove—

(a) that he did not know and had no reasonable cause to suspect that the disclosure or interference was likely to affect a terrorist investigation, or

(b) that he had a reasonable excuse for the disclosure or interference.

Terrorism Act 2000, s 39(5)

In relation to the defence in section 39(5)(a), section 118 of the Terrorism Act 2000 shifts the burden of proof to the prosecution where the defendant adduces evidence that is sufficient to raise this defence (for details see **4.3.10**). This does not apply to the defence in section 39(5)(b).

Police powers

If suspected terrorist:

Power of arrest under TACT (see **5.3.1**)

Power to stop and search under TACT (see **5.2.1**)

If the person is not suspected of being a terrorist consider using PACE powers (such as ss 24, 17, 18, and 32 of PACE) but see **5.3.1** for drawbacks on using PACE powers for potential terrorists.

Notes

(a) No offence is committed where the disclosure is made by a professional legal adviser either to his client or his client's representative when giving legal advice to the client or to another person for the purpose of actual or contemplated proceedings, and without a view to furthering a criminal purpose (Terrorism Act 2000, s 39(6)).

(b) No offence is committed where the disclosure is of a matter within section 21D(2) or (3)(a) (terrorist property: tipping off, see **4.4.11**), and the information on which the disclosure is based came to the person in the course of a business in the regulated sector. For the meaning of 'business in the regulated sector', see **4.4.9**.

(c) The provisions on post-charge questioning apply to this offence, see **4.2.2 note (g)**.

(d) See also section 19 of the Terrorism Act 2000 which creates a duty to disclose information relating to certain financial offences under the Act and an offence of failing to do so (see **4.4.6**), as well as further provisions on disclosure in sections 20–21B and 38B (see **4.4.7–4.4.10, 5.1.9**).

(e) Sections 19–21 of the Counter-Terrorism Act 2008 make provisions on the disclosure of information and the intelligence services (see PNLD reference numbers D23724, D23725, and D23726).

(f) This offence can be tried in any place in the UK if it was committed in the UK (Counter-Terrorism Act 2008, s 28).

PNLD reference numbers

H3774, H3775, H3776, H3777, D8727

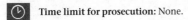 **DPP/AG consent required:** Terrorism Act 2000, s 117 (see **5.7.4**).

🕐 **Time limit for prosecution:** None.

♿ **Summary:** Maximum six months' imprisonment and/or fine not exceeding the statutory maximum.

🏛 **Indictment:** Maximum five years' imprisonment and/or fine.

5.1.9 **Fail to disclose information about acts of terrorism**

Section 38B of the Terrorism Act 2000 provides for the offence of failing to disclose information about acts of terrorism which may be of material assistance.

(1) This section applies where a person has information which he knows or believes might be of material assistance—

(a) in preventing the commission by another person of an act of **terrorism**, or

   (b) in securing the apprehension, prosecution or conviction of another person, in the United Kingdom, for an offence involving the commission, preparation or instigation of **an act of terrorism**.

(2) The person commits an offence if he does not disclose the information as soon as reasonably practicable in accordance with **subsection (3)**.

Terrorism Act 2000, s 38B(1) and (2)

Points to prove

✓ date and location
✓ knowing/believing
✓ that you had information
✓ which might be of material assistance in
✓ preventing the commission by another person of an act of terrorism *or*
  securing the apprehension/prosecution/conviction of another person in the UK
✓ for an offence involving the commission/preparation/instigation of an act of terrorism
✓ failed to disclose that information
✓ as soon as reasonably practicable
✓ to a constable

Meanings

Terrorism (see **4.1.1**)

Act of terrorism (see **4.1.2**)

Subsection (3)

Means disclosure made to a constable.

Police powers

If suspected terrorist:

Power of arrest under TACT (see **5.3.1**)

Power to stop and search under TACT (see **5.2.1**)

If the person is not suspected of being a terrorist then consider using PACE powers of arrest but see **5.3.1** for drawbacks on using PACE powers for potential terrorists.

Defence

(4) It is a defence for a person charged with an offence under subsection (2) to prove that he had a reasonable excuse for not making the disclosure.

Terrorism Act 2000, s 38B(4)

Notes

(a) For non terrorism-related offences there is no legal duty to report information to the police, only a moral one. This section creates a legal duty to report information to the police. However, the person must *know* or *believe* that the information will be of material assistance so suspicion is not enough to commit the offence.

(b) The information must also relate to the possible prevention of an act of terrorism or to the apprehension, prosecution, or conviction of a person involved in the commission, instigation, or preparation of an act of terrorism. This points to the fact that there must be an act of terrorism that has or is going to occur.

(c) Home Office Circular 7/2002 provides that this duty relates to every person and having a familial and legal relationship with a person does not grant immunity from the obligation to disclose information. This would cover family members who are not involved in terrorism but know or believe that a family member is and even includes the relationship between a client and a solicitor.

(d) This offence could be committed in a number of ways: by failing to tell the police anything at all, by refusing to answer questions, or by relating false information.

(e) Charges under this offence could be possible in four different scenarios. First, where there is evidence that an accomplice or conspirator is involved in an act of terrorism and the evidence against them is weak, section 38B could be used. Secondly, where the police have discovered an active terrorist organization, section 38B could be used to prosecute those less involved. Thirdly, where evidence in a terrorist plot is not enough to charge the main offenders, section 38B could be used for those less involved. Fourthly, those persons who have been coerced into aiding terrorists, for example by loaning cars, section 38B could be considered (Clive Walker, *Blackstone's Guide to the Anti-Terrorism Legislation*, 2002).

(f) Sections 19–21 of the Counter-Terrorism Act 2008 make provision for the disclosure of information and the intelligence services. See PNLD reference numbers D23724, D23725, and D23726.

(g) *Extra-territorial jurisdiction*—proceedings for an offence can be taken, and the offence can be regarded as having been committed, in any place where the person to be charged is or has been since he first believed or knew about information that might be of assistance in the prevention of terrorism or bringing a terrorist to justice (Terrorism Act 2000, s 38B(6)). This allows a person resident in the UK to be charged with the offence even if he was outside the UK at the time he became aware of the information.

(h) This offence can be tried in any place in the UK if it was committed in the UK (Counter-Terrorism Act 2008, s 28).

(i) Notification requirements apply (see **5.7.5**).

(j) The provisions on post-charge questioning apply to this offence, see **4.2.2 note (g)**.

PNLD reference numbers

H3571, D10405

 Time limit for prosecution: None.

 Summary: Maximum six months' imprisonment and/or a fine not exceeding the statutory maximum.

 Indictment: Maximum five years' imprisonment and/or a fine.

5.2 Stop and Search and Other Powers

This part sets out officers' powers in relation to stopping and searching people and vehicles and powers relating to placing cordons and parking restrictions under the Terrorism Act 2000.

5.2.1 Power to stop and search

Section 43 of the Terrorism Act 2000 provides a police officer with a power to stop and search anyone (and their vehicle) whom he reasonably suspects is a terrorist or search anyone who has been arrested under section 41 (see **5.3.1**). Section 43A provides a power for a police officer to stop and search a vehicle, including its driver, any passengers, and anything in or on the vehicle, if he reasonably suspects the vehicle is being used for the purposes of terrorism (see **5.3.1**).

Police powers

(1) A constable may stop and search a person whom he reasonably suspects to be a **terrorist** to discover whether he has in his possession anything which may constitute evidence that he is a terrorist.

(2) A constable may search a person arrested under section 41 to discover whether he has in his possession anything which may constitute evidence that he is a terrorist.

(4A) Subsection (4B) applies if a constable, in exercising the power under subsection (1) to stop a person whom the constable reasonably suspects to be a terrorist, stops a vehicle (see section 116(2)).

(4B) The constable—

    (a) may search the vehicle and anything in or on it to discover whether there is anything which may constitute evidence that the person concerned is a terrorist, and

    (b) may seize and retain anything which the constable—

        (i) discovers in the course of such a search, and

        (ii) reasonably suspects may constitute evidence that the person is a terrorist.

Terrorism Act 2000, s 43(1), (2), (4A), and (4B)

(1) Subsection (2) applies if a constable reasonably suspects that a vehicle is being used for the purposes of terrorism.

(2) The constable may stop and search—

    (a) the vehicle;

    (b) the **driver** of the vehicle;

    (c) a passenger in the vehicle;

    (d) anything in or on the vehicle or carried by the driver or a passenger;

to discover whether there is anything which may constitute evidence that the vehicle is being used for the purposes of terrorism.

Terrorism Act 2000, s 43A(1) and (2)

Meanings

Terrorist (see **4.1.3**)

Driver

In relation to an aircraft, hovercraft, or vessel, means the captain, pilot, or other person with control of the aircraft, hovercraft, or vessel or any member of its crew and, in relation to a train, includes any member of its crew (Terrorism Act 2000, s 43A(5)).

Notes

(a) Sections 43(1) and 43A(1) are very wide-ranging powers, they are much wider than the powers under section 1 of the Police and Criminal Evidence Act 1984 as no reason is needed other than a reasonable suspicion that the person is a terrorist (as defined by section 40, see **4.1.3**) which is a very low-level requirement and covers many possibilities.

(b) Any material that the constable believes is evidence that the person is a terrorist or that the vehicle is being used for the purposes of terrorism can be seized and retained (Terrorism Act 2000, s 43(4) and s 43A(3)). This material can be taken away and examined elsewhere (Criminal Justice and Police Act 2001, s 51) see **5.1.2 note (g)**.

(c) This power can be used in any part of the UK (s 43(5) and s 43A(4)).

(d) These sections do not limit where the power can be used but if it is in a private place then the constable would have to have some other lawful reason or consent for being on the premises.

(e) Home Office Circular 12/2009 'Photography and Counter-Terrorism Legislation' provides information on photography and the use of section 43 often in combination with section 58A (PNLD reference number D21572).

PNLD reference number

D8731, D29908

5.2.2 Powers to stop and search in specified areas and places

Section 47A of the Terrorism Act 2000 makes provision for a senior police officer to give an authorization to allow the stop and search of vehicles (including drivers of vehicles, passengers, and anything found in or on a vehicle) and pedestrians (including anything carried by a pedestrian), to search for anything that may constitute evidence that a person is a terrorist, or the vehicle is being used for the purposes of terrorism. The senior officer must reasonably suspect that an act of terrorism will take place and reasonably consider that the authorization is necessary to prevent such an act and that the area or place specified in the authorization is no greater than necessary and the duration of the authorization is no longer than necessary. Once the authorization has been given, a constable does not need any reasonable suspicion in order to exercise the powers. Schedule 6B to the Terrorism Act 2000 provides supplementary provisions in relation to the power under section 47A. There is also a Code of Practice, 'Code of Practice (England, Wales and Scotland) for the Authorisation and Exercise of Stop and Search Powers Relating to Section 47A of, and Schedule 6B to, the Terrorism Act 2000', for the full text see **Appendix 8**.

Note

See also Police and Criminal Evidence Act 1984 Code A, paragraphs 2.19–2.26 and 4.4.

PNLD reference numbers

D29909, D29674, D29917, S2057

5.2.3 **Cordons**

Section 34 of the Terrorism Act 2000 provides for the police to place a cordon around an area for the purposes of a terrorist investigation.

Police powers

Subject to subsections 34(1A), (1B) and (2), a designation under section 33 may only be made where the area is outside Northern Ireland and is wholly or partly within a police area, by an officer for the police area who is of at least the rank of superintendent.

Terrorism Act 2000, s 34(1)

Meanings

Subject to subsections 34(1A), (1B)

Is reference to the fact that the British Transport Police and the Ministry of Defence Police can only authorize cordons in or in the vicinity of premises policed by them. Also, in the case of the Ministry of Defence, they can police any area covered by the Ministry of Defence Police Act 1987. They cannot cordon areas under any other circumstances (Terrorism Act 2000, s 34(1C)).

Subject to subsections 34(2)

A constable of any rank can place a cordon if he considers it necessary by reason of urgency.

A designation under section 33

Means that an area can be cordoned off for the purposes of a **terrorist investigation** if the person making it considers it expedient to do so.

Terrorist investigation (see 5.1)

Notes

(a) A cordon gives the police powers to cordon off an area involved in a terrorist incident or one that they believe may be or become involved in one. Whilst it is a wide-ranging power, the benefits of stopping terrorist acts, protecting the public, and preventing the loss or contamination of any potential evidence at the scene must outweigh the inconvenience and draconian measure of the cordon.

(b) If a constable makes a designation under section 34(2) then he must do so in writing and also inform an officer of at least the rank of Superintendent as soon as possible. The officer who is told of the designation can confirm or cancel it. If it is cancelled it must be done in writing, giving the reasons for the cancellation (s 34(3) and (4)).

(c) A designation can be made orally but must be confirmed in writing as soon as practicable (s 33(3)).

(d) Whosoever makes the designation should arrange for the area to be cordoned off with tape marked with 'police' or in any other appropriate way (s 33(4)).

(e) The initial cordon cannot last for a period longer than 14 days. The person who made the designation or another person who is authorized to do so can extend the period of designation in writing but cannot extend it for a period longer than 14 days, giving a total period of 28 days (s 35).

(f) See **5.2.5** for offences related to cordons.

(g) There is a power to authorize a search of premises in a cordoned area (see **5.2.4**).

(h) Section 116 of the Terrorism Act 2000 provides an additional offence of failing to stop a vehicle when requested to do so by an officer. This offence can be tried in any place in the UK if it was committed in the UK (Counter-Terrorism Act 2008, s 28).

PNLD reference numbers

D8723, D8724

5.2.4 **Police power to search and enter in cordoned area**

Paragraph 3 of Schedule 5 to the Terrorism Act 2000 provides specific powers to enter and search premises, search persons, and seize and retain relevant material which applies to premises in a cordoned area.

(1) Subject to sub-paragraph (2), a police officer of at least the rank of superintendent may by written authority signed by him authorise a search of specified premises which are wholly or partly within a **cordoned area**.

(3) An authorisation under this paragraph shall authorise any constable—

   (a) to enter the premises specified in the authority,
   (b) to search the premises and any person found there,
   (c) to seize and retain any **relevant material** (within the meaning of paragraph 1(3) which is found on a search under paragraph (b).

(6) An authorisation under this paragraph shall not be given unless the person giving it has reasonable grounds for believing that there is material to be found on the premises which—

   (a) is likely to be of substantial value, whether by itself or together with other material, to a terrorist investigation, and
   (b) does not consist of or include **excepted material**.

Terrorism Act 2000, Sch 5, para 3(1), (3), and (6)

Meanings

Cordoned area (see **5.2.3**)

Material is relevant

If the constable has reasonable grounds for believing that—

(a) it is likely to be of substantial value, whether by itself or together with other material, to a terrorist investigation, and
(b) it must be seized in order to prevent it from being concealed, lost, damaged, altered or destroyed (Terrorism Act 2000, Sch 5, para 1(3)).

Excepted material (see **5.1.1**)

Notes

(a) *Urgency*—a constable who is not of at least the rank of Superintendent may give an authorization under paragraph 3 if he considers it necessary by reason of urgency (Terrorism Act 2000, Sch 5, para 3(2)).

(b) *Duration*—the powers to enter and search premises and persons found there may be exercised on one or more occasions and at any time during the period when the designation of the cordoned area under section 33 of the Terrorism Act 2000 has effect (see **5.2.3**) (Terrorism Act 2000, Sch 5, para 3(4)).

(c) *Items subject to legal privilege*—the seizure and retention of such items (see **5.1.1**) cannot be authorized by a warrant under this provision (Terrorism Act 2000, Sch 5, para 3(5)(a)). Where access to excluded or special procedure material is required, see **5.1.4** and **5.1.5**.

(d) *Removal of clothing*—under this provision a constable may only require a person to remove headgear, footwear, an outer coat, a jacket, or gloves (Terrorism Act 2000, Sch 5, para 3(5)(b)).

(e) *Use of force*—a constable may, if necessary, use reasonable force for the purpose of exercising a power of entry, search, or seizure (Terrorism Act 2000, s 114(2)).

(f) *Additional powers*—the power to seize and retain materials attracts additional powers under the Criminal Justice and Police Act 2001, sections 50, 51, and 55, namely additional powers of seizure from premises and additional powers of seizure from the person; there is an obligation to return excluded and special procedure material. For details see **5.1.2 note (g)**.

(g) Section 21 of the Police and Criminal Evidence Act 1984 provides a person from whom material has been lawfully seized by the police, with certain rights to access to and/or copies of it.

(h) Section 22 of the Police and Criminal Evidence Act 1984 provides directions and powers in relation to items that have been seized by the police.

(i) *Offence*—it is an offence to wilfully obstruct a search under paragraph 3 (summary, maximum three months' imprisonment and/or fine not exceeding level 4 on the standard scale) (Terrorism Act 2000, Sch 5, para 3(7) and (8)).

PNLD reference number
D8765

5.2.5 **Offences related to cordons**

Section 36 of the Terrorism Act 2000 provides police powers and offences related to cordons.

Police powers

A constable in uniform may—

(a) order a person in a cordoned area to leave it immediately;
(b) order a person immediately to leave premises which are wholly or partly in or adjacent to a cordoned area;
(c) order the driver or person in charge of a vehicle in a cordoned area to move it from the area immediately;
(d) arrange for the removal of a vehicle from a cordoned area;
(e) arrange for the movement of a vehicle within a cordoned area;
(f) prohibit or restrict access to a cordoned area by pedestrians or vehicles.

Terrorism Act 2000, s 36(1)

Offence

(2) A person commits an offence if he fails to comply with an order, prohibition or restriction imposed by virtue of subsection (1).

Terrorism Act 2000, s 36(2)

Points to prove

Section 36(1)(a)

✓ date and location
✓ failed to comply when ordered by a constable in uniform
✓ to leave
✓ a cordoned area immediately

Section 36(1)(b)

✓ date and location
✓ failed to comply with an order by a constable in uniform
✓ to leave premises
✓ wholly/partly within/adjacent to
✓ a cordoned area immediately

Section 36(1)(c)

✓ date and location
✓ being the driver/person in charge of a vehicle
✓ within a cordoned area
✓ failed to move the vehicle immediately
✓ when ordered to do so by a constable in uniform

Section 36(1)(f)

✓ date and location
✓ being a pedestrian/driver of a vehicle

> ✓ failed to comply with
> ✓ a prohibition/restriction of access to a cordoned area
> ✓ imposed by a constable in uniform

Meanings

Order, prohibition or restriction imposed by virtue of subsection (1)

See **Police powers** earlier in this section.

Defence

(3) It is a defence for a person charged with an offence under subsection (2) to prove that he had a reasonable excuse for his failure.

Terrorism Act 2000, s 36(3)

Police powers in respect of offence in section 36(2)

If suspected terrorist:

Power of arrest under TACT (see 5.3.1)

Power to stop and search under TACT (see 5.2.1)

If the person is not suspected to be a terrorist, consider using PACE powers (such as ss 24, 17, 18, and 32 of PACE) but see **5.3.1** for drawbacks on using PACE powers for potential terrorists.

Notes

(a) A community support officer has the same powers as a constable under this section (Police Reform Act 2002, Sch 4, para 14).

(b) A cordon gives the police powers to cordon off an area involved in a terrorist incident or one that they believe may be or become involved in one. Whilst it is a wide-ranging power, the benefits of stopping terrorist acts and preventing the loss of any potential scene and evidence must outweigh the inconvenience and draconian measure of the cordon.

PNLD reference numbers

H3782, H3783, H3784, H3794, D8726

 Time limit for prosecution: Six months.

 Summary: Maximum three months' imprisonment and/or a fine not exceeding level four on the standard scale.

5.2.6 **Power to restrict parking**

Section 48 of the Terrorism Act 2000 provides the police with a power to restrict parking in specified areas.

Police powers

An authorisation under this section authorises any constable in uniform to prohibit or restrict the **parking** of **vehicles** on a **road** specified in the authorisation.

Terrorism Act 2000, s 48(1)

A constable exercising the power conferred by an authorisation under section 48 may suspend a parking place.

Terrorism Act 2000, s 49(2)

Meanings

Parking

Means leaving a vehicle or permitting it to remain at rest (Terrorism Act 2000, s 52).

Vehicle

Means any vehicle, whether or not it is in a fit state for use on roads, and includes any chassis or body, with or without wheels, appearing to have formed part of such a vehicle, and any load carried by, and anything attached to, such a vehicle (Road Traffic Regulation Act 1984, s 99(5)).

Road

Means any highway and any other road to which the public has access, and includes bridges over which a road passes. It always includes obvious public highways, footpaths, and bridleways maintained by government agencies or local authorities (Road Traffic Act 1988, s 192(1)).

Notes

(a) An authorization under this section may only be given if it is considered expedient to prevent acts of terrorism (s 48(2)).

(b) The authorization may be given by an officer of at least the rank of Assistant Chief Constable or a Commander for the Metropolitan and City of London Police (s 48(3)).

(c) An authorization may be given orally but if it is, it should be confirmed in writing as soon as practicable (s 48(4)).

(d) The power under this section shall be exercised by the placing of a traffic sign on the road concerned (s 49(1)). Traffic sign has been given the same meaning as that in the Road Traffic Regulation Act 1984 (s 64) which is any object or device (whether fixed or portable) for conveying to traffic on roads or any specified class of traffic, warnings, information, requirements, restrictions, or prohibitions of any description (specified by regulations or authorized by the Secretary of State) and any line or mark on a road for so conveying such warnings, information, requirements, restrictions, or prohibitions.

(e) If a constable suspends a parking place under s 49(2) then any vehicle contravening this can be towed away (s 49(3)).

(f) The period specified in this section cannot exceed 28 days but can be renewed in writing by the person who gave the authorization or who is authorized to do so (s 50(2) and (3)).

(g) There are also the powers to divert traffic for the purposes of preventing terrorism under section 22C of the Road Traffic Regulation Act 1984.

PNLD reference numbers

D8736, D8737

5.2.7 **Offences related to parking restrictions**

Section 51 of the Terrorism Act 2000 creates the offences related to parking where parking is prohibited or restricted for the prevention of acts of terrorism.

Offence

(1) A person commits an offence if he parks a **vehicle** in contravention of a prohibition or restriction imposed by virtue of **section 48**.

(2) A person commits an offence if—

    (a) he is the **driver** or other person in charge of a vehicle which has been permitted to remain at rest in contravention of any prohibition or restriction imposed by virtue of section 48, and

    (b) he fails to move the vehicle when ordered to do so by a constable in uniform.

Terrorism Act 2000, s 51(1) and (2)

Points to prove

Section 51(1)

✓ date and location
✓ park vehicle
✓ in contravention of prohibition/restriction under section 48

Section 51(2)

✓ date and location
✓ driver/person in charge of vehicle
✓ permitted to rest on a road
✓ in contravention of prohibition/restriction under section 48
✓ failed to move the vehicle
✓ when ordered by constable in uniform

Meanings

Vehicle (see 5.2.6)

Section 48 (see 5.2.6)

Driver

Means, in relation to a vehicle which has been left on any road, the person who was driving it when it was left there (Terrorism Act 2000, s 52).

Defence

(3) It is a defence for a person charged with an offence under this section to prove that he had a reasonable excuse for the act or omission in question.

Terrorism Act 2000, s 51(3)

It will be for the court to decide what constitutes a reasonable excuse.

Displaying a disabled badge does not in itself constitute a reasonable excuse (Terrorism Act 2000, s 51(4)).

Police powers

If suspected terrorist:

Power of arrest under TACT (see **5.3.1**)

Power to stop and search under TACT (see **5.2.1**)

If the person is not suspected of being a terrorist then consider using PACE powers (such as ss 24, 17, 18, and 32 of PACE) but see **5.3.1** for drawbacks on using PACE powers for potential terrorists.

PNLD reference numbers

H3569, H3570, D8738

 Time limit for prosecution: Six months.

 Summary: Section 51(1): a fine not exceeding level four on the standard scale.

Summary: Section 51(2): maximum three months' imprisonment and/or a fine not exceeding level four on the standard scale.

5.3 **Arrest and Detention**

Section 41 of and Schedule 8 to the Terrorism Act 2000 deal with the arrest and detention of suspected terrorists. Police and Criminal Evidence Act 1984 Code of Practice H deals with the detention, treatment, and questioning by police officers of persons arrested under section 41 of the Terrorism Act 2000 and detained in police custody under section 41 of and Schedule 8 to the Act. Code H can be found in full at **Appendix 4**. Code H is primarily based on Code C: in each of the 'Notes' sections the relevant differences between Code C and Code H are summarized.

5.3.1 **Arrest without warrant**

Section 41 of the Terrorism Act 2000 creates a power of arrest for those suspected to be terrorists. There is no need to satisfy the necessity test but an officer must have reasonable suspicion that the person is a terrorist.

Police powers

A constable may arrest without a warrant a person whom he reasonably suspects to be a **terrorist**.

Terrorism Act 2000, s 41(1)

Meanings

Terrorist

Means a person who is or has been concerned in the commission, preparation, or instigation of acts of terrorism or has committed one of a list of offences (eg weapons training, money laundering, directing a terrorist organization) (see **4.1.3** for full details).

Notes

(a) This is a very broad power of arrest and there is no need for the necessity test to be fulfilled as with those arrested under the Police and Criminal Evidence Act 1984: the only requirement is to reasonably suspect that the person is a terrorist. This means that an arrest can be made at a time when the police believe it should be made even though under PACE provisions there may not be enough evidence to arrest a person in connection with a specific offence. The advantage of the use of the term 'terrorism' is that the basis for the arrest may be more speculative in terms of a range of possible offences. But the term 'terrorism' should still be conceived as being equivalent to criminality; otherwise it may be challenged as an incursion into liberty which lacks legal certainty.

(b) Section 43 of the Terrorism Act 2000 provides a power of search for a person arrested under section 41 (see **5.2.1**). A warrant under Schedule 5 is required in order to search premises (see **5.1.1**).

(c) A person can be detained on the authority of the police under this section for 48 hours from the time of arrest (Terrorism Act 2000, s 41(3))—if no extensions are sought under Schedule 8 (see **5.3.11**) then the person must be released. For those detained initially under Schedule 7 and subsequently arrested under section 41 the time begins when the examination under that Schedule began (see **5.4.1**).

(d) If a person suspected of being a terrorist is arrested using PACE provisions, the provisions under the Terrorism Act (TACT) will not be available unless further offences are disclosed. If there is any reasonable suspicion that the person is involved in terrorism, it is advisable to use the power of arrest under section 41 and not section 24 of PACE, for two reasons. First, once arrested, due to the very sensitive nature of this type of investigation, there is no requirement that the suspect be given detailed information of the reasons for the arrest; both the suspect and any representatives need only be informed of legal grounds and basic factual details (eg you are suspected of being a terrorist and have been arrested and detained under section 41 of the Terrorism Act 2000 (see **note (g)**). Not having to give full details allows greater flexibility in the investigation and the tactics of interrogation. Secondly, suspects arrested under TACT are subject to extra powers of detention after arrest—up to 14 days rather than 96 hours (see **5.3.5**, **5.3.10**, and **5.3.11**).

(e) This power of arrest is not to be used indiscriminately; there must be real and reasonable suspicion (see **Related cases**) and it is normally exercised only against terrorism related to Irish or international causes.

(f) When arresting anyone under this section, it is advisable, for safety reasons, to give the terrorist suspect another identification number other than a collar number, such as the number on the back of the warrant card, from which it is much more difficult to identify a person (check force policy for local procedures). Also, when talking to colleagues in the company of a terrorist suspect, do not use any personal details such as nicknames or first names which could possibly lead to identification, instead it might be advisable to address colleagues by rank (check force policy for local procedures).

(g) *Code H*—Code H states that the custody record shall record, and the detained person shall be informed, that the person was arrested under section 41 and the grounds for the arrest. However, where the grounds of arrest are reasons of a sensitive nature, the grounds can initially be recorded that the person is a terrorist in line with section 40(1)(a) or (b), (see **4.1**). However, Article 5.2 of the European Convention allows only a few hours' delay in giving some indication as to the nature of the offences and charges, but those details may be deduced from a later interrogation (for Code H in full see **Appendix 4**).

(h) This power of arrest can be used across the UK (Terrorism Act 2000, s 41(9)).

(i) Lord Carlile, the independent reviewer of terrorism stated in his report into Operation Pathway that the police and the CPS should take immediate steps to ensure that their procedures reflect the need for legal advice to the police at an early stage. CPS expert, vetted lawyers should be informed, well before arrests take place, of ongoing enquiries likely to result in arrests. They should be asked to advise on the state of the intelligence, information, and evidence as the enquiry in question progresses, with an eye on the implications and challenges post-arrest.

(j) The rest of section 41 deals with the detention of a suspect which is covered in **5.3.8**, **5.3.9**, and **5.3.11**.

(k) If a person is arrested and detained under section 24 of PACE, and a subsequent search of premises uncovers evidence of a terrorism offence, that person should be further arrested using either section 24 of PACE or section 41 of the Terrorism Act 2000. The detention clock for the terrorism offence will start from the same time as for the original offence.

(l) See **5.4** for those detained at ports who could be later arrested under section 41.

Related cases

O'Hara v Chief Constable of the Royal Ulster Constabulary [1997] AC 286 The test for whether a police officer had reasonable suspicion for arrest (under previous terrorism legislation) was a simple one—what was in the mind of the officer when the arrest was made. The components involve both a genuine and subjective suspicion in the mind of the arresting officer that the arrestee has been concerned in acts of terrorism and also objectively reasonable grounds for forming such a suspicion. Thus, there is an objective element to the test in that the grounds must be reasonable. Reasonable suspicion can be formed by the officer based on information he has been told either by a superior officer or an informant, there is no need for the arresting officer first to establish that the information was true but it must be genuinely believed. Reasonable grounds for suspicion must be taken in light of the whole situation which includes the information and the context in which it was received.

Raissi v Metropolitan Police Commissioner [2007] EWHC 2842 (QB), [2007] All ER (D) 494 (Nov) QBD A was arrested as a suspected terrorist. She was the wife of a prime suspect thought to be involved in the bombings on 11 September 2001, and she had been with him in a foreign country when it was believed that he may have undergone terrorist training (at the same time and location of one of the perpetrators of the bombings). It was reasonable for the officer to suspect that she may be a terrorist. B was also arrested as a suspected terrorist; he was the brother of the prime suspect, thought by the officer to be a close brother who lived nearby. The officer had also been influenced by the fact that he had been informed that family links played a part in terrorist activity. This did not pass the threshold of reasonable suspicion and the arrest of the brother was unlawful. The Commissioner appealed but the appeal was dismissed ([2008] EWCA Civ 1237).

PNLD reference numbers

D8729, C417, C1529

5.3.2 Warrants—enter and search of premises for purposes of arrest

Section 42 of the Terrorism Act 2000 sets out the procedure to follow when making an application to a justice of the peace for the issue of a warrant to search premises in order to make an arrest under section 41 of the Act (see **5.3.1**).

(1) A justice of the peace may on the application of a constable issue a warrant in relation to specified premises if he is satisfied that there are reasonable grounds for suspecting that a person whom the constable reasonably suspects to be a **person falling within section 40(1)(b)** is to be found there.

(2) A warrant under this section shall authorise any constable to enter and search the specified premises for the purpose of arresting the person referred to in subsection (1) under section 41 *[arrest without warrant]*.

Terrorism Act 2000, s 42(1) and (2)

Meanings

Person falling within section 40(1)(b)

Is a person who is or has been concerned in the commission, preparation, or instigation of **acts of terrorism**.

Acts of terrorism (see **4.1.2**)

Notes

(a) For arrest without warrant under section 41, see **5.3.1**.

(b) Schedule 5 to the Terrorism Act 2000 contains provisions to obtain a warrant to search premises for those arrested under section 41 (see **5.1.2**).

PNLD reference number

D8730

5.3.3 **Places of detention and methods of identification**

Paragraphs 1 and 2 of Schedule 8 to the Terrorism Act 2000 provide for places of detention for those arrested under section 41 or detained under Schedule 7 and the means to identify them.

1(1) The Secretary of State shall **designate places** at which persons may be detained under **Schedule 7** or section 41.
2(1) An **authorised person** may take any steps which are reasonably necessary for—
  (a) photographing the detained person,
  (b) measuring him, or
  (c) identifying him.

Terrorism Act 2000, Sch 8, paras 1(1) and 2(1)

Meanings

Designated places

In England and Wales, there has been the designation of any police station or prison or (additionally for persons under 18) any Young Offender Institution, Secure Training Centre, or other place of safety. In practice, a number of police stations in Britain have been equipped to hold terrorist suspects in conditions of sufficient security—most notably at Paddington Green Police Station in London and the Antrim Serious Crime Suite in Northern Ireland. In Britain, persons are transferred to prison accommodation after 14 days' detention but will be returned to a police station for interrogation purposes.

Schedule 7

Refers to those detained at ports (see **5.4.1**).

Authorised person

Means a constable, a prison officer, a person authorized by the Secretary of State, and in the case of a person detained under Schedule 7 an examining officer (ie a constable, an immigration officer, or a customs officer (see **5.4.1**)).

Notes

(a) A constable must take a person arrested under section 41 as soon as is reasonably practicable to the police station he considers most appropriate (para 1(4)). Most forces will have police stations designated for terrorist suspects and those should be used. Where it is considered appropriate, in the best interests of all concerned and after risk assessments have been carried out, a terrorist suspect could be taken to cells in another force area if the arresting force does not have the correct facilities.

(b) *Custody area*—the custody area should be completely sterile and contain no files, newspapers, radios, or televisions. Terrorist suspects should be placed in forensically sealed cells where they will undergo a thorough forensic examination. The custody record should be all on paper and not on the normal computer system used for PACE prisoners (unless force policy dictates otherwise). Normally, there should not be any computer terminals in the cell area; this is because the information contained therein is very sensitive.

(c) *Review*—a review (under Sch 8, para 21) of the detention must be done **first** before anything else, detention must be authorized in person by the review officer (see **5.3.8**) present at the police station before any other steps are taken. If appropriate, it could be done from outside the cell. Failure to authorize detention could lead to valuable evidence being found inadmissible. If a review is not done first there must be a justifiable reason.

(d) *Welfare*—the welfare of the detained person is paramount and is an area that will be open to legal challenges. The detained person by the very nature of their arrest and detention is a vulnerable person and consideration should be given to constant supervision (CCTV) to ensure their welfare.

(e) *Code H key points*—there is **no** provision for bail before charge for anyone detained under section 41 (para 1.6). If a detainee is taken to hospital to receive medical treatment, unlike under PACE, the clock does not stop (Note 1L). The review officer (at this point an Inspector not involved in the investigation) (see **5.3.10**), not the custody officer, is responsible for authorizing detention (Note 3H). Where practicable, provisions should be made to allow a detained person to practise their religion (separate prayer room, appropriate food and clothing, and religious books) (para 8.8 and Note 8D). This is an important part of a detained person's welfare and forces should ensure that religious observances are followed, such as uncontaminated religious books, allowing the person to pray at the appropriate times, and even waking them up during the rest period if they so request. Reading material (including main religious texts) should be made available to the detained person where practicable unless it interferes with the investigation or prevents or hinders statutory duties or those under this Code (para 8.10).

(f) *Code H continued*—the record of arrest need not show a specific offence, only that the person has been arrested under section 41 (para 3.4 and Note 3G). Risk assessments do not form part of the custody record and should not be shown to the detained person or their legal representative (para 3.8). It is advisable to keep these in a completely separate location and not as part of the custody package. If practicable, brief outdoor exercise should be offered; where this is not possible and where facilities exist, indoor exercise should be offered instead (para 8.7). Exercise should be offered on each occasion even if it has been refused previously and the custody record updated. Detained persons must be visited every hour by custody staff. At least once every 24 hours, the detained person who is held for more than 96 hours should be visited by a health care professional (para 9.1). Some forces use designated doctors to carry out these visits; check force policy. There is no requirement for the identity of officers or police staff to be disclosed in terrorism cases (para 2.8) (see also **note (i)**).

(g) Reasonable force may be used where appropriate in order to photograph, identify, or measure the detained person (Terrorism Act 2000, s 114(2)).

(h) If a person is arrested in one part of the UK but all or part of his detention takes place in another then he shall be detained in accordance with the parts of Schedule 8 applicable to the part of the country in which he is in detention (para 1(6)). There are slight differences in the law for Scotland and Northern Ireland, so if in the unusual circumstance that a person is arrested in Scotland but detained in England, the law relating to England should be adhered to.

(i) When arresting anyone under this section, it is advisable, for safety reasons, to give the terrorist suspect another identification number other than a collar number, such as the number on the back of the warrant card, from which it is much more difficult to identify a person (check force policy for local procedures). Also, when talking to colleagues in the company of a terrorist suspect, do not use any personal details such as nicknames or first names which could possibly lead to identification, instead it might be advisable to address colleagues by rank (check force policy for local procedures).

(j) Under paragraph 2 of Schedule 8 there is no power to fingerprint or take samples only to measure, identify, and photograph (see also Code H 3.12–3.13.). The power to take samples is under paragraphs 10 and 12 of Schedule 8 (see **5.3.6**).

(k) There is nothing in Schedule 8 to prevent a detained person being taken elsewhere to be measured, identified, and photographed.

(l) If a person is detained under Schedule 7 (those detained at ports, see **5.4.1**), he may be transported to other places in order to examine him, establish his nationality or citizenship, or make arrangements for him to be sent to another country or territory outside the UK (para 1(3)).

PNLD reference number

D8786

5.3.4 **Recording of interviews and codes of practice**

Paragraphs 3 and 4 of Schedule 8 to the Terrorism Act 2000 detail how interviews shall be recorded. These paragraphs state that there shall be a code of practice (see Terrorism Act 2000 (Video Recording with Sound of Interviews and Associated Code of Practice) Order 2012 (SI 2012/1792) see **Appendix 7** for the full code of practice) for the video recording of interviews with terrorist suspects and any interviews conducted must abide by that code.

Notes

(a) A breach of the code of practice by a constable is not an offence in itself, nor will it leave him open to civil proceedings (para 4(6)).

(b) The codes of practice are, however, admissible in any criminal and civil proceedings and can be taken into account where considered to be appropriate (para 4(7)).

(c) *Code H*—an appropriate adult could be required to leave the interview if the interviewing officer considers that their behaviour is hindering the interview. A Superintendent, or if one is not readily available an Inspector, should be consulted (para 11.10). Officers should consider the effect of prolonged detention on any information provided by the detained person, particularly if it has not been mentioned previously when asked (Note 11D). Detained persons and their legal representatives should, where practicable, be made aware of the general reasons why there are extended periods (over 24 hours) between interviews (para 12.9 and Note 12C).

PNLD reference number

D8787

5.3.5 **Detained person—status and rights**

Paragraphs 5–9 of Schedule 8 to the Terrorism Act 2000 set out a detained person's status and his rights.

5 A detained person shall be deemed to be in **legal custody** throughout the period of his detention.

6(1) Subject to paragraph 8, **a person detained under Schedule 7** or **section 41** at a police station in England or Wales shall be entitled, if he so requests, to have one named person informed as soon as is reasonably practicable that he is being detained there.

7(1) Subject to paragraphs 8 and 9, a person detained under Schedule 7 or section 41 at a police station in England or Wales shall be entitled, if he so requests, to consult a solicitor as soon as is reasonably practicable, privately and at any time.

Terrorism Act 2000, Sch 8, paras 5, 6(1), and 7(1)

Meanings

Legal custody

Means from arrival at the police station.

A person detained under Schedule 7

Means a person detained at a port (see **5.4**).

A person detained under section 41

Means a person arrested as a suspected terrorist (see **5.3.1**).

Police powers

8(1) Subject to sub-paragraph (2), an officer of at least the rank of superintendent may authorise a delay—

  (a) in informing the person named by a detained person under paragraph 6;

  (b) in permitting a detained person to consult a solicitor under paragraph 7.

9(1) A direction under this paragraph may provide that a detained person who wishes to exercise the right under paragraph 7 may consult a solicitor only in the sight and hearing of a qualified officer *[see **note 1** for meaning of qualified officer]*.

9(2) A direction under this paragraph may be given where the person is detained at a police station in England or Wales, by an officer of at least the rank of Commander or Assistant Chief Constable.

Terrorism Act 2000, Sch 8, paras 8(1) and 9(1) and (2)

Notes

(a) A person who can be informed under paragraph 6 must be a friend, relative, or someone who would have an interest in the welfare of the detained person (para 6(2)). If the person is transferred to another police station he has the right to have a person informed of the transfer (para 6(3)).

(b) A detained person also has the right, subject to certain conditions, to be able to consult a solicitor privately and at any time (para 7(1)). Such a request and the time it was made must be recorded (para 7(2)).

(c) A Superintendent can delay the right to have someone informed or the right to consult a solicitor (para 8(1)). Where a person is detained under section 41 he must be allowed to exercise his right to inform a person of his whereabouts and to consult a solicitor within 48 hours (para 8(2)). The right to consult with a lawyer is viewed by the courts as very important in any consideration of whether the person has been treated fairly. The police should also consider whether the reasons for refusal in relation to one lawyer might apply to another lawyer.

(d) A Superintendent can only give an authorization to delay these rights if he has reasonable grounds for *believing* that to allow the suspect to exercise these rights will have any of the following consequences (para 8(5)):
   • interference with or harm to evidence of a serious offence (indictable offence or an offence, or conspiracy or attempt to commit an offence under section 40(1)(a) (see **4.1**));
   • interference with or physical injury to any person;
   • alerting of persons suspected of, but not yet arrested for, a serious offence;
   • hindering of recovering property obtained as a result of a serious offence or in respect of which a forfeiture order could be made under section 23 or 23A of the Terrorism Act 2000 (see **4.4.12**);

- interference with the gathering of information about the commission, instigation, or preparation of acts of terrorism;
- alerting of a person making it more difficult to prevent an act of terrorism (see **4.1**); and
- alerting of a person making it more difficult to secure a(ny) person's apprehension, prosecution, or conviction in connection with the commission, instigation, or preparation of an act of terrorism (para 8(4)).

(e) A Superintendent can also delay these rights if he has reasonable grounds for believing that the detained person has benefited from his criminal conduct (obtained property or pecuniary advantage) or that the recovery of property constituting the benefit will be hindered by informing a named person or allowing the person to seek advice from a solicitor (para 8(5)).

(f) Where an authorization is given orally, it must be confirmed in writing as soon as reasonably practicable and the detained person should also be informed as soon as reasonably practicable (para 8(6) and (7)).

(g) If the reason for the delay ceases to exist then there must be no further delay in allowing the detained person his rights (para 8(8)).

(h) *Code H* (see **Appendix 4** for the full Code)—where appropriate, the detained person should be allowed to receive visitors, friends, family, or others likely to be concerned with his welfare. Risk assessments and close liaison with the investigating team should always be carried out prior to this occurring (para 5.4 and Note 5B). Official visitors should also be permitted, as long as the detained person consents and after consultation with the officer with overall responsibility for the investigation. An official visitor must not compromise safety or security or unduly delay the investigation (Note 5C includes examples of official visitors). Officers must consider the risk of the detained person passing on information to associates if permitted to have writing materials or allowed to communicate via telephone (para 5.6 and Note 5G).

(i) Paragraph 9(1) of Schedule 8, which allows for a consultation to occur between legal representative and his client in the hearing of a police officer, is a controversial one and could undermine one of the most important rights a detained person has—the right to seek independent legal advice. Home Office Circular 42/2003, which was produced after the case of **Brennan** (see **Related case**) states that this power should only be used exceptionally after a careful assessment encompassing applicability and proportionality (see also Code H, para 6.5).

(j) The Home Office Circular also states that even if the police believe that such consequences will occur, the restriction should only be imposed if it is proportionate to do so in light of all the circumstances of the case. Factors that should be taken into account in reaching this evaluation are:

- whether the suspect has been initially cooperative and has been answering questions: if the suspect has been cooperating and making admissions that could prejudice his defence, it may indicate that the suspect is in need of legal advice and as such requires uninhibited access to his solicitor;
- whether the suspect could be considered vulnerable: a court could rule that a vulnerable suspect has more need of solicitor access. A suspect may have an obvious vulnerability such as a physical or sensory disability. Equally, he may be made vulnerable through restricted language ability and cultural differences. However, there will equally be cases when the vulnerability of the suspect is not immediately obvious but could be deduced from behavioural and response patterns. Such vulnerabilities would need careful assessment and might include some form of mental impairment, drug dependency, or a condition that is controlled by medication. Further, overwhelming or prolonged emotional distress might be interpreted as vulnerability (para 15 of HOC 42/2003).

(k) If the police choose to exercise this power (to have a police officer within hearing of legal consultation), it is essential that they can show that one of the consequences in paragraph 8(4) (see **note (d)**) would occur if a police officer was not present during the detained person's consultation with his solicitor or that the detained person has benefited from his criminal conduct and that, unless the direction is given, the exercise of the right by the detained person will hinder the recovery of the value of the property constituting the benefit (para 14 of HOC 42/2003 and Sch 8, para 9(3)).

(l) A qualified officer for the purposes of paragraph 9 is a uniformed Inspector of the force concerned, with no connection to the detained person's case (Sch 8, para 9(4)).

(m) Once the reason for the direction under paragraph 9 ceases to exist then the detained person can consult with his solicitor in private (para 9(5)).

Related case

Brennan v UK (2002) 34 EHRR 18 This is a Northern Ireland case and the power exercised was under section 45 of the Northern

Ireland (Emergency Provisions) Act 1991 which is a similar provision to paragraph 9 of Schedule 8 to the Terrorism Act 2000. The European Court of Human Rights held that there had been a breach of Article 6(3)(c) (right to legal assistance) because the defendant's first consultation with his solicitor was in the hearing of a police officer and would have prevented him from speaking freely. However, it was held that access to a solicitor may be restricted subject to the police showing good reason (see **notes (i) and (j)**).

PNLD reference numbers

D8788, D8789, D19341

5.3.6 **Taking of fingerprints and samples**

Paragraphs 10–13 of Schedule 8 to the Terrorism Act 2000 provide for the taking of samples from terrorist suspects and what may be done with them when they have been taken.

Police powers

10(2) **Fingerprints** may be taken from the detained person only if they are taken by a constable—
  (a) with the **appropriate consent** given in writing, or
  (b) without that consent under sub-paragraph (4).

10(3) A **non-intimate** sample may be taken from the detained person only if it is taken by a constable—
  (a) with the appropriate consent given in writing, or
  (b) without that consent under sub-paragraph (4).

10(4) Fingerprints or a non-intimate sample may be taken from the detained person without the appropriate consent only if—
  (a) he is detained at a police station and a police officer of at least the rank of superintendent authorises the fingerprints or sample to be taken, or
  (b) he has been convicted of a **recordable offence** and, where a non-intimate sample is to be taken, he was convicted of the offence on or after 10th April 1995.

10(5) An **intimate sample** may be taken from the detained person only if—
  (a) he is detained at a police station,
  (b) the appropriate consent is given in writing,
  (c) a police officer of at least the rank of superintendent authorises the sample to be taken, and

(d) subject to paragraph 13(2) and (3), the sample is taken by a constable.

Terrorism Act 2000, Sch 8, para 10(2)–(5)

Meanings

Fingerprints

In relation to any person, means a record (in any form and produced by any method) of the skin pattern and other physical characteristics or features of any of that person's fingers or either of his palms (Police and Criminal Evidence Act 1984 (PACE), s 65).

Appropriate consent

Means—

(a) in relation to a person who has attained the age of 17 years, the consent of that person;

(b) in relation to a person who has not attained that age but has attained the age of 14 years, the consent of that person and his parent or guardian; and

(c) in relation to a person who has not attained the age of 14 years, the consent of his parent or guardian (PACE, s 65).

Non-intimate sample

Means—

(a) a sample of hair other than pubic hair;

(b) a sample taken from a nail or from under a nail;

(c) a swab taken from any part of a person's body other than a part from which a swab taken would be an intimate sample;

(d) saliva;

(e) a skin impression—which in relation to any person, means any record (other than a fingerprint) which is a record (in any form and produced by any method) of the skin pattern and other physical characteristics or features of the whole or any part of his foot or of any other part of his body (PACE, s 65).

Recordable offence

Means any offence punishable with a term of imprisonment and some other non-imprisonable offences specified by the Secretary of State, for example firearms, begging, public order, and fail to provide a specimen of breath (PACE, s 118).

Intimate sample

Means—

(a) a sample of blood, semen, or any other tissue, fluid, urine, or pubic hair;

(b) a dental impression;

(c) a swab taken from any part of a person's genitals (including pubic hair) or from a person's body orifice other than the mouth (PACE, s 65).

Notes

(a) An intimate sample may only be taken with consent (in writing) and the authorization of an officer of at least the rank of Superintendent. This is mainly because intimate samples (except for a urine sample) require a third party professional to take them and their ethical codes will not permit them to take a sample by force. If an intimate sample is refused without good cause, adverse inferences can be drawn by the courts (para 13(1)). Intimate samples, other than urine, must be taken by a registered medical practitioner or dentist on the authority of a constable (para 13(2) and (3)).

(b) For an authorization to be given for the taking of fingerprints and non-intimate samples without consent, an officer must be satisfied that the fingerprints of the detained person will facilitate the ascertainment of that person's identity; and that person has refused to identify himself or the officer has reasonable grounds for suspecting that that person is not who he claims to be (para 10(6A)). Further, an officer may also only give such an authorization if—

   (i) in the case of a person detained under section 41, the officer reasonably suspects that the person has been involved in an offence under any of the provisions mentioned in section 40(1)(a) (see **4.1**), and the officer reasonably believes that the fingerprints or sample will tend to confirm or disprove his involvement; or

   (ii) in any case, the officer is satisfied that the taking of the fingerprints or sample from the person is necessary in order to assist in determining whether he falls within section 40(1)(b) (commission, preparation, or instigation of acts of terrorism) (para 10(6)).

(c) If an authorization is given orally, it should be confirmed in writing as soon as reasonably practicable (para 10(7)).

(d) Before fingerprints are taken under this paragraph, the detained person shall be informed that they may be used for the purposes of a speculative search under section 63(A) of PACE and also paragraph 14(4) of Schedule 8 (see **5.3.7**) and if they were taken with consent or under para 10(4)(b) (convicted of a recordable offence) the reason that they were taken (para 11(1)).

(e) If the samples (non-intimate and fingerprints) are to be taken without consent, the detained person shall be told that authorization has been given, why it has been given and, where relevant, the nature of the offence he is suspected of being involved in (para 11(2)).

(f) After the samples have been taken, it shall be recorded (as soon as reasonably practicable) that the person has been told what will happen to the samples and, where authorization was given, the fact it was given and the reasons why and that appropriate consent was given (para 11(3)).

(g) Where a sample of hair (other than pubic) is to be taken, they can be taken by either cutting or plucking hair from roots as long as no more are taken than is necessary for a sufficient sample (para 13(4)).

(h) Reasonable force may be used where appropriate in order to take samples (other than intimate) under this paragraph (Terrorism Act 2000, s 114(2)).

(i) If two or more non-intimate samples have been taken under paragraph 10 and they have proved to be insufficient and the person has been released from custody, an intimate sample may be taken (with consent in writing and authorization from a Superintendent) by a constable or medical practitioner or dentist (para 12(2)). **Notes (c), (d), and (e)** apply to any sample taken under paragraph 12(2).

PNLD reference numbers

D8790, D8791

5.3.7 **Checking of fingerprints and samples**

Paragraph 14 of Schedule 8 to the Terrorism Act 2000 states what can be done with fingerprints taken under paragraphs 10 and 12.

14(1) This paragraph applies to—
    (a) **fingerprints** or **samples** taken under **paragraph 10** or **12**, and
    (b) information derived from those samples.

14(2) The fingerprints and samples may be retained but shall not be used by any person except for the purposes of a terrorist investigation or for purposes related to the prevention or

detection of **crime**, the investigation of an offence or the
conduct of a prosecution.

Terrorism Act 2000, Sch 8, para 14(1) and (2)

Meanings

Fingerprints (see **5.3.6**)

Samples (see **5.3.6**)

Paragraph 10 or 12 (see **5.3.6**)

Crime

Means—

(a) a reference to crime includes a reference to any conduct which—
   (i) constitutes one or more criminal offences (whether under
       the law of a part of the UK or of a country or territory
       outside the UK); or
   (ii) is, or corresponds to, any conduct which, if it all took place
       in any one part of the UK, would constitute one or more
       criminal offences; and
(b) the references to an investigation and to a prosecution include
    references, respectively, to any investigation outside the
    United Kingdom of any crime or suspected crime and to a
    prosecution brought in respect of any crime in a country or
    territory outside the UK (Terrorism Act 2000, Sch 8, para
    14(4A)).

Notes

(a) Paragraph 14(2)–(3) provides that samples taken under
    paragraphs 10 and 12 can be checked against those taken
    under section 63A(1) of the Police and Criminal Evidence Act
    1984 and those taken under previous terrorism provisions
    (s 15(9) of, or para 7(5) of Sch 5 to the Prevention of Terrorism
    (Temporary Provisions) Act 1989) as long as they are for the
    purposes of a terrorist investigation or for the purposes related
    to the prevention or detection of crime, the investigation of an
    offence, or the conduct of a prosecution. Intelligence checks
    could be carried out as this would be covered by the prevention
    and detection of crime but those to identify a person cannot be
    made under this paragraph and must be made under paragraph
    10 (see **5.3.6 note (b)**).

(b) The *Protection of Freedoms Act 2012* repeals paragraph 14 of
    Schedule 8 and replaces it with paragraphs 20A to 20I.
    Generally, material must be destroyed unless it is retained
    under a power conferred under paragraphs 20B–20E; except in

the case of samples which must be destroyed as soon as a DNA profile has been satisfactorily derived from the sample and in any event within six months of taking the sample (para 20G). Paragraphs 20(6)–20(13) provide that samples may be retained for a longer period than six months in certain circumstances. Where, following detention under section 41 or Schedule 7, the person is convicted of a recordable offence (or where the person already has such a conviction, other than an exempt conviction), the material need not be destroyed and may be retained indefinitely. See PNLD reference number S399 to check whether these amendments are in force.

(c) This paragraph (other than sub-para (4)) applies to fingerprints or samples (including information derived from those samples) taken under section 15(9) of, or paragraph 7(5) of Schedule 5 to the Prevention of Terrorism (Temporary Provisions) Act 1989 (no longer in force) as it applies to fingerprints or samples (including information derived from those samples) taken under paragraph 10 or 12 (para 14(5)).

(d) *Counter-Terrorism Act 2008*—section 14 amends the Police and Criminal Evidence Act 1984 (s 63A) to allow checks to be made, by those with access, to fingerprints and samples held by the Security Service and the Secret Intelligence Service. See PNLD reference number S2 to check whether these amendments are in force.

PNLD reference number

D8792

5.3.8 **Reviews of detention**

Paragraphs 21 and 22 of Schedule 8 to the Terrorism Act 2000 provide details of when reviews should be carried out and when they can be postponed.

21(1) A person's detention shall be periodically reviewed by a **review officer**.

21(2) The first review shall be carried out as soon as is reasonably practicable after the time of the person's arrest.

21(3) Subsequent reviews shall, subject to **paragraph 22**, be carried out at intervals of not more than 12 hours.

21(4) No review of a person's detention shall be carried out after **a warrant extending his detention has been issued under Part III**.

Terrorism Act 2000, Sch 8, para 21(1)–(4)

Meanings

Review officer (see 5.3.10)

Paragraph 22 (see notes (d), (e), and (f))

A warrant extending detention under Part III (see 5.3.11)

Notes

(a) Paragraph 21(4) is an important paragraph in that it provides that after 48 hours (the initial detention period) strictly speaking no reviews need be carried out. However, to ensure the welfare of the detained person is maintained it would be advisable to ensure the reviews continue. These reviews are not statutory reviews as these have now been passed on to a higher authority (the courts) but become reviews of the detained person's welfare and would be more than likely to be done by the custody officer.

(b) The review must be done **first** before anything else. Detention must be authorized before any other steps are taken. If appropriate, it could be done from outside the cell. Failure to authorize detention could lead to valuable evidence being found inadmissible. If a review is not done first there must be a justifiable reason.

(c) Reviews of those detained for terrorism offences must be done in person and cannot be carried out by telephone.

(d) Reviews can be postponed if at the time the review is supposed to go ahead, the detained person is being interviewed by police officers and the review officer feels that the investigation may be prejudiced if the review was carried out, or if there is no review officer available, or if it is not practicable for any other reason to carry out the review (para 22(1)).

(e) Where a review has been postponed, it shall be carried out as soon as reasonably practicable (para 22(2)).

(f) In order to calculate when the next review should take place, a postponed review will be deemed to have taken place at the latest time in accordance with paragraph 21 (para 22(3)).

(g) *Code H*—when reviewing a detained person's detention, no officer should question the detained person about his involvement in any offence or with regards to any comments he may make with regards to his continued detention (para 14.2).

PNLD reference number

D8793

5.3.9 **Grounds for continued detention**

Paragraph 23 of Schedule 8 to the Terrorism Act 2000 sets out when detention can be continued for those held under section 41.

Police powers

A **review officer** may authorise a person's continued detention only if satisfied that it is necessary—

(a) to obtain **relevant evidence** whether by questioning him or otherwise,

(b) to preserve relevant evidence,

(ba) pending the result of an examination or analysis of any relevant evidence or, of anything the examination or analysis of which is to be or is being carried out with a view to obtaining relevant evidence,

(c) pending a decision whether to apply to the Secretary of State for a **deportation notice** to be served on the detained person,

(d) pending the making of an application to the Secretary of State for a deportation notice to be served on the detained person,

(e) pending consideration by the Secretary of State whether to serve a deportation notice on the detained person, or

(f) pending a decision whether the detained person should be charged with an offence.

Terrorism Act 2000, Sch 8, para 23(1)

Meanings

Review officer (see **5.3.10**)

Relevant evidence

Means evidence which—

(a) relates to the commission by the detained person of an offence under any of the provisions mentioned in section 40(1)(a) (see **4.1**) or

(b) indicates that the detained person falls within section 40(1)(b) (Terrorism Act 2000, Sch 8, para 23(4)).

Deportation notice

Means notice of a decision to make a deportation order under the Immigration Act 1971 (Terrorism Act 2000, Sch 8, para 23(5)).

Notes

(a) The review officer must ensure that before he authorizes continued detention under this paragraph (all subsections except (ba)) that the procedure/investigation is being carried out diligently and expeditiously (para 23(2)).

(b) Reviews of those detained for terrorism offences must be done in person and cannot be carried out by telephone.

PNLD reference number

D8794

5.3.10 Detention—review officer, representations, and record of review

Paragraphs 24–28 of Schedule 8 to the Terrorism Act 2000 deal with the review officer and the procedures he must carry out when reviewing detention.

24(1) The review officer shall be an officer who has not been directly involved in the investigation in connection with which the person is detained.

24(2) In the case of a review carried out within the period of 24 hours beginning with the time of arrest, the review officer shall be an officer of at least the rank of inspector.

24(3) In the case of any other review, the review officer shall be an officer of at least the rank of superintendent.

26(1) Before determining whether to authorise a person's continued detention, a review officer shall give either of the following persons an opportunity to make representations about the detention—

   (a) the detained person, or

   (b) a solicitor representing him who is available at the time of the review.

27(1) Where a review officer authorises continued detention he shall inform the detained person—

   (a) of any of his rights under **paragraphs 6 and 7** which he has not yet exercised, and

   (b) if the exercise of any of his rights under either of those paragraphs is being delayed in accordance with the provisions of paragraph 8, of the fact that it is being so delayed.

28(1) A review officer carrying out a review shall make a written record of the outcome of the review and of any of the following which apply—

    (a) the grounds upon which continued detention is authorised,

    (b) the reason for postponement of the review,

    (c) the fact that the detained person has been informed as required under paragraph 27(1),

    (d) the officer's conclusion on the matter considered under paragraph 27(2)(a),

    (e) the fact that he has taken action under paragraph 27(2)(b), and

    (f) the fact that the detained person is being detained by virtue of section 41(5) or (6).

Terrorism Act 2000, Sch 8, paras 24(1), (2), (3), 26(1), 27(1), and 28(1)

Meanings

Paragraphs 6 and 7

Means the right to have someone informed and the right to legal advice (see **5.3.5**).

Notes

(a) *Review officer*—where the review officer is an officer below the rank of Superintendent, and a higher ranking officer gives him directions relating to the detained person which contradict his duties under Schedule 8, the review officer must refer the matter to an officer of at least the rank of Superintendent without delay (para 25(1) and (2)).

(b) *Representations*—these may be made orally or in writing (para 26(2)) and the review officer can refuse to hear oral representations from the detained person if he considers that he is unfit because of his condition or behaviour (para 26(3)).

(c) *Rights*—where a review officer authorizes continued detention and the detained person has had his rights under paragraphs 6 and 7 delayed (right to have someone informed and right to legal advice), he shall consider whether the reasons for the delay continue and if he believes they no longer exist he shall inform the officer who authorized the delay of his opinion (unless it was he who made the decision) (para 27(2)).

(d) *Written record*—a written record of the outcome must be made in the presence of the detained person and he must be informed whether the review officer is authorizing detention and, if so, on what grounds. If the detained person is incapable of understanding what is being said to him, is violent, or is likely to become so, or is in need of medical attention then this does not apply (para 28(2), (3)).

(e) Reviews of those detained for terrorism offences must be done in person and cannot be carried out by telephone.

PNLD reference numbers

D8795, D8796, D8797

5.3.11 **Warrant of further detention**

Paragraphs 29–37 of Schedule 8 to the Terrorism Act 2000 set out the procedure for extending detention under section 41.

29(2) A warrant of further detention—
    (a) shall authorise the further detention under **section 41** of a specified person for a specified period, and
    (b) shall state the time at which it is issued.

30(1) An **application for a warrant shall be made**—
    (a) during the **period mentioned in section 41(3)**, or
    (b) within six hours of the end of that period.

31 An application for a warrant may not be heard unless the person to whom it relates has been given a notice stating—
    (a) that the application has been made,
    (b) the time at which the application was made,
    (c) the time at which it is to be heard, and
    (d) the grounds upon which further detention is sought.

32(1) A **judicial authority** may issue a warrant of further detention only if satisfied that—
    (a) there are reasonable grounds for believing that the further detention of the person to whom the application relates is necessary as mentioned in **subparagraph (1A)**, and
    (b) the investigation in connection with which the person is detained is being conducted diligently and expeditiously.

33(1) The person to whom an application relates shall—
    (a) be given an opportunity to make oral or written representations to the judicial authority about the application, and
    (b) subject to **sub-paragraph (3)**, be entitled to be legally represented at the hearing.

34(1) The person who has made an application for a warrant may apply to the judicial authority for an order that specified information upon which he intends to rely be withheld from—

    (a) the person to whom the application relates, and
    (b) anyone representing him.
Terrorism Act, Sch 8, paras 29(2), 30(1), 31, 32(1), 33(1), and 34(1)

Meanings

Section 41 (see 5.3.1)

Application for a warrant shall be made

An application for a warrant is made when written or oral notice of an intention to make the application is given to a judicial authority (Terrorism Act, Sch 8, para 30(3)).

Period mentioned in section 41(3)

This is 48 hours.

Judicial authority

Means in England and Wales, a District Judge (magistrates' courts) who is designated for the purpose of this Part by the Lord Chief Justice of England and Wales (Terrorism Act, Sch 8, para 29(4)).

Sub-paragraph (1A)

See note (d).

Sub-paragraph (3)

See note (e) and Related cases for more information.

Notes

(a) *Warrant of further detention*—a Crown Prosecutor or a police officer of at least the rank of Superintendent may apply for a warrant of further detention (para 29(1)). A warrant of further detention shall be issued for a period of **seven days** (see **note (i)**). The seven days shall start at the time the person was arrested under section 41 or if he was detained under Schedule 7 (see **5.4.1**) the time when his examination under that Schedule began (para 29(3)). A warrant of further detention may be for a shorter period if the application so requests or if the judicial authority is satisfied that it would be inappropriate for it to be for a period of seven days (para 29(3A)). For further extensions see **note (i)**.

(b) *Time limits*—an application must be made within 54 hours (48 hours plus six hours) (para 30(1), the extra six hours given for the practicalities of getting a high-security detainee to court) and a judicial authority hearing an application after 48 hours shall dismiss it if he considers that it would have been reasonably practicable to make it within 48 hours (para 30(1), (2)).

(c) *Notice*—notice must be given to the detained person and the application shall not be heard unless this has been done (para 31).

(d) *Grounds for extension*—the further detention of a person is necessary as mentioned in this sub-paragraph if it is necessary—

   (i) to obtain relevant evidence whether by questioning him or otherwise;

   (ii) to preserve relevant evidence; or

   (iii) pending the result of an examination or analysis of any relevant evidence or of anything the examination or analysis of which is to be or is being carried out with a view to obtaining relevant evidence (para 32(1A)). Relevant evidence means evidence which relates to any of the offences mentioned in section 40(1)(a) (see **4.1**) or which indicates that he is or has been involved in the commission, preparation, or instigation of acts of terrorism (see **4.1**) (para 32(2)).

(e) *Representation*—a judicial authority shall adjourn the hearing of an application if the person is not legally represented, is entitled to be, and wishes to be (para 33(2)). A judicial authority may exclude from any part of the hearing the person to whom the application relates or anyone representing him (para 33(3)), see **Related case**.

(f) *Hearing*—a judicial authority may, after giving the opportunity for representations to be made by the applicant (police or CPS) and/or by or on behalf of the detained person, direct that the hearing shall go ahead not in the presence of the detained person or his representative but by some other means so that they can see and be seen by the judicial authority (eg by live television link) (para 33(4) and (5)). If the detained person wishes to make representations about such a direction then he must do so using the means specified in the direction (live link etc) (para 33(6)). A judicial authority shall adjourn the hearing of a direction under this sub-paragraph if the person is not legally represented, is entitled to be, and wishes to be (para 33(7)). A judicial authority is only able to make such a direction if he has been notified (and it has not been withdrawn) by the Secretary of State that there are the facilities available at the place where the person is detained (para 33(8)). If the judicial authority is able to make such a direction but chooses not to do so, it shall state the reasons why (para 33(9)). It is presumed under paragraph 33(9) that the hearing will be conducted by video link. If so, the police must arrange for a secure and distinct area in the police station which can become a courtroom for those purposes (including no photography).

(g) *Information*—the police or CPS can apply for an order to withhold certain information from the detained person and his legal representative. The judicial authority will grant the order only if he is satisfied that one of the following will occur if the information was disclosed—

   (i) evidence of an offence under any of the provisions mentioned in section 40(1)(a) (see **4.1**) would be interfered with or harmed;

   (ii) the recovery of property obtained as a result of an offence under any of those provisions would be hindered;

   (iii) the recovery of property in respect of which a forfeiture order could be made under section 23 or 23A (of the Terrorism Act 2000, see **4.4.12**) would be hindered;

   (iv) the apprehension, prosecution, or conviction of a person who is suspected of falling within section 40(1)(a) or (b) would be made more difficult as a result of his being alerted;

   (v) the prevention of an act of terrorism (see **4.1**) would be made more difficult as a result of a person being alerted;

   (vi) the gathering of information about the commission, preparation, or instigation of an act of terrorism would be interfered with; or

   (vii) a person would be interfered with or physically injured (para 34(2)).

A judicial authority may also make such an order if he is satisfied that the person has benefited from his criminal conduct and if that information was disclosed, recovery of the benefit would be hindered (para 34(3)). The judicial authority shall direct that the detained person and his legal representative be excluded from the hearing of the application under this paragraph (para 34(4)). See also **Related case**.

(h) *Adjournment*—an adjournment for the application of a warrant of further detention can only be given if the hearing is adjourned to a date before the end of the 48-hour period from when the person was arrested but this does not apply to an adjournment under para 33(2) (an adjournment for the detained person to obtain legal representation if he so wishes) (para 35).

(i) *Extensions of warrants*—a Superintendent or above or a Crown Prosecutor may apply for an extension of a warrant of further detention (para 36(1)). A judicial authority (District Judge, magistrates' court) will hear the application (para 36(1) and (1A). Warrants of detention can be extended for a maximum period of seven days at any one time and for a total period of 14 days (para 36(3)). The judicial authority can make the warrant for a shorter period of time than seven days, if the applicant requests it or if they feel it would be inappropriate to extend it for the length of time requested (para 36(3AA)). **Notes (c) and (d)** apply to extensions to warrants of further detention as they do to warrants of further detention. The warrant should be endorsed with the new specified period of time of detention (para 36(2)). A hearing for an application to extend detention may only be adjourned if it is to a date before the expiration of the specified time in the warrant; this does not apply to an adjournment under para 33(2) (an adjournment for the detained person to obtain legal representation if he so wishes) (para 36(5) and (6)) (see also **note (h)** at **5.3.1**).

(j) *Code H* (full Code H can be found at **Appendix 4**)—if the Detention of Terrorists Suspects (Temporary Extension) Bill is enacted and in force, a High Court judge may extend or further extend a warrant of further detention to authorize a person to be detained beyond a period of 14 days from the time of their arrest (or if they were being detained under TACT, Sch 7, from the time at which their examination under Sch 7 began). The provisions of Annex J will apply when a warrant of further detention is so extended or further extended (para 14.5).

(k) If it appears to the police officer in charge of the detained person's detention that any of the matters (obtain evidence by questioning or preserve evidence) on which the last detention was based, have changed then he must release the person from custody immediately or tell the person who does have custody of the detained person and they in turn must release them immediately (para 37).

Related case

Ward v Police Service of Northern Ireland [2007] UKHL 50 A detained person and his solicitor were excluded from part of a hearing for a warrant of further detention so that the judge could question the police with regard to the remaining topics on which they wished to interview the detained person. The detained person and his legal representative were not informed of the information that had been discussed. This was permitted within the parameters of paragraph 33 and was also of benefit to the detained person so that the judge could satisfy himself that the police did have grounds to detain him further.

PNLD reference numbers

D8786–D8799, D8951, D8952, C1558

5.4 **Ports Control**

Section 53 of and Schedule 7 to the Terrorism Act 2000 provide powers for the control of ports (airports and seaports). The port controls are in addition to any powers under the Immigration Act 1971 which regulates entry into and stay in the UK generally (not included in this book). Unlike the immigration control, the security controls at ports do not give examining officers power on their own authority to refuse entry and place no requirements on travellers to obtain leave to enter the country. Another difference from the immigration powers is that these measures can apply to travel within the UK (see **5.4.1 note (g)**).

Further police powers are set out in the Aviation Security Act 1982 and the Immigration, Asylum and Nationality Act 2006. Offences relating to the security of airports and aircraft can be found in the Aviation Security Act 1982 and the Air Navigation Order 2009 which also provide police powers. The Aviation and Maritime Security Act 1990 is concerned with the security of ships and harbours and the offence of trespass on an aerodrome is set out in the Civil Aviation Act 1982. For measures aimed at enhancing the security of ships and ports see the Ship and Port Facility (Security) Regulations 2004 (as amended) (not included in this book).

See case study on Glasgow Operation Seagram (see **2.5**).

5.4.1 **Power to stop, question, and detain**

Schedule 7 to the Terrorism Act 2000 allows examining officers (constables, immigration and designated customs officers) to stop, question, and detain persons at ports for up to nine hours to determine whether the person is or has been concerned in the commission, preparation, or instigation of acts of terrorism.

Powers

2(1) An **examining officer** may question a person to whom this paragraph applies for the purpose of determining whether he appears to be a **person falling within section 40(1)(b)**.

2(2) This paragraph applies to a person if—

   (a) he is at a **port** or in **the border area**, and

   (b) the examining officer **believes** that the person's presence at the port or in the area is connected with his entering or leaving Great Britain or Northern Ireland or his travelling by air within Great Britain or within Northern Ireland.

2(3) This paragraph also applies to a person on a **ship** or aircraft which has arrived at any place in Great Britain or Northern Ireland (whether from within or outside Great Britain or Northern Ireland).

2(4) An examining officer may exercise his powers under this paragraph whether or not he has grounds for suspecting that a person falls within section 40(1)(b).

5 A person who is questioned under paragraph 2 or 3 must—
   (a) give the examining officer any information in his possession which the officer requests;
   (b) give the examining officer on request either a valid passport which includes a photograph or another document which establishes his identity;
   (c) declare whether he has with him documents of a kind specified by the examining officer;
   (d) give the examining officer on request any document which he has with him and which is of a kind specified by the officer.

Terrorism Act 2000, Sch 7, paras 2 and 5

Meanings

Examining officer

Means any of the following—

(a) a constable,
(b) an **immigration officer**, and
(c) a **customs officer** who is designated for the purpose of this Schedule by the Secretary of State and the Commissioners of Customs and Excise (Terrorism Act 2000, Sch 7, para 1(1)).

Immigration officer

Means a person appointed as an immigration officer under paragraph 1 of Schedule 2 to the Immigration Act 1971 (Terrorism Act 2000, s 121).

Customs officer

Means an officer of Revenue and Customs (Terrorism Act 2000, s 121).

Note: most port control powers provided in Schedule 7 to the Terrorism Act 2000 are available to police officers, immigration officers, and designated customs officers.

However, according to the Code of Practice for Examining Officers (see **5.4.9**) immigration and customs officers should only exceptionally exercise their functions and only when a police officer is not readily available or on specific request by a police officer (rank of sergeant or above); such action should be authorized by an officer of a certain rank (for details see Code of Practice, para 6, see **Appendix 6**).

A person falls within section 40(1)(b)

If he is or has been concerned in the commission, preparation, or instigation of **acts of terrorism**.

Acts of terrorism (see **4.1.2**)

Port

Includes an airport and a hoverport (Terrorism Act 2000, Sch 7, para 1(2)).

And a place shall be treated as a port in relation to a person if an examining officer believes that the person—

(a) has gone there for the purpose of embarking on a ship or aircraft, or
(b) has arrived there on disembarking from a ship or aircraft (Terrorism Act 2000, Sch 7, para 1(3)).

It also includes a railway station or other places where—

(a) persons embark or disembark or
(b) goods are loaded or unloaded,

on or from a through train (international services) or shuttle train (trains carrying road traffic between England and France), as the case may be (Channel Tunnel (International Arrangements) Order 1993, Sch 4 (SI 1993/1813), see **note (w)**).

The border area

Refers to the area no more than one mile from the border between Northern Ireland and the Republic of Ireland (Terrorism Act 2000, Sch 7, para 4).

Belief

Should be justifiable (ie based on factors relevant to terrorism) and will depend on the individual circumstances (see **note (g)**). However, there is no need to establish reasonable suspicion (Terrorism Act 2000, Sch 7, para 2(4)).

Ship

Includes a hovercraft (Terrorism Act 2000, Sch 7, para 1(2)).

Notes

(a) *The purpose of questioning* and associated powers is to determine whether a person appears to be someone who is or has been concerned in the commission, preparation, or instigation of acts of terrorism. The powers must not be used for any other purpose. They are in addition to the power of arrest under section 41 of the Terrorism Act 2000 (see **5.3.1**). Unless a person is arrested he does not have to be cautioned. Because there is no need for reasonable suspicion that the person is concerned in the commission, preparation, or instigation of acts of terrorism, the power can be exercised more widely than normal powers available to police, immigration or customs officers, as well as allowing for more specific operations.

(b) *Examination* begins after initial screening questions have been asked. Screening questions do not form part of the examination and these questions do not need to be recorded nor does the National Joint Unit (NJU) need to be informed. The screening questions are: destination; identification; provenance; and method/purpose of travel (more detail can be found in Guidance on Schedule 7 issued by NPIA—see < http://www.npia.police.uk/en/14749.htm >).

(c) *Referral to the police*—once initial screening questions have been asked by an immigration or customs officer and it appears necessary to continue the examination, the person should be referred to a police officer. For details see paragraph 12 of the Code of Practice for Examining Officers (see **Appendix 6**).

(d) *Legal advice/right to have someone informed*—an examinee (not under detention) can request to consult a solicitor or request to have someone informed. The solicitor will not be provided at public expense and the examination will not be delayed pending the arrival of a solicitor. (See also Annex B to **Appendix 6**.) These requests may be allowed at the discretion of the examining officer. Once a person is detained, they can have full access to a solicitor (see **5.3.5**).

(e) *Offence*—the examining officer must specify the information and/or documentation that he is requesting (Sch 7, para 5). Where a person fails to comply with a duty imposed under or by virtue of the Schedule or wilfully obstructs or seeks to frustrate a search or examination under or by virtue of this Schedule then he commits an offence (see **5.4.8**). For the offence to be committed, the examining officer must have stated the information or document he requires and the person must have failed to comply with the request or obstructed or frustrated the search or examination. Examples of scenarios involved here may be where a person wishes to remain silent for all or part of the examination. The examinee may say that he does not have a document of a kind specified by the examining officer when requested, but such a document is found when the examinee's property is searched. The examinee may refuse to hand over the PIN for any device that stores electronic data (eg mobile phone, etc) and that is in his possession.

(f) *Examination/detention*—examination is a form of checking travellers distinct from detention and arrest. Examination and examination whilst under detention are two separate procedures. Examination may or may not involve formal detention or arrest; in most cases examination will not require detention. Detention might be necessary where the person does not cooperate or insists on leaving. If there is reasonable suspicion of the person being a terrorist, then the power of arrest under section 41 (see **5.3.1**) is likely to be more appropriate.

(g) *Application*—the examining officer must believe that a person's presence at the port is connected with his entering or leaving Great Britain or his travelling by air within Great Britain. For examples see paragraph 7 of the Code of Practice for Examining Officers (see **Appendix 6**). The powers also apply to a person on a ship or an aircraft which has arrived at any place in Great Britain. Note that the powers in Schedule 7 cannot be used if someone is travelling within Great Britain unless the person is travelling by air. Note also that people travelling within the Common Travel Area (UK, Republic of Ireland, Channel Islands, and the Isle of Man) may not routinely carry passports as a primary means of identification.

(h) *Exercise of power*—the power to stop, question, and detain must be exercised in a way that causes as little embarrassment or offence as possible. Bear in mind that there is no need for reasonable suspicion of a person's involvement in terrorism. Also avoid discriminating against persons on the grounds of race, colour, religion, creed, gender, or sexual orientation (see also Code of Practice for Examining Officers, para 10 and notes for guidance, **Appendix 6**).

(i) *Once an examination lasts for one hour*, notice of examination should be served by the examining officer on the person as set out in Annex A to the Code of Practice (see **Appendix 6**) and explained to him. NJU should be notified where an examination lasts for more than one hour and where an examinee is detained under Schedule 7. No combination of examination and/or examination with detention shall exceed nine hours (see **note (s)**).

(j) *Certain information* should be given to a detained person:
- that he is not under arrest or caution, but detained under the provisions of Schedule 7 to the Terrorism Act 2000;
- that this does not mean he is suspected of being involved in terrorism, but that the purpose of the questioning is to establish whether he appears to be such a person;
- that he is under a duty to give all information in his possession which is requested by the officer;
- that failure to comply is an offence (see **5.4.8**).

See also paragraph 35 of the Code of Practice for Examining Officers and Annex A (Form of notice of duties and rights) (see **Appendix 6**).

(k) *Refreshments*—depending on the length of the examination, ensure that refreshments are available at regular intervals.

(l) *Juveniles and other vulnerable people* should only be questioned after special consideration. They should be questioned in the presence of a parent, guardian, or responsible person, and if travelling on their own, of a social worker or other person not connected to the police. Bear in mind that children, especially if on their own, may be easily intimidated; on the other hand, they may be vulnerable to exploitation by adults using them for terrorist aims. For further details refer to paragraphs 15–18 of the Code of Practice for Examining Officers (see **Appendix 6**).

(l) *Video recording*—interviews with a person detained under Schedule 7 do not have to be audio or video recorded, unless they take place at a police station. The Code of Practice on Video Recording of Interviews (see **Appendix 7**) applies to interviews by a constable of a person detained under Schedule 7 or section 41 if the interview takes place in a police station (see **5.3.4**). PACE Code of Practice E does not apply to such interviews.

(m) *'Information'* requested by an examining officer includes information stored in electronic devices and data and passwords to access that data. Where the information is located elsewhere, for example on another server, and is accessed via a mobile phone or internet connection, further authority, such as a warrant, would be required (see note on para 25 of the Code of Practice for Examining Officers, **Appendix 6**).

(n) *Additional powers*—where an examining officer exercises the power to question under paragraph 2 he may stop a person or vehicle, and detain a person. For the purpose of detaining a person, an examining officer may authorize the person's removal from a ship, aircraft, or vehicle (this includes a train, Sch 7, para 1(2)) (Sch 7, para 6). There is also a power of search (see **5.4.2**).

(o) *Vehicle/ship/aircraft*—an examining officer may also enter a vehicle (which does not include aircraft, hovercraft, train, or vessel for the purposes of Schedule 7) for the purpose of stopping, questioning, or detaining a person (Terrorism Act 2000, Sch 14, para 2). However, an examining officer may search a ship or aircraft; search anything on a ship or aircraft; search anything which he reasonably believes has been, or is about to be, on a ship or aircraft in order to satisfy himself whether there are persons on board whom he may wish to question under paragraph 2 (Terrorism Act 2000, Sch 7, para 7).

(p) *Reasonable force*—an examining officer may *not* use reasonable force for the purpose of exercising a power under paragraph 2, that is, questioning a person. The use of force is expressly excluded in this instance in section 114(2) which allows the use of reasonable force in the exercise of other powers under the Act. However, if a person fails to cooperate when stopped and questioned this might lead to sufficient suspicion for an arrest under section 41 of the Terrorism Act 2000 (see **5.3.1**).

(q) *Treatment of detained person*—where a person is detained under this power he has to be treated in the same way as a person arrested and detained under section 41 of the Terrorism Act 2000, the provisions of Part 1 of Schedule 8 to the Terrorism Act 2000 apply (Sch 7, para 6(3)). This means that the powers provided in Schedule 8 also apply, so that, for example, a person who is being examined whilst in detention may be photographed, measured, and identified (Sch 8, para 2). For details, rights of the detained person and police powers see **5.3.5**.

(r) *Fingerprints* may be taken at the port of entry with the consent of the individual. However, where consent has been refused the person should be taken to a police station (see **5.3.6**).

(s) *Duration*—a person may be detained and/or examined under this power for up to nine hours. The relevant time begins when his examination begins (Sch 7, para 6(4)). An examination begins as soon as a person or vehicle has been stopped and screening questions (used to identify the individual and his travel patterns) have been asked. A longer detention is only possible if the person is arrested (see also **Related cases**). Note that if a person is later arrested under section 41 of the Terrorism Act 2000 or under section 24 of the Police and Criminal Evidence Act 1984, the relevant time is still counted from the time when his examination under Schedule 7 has begun (see also **5.3.1** and **Appendix 6**).

(t) *Detention of property*—any document that has been given to the examining officer in accordance with paragraph 5(d) may be detained (see **5.4.3**).

(u) *Records* should be made of all examinations. For details see paragraphs 13–14 of the Code of Practice for Examining Officers (see **Appendix 6**).

(v) *Supply information to other authorities*—where an examining officer acquires information in the exercise of the power to question a person, this information may be supplied to the Secretary of State for use in relation to immigration, to the Commissioners for Customs and Excise or a customs officer, to a constable, to the Director of the Serious Organised Crime Agency, and to a person specified by order of the Secretary of State for use of a kind specified in the order. A customs or immigration officer may supply such information to an examining officer (Sch 14, para 4).

(w) *Channel Tunnel*—the powers also apply to persons embarking on or disembarking from trains that have arrived in Great Britain through the Channel Tunnel System, international trains (through trains; eg from Brussels to London) as well as so-called shuttle trains which carry road traffic between England and France (Channel Tunnel (International Arrangements) Order 1993 (SI 1993/1813)).

Related cases

Breen v Chief Constable of Dumfries and Galloway [1997] SLT 826 The time limit for detention must not be exceeded for the purpose of considering the case.

CC v Commissioner of Police of the Metropolis [2011] EWHC 3316 (Admin) This case determines the scope and extent of the powers laid down in Schedule 7 to the Terrorism Act 2000: Schedule 7 powers may to be used to make a determination as to whether a person appears to be a terrorist, but not to gain intelligence about overseas activities once it is already determined that the person is considered to be a terrorist.

PNLD reference numbers

D8776, D8777, C2978

5.4.2 **Searches**

In order to check whether there are persons that an examining officer (constable, immigration and designated customs officer) might want to question under paragraph 2 of Schedule 7 to the Terrorism Act 2000 (see **5.4.1**) an examining officer or an authorized person (see **note (j)**) may search ships or aircraft. If a person is questioned under this Schedule there is a power to search the person, his belongings, the ship or aircraft or vehicles. There is also a power to examine unaccompanied baggage or goods to determine whether they have been used in the commission, preparation, or instigation of acts of terrorism.

Powers

7 For the purpose of satisfying himself whether there are any persons whom he may wish to question under paragraph 2 an **examining officer** may—

(a) search a **ship** or aircraft;

(b) search anything on a ship or aircraft;

(c) search anything which he reasonably believes has been, or is about to be, on a ship or aircraft.

8(1) An examining officer who questions a person under paragraph 2 may, for the purpose of determining whether he falls within section 40(1)(b)—

(a) search the person;

(b) search anything which he has with him, or which belongs to him, and which is on a ship or aircraft;

(c) search anything which he has with him, or which belongs to him, and which the examining officer reasonably believes has been, or is about to be, on a ship or aircraft;

(d) search a ship or aircraft for anything falling within paragraph (b);

(e) search a **vehicle** which is on a ship or aircraft;

(f) search a vehicle which the examining officer reasonably believes has been, or is about to be, on a ship or aircraft.

9(1) An examining officer may examine goods to which this paragraph applies for the purpose of determining whether they have been used in the commission, preparation or instigation of acts of terrorism.

9(2) This paragraph applies to—

(a) **goods** which have arrived in or are about to leave Great Britain or Northern Ireland on a ship or vehicle, and

(b) goods which have arrived at or are about to leave any place in Great Britain or Northern Ireland on an aircraft (whether the place they have come from or are going to is within or outside Great Britain or Northern Ireland).

9(4) An examining officer may board a ship or aircraft or enter a vehicle for the purpose of determining whether to exercise his power under this paragraph.

Terrorism Act 2000, Sch 7, paras 7, 8(1), and 9(1), (2), and (4)

Meanings

Examining officer

Means constable, immigration officer, and designated customs officer (see **5.4.1**).

Ship

Includes a hovercraft (Terrorism Act 2000, Sch 7, para 1(2)).

Vehicle

Includes a train (Terrorism Act 2000, Sch 7, para 1(2)).

Goods

Includes property of any description, and containers (Terrorism Act 2000, Sch 7, para 9(3)).

Notes

(a) These powers of search must not be used for any other purpose than to determine whether the person appears to be someone who is, or has been, involved in the commission, preparation, or instigation of terrorism. However, searches may be carried out for other purposes under other powers, for example under section 43 of the Terrorism Act 2000 (see **5.2.1**) or under the Police and Criminal Evidence Act 1984.

(b) An examining officer may enter a *vehicle*, aircraft, hovercraft, train, or vessel for the purpose of a search (Sch 14, para 2).

(c) An examining officer may *use reasonable force* for the purpose of a search if necessary (Sch 14, para 3).

(d) The Code of Practice for Examining Officers applies to searches under Schedule 7 (see **Appendix 6**). Note that PACE Code A does not apply to such searches.

(e) The search of the person must be carried out by someone of the same sex (Sch 7, para 8(3)).

(f) *Baggage*—searches of baggage do not have to be carried out by a person of the same sex, but should be if the person objects; see further paragraph 23 of the Code of Practice for Examining Officers (see **Appendix 6**).

(g) As when questioning a person, every effort should be made to avoid potential embarrassment (see **5.4.1 note (h)** and paras 23–24 of the Code of Practice) (see **Appendix 6**).

(h) Where an officer searches a person and is not in uniform he should show evidence of his authority, such as a warrant card. If requested, sufficient information to identify the officer in case of a query or complaint should be given, such as collar number and location. It is not necessary to give a name; and in certain circumstances it might be appropriate not to do so. See further paragraphs 26–27 of the Code of Practice (see **Appendix 6**).

(i) *Strip searches* (searches involving the removal of more than outer clothing) should not be undertaken routinely and should only be considered necessary where the person is in police custody as result of detention under Schedule 7. However, if the examining officer has reasonable grounds to suspect that a person has concealed something which may be evidence that the person is involved in terrorism or which might have been used for such a purpose a strip search may take place at a port. For details on how to conduct a strip search refer to paragraphs 30–32 of the Code of Practice for Examining Officers (see **Appendix 6**).

(j) An examining officer may authorize a person to carry out on his behalf a search or examination under any of paragraphs 7–9. The authorized person may also board a ship or an aircraft in accordance with paragraph 9(4) (Sch 7, para 10).

(k) Anything searched or found during a search or examined may be detained (see **5.4.3**).

(l) As a result of a search, offences other than terrorism offences may be discovered, for example in relation to drugs. These can be dealt with using general police powers.

(m) Where an examining officer acquires information in the exercise of the power to search this information may be supplied to others (for details see **5.4.1 note (v)**).

(n) The powers also apply to trains that have arrived in Great Britain through the Channel Tunnel System, international trains (through trains; eg from Brussels to London) as well as so-called shuttle trains which carry road traffic between England and France (Channel Tunnel (International Arrangements) Order 1993 (SI 1993/1813)).

PNLD reference number

D8778

5.4.3 **Detention of property**

During controls at ports certain property may be detained by an examining officer (constable, immigration and designated customs officer) for future examination, as evidence, or in connection with deportation orders. This power covers any property which has been searched or found during a search under paragraph 8 or examined under paragraph 9 (see **5.4.2**). It also applies to documents which have been given to the examining officer under Schedule 7, paragraph 5(d) to the Terrorism Act 2000 (see **5.4.1**).

Powers

(1) This paragraph applies to anything which—
   (a) is given to an **examining officer** in accordance with paragraph 5(d) *[ie documents requested by the officer when questioning under paragraph 2]*,
   (b) is searched or found on a search under paragraph 8, or
   (c) is examined under paragraph 9.
(2) An examining officer may detain the thing—
   (a) for the purpose of examination, for a period not exceeding seven days beginning with the day on which the detention commences,
   (b) while he believes that it may be needed for use as evidence in criminal proceedings, *or*
   (c) while he believes that it may be needed in connection with a decision by the Secretary of State whether to make a deportation order under the Immigration Act 1971.

Terrorism Act 2000, Sch 7, para 11

Meanings

Examining officer

Means constable, immigration officer and designated customs officer (see **5.4.1**).

Notes

(a) This power may be exercised by an examining officer or by a person authorized by an examining officer to carry out a search or examination on his behalf under paragraphs 7–9 (Sch 7, para 10).
(b) An examining officer may if necessary use *reasonable force* for the purpose of exercising this power (Sch 14, para 3).
(c) The powers also apply to trains that have arrived in Great Britain through the Channel Tunnel System, international trains (through trains, eg from Brussels to London) as well as so-called shuttle trains which carry road traffic between England and France (Channel Tunnel (International Arrangements) Order 1993 (SI 1993/1813)).

PNLD reference number

D8779

5.4.4 Designated ports

Paragraph 12 of Schedule 7 to the Terrorism Act 2000 provides that ships and aircraft on journeys between Great Britain, Northern Ireland, the Isle of Man, and the Channel Islands may only use designated ports for the embarking or disembarking of passengers unless a different arrangement is approved by an examining officer. Captains of aircraft carrying passengers other than for reward may allow their passengers to embark from, or disembark at, non-designated airports provided they give 12 hours' notice to a constable in the relevant area.

(1) This paragraph applies to a journey—
   (a) to Great Britain from the Republic of Ireland, Northern Ireland or any of the Islands,
   (b) from Great Britain to any of those places,
   (c) to Northern Ireland from Great Britain, the Republic of Ireland or any of the Islands, or
   (d) from Northern Ireland to any of those places.
(2) Where a **ship** or aircraft is employed to carry passengers for reward on a journey to which this paragraph applies the owners or agents of the ship or aircraft shall not arrange for it to call at a **port** in Great Britain or Northern Ireland for the purpose of disembarking or embarking passengers unless—
   (a) the port is a **designated port**, or
   (b) an **examining officer** approves the arrangement.
(3) Where an aircraft is employed on a **journey** to which this paragraph applies **otherwise than to carry passengers for reward**, the **captain** of the aircraft shall not permit it to call at or leave a port in Great Britain or Northern Ireland unless—
   (a) the port is a designated port, or
   (b) he gives at least 12 hours' notice in writing to a constable for the police area in which the port is situated (or, where the port is in Northern Ireland, to a member of the Police Service of Northern Ireland).

Terrorism Act 2000, Sch 7, para 12(1)–(3)

Meanings

Ship

Includes a hovercraft (Terrorism Act 2000, Sch 7, para 1(2)).

Port

Includes an airport and a hoverport (Terrorism Act 2000, Sch 7, para 1(2)).

Designated port

Is a port which appears in the table in Schedule 7 (see **note (b)**).

Examining officer

Means constable, immigration officer, and designated customs officer (see **5.4.1**).

Journey otherwise than to carry passengers for reward

May include, for example, when costs are shared between the pilot and up to three passengers, passengers who are joint owners of the aircraft, charity flights, and instructional flights (trial lessons).

Captain

Means master of a ship or commander of an aircraft (Terrorism Act 2000, Sch 7, para 1(2)).

Notes

(a) A designated port is a port which appears in the table included in Schedule 7 (see **note (b)**). This table includes many air and sea ports used for commercial passenger and freight traffic. These are mainly ports with journeys to and from Ireland. Some ports are not listed, such as Dover. In such ports, normal border controls apply. However, much of the provision of Schedule 7 to the Terrorism Act 2000 still applies whether the port is designated or not.

(b) The following are designated seaports and airports in England and Wales:

Seaports

Fishguard

Fleetwood

Heysham

Holyhead

Pembroke Dock

Plymouth

Poole Harbour

Port of Liverpool

Portsmouth Continental Ferry Port

Southampton

Swansea

Torquay

Weymouth

Airports

Biggin Hill

Birmingham

Blackpool

Bournemouth (Hurn)

Bristol

Cambridge

Cardiff

Carlisle

Coventry

East Midlands

Exeter

Gloucester/Cheltenham (Staverton)

Humberside

Leeds/Bradford

Liverpool

London-City

London-Gatwick

London-Heathrow

Luton

Lydd

Manchester

Manston

Newcastle

Norwich

Plymouth

Sheffield City

Southampton

Southend

Stansted

Teesside

(c) Contravention of the prohibitions in paragraphs 12(2) and 12(3) is an offence (see **5.4.8**).

PNLD reference numbers

D8780, D8785

5.4.5 **Embarkation and disembarkation**

Paragraphs 13–15 of Schedule 7 to the Terrorism Act 2000 provide controls for the embarkation and disembarkation of passengers at ports, including airports and hoverports.

Notes

(a) The Secretary of State may give a written notice to the owners or agents of ships and aircraft in order to designate control areas in any port in the UK and specify conditions on and restrictions for the embarkation or disembarkation of passengers in a control area. The receiver of such a notice has to take all reasonable steps to ensure that passengers do not (dis)embark at the port outside that control area and that all conditions and restrictions specified in the notice are complied with (Sch 7, para 13). Failure to comply is an offence (see **5.4.8**).

(b) A control area in a port is designated by the Secretary of State by giving a written notice to the ports managers (ie the persons concerned with the management of a port). The notice may require that the port manager provides specified facilities in the control area for the (dis)embarkation and examination of passengers under Schedule 7. The notice can also contain conditions and restrictions relating to the (dis)embarkation of passengers in a control area and require that notices with specified information about the ports and border controls under the Terrorism Act 2000 are displayed in specified locations in a certain form.

(c) Port managers have to take all reasonable steps to comply with requirements set out in such a notice; failure to comply is an offence (Sch 7, para 14) (see **5.4.8**).

(d) Currently, no control areas have been designated.

(e) Paragraph 15 of Schedule 7 to the Terrorism Act 2000 provides that where a ship which is employed to carry passengers for reward, or an aircraft arrives in or leaves Great Britain from or for the Republic of Ireland, Northern Ireland, or any of the Islands (the so-called Common Travel Area or CTA), the captain shall ensure—

    (i) that passengers and members of the crew do not disembark at a port unless either they have been examined by an examining officer or they disembark in accordance with arrangements approved by an examining officer;

    (ii) that passengers and members of the crew do not embark at a port except in accordance with arrangements approved by an examining officer;

    (iii) where a person is to be examined under this Schedule on board the ship or aircraft, that he is presented for examination in an orderly manner (Sch 7, para 15(2)).

    Failure to comply is an offence (see **5.4.8**).

(f) Where the disembarkation requirements on arrival in the UK under paragraph 27 of Schedule 2 to the Immigration Act 1971 apply (ie the 'normal' immigration requirements re examination of passengers by immigration officers), the requirements of paragraph (2)(a) are in addition to the requirements of paragraph 27 of that Schedule.

(g) The controls on embarkation and disembarkation also apply to trains that have arrived in Great Britain through the Channel Tunnel System, international trains (through trains, eg from Brussels to London) as well as so-called shuttle trains which carry road traffic between England and France (Channel Tunnel (International Arrangements) Order 1993 (SI 1993/1813)).

PNLD reference number

D8781

5.4.6 **Carding**

Paragraph 16 of Schedule 7 to the Terrorism Act 2000 provides for a landing and embarkation card scheme for passengers. This process is known as 'carding' and allows for basic information to be collected directly from passengers, aside from the information provided by the carrier (see **5.4.7**).

This scheme applies to persons who (dis)embark in Great Britain from ships, including hovercraft, and aircraft which have come from or are going to the Republic of Ireland, Northern Ireland, the Channel Islands, or the Isle of Man—and equally in Northern Ireland for ships and aircraft coming from or going to Great Britain, the Republic of Ireland, or any of the Islands (CTA).

For other journeys the normal border controls apply such as under section 32 of the Immigration, Asylum and Nationality Act 2006 (see **5.4.11**), and under paragraph 17 of Schedule 7 to the Terrorism Act 2000 (see **5.4.7**).

Notes

(a) If required by an examining officer (constable, immigration officer, and designated customs officer, see **5.4.1**) persons have to complete a card and produce it to the officer. The form of the card and the required information is set out in Parts 1 (Landing Card) and 2 (Embarkation Card) of the Schedule to the Terrorism Act 2000 (Carding) Order 2001 (SI 2001/426). An example of a landing/embarkation card can be found in Annex C of the Home Office Circular 3/2001. Cards have to be supplied by the police.

(b) A landing/embarkation card may be required whether or not the examining officer suspects the person is involved in terrorism. As with questioning, avoid discrimination or causing embarrassment or offence (see **5.4.1 note (h)**).

(c) Passengers not travelling within the CTA are not required to complete cards. However, they might be asked to provide information by other means, for example questioning, if they are subject to an examination under paragraph 2 of Schedule 7 (see **5.4.1**).

(d) Under paragraph 18 of Schedule 7 to the Terrorism Act 2000 it is an offence wilfully to fail to comply with this requirement (see **5.4.8**).

(e) Where an examining officer acquires information under the carding provisions this may be supplied to others, for details see **5.4.1 note (v)**.

(f) Carding does not apply to the Channel Tunnel.

PNLD reference numbers

D8782, D10141, D3152

5.4.7 **Provision of passenger information**

Paragraph 17 of Schedule 7 to the Terrorism Act 2000 allows examining officers (constables, immigration and designated customs officers) to require owners and agents of ships and aircraft to provide certain passenger information. Passengers and members of the crew have to provide information as required to the agent or owner.

(1) This paragraph applies to a **ship** or aircraft which—

    (a) arrives or is expected to arrive in any place in the United Kingdom (whether from another place in the United Kingdom or from outside the United Kingdom), or

    (b) leaves or is expected to leave the United Kingdom.

(2) If an **examining officer** gives the owners or agents of a ship or aircraft to which this paragraph applies a written request to provide **specified information**, the owners or agents shall comply with the request as soon as is reasonably practicable.

(3) A request to an owner or agent may relate—
    (a) to a particular ship or aircraft,
    (b) to all ships or aircraft of the owner or agent to which this paragraph applies, or
    (c) to specified ships or aircraft.

(4) Information may be specified in a request only if it is of a kind which is prescribed by order of the Secretary of State and which relates—
    (a) to passengers,
    (b) to crew,
    (c) to vehicles belonging to passengers or crew, or
    (d) to goods.

(5) A passenger or member of the crew on a ship or aircraft shall give the **captain** any information required for the purpose of enabling the owners or agents to comply with a request under this paragraph.

Terrorism Act 2000, Sch 7, para 17(1)–(5)

Meanings

Ship

Includes a hovercraft (Terrorism Act 2000, Sch 7, para 1(2)).

Examining officer

Means constable, immigration officer, and designated customs officer (see **5.4.1**).

Specified information

1 The following information about passengers or crew, namely—
    (a) the person's—
        (i) full name,
        (ii) gender,
        (iii) date and place of birth,
        (iv) home address, and
        (v) nationality; and
    (b) where the person has a travel document—
        (i) the type of document,
        (ii) its number,
        (iii) its country of issue, and
        (iv) its expiry date.

2 The number of items that a passenger has placed in the hold of
an aircraft.

3 The following information about any vehicle belonging to
passengers or crew, namely, its registration number.

4 The following information about goods carried on a vehicle,
namely—

(a) a brief description of them,

(b) the address from which the goods were collected,

(c) the address to which the goods are to be delivered, and

(d) the registration number of that vehicle.

5 The following information about goods which are not carried
on a vehicle, namely—

(a) a brief description of them,

(b) the method of payment for the carriage of the goods,
and

(c) the name or number of any container in which the goods
are placed. (Schedule 7 to the Terrorism Act 2000
(Information) Order 2002, Sch)

Captain

Means master of a ship or commander of an aircraft (Terrorism Act
2000, Sch 7, para 1(2)).

Notes

(a) Information provided by shippers and carriers is of great value
to port officers. Knowing who is or what is carried on aircraft or
ships may enable the police to make further important
enquiries. It is therefore essential that the information
provided is accurate, adequate, and given a high level of
importance by transport operators.

(b) Failure of the owner, agent, passengers, or members of the
crew to comply with a request for information is an offence
(see **5.4.8**).

(c) Where an examining officer acquires information in the
exercise of the power to search this information may be
supplied to others, for details see **5.4.1 note (v)**.

(d) The requirements for the provision of passenger information
under paragraph 17 of Schedule 7 to the Terrorism Act 2000 do
not apply to the Channel Tunnel.

PNLD reference numbers

D8783, D10142

5.4.8 **Offences in relation to ports controls**

Paragraph 18 of Schedule 7 to the Terrorism Act 2000 creates a range of offences in relation to ports controls under that Schedule. There are three different offences: failure to comply with a duty; contravention of a prohibition; and obstruction of a search or examination.

Offences

A person commits an offence if he—
(a) wilfully fails to comply with a duty imposed under or by virtue of this Schedule,
(b) wilfully contravenes a prohibition imposed under or by virtue of this Schedule, or
(c) wilfully obstructs, or seeks to frustrate, a search or examination under or by virtue of this Schedule.

Terrorism Act 2000, Sch 7, para 18(1)

Points to prove

Paragraph 18(1)(a) of Schedule 7

✓ date and location
✓ wilfully
✓ failed to comply with a duty imposed by Schedule 7 to the Terrorism Act 2000

Paragraph 18(1)(b) of Schedule 7

✓ date and location
✓ wilfully
✓ contravened
✓ a prohibition imposed under/by virtue of Schedule 7 to the Terrorism Act 2000

Paragraph 18(1)(c) of Schedule 7

✓ date and location
✓ wilfully
✓ obstructed/sought to frustrate
✓ a search/examination under/by virtue of Schedule 7 to the Terrorism Act 2000

Police powers

If suspected terrorist:

Power of arrest under TACT (see **5.3.1**)

Power to stop and search under TACT (see **5.2.1**)

If the person is not suspected to be a terrorist, consider using PACE powers (such as ss 24, 17, 18, and 32 of PACE) but see **5.3.1** for drawbacks on using PACE powers for potential terrorists.

Notes

(a) The following duties are set out in Schedule 7 of the Terrorism Act 2000:

- give information/passport/document to examining officer on request, paragraph 5 (see **5.4.1**);
- owner/agent of ship/aircraft ensure that passengers do not (dis)embark outside control area/that specified conditions/ restrictions are met/complied with, paragraph 13(2) (see **5.4.5**);
- ports manager comply with notice, paragraph 14(2) (see **5.4.5**);
- captain to ensure that passengers/crew do not (dis)embark other than arranged with examining officer/that person who is examined is presented in orderly manner, paragraph 15(2) (see **5.4.5**);
- owner/agent of ship/aircraft to supply passengers with cards as specified, paragraph 16(2) (see **5.4.6**);
- owner/agent of ship/aircraft to comply with request, paragraph 17(2) (see **5.4.7**);
- passenger/member of crew give captain information as required, paragraph 17(5) (see **5.4.7**).

(b) The following prohibitions are set out in Schedule 7 of the Terrorism Act 2000:

- owner/agent of ship/aircraft must not arrange for ship/ aircraft to call at port unless designated port/arrangement with examining officer, paragraph 12(2) (see **5.4.4**);
- captain of aircraft must not permit aircraft to call at/leave a port unless designated port/giving 12 hours' notice, paragraph 12(3) (see **5.4.4**).

(c) For searches and examinations under Schedule 7 see **5.4.1** and **5.4.2**.

(d) The offence requires that the person acted 'wilfully' not just 'knowingly'. That means that the offence might not be committed if, for example, a carrier makes every effort to collect the requested information but it is simply not possible for some reason, even within a reasonable timescale.

(e) The provisions on post-charge questioning apply to this offence (see **4.2.2 note (g)**).

(f) This offence can be tried in any place in the UK if it was committed in the UK (Counter-Terrorism Act 2008, s 28).

PNLD reference numbers

H3797, H3798, H3799, D8784

 Time limit for prosecution: Six months.

 Summary: Maximum three months' imprisonment and/or fine not exceeding level four on the standard scale.

5.4.9 Code of Practice for Examining Officers

The Code of Practice for Examining Officers issued under Schedule 14 to the Terrorism Act 2000 applies to all examining officers—that is, constables, immigration officers, and designated customs officers (see **5.4.1**) exercising functions under the Terrorism Act 2000 (see **5.4.1–5.4.7**). It does not apply in the exercise of powers under other Acts, for example under the Immigration Act 1971, the Customs and Excise Management Act 1979, or the Immigration, Asylum and Nationality Act 2006.

Notes

(a) The code should be available at all police stations and at police offices at ports where the powers are, or are likely to be, used, for consultation by the police and the public.

(b) Failure by an officer to observe a provision of a code does not of itself make him liable to criminal or civil proceedings (Terrorism Act 2000, Sch 14, para 6(2)).

(c) The National Policing Improvement Agency have issued guidance on this matter—Practice Advice on Schedule 7 of the Terrorism Act 2000 (see <http://www.npia.police.uk/en/14749.htm>). The Practice Advice especially accords much fuller emphasis to community engagement which it views as 'essential'.

(d) For the full text of the Code see **Appendix 6**.

PNLD reference numbers

S1127, D8956

5.4.10 **Police powers to stop and search in airports**

The policing of airports is provided for in Part III (sections 24B–31) of the Aviation Security Act 1982. It gives police officers powers to stop and search persons, vehicles, and aircraft for stolen or prohibited articles in any airport. It also deals with the policing of relevant aerodromes.

Power to stop and search at aerodromes

(1) Subject to subsection (2) below, a constable may search—
    (a) any person, vehicle or aircraft in an **aerodrome**, or
    (b) anything which is in or on such a vehicle or aircraft, for stolen or **prohibited articles**.

(2) This section does not give a constable power to search a person, vehicle or aircraft, or anything in or on a vehicle or aircraft, unless he has reasonable grounds for suspecting that he will find stolen or prohibited articles.

(3) For the purposes of exercising the power conferred by subsection (1) above, a constable may—
    (a) enter any part of an aerodrome;
    (b) detain a person, vehicle or aircraft;
    (c) board an aircraft.

Aviation Security Act 1982, s 24B(1)–(3)

Meanings

Aerodrome

Means the aggregate of the land, buildings, and works comprised in an aerodrome within the meaning of the Civil Aviation Act 1982 and (if and so far as not comprised in an aerodrome as defined in that Act) any land, building, or works situated within the boundaries of an area designated, by an order made by the Secretary of State which is for the time being in force, as constituting the area of an aerodrome for the purposes of this Act (Aviation Security Act 1982, s 38(1)).

Aerodrome within the meaning of the Civil Aviation Act 1982

Means any area of land or water designed, equipped, set apart, or commonly used for affording facilities for the landing and departure of aircraft and includes any area or space, whether on the ground, on the roof of a building or elsewhere, which is designed, equipped, or set apart for affording facilities for the landing and departure of aircraft capable of descending or climbing vertically (Civil Aviation Act 1982, s 105).

The term aerodrome is used rather than airport, as it has wider meaning and covers major airports as well as airfields used only by private flying clubs.

Prohibited article

An article is prohibited if it is an article—

(a) made or adapted for use in the course of or in connection with **criminal conduct**, or
(b) intended by the person having it with him for such use by him or by some other person (Aviation Security Act 1982, s 24B(5)).

Criminal conduct

Means conduct which—

(a) constitutes an offence in the part of the UK in which the aerodrome is situated, or
(b) would constitute an offence in that part of the UK if it occurred there (Aviation Security Act 1982, s 24B(6)).

Notes

(a) *Power to seize articles*—if a constable discovers an article which he has reasonable grounds for suspecting to be a stolen or prohibited article, he may seize it (Aviation Security Act 1982, s 24B(4)).
(b) A warrant is not necessary to exercise the powers under this section (Aviation Security Act 1982, s 24B(8)).
(c) This section does not authorize a constable to enter a dwelling (Aviation Security Act 1982, s 24B(9)).
(d) Further police powers are available at relevant aerodromes under sections 25AA–29E of the Aviation Security Act 1982. They apply only to relevant aerodromes which essentially include all of the major airports in the UK. Constables may enter any part of such an airport, section 26, and have powers to stop and search to prevent theft, section 27.

PNLD reference number

D20441

5.4.11 Police powers regarding passenger and crew information

Section 32 of the Immigration, Asylum and Nationality Act 2006 provides police powers to gather information in respect of ships and aircraft arriving (or expected to arrive) or leaving (or expected to leave) the UK. A police officer of at least the rank of superintendent may request passenger or crew information or information about the flight from the owner or agent of a ship or aircraft.

(1) This section applies to ships and aircraft which are—
   (a) arriving, or expected to arrive, in the United Kingdom, or
   (b) leaving, or expected to leave, the UK.
(2) The owner or agent of a ship or aircraft shall comply with any requirement imposed by a constable of the rank of superintendent or above to provide **passenger or service information**.
(3) A passenger or member of crew shall provide to the owner or agent of a ship or aircraft any information that he requires for the purpose of complying with a requirement imposed by virtue of subsection (2).

   Immigration, Asylum and Nationality Act 2006, s 32(1)–(3)

Meanings

Passenger or service information

Relates to passengers, members of crew or a voyage or flight and is specified in Schedules 3 and 4 to the Immigration and Police (Passenger, Crew and Service Information) Order 2008 (SI 2008/5) (s 32(5)). Examples of what is listed in the Schedule include: information as provided on the passenger's or member of crew's travel document (full name, gender, date of birth, nationality, etc), the vehicle registration number of any vehicle in which the passenger is travelling, flight numbers, ship name, name of carrier, scheduled departure and arrival times.

Notes

(a) A requirement to provide information under section 32(2) may only be imposed by a police officer if he thinks it necessary for police purposes (Immigration, Asylum and Nationality Act 2006, s 32(4)). Police purposes means any of the following—

   (i) the prevention, detection, investigation, or prosecution of criminal offences;
   (ii) safeguarding national security;
   (iii) such other purposes as may be specified (Immigration and Asylum Act 1999, s 21(3)).

(b) A requirement to provide information under section 32(2)—

   (i) must be in writing;
   (ii) may apply generally or only to one or more specified ships or aircraft;

(iii) must specify a period, not exceeding six months and beginning with the date on which it is imposed, during which it has effect;

(iv) must state—
- the information required, and
- the date or time by which it is to be provided (s 32(6)).

(c) These powers also apply to trains that have arrived in Great Britain through the Channel Tunnel System, international trains (through trains; eg from Brussels to London) as well as so-called shuttle trains which carry road traffic between England and France (Channel Tunnel (International Arrangements) Order 1993 (SI 1993/1813)).

(d) Failure to comply with a requirement imposed under section 32(2) or (3) is an offence (summary, penalty maximum three months' imprisonment and/or fine not exceeding level 4 on the standard scale).

PNLD reference numbers

H9304, H9303, D21703, D21705

5.4.12 Hijacking aircraft

Section 1 of the Aviation Security Act 1982 creates the offence of hijacking an aircraft in flight.

Offence

A person on board an aircraft in flight who unlawfully, by the use of force or by threats of any kind, seizes the aircraft or exercises control of it commits the offence of hijacking, whatever his nationality, whatever the State in which the aircraft is registered and whether the aircraft is in the United Kingdom or elsewhere, but subject to subsection (2) below.

Aviation Security Act 1982, s 1(1)

Points to prove

✓ date and location
✓ being on board an aircraft in flight
✓ unlawfully
✓ by use of force/threats
✓ seized/exercised control of aircraft

Meanings

In flight

The period during which an aircraft is in flight shall be deemed to include any period from the moment when all its external doors are closed following embarkation until the moment when any such door is opened for disembarkation, and, in the case of a forced landing, any period until the competent authorities take over responsibility for the aircraft and for persons and property on board, and anything done on board an aircraft while in flight over any part of the UK shall be treated as done in that part of the UK (Aviation Security Act 1982, s 38(3)).

Defence

See Related case.

Police powers

If suspected terrorist:

Power of arrest under TACT (see 5.3.1)

Power to stop and search under TACT (see 5.2.1)

If the person is not suspected of being a terrorist consider using PACE powers (such as ss 24, 17, 18, and 32 of PACE) but see 5.3.1 for drawbacks on using PACE powers for potential terrorists.

Power of arrest—section 7(1) of the Aviation Security Act 1982:

Where a constable has reasonable cause to suspect that a person about to embark on an aircraft in the UK, or a person on board such an aircraft, intends to commit, in relation to the aircraft, an offence under any of the preceding provisions of this Part of this Act (other than section 4), the constable may prohibit him from travelling on board the aircraft, and for the purpose of enforcing that prohibition the constable—

(a) may prevent him from embarking on the aircraft or, as the case may be, may remove him from the aircraft; and

(b) may arrest him without warrant and detain him for so long as may be necessary for that purpose.

Aviation Security Act 1982, s 7(1)

It is an offence to intentionally obstruct a person acting in the exercise of this power (Aviation Security Act 1982, s 7(2), either way, summary: maximum fine not exceeding the statutory maximum, on indictment: maximum two years' imprisonment and/or fine).

Powers of commander of the aircraft—section 94 of the Civil Aviation Act 1982:

The commander of an aircraft in flight (that means from the time the external doors are closed following embarkation until doors are opened for disembarkation) has certain powers, for example to restrain persons on board whose actions jeopardize the safety of the aircraft or persons on board. Police officers may use these powers at the request or with the authority of the commander of the aircraft. For details see section 94 of the Civil Aviation Act 1982 (not reproduced here).

Notes

(a) This offence applies to acts done outside the UK regardless of the nationality of the offender or the place of registration of the aircraft with two exceptions: the offence does not apply if the aircraft is used in **military**, customs, or police service, or both the place of take-off and the place of landing are in the **territory** of the state in which the aircraft is registered, unless—

   (i) the person seizing or exercising control of the aircraft is a **UK national**; or

   (ii) his act is committed in the UK; or

   (iii) the aircraft is registered in the UK or is used in the military or customs service of the UK or in the service of any police force in the UK (Aviation Security Act 1982, s 1(2)).

Military service includes naval and air force service (Aviation Security Act 1982, s 38(1)). And the territorial waters of any state shall be treated as part of its *territory* (Aviation Security Act 1982, s 1(5)).

UK national means an individual who is—

   (a) a British citizen, a British overseas territories citizen, a British National (Overseas) or a British Overseas citizen;

   (b) a person who under the British Nationality Act 1981 is a British subject; or

   (c) a British protected person (within the meaning of that Act) (Aviation Security Act 1982, s 38(1)).

(b) Certain acts committed in connection with the offence of hijacking are also offences under UK law independent of the nationality of the offender or the place where they are committed.

Without prejudice to section 92 of the Civil Aviation Act 1982 (application of criminal law to aircraft) or to section 2(1)(b) of this Act, where a person (of whatever nationality) does on board any aircraft (wherever registered) and while outside the UK any act which, if done in the UK would constitute the offence of murder (see **5.8.4.1**), attempted murder, manslaughter (**5.8.4.3**), culpable homicide or assault or an offence under section 18 (wounding with intent), 20 (wounding), 21 (attempting to choke), 22 (using chloroform), 23 (maliciously administer poison), 28 (causing grievous bodily harm by gunpowder) or 29 (corrosive substances) of the Offences Against the Person Act 1861 or section 2 of the Explosive Substances Act 1883 (cause explosion likely to endanger life or property, see **5.8.1.1**), his act shall constitute that offence if it is done in connection with the offence of hijacking committed or attempted by him on board that aircraft (Aviation Security Act 1982, s 6(1)).

That means that apart from the offence of hijacking, the offender may have committed any of the offences mentioned in section 6(1) even if the act did not take place in the UK. In addition to this, the offender might have committed further offences under UK law if the aircraft was travelling to the UK (Civil Aviation Act 1982, s 92), or the offence of endangering the safety of aircraft, section 2(1)(b) (see **5.4.13**).

(c) It is also an offence to induce someone to commit this offence outside the UK despite the exception in section 1(2) (Aviation Security Act 1982, s 6) (see **5.4.15**).

(d) For the liability of company directors etc see section 37 of the Aviation Security Act 1982 (see **5.7.2**).

Related cases

R v Abdul-Hussain (Mustafa Shakir) [1998] EWCA Crim 3528
Shi'ite Muslims had hijacked a plane and claimed to have done so in order to escape death at hands of Iraqi authorities. The court stated that the defence of duress is available in relation to this offence and the defendants were acquitted on appeal and granted asylum. However, the terror induced in innocent passengers will generally raise issues of proportionality; imminent peril of death or serious injury to the defendant or his dependants has to operate on the mind of the defendant at the time he commits the act so as to overbear his will, but the execution of the threat need not be immediately in prospect. The period of time between the beginning of the peril and the defendant's act is a relevant but not determinative factor; all circumstances of the peril, including the number, identity, and status of those creating it, and the opportunities (if any) to avoid it are relevant, initially for the judge and, in appropriate cases, for the

jury, when assessing whether the defendant's mind is affected so as to overbear his will.

R v Safi [2003] EWCA Crim 1809 The defendants hijacked an aircraft from Afghanistan, which flew via Moscow to the UK, and claimed to have done so in order to escape capture, torture, and death by the ruling party in Afghanistan, due to the fact that they were members of an opposing organization. They claimed that they continued to act under duress in Moscow and the UK to avoid deportation or being killed by police or soldiers; however, evidence was adduced that there was no risk of the defendants being deported from the UK. It was held that the defence of duress was available to the defendants and they were acquitted. The court stated that it was not necessary for there to be a threat in fact before the defence of duress could be invoked, simply that a defendant reasonably believed there was a threat.

PNLD reference numbers

H8550, D4310, D4319, D3583, C3036, C3037

AG✓	**AG consent required:** Aviation Security Act 1982, s 8(1).
🕐	**Time limit for prosecution:** None.
▦	**Indictment:** Maximum life imprisonment.

5.4.13 Destroy, damage, endanger safety of aircraft

Section 2 of the Aviation Security Act 1982 creates the offences of unlawfully destroying or damaging aircraft in flight or in service and unlawfully and intentionally placing or causing to be placed on an aircraft in service or in flight any device or substance likely to destroy the aircraft or endanger its safety.

> **Offences**
>
> (1) It shall, subject to subsection (4) below, be an offence for any person **unlawfully** and intentionally—
>
>   (a) to destroy an **aircraft in service** or so to damage such an aircraft as to render it incapable of flight or as to be likely to endanger its safety in flight; or
>
>   (b) to commit on board an **aircraft in flight** any **act of violence** which is likely to endanger the safety of the aircraft.

(2) It shall also, subject to subsection (4) below, be an offence for any person unlawfully and intentionally to place, or cause to be placed, on an aircraft in service any device or substance which is likely to destroy the aircraft, or is likely so to damage it as to render it incapable of flight or as to be likely to endanger its safety in flight; but nothing in this subsection shall be construed as limiting the circumstances in which the commission of any act—

(a) may constitute an offence under subsection (1) above, or

(b) may constitute attempting or conspiring to commit, or aiding, abetting, counselling or procuring, or being art and part in, the commission of such an offence.

Aviation Security Act 1982, s 2(1) and (2)

Points to prove

Destroy aircraft

✓ date and location
✓ unlawfully and intentionally
✓ destroyed an aircraft in service

Damage aircraft

✓ date and location
✓ unlawfully and intentionally
✓ damaged an aircraft in service
✓ as to render it incapable of flight/be likely to endanger its safety in flight

Endangering aircraft

✓ date and location on board an aircraft in flight
✓ unlawfully and intentionally
✓ committed an act of violence likely to endanger the safety of the aircraft

Placing device on aircraft

✓ date and location
✓ unlawfully and intentionally
✓ placed/caused to be placed on an aircraft
✓ a device/substance which was likely to destroy the aircraft/so to damage it as to render it incapable of flight/as to be likely to endanger its safety in flight

Meanings

Unlawfully

(a) in relation to the commission of an act in the UK, means so as (apart from this Act) to constitute an offence under the law of the part of the UK in which the act is committed, and

(b) in relation to the commission of an act outside the UK, means so that the commission of the act would (apart from this Act) have been an offence under the law of England and Wales if it had been committed in England and Wales or of Scotland if it had been committed in Scotland (Aviation Security Act 1982, s 2(6)).

Aircraft in service/in flight

(a) The period during which an aircraft is in flight shall be deemed to include any period from the moment when all its external doors are closed following embarkation until the moment when any such door is opened for disembarkation, and, in the case of a forced landing, any period until the competent authorities take over responsibility for the aircraft and for persons and property on board; and

(b) an aircraft shall be taken to be in service during the whole of the period which begins with the pre-flight preparation of the aircraft for a flight and ends 24 hours after the aircraft lands having completed that flight, and also at any time (not falling within that period) while, in accordance with the preceding paragraph, the aircraft is in flight,

and anything done on board an aircraft while in flight over any part of the UK shall be treated as done in that part of the UK (Aviation Security Act 1982, s 38(3)).

Act of violence

Means—

(a) any act done in the UK which constitutes the offence of murder (see **5.8.4.1**), attempted murder, manslaughter (**5.8.4.3**), culpable homicide or assault or an offence under section 18 (wounding with intent), 20 (wounding), 21 (attempting to choke), 22 (using chloroform), 23 (maliciously administer poison), 24 (administer poison to injure), 28 (causing grievous bodily injury by gunpowder), or 29 (causing gunpowder to explode with intent) of the Offences Against the Person Act 1861 or under section 2 of the Explosive Substances Act 1883 (causing explosion likely to endanger life or property, see **5.8.1.1**), and

(b) any act done outside the UK which, if done in the UK, would constitute such an offence as is mentioned in paragraph (a) (Aviation Security Act 1982, s 2(7)).

Police powers

If suspected terrorist:

Power of arrest under TACT (see **5.3.1**)

Power to stop and search under TACT (see **5.2.1**)

If the person is not suspected to be a terrorist consider using PACE powers (such as ss 24, 17, 18, and 32 of PACE) but see **5.3.1** for drawbacks on using PACE powers for potential terrorists.

Power of arrest—section 7(1) of the Aviation Security Act 1982 (see **5.4.12**), includes power to prohibit from travelling on board the aircraft, to prevent from embarking on or remove from aircraft, arrest and detain.

Powers of commander of the aircraft—section 94 of the Civil Aviation Act 1982 (see **5.4.12**)

Notes

(a) This offence applies to acts done outside the UK regardless of the nationality of the offender and the State in which the aircraft is registered (Aviation Security Act 1982, s 2(3)) with the following exceptions. The offences do not apply to any act committed in relation to an aircraft used in **military**, customs, or police service unless the act is committed in the UK, or where the act is committed outside the UK, the person committing it is a **UK national** (Aviation Security Act 1982, s 2(3) and (4)). *Military service* includes naval and air force service (Aviation Security Act 1982, s 39(1)). *UK national* (see **5.4.12**).

(b) It is also an offence to induce someone to commit this offence outside the UK despite the exception in section 2(4) (Aviation Security Act 1982, s 6) (see **5.4.15**).

(c) For the liability of company directors, etc see section 37 of the Aviation Security Act 1982 (see **5.7.2**).

(d) It is also an offence to destroy or damage property associated with air navigation facilities where the destruction or damage is likely to endanger the safety of aircraft in flight; and also to communicate false information where that information endangers the safety of aircraft in flight (Aviation Security Act 1982, s 3).

PNLD reference numbers

H8551, H8552, H8553, H8554, D4311

AG✓   **AG consent required:** Aviation Security Act 1982, s 8(1).

🕐   **Time limit for prosecution:** None.

▦   **Indictment:** Maximum life imprisonment.

5.4.14 Possession of dangerous articles on aircraft or in aerodrome

Section 4 of the Aviation Security Act 1982 makes it an offence for a person to have with him or in his baggage dangerous articles, such as firearms, imitation firearms, and explosives, in an aircraft, aerodrome, or air navigation installation.

Offence

(1) It shall be an offence for any person without lawful authority or reasonable excuse (the proof of which shall lie on him) **to have with him—**

    (a) in any **aircraft registered in the United Kingdom**, whether at a time when the aircraft is in the United Kingdom or not, or

    (b) in any other aircraft at a time when it is in, or in flight over, the United Kingdom, or

    (c) in any part of an **aerodrome** in the United Kingdom, or

    (d) in any **air navigation installation** in the United Kingdom which does not form part of an aerodrome,

any article to which this section applies.

(2) This section applies to the following **articles**, that is to say—

    (a) any **firearm**, or any article having the appearance of being a firearm, whether capable of being discharged or not;

    (b) any **explosive**, any article manufactured or adapted (whether in the form of a bomb, grenade or otherwise) so as to have the appearance of being an explosive, whether it is capable of producing a practical effect by explosion or not, or any article marked or labelled so as to indicate that it is or contains an explosive; and

    (c) any article (not falling within either of the preceding paragraphs) made or adapted for use for causing injury to or incapacitating a person or for destroying or damaging **property**, or intended by the person having it with him for such use, whether by him or by any other person.

Aviation Security Act 1982, s 4(1) and (2)

Points to prove

✓ date and location
✓ without lawful authority/reasonable excuse had with you
✓ in an aircraft registered in the UK *or*
✓ in any aircraft at a time when it is in, or in flight over, the UK *or*
  in any part of an aerodrome *or*
  in any air navigation installation
✓ a firearm *or*
  an article having the appearance of being a firearm *or*
  an explosive *or*
  an article manufactured/adapted so as to have the appearance of being an explosive whether capable of producing a practical effect by explosion or not *or*
  an article marked/labelled so as to indicate that it is/ contains an explosive *or*
  an article made/adapted for use for causing injury to/ incapacitating any person *or*
  an article made/adapted for use for destroying/damaging property *or*
  an article intended for use by you/any other person/for causing injury to/incapacitating a person *or*
  an article intended for use by you/any other person for destroying/damaging property

Meanings

To have with him

Is explained in section 4(3) and (5) (see **note (a)**).

Aircraft registered or operating in the UK

Means any aircraft which is either—

(a) an aircraft registered in the UK, or
(b) an aircraft not so registered which is for the time being allocated for use on flights which (otherwise than in exceptional circumstances) include landing at or taking off from one or more aerodromes in the UK (Aviation Security Act 1982, s 38(1)).

Aerodrome (see **5.4.10**)

Air navigation installation

Means any building, works, apparatus, or equipment used wholly or mainly for the purpose of assisting air traffic control or as an aid to air navigation, together with any land contiguous or adjacent to any such building, works, apparatus or equipment and used wholly or mainly for purposes connected therewith (Aviation Security Act 1982, s 38(1)).

Firearm

Includes an airgun or air pistol (Aviation Security Act 1982, s 38(1)).

Explosive

Means any article manufactured for the purpose of producing a practical effect by explosion, or intended for that purpose by a person having the article with him (Aviation Security Act 1982, s 38(1)).

Article

Includes any substance, whether in solid or liquid form or in the form of a gas or vapour (Aviation Security Act 1982, s 38(1)).

Property

Includes any land, buildings, or works, any aircraft or vehicle and any baggage, cargo, or other article of any description (Aviation Security Act 1982, s 38(1)).

Police powers

If suspected terrorist:

Power of arrest under TACT (see 5.3.1)

Power to stop and search under TACT (see 5.2.1)

If the person is not suspected to be a terrorist consider using PACE powers (such as ss 24, 17, 18, and 32 of PACE) but see **5.3.1** for drawbacks on using PACE powers for potential terrorists.

Power of arrest—section 7(1) of the Aviation Security Act 1982 (see 5.4.12), includes power to prohibit from travelling on board the aircraft, to prevent from embarking on or remove from aircraft, arrest and detain

Powers of commander of the aircraft—section 94 of the Civil Aviation Act 1982 (see 5.4.12)

Notes

(a) A person is regarded as 'having baggage with him' even if he is not actually carrying an item himself, but the baggage is, for example, already checked in. Section 4(3) explains this, but does not limit it to these circumstances (s 4(5)):

(3) For the purposes of this section a person who is for the time being in an aircraft, or in part of an aerodrome, shall be treated as having with him in the aircraft, or in that part of the aerodrome, as the case may be, an article to which this section applies if—

   (a) where he is in an aircraft, the article, or an article in which it is contained, is in the aircraft and has been caused (whether by him or by any other person) to be brought there as being, or as forming part of, his baggage on a flight in the aircraft or has been caused by him to be brought there as being, or as forming part of, any other property to be carried on such a flight, or

   (b) where he is in part of an aerodrome (otherwise than in an aircraft), the article, or an article in which it is contained, is in that or any other part of the aerodrome and has been caused (whether by him or by any other person) to be brought into the aerodrome as being, or as forming part of, his baggage on a flight from that aerodrome or has been caused by him to be brought there as being, or as forming part of, any other property to be carried on such a flight on which he is also to be carried, notwithstanding that the circumstances may be such that (apart from this subsection) he would not be regarded as having the article with him in the aircraft or in a part of the aerodrome, as the case may be.

(5) Nothing in subsection (3) above shall be construed as limiting the circumstances in which a person would, apart from that subsection, be regarded as having an article with him as mentioned in subsection (1) (Aviation Security Act 1982, s 4(3) and (5)).

(b) The burden of proof that the defendant had lawful authority or reasonable excuse for having an article with him lies on the defendant.

(c) For the liability of company directors, etc see section 37 of the Aviation Security Act 1982 (see **5.7.2**).

Related case

DPP v Hynde [1998] 1 All ER 649 A butterfly knife by its very design is necessarily made for the purpose of injury to the person.

PNLD reference numbers

H8142, H8143, H8144, D4313, D4314

Time limit for prosecution: None.

 Summary: Maximum three months' imprisonment and/or fine not exceeding the statutory maximum.

 Indictment: Maximum five years' imprisonment and/or fine.

5.4.15 Induce or assist commission of offence re aircraft

Section 6 of the Aviation Security Act 1982 makes it an offence to induce or assist the commission of other offences under this Act where this would otherwise not be an offence under UK law.

Offence

It shall be an offence for any person in the United Kingdom to induce or assist the commission outside the United Kingdom of any act which—

(a) would, but for subsection (2) of section 1 *[hijacking]* of this Act, be an offence under that section; or

(b) would, but for subsection (4) of section 2 *[destroy/damage/endanger safety of aircraft]* of this Act, be an offence under that section; or

(c) would, but for subsection (5) or (6) of section 3 *[destroy or damage property likely to endanger aircraft]* of this Act, be an offence under that section.

Aviation Security Act 1982, s 6(2)

Points to prove

✓ date and location
✓ induced the commission outside the UK of an act of
✓ hijacking under s 1(1) of the Aviation Security Act 1982 *or*
destroying/damaging/endangering the safety of an aircraft under s 2(1) of the Act *or*
destroying/damaging/interfering with the operation of property used for the provision of air navigation facilities under s 3(1) of the Act

---

Police powers

If suspected terrorist:

Power of arrest under TACT (see **5.3.1**)

Power to stop and search under TACT (see **5.2.1**)

If the person is not suspected of being a terrorist consider using PACE powers (such as ss 24, 17, 18, and 32 of PACE) but see **5.3.1** for drawbacks on using PACE powers for potential terrorists.

Power of arrest—section 7(1) of the Aviation Security Act 1982 (see **5.4.12**), includes power to prohibit from travelling on board the aircraft, to prevent from embarking on or remove from aircraft, arrest and detain

Powers of commander of the aircraft—section 94 of the Civil Aviation Act 1982 (see **5.4.12**)

Notes

(a) The offences of hijacking, section 1 (see **5.4.12**), destroying, damaging, or endangering the safety of aircraft, section 2 (**5.4.13**), and destroying or damaging property used for the provision of air navigation facilities likely to endanger aircraft, section 3, are all subject to some exceptions, for example if committed outside the UK by a non-UK national. The purpose of section 6(2) is to ensure that a person can be prosecuted if he, while in the UK, induces or assists another person outside the UK who is not a UK national and who therefore does not commit an offence under UK law himself.

(b) Section 8 of the Accessories and Abettors Act 1861 does apply to the offences under sections 1, 2, and 3; the normal rules on aiding and abetting therefore apply to these offences in addition to section 6 (see **5.8.5.4**).

(c) For the liability of company directors, etc see section 37 of the Aviation Security Act 1982 (see **5.7.2**).

PNLD reference numbers

H8561, D4318

AG✓ **AG consent required:** Aviation Security Act 1982, s 8(1).

⏱ **Time limit for prosecution:** None.

▦ **Indictment:** Maximum life imprisonment.

5.4.16 Unauthorized presence in security restricted area of an airport

Section 21C of the Aviation Security Act 1982 makes it an offence for a person without lawful authority or reasonable excuse to go onto any part of a security restricted area of an aerodrome or air navigation installation without appropriate authorization, or to remain there.

Offence

A person shall not—

(a) go, with or without a vehicle, onto any part of a **security restricted area** of—

    (i) an **aerodrome**, or

    (ii) an **air navigation installation** which does not form part of an aerodrome, except with the permission of the manager of the aerodrome, the authority responsible for the air navigation installation or a person acting on behalf of that **manager** or authority, and in accordance with any conditions subject to which that permission is for the time being granted, or

(b) remain on any part of such a security restricted area after being requested to leave by the manager of the aerodrome, the authority responsible for the air navigation installation or a person acting on behalf of that manager or authority.

Aviation Security Act 1982, s 21C(1)

Points to prove

Enter restricted zone without permission

- ✓ date and location
- ✓ without lawful authority/reasonable excuse
- ✓ went on to part of the security restricted area of an aerodrome/of an air navigation installation not forming part of an aerodrome
- ✓ without the permission
- ✓ of the manager/person acting on behalf of manager

Breach entry of restricted zone

- ✓ date and location
- ✓ without lawful authority/reasonable excuse

> ✓ went onto part of a security restricted area of an aerodrome/
> of an air navigation installation not forming part of an
> aerodrome
> ✓ in breach of condition subject to which you had been granted
> permission to enter the security restricted area
> ✓ by the manager of the aerodrome/person acting on behalf of
> manager
>
> **Fail to leave restricted zone on request**
> ✓ date and location
> ✓ without lawful authority/reasonable excuse
> ✓ remained on part of a security restricted area of an aerodrome/
> of an air navigation installation not forming part of an
> aerodrome
> ✓ when requested to leave
> ✓ by the manager/person acting on behalf of manager

Meanings

Security restricted area

Means that area of airside where, in addition to access being
restricted, other aviation security standards are applied; and *airside*
means the movement area of an airport, adjacent terrain and buildings or portions thereof, access to which is restricted (Aviation Security Act 1982, s 24A(1), and Regulation (EC) No 300/2008 of the
European Parliament and of the Council of 11 March 2008 on common rules in the field of civil aviation security, Art 3).

Aerodrome (see **5.4.10**)

Air navigation installation (see **5.4.14**)

Manager

In relation to an aerodrome, means the person (whether the Civil
Aviation Authority, a local authority, or any other person) by whom
the aerodrome is managed (Aviation Security Act 1982, s 38).

Police powers

Power of arrest under TACT (see **5.3.1**)

Power to stop and search under TACT (see **5.2.1**)

A constable, the manager of an aerodrome, or a person acting on his
behalf may use reasonable force to remove a person who fails to
comply with a request under section 21C(1)(b) (Aviation Security
Act 1982, s 21C(4)).

If the person is not suspected to be a terrorist, consider using PACE powers (such as ss 24, 17, 18, and 32 of PACE) but see **5.3.1** for drawbacks on using PACE powers for potential terrorists.

Notes

(a) The offences in section 21C(1)(a) do not apply unless it is proved that, at the material time, notices stating that the area concerned was a security restricted area were posted so as to be readily seen and read by persons entering the security restricted area (s 21C(2)). 'Security restricted areas' used to be called 'restricted zones', and a notice stating that the area concerned was a restricted zone is to be treated as a notice stating that the area concerned was a security restricted area (s 21C(2A)).

(b) A person is permitted to have access to a security restricted area of an aerodrome or air navigation installation if he is permitted to enter that area or if arrangements exist for permitting any of his employees or agents to enter that area (s 24A(2)).

(c) For the liability of company directors, etc see section 37 of the Aviation Security Act 1982 (see **5.7.2**).

(d) See also the offences of unauthorized presence on board an aircraft (**5.4.17**).

PNLD reference numbers

H10835–H10840, D4330

 Time limit for prosecution: Six months.

 Summary: Fine not exceeding level five on the standard scale.

5.4.17 Unauthorized presence on board an aircraft

Section 21D of the Aviation Security Act 1982 creates the offence of unauthorized presence on board an aircraft.

Offence

(1) A person shall not—
   (a) get into or onto an aircraft at an aerodrome in the United Kingdom except with the permission of the operator of the aircraft or a person acting on his behalf, or
   (b) remain on an aircraft at such an aerodrome after being requested to leave by the operator of the aircraft or a person acting on his behalf.
(2) A person who contravenes subsection (1) above without lawful authority or reasonable excuse shall be guilty of an offence . . .

Aviation Security Act 1982, s 21D(1) and (2)

Points to prove

Board aircraft without permission

✓ date and location
✓ without lawful authority/reasonable excuse
✓ at an aerodrome
✓ got into/onto an aircraft
✓ without the permission
✓ of the operator of the aircraft/person acting on operator's behalf

Fail/refuse to leave aircraft on request

✓ date and location
✓ without lawful authority/reasonable excuse
✓ at an aerodrome
✓ remained on an aircraft
✓ after being requested to leave by
✓ operator of aircraft/person acting on operator's behalf

Meanings

Aerodrome (see 5.4.10)

Operator

In relation to an aircraft, means the person having the management of the aircraft for the time being or, in relation to a time, at that time (Civil Aviation Act 1982, s 105).

Police powers

If suspected terrorist:

Power of arrest under TACT (see **5.3.1**)

Power to stop and search under TACT (see **5.2.1**)

A constable, the operator of an aircraft, or a person acting on his behalf may use reasonable force to remove a person who fails to comply with a request under section 21D(1)(b) (Aviation Security Act 1982, s 21D(3)).

If the person is not suspected to be a terrorist, consider using PACE powers (such as ss 24, 17, 18, and 32 of PACE) but see **5.3.1** for drawbacks on using PACE powers for potential terrorists.

Notes

(a) For the liability of company directors, etc see section 37 of the Aviation Security Act 1982 (see **5.7.2**).

(b) See also the offences of unauthorized presence in a security restricted area of an aerodrome (**5.4.16**).

PNLD reference numbers

H4231, H4232, D4331

 Time limit for prosecution: Six months.

 Summary: Fine not exceeding level five on the standard scale.

5.4.18 Obstruction or impersonation of authorized person

Section 21E of the Aviation Security Act 1982 provides the offences of intentionally obstructing an authorized person in the execution of his duties and of falsely pretending to be an authorized person.

> ### Offence
>
> (1) A person who—
>
>   (a) intentionally obstructs an **authorised person** acting in the exercise of a power conferred on him by or under this Part of this Act, or
>
>   (b) falsely pretends to be an authorised person, commits an offence.
>
> *Aviation Security Act 1982, s 21E(1)*

> **Points to prove**
>
> ✓ date and location
> ✓ intentionally obstructed/falsely pretended to be
> ✓ an authorized person acting in exercise of power under Aviation Security Act 1982

Meanings

Authorised person

Means a person authorized in writing by the Secretary of State for the purposes of Part II of the Aviation Security Act 1982 (Protection of Aircraft, Aerodromes and Air Navigation Installations Against Acts of Violence, ss 10–24A) (Aviation Security Act 1982, s 24A).

Police powers

If suspected terrorist:

Power of arrest under TACT (see 5.3.1)

Power to stop and search under TACT (see 5.2.1)

If the person is not suspected to be a terrorist, consider using PACE powers (such as ss 24, 17, 18, and 32 of PACE) but see **5.3.1** for drawbacks on using PACE powers for potential terrorists.

PNLD reference numbers

H4233, H4234, D4332

Obstruct authorized person

 Time limit for prosecution: None.

 Summary: Fine not exceeding statutory maximum.

 Indictment: Maximum two years' imprisonment and/or fine.

Pretend to be authorized person

 Time limit for prosecution: Six months.

 Summary: Fine not exceeding level five on the standard scale.

5.4.19 **Endangering safety of an aircraft, a person, or property**

Article 137 of the Air Navigation Order 2009 (SI 2009/3015) creates the offence of endangering the safety of an aircraft.

Offence

A person shall not recklessly or negligently act in a manner likely to endanger an aircraft, or any person therein.

Air Navigation Order 2009, art 137

Points to prove

✓ date and location
✓ recklessly act in a manner
✓ likely to endanger an aircraft/person in an aircraft

Police powers

If suspected terrorist:

Power of arrest under TACT (see **5.3.1**)

Power to stop and search under TACT (see **5.2.1**)

If the person is not suspected to be a terrorist, consider using PACE powers (such as ss 24, 17, 18, and 32 of PACE) but see **5.3.1** for drawbacks on using PACE powers for potential terrorists.

Powers of commander of the aircraft—section 94 of the Civil Aviation Act 1982 (see **5.4.12**)

Note

The offence applies to offences committed in the UK, and to acts committed on aircraft which are UK-registered or which are foreign-registered but within the UK or over UK territorial waters, regardless of the nationality of the offender, for details see articles 248 and 249 of the Air Navigation Order 2009.

PNLD reference numbers

H9014, D25024

Time limit for prosecution: None.

 Summary: Fine not exceeding the statutory maximum.

 Indictment: Maximum five years' imprisonment and/or fine.

5.4.20 **Cause or permit aircraft to endanger person or property**

Article 138 of the Air Navigation Order 2009 (SI 2009/3015) creates the offence of causing or permitting an aircraft to endanger the safety of any person or property.

> **Offence**
>
> A person shall not recklessly or negligently act in a manner likely to endanger an aircraft, or any person therein.
>
> *Air Navigation Order 2009, art 138*

Points to prove

✓ date and location
✓ recklessly/negligently
✓ caused/permitted an aircraft
✓ to endanger persons/property

Police powers

If suspected terrorist:

Power of arrest under TACT (see **5.3.1**)

Power to stop and search under TACT (see **5.2.1**)

If the person is not suspected to be a terrorist, consider using PACE powers (such as ss 24, 17, 18, and 32 of PACE) but see **5.3.1** for drawbacks on using PACE powers for potential terrorists.

Powers of commander of the aircraft—section 94 of the Civil Aviation Act 1982 (see **5.4.12**)

Note

The offence applies to offences committed in the UK, and to acts committed on aircraft which are UK-registered or which are foreign-registered but within the UK or over UK territorial waters, regardless of the nationality of the offender, see articles 248 and 249 of the Air Navigation Order 2009.

PNLD reference numbers

H9015, H9016, D25025

 Time limit for prosecution: None.

 Summary: Fine not exceeding the statutory maximum.

 Indictment: Maximum two years' imprisonment and/or fine.

5.4.21 Endangering safety at aerodromes

Section 1 of the Aviation and Maritime Security Act 1990 creates offences of endangering safety at aerodromes.

Offence

(1) It is an offence for any person by means of any device, substance or weapon intentionally to commit at an **aerodrome** serving international civil aviation any **act of violence** which—

  (a) causes or is likely to cause death or serious personal injury, and

  (b) endangers or is likely to endanger the safe operation of the aerodrome or the safety of persons at the aerodrome.

(2) It is also, subject to subsection (4) below, an offence for any person by means of any device, substance or weapon **unlawfully** and intentionally—

  (a) to destroy or seriously to damage—

   (i) property used for the provision of any facilities at an aerodrome serving international civil aviation (including any apparatus or equipment so used), or

   (ii) any aircraft which is at such an aerodrome but is not in service, or

  (b) to disrupt the services of such an aerodrome, in such a way as to endanger or be likely to endanger the safe operation of the aerodrome or the safety of persons at the aerodrome.

Aviation and Maritime Security Act 1990, s 1(1) and (2)

Points to prove

Section 1(1)

✓ date and location
✓ by means of device(s)/substance(s)/weapon(s)
✓ at an aerodrome serving international civil aviation
✓ intentionally
✓ committed an act of violence
✓ which caused serious personal injury/death/which was likely to cause death/serious personal injury
✓ and endangered/was likely to endanger
✓ the safe operation of/safety of persons at aerodrome

Section 1(2)

✓ date and location
✓ by means of device(s)/substance(s)/weapon(s)
✓ at an aerodrome serving international civil aviation
✓ unlawfully and intentionally
✓ disrupted the services of the aerodrome in such way as to or
✓ destroyed/seriously damaged property used for provision of facilities/aircraft not in service at that aerodrome in such way as to
✓ endanger/be likely to endanger safe operation of aerodrome/safety of persons at aerodrome

Meanings

Aerodrome

Has the same meaning as in the Civil Aviation Act 1982 (see **5.4.10**).

Act of violence

Means—

(a) any act done in the UK which constitutes the offence of murder (see **5.8.4.1**), attempted murder, manslaughter (see **5.8.4.3**), culpable homicide, or assault or an offence under section 18 (*wounding with intent*), 20 *(wounding)*, 21 (*attempting to choke*), 22 (*using chloroform*), 23 (*maliciously administer poison*), 24 (*administer poison to injure*), 28 (*causing grievous bodily harm by gunpowder*), or 29 (*corrosive substance*) of the Offences Against the Person Act 1861 or under section 2 of the Explosive Substances Act 1883 (see **5.8.1.1**), and

(b) any act done outside the UK which, if done in the UK, would constitute such an offence as is mentioned in paragraph (a) (Aviation and Maritime Security Act 1990, s 1(9)).

Unlawfully

Means—

(a) in relation to the commission of an act in the UK, means so as (apart from this section) to constitute an offence under the law of the part of the UK in which the act is committed, and

(b) in relation to the commission of an act outside the UK, means so that the commission of the act would (apart from this section) have been an offence under the law of England and Wales if it had been committed in England and Wales or of Scotland if it had been committed in Scotland (Aviation and Maritime Security Act 1990, s 1(9)).

Police powers

If suspected terrorist:

Power of arrest under TACT (see 5.3.1)

Power to stop and search under TACT (see 5.2.1)

If the person is not suspected to be a terrorist, consider using PACE powers (such as ss 24, 17, 18, and 32 of PACE) but see **5.3.1** for drawbacks on using PACE powers for potential terrorists.

Note

This offence applies to acts done outside the UK regardless of the nationality of the offender with one exception: subsection (2)(a)(ii) does not apply to any act committed in relation to an aircraft used in **military**, customs, or police service unless—

(i) the act is committed in the UK, or

(ii) where the act is committed outside the UK, the person committing it is a **UK national** (Aviation and Maritime Security Act 1990, s 1(3) and (4)).

Military service

Includes naval and air force service (Aviation Security Act 1982, s 38(1)).

UK national

Means an individual who is—

(a) a British citizen, a British overseas territories citizen, a British National (Overseas) or a British Overseas citizen;

(b) a person who under the British Nationality Act 1981 is a British subject; or

(c) a British protected person (within the meaning of that Act) (Aviation Security Act 1982, s 38(1)).

(d) Section 50 of the Aviation and Maritime Security Act 1990 provides for offences committed by a body corporate (see **5.7.2**).

(e) The Aviation and Maritime Security Act 1990 contains further offences regarding the safety of ships and fixed platforms, such as hijacking of ships (s 9), seizing or exercising control of fixed platforms (s 10), and endangering safe navigation (s 12). In addition to this, the Act provides powers for the protection of ships and harbour areas against acts of violence; the Secretary of State may, for example, impose restrictions on ships (s 21) or require other persons to carry out searches in harbour areas (ss 22 and 23).

PNLD reference numbers

D4315, H4211, H4212, H4454, H4455, H4456

 AG consent required: Aviation and Maritime Security Act 1990, s 1(7).

 Time limit for prosecution: None.

 Indictment: Maximum life imprisonment.

5.4.22 Trespass on licensed aerodromes

Section 39 of the Civil Aviation Act 1982 creates the offence of trespassing on licensed aerodromes.

Offence

Subject to subsection (2) below, if any person trespasses on any land forming part of an **aerodrome licensed** in pursuance of an **Air Navigation Order**, he shall be liable on summary conviction to a fine not exceeding level 3 on the standard scale.

Civil Aviation Act 1982, s 39(1)

Points to prove

✓ date and location
✓ trespassed
✓ on land forming part of a licensed aerodrome

Meanings

Subject to subsection (2) below (see **Defence**)

Aerodrome

Means any area of land or water designed, equipped, set apart, or commonly used for affording facilities for the landing and departure of aircraft and includes any area or space, whether on the ground, on the roof of a building or elsewhere, which is designed, equipped, or set apart for affording facilities for the landing and departure of aircraft capable of descending or climbing vertically (Civil Aviation Act 1982, s 105(1)).

Licensed aerodromes

Means licensed under article 211 of the Air Navigation Order 2009 (SI 2009/3015).

Air Navigation Order

Means an Order in Council under section 60 of the Civil Aviation Act 1982, the most relevant being the Air Navigation Order 2009 (Civil Aviation Act 1982, s 105(1)).

Defence

(2) No person shall be liable under this section unless it is proved that, at the material time, notices warning trespassers of their liability under this section were posted so as to be readily seen and read by members of the public, in such positions on or near the boundary of the aerodrome as appear to the court to be proper.

Civil Aviation Act 1982, s 39(2)

Police powers

Power of arrest under TACT (see **5.3.1**)

Power to stop and search under TACT (see **5.2.1**)

If the person is not suspected of being a terrorist consider using PACE powers (such as ss 24, 17, 18, and 32 of PACE) but see **5.3.1** for drawbacks on using PACE powers for potential terrorists.

Note

See also the offence of unauthorized presence in security restricted area of an airport (see **5.4.16**).

PNLD reference number

D4347

Time limit for prosecution: Six months.

 Summary: Fine not exceeding level three on the standard scale.

5.5 **Chemical, Biological, Radiological, and Nuclear**

Various Acts contain provisions dealing with chemical, biological, radioactive, and nuclear weapons and/or material. The Terrorism Act 2006 creates offences relating to radioactive devices and materials and nuclear facilities. The Anti-terrorism, Crime and Security Act 2001 creates offences relating to the use of nuclear weapons and pathogens and toxins. Further provisions deal with the security of the nuclear industry, trespassing on nuclear sites, the use of noxious substances, and biological and chemical weapons. The offence of public nuisance can be utilized whenever the precise nature of the substance is not clear as chemical, biological, radiological, or nuclear (and might not even be viable as a weapon of any kind).

5.5.1 **Making and possession of radioactive devices or materials**

Section 9 of the Terrorism Act 2006 creates the offence of making or possessing radioactive devices or materials. This offence is specifically terrorism-related and adds to other offences relating to nuclear weapons and other nuclear material which are not terrorism-related.

Offence

(1) A person commits an offence if—
   (a) he makes or has in his possession a **radioactive device**, or
   (b) he has in his possession **radioactive material**,

   with the intention of using the **device** or **material** in the course of or in connection with the commission or preparation of an act of terrorism or for the purposes of terrorism, or of making it available to be so used.

   Terrorism Act 2006, s 9(1)

Points to prove

✓ date and location
✓ made/possessed radioactive device/material
✓ intending to use it in the course of/in connection with the commission/preparation of an act of terrorism *or* for the purposes of terrorism *or* to make it available to be so used

Meanings

Radioactive device

Means—

(a) a nuclear weapon or other nuclear explosive device;
(b) a radioactive material dispersal device;
(c) a radiation-emitting device.

Radioactive material

Means nuclear material or any other radioactive substance which—

(a) contains nuclides that undergo spontaneous disintegration in a process accompanied by the emission of one or more types of ionising radiation, such as alpha radiation, beta radiation, neutron particles or gamma rays; and
(b) is capable, owing to its radiological or fissile properties, of—
    (i) causing serious bodily injury to a person;
    (ii) causing serious damage to property;
    (iii) endangering a person's life; or
    (iv) creating a serious risk to the health or safety of **the public** (Terrorism Act 2006, s 9(4)).

This definition can include (under 'radioactive material dispersal device') a 'dirty bomb' in which an explosive causes radioactive material to disperse, with the effect that the radiation causes danger.

The public

Means the public of any part of the UK or of a country or territory outside the UK, or any section of the public (Terrorism Act 2006, s 20(3)).

Device

Includes any of the following, whether or not fixed to land, namely, machinery, equipment, appliances, tanks, containers, pipes, and conduits (Terrorism Act 2006, s 9(5)).

Nuclear material

Has the same meaning as in the Nuclear Material (Offences) Act 1983 (Terrorism Act 2006, 9(5)). Section 6 of the Nuclear Material (Offences) Act 1983 defines 'nuclear material' as material which, within the meaning of the Convention on the Physical Protection of Nuclear Material, is nuclear material used for peaceful purposes. It covers particular types of plutonium and uranium, such as uranium-233 and any material containing such uranium or plutonium.

Terrorism/act of terrorism (see **4.1**)

Police powers

Power of arrest under TACT (see **5.3.1**)

Power to stop and search under TACT (see **5.2.1**)

Notes

(a) It is irrelevant whether the act of terrorism to which an intention relates is a particular act of terrorism, an act of terrorism of a particular description, or an act of terrorism generally (s 9(2)).

(b) *Extra-territorial jurisdiction*—this offence applies to acts done outside the UK regardless of the nationality of the offender (Terrorism Act 2006, s 17, see **5.7.1.1**).

(c) This offence can be tried in any place in the UK if it was committed in the UK (Counter-Terrorism Act 2008, s 28).

(d) Notification requirements apply (see **5.7.5**).

(e) The provisions on post-charge questioning apply to this offence (see **4.2.2 note (g)**).

(f) *Forfeiture*—section 11A of the Terrorism Act 2006 provides that the court on conviction of this offence may order the forfeiture of any radioactive device or radioactive material, or any nuclear facility, made or used in committing this offence. Also, section 23A of the Terrorism Act 2000 provides that the court can order the forfeiture of money or other property, on conviction for this and other offences, if the money or property was in the possession or control of the person convicted and it had been used for terrorism purposes, was intended for that use, or the court believed it would be used for that purpose unless forfeited (see **4.4.12**). For forfeiture of terrorist cash in general, see **4.4.17**.

(g) *Corporate liability*—for the liability of company directors, etc see section 18 of the Terrorism Act 2006 (see **5.7.2.1**).

(h) Also consider the offences of 'misuse of radioactive devices or material and misuse and damage of facilities' (see **5.5.2**) and 'terrorist threats relating to radioactive devices, material or facilities' (see **5.5.3**), the offences concerning nuclear weapons, section 47 of the Anti-terrorism, Crime and Security Act 2001 (see **5.5.4**), and the offences in the Nuclear Material (Offences) Act 1983 (offences relating to damage to the environment, s 1B, importing or exporting nuclear material, s 1C, etc).

PNLD reference numbers

H8460, H8465, D18580

 DPP/AG consent required: Terrorism Act 2006, s 19 (see **5.7.4**).

 Time limit for prosecution: None.

 Indictment: Maximum life imprisonment.

5.5.2 **Misuse of radioactive devices and materials and misuse or damage of facilities**

Section 10 of the Terrorism Act 2006 makes it an offence to misuse radioactive devices or material and to misuse or damage nuclear facilities in connection with terrorism. It adds to other offences in relation to nuclear weapons (see **5.5.4**).

Offences

(1) A person commits an offence if he uses—
   (a) a radioactive device, or
   (b) **radioactive material**, in the course of or in connection with the commission of an **act of terrorism** or for the purposes of **terrorism**.
(2) A person commits an offence if, in the course of or in connection with the commission of an act of terrorism or for the purposes of terrorism, he uses or damages a **nuclear facility** in a manner which—
   (a) causes a release of radioactive material; or
   (b) creates or increases a risk that such material will be released.

Terrorism Act 2006, s 10(1) and (2)

Points to prove

Section 10(1)

✓ date and location

✓ used a radioactive device/radioactive material

✓ in the course of/in connection with the commission of an act of terrorism/for the purposes of terrorism

Section 10(2)

✓ date and location

✓ used/damaged a nuclear facility

✓ in a manner which caused a release of radioactive material *or* created/increased a risk that radioactive material would be released

✓ in the course of/in connection with the commission of an act of terrorism/for the purposes of terrorism

Meanings

Radioactive device and radioactive material (see **5.5.1**)

Terrorism/act of terrorism (see **4.1**)

Nuclear facility

Means—

(a) a **nuclear reactor**, including a reactor installed in or on any **transportation device** for use as an energy source in order to propel it or for any other purpose; or

(b) a plant or conveyance being used for the production, storage, processing or transport of radioactive material (Terrorism Act 2006, s 10(4)).

Nuclear reactor

Means any plant (including any machinery, equipment, or appliance, whether affixed to land or not) designed or adapted for the production of atomic energy by a fission process in which a controlled chain reaction can be maintained without an additional source of neutrons (Terrorism Act 2006, s 10(5), and Nuclear Installations Act 1965, s 26).

Transportation device

Means any vehicle or any space object (that includes the component parts of a space object, its launch vehicle, and the component parts of that) (Terrorism Act 2006, s 10(5), and Outer Space Act 1986, s 13(1)).

Police powers

Power of arrest under TACT (see **5.3.1**)

Power to stop and search under TACT (see **5.2.1**)

Notes

(a) *Extra-territorial jurisdiction*—this offence applies to acts done outside the UK regardless of the nationality of the offender (Terrorism Act 2006, s 17, see **5.7.1.1**).

(b) This offence can be tried in any place in the UK if it was committed in the UK (Counter-Terrorism Act 2008, s 28).

(c) Notification requirements apply (see **5.7.5**).

(d) The provisions on post-charge questioning apply to this offence (see **4.2.2 note (g)**).

(e) *Forfeiture*—section 11A of the Terrorism Act 2006 provides that the court on conviction of this offence may order the forfeiture of any radioactive device or radioactive material, or any nuclear facility, made or used in committing this offence. Also, section 23A of the Terrorism Act 2000 provides that the court can order the forfeiture of money or other property, on conviction for this and other offences, if the money or property was in the possession or control of the person convicted and it had been used for terrorism purposes, was intended for that use, or the court believed it would be used for that purpose unless forfeited (see **4.4.12**). For forfeiture of terrorist cash in general see **4.4.17**.

(f) *Corporate liability*—for the liability of company directors, etc see section 18 of the Terrorism Act 2006 (see **5.7.2.1**).

(g) Also see the offences of 'making and possession of radioactive devices or material' (see **5.5.1**) and 'terrorist threats relating to radioactive devices, material or facilities' (see **5.5.3**) and the offences concerning nuclear weapons under section 47 of the Anti-terrorism, Crime and Security Act 2001 (see **5.5.4**).

PNLD reference numbers

H8461, H8463, D18581

DPP✓ AG✓ **DPP/AG consent required:** Terrorism Act 2006, s 19 (see **5.7.4**).

🕐 **Time limit for prosecution:** None.

▦ **Indictment:** Maximum life imprisonment.

5.5.3 **Terrorist threats relating to radioactive devices and materials or facilities**

Section 11 of the Terrorism Act 2006 creates offences concerning the making of threats relating to radioactive devices, radioactive material, or nuclear facilities in connection with terrorism. It adds to the offences under section 113 of the Anti-terrorism, Crime and Security Act 2001 in relation to noxious substances or things (see **5.5.15**).

Offences

(1) A person commits an offence if, in the course of or in connection with the commission of an **act of terrorism** or for the purposes of **terrorism**—

  (a) he makes a demand—

    (i) for the supply to himself or to another of a **radioactive device** or of **radioactive material**;

    (ii) for a **nuclear facility** to be made available to himself or to another; or

    (iii) for access to such a facility to be given to himself or to another;

  (b) he supports the demand with a threat that he or another will take action if the demand is not met; and

  (c) the circumstances and manner of the threat are such that it is reasonable for the person to whom it is made to assume that there is real risk that the threat will be carried out if the demand is not met.

(2) A person commits an offence if—

  (a) he makes a threat falling within subsection (3) in the course of or in connection with the commission of an act of terrorism or for the purposes of terrorism; and

  (b) the circumstances and manner of the threat are such that it is reasonable for the person to whom it is made to assume that there is real risk that the threat will be carried out, or would be carried out if demands made in association with the threat are not met.

(3) A threat falls within this subsection if it is—

  (a) a threat to use radioactive material;

  (b) a threat to use a radioactive device; or

  (c) a threat to use or damage a nuclear facility in a manner that releases radioactive material or creates or increases a risk that such material will be released.

Terrorism Act 2006, s 11(1)–(3)

Points to prove

Section 11(1)

- ✓ date and location
- ✓ in the course of/in connection with the commission of an act of terrorism/for the purposes of terrorism
- ✓ made a demand
- ✓ for the supply to yourself/another of a radioactive device/material *or*

  for a nuclear facility to be made available to yourself/another *or*

  for access to a nuclear facility to be given to yourself/another *and*
- ✓ supported the demand with a threat
- ✓ that you/another would take action if the demand was not met *and*
- ✓ the circumstances and manner of the threat were such
- ✓ that it was reasonable for the person to whom it was made
- ✓ to assume that there was a real risk
- ✓ that the threat would be carried out if the demand was not met

Section 11(2)

- ✓ date and location
- ✓ made a threat
- ✓ to use radioactive material/radioactive device *or*

  to use/damage a nuclear facility in a manner that releases radioactive material/creates/increases a risk that such material would be released
- ✓ in the course of/in connection with the commission of an act of terrorism/for the purposes of terrorism
- ✓ the circumstances and manner of the threat were such
- ✓ that it was reasonable for the person to whom it was made
- ✓ to assume that there was a real risk
- ✓ that the threat would be carried out if the demand was not met

Meanings

Terrorism/act of terrorism (see 4.1)

Radioactive device and radioactive material (see 5.5.1)

Nuclear facility (see 5.5.2)

Police powers

Power of arrest under TACT (see 5.3.1)

Power to stop and search under TACT (see 5.2.1)

Notes

(a) The offences are similar to blackmail. Both offences are completed by making the threat alone. No radioactive device or material actually needs to exist.

(b) The offences can only be committed in relation to terrorism, not Convention offences (see **5.7.3**). Also, they can be committed 'in the course of or in connection with' acts of terrorism, but not in preparation for acts of terrorism.

(c) The offence only takes place if the threat is credible looking at the circumstances and manner in which it was made.

(d) *Extra-territorial jurisdiction*—the offences apply to acts done outside the UK regardless of the nationality of the offender (Terrorism Act 2006, s 17, see **5.7.1.1**).

(e) This offence can be tried in any place in the UK if it was committed in the UK (Counter-Terrorism Act 2008, s 28).

(f) Notification requirements apply (see **5.7.5**).

(g) The provisions on post-charge questioning apply to this offence (see **4.2.2 note (g)**).

(h) *Forfeiture*—section 11A of the Terrorism Act 2006 provides that the court on conviction of this offence may order the forfeiture of any radioactive device or radioactive material, or any nuclear facility, made or used in committing this offence. Also, section 23A of the Terrorism Act 2000 provides that the court can order the forfeiture of money or other property, on conviction for this and other offences, if the money or property was in the possession or control of the person convicted and it had been used for terrorism purposes, was intended for that use, or the court believed it would be used for that purpose unless forfeited (see **4.4.12**). For forfeiture of terrorist cash in general see **4.4.17**.

(i) Also see the offences of 'making and possession of radioactive devices or material' (see **5.5.1**) and 'misuse of radioactive devices or material and misuse and damage of facilities' (see **5.5.2**), the offences concerning nuclear weapons under section 47 of the Anti-terrorism, Crime and Security Act 2001 (see **5.5.4**) and the offences under section 113 of the Anti-terrorism, Crime and Security Act 2001 in relation to noxious substances or things (see **5.5.7**).

(j) *Corporate liability*—for the liability of company directors, etc
see section 18 of the Terrorism Act 2006 (see **5.7.2.1**).

PNLD reference numbers

H8462, H8464, D18582

 DPP/AG consent required: Terrorism Act 2006, s 19
(see **5.7.4**).

 Time limit for prosecution: None.

Indictment: Maximum life imprisonment.

5.5.4 **Use, etc of nuclear weapons**

Section 47 of the Anti-terrorism, Crime and Security Act 2001 creates offences regarding the use of nuclear weapons.

Offence

A person who—

(a) knowingly causes a **nuclear weapon** explosion;
(b) develops or produces, or **participates in the development or
production** of, a nuclear weapon
(c) has a nuclear weapon in his possession;
(d) **participates in the transfer of a nuclear weapon**; or
(e) engages in military preparations, or in preparations of a military
nature, intending to use, or threaten to use, a nuclear weapon,
is guilty of an offence.

Anti-terrorism, Crime and Security Act 2001, s 47(1)

Points to prove

Section 47(1)(a)

✓ date and location
✓ knowingly
✓ caused
✓ a nuclear weapon explosion

Section 47(1)(b)

✓ date and location
✓ developed/produced or

> ✓ participated in the development/production of
> ✓ a nuclear weapon
>
> ### Section 47(1)(c)
>
> ✓ date and location
> ✓ possessed
> ✓ a nuclear weapon
>
> ### Section 47(1)(d)
>
> ✓ date and location
> ✓ participated in the transfer of
> ✓ a nuclear weapon
>
> ### Section 47(1)(e)
>
> ✓ date and location
> ✓ engaged in military preparations/in preparations of a military nature
> ✓ intending to use/threatening to use
> ✓ a nuclear weapon

Meanings

Nuclear weapon

Includes a nuclear explosive device that is not intended for use as a weapon (Anti-terrorism, Crime and Security Act 2001, s 47(6)). In this way, a 'dirty bomb' is covered.

A person participates in the development or production of a nuclear weapon

If he does any act which—

(a) facilitates the development by another of the capability to produce or use a nuclear weapon, or
(b) facilitates the making by another of a nuclear weapon, knowing or having reason to believe that his act has (or will have) that effect (Anti-terrorism, Crime and Security Act 2001, s 47(3)).

A person participates in the transfer of a nuclear weapon

If—
(a) he buys or otherwise acquires it or agrees with another to do so;
(b) he sells or otherwise disposes of it or agrees with another to do so; or

(c) he makes arrangements under which another person either acquires or disposes of it or agrees with a third person to do so (Anti-terrorism, Crime and Security Act 2001, s 47(4)).

Defence

(1) In proceedings for an offence under section 47(1)(c) or (d) relating to an object it is a defence for the accused to show that he did not know and had no reason to believe that the object was a nuclear weapon.

(2) But he shall be taken to have shown that fact if—
   (a) sufficient evidence is adduced to raise an issue with respect to it; and
   (b) the contrary is not proved by the prosecution beyond reasonable doubt.

(3) In proceedings for such an offence it is also a defence for the accused to show that he knew or believed that the object was a nuclear weapon but, as soon as reasonably practicable after he first knew or believed that fact, he took all reasonable steps to inform the Secretary of State or a constable of his knowledge or belief.

Anti-terrorism, Crime and Security Act 2001, s 48 (1)–(3)

Police powers

Power of entry to search for evidence relating to nuclear weapons, etc—section 52 of the Anti-terrorism, Crime and Security Act 2001 (see 5.5.6)

If suspected terrorist:

Power of arrest under TACT (see 5.3.1)

Power to stop and search under TACT (see 5.2.1)

If the person is not suspected to be a terrorist, consider using PACE powers (such as ss 24, 17, 18, and 32 of PACE) but see **5.3.1** for drawbacks on using PACE powers for potential terrorists.

Notes

(a) Section 48 of the Anti-terrorism, Crime and Security Act 2001 makes exceptions for actions carried out in the course of an armed conflict or for actions authorized by the Secretary of State.

(b) *Extra-territorial jurisdiction*—the offence applies to acts done outside the UK, but only if they are done by a **UK person** (Anti-terrorism, Crime and Security Act 2001, s 47(7)).

UK person

Means a **UK national**, a Scottish partnership, or a body
incorporated under the law of a part of the UK.

UK national

Is an individual who is—

(a) a British citizen, a British overseas territories citizen, a
British National (Overseas), or a British Overseas citizen;
(b) a person who under the British Nationality Act 1981 is a
British subject; or
(c) a British protected person within the meaning of that Act
(Anti-terrorism, Crime and Security Act 2001, s 56).

Where the offence is committed outside the UK proceedings
may be taken, and the offence may for incidental purposes
be treated as having been committed, in any part of the UK
(Anti-terrorism, Crime and Security Act 2001, s 51(1)).

Where a person aids, abets, counsels or procures, or incites, a
person who is not a UK person to commit this offence
outside the UK, see **5.5.5**.

(c) *Revenue and Customs prosecutions*—proceedings for this offence
(including an offence of aiding, abetting, counselling or
procuring the commission of, or attempting or conspiring to
commit this offence, or an offence of encouraging or assisting
crime under the Serious Crime Act 2007) may be instituted by
the Director of Revenue and Customs Prosecutions or by order
of the Commissioners for Her Majesty's Revenue and Customs
if it appears to the Director or to the Commissioners that the
offence has involved—
   (i) the development or production outside the UK of a
   nuclear weapon;
  (ii) the movement of a nuclear weapon into or out of any
   country or territory;
 (iii) any proposal or attempt to do anything falling within
   paragraph (a) or (b) (Anti-terrorism, Crime and Security
   Act 2001, s 53).
(d) *Corporate liability*—see section 54(3) of the Anti-terrorism,
Crime and Security Act 2001 (see **5.7.2.2**).

PNLD reference numbers

H4752, H4753, H4754, H4755, H4756, D10327

AG✓ **AG consent required:** Anti-terrorism, Crime and Security Act 2001, s 55.

🕐 **Time limit for prosecution:** None.

🏛 **Indictment:** Maximum life imprisonment.

5.5.5 **Assisting or inducing certain weapons-related acts overseas**

Section 50 of the Anti-terrorism, Crime and Security Act 2001 makes it an offence to aid, abet, counsel, or procure, or encourage or assist offences relating to nuclear weapons, chemical weapons, or biological agents and toxins outside the UK.

Offence

A person who aids, abets, counsels or procures, or **incites**, a person who is not a **United Kingdom person** to do **a relevant act** outside the United Kingdom is guilty of an offence.

Anti-terrorism, Crime and Security Act 2001, s 50(1)

Points to prove

✓ date and location
✓ aided, abetted, counselled or procured
✓ person who is not a UK person
✓ to do an act
✓ outside the UK
✓ which, if committed by a UK person, would constitute a contravention of
✓ section 1 of the Biological Weapons Act 1974 *or*
✓ section 2 of the Chemical Weapons Act 1996 *or*
✓ section 47 of the Anti-terrorism, Crime and Security Act 2001

Meanings

Incites

Refers to the offences of encouraging or assisting crime under the Serious Crime Act 2007.

UK person (see **5.5.4**)

A relevant act

Is an act that, if done by a UK person, would contravene any of the following provisions—

(a) section 1 of the Biological Weapons Act 1974 (offences relating to biological agents and toxins, see **5.5.17**);
(b) section 2 of the Chemical Weapons Act 1996 (offences relating to chemical weapons, see **5.5.18**); or
(c) section 47 (offences relating to nuclear weapons, see **5.5.4**).

Defence

A person accused of an offence under this section in relation to a relevant act which would contravene a provision mentioned in subsection (2) may raise any defence which would be open to a person accused of the corresponding offence ancillary to an offence under that provision.

Anti-terrorism, Crime and Security Act 2001, s 50(4)

Police powers

Power of entry to search for evidence relating to nuclear weapons, etc—section 52 of the Anti-terrorism, Crime and Security Act 2001 (see **5.5.6**)

If suspected terrorist:

Power of arrest under TACT (see **5.3.1**)

Power to stop and search under TACT (see **5.2.1**)

If the person is not suspected to be a terrorist, consider using PACE powers (such as ss 24, 17, 18, and 32 of PACE) but see **5.3.1** for drawbacks on using PACE powers for potential terrorists.

Notes

(a) *Extra-territorial jurisdiction*—this offence applies to acts done outside the UK, but only if they are done by a UK person (Anti-terrorism, Crime and Security Act 2001, s 50(6)). Where the offence is committed outside the UK proceedings may be taken, and the offence may for incidental purposes be treated as having been committed, in any part of the UK (Anti-terrorism, Crime and Security Act 2001, s 51(1)).

(b) *Revenue and Customs prosecutions*—proceedings for this offence may be instituted by the Director of Revenue and Customs Prosecutions or by order of the Commissioners for Her

Majesty's Revenue and Customs, for details see **5.5.4**
(Anti-terrorism, Crime and Security Act 2001, s 53).

(c) *Corporate liability*—see section 54(3) of the Anti-terrorism,
Crime and Security Act 2001 (**5.7.2.2**).

PNLD reference numbers

H4757, H4758, D10330

 AG consent required: Anti-terrorism, Crime and Security
Act 2001, s 55.

 Time limit for prosecution: None.

 Indictment: Maximum life imprisonment.

5.5.6 Power of entry to search for evidence relating to nuclear weapons, etc

Section 52 of the Anti-terrorism, Crime and Security Act 2001 provides powers of entry under warrant to authorized officers of the
Secretary of State and accompanying police officers to search for
evidence for the commission of an offence under sections 47 and 50
(see **5.5.4** and **5.5.5**).

Powers

(1) If—
   (a) a justice of the peace is satisfied on information on oath
       that there are reasonable grounds for suspecting that
       evidence of the commission of an offence under section 47
       [use etc. of nuclear weapons, see 5.5.4] or 50 *[assisting or
       inducing certain weapons-related acts overseas, see 5.5.5]* is to
       be found on any premises;
   (b) *[Scotland only.]*

   he may issue a warrant authorising an **authorised officer** to
   enter the premises, if necessary by force, at any time within
   one month from the time of the issue of the warrant and to
   search them.

(2) The powers of a person who enters the premises under the
    authority of the warrant include power—
   (a) to take with him such other persons and such equipment
       as appear to him to be necessary;

(b) to inspect, seize and retain any substance, equipment or document found on the premises;

(c) to require any document or other information which is held in electronic form and is accessible from the premises to be produced in a form—

 (i) in which he can read and copy it; or

 (ii) from which it can readily be produced in a form in which he can read and copy it;

(d) to copy any document which he has reasonable cause to believe may be required as evidence for the purposes of proceedings in respect of an offence under section 47 or 50.

(3) A constable who enters premises under the authority of a warrant or by virtue of subsection (2)(a) may—

(a) give such assistance as an authorised officer may request for the purpose of facilitating the exercise of any power under this section; and

(b) search or cause to be searched any person on the premises who the constable has reasonable cause to believe may have in his possession any document or other thing which may be required as evidence for the purposes of proceedings in respect of an offence under section 47 or 50.

Anti-terrorism, Crime and Security Act 2001, s 52(1)–(3)

Meanings

Authorised officer

Means an authorized officer of the Secretary of State (Anti-terrorism, Crime and Security Act 2001, s 52(8)).

Notes

(a) There is no provision for the police to obtain a warrant directly, but they may be permitted to accompany authorized officers.

(b) The powers conferred by a warrant under this section shall only be exercisable, if the warrant so provides, in the presence of a constable (Anti-terrorism, Crime and Security Act 2001, s 52(5)).

(c) No constable shall search a person of the opposite sex (Anti-terrorism, Crime and Security Act 2001, s 52(4)).

(d) It is an offence to wilfully obstruct an authorized officer in the exercise of a power conferred by a warrant under section 52, or to fail without reasonable excuse to comply with a reasonable request made by an authorized officer or a constable for the purpose of facilitating the exercise of such a power (either way, summary: fine not exceeding the statutory maximum, on indictment: maximum two years' imprisonment and/or fine (Anti-terrorism, Crime and Security Act 2001, s 52(6) and (7))).

(e) *Counter-Terrorism Act 2008*—sections 1–9 of the Act provide further powers to remove documents for examination etc for searches under section 52(1) or (3)(b). See PNLD reference number S1136 to check whether these sections are in force.

PNLD reference numbers

H4759, H4760, D10332

5.5.7 Security of nuclear industry

Section 79 of the Anti-terrorism, Crime and Security Act 2001 makes it an offence to disclose information which might prejudice the security of a nuclear site or nuclear material.

Offence

A person is guilty of an offence if he **discloses** any information or thing the **disclosure** of which might prejudice the security of any **nuclear site** or of any **nuclear material**—

(a) with the intention of prejudicing that security; or

(b) being reckless as to whether the disclosure might prejudice that security.

Anti-terrorism, Crime and Security Act 2001, s 79(1)

Points to prove

✓ disclosed

✓ information/thing

✓ the disclosure of which might prejudice

✓ the security of any nuclear site/material

✓ with the intention of prejudicing that security *or* being reckless as to whether the disclosure might prejudice that security

Meanings

Disclose and disclosure

In relation to a thing, include parting with possession of it (Anti-terrorism, Crime and Security Act 2001, s 79(4)).

Nuclear site

Means a site in the UK (including a site occupied by or on behalf of the Crown) which is (or is expected to be) used for any purpose mentioned in section 1(1) of the Nuclear Installations Act 1965 (such as the installation or operating of a nuclear reactor or other installation designed or adapted for the production or use of atomic energy storage or the processing or disposal of nuclear fuel).

Nuclear material

Means—

(a) any fissile material in the form of—
    (i) uranium metal, alloy, or chemical compound; or
    (ii) plutonium metal, alloy, or chemical compound;
(b) any other fissile material prescribed by regulations made by the Secretary of State (Energy Act 2004, s 71(1)).

A reference to nuclear material

Is a reference to—

(a) nuclear material which is being held on any nuclear site, or
(b) nuclear material anywhere in the world which is being transported to or from a nuclear site or carried on board a **British ship** (including nuclear material which is expected to be so held, transported, or carried) (Anti-terrorism, Crime and Security Act 2001, s 79(2)).

British ship

Means a ship (including a ship belonging to Her Majesty) which is registered in the UK (Anti-terrorism, Crime and Security Act 2001, s 79(4)).

Police powers

If suspected terrorist:

Power of arrest under TACT (see 5.3.1)

Power to stop and search under TACT (see 5.2.1)

If the person is not suspected to be a terrorist, consider using PACE powers (such as ss 24, 17, 18, and 32 of PACE) but see **5.3.1** for drawbacks on using PACE powers for potential terrorists.

Notes

(a) Unlike under most sections of the Official Secrets Act 1989, section 79 makes no reference to whether the information is already in the public domain or whether it might be in the wider public interest to disclose it.

(b) *Extra-territorial jurisdiction*—the offence applies to acts done outside the UK, but only if they are done by a UK person. And proceedings for an offence committed outside the UK may be taken, and the offence may for incidental purposes be treated as having been committed, in any place in the UK (Anti-terrorism, Crime and Security Act 2001, s 79(5) and (6)). 'UK person' means a UK national, a Scottish partnership, or a body incorporated under the law of any part of the UK. For this purpose, a UK national is an individual who is—

   (i) a British citizen, a British overseas territories citizen, a British National (Overseas), or a British Overseas citizen;
   (ii) a person who under the British Nationality Act 1981 is a British subject; or
   (iii) a British protected person within the meaning of that Act (Anti-terrorism, Crime and Security Act 2001, s 81(2) and (3)).

(c) Section 80 of the Anti-terrorism, Crime and Security Act 2001 creates a similar offence in relation to disclosures of uranium enrichment technology (either way offence, maximum penalty on summary conviction imprisonment of six months and/or fine not exceeding the statutory maximum, on indictment seven years imprisonment and/or fine). See also the Uranium Enrichment Technology (Prohibition on Disclosure) Regulations 2004 (SI 2004/1818) which make it an offence to make disclosures of uranium enrichment technology unless such disclosures are exempt.

(d) Further provisions dealing with the security of nuclear premises and of transport of nuclear material and the security of sensitive nuclear information can be found in the Nuclear Industries Security Regulations 2003 (SI 2003/403, as amended by SI 2006/2815).

PNLD reference numbers

H4764, D10355, H4765, D10356

 AG consent required: Anti-terrorism, Crime and Security Act 2001, s 81(1).

 Time limit for prosecution: None.

 Summary: Maximum six months' imprisonment and/or fine not exceeding the statutory maximum.

 Indictment: Maximum seven years' imprisonment and/or fine.

5.5.8 **Trespassing on a nuclear/designated site**

Section 128 of the Serious Organised Crime and Police Act 2005 creates the offence of trespassing on a nuclear or designated site.

Offence

A person commits an offence if he enters, or is on, any protected site in England and Wales or Northern Ireland as a **trespasser**.

Serious Organised Crime and Police Act 2005, s 128(1)

Points to prove

✓ date and location
✓ as a trespasser
✓ entered/were on
✓ a nuclear site *or*
   a designated site designated by the Secretary of State

Meanings

Protected site

Means a **nuclear site** or a **designated site** (Serious Organised Crime and Police Act 2005, s 128(1A)).

Nuclear site

Means (all licensed nuclear sites)—

(a) so much of any premises in respect of which a nuclear site licence (within the meaning of the Nuclear Installations Act 1965) is for the time being in force as lies within the outer perimeter of the protection provided for those premises; and

(b) so much of any other premises of which premises falling within paragraph (a) form a part as lies within that outer perimeter (Serious Organised Crime and Police Act 2005, s 128(1B)).

Designated site

Means a site designated by the Secretary of State (Serious Organised Crime and Police Act 2005, s 128(2)). Examples of current designated sites are RAF bases, Buckingham Palace, Thames House, St James's Palace, 10 Downing Street, and the Palace of Westminster. A full list for England and Wales can be found in the Serious Organised

Crime and Police Act 2005 (Designated Sites (under Section 128) Order 2007 (SI 2007/930)).

Trespasser

Means a person who is on any premises without the owner or occupier's consent or without lawful excuse.

Police powers

If suspected terrorist:
Power of arrest under TACT (see **5.3.1**)

Power to stop and search under TACT (see **5.2.1**)

If the person is not suspected to be a terrorist, consider using PACE powers (such as ss 24, 17, 18, and 32 of PACE) but see **5.3.1** for drawbacks on using PACE powers for potential terrorists.

Defence

(4) It is a defence for a person charged with an offence under this section to prove that he did not know, and had no reasonable cause to suspect, that the site in relation to which the offence is alleged to have been committed was a protected site.

Serious Organised Crime and Police Act 2005, s 128(4)

It is for the defendant to prove this defence. This is viewed as appropriate because in such a case the facts to be proved would be within the defendant's own knowledge (Home Office Circular 18/2007).

Notes

(a) A person who is on any protected site as a trespasser does not cease to be a trespasser by virtue of being allowed time to leave the site (Serious Organised Crime and Police Act 2005, s 128(7)).

(b) Home Office Circular 18/2007 provides some additional guidance. The background to this offence being created is the high-profile security breaches at Buckingham Palace and Windsor Castle after which it was felt that a specific offence in such cases was needed to give officers a power of arrest where no other offences had been committed. It also provides that good practice when encountering a trespasser at such sites would be to warn the individual verbally that the site is a protected site under section 128 of the Serious Organised

Crime and Police Act 2005 and that trespass on the site is a criminal offence. This would ensure that even if the individual could prove he met the defence in respect of original entry to the site, he could still be proceeded against if he did not subsequently leave the site following the warning.

(c) Section 131(1) of the Serious Organised Crime and Police Act 2005 provides that the rights with regards to freedom to roam do not apply to protected sites.

(d) The Secretary of State (with the consent of the landowner) may display any signs he considers appropriate to inform the public with regards to the designated site (Serious Organised Crime and Police Act 2005, s 131).

PNLD reference numbers

H6614, D16684, D20007

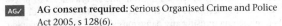 **AG consent required:** Serious Organised Crime and Police Act 2005, s 128(6).

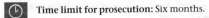 **Time limit for prosecution:** Six months.

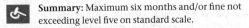 **Summary:** Maximum six months and/or fine not exceeding level five on standard scale.

5.5.9 Pathogens and toxins

Part 7 (ss 58–75) of the Anti-terrorism, Crime and Security Act 2001 deals with the control of pathogens and toxins. Section 58 and Schedule 5 set out to which pathogens and toxins the requirements under Part 7 apply.

The list in Schedule 5 (not reproduced here; see also the amendments made to the list by SI 2007/929 and SI 2012/1466) comprises the pathogens and toxins that potentially pose the greatest risk to human life if misused by terrorists. The list includes viruses (organisms that can only reproduce within the cells of other organisms, such as the Ebola virus, pandemic strains of influenza viruses, the Polio virus, the rabies virus), rickettsiae (bacteria which cannot survive outside the cells of animals), bacteria (single-celled organisms that multiply by cell division an do not possess a nucleus, such as anthrax), and toxins (poisonous agents especially a poisonous substance produced by a living organism including a genetically modified organism, such as ricin).

The provisions in Part 7 use the term 'dangerous substance'.

Meaning

Dangerous substance

Means—

(a) anything which consists of or includes a substance for the time being mentioned in Schedule 5; or
(b) anything which is infected with or otherwise carries any such substance (Anti-terrorism, Crime and Security Act 2001, s 58(4)).

PNLD reference numbers

D10337, D10396

5.5.10 **Duty to notify Secretary of State**

Section 59 of the Anti-terrorism, Crime and Security Act 2001 places a duty on the occupiers of premises to notify the Secretary of State before keeping or using any dangerous substance there. Occupiers of premises holding these substances must notify the Secretary of State within one month.

(1) The **occupier** of any premises must give a notice to the Secretary of State before any **dangerous substance** is kept or used there.
(4) A notice under this section must—
   (a) identify the premises in which the substance is kept or used;
   (b) identify any building or site of which the premises form part; and
   (c) contain such other particulars (if any) as may be prescribed.
   Anti-terrorism, Crime and Security Act 2001, s 59(1) and (4)

Meanings

Occupier

Includes a partnership or unincorporated association and, in relation to premises that are unoccupied, means any person entitled to occupy the premises (Anti-terrorism, Crime and Security Act 2001, s 74(1)).

Dangerous substance (see 5.5.9)

Notes

(a) The occupier of any premises in respect of which a notice has been given may withdraw the notice if no dangerous substance is kept or used there (Anti-terrorism, Crime and Security Act 2001, s 59(3)).

(b) Where a substance which is kept or used in any premises becomes a dangerous substance by virtue of a modification of Schedule 5, but no other dangerous substance is kept or used there, the occupier of the premises must give a notice under section 59 within one month beginning with the day on which that modification comes into force (Anti-terrorism, Crime and Security Act 2001, s 59(6)).

(c) The police may require information about the security of dangerous substances and about persons with access to such substances from the owner of premises in respect of which a notice under section 59 is in force (see **5.5.11**).

(d) Failure to comply with this duty is an offence (see **5.5.14**).

PNLD reference number

D10338

5.5.11 **Information about security of dangerous substances and about persons with access to such substances**

Sections 60 and 61 of the Anti-terrorism, Crime and Security Act 2001 give the police the power to require information about the security of dangerous substances and about persons with access to such substances.

Police power

Information about security of dangerous substances:

(1) A constable may give to the **occupier** of any **relevant premises** a notice requiring him to give the **chief officer of police** such information as is specified or described in the notice by a time so specified and in a form and manner so specified.

(2) The required information must relate to—
  (a) any **dangerous substance** kept or used in the premises; or
  (b) the **measures taken** (whether by the occupier or any other person) **to ensure the security of any such substance**.

Anti-terrorism, Crime and Security Act 2001,
s 60(1) and (2)

Information about persons with access to dangerous substances:

(1) A police officer of at least the rank of inspector may give to the **occupier** of any **relevant premises** a notice requiring him to give the chief officer of police a list of—
  (a) each person who has access to any dangerous substance kept or used there;
  (b) each person who, in such circumstances as are specified or described in the notice, has access to such part of the premises as is so specified or described;
  (c) each person who, in such circumstances as are specified or described in the notice, has access to the premises; or
  (d) each person who, in such circumstances as are specified or described in the notice, has access to any building or site of which the premises form part.

(7) Any list under this section must—
  (a) identify the access which the person has, or is proposed to have;
  (b) state the full name of that person, his date of birth, his address and his nationality; and
  (c) contain such other matters (if any) as may be prescribed.
        Anti-terrorism, Crime and Security Act 2001, s 61(1) and (7)

Meanings

Occupier (see 5.5.10)

Relevant premises

Means any premises—
(a) in which any dangerous substance is kept or used, or
(b) in respect of which a notice under section 59 (see **5.5.10**) is in force (Anti-terrorism, Crime and Security Act 2001, s 60(4)).

Chief officer of police

Means the chief officer of police for the area in which the premises are situated (Anti-terrorism, Crime and Security Act 2001, s 74(1)).

Dangerous substance (see 5.5.9)

Measures taken to ensure the security of any dangerous substance kept or used in any relevant premises

Include—
(a) measures taken to ensure the security of any building or site of which the premises form part; and
(b) measures taken for the purpose of ensuring access to the substance is given only to those whose activities require access

and only in circumstances that ensure the security of the substance (Anti-terrorism, Crime and Security Act 2001, s 60(3)).

Notes

(a) A list under section 61(1) must be given before the end of the period of one month beginning with the day on which the notice is given (Anti-terrorism, Crime and Security Act 2001, s 61(2)).

(b) Where a list under section 61(1) is given, the occupier of the premises must secure that only persons mentioned in the list are given the access identified in the list relating to them. A supplementary list may be given of other persons to whom it is proposed to give access. Where a supplementary list is given, the occupier of the premises must secure that persons mentioned in that list do not have the proposed access relating to them until the end of the period of 30 days beginning with the day on which that list is given. But the chief officer of police may direct that a person may have such access before the end of that period (Anti-terrorism, Crime and Security Act 2001, s 61(3), (4), and (5)).

(c) A person who is required to do an act in response to a notice under section 60 may appeal to the magistrates' court, on the grounds that it is unreasonable to do the act (Anti-terrorism, Crime and Security Act 2001, s 71).

(d) Failure of the occupier of the premises to comply with a request by the police is an offence (see **5.5.14**).

PNLD reference numbers

D10339, D10340

5.5.12 Directions requiring security measures, disposal of dangerous substances, and denial of access

Sections 62–64 of the Anti-terrorism, Crime and Security Act 2001 enable the police to require the occupier of premises holding dangerous substances to make improvements to the security arrangements operating there. Further, they give the Secretary of State the power to require the disposal of dangerous substances and denial of access to such premises.

Police power

(1) A constable may give directions to the **occupier** of any **relevant premises** requiring him to take such measures to ensure the security of any **dangerous substance** kept or used there as are specified or described in the directions by a time so specified.

(2) The directions may—

    (a) specify or describe the substances in relation to the security of which the measures relate; and

    (b) require the occupier to give a notice to the **chief officer of police** before any other dangerous substance specified or described in the directions is kept or used in the premises.

Anti-terrorism, Crime and Security Act 2001, s 62

Meanings

Occupier (see **5.5.10**)

Relevant premises (see **5.5.11**)

Measures taken to ensure the security of any dangerous substance

These are to be construed in accordance with section 60 (see **5.5.11**, Anti-terrorism, Crime and Security Act 2001, s 74(2))

Dangerous substance (see **5.5.9**)

Chief officer of police (see **5.5.11**)

Notes

(a) Where the Secretary of State has reasonable grounds for believing that adequate measures to secure the security of any dangerous substance kept or used in any relevant premises are not being taken and are unlikely to be taken, he may give a direction to the occupier requiring the disposal of the substance (s 63).

(b) The Secretary of State may also give directions to the occupier of relevant premises requiring that certain persons must not have access to dangerous substances, to (certain parts of) the premises or buildings or sites which form part of the premises if he believes that the direction is necessary in the interest of national security (s 64).

(c) Where a direction is given under section 64 denying access an appeal may be made to the Pathogens Access Appeal Commission (s 70 and Sch 6).

(d) A person who is required to do an act in response to directions under section 62 or 63 may appeal to the magistrates' court, on the grounds that it is unreasonable to do the act (s 71).

(e) Failure to comply with a direction under this section is an offence (see **5.5.14**).

PNLD reference numbers

D10341, D10342, D10343

5.5.13 **Powers of entry to assess security measures, and search warrants**

Sections 65 and 66 of the Anti-terrorism, Crime and Security Act 2001 provide for powers of entry to premises on which dangerous substances are kept.

Police power

(1) A constable may, on giving notice under this section, enter any **relevant premises**, or any building or site of which the premises form part, at a reasonable time for the purpose of assessing the **measures taken to ensure the security of any dangerous substance** kept or used in the premises.

(4) A constable who has entered any premises, building or site by virtue of subsection (1) may for the purpose mentioned in that subsection—

(a) search the premises, building or site;

(b) require any person who appears to the constable to be in charge of the premises, building or site to facilitate any such inspection; and

(c) require any such person to answer any question.

Anti-terrorism, Crime and Security Act 2001, s 65(1) and (4)

Search warrant

(1) If, in England and Wales or Northern Ireland, on an application made by a constable a justice of the peace is satisfied that there are reasonable grounds for believing—

(a) that a dangerous substance is kept or used in any premises but that no notice under section 59 *[see **5.5.10**]* is in force in respect of the premises, or

(b) that the occupier of any relevant premises is failing to comply with any direction given to him under section 62 or 63 *[see 5.5.12]*,

and that any of the conditions mentioned in subsection (4) apply, he may issue a warrant authorising a constable to enter the premises, if necessary by force, and to search them.

(3) A constable may seize and retain anything which he believes is or contains a dangerous substance.

(4) The conditions mentioned in subsection (1) are—

   (a) that it is not practicable to communicate with any person entitled to grant entry to the premises;

   (b) that it is practicable to communicate with a person entitled to grant entry to the premises but it is not practicable to communicate with any person entitled to grant access to any substance which may be a dangerous substance;

   (c) that entry to the premises will not be granted unless a warrant is produced;

   (d) that the purpose of a search may be frustrated or seriously prejudiced unless a constable arriving at the premises can secure immediate entry to them.

   Anti-terrorism, Crime and Security Act 2001, s 66(1), (3) and (4)

Meanings

Relevant premises (see 5.5.11)

Measures taken to ensure the security of any dangerous substance (see 5.5.11)

Dangerous substance (see 5.5.9)

Notes

(a) The notice must be given to the occupier of the premises, or (as the case may be) the occupier of the building or site of which the premises form part, at least two working days before the proposed entry (s 65(2)). For the meaning of 'occupier' see 5.5.10.

(b) The notice must set out the purpose mentioned in subsection (1) (s 65(3)).

(c) Under this section a constable may take with him such other persons as appear to him to be necessary (s 65(5)). In practice, the work is carried out by Police Counter Terrorism Security Advisers whose work is coordinated and directed by the National Counter Terrorism Security Office.

PNLD reference numbers

D10344, D10345

5.5.14 Offences relating to pathogens and toxins

Section 67 of the Anti-terrorism, Crime and Security Act 2001 makes it an offence for occupiers of premises to fail, without reasonable excuse, to comply with any duty or directions imposed by this Part 7 (ss 58–75) of the Act in relation to the security of pathogens and toxins.

Offences

(1) An **occupier** who fails without reasonable excuse to comply with any **duty or direction imposed** on him by or under this **Part** is guilty of an offence.

(2) A person who, in giving any information to a person exercising functions under this Part, knowingly or recklessly makes a statement which is false or misleading in a material particular is guilty of an offence.

Anti-terrorism, Crime and Security Act 2001, s 67(1) and (2)

Points to prove

Section 67(1)

✓ date and location

✓ being the occupier of premises

✓ failed without reasonable excuse

✓ to comply with a duty/direction imposed by or under Part 7 of the Anti-terrorism, Crime and Security Act 2001

Section 67(2)

✓ date and location

✓ made a statement

✓ which was false/misleading in a material particular

✓ when providing information

✓ to a person exercising functions under Part 7 of the Anti-terrorism, Crime and Security Act 2001

Meanings

Occupier (see **5.5.10**)

Duty or direction imposed on him by or under this Part
[Part 7, ss 58–75]

Duty to notify the Secretary of State before keeping or using any dangerous substance (see **5.5.11**); duty to give information about security of dangerous substances (see **5.5.11**); duty to give information about persons with access to dangerous substances (see **5.5.11**); duty to take security measures re/to dispose of dangerous substances/to deny access (see **5.5.12**).

Police powers

If suspected terrorist:

Power to arrest under TACT (see **5.3.1**)

Power to stop and search under TACT (see **5.2.1**)

If the person is not suspected to be a terrorist, consider using PACE powers (such as ss 24, 17, 18, and 32 of PACE) but see **5.3.1** for drawbacks on using PACE powers for potential terrorists.

Notes

(a) The offence in section 67(2) may be relevant where a person gives information under section 59 (duty to notify Secretary of State about dangerous substances, see **5.5.10**) or under sections 60 and 61 (information about security of dangerous substances and persons with access to such substances, see **5.5.11**).

(b) *Corporate liability*—for the liability of company directors, etc see section 68 of the Anti-terrorism, Crime and Security Act 2001 (see **5.7.2.3**).

(c) Proceedings for an offence alleged to have been committed by a partnership or an unincorporated association must be brought in the name of the partnership or association; for details see section 69 of the Anti-terrorism, Crime and Security Act 2001 (not reproduced here).

PNLD reference numbers

H4762, H4763, D10346

 Time limit for prosecution: None.

 Summary: Maximum six months' imprisonment and/or fine not exceeding the statutory maximum.

Indictment: Maximum five years' imprisonment and/or fine.

5.5.15 Use of noxious substances or things to cause harm and intimidate

Sections 113, 113A, and 113B of the Anti-terrorism, Crime and Security Act 2001 deal with the offence of using noxious substances or things to cause harm and intimidate.

Offence

(1) A person who takes any **action** which—
   (a) involves the use of a noxious **substance** or other noxious thing;
   (b) has an effect falling within subsection (2); and
   (c) is designed to influence **the government** or international governmental organisation or to intimidate the public or a section of **the public**,
is guilty of an offence.

(3) A person who—
   (a) makes a threat that he or another will take any action falling within subsection (1); and
   (b) intends thereby to induce in a person anywhere in the world the fear that the threat is likely to be carried out,
is guilty of an offence.

Anti-terrorism, Crime and Security Act 2001, s 113(1) and (3)

Points to prove

Use noxious substance/thing to cause violence/damage (s 113(1))

- ✓ date and location
- ✓ committed an act
- ✓ anywhere in the world
- ✓ designed to influence the government/an international governmental organization/to intimidate the public/a section of the public
- ✓ which caused/was likely to cause
- ✓ serious violence against a person/serious damage to real/personal property
- ✓ which involved the use of a noxious substance/thing

Commit act to induce fear/endanger life or health (s 113(1))

✓ date and location
✓ committed an act
✓ anywhere in the world
✓ designed to influence the government/an international governmental organization/to intimidate the public/a section of the public
✓ had/was likely to have the effect of
✓ endangering human life/creating a serious risk to the health/safety
✓ of the public/a section of the public
✓ which involved the use of a noxious substance/thing

Threaten use of noxious substance (s 113(3))

✓ date and location
✓ made a threat that you/another
✓ designed to influence the government/an international governmental organization/to intimidate the public/section of the public
✓ that you/another would take action
✓ involving the use of a noxious substance/thing
✓ to cause serious violence against a person anywhere in the world *or*

   to cause serious damage to real or personal property anywhere in the world *or*

   have the effect of endangering human life *or*

   creating a serious risk to the health/safety of the public/section of the public *or*

   have the effect of inducing in members of the public
✓ the fear that the action was likely to endanger their lives *or* create a serious risk to their health or safety and
✓ intending thereby to induce in a person
✓ anywhere in the world
✓ the fear that the threat was likely to be carried out

Meanings

Action

Has an effect falling within this subsection if it—

(a) causes serious violence against a person anywhere in the world;

(b) causes serious damage to real or personal property anywhere in the world;

(c) endangers human life or creates a serious risk to the health or safety of the public or a section of the public; or

(d) induces in members of the public the fear that the action is likely to endanger their lives or create a serious risk to their health or safety;

but any effect on the person taking the action is to be disregarded (Anti-terrorism, Crime and Security Act 2001, s 113(2)).

Substance

Includes any biological agent and any other natural or artificial substance (whatever its form, origin, or method of production) (Anti-terrorism, Crime and Security Act 2001, s 115).

The government

Means the government of the UK, a part of the UK, or of a country other than the UK (Anti-terrorism, Crime and Security Act 2001, s 113(5)).

The public

Includes the public of a country other than the UK (Anti-terrorism, Crime and Security Act 2001, s 113(5)).

Police powers

If suspected terrorist:

Power of arrest under TACT (see 5.3.1)
Power to stop and search under TACT (see 5.2.1)

If the person is not suspected to be a terrorist, consider using PACE powers of arrest but see **5.3.1** for drawbacks on using PACE powers for potential terrorists.

Power to stop and search—section 43 of the Terrorism Act 2000 (see 5.2.1)

Notes

(a) The offence—the action or threat—must originate in the UK even if its effect is felt outside the UK.

(b) This section is designed to cover those individuals who seek to cause havoc by, for example, sending anthrax through the post, or damaging fields or polluting water supplies. The scope of the offences includes someone acting or threatening to act in the UK at the time; for example, sending a parcel containing anthrax from the UK to someone in France with the intention of causing harm there.

(c) For a person to be guilty of an offence under section 113(3) it is not necessary for him to have any particular person in mind.

(d) The provisions on post-charge questioning apply to this offence (see **4.2.2 note (g)**).

(e) *Extra-territorial jurisdiction*—this offence applies to conduct done within the UK and also to conduct done outside of the UK providing two conditions are satisfied. The first condition is that the conduct is done for the purpose of advancing a political, religious, racial, or ideological cause.
The second condition is that the conduct is by a UK national or a UK resident; or by any person done to, or in relation to, a UK national, a UK resident, or a protected person; or by any person done in circumstances which fall within section 63D(1)(b) and (c) or (3)(b) and (c) of the Terrorism Act 2000 (commission of offences abroad see **5.7.1**). For the purposes of this section it is immaterial whether a person knows that another is a UK national, a UK resident, or a protected person (Anti-terrorism, Crime and Security Act 2001, s 113A(1)–(3) and (5)).

(f) Proceedings for an offence committed under section 113 outside the UK may be taken, and the offence may for incidental purposes be treated as having been committed, in any part of the UK (Anti-terrorism, Crime and Security Act 2001, s 113B(1) and (2)).

(g) This offence can be tried in any place in the UK if it was committed in the UK (Counter-Terrorism Act 2008, s 28).

PNLD reference numbers

H4766-4769, H4781, D10365, D12307, D12308

| AG✓ | **AG consent required:** Anti-terrorism, Crime and Security Act 2001, s 113B (where offence committed outside UK). |

🕐 **Time limit for prosecution:** None.

Summary: Maximum six months' imprisonment and/or fine not exceeding the statutory maximum.

Indictment: Maximum 14 years' imprisonment and/or fine.

5.5.16 Hoaxes involving noxious substances or things

Section 114 of the Anti-terrorism, Crime and Security Act 2001 creates similar offences for biological, chemical, and nuclear hoaxes.

Offences

(1) A person is guilty of an offence if he—
   (a) places any **substance** or other thing in any place whatever; or
   (b) sends any substance or other thing from one place to another (by post, rail or any other means whatever);

with the **intention** of inducing in a person anywhere in the world a belief that it is likely to be (or contain) a noxious substance or other noxious thing and thereby endanger human life or create a serious risk to human health.

(2) A **person** is guilty of an offence if he communicates any information which he knows or believes to be false with the intention of inducing in a person anywhere in the world a belief that a noxious substance or other noxious thing is likely to be present (whether at the time the information is communicated or later) in any place and thereby endanger human life or create a serious risk to human health.

Anti-terrorism, Crime and Security Act 2001, s 114(1) and (2)

Points to prove

Section 114(1)

✓ date and location
✓ placed/sent
✓ a substance/thing
✓ intending
✓ to induce in a person
✓ a belief that it is likely to be/contain a noxious substance/thing
✓ thereby endanger human life/create a serious risk to human health

Section 114(2)

✓ date and location
✓ communicated information
✓ which you knew/believed to be false
✓ intending
✓ to induce in a person
✓ anywhere in the world
✓ a belief that a noxious substance/thing
✓ was likely to be present in any place
✓ thereby endanger human life/create a serious risk to human health

---

Meanings

Substance

Includes any biological agent and any other natural or artificial substance (whatever its form, origin, or method of production) (Anti-terrorism, Crime and Security Act 2001, s 115).

Intention

Is not defined but has to be proved. It can be proved by drawing on two sources of information or by a combination of both.

1. By admissions made by the defendant in interview with reference to his state of mind at the time of commission of the offence and his answers to questions with regard to his actions and intentions at the time of the offence.
2. By inference from the circumstances of the offence, any evidence from witnesses, the defendant's actions and property found on him or in his control, such as a motor vehicle for transporting property. To prove intent, an officer needs to take all this into account, the important thing is that he has to prove the defendant's state of mind at the time.

Person

It is not necessary to have any particular person in mind.

Police powers

If suspected terrorist:

Power of arrest under TACT (see 5.3.1)

Power to stop and search under TACT (see 5.2.1)

If the person is not suspected to be a terrorist, consider using PACE powers of arrest but see **5.3.1** for drawbacks on using PACE powers for potential terrorists.

Notes

(a) A related offence is food contamination contrary to section 38 of the Public Order Act 1986. It is an offence under section 38(1) to intend to cause alarm, injury, or loss by contamination or interference with goods or by making it appear that goods have been contaminated or interfered with in a place where goods of that description are consumed, used, sold, or otherwise supplied. It is also an offence under section 38(2) to make threats or claims relating to along these lines (s 38(2)) or to possess materials under section 38(3) with a view to the committing of a section 38(1) offence (s 38(3)). Section 38 responded to a small number of well-publicized incidents of 'consumer terrorism', a minority of which could involve animal rights activists or an individual trying to blackmail a manufacturer or supermarket chain. Goods includes substances whether natural or manufactured and whether or not incorporated in or mixed with other goods. The court should be made aware of the disruptions and anxiety that was caused by the hoax, for example how much time and expense was wasted by the hoax.

(b) Consider also the more general offence of bomb hoaxes in section 51 of the Criminal Law Act 1977 (see **5.8.2**).

PNLD reference numbers

H4771, H4772, D10366, D436

 Time limit for prosecution: None.

 Summary: Maximum six months' imprisonment and/or a fine not exceeding the statutory maximum.

 Indictment: Maximum seven years' imprisonment.

5.5.17 **Biological weapons**

Section 1 of the Biological Weapons Act 1974 makes it an offence to develop, produce, stockpile, acquire, retain, or transfer biological agents, toxins, and weapons.

Offences

(1) No person shall develop, produce, stockpile, acquire or retain—

    (a) any **biological agent** or **toxin** of a type and in a quantity that has no justification for **prophylactic**, protective or other peaceful purposes; or

    (b) any weapon, equipment or means of delivery designed to use biological agents or toxins for hostile purposes or in armed conflict.

(1A) A person shall not—

    (a) transfer any biological agent or toxin to another person or enter into an agreement to do so, or

(b) make arrangements under which another person transfers any biological agent or toxin or enters into an agreement with a third person to do so,

if the biological agent or toxin is likely to be kept or used (whether by the transferee or any other person) otherwise than for prophylactic, protective or other peaceful purposes and he knows or has reason to believe that that is the case.

Biological Weapons Act 1974, s 1(1)–(1A)

Points to prove

Section 1(1)

✓ date and location

✓ developed/produced/stockpiled/acquired/retained

✓ a biological agent/toxin of a type and in a quantity that has no justification for prophylactic/protective/other peaceful purpose *or*

a weapon/equipment/means of delivery designed to use biological agents/toxins for hostile purposes/in armed conflict

Section 1(1A)(a)

✓ date and location

✓ transferred/entered into an agreement to transfer

✓ a biological agent/toxin

✓ to another person

✓ when the biological agent/toxin was likely to be kept or used (whether by the transferee or any other person) otherwise than for prophylactic/protective/other peaceful purposes

✓ knowing/having reason to believe that that was the case

Section 1(1A)(b)

✓ date and location

✓ made arrangements under which another person transferred a biological agent/toxin

or

entered into an agreement with a third person to transfer a biological agent/toxin

✓ when the biological agent/toxin was likely to be kept or used (whether by the transferee or any other person) otherwise than for prophylactic/protective/other peaceful purposes

✓ knowing/having reason to believe that that was the case

Meanings

Biological agent

Means any microbial or other biological agent.

Toxin

Means any toxin, whatever its origin or method of production.

Prophylactic

Intended to prevent disease.

Police powers

If suspected terrorist:

Power of arrest under TACT (see 5.3.1)

Power to stop and search under TACT (see 5.2.1)

If the person is not suspected to be a terrorist, consider using PACE powers of arrest but see **5.3.1** for drawbacks on using PACE powers for potential terrorists.

Power of entry and search under section 4 of the Biological Weapons Act 1974:

(1) If a justice of the peace is satisfied by information on oath, or in Scotland the sheriff or a magistrate or justice of the peace is satisfied by evidence on oath, that there is reasonable ground for suspecting that an offence under section 1 of this Act has been, or is about to be, committed, he may grant a search warrant authorising a constable—

   (a) to enter, at any time within three months from the date of the warrant, any premises or place named therein, if necessary by force, and to search the premises or place and every person found therein;

   (b) to inspect any document found in the premises or place or in the possession of any person found therein, and to take copies of, or seize or detain any such document;

   (c) to inspect, seize and detain any equipment so found; and

   (d) to inspect, sample, seize and detain any substance so found.

(2) A warrant issued under subsection (1) above, authorising a constable to take the steps mentioned in that subsection, may also authorise any person named in the warrant to accompany the constable and assist him in taking any of those steps.

Biological Weapons Act 1974, s 4

Notes

(a) *Extra-territorial jurisdiction*—section 1A of the Biological Weapons Act 1974 extends the application of section 1 to acts done outside the UK by UK persons. If a person does anything outside the UK as an act of terrorism or for the purposes of terrorism and his action would have constituted the commission of an offence under this section, he is guilty of an offence (Terrorism Act 2000, s 62, see **5.7.1.2**).

(b) *Revenue and Customs prosecutions*—Commissioners for Her Majesty's Revenue and Customs can prosecute offences under this section (Biological Weapons Act 1974, s 1B).

(c) *Corporate liability*—where an offence under this section has been committed by a body corporate, with the knowledge or negligence of any director, manager, secretary, etc then both shall be guilty and liable to prosecution (Biological Weapons Act 1974, s 3).

PNLD reference numbers

D15596–98, D15600, D15601

AG✓ AG consent required: Biological Weapons Act 1974, s 2.

🕐 Time limit for prosecution: None.

▦ Indictment: Life imprisonment.

5.5.18 **Chemical weapons**

Section 2 of the Chemical Weapons Act 1996 sets out offences related to chemical weapons.

Offence

(1) No person shall—
    (a) use a **chemical weapon;**
    (b) develop or produce a chemical weapon;
    (c) have a chemical weapon in his possession;
    (d) participate in the **transfer** of a chemical weapon;
    (e) engage in military preparations, or in preparations of a military nature, intending to use a chemical weapon.

Chemical Weapons Act 1996, s 2(1)

Points to prove

Section 2(1)(a)–(d)

✓ date and location
✓ use/develop/produce/possess/participate in transfer of
✓ a chemical weapon

Section 2(1)(e)

✓ date and location
✓ engaged in military preparations/preparations of a military nature
✓ with the intention
✓ to use
✓ a chemical weapon

Meanings

Chemical weapon

Means—

(a) toxic chemicals and their **precursors**;
(b) munitions and other devices designed to cause death or harm through the toxic properties of toxic chemicals released by them;
(c) equipment designed for use in connection with munitions and devices falling within paragraph (b) (Chemical Weapons Act 1996, s 1(1)).

A *precursor* is a chemical reactant which takes part at any stage in the production (by whatever method) of a toxic chemical (Chemical Weapons Act 1996, s 1(6)).

Transfer

A person participates in the transfer of an object if he acquires or disposes of the object or enters into a contract to acquire or dispose of it, or he makes arrangements under which another person acquires or disposes of the object or another person enters into a contract to acquire or dispose of it. To acquire an object is to buy it, hire it, borrow it, or accept it as a gift; to dispose of an object is to sell it, let it on hire, lend it, or give it (Chemical Weapons Act 1996, s 2(4) and (5)).

Police powers

If suspected terrorist:

Power of arrest under TACT (see **5.3.1**)
Power to stop and search under TACT (see **5.2.1**)

If the person is not suspected to be a terrorist, consider using PACE powers (such as ss 24, 17, 18, and 32 of PACE) but see **5.3.1** for drawbacks on using PACE powers for potential terrorists.

Defence

(6) In proceedings for an offence under subsection (1)(a), (c) or (d) relating to an object it is a defence for the accused to prove—

    (a) that he neither knew nor suspected nor had reason to suspect that the object was a chemical weapon, or

    (b) that he knew or suspected it to be a chemical weapon and as soon as reasonably practicable after he first so knew or suspected he took all reasonable steps to inform the Secretary of State or a constable of his knowledge or suspicion.

(7) Nothing in subsection (6) prejudices any defence which it is open to a person charged with an offence under this section to raise apart from that subsection.

Chemical Weapons Act 1996, s 2(6) and (7)

Notes

(a) For the purposes of section 2(1), an object will not be a chemical weapon if it is used or a person does an act with the intention that the object will be used only for permitted purposes. Permitted purposes are: peaceful purposes; purposes related to protection against toxic chemicals; legitimate military purposes; purposes of enforcing the law. Legitimate military purposes are all military purposes except those which depend on the use of the toxic properties of chemicals as a method of warfare in circumstances where the main object is to cause death, permanent harm, or temporary incapacity to humans or animals. A toxic chemical is a chemical which through its chemical action on life processes can cause death, permanent harm, or temporary incapacity to humans or animals; and the origin, method of production, and place of production are immaterial. As to whether or not something falls within permitted purposes the types and quantities of objects will be taken into account (Chemical Weapons Act 1996, ss 1(3)–(5) and 2(2) and (3)).

(b) *Extra-territorial jurisdiction*—this offence applies to acts done within and outside the UK (Chemical Weapons Act 1996, s 3).

If a person does anything outside the UK as an act of terrorism or for the purposes of terrorism and his action would have constituted the commission of an offence under this section, he is guilty of an offence (Terrorism Act 2000, s 62, see **5.7.1.2**).

(c) There are other offences in the Act that have not been reproduced here. The most serious offences of use of chemical weapons, and creating chemical weapons production facilities under sections 2 (in this chapter) and 11, which are punishable by life imprisonment. The middle range offences of providing false or misleading information under sections 9, 17, 20, 21, 22, and 23, disclosure of confidential information under section 32, and use of Schedule 1 chemicals under section 19 are each punishable by a fine, imprisonment, or both. The lesser offences of failure to provide information under section 9, failure to comply with a notice under section 22, failure to comply with a regulation under section 23, offences connected with inspections under section 26, and destruction of objects, etc, under section 17 attract a fine alone.

PNLD reference numbers

H5251–55, D11802

 AG consent required: Chemical Weapons Act 1996, s 31(1).

 Time limit for prosecution: None.

 Indictment: Life imprisonment.

5.6 Terrorism Prevention and Investigation Measures Notices

The Terrorism Prevention and Investigation Measures Act 2011 repealed the Prevention of Terrorism Act 2005 and therefore control orders and replaced them with Terrorism Prevention and Investigation Measures Notices (TPIM notices).

Section 3 of the Terrorism Prevention and Investigation Measures Act 2011 sets out the five conditions that have to be met in order for a TPIM notice to be issued by the Secretary of State.

3(1) Condition A is that the Secretary of State reasonably believes that the individual is, or has been, involved in **terrorism-related activity** (the 'relevant activity').

3(2) Condition B is that some or all of the relevant activity is **new terrorism-related activity**.

3(3) Condition C is that the Secretary of State reasonably considers that it is necessary, for purposes connected with protecting members of the public from a risk of terrorism, for **terrorism prevention and investigation measures** to be imposed on the individual.

3(4) Condition D is that the Secretary of State reasonably considers that it is necessary, for purposes connected with preventing or restricting the individual's involvement in terrorism-related activity, for the specified terrorism prevention and investigation measures to be imposed on the individual.

3(5) Condition E is that—

    (a) the court gives the Secretary of State permission under section 6, or

    (b) the Secretary of State reasonably considers that the urgency of the case requires terrorism prevention and investigation measures to be imposed without obtaining such permission.

Terrorism Prevention and Investigation Measures Act 2011, s 3

Offence

(1) An individual is guilty of an offence if—

    (a) a **TPIM notice** is in force in relation to the individual, and

    (b) the individual contravenes, without reasonable excuse, any measure specified in the TPIM notice.

Terrorism Prevention and Investigation Measures Act 2011, s 23(1)

Points to prove

✓ date and location
✓ contravened without reasonable excuse
✓ a measure
✓ specified in a TPIM notice
✓ which was in force in relation to the individual

Meanings

Terrorism-related activity

For the purposes of this Act, involvement in terrorism-related activity is any one or more of the following—

(a) the commission, preparation or instigation of acts of terrorism;

(b) conduct which facilitates the commission, preparation or instigation of such acts, or which is intended to do so;

(c) conduct which gives encouragement to the commission, preparation or instigation of such acts, or which is intended to do so;

(d) conduct which gives support or assistance to individuals who are known or believed by the individual concerned to be involved in conduct falling within paragraphs (a) to (c);

and for the purposes of this Act it is immaterial whether the acts of terrorism in question are specific acts of terrorism or acts of terrorism in general (Terrorism Prevention and Investigation Measures Act 2011, s 4).

New terrorism-related activity

Means—

(a) if no TPIM notice relating to the individual has ever been in force, terrorism-related activity occurring at any time (whether before or after the coming into force of this Act);

(b) if only one TPIM notice relating to the individual has ever been in force, terrorism-related activity occurring after that notice came into force; or

(c) if two or more TPIM notices relating to the individual have been in force, terrorism-related activity occurring after such a notice came into force most recently (Terrorism Prevention and Investigation Measures Act 2011, s 3(6)).

Terrorism prevention and investigation measures

Means requirements, restrictions and other provision which may be made in relation to an individual by virtue of Schedule 1 (terrorism prevention and investigation measures) (Terrorism Prevention and Investigation Measures Act 2011, s 2(2)).

TPIM notice

Means a notice where specified terrorism prevention and investigation measures are imposed on an individual if conditions A–E in section 3 (see earlier) are met (Terrorism Prevention and Investigation Measures Act 2011, s 2(1)).

Notes

(a) Schedule 1 to the Terrorism Prevention and Investigation Measures Act 2011 provides an exhaustive list of measures that can be imposed by the Secretary of State; only the measures that are within Schedule 1 can be imposed.

- *Overnight residence measure*—restrictions with regards to the residence in which the individual resides.
- *Travel measure*—restrictions on an individual leaving the UK, or Great Britain if that is the individual's place of residence, or Northern Ireland if that is his or her place of residence.
- *Exclusion measure*—excludes the individual from certain streets, areas or towns, for example an area where it is believed that extremists' contacts are present.
- *Movement directions measure*—requires that the individual comply with directions in relation to his movements given by a constable. For example, requiring the individual to be escorted to his place of residence in order to fit him with an electronic tag.
- *Financial services measure*—requirements on an individual's access to bank accounts and cash.
- *Property measure*—requirements relating to the transfer of property to or by the individual or in relation to the disclosure of property.
- *Electric communication device measure*—restrictions on the possession or use of electronic communication devices by the individual or by other persons in the individual's residence.
- *Association measure*—the Secretary of State may impose restrictions on the individual's association or communication with other persons.
- *Work or studies measure*—restrictions on the individual's work or studies.
- *Reporting measure*—a requirement for the individual to report to a police station and comply with any direction given by a constable in relation to such reporting.
- *Photography measure*—a requirement for the individual to allow photographs to be taken of them at such locations and times as required.
- *Monitoring measure*—a requirement for the individual to cooperate with specified arrangements for enabling the individual's movements, communications, or other activities to be monitored by electronic or other means.

(b) *Powers of entry, search and seizure*—there are powers of entry with and without a warrant. Without a warrant a constable may enter and search premises for the purposes of locating an individual in order to serve a notice, search premises in order to ascertain whether an individual subject to a TPIM notice has absconded, and search an individual subject to a TPIM notice for the purposes of public safety. With a warrant it is possible to search an individual or premises in order to ascertain whether they are complying with the TPIM notice (Sch 5).

(c) *Fingerprints and samples*—Schedule 6 makes provisions for the taking and retention of fingerprints and samples of a person subject to a TPIM notice.

(d) *Time limit*—a TPIM notice remains in force for one year beginning on the date on which it is served, or at a later date specified in the notice. The TPIM notice may be extended for a further year, but this can only be done once (s 5).

(e) *Prior permission of the court*—the court has certain powers and functions in relation to TPIM notices and these can be found in section 6. There are provisions in Schedule 2 for urgent cases where the prior permission of the court has not been obtained.

(f) *Criminal investigation into terrorism-related activity*—the Secretary of State must consult with the chief officer of the police force concerned on whether there is any evidence that could be used to prosecute the individual. The chief officer of police is then under a statutory duty to consult with the CPS. The chief officer must also review the investigation into the individual with a view to bringing a prosecution for a terrorism-related offence and must report on this to the Secretary of State (s 10).

PNLD reference numbers

H7967, S1461

 Time limit for prosecution: None.

 Summary: Maximum six months' imprisonment and/or a fine not exceeding the statutory maximum.

 Indictment: Maximum five years' imprisonment and/or a fine.

5.7 Other Issues

5.7.1 Commission of offence abroad

Generally, a person can only be prosecuted in the UK for acts done on UK territory. However, there are some exceptions to this rule. Certain offences or Acts include provisions that extend offences to acts done by UK citizens abroad. Others even extend the offence to acts done by anyone in any place; see for example the offence of hijacking aircraft (see **5.4.12**). Most of the time, the extent of each offence is provided for in the section or Act creating the offence. If a particular offence can be committed abroad, this is set out in the notes to each offence in this Handbook.

There are some provisions that extend UK jurisdiction to acts done abroad for a number of offences. These are explained in this chapter, namely section 17 of the Terrorism Act 2006 and sections 62–63E of the Terrorism Act 2000.

Note

Notification requirements apply to offences in respect of which there is jurisdiction by virtue of any of sections 62–63D of the Terrorism Act 2000 and section 17 of the Terrorism Act 2006 (see **5.7.5**).

5.7.1.1 Section 17 of the Terrorism Act 2006

Section 17 of the Terrorism Act 2006 provides extra-territorial jurisdiction in relation to a number of offences relating to terrorism regardless of the nationality of the offender.

(1) If—
  (a) a person does anything outside the United Kingdom, and
  (b) his action, if done in a part of the United Kingdom, would constitute an **offence falling within subsection (2)**,
  he shall be guilty in that part of the United Kingdom of the offence.
(3) Subsection (1) applies irrespective of whether the person is a British citizen or, in the case of a company, a company incorporated in a part of the United Kingdom.

Terrorism Act 2006, s 17(1) and (3)

Meanings

Offences falling within subsection (2)

Offences under the Terrorism Act 2006:

- encouragement of terrorism, s 1 (see **4.3.1**);
- training for terrorist acts, s 6 (see **4.3.7**);
- attendance at a place used for terrorist training, s 8 (see **4.3.8**);
- making and possession of radioactive devices and material, s 9 (see **5.5.1**);
- misuse of radioactive devices and materials and misuse or damage of facilities, s 10 (see **5.5.2**);
- terrorist threats relating to radioactive devices and materials or facilities, s 11 (see **5.5.3**).

Offences under the Terrorism Act 2000:

- membership of proscribed organizations, s 11(1) (see **4.2.2**);
- weapons training, s 54 (see **4.3.9**);
- conspiracy to commit an offence falling within this subsection (see **5.8.5.2**);
- encouraging/assisting an offender (see **5.8.5.1**);
- attempting to commit such an offence (see **5.8.5.5**);
- aiding, abetting, counselling, or procuring the commission of such an offence (see **5.8.5.4**).

Notes

(a) Extra-territorial jurisdiction applies irrespective of whether or not the person is a British citizen or, in the case of a company, a company incorporated in a part of the UK (s 17(3)).

(b) If one of the offences listed in the previous **Meanings** section is committed wholly or partly outside the UK, proceedings for the offence may be taken at any place in the UK; and the offence may for all incidental purposes be treated as having been committed at any such place (s 17(4)).

(c) The extra-territorial jurisdiction set out in this section is required to give effect to a number of international treaties which require the UK and other states which are party to the treaty to take jurisdiction in respect of offences committed anywhere by nationals of any state and of anyone present on UK territory if the UK does not extradite that person to the state where the offence was committed. The main purpose of this is to avoid the situation where a criminal can hide in another country, for example the UK, if the country where he committed the offence does not, for whatever reason, conduct a prosecution and/or request his extradition.

(d) At present, even though there is an International Criminal Court, its jurisdiction does not explicitly refer to terrorism, so terrorism-related offences would still be prosecuted by national authorities. Theoretically, anyone suspected of having committed any of the offences listed in section 17(2) anywhere in the world could be prosecuted in the UK. In the view of Lord Carlile, the independent reviewer of the Terrorism Act 2000 and other anti-terrorist legislation, it could hardly be considered wrong to arrest and prosecute a major international terrorist if he happened to transit through the UK and be apprehended here; or a UK national involved in terrorism offences in other parts of the world. In this way, terrorism offences are made into international crimes, though that position has not been adopted by international law or most other national jurisdictions except for some international offences, such as the hijacking of aircraft (see Aviation Security Act 1982), hostage-taking (see Taking of Hostages Act 1982), or attacks on diplomats (see Internationally Protected Persons Act 1978). The discretion whether or not to prosecute is important and sensitive in this context since some might view armed resistance to oppressive regimes as being justified. See also 'Consents to prosecution', **5.7.4.**

(e) The provisions on post-charge questioning apply to offences in respect of which there is jurisdiction by virtue of this section (see **4.2.2 note (g)**).

5.7.1.2 Section 62 of the Terrorism Act 2000

Section 62 of the Terrorism Act 2000 provides extra-territorial jurisdiction in relation to a number of terrorism-related bombing offences.

(1) If—
   (a) a person does anything outside the United Kingdom as an act of terrorism or for the purposes of terrorism, and
   (b) his action would have constituted the commission of one of the **offences listed in subsection (2)** if it had been done in the United Kingdom,
   he shall be guilty of the offence.

Terrorism Act 2000, s 62(1)

Meanings

Offences listed in subsection (2)

Means—

Offences under the Explosive Substances Act 1883:

- cause explosion endangering life or property, section 2 (see **5.8.1.1**);
- do act/conspire/possess to cause explosion endangering life or property, section 3 (see **5.8.1.2**);
- punishment of accessories, section 5 (see **5.8.1.1**).

Offences under the Biological Weapons Act 1974:
- develop/produce, etc biological weapons, section 1 (see **5.5.17**).

Offences under the Chemical Weapons Act 1996:
- use of chemical weapons, section 2 (see **5.5.18**) (Terrorism Act 2000, s 62(2)).

Notes

(a) This applies irrespective of whether the person is a British citizen or not or, in the case of a company, a company incorporated in a part of the UK.

(b) The extra-territorial jurisdiction set out in this section was required to enable the UK to ratify the United Nations Convention for the Suppression of Terrorist Bombings 1997. It enables the UK to meet its obligations under the Convention either to extradite the suspect or to prosecute him. Where, for example, a foreign national cannot be extradited to another country (granted asylum in the UK, threat of torture abroad) he may be prosecuted in the UK under this provision.

(c) The provisions on post-charge questioning apply to offences in respect of which there is jurisdiction by virtue of this section (see **4.2.2 note (g)**).

5.7.1.3 Section 63 of the Terrorism Act 2000

Section 63 of the Terrorism Act 2000 provides for extra-territorial jurisdiction for certain terrorist finance offences (see **4.4.2–4.4.5**).
(1) If—
    (a) a person does anything outside the United Kingdom, and
    (b) his action would have constituted the commission of an **offence under any of sections 15 to 18** if it had been done in the United Kingdom,
he shall be guilty of the offence.

Terrorism Act 2000, s 63(1)

Meanings

Offences under any of sections 15 to 18

These are fundraising (s 15, see **4.4.2**), use and possession of money or property (s 16, see **4.4.3**), arranging funds or property (s 17, see **4.4.4**), and money laundering (s 18, see **4.4.5**).

Notes

(a) Extra-territorial jurisdiction applies irrespective of whether the person is a British citizen or, in the case of a company, a company incorporated in a part of the UK.

(b) This provision is based on the United Nations Convention for the Suppression of the Financing of Terrorism 1999. It allows the UK either to extradite a suspect or to prosecute in the UK where extradition might not be possible or desired.

(c) The provisions on post-charge questioning apply to offences in respect of which there is jurisdiction by virtue of this section (see **4.2.2 note (g)**).

5.7.1.4 Section 63A of the Terrorism Act 2000

Section 63A of the Terrorism Act 2000 provides for extra-territorial jurisdiction for the terrorism-related offences in sections 56–61 of the Terrorism Act 2000 where these are committed by UK residents or UK nationals.

If—

(a) a **United Kingdom national** or a **United Kingdom resident** does anything outside the United Kingdom, and

(b) his action, if done in any part of the United Kingdom, would have constituted an **offence under any of sections 56 to 61,**

he shall be guilty in that part of the United Kingdom of the offence.

Terrorism Act 2000, s 63A(1)

Meanings

United Kingdom national

Means an individual who is—

(a) a British citizen, a British overseas territories citizen, a British National (Overseas) or a British Overseas citizen,

(b) a person who under the British Nationality Act 1981 is a British subject, or

(c) a British protected person within the meaning of that Act (Terrorism Act 2000, s 63A(2)).

United Kingdom resident

Means an individual who is resident in the UK (Terrorism Act 2000, s 63A(3)).

Offences under any of sections 56 to 61

These are directing a terrorist organization (s 56, see **4.2.5**), possession of articles for terrorist purpose (s 57, see **4.3.10**), collection of information (s 58, see **4.3.11**), eliciting, publishing, or communicating information about members of the armed forces, etc (s 58A, see **4.3.12**), and inciting terrorism overseas (s 59 for England and Wales, see **4.3.5**, ss 60 and 61 for Northern Ireland and Scotland).

Notes

(a) The effect of this section is that acts committed outside the UK by UK nationals or residents can be prosecuted in the UK. (This section and sections 63B–63E implement the European Union Framework Decision of 13 June 2002 on combating terrorism.)

(b) Where such an extra-territorial offence is created, extra-territorial jurisdiction is automatically taken over secondary and inchoate offences, such as aiding, abetting, attempting, inciting, conspiring, counselling, or procuring. That means that not only could the principal offender be prosecuted, but also someone who aided and abetted, etc.

(c) The provisions on post-charge questioning apply to offences in respect of which there is jurisdiction by virtue of this section (see **4.2.2 note (g)**).

5.7.1.5 Section 63B of the Terrorism Act 2000

Section 63B of the Terrorism Act 2000 provides for extra-territorial jurisdiction where terrorist attacks are committed abroad by UK nationals or residents.

(1) If—

(a) a **United Kingdom national** or a **United Kingdom resident** does anything outside the United Kingdom as an **act of terrorism** or for the purposes of terrorism, and

(b) his action, if done in any part of the United Kingdom, would have constituted an **offence listed in subsection (2)**,

he shall be guilty in that part of the United Kingdom of the offence.

Terrorism Act 2000, s 63B(1)

Meanings

United Kingdom national (see 5.7.1.4)

United Kingdom resident see 5.7.1.4)

Act of terrorism (see 4.1.2)

Offence listed in subsection (2)

(a) murder (see **5.8.4**), manslaughter (see **5.8.4**), culpable homicide, rape, assault causing injury, assault to injury, kidnapping (see **5.8.3.2**), abduction, or false imprisonment;

(b) an offence under section 4, 16 (see **5.8.3.1**), 18, 20, 21, 22, 23, 24, 28, 29, 30, or 64 of the Offences Against the Person Act 1861;

(c) an offence under any of sections 1–5 of the Forgery and Counterfeiting Act 1981;

(d) the uttering of a forged document or an offence under section 46A of the Criminal Law (Consolidation) (Scotland) Act 1995;

(e) an offence under section 1 or 2 of the Criminal Damage Act 1971;

(f) an offence under article 3 or 4 of the Criminal Damage (Northern Ireland) Order 1977;

(g) malicious mischief;

(h) wilful fire-raising (Terrorism Act 2000, s 63B(2)).

Notes

(a) These offences could normally not be prosecuted in the UK, even though committed by UK nationals or residents; the effect of this section is that a prosecution for such offences in the UK is possible where they are related to a terrorist attack.

(b) The provisions on post-charge questioning apply to offences in respect of which there is jurisdiction by virtue of this section (see **4.2.2 note (g)**).

AG✓ **AG consent required:** Terrorism Act 2000, s 63E(1).

5.7.1.6 Sections 63C and 63D of the Terrorism Act 2000

Sections 63C and 63D of the Terrorism Act 2000 make further provision for extra-territorial jurisdiction for a number of terrorism-related offences. Section 63C concerns offences committed against UK nationals or residents and 'protected persons' outside the UK as an act of terrorism or for the purposes of terrorism. The nationality or residence of the offender is irrelevant. 'Protected persons' include all diplomatic and consular staff, whether UK nationals or not; they are defined in section 63C(3). The offences are listed in section

63C(2) and include murder (see **5.8.4**), manslaughter, kidnapping, and a number of offences under the Offences Against the Person Act 1861 and under the Forgery and Counterfeiting Act 1981. Section 63D gives UK jurisdiction over the offence of criminal damage or threat of criminal damage (Criminal Damage Act 1971, ss 1 and 2) where it is committed as a terrorist attack or threatened attack against the residential or working premises or vehicles of protected persons when a protected person is in, or likely to be, on the premises or in the vehicle. For the purposes of sections 63C and 63D, it is immaterial whether a person knows that another person is a UK national or resident or a protected person (Terrorism Act 2000, s 63E(3)). Proceedings may only be started by or with the consent of the Attorney General, unless the offence is under one of the following Acts: the Internationally Protected Persons Act 1978, the Suppression of Terrorism Act 1978, the Nuclear Material (Offences) Act 1983, the United Nations Personnel Act 1997 (Terrorism Act 2000, s 63E(1) and (2)). The provisions on post-charge questioning apply to offences in respect of which there is jurisdiction by virtue of one of these sections (see **4.2.2 note (g)**).

PNLD reference numbers

D18583, D8746, D8747, D12302, D12303, D12304, D12305, D12306

5.7.2 **Company directors' liability**

Certain offences may not only be committed by individuals, but also by companies. The following provisions set out the liability of company directors, managers, secretaries, and other similar officers of a body corporate for certain terrorism-related offences.

5.7.2.1 **Section 18 of the Terrorism Act 2006**

(1) Where an **offence under this Part** *[Part 1, sections 1–20]* is committed by a body corporate and is proved to have been committed with the consent or connivance of—

    (a) a **director**, manager, secretary or other similar officer of the **body corporate**, or

    (b) a person who was purporting to act in any such capacity,

    he (as well as the body corporate) is guilty of that offence and shall be liable to be proceeded against and punished accordingly.

Terrorism Act 2006, s 18(1)

Meanings

Offences under Part 1 of the Terrorism Act 2006

- encouragement of terrorism, s 1 (see **4.3.1**);
- dissemination of terrorist publications, s 2 (see **4.3.2**);
- preparation of terrorist acts, s 5 (see **4.3.6**);
- training for terrorist acts, s 6 (see **4.3.7**);
- attendance at a place used for terrorist training, s 8 (see **4.3.8**;
- making and possession of radioactive devices and material, s 9 (see **5.5.1**);
- misuse of radioactive devices and materials and misuse or damage of facilities, s 10 (see **5.5.2**);
- terrorist threats relating to radioactive devices and materials or facilities (s 11, see **5.5.3**).

Body corporate

Is the legal term for a corporation. It is distinct from a natural person, although it has many of the same legal rights.

Director

In relation to a body corporate whose affairs are managed by its members, means a member of the body corporate (Terrorism Act 2006, s 18(3)).

Note

Of the offences in sections 1–20 of the Terrorism Act 2006, a corporate body is most likely to be prosecuted for an offence under section 2 for disseminating terrorist publications. Both the senior officer (or officers, if consent, connivance, or neglect can be proved against each) and the body corporate will be liable for the offence.

5.7.2.2 Section 54 of the Anti-terrorism, Crime and Security Act 2001 (weapons of mass destruction)

Section 54 of the Anti-terrorism, Crime and Security Act 2001 lays out individual liability of the relevant senior office holder in a body corporate, in addition to corporate responsibility, in relation to certain offences concerning weapons of mass destruction.

(3) Where an **offence under section 47, 50 or subsection (1) above** committed by a body corporate is proved to have been committed with the consent or connivance of, or to be attributable to any neglect on the part of—

(a) a **director**, manager, secretary or other similar officer of the body corporate; or

(b) any person who was purporting to act in any such capacity,

he as well as the body corporate shall be guilty of that offence and shall be liable to be proceeded against and punished accordingly.

Anti-terrorism, Crime and Security Act 2001, s 54(3)

Meanings

Offence under section 47, 50 or subsection (1) above

- use, etc of nuclear weapon, section 47 (see **5.5.4**);
- assisting or inducing certain weapons-related acts overseas, section 50 (see **5.5.5**);
- make false/misleading statement re section 47/50 statement, section 54(1).

Director

In relation to a body corporate whose affairs are managed by its members, means a member of the body corporate (Anti-terrorism, Crime and Security Act 2001, s 54(4)).

5.7.2.3 Section 68 of the Anti-terrorism, Crime and Security Act 2001 (security of pathogens and toxins)

Section 68 of the Anti-terrorism, Crime and Security Act 2001 concerns offences committed by a body corporate, as the occupier of premises under Part 7 which deals with the security of pathogens and toxins. It enables the prosecution of certain officers or employees, in addition to the body corporate.

(1) If an offence under this **Part *[Part 7, sections 58–75]*** committed by a body corporate is shown to have been committed with the consent or connivance of, or to be attributable to any neglect on the part of—

(a) any **officer**, or

(b) any other employee of the body corporate who is in charge of any relevant premises or the access to any dangerous substance kept or used there,

he, as well as the body corporate, is guilty of the offence and liable to be proceeded against and punished accordingly.

Anti-terrorism, Crime and Security Act 2001, s 68(1)

Meanings

Offences under Part 7 of the Anti-terrorism, Crime and Security Act 2001

Failure of occupier of premises to comply with duty/direction or making false/misleading statement when giving information, section 67 (see **5.5.14**).

Officer

In relation to a body corporate, means—

(a) any director, manager, secretary, or other similar officer of the body corporate; or

(b) any person purporting to act in any such capacity
(Anti-terrorism, Crime and Security Act 2001, s 68(2)).

Notes

(a) Where the affairs of a body corporate are managed by its members, this section applies in relation to the acts and defaults of a member in connection with his functions of management as if he were a director of the body corporate (s 68(3)).

(b) Section 69 clarifies how the provisions relating to offences apply to an unincorporated association or partnership where it is the occupier of the premises.

5.7.2.4 Further provisions

Section 37 of the Aviation Security Act 1982 makes provisions for the commission of offences under that Act by bodies corporate, as does section 50 of the Aviation and Maritime Security Act 1990 for offences committed under that Act. Paragraph 8 of Schedule 6 to the Terrorism Act 2000 deals with offences committed by a financial institution under paragraph 1(3) (failure to comply with requirement re financial information, see **4.4.15**).

A further provision dealing with the commission of offences by a body corporate is included in Schedule 3 to the Anti-terrorism, Crime and Security Act 2001 (para 9, re freezing orders); paragraph 9 states that a freezing order may provide that where an offence has been committed by a body corporate with the consent, connivance, or by neglect of a director, manager, secretary, or other similar officer, then he is also liable for the offence.

PNLD reference numbers

D18584, D10334, D10347, D4338, D12876

5.7.3 **Convention offences**

The term '**Convention offences**' is used in a number of offences created by the Terrorism Act 2006. They are intended to cover the terrorist offences in the Council of Europe Convention for the Prevention of Terrorism 2005. The offences in the Terrorism Act 2006 cover actions that relate to acts of terrorism **and** Convention offences.

Meanings

Convention offence

Means an offence listed in Schedule 1 to the Terrorism Act 2006 or an equivalent offence under the law of a country or territory outside the UK (Terrorism Act 2006, s 20).

Schedule 1 to the Terrorism Act 2006 contains a list of Convention offences:

Explosives offences under the Offences Against the Person Act 1861—

- causing injury by explosion, section 28;
- causing explosions, section 29;
- handling or placing explosives, section 30.

Explosives offences under the Explosive Substances Act 1883–

- causing an explosion likely to endanger life, section 2 (see **5.8.1.1**);
- preparation of explosives, section 3 (see **5.8.1.2**);
- ancillary offences, section 5.

Biological weapons offences under the Biological Weapons Act 1974—

- development, etc of biological weapons, section 1 (see **5.5.17**).

Offences against internationally protected persons under the Internationally Protected Persons Act 1978—

- attacks against protected persons committed outside the UK (s 1(1)(a)), if the offence is committed (whether in the UK or elsewhere) in relation to a protected person;
- attacks on relevant premises, etc (s 1(1)(b)), if the offence is committed (whether in the UK or elsewhere) in connection with an attack on relevant premises or on a vehicle ordinarily used by a protected person, and at a time when a protected person is in or on the premises or vehicle;
- threats, etc in relation to protected persons, section 1(3).

Hostage-taking under the Taking of Hostages Act 1982—

• hostage-taking, section 1.

Hijacking and other offences against aircraft under the Aviation Security Act 1982—

• hijacking, section 1 (see **5.4.12**);

• destroying, damaging, or endangering safety of aircraft, section 2 (see **5.4.13**);

• other acts endangering or likely to endanger safety of aircraft, section 3;

• ancillary offences, section 6(2) (see **5.4.15**).

Offences involving nuclear material or nuclear facilities under the Nuclear Material (Offences) Act 1983—

• offences in relation to nuclear material committed outside the UK, section 1(1)(a) to (d), if the offence is committed (whether in the UK or elsewhere) in relation to or by means of nuclear material;

• offences in section 1(1)(a) or (b) where the act making the person guilty of the offence (whether in the UK or elsewhere) is directed at a nuclear facility or interferes with the operation of such a facility, and causes death, injury, or damage resulting from the emission of ionising radiation or the release of radioactive material;

• offences relating to damage to environment, section 1B;

• offences of importing or exporting etc nuclear material, section 1C;

• offences involving preparatory acts and threats in relation to nuclear material, section 2.

Offences under the Customs and Excise Management Act 1979—

• improper importation of goods, section 50(2) and (3), in connection with a prohibition or restriction relating to the importation of nuclear material;

• exportation of prohibited or restricted goods, section 68(2), in connection with a prohibition or restriction relating to the exportation or shipment as stores of nuclear material;

• fraudulent evasion of duty, section 170(1) or (2), in connection with a prohibition or restriction relating to the importation, exportation, or shipment as stores of nuclear material.

Offences under the Aviation and Maritime Security Act 1990—

- endangering safety at aerodromes, section 1 (see **5.4.21**);
- hijacking of ships, section 9;
- seizing or exercising control of fixed platforms, section 10;
- destroying ships or fixed platforms or endangering their safety, section 11;
- other acts endangering or likely to endanger safe navigation, section 12;
- offences involving threats relating to ships or fixed platforms, section 13;
- ancillary offences, section 14.

Offences involving chemical weapons under the Chemical Weapons Act 1996—

- use, development etc of chemical weapons, section 2 (see **5.5.18**).

Offences relating to terrorist funds under the Terrorism Act 2000—

- terrorist fundraising, section 15 (see **4.4.2**);
- use or possession of terrorist funds, section 16 (see **4.4.3**);
- funding arrangements for terrorism, section 17 (see **4.4.4**);
- money laundering of terrorist funds, section 18 (see **4.4.5**).

Offences relating to directing terrorist organizations under the Terrorism Act 2000—

- directing a terrorist organization, section 56 (see **4.2.5**).

Offences involving nuclear weapons under the Anti-terrorism, Crime and Security Act 2001—

- use, development etc of nuclear weapons, section 47 (see **5.5.4**).

Conspiracy, etc—

- conspiracy to commit a Convention offence;
- inciting the commission of a Convention offence;
- attempting to commit a Convention offence;
- aiding, abetting, counselling, or procuring the commission of a Convention offence (see **5.8.5**).

PNLD reference number

D18590

5.7.4 **Consents to prosecution**

The prosecution of a number of terrorism-related offences requires the consent of either the (DPP) or the Attorney General (AG).

The main provisions setting out consent to prosecution are section 117 of the Terrorism Act 2000 and section 19 of the Terrorism Act 2006. They provide that for certain offences proceedings for the offence shall not be instituted in England and Wales without the consent of the DPP; but if it appears to the DPP that such an offence has been committed outside the UK or for a purpose wholly or partly connected with the affairs of a country other than the UK, his consent for the purposes of this section may be given only with the permission of the AG.

A number of other Acts make similar provision, for example section 8(1) of the Aviation Security Act 1982 provides that for most of the offences under that Act the consent of the AG is required.

Where consent is required for the prosecution of a particular offence, this is stated in this Handbook for each offence with an icon at the end of the chapter.

PNLD reference numbers

D8751, D18585

5.7.5 **Notification requirements**

Sections 40–61 of and Schedules 4–6 to the Counter-Terrorism Act 2008 provide a notification scheme that applies to all offenders sentenced (or made subject of a hospital order) in respect of terrorism offences or offences having a terrorist connection. The requirements are similar to those for sex offenders in sections 80–92 of the Sexual Offences Act 2003.

Notes

(a) The notification requirements basically apply to persons convicted of terrorism(-related) offences who are aged 16 or over on the day they are being dealt with (s 44) and who are made subject to a sentence or order which triggers the notification requirements (set out in s 45). The requirements are automatically imposed—there need be no specific consideration by the sentencing court.

(b) The system applies to British nationals and to foreign nationals, in the latter case in addition to powers to refuse entry under paragraph 21 of Schedule 2 to the Immigration Act 1971, or the enhanced controls of special immigration status under Part 10 (ss 130–137) of the Criminal Justice and Immigration Act 2008.

(c) The Counter-Terrorism Act 2008 (Foreign Travel Notification Requirements) Regulations 2009 provide details of the notification requirements for foreign travel.

(d) There is an initial notification (s 47), changes which need to be notified (s 48), and also a periodic re-notification (s 49) and a notification on return after absence from the UK (s 56).

(e) For the method of notification, see section 50. The period for which the notification requirements apply is set out in section 53.

(f) It is an offence to fail to comply with the notification requirement, and also to give false information. The offence is an either way offence and the penalties are, summary— maximum six months' imprisonment and/or fine not exceeding the statutory maximum, on indictment—maximum five years' imprisonment and/or fine (s 54).

(g) Where the person subject to notification requirements is abroad or returns from abroad, see sections 55 and 56.

(h) Notification requirements also apply to persons who have been sentenced, etc outside the UK (s 57 and Sch 4).

(i) Foreign travel restriction orders may prohibit persons subject to notification requirements from travelling abroad (s 58 and Sch 5).

(j) There is also provision for the application of the notification requirements in respect of service offences (s 59 and Sch 6).

PNLD reference numbers

D23737–D23757, D23840, D23613–D23617, D23618–D23627, D23842, D23845–D23846, D23848–D23850

5.8 Alternative Offences

The following section deals with alternative criminal offences to the specific terrorism-related offences. This section contains only the information that is relevant to a terrorist investigation. Consider also offences such as criminal damage, arson, etc.

Also bear in mind that courts have to treat the fact that an offence has a terrorist connection as an aggravating factor when sentencing (Counter-Terrorism Act 2008, s 30); this requires that relevant material must be before the court.

5.8.1 Explosives offences

The Explosive Substances Act 1883 creates offences relating to causing explosions.

5.8.1.1 Cause explosion likely to endanger life or property

Section 2 of the Explosive Substances Act 1883 creates the offence of causing an explosion likely to endanger life or property.

Offence

A person who in the United Kingdom or (being a citizen of the United Kingdom and Colonies) or in the Republic of Ireland **unlawfully** and **maliciously** causes by any **explosive substance** an explosion of a nature likely to endanger life or to cause serious injury to property shall, whether any injury to person or property has been actually caused or not, be guilty of an offence.

Explosive Substances Act 1883, s 2

Points to prove

✓ date and location
✓ unlawfully and maliciously
✓ cause by an explosive substance
✓ an explosion
✓ of a nature likely to
✓ endanger life/cause serious injury to property

Meanings

Unlawfully

Means without excuse or justification at law.

Maliciously

Means malice (ill-will or an evil motive) must be present. 'Maliciously requires either an actual intention to do the particular kind of harm that was done or recklessness whether any such harm should occur or not; it is neither limited to, nor does it require, any ill-will towards the person injured' (**R v Cunningham [1957] 2 All ER 412, CA**).

Explosive substance

Shall be deemed to include any materials for making any **explosive** substance; also any apparatus, machine, implement, or materials used, or intended to be used, or adapted for causing, or aiding in causing, any explosion in or with any explosive substance; also any part of any such apparatus, machine, or implement (Explosive Substances Act 1883, s 9).

In **R v Wheatley [1979] 1 All ER 954** it was also held that this definition should incorporate that found in section 3 of the Explosives Act 1875.

Explosive

(1) Means gunpowder, nitro-glycerine, dynamite, gun-cotton, blasting powders, fulminate of mercury or of other metals, coloured fires, and every other substance, whether similar to those above-mentioned or not, used or manufactured with a view to produce a practical effect by explosion or a pyrotechnic effect; and

(2) Includes fog-signals, fireworks, fuses, rockets, percussion caps, detonators, cartridges, ammunition of all descriptions, and every adaptation or preparation of an explosive as above defined (Explosives Act 1875, s 3).

Police powers

Power of arrest—section 24 of the Police and Criminal Evidence Act 1984

Powers of entry and search—sections 17, 18, and 32 of the Police and Criminal Evidence Act 1984

Section 73 of the Explosives Act 1875 provides a constable with a power of entry, search, and seizure where he believes an offence under the Explosives Act 1875 or the Explosive Substances Act 1883 has been or is being committed.

Where any of the following officers—namely, any . . . constable, if such constable or officer is specially authorised either

(a) by warrant of a justice (which warrant such justice may grant upon reasonable ground being assigned on oath), or

(b) (where it appears to a superintendent or other officer of police of equal or superior rank, or to a Government inspector, that the case is one of emergency and that the delay in obtaining a warrant would be likely to endanger life), by a written order from such superintendent, officer or inspector—

has reasonable cause to believe that any offence has been or is being committed with respect to an explosive in any place (whether a building or not, or a carriage, boat or ship), or that any explosive is in any such place in contravention of this Act, or that the provisions of this Act are not duly observed in any such place, such officer may, on producing, if demanded, . . ., in the case of any other officer his authority, enter at any time, and if needs be by force, and as well on Sunday as on other days, the said place, and every part thereof, and examine the same, and search for explosives therein, and take samples of any explosive and ingredient of an explosive therein, and any substance reasonably supposed to be an explosive, or such ingredient which may be found therein.

Explosives Act 1875, s 73

Notes

(a) Forensic evidence is very important in these cases and should be gathered with great care so as to avoid arguments about origin or contamination.

(b) For this offence to be committed there is no requirement that actual injury be caused, just that the explosion was of a nature that could have caused serious injury to people or property.

(c) *Extra-territorial jurisdiction*—if a person does anything outside the UK as an act of terrorism or for the purposes of terrorism and his action would have constituted the commission of an offence under this section or section 5 (see **note (d)**), he is guilty of an offence (Terrorism Act 2000, s 62, see **5.7.1.2**).

(d) Any person (who is a British citizen) who assists in the commission of an offence in this Act in any way shall be treated as a principal (main offender) (Explosive Substances Act 1883, s 5).

(e) Any person who obstructs a constable or refuses him admission to the place he wishes to enter and search using his powers under section 73 of the Explosives Act 1875, commits an offence. It is an either way offence, the penalty is a fine and the defendant shall also forfeit all explosives and ingredients that were in his possession or under his control at the time.

(f) If the constable enters under section 73 using a written order from a Superintendent, the Superintendent must send a report to the Secretary of State detailing everything the constable did under the order.

PNLD reference numbers

H4477, D3740

AG√ **AG consent required:** Explosive Substances Act 1883, s 7.

🕐 **Time limit for prosecution:** None.

▦ **Indictment:** Life imprisonment.

5.8.1.2 Preparation of explosives

Section 3 of the Explosive Substances Act 1883 sets out four offences in relation to explosive substances.

Offences

(1) A person who in the United Kingdom or a **dependency** or (being a citizen of the United Kingdom and Colonies) elsewhere **unlawfully** and **maliciously**—
   (a) does any act with **intent** to cause, or conspires to cause, by an **explosive substance** an explosion of a nature likely to endanger life, or cause serious injury to property, whether in the United Kingdom or elsewhere, or
   (b) makes or has in his possession or under his control an explosive substance with intent by means thereof to endanger life, or cause serious injury to property, whether in the United Kingdom or elsewhere, or to enable any other person so to do,

shall, whether any explosion does or does not take place, and whether any injury to person or property is actually caused or not, be guilty of an offence, and the explosive substance shall be forfeited.

Explosive Substances Act 1883, s 3(1)

Points to prove

Section 3(1)(a)
✓ date and location
✓ unlawfully and maliciously

✓ did an act
✓ with intent
✓ to cause an explosion likely to
✓ endanger life/cause serious injury to property

Section 3(1)(a)

✓ date and location
✓ unlawfully and maliciously
✓ conspired
✓ to cause an explosion likely to
✓ endanger life/cause serious injury to property

Section 3(1)(b)

✓ date and location
✓ unlawfully and maliciously
✓ made
✓ an explosive substance
✓ with intent
✓ to endanger life/cause serious injury to property or
✓ enable another so to do

Section 3(1)(b)

✓ date and location
✓ unlawfully and maliciously
✓ had in your possession *or*
  under your control
✓ an explosive substance
✓ with intent
✓ to endanger life *or*
  cause serious injury to property *or*
  enable another so to do

Meanings

Dependency

Means the Channel Islands, the Isle of Man, and any colony, other than a colony for whose external relations a country other than the UK is responsible.

Unlawfully (see 5.8.1.1)

Maliciously (see 5.8.1.1)

Intent

Intention is not defined but has to be proved. It can be proved by drawing on two sources of information or by a combination of both.

1. By admissions made by the defendant in interview with reference to his state of mind at the time of commission of the offence and his answers to questions with regard to his actions and intentions at the time of the offence.
2. By inference from the circumstances of the offence, any evidence from witnesses, the defendant's actions and property found on him or in his control, such as a motor vehicle for transporting property. To prove intent, an officer needs to take all this into account, the important thing is that he has to prove the defendant's state of mind at the time.

Explosive substance (see **5.8.1.1**)

Police powers

Power of arrest—section 24 of the Police and Criminal Evidence Act 1984

Powers of entry and search—sections 17, 18, and 32 of the Police and Criminal Evidence Act 1984

See also at **5.8.1.1** powers under the Explosives Act 1875.

Notes

(a) For this offence to be committed there is no requirement that actual injury be caused, just that the explosion was of a nature that could have caused serious injury to people or property.

(b) Forensic evidence is very important in these cases and should be gathered with great care so as to avoid arguments about origin or contamination.

(c) *Extra-territorial jurisdiction*—if a person does anything outside the UK as an act of terrorism or for the purposes of terrorism and his action would have constituted the commission of an offence under this section or section 5 (see **note (d)**), he is guilty of an offence (Terrorism Act 2000, s 62, see **5.7.1.2**).

(d) Any person (who is a British citizen) who assists in the commission of an offence in this Act in any way shall be treated as a principal (main offender) (Explosive Substances Act 1883, s 5).

PNLD reference numbers

H4468, H4469, H4478, H4479, D3741

 AG consent required: Explosive Substances Act 1883, s 7.

 Time limit for prosecution: None.

 Indictment: Life imprisonment.

5.8.1.3 Making or possessing an explosive substance in suspicious circumstances

Section 4 of the Explosive Substances Act 1883 sets out the offence of making or possessing explosive substances in suspicious circumstances.

Offence

Any person who makes or knowingly has in his possession or under his control any **explosive substance**, under such circumstances as to give rise to a reasonable suspicion that he is not making it or does not have it in his possession or under his control for a lawful object, shall, unless he can show that he made it or had it in his possession or under his control for a **lawful object**, be guilty of **felony**, and, on conviction, shall be liable to **penal servitude** for a term not exceeding fourteen years, or to imprisonment for a term not exceeding two years with or without **hard labour**, and the explosive substance shall be forfeited.

Explosive Substances Act 1883, s 4(1)

Points to prove

Made explosive substance

✓ date and location
✓ made explosive substance
✓ under circumstances giving reasonable suspicion
✓ not making it for a lawful object

Possessed or had explosive substance under his control

✓ date and location
✓ knowingly
✓ possessed/had under his/her control explosive substance
✓ under circumstances giving reasonable suspicion
✓ not for lawful object

Meanings

Explosive substance (see **5.8.1.1**)

Lawful object

Means lawful purpose.

Felony, penal servitude, and hard labour

These are historical terms that are no longer current. The penalty is imprisonment only, there is no hard labour. See the end of this section for maximum sentence.

Police powers

Power of arrest—section 24 of the Police and Criminal Evidence Act 1984

Powers of entry and search—sections 17, 18, and 32 of the Police and Criminal Evidence Act 1984

See also at **5.8.1.1** powers under the Explosives Act 1875.

Note

Any person (who is a British citizen) who assists in the commission of an offence in this Act in any way shall be treated as a principal (main offender) (Explosive Substances Act 1883, s 5).

Related cases

R v Berry [1994] 2 All ER 913 It is the responsibility of the prosecution to prove that the accused 'knowingly' was in possession of a substance and knew it was an explosive substance as defined and that he possessed it under such circumstances as to give rise to reasonable suspicion that he did not have it for a lawful object. The accused then has to show that he possessed it for a lawful object.

A-G's Reference (No 2 of 1983) [1984] 1 All ER 988 The term 'lawful object' could include, in limited circumstances, possession of explosive substances for the purpose of self-defence.

PNLD reference numbers

H1722, H2166, D3742, C691

 AG consent required: Explosive Substances Act 1883, s 7.

 Time limit for prosecution: None.

 Indictment: Maximum 14 years' imprisonment.

5.8.2 **Bomb hoaxes**

Section 51 of the Criminal Law Act 1977 provides the offences related to bomb hoaxes.

Offences

(1) A person who—
    (a) places any **article** in any place whatever; or
    (b) dispatches any article by post, rail or any other means whatever of sending things from one place to another,

with the **intention** (in either case) of inducing in some other **person** a belief that it is likely to explode or ignite and thereby cause personal injury or damage to property is guilty of an offence.

(2) A person who communicates any information which he knows or believes to be false to another person with the intention of inducing in him or any other person a false belief that a bomb or other thing liable to explode or ignite is present in any place or location whatever is guilty of an offence.

Criminal Law Act 1977, s 51(1)–(2)

Points to prove

Section 51(1)

✓ date and location
✓ placed in any place or dispatched by post/rail/other means of sending things
✓ an article
✓ with intent
✓ to induce in another the belief
✓ that the article
✓ was likely to explode/ignite
✓ and cause personal injury/damage to property

Section 51(2)

✓ date and location
✓ communicated
✓ information
✓ you knew/believed to be false
✓ to another person
✓ with intent
✓ of inducing a false belief in that person/any other person
✓ that bomb/thing was in place or location and
✓ was liable to explode/ignite at that place/location was present

Meanings

Article

This includes substances.

Intention

Intention is not defined but has to be proved. It can be proved by drawing on two sources of information or by a combination of both.

1. By admissions made by the defendant in interview with reference to his state of mind at the time of commission of the offence and his answers to questions with regard to his actions and intentions at the time of the offence.
2. By inference from the circumstances of the offence, any evidence from witnesses, the defendant's actions and property found on him or in his control, such as a motor vehicle for transporting property. To prove intent, an officer needs to take all this into account, the important thing is that he has to prove the defendant's state of mind at the time.

Person

It is not necessary to have any particular person in mind.

Police powers

Power of arrest—section 24 of the Police and Criminal Evidence Act 1984

Powers of entry and search—sections 17, 18, and 32 of the Police and Criminal Evidence Act 1984

Notes

(a) Section 51(1) concerns the placing or dispatching of articles with the intention that people believe that the articles are bombs or explosive devices, whereas section 51(2) concerns people who communicate false information intending others to believe that there is a bomb or explosive device likely to explode.

(b) This section does not require a specific place or location to be given.

Related case

R v Webb [1995] 27 LS Gaz R 31, CA The hoax message does not have to give a specific place or location.

PNLD reference numbers

H2056, H2057, H2102, D1420, C376

 Time limit for prosecution: None.

 Summary: Maximum six months' imprisonment and/or a fine not exceeding the statutory maximum.

 Indictment: Maximum seven years' imprisonment.

5.8.3 **Threats to kill and kidnap**

The explanations about the following offences have been modified to include only the information considered relevant for a terrorist investigation. Also consider the offences in sections 18, 20, and 47 of the Offences Against the Person Act 1861 (not reproduced here).

5.8.3.1 **Threats to kill**

Section 16 of the Offences Against the Person Act 1861 provides the offence of threats to kill.

Offence

A person who, without lawful excuse makes to another a threat **intending** that the other would fear it would be carried out, to kill that other or a third person shall be guilty of an offence.

Offences Against the Person Act 1861, s 16

Points to prove

✓ date and location
✓ without lawful excuse
✓ made threat to kill
✓ intending to cause fear threat would be carried out

Meanings

Intending (see **Intent** at 5.8.2).

Police powers

Power of arrest—section 24 of the Police and Criminal Evidence Act 1984

Powers of entry and search—sections 17, 18, and 32 of the Police and Criminal Evidence Act 1984

Notes

(a) There is no need to show that the defendant intended to kill anyone. The relevant intent has to be that the person receiving the threat would fear the threat (to kill them or a third person) would be carried out.

(b) The onus is on the prosecution to prove that there was no lawful excuse for making a threat. The jury should be directed to any facts that could give rise to a defence of lawful excuse which was reasonable. It is for the jury to decide what is reasonable and what amounts to a threat.

(c) Consider hearsay and bad character admissibility under the Criminal Justice Act 2003.

(d) Proof of the mens rea ('guilty mind'), is required, that means the intention that the other person would fear the threat would be carried out to kill that person or a third person.

(e) Evidence of previous history between the parties is admissible as tending to prove that the defendant intended his words to be taken seriously.

(f) Detail in file and witness statements the following points:

- nature of the threats made—exact words used and in what context, include any previous threats made;
- the fact that the threat was understood by the person to whom it was made and that the person feared the threat would be carried out;
- describe the full circumstances of the incident, antecedent history, details of the relationship between the defendant and complainant.

(g) Does the defendant have a lawful excuse (defence) for making the threat?

(h) Consider whether or not there are any 'aggravating' circumstances such as racial or religious motivation or terrorism.

Defences

The specific statutory defence to this offence is having a lawful excuse. Such excuse could arise from a number of sources, including the prevention of crime or self-defence.

The defence will only apply if it was reasonable in all the circumstances to make the threat.

Related cases

R v Rizwan Mawji [2003] EWCA Crim 3067, CA Where a threat to kill was made to a victim by email and he printed that email, it could be adduced in evidence after he had given oral evidence without offending the rules of hearsay.

R v Williams (Clarence Ivor) (1987) 84 Cr App R 299, CA On a charge of threats to kill, evidence of a previous assault is admissible by the judge as it went to the seriousness of the threat and tended to prove that the accused intended his victim to take the threat seriously.

R v Cousins [1982] 2 All ER 115, CA A lawful excuse can exist if a threat to kill is made for the prevention of crime or for self-defence, provided that it is reasonable in the circumstances to make such a threat.

PNLD reference numbers

H2144, D6785, C1977, C1978, C2803

 Time limit for prosecution: None.

 Summary: Maximum six months' imprisonment and/or a fine not exceeding the statutory maximum.

Indictment: Maximum ten years' imprisonment.

5.8.3.2 Kidnap

Kidnapping is an offence at common law.

Offence

The taking or carrying away of one person by another, by force or **fraud**, without the consent of the person so taken or carried away, and without lawful excuse.

Points to prove

✓ date and location
✓ without lawful excuse
✓ by force/fraud
✓ took/carried away
✓ another person
✓ without his consent

Meanings

Fraud

Means deceit/guile/trick. It should not be confused with the narrower meaning given to it for the purposes of consent in sexual offences.

Notes

(a) The important points to prove are the deprivation of liberty and carrying away even where a short distance is involved—and the absence of consent.

(b) In the case of a child, it is the child's consent that should be considered (rather than the parent/guardian) and in the case of a very young child, absence of consent may be inferred.

Defences

Consent or lawful excuse.

Related cases

R v Hendy-Freegard [2007] EWCA Crim 1236, CA The victim must have been deprived of their liberty by the kidnapper for the offence to be made out. Inducing a person by deception to move from one place to another unaccompanied by the 'kidnapper' could not constitute a taking and carrying away or deprivation of liberty.

R v Wellard [1978] 3 All ER 161, CA The defendant purported to be a police officer and escorted/placed a female victim into his car a short distance away. It was held that the ingredients of the offence of kidnapping are: that the victim was deprived of their liberty; and carried away from the place where they wanted to be without lawful excuse.

R v Cort [2003] 3 WLR 1300, CA The defendant went to bus stops telling lone women that the bus they were waiting for had broken down and offering/providing lifts in his vehicle. The fact that the defendant had lied about the absence of the buses meant that, although they had got into the car voluntarily, the women had not given true consent to the journey and the offences of kidnap (and attempts) were complete.

PNLD reference numbers

H2156, H5104, D489, C1520, C135

 Time limit for prosecution: None.

 Indictment: Life imprisonment and/or unlimited fine.

5.8.4 **Murder and manslaughter**

5.8.4.1 Murder

The offence of murder comes under the common law and is defined as:

Offence (at common law)

Where a person of **sound mind and discretion** unlawfully kills any reasonable creature in being and under the Queen's peace, with intent to kill or cause grievous bodily harm.

Points to prove

✓ date and location
✓ unlawfully
✓ killed
✓ a human being
✓ with intent to kill or cause grievous bodily harm

Meanings

Sound mind and discretion

Every person of the age of discretion is presumed to be sane and accountable for his actions, unless the contrary is proved. This means anyone who is not insane or is under ten years old.

Unlawfully

Means without lawful authority, legal justification, or excuse.

Kills

This is 'the act' ('actus reus') which is the substantial cause of death (stabbed, shot, strangled, suffocated, poisoned, etc).

Reasonable creature in being

Any human being, including a baby born alive having an independent existence from its mother.

Under the Queen's peace

This is meant to exclude killing in the course of war. A British subject takes the Queen's peace with them everywhere in the world.

Intent

Intention is not defined but has to be proved, see **5.8.2**.

Cause/causation

If there is an 'intervening factor' between the defendant's actions and the death of the victim, the jury will consider whether the defendant's act contributed significantly to the death.

Grievous bodily harm

Means 'serious or really serious harm' (**R v Saunders [1985] Crim LR 230, CA**). Bodily harm can include inflicting/causing a psychiatric harm/illness (silent/heavy breathing/menacing telephone calls—**R v Ireland [1998] AC 147, HL**). It could include psychiatric injury, in serious cases, as well as physical injury (stalking victim—**R v Burstow [1997] 4 All ER 225, HL**).

Police powers

Power of arrest—section 24 of the Police and Criminal Evidence Act 1984

Powers of entry and search—sections 17, 18, and 32 of the Police and Criminal Evidence Act 1984

Notes

(a) If a defendant wishes to plead insanity, they will be judged on M'Naghten Rules from **M'Naghten's Case (1843) 10 Cl & F 200**. This examines the extent to which, at the time of the commission of the offence, the person was 'labouring under such defect of reason from disease of the mind that either: (a) the defendant did not know what he was doing, or (b) he did know what he was doing but did not know it was wrong.'

(b) The onus is on the prosecution to prove that the killing was unlawful.

(c) If a person intentionally causes grievous bodily harm and the victim subsequently dies as a result, he is guilty of murder.

(d) Traditionally, it required 'malice aforethought', but practically it is the relevant intent that will determine whether an unlawful killing is murder or manslaughter.

(e) The jury will consider whether the defendant's act contributed significantly to the death by applying the 'substantial test' as set out in **R v Smith [1959] 2 All ER 193, Court Martial CA**.

(f) Whether the defendant intended or foresaw the results of his actions will be determined by a number of factors.

(g) The defendant's act must be the substantial cause of death.

(h) The killing must be causally related to the acts of the defendant and not through an intervening factor which breaks the chain of causation. If there is doubt whether death was caused by some supervening event (eg medical negligence when treated), the prosecution does not have to prove that the supervening event was not a significant cause of death.

(i) Intention has to be proved (see **Meanings**).

(j) The date of the offence is the actual date of death.

(k) If a person is suffering from a terminal disease and receives a wound that hastens their death, this killing would (with the required intent) be murder or manslaughter.

(l) A murder or manslaughter committed by a British citizen outside the UK may be tried in this country as if it had been committed here (Offences Against the Person Act 1861, s 9, and the British Nationality Act 1948, s 3).

(m) Motivation will form a key part of any prosecution and will also be relevant in considering the availability of special or general defences. Motivation, such as revenge, would mean that a person has had time to think/reflect so negating the defence of provocation (no sudden and temporary loss of self-control) and increasing the likelihood that the defendant foresaw the consequences of his actions and therefore that he intended them to happen.

(n) The only mens rea that will suffice for attempted murder is intent to kill and the defence of diminished responsibility cannot be used in answer to such a charge.

(o) For incitement of terrorism overseas, where the act of terrorism would constitute murder, see **4.3.5**.

(p) Section 2 of the Suicide Act 1961 deals with encouraging or assisting suicide, whereby a person commits an offence if they do an act capable of encouraging or assisting the suicide or attempted suicide of another person, and the act was intended to encourage or assist suicide or an attempt at suicide.

Defences to murder

Insanity

See the meaning of 'sound mind and discretion' and explanatory notes as to 'insanity'.

Lawful killing

Means with lawful authority; legal justification or excuse.

Self-defence

Use of reasonable force to defend oneself.

At war

This is self-explanatory, not being under the 'Queen's peace' (see **Meanings**).

Specific defences

Loss of control

Where a person (D) kills or is a party to the killing of another (V), D is not to be convicted of murder if—

(a) D's acts and omissions in doing or being a party to the killing resulted from D's loss of self-control,

(b) the loss of self-control had a qualifying trigger, and

(c) a person of D's sex and age, with a normal degree of tolerance and self-restraint and in the circumstances of D, might have reacted in the same or in a similar way to D.

Coroners and Justice Act 2009, s 54(1)

Diminished responsibility

(1) A person (D) who kills or is a party to the killing of another is not to be convicted of murder if D was suffering from an abnormality of mental functioning which—

   (a) arose from a recognised medical condition,

   (b) substantially impaired D's ability to do one or more of the things mentioned in subsection (1A), and

   (c) provides an explanation for D's acts and omissions in doing or being a party to the killing.

(1A) Those things are—

   (a) to understand the nature of D's conduct;

   (b) to form a rational judgement;

   (c) to exercise self-control.

Homicide Act 1957, s 2

Suicide pact

Means a common agreement between two or more persons having for its object the death of all of them, whether or not each is to take his own life, but nothing done by a person who enters into a suicide pact shall be treated as done by him in pursuance of the pact unless it is done while he has the settled intention of dying in pursuance of the pact (Homicide Act 1957, s 4(3)).

Related cases

R v Rahman and others [2008] UKHL 45, HL Victim died from a stab wound to the back during an attack by a number of people all armed with various weapons, but the identity of the person who had inflicted the fatal wound was unknown. This was joint unlawful enterprise to inflict unlawful violence, where a principal killed with an intention to kill which was unexpected and unforeseen by the others. The case gave a test to be applied as to liability.

R v Smith [1959] 2 All ER 193, Court Martial CA Only if the second cause is so overwhelming as to make the original wound merely part of the history can it be said that the death does not flow from the wound.

R v Moloney [1985] 1 All ER 1025, HL The jury has to decide whether the defendant intended to kill or cause grievous bodily harm.

PNLD reference numbers

H2172, H2173, D6753–D6763, C342, C1438

 AG consent required: Consent of the Attorney General is required where the injury was sustained more than three years before death; or the accused has been previously convicted of the offence alleged to be connected with the death.

🕐 **Time limit for prosecution:** None.

 Indictment: Life imprisonment.

5.8.4.2 Soliciting to commit murder

Section 4 of the Offences Against the Person Act 1861 sets out the offence of soliciting to commit murder.

Offence

Whosoever shall **solicit**, encourage, persuade or **endeavour** to persuade, or shall propose to any person, to **murder** any other person, whether he be a **subject of her Majesty** or not, and whether he be within the **Queen's dominions** or not, shall be guilty of an offence.

Offences Against the Person Act 1861, s 4

Points to prove

✓ date and location
✓ solicited/encouraged/persuaded/endeavour to persuade/proposed to murder another person

---

Meanings

Solicit

The *Oxford Dictionary* defines it as 'ask for or try to obtain (something) from someone, ask for something from'.

Endeavour

The *Oxford Dictionary* defines it as 'try hard to do or achieve something'.

Murder (see 5.8.4.1)

Subject of her Majesty

Means a British subject.

Queen's dominions

Means within independent countries under sovereign authority (eg Australia).

Police powers

Power of arrest—section 24 of the Police and Criminal Evidence Act 1984

Powers of entry and search—sections 17, 18, and 32 of the Police and Criminal Evidence Act 1984

Notes

(a) To constitute soliciting there must be some communication between the accused and the person solicited; however, it is not necessary to prove that the mind of the person solicited was affected by the soliciting. In the absence of actual communication, there may be a conviction of attempted solicitation. In the case of **R v Banks (1873) 12 Cox 393** the solicitation was by letter with no evidence of it having been received by the person solicited.

(b) The publication and circulation of an article in a newspaper may be an encouragement, or endeavour to persuade to murder, even though not addressed to any person in particular.

(c) The intended victim need not be identified, need not be a British subject, and need not even be in the country. Solicitation against a particular class is sufficient, for example a particular race or religion.

Related cases

R v Winter [2007] EWCA Crim 3493 Section 4 of the Offences Against the Person Act 1861 was sufficiently wide enough to include soliciting a person to act as a secondary party to murder. Such an offence can be committed by numerous persons playing their part, it matters not whether they played no part in the actual killing. There is a difference between soliciting and assisting murder and for solicitation the jury must be satisfied that someone had formed a plan in advance of encouraging others to join in.

R v Abu Hamza [2006] EWCA Crim 2918 The common law principle is that an inchoate offence could not be committed unless the conduct planned or incited would, if enacted, be an indictable offence in England, but section 4 of the Offences Against the Person Act 1861 was an exception to the rule. The loophole that Parliament sought to close when enacting this section was to deal with the conduct of visitors in England in relation to murders or attempted murders outside the jurisdiction. In light of this, it would not be sensible to restrict the offence to murderers who were British citizens. Section 4 does not imply that conspirators or those incited should be British citizens either. Murder is such a grave crime that it would be absurd to distinguish between inciting a British citizen within the English jurisdiction to commit it and inciting a foreigner to do so.

PNLD reference numbers

H9210, H9211, D6784, C1547, C1490

Time limit for prosecution: None.

Indictment: Life imprisonment, although case law shows that seven years' imprisonment has been the common maximum penalty.

5.8.4.3 Manslaughter

Manslaughter is an offence at common law and is defined as:

> **Offence**
>
> Manslaughter is the **unlawful killing** of another human being which can either be a **voluntary** or **involuntary manslaughter** offence.

Points to prove

✓ date and location
✓ unlawful act or gross negligence
✓ killed
✓ a human being

Meanings

Unlawful killing (see **Murder** at **5.8.4.1**)

Voluntary manslaughter

This occurs when a murder charge is reduced to voluntary manslaughter by reason of one of the specific defences to murder (see **5.8.4.1**).

Involuntary manslaughter

Is an unlawful killing without an intention to kill or cause grievous bodily harm. Apart from the required intent, the elements of the offence are the same as for murder (see **5.8.4.1**). Manslaughter can be caused by:

- unlawful act (not omission): the unlawful act must be unlawful in itself (eg another criminal offence such as an assault or a threat to kill) and must involve a risk that someone would be harmed by it;
- gross negligence (involving breach of duty): gross negligence manslaughter requires a breach of a duty of care owed by the defendant to the victim under circumstances where the defendant's conduct was serious enough to amount to a crime.

Police powers

Power of arrest—section 24 of the Police and Criminal Evidence Act 1984

Powers of entry and search—sections 17, 18, and 32 of the Police and Criminal Evidence Act 1984

Notes

(a) Previous convictions or past behaviour of the defendant in homicide cases may well be relevant, both to the issue of mens rea/intent and also to sentence.

(b) The burden of proof in relation to claiming diminished responsibility or acting in pursuance of a suicide pact lies with the defendant.

(c) Acts having fatal consequences for another person can arise in a number of forms—from workplace accidents to calculated acts of violence.

(d) Motivation will form a key part of any prosecution and will also be relevant in considering the availability of special or general defences.

(e) The only mens rea that will suffice for attempted murder is an intention to kill.

(f) Section 2(1) of the Suicide Act 1961 deals with encouraging or assisting suicide, whereby a person commits an offence if they do an act capable of encouraging or assisting the suicide or attempted suicide of another person, and the act was intended to encourage or assist suicide or an attempt at suicide.

Related cases

R v Roberts, Day I and Day M [2001] EWCA Crim 1594 An intent to cause GBH is murder but an intention only to do some lesser harm is manslaughter.

R v Prentice, and Hollaway Adomako Sulman [1993] 4 All ER 935, HL Manslaughter by gross negligence requires—

- that the defendant owed a duty of care to the victim;
- a breach of that duty;
- which caused the victim's death; and
- in circumstances where the defendant's conduct was so bad as to amount to a criminal act.

PNLD reference numbers

H2169, H2097, D6780, D6781, D6782, C236, C673

 Time limit for prosecution: None.

 Indictment: Life imprisonment.

5.8.5 Encouraging or assisting an offence, conspiracy, aid and abet, and attempt

5.8.5.1 Encouraging or assisting an offence

Sections 44–46 of the Serious Crime Act 2007 provide for the offences of encouraging or assisting an offence. These offences replace the common law offence of incitement.

> **Offences**
>
> 44(1) A person commits an offence if—
> (a) he does an **act capable of encouraging or assisting the commission of an offence**; and
> (b) he intends to encourage or assist its commission.

45 A person commits an offence if—
  (a) he does an act capable of encouraging or assisting the commission of an offence; and
  (b) he believes—
    (i) that the offence will be committed; and
    (ii) that his act will encourage or assist its commission.

46(1) A person commits an offence if—
  (a) he does an act capable of encouraging or assisting the commission of one or more of a number of offences; and
  (b) he believes—
    (i) that one or more of those offences will be committed (but has no belief as to which); and
    (ii) that his act will encourage or assist the commission of one or more of them.

Serious Crime Act 2007, ss 44(1), 45, and 46(1)

Meanings

An act capable of encouraging or assisting the commission of an offence

A person doing an act that is capable of encouraging the commission of an offence includes a reference to his doing so by threatening another person or otherwise putting pressure on another person to commit the offence.

A person doing an act that is capable of encouraging or assisting the commission of an offence includes a reference to his doing so by—

(a) taking steps to reduce the possibility of criminal proceedings being brought in respect of that offence;
(b) failing to take reasonable steps to discharge a duty.

But a person is not to be regarded as doing an act that is capable of encouraging or assisting the commission of an offence merely because he fails to respond to a constable's request for assistance in preventing a breach of the peace (Serious Crime Act 2007, s 65).

Defences

(1) A person is not guilty of an offence under this Part *[Part 2 (sections 44–67)]* if he proves—
  (a) that he knew certain circumstances existed; and
  (b) that it was reasonable for him to act as he did in those circumstances.
(2) A person is not guilty of an offence under this part if he proves—
  (a) that he believed certain circumstances to exist;

> (b) that his belief was reasonable; and
> (c) that it was reasonable for him to act as he did in the circumstances as he believed them to be.
>
> *Serious Crime Act 2007, s 50(1) and (2)*

Factors that are to be taken into account when assessing reasonableness are: the seriousness of the anticipated offence (or, in the case of an offence under section 46, the offences specified in the indictment); any purpose for which he claims to have been acting; any authority by which he claims to have been acting (Serious Crime Act 2007, s 50(3)).

Police powers

Power of arrest—section 24 of the Police and Criminal Evidence Act 1984

Powers of entry and search—sections 17, 18, and 32 of the Police and Criminal Evidence Act 1984

If suspected terrorist then:

Power of arrest under TACT (see **5.3.1**)

Powers to stop and search under TACT (see **5.2.1**)

Note

There are details for the requirement of proof and other provisions for these offences contained in sections 47–49 of the Serious Crime Act 2007 (not reproduced here).

PNLD reference numbers

D21841–D21847

Penalty: As per the anticipated or reference offence.

5.8.5.2 Conspiracy

Section 1 of the Criminal Law Act 1977 sets out the offence of conspiracy.

> **Offence**
>
> 1(1) If a person agrees with any other person or persons that a **course of conduct** shall be pursued which, if the agreement is carried out in accordance with their intentions either—

(a) will necessarily amount to or involve the commission of any offence
   or offences by one or more of the parties to the agreement; or
(b) would do so but for the existence of facts which render the
   commission of the offence or any of the offences impossible,
he is guilty of **conspiracy** to commit the offence or offences in
question.

Criminal Law Act 1977, s 1(1)

Points to prove
✓ date and location
✓ conspired
✓ with person(s)
✓ to commit an offence

Meanings

Course of conduct

It is the course of conduct agreed upon that is critical. If that course
involves an act to be carried out by an innocent party, the fact that
he does not carry it out and thereby prevents the commission of the
substantive offence, does not absolve the other parties to the agreement from liability (**R v Bolton (1992) 94 Cr App R 74**).

A course of conduct may be actual physical acts which the parties
propose shall be done or it might include the consequences which
they intend to follow from their conduct and the relevant circumstances which they know or believe or intend to exist. If it goes outside their intentions, there is no conspiracy. But there will still be
primary liability for the consequences, for example A and B agree to
cause GBH to X. X dies as a result. They are guilty of conspiracy to
commit GBH. They are not guilty of conspiracy to murder. But they
are guilty of murder.

Conspiracy

Means to agree together to plot, to scheme together, to devise
together.

Police powers

Power of arrest—section 24 of the Police and Criminal Evidence Act 1984

Powers of entry and search—sections 17, 18, and 32 of the Police and Criminal Evidence Act 1984

Notes

(a) The offence of conspiracy lies between incitement (now abolished) and attempt and to some extent is a form of preventive measure to enable a legal intervention in a series of conduct to be carried out at an early stage to prevent a crime being committed.

(b) Conspiracy is a preliminary phase to the commission of many crimes but it is also a crime in its own right. The essence of the offence of conspiracy is an agreement. To constitute the offence, what occurs must go beyond the negotiation stage or intention and become a matter of agreement. This agreement could be indicated by letter, telephone, handshake, nod, or bodily movement. Negotiations prior to a conspiracy could involve incitements by the parties to the negotiation. Therefore if a person pulls out at the planning stage before an agreement, there is no conspiracy. For example, a man is approached by a gang and asked if he knows anyone who is interested in taking part in a payroll robbery. He introduces a man to the gang who initially says he is interested but after discussion he refuses to take part and pulls out. This is only negotiation. An agreement had not been reached—**R v Walker [1962] Crim LR 458**.

(c) Nothing needs be done in pursuit of an agreement. The offence is complete with the agreement.

(d) Repentance, lack of opportunity, or failure are all immaterial. The fact that a person withdraws from the agreement can only be used as mitigation.

(e) Section 1(1)(b) is very similar to the 'impossibility rule' in criminal attempts.

(f) Where the substantive offence includes an element of intent, it is advisable to specify this in the charge even though it may appear superfluous, for example: Conspired together with *[specify person]* to wound *[specify person]* with intent to do him grievous bodily harm.

(g) *Practical examples*—in relation to subsection 1(1)(a):

    (i) Two men agree to go out and break into a jeweller's to steal. Will their conduct necessarily amount to the commission of an offence by at least one of them? Yes, burglary; therefore once the agreement is reached a conspiracy exists.

    (ii) Two men agree to embark on a simple burglary; unknown to his accomplice one of the men has with him a firearm. Is there a conspiracy? Yes, but only to burglary not aggravated burglary. The course of conduct agreed upon did not include the taking of a firearm.

Practical examples—in relation to subsection 1(1)(b):

(i) Two men agree to rape a woman. They go to her home but find she is no longer there. Conspiracy.

(ii) Two men agree to go on a safe-blowing expedition, but when they arrive they find their explosives are not capable of blowing the safe. Conspiracy.

(iii) Two men agree to extract cocaine from a substance they have acquired from C. Though the substance contains no cocaine, they are guilty of conspiracy to produce controlled drugs (since they are guilty in light of the facts as they believed them to be)—**DPP v Nock [1978] AC 979**.

Consider the situation where two men agree to a burglary at a house but on arrival discover the police and fire brigade are present as a result of a fire next door.

Do these circumstances fit para (b) the 'impossible'? No, the offence still could be committed and would come under para (a).

(h) Where liability for any offence may be incurred without knowledge on the part of the person committing it of any particular fact or circumstances necessary for the commission of the offence, a person shall nevertheless not be guilty of conspiracy to commit that offence by virtue of subsection (1) unless he and at least one other party to the agreement intend or know that that fact or circumstance shall or will exist at the time when the conduct constituting the offence is to take place.

For example, A and B agree to have intercourse with X unsure as to whether she consents. X does not consent. A and B are guilty of rape since recklessness as to consent is sufficient mens rea. But they are not guilty of conspiracy since they do not have knowledge or belief as to lack of consent.

It may not be necessary to show that the persons accused of conspiracy were in direct communication with each other. Provided they have a common design then it may be proper that they be indicted even if they have not been in touch with each other until they stand in the dock (**R v Meyrick and Rubiffi (1929) 21 Cr App R 94**).

It is quite possible for a number of conspirators to deal only with one person at the hub and for them all to be members of the same conspiracy. The issue in such a situation is whether they were aware that the scheme to which they attached themselves went beyond their agreement with the person at the hub. Equally, it is possible for there to be but one conspiracy where A agrees with B, B agrees with C, and so on. These are referred to as 'wheel' and 'chain' conspiracies respectively.

For example, A (the brains) knows B (a good villain) who knows C (a driver) who knows D (the heavy) who knows E (a gun dealer) who knows F (a farmer whose premises they can use after the job), etc. Each one only knows one and does not meet the others (chain conspiracy). Each of the conspirators by entering into a common agreement makes the others his agents. The agreement must be a shared 'common' one and not two or more distinct conspiracies in relation to different persons or property as was arguably the case in Meyrick.

(i) Consider also the offence of preparation of terrorist acts (**4.3.6**).

Related case

R v Kenning and others [2008] EWCA Crim 1534 Agreement to aid and abet is not capable of being a criminal conspiracy in law. It was, however, possible for persons to agree to aid and abet an offence that they intended or expected would be committed by someone who was not a party to the agreement but it was difficult to regard such an agreement as constituting a criminal conspiracy for the purpose of section 1(1) of the Criminal Law Act 1977.

PNLD reference numbers

D5906, C1924

 DPP consent required: DPP consent required for conspiracy to commit summary offence, Criminal Law Act 1977, s 4.

 Indictment: As for the substantive offence, for details see section 3 of the Criminal Law Act 1977.

5.8.5.3 Conspiracy to commit offences outside England and Wales

Section 1A of the Criminal Law Act 1977 provides the offence of conspiring to commit offences outside England and Wales. In order for this offence to be committed, four conditions must be satisfied.

1. That the pursuit of the agreed course of conduct would at some stage involve an act by one or more of the parties or the happening of some other event intended to take place outside England and Wales.
2. That the act or event is an offence in that place.
3. That the agreement would satisfy section 1(1) of the Criminal Law Act 1977 but for the fact that the offence would be an offence triable in England and Wales if carried out as intended.

4. That—
   (i) a party to the agreement (or an agent) did anything in relation to the agreement in England and Wales before its formation; or
   (ii) a party to the agreement became a party in England and Wales (by joining in person or through an agent); or
   (iii) a party to the agreement (or a party's agent), did or omitted anything in England and Wales in pursuance of the agreement (Criminal Law Act 1977, s 1A).

Note

A reference to an offence is to be read as a reference to what would be the offence in question but for the fact that it is not an offence triable in England and Wales (s 1A(6)).

PNLD reference numbers

D5906, D5907, D5912

 **AG consent required:** Criminal Law Act 1977, s 4(5).

Time limit for prosecution: As per substantive offence.

Summary: As per substantive offence.

5.8.5.4 Aid and abet

Section 8 of the Accessories and Abettors Act 1861 creates the offence of aiding and abetting for indictable offences and section 44 of the Magistrates' Courts Act 1980 creates the offence for summary and either way offences.

Offences

Whosoever shall **aid**, **abet**, **counsel** or **procure** the commission of any indictable offence whether the same be an offence at common law or by virtue of any Act passed or to be passed, shall be liable to be tried, indicted and punished as a **principal offender**.

Accessories and Abettors Act 1861, s 8

(1) A person who aids, abets, counsels or procures the commission by another person of a summary offence shall be guilty of the like offence and may be tried (whether or not he is charged as a principal) either by a court having jurisdiction to try that other person or by a court having by virtue of his own offence jurisdiction to try him.

(2) Any offence consisting in aiding, abetting, counselling or procuring the commission of an offence triable either way (other than an

> offence listed in **Schedule 1** to this Act) shall by virtue of this
> subsection be triable either way.
>
> *Magistrates' Courts Act 1980, s 44*

Meanings

Aid

Means to provide help or assistance to a principal offender, whether
before or at the time of commission of the offence.

Abet

Is difficult to describe, but such an activity could include where an
individual incites, instigates, or encourages the principal to commit
the offence.

Counsel

Means to advise or solicit the commission of an offence.

Procure

Means 'obtaining by care and effort'. A course of action is procured
by setting out to see that it happens and taking the appropriate steps
to produce that happening. A causal link must be established
between what the procurer did and what the principal did.

Principal offender

Means the party whose act is the most immediate cause of the guilty
deed.

Offence listed in Schedule 1

A full list can be found on PNLD at D9821, examples are section 20
of the Offences Against the Person Act 1861, common law offences
of public nuisance and outraging public decency and section 1 of
the Perjury Act 1911.

Police powers

Power of arrest—section 24 of the Police and Criminal Evidence Act 1984

Powers of entry and search—sections 17, 18, and 32 of the Police and Criminal Evidence Act 1984

Note

To be convicted as an 'aider or abettor' a person must have knowledge of all the circumstances which constitute the offence. Whether

the 'aider' realizes that the particular circumstances constitute an offence is immaterial.

Related cases

R v Kenning and others [2008] EWCA Crim 1534 Agreement to aid and abet is not capable of being a criminal conspiracy in law. There could be no conviction for aiding, abetting, counselling, or procuring an offence unless the actus reus (criminal conduct) of the substantive offence actually occurred and under section 1(4)(b) of the Criminal Attempts Act 1981 there was no offence of attempting to aid, abet, counsel, or procure the commission of an offence. It was, however, possible for persons to agree to aid and abet an offence that they intended or expected would be committed by someone who was not a party to the agreement but it was difficult to regard such an agreement as constituting a criminal conspiracy for the purpose of section 1(1) of the 1977 Act.

R v Loukes [1996] Crim LR 341 Offence must have occurred for it to be aided and abetted.

PNLD reference numbers

D920, D923, D9256, C1924, C425

 Time limit for prosecution: As per principal offence.

 Summary: As per principal offence.

 Indictment: As per principal offence.

5.8.5.5 **Attempts**

Section 1 of the Criminal Attempts Act 1981 provides the offence of attempting to commit a criminal offence.

Offence

1(1) If, with **intent to commit an offence to which this section applies**, a person does an act which is **more than merely preparatory** to the commission of the offence, he is guilty of attempting to commit the offence.

Criminal Attempts Act 1981, s 1(1)

Meanings

Intent

Intention is not defined but has to be proved (see **5.8.2**).

An offence to which this section applies

All indictable offences, except for conspiracy, aiding and abetting, and assisting offender offences and encouraging and assisting suicide (Criminal Attempts Act 1981, s 1(4)).

More than merely preparatory

The offence of attempt is complete if he does an act which is a step towards the commission of the specific crime, which is immediately and not remotely connected with the commission of it, and the doing of which cannot reasonably be regarded as having any other purpose than the commission of the specific crime. The main point to remember is that an attempt is not the same as the intent to commit an offence. If an act is merely preparatory (eg obtaining an insurance claim form to make a false claim), then it is not an attempt. There would have to be some other act, such as actually filling the form out and posting it. Mere intent is not enough. See **Related cases** for more detail.

Police powers

Power of arrest—section 24 of the Police and Criminal Evidence Act 1984

Powers of entry and search—sections 17, 18, and 32 of the Police and Criminal Evidence Act 1984

Notes

(a) Criminal attempt offences are only possible where the principal offence is either an indictable offence or one that is triable either way. Attempts to commit summary offences are not recognized in law. However, an anomaly exists in that criminal damage is an either way offence which, if the amount damaged totals under £5,000, can be treated by magistrates as a summary offence. Such an attempt is still an either way offence (which can be tried summarily), it is not a purely summary offence in the normal sense (**R v Bristol Justices, ex p Edgar (1998)**). A suspect can be charged with attempting to damage property under £5,000.

(b) Consider also the offence of preparation of terrorist acts (**4.3.6**).

Related cases

Davey v Lee [1967] 2 All ER 423 An attempt to commit a crime is an act done with intent to commit that crime, and forming part of a series of acts which would constitute the actual commission if it were not interrupted. The Lord Chief Justice also stated that the test that should be applied was the one set out in *Archbold* which is 'the actus reus necessary to constitute an attempt is complete if the prisoner does an act which is a step towards the commission of the specific crime, which is immediately and not merely remotely connected with the commission of it, and the doing of which cannot reasonably be regarded as having any other purpose than the commission of the specific crime.'

R v Geddes [1996] Crim LR 894 G was seen by a teacher in the boys' lavatory block at a school. A cider can with G's fingerprints was in one of the cubicles. His rucksack, containing a large kitchen knife, some rope and a roll of masking tape, was found in nearby bushes. He was charged and convicted of attempted child abduction, the prosecution putting forward the argument that G had been hiding in the lavatories to abduct a child. G appealed on the grounds that he had not attempted to commit the offence. The appeal was upheld and G's conviction quashed. The difference between a 'preparatory act' and an 'attempt' is not always easy to define. In this case, G's intentions were not really in doubt; he had made preparations, equipped himself, and put himself in a position where he could carry out the attack. However, the statutory test for an attempt requires an answer to the question:

Has the defendant actually tried to commit the offence in question? G had never had any communication with, nor had he confronted, any schoolboy. In view of this, the court had to conclude that he had not reached the stage where he could have been said to attempt an abduction.

PNLD reference numbers

D20, D162, D161, C443, C172

 Time limit for prosecution: As per principal offence.

 Summary: As per principal offence.

 Indictment: As per principal offence.

Appendix 1
List of Proscribed Terrorist Organizations

The list of proscribed organizations and the names of outlawed groups may change. To keep updated on the current list of proscribed terrorist groups in the UK, access the Home Office website following the links at: <http://www.homeoffice.gov.uk>.

Part A: List of Proscribed International Groups

17 November Revolutionary Organisation (N17)

Abu Nidal Organisation (ANO)

Abu Sayyaf Group (ASG)

Al-Gama'at al-Islamiya (GI)

Al Ghurabaa

Al Ittihad Al Islamia (AIAI)

Al Qa'ida (AQ)

Al Shabaab

Ansar Al Islam (AI)

Ansar Al Sunna (AS)

Armed Islamic Group (Groupe Islamique Armée) (GIA)

Asbat Al-Ansar ('League of Partisans' or 'Band of Helpers')

Babbar Khalsa (BK)

Basque Homeland and Liberty (Euskadi ta Askatasuna) (ETA)

Baluchistan Liberation Army (BLA)

Egyptian Islamic Jihad (EIJ)

Groupe Islamique Combattant Marocain (GICM)

Hamas Izz al-Din al-Qassem Brigades

Harakat-Ul-Jihad-Ul-Islami (HUJI)

Harakat-Ul-Jihad-Ul-Islami (Bangladesh) (HUJI-B)

Harakat-Ul-Mujahideen/Alami (HuM/A) and Jundallah

Harakat Mujahideen (HM)

Hezb-E Islami Gulbuddin (HIG)

Hizballah Military Wing

International Sikh Youth Federation (ISYF)

Islamic Army of Aden (IAA)

Islamic Jihad Union (IJU)

Islamic Movement of Uzbekistan (IMU)

Jaish e Mohammed (JeM)

Jammat-ul Mujahideen Bangladesh (JMB)

Jeemah Islamiyah (JI)

Khuddam Ul-Islam (KuI) and splinter group **Jamaat Ul-Furquan** (JuF)

Kongra Gele Kurdistan (PKK)

Lashkar e Tayyaba (LT)

Liberation Tigers of Tamil Eelam (LTTE)

Libyan Islamic Fighting Group (LIFG)

Palestinian Islamic Jihad—Shaqaqi (PIJ)

Revolutionary Peoples' Liberation Party—Front (Devrimci Halk Kurtulus Partisi—Cephesi) (DHKP-C)

Salafist Group for Call and Combat (Groupe Salafiste pour la Predication et le Combat) (GSPC)

Saved Sect or **Saviour Sect**

Sipah-E Sahaba Pakistan (SSP) (aka **Millat-E Islami Pakistan** (MIP) (Note: SSP was renamed MIP in April 2003 but is still referred to as SSP) and splinter group **Lashkar-E Jhangvi** (LeJ))

Tehrik Nefaz-e Shari'at Muhammadi (TNSM)

Tehrik-e Taliban Pakistan (TTP)

Teyre Azadiye Kurdistan (TAK) (Note: Mujaheddin e Khalq (MeK) was removed from the list of proscribed organisations in June 2008, as a result of judgments of the Proscribed Organisations Appeals Commission and the Court of Appeal)

Part B: List of Proscribed Northern Irish Groups

Continuity Army Council

Cumann na mBan

Fianna na hEireann

Irish National Liberation Army

Irish People's Liberation Organisation

Irish Republican Army

Loyalist Volunteer Force

Appendix 1: List of Proscribed Terrorist Organizations

Orange Volunteers
Red Hand Commandos
Red Hand Defenders
Saor Eire
Ulster Defence Association
Ulster Freedom Fighters
Ulster Volunteer Force

Appendix 2
Profiles of Proscribed Terrorist Groups

The following list of terrorist organizations are currently proscribed under UK legislation, and therefore outlawed in the UK. There are 47 international terrorist organizations proscribed under the provisions of Schedule 2 to the Terrorism Act 2000. Of these, two organizations are proscribed under powers introduced in the Terrorism Act 2006, as glorifying terrorism. There are 14 organizations in Northern Ireland proscribed under previous anti-terror legislation.

The list of proscribed organizations and the names of terrorist groups may change. To keep updated on the current list of outlawed organizations in the UK, access the Home Office website following the links at: <http://www.homeoffice.gov.uk>.

17 November Revolutionary Organisation (N17)

November 17 aims to highlight and protest at what it deems to be imperialist and corrupt actions of the Greek Military Junta. The group holds an anti-US view blaming the US for supporting the Junta. November 17 was formed in 1974 and is a radical leftist group following a Marxist ideology. Members believe that capitalism is based on the exploitation of workers and so are committed to a 'workers' revolution'. November 17, which is often referred to as 'N17', opposes the Greek Government and Western interests. The group's name refers to the final day of the 1973 Athens Polytechnic uprising in which a series of protests against the Greek Military Junta ended when security forces stormed the Polytechnic campus.

Abu Nidal Organisation (ANO)

The principal aim of the Abu Nidal Organisation terrorist group is the destruction of the State of Israel. It is also hostile to 'reactionary' Arab regimes and states supporting Israel. Abu Nidal was a Palestinian political leader. During the height of his reign in the 1970s and 1980s, he was widely regarded as the world's most dangerous terrorist. Following the rejection of a peace settlement with Israel, the Abu Nidal Organisation, which is often referred to as 'ANO', was established following a split with the Palestine Liberation Organisation (PLO) in 1974.

Abu Sayyaf Group (ASG)

The aim of the Abu Sayyaf Group (ASG) is to fight for an independent Islamic state in the Southern Philippine island of Mindanao. ASG is one of a number of militant separatist groups based in and around the southern islands of the Philippines where groups have been engaged in an insurgency to create a state independent of the predominantly Catholic Philippines. ASG emerged as a splinter group during 1990 composed of former Moro National Liberation Front (MNLF) fighters.

Al-Gama'at al-Islamiya (GI)

The main aim of the proscribed terrorist group, Al-Gama'at al-Islamiya (GI), is to overthrow the Egyptian Government and replace it with an Islamic state. Some members of GI also wish to achieve the removal of Western influence from the Arab world. GI was formally organized during 1973 in the Upper Nile regions of Al-Minya, Asyu't, Qina, and Sohaj in Egypt. It is Egypt's largest militant group, having several thousand members at the height of its notoriety. Sheikh Omar Abdel a-Rahman, commonly known as the 'Blind Sheikh', became the spiritual leader of GI providing the moral grounds for the group's criminal and terrorist activity.

Al Ghurabaa (AG)

Al Ghurabaa (AG) is a splinter group of Al-Muhajiroun (ALM) and disseminates materials that glorify acts of terrorism. On 17 July 2006, AG was outlawed in the UK under new provisions of the Terrorism Act 2006 for glorifying terrorism. AG is a UK-based organization believed to be a splinter group from Al-Muhajiroun, a former organization led by the radical cleric, Omar Backri Mohammed. AG was proscribed as a terrorist group following its organization of a protest on 3 February 2006 in response to the Danish cartoons depicting the Prophet Mohammed.

Al Ittihad Al Islamia (AIAI)

The main aims of Al Ittihad Al Islamia (AIAI) are to establish a radical Sunni Islamic state in Somalia and to regain the Ogaden region of Ethiopia as Somali territory via an insurgent campaign. AIAI is Somalia's largest militant Islamic organization, rising to power in the early 1990s following the collapse of the Siad Barre regime. It is reported that the former leader of al Qa'ida, Usama bin Laden, assisted in funding AIAI with the goal of creating an Islamist state in the Horn of Africa.

Al Qa'ida (AQ)

The core aim of al Qa'ida (AQ) is to establish an Islamic Caliphate throughout the world by working with allied Islamic extremist groups to overthrow apostate regimes and expelling Westerners and non-Muslims from Muslim countries. AQ, translated in Arabic as 'the base', is an international terrorist network formerly led by Usama bin Laden. Established around 1988 by bin Laden, AQ helped finance, recruit, transport, and train thousands of fighters from dozens of countries to be part of an Afghan resistance to defeat the Soviet Union invasion of Afghanistan during the 1980s.

Al Shabaab (AS)

The principal aim of Al Shabaab is to establish a fundamentalist Islamic state in Somalia. Al Shabaab has previously declared its allegiance to Usama bin Laden announcing its intention to combine violent campaigns in the Horn of Africa with al Qa'ida's global jihad. Al Shabaab, which is also referred to as Harakat al-Shabaab Mujahedeen, is translated as the 'Movement of Warrior Youth'. Al Shabaab is an insurgent group within Somalia waging a violent campaign against the Somali Transitional Federal Government and African Union peacekeeping forces since 2007. They have declared war on the United Nations and also Western non-governmental organizations that distribute food aid in Somalia.

Ansar Al Islam (AI)

Ansar Al Islam (AI) is a radical Sunni Salafi group from the northeast of Iraq around Halabja. The group is anti-Western and opposes the influence of the US in Iraqi Kurdistan and the relationship between the Kurdistan Democratic Party (KDP), the Patriotic Union of Kurdistan (PUK), and the US Government. AI, translated in Arabic as 'Supporters' or 'Partisans' of Islam, is one of a number of Sunni Islamist groups based in the Kurdish-controlled northern provinces of Iraq. AI promotes a radical interpretation of Islam, close to the official Saudi ideology of Wahhabism applying strict Sharia law.

Ansar Al Sunna (AS)

Ansar Al Sunna (AS) is a fundamentalist Sunni Islamist extremist group based in Iraq whose aim is to expel all foreign influences from Iraq and to create a fundamentalist Islamic state. AS was founded on 20 September 2003 after declaring its existence on the internet. AS is believed to contain Kurdish Ansar Al Islam operatives, foreign al Qa'ida terrorists and Iraqi Sunnis. AS adheres to a rigid Salafi ideology which calls upon Muslims to support its activities in Iraq describing it as their duty to do so. AS has claimed responsibility for numerous suicide bombings.

Armed Islamic Group (Groupe Islamique Armée) (GIA)

The aim of the GIA is to create an Islamic state in Algeria using all necessary means, including violence.

Asbat Al-Ansar (AAA)

The aim of Asbat Al-Ansar is to overthrow the government in Lebanon and enforce its extremist interpretation of Islamic law within Lebanon. Asbat Al-Ansar, translated in Arabic as 'League of Partisans' or 'Band of Helpers' sometimes uses the aliases of 'The Abu Muhjin' or 'Jama'at Nour'. Asbat Al-Ansar is based in Lebanon, and is a Sunni extremist group composed primarily of Palestinians. The group follows an extremist interpretation of Islam that justifies violence against civilian targets to achieve political ends. Some of those goals include overthrowing the Lebanese Government and thwarting perceived anti-Islamic and pro-Western influences in the country.

Babbar Khalsa (BK)

Babbar Khalsa (BK) is a Sikh movement that aims to establish an independent Sikh state called 'Khalistan' within the Punjab region of India. BK fights for the liberation of Khalistan, the Sikh homeland in Punjab Province, which declared its independence in 1987. BK conducts attacks in India which are mounted against Indian officials and facilities as well as civilians. BK was most active during the 1970s and 1980s. Prior to the 9/11 attacks in the US, BK was attributed as conducting the world's worst terrorist attack, bombing Air India Flight 182 on 23 June 1985.

Basque Homeland and Liberty, (Euskadi ta Askatasuna) (ETA)

The aim of Euskadi ta Askatasuna is to create an independent socialist Basque country. Their core objectives were outlined in the 'Democratic Alternative' paper published in 1995 which states that they seek to force the governments of Spain and France to recognize the rights of the Basque country ensuring that Basque citizens are also uniquely recognized whilst providing an amnesty for all of its members, prisoners, and those currently exiled. They also seek respect for a democratic process offering a total ceasefire when all conditions have been met. Euskadi ta Askatasuna, commonly known as 'ETA', was founded in 1959 to fight for an independent homeland, principally in Spain's Basque region.

Baluchistan Liberation Army (BLA)

The Baluchistan Liberation Army (BLA) comprises tribal groups based in the Baluchistan area of Eastern Pakistan. It aims to establish an independent nation encompassing the Baluch-dominated areas of Pakistan, Afghanistan, and Iran. BLA was listed as a proscribed organization together with other international terrorist groups by the Government on 17 July 2006. Targets of BLA include civilians, specifically those of Punjabi origin. During June 2000 a series of bomb attacks were conducted by BLA terrorists in the region of Quetta in Pakistan which is an area frequented by Pakistani military personnel. The attacks resulted in the deaths of 31 people, 26 of whom were soldiers.

Continuity Army Council (CAC)

The aim of the Continuity Army Council is to lend support to those persons or organizations who seek to unify Ireland. The Continuity Army Council was formed following an Irish Republican Army (IRA) General Army Convention (GAC) meeting which was conducted in September 1986. The GAC is the IRA's highest decision-making body and this was the first time in 16 years they had met. The meeting was called to discuss the constitution of the IRA. As a result of the discussions, a number of IRA members who were opposed to some of the changes to be made to the IRA constitution established a new IRA Executive calling themselves the Continuity Army Council (CAC).

Cumann na mBan

The primary aim of Cumann na mBan is to advance the cause of Irish liberty devoted to unifying Ireland. Cumann na mBan is translated from Irish meaning 'Union of Women' or the 'League of Women' who were established in 1914 as an auxiliary of the Irish Volunteers. Throughout the struggles in Ireland, especially during the Easter Rising in 1916, the women of Cumann na mBan directly assisted the Irish Volunteers playing a vital role. They worked at first aid posts tending to the wounded, prepared and delivered meals, gathered intelligence on scouting expeditions, carried messages, and transferred arms.

Egyptian Islamic Jihad (EIJ)

The main aim of Egyptian Islamic Jihad (EIL) is to overthrow the Egyptian Government and replace it with an Islamic state. It also shares the ideology promoted by al Qa'ida aiming to establish an Islamic Caliphate throughout the world by working with allied

Islamic extremist groups to overthrow apostate regimes and expelling Westerners and non-Muslims from Muslim countries. EIJ is a militant Islamist group that was established in 1973 and originally conducted armed attacks against the Egyptian Government. During June 2001, EIJ merged with al Qa'ida and that served to broaden its aims. EIJ has now largely been absorbed by al Qa'ida. The leader of EIJ, Ayman al-Zawahiri, is now the spiritual leader of al Qa'ida.

Fianna na hEireann

The primary aim of Fianna na hEireann is to promote the objectives, principles, and exercises of scouting among the boys and girls of Ireland to 'cultivate, train and develop all faculties physical, intellectual and spiritual; to implant them with respect for themselves and a desire to give service to others, that may in the fullness of manhood grow into useful, honest, upright citizens, worthy of the land that bore them devoted to the unification of Ireland.' The Fianna na hEireann, translated as the 'Soldiery of Ireland' or the 'Warriors of Ireland', was founded in 1909 as a scouting organization that emphasized Irish nationalism.

Groupe Islamique Combattant Marocain (GICM)

The Groupe Islamique Combattant Marocain's (GICM) primary objective is the installation of a governing system of the Caliphate to replace the governing Moroccan monarchy. The group also has an al Qa'ida-inspired global extremist agenda. GICM was listed as a proscribed organization on 10 October 2005. GICM is one of a small number of North African terrorist groups growing out of Afghanistan during the tenure of the Taliban in the mid-1990s.

Hamas Izz al-Din al-Qassem Brigades

The aim of Hamas Izz al-Din al-Qassem Brigades is to end Israeli occupation in Palestine and to establish an Islamic state. Hamas Izz al-Din al-Qassem Brigades, often referred to as 'Hamas IDQ', is a military wing of the Palestinian Group Hamas. This specific brigade was established in 1992 to provide a coordinated military response for Hamas. A number of Palestinian groups emerged in the late 1980s to pursue the goal of establishing an Islamic Palestinian state in place of Israel. Hamas IDQ have been responsible for many attacks against Israeli civilian and military targets including the kidnapping of Israeli soldier, Gilad Shalit, during 2006.

Harakat-Ul-Jihad-Ul-Islami (HUJI)

The aim of Harakat-Ul-Jihad-Ul-Islami (HUJI) is to achieve accession of all Kashmir to Pakistan. HUJI is translated in Arabic as 'The Islamic Holy War' and was established in 1984 by Fazalur Rehman Khalil and Qari Saifullah Akhtar. HUJI is widely recognized to be the first Pakistan-based militant Islamist terrorist group formed during the Afghan-Soviet conflict. Following the withdrawal of Soviet forces from Afghanistan in 1989, HUJI merged with Harkat-ul-Mujahideen (HuM), another Pakistani militant group. HUJI aims to establish Islamic rule by waging war. Its beliefs derive from the Deobandi ideology, its recruits being indoctrinated in an extreme and radical interpretation of Islam.

Harakat-Ul-Jihad-Ul-Islami (Bangladesh) (HUJI-B)

The primary aim of Harakat-Ul-Jihad-Ul-Islami (Bangladesh) (HUJI-B) is to establish Islamic rule in Bangladesh. HUJI-B drew its inspiration from Usama bin Laden and so broadly follows the ideology promoted by al Qa'ida. HUJI-B has a strong Wahabi and Taliban influence. Members of HUJI-B oppose both Indian and Western influence in Bangladesh believing that Hindu and Christian cultural influences are damaging the Islamic culture. HUJI-B was established in 1992 and like Harakat-Ul-Jihad-Ul-Islami (HUJI) is reported to have received assistance and guidance from Usama bin Laden.

Harakat-Ul-Mujahideen/Alami (HuM/A) and Jundallah

The aim of both Harakat-Ul-Mujahideen/Alami (HuM/A) and Jundallah is the rejection of democracy and to establish a caliphate based on Sharia law. Harakat-Ul-Mujahideen/Alami and Jundallah also aims to achieve accession of all Kashmir to Pakistan. HuM/A is a Pakistani militant group being established in 1985 to oppose the Soviet invasion of Afghanistan. Translated in Arabic as the 'Order for Holy Warriors', the initial objectives of HuM/A were the provision of food and shelter for the Afghan refugees in the North-West Frontier Province in Pakistan. Following the withdrawal of Soviet forces in 1989, HuM/A has continued to wage violent jihad against secular Muslim governments and the West.

Harakat Mujahideen (HM)

The primary aim of Harakat Mujahideen (HM) is to seek independence for Indian-administered Kashmir. Formerly known as Harakat ul-Ansar (HuA), HM formed as the result of a merger between Harkat-Ul-Mujahideen (HuM) and Harkat ul-Jihad-al-Islami (HuJI). HuA was established in Karachi during 1980 primarily to send volunteers to Afghanistan to assist Afghan rebels to fight against Soviet forces. The headquarters of HuA were located in Punjab where they followed the Deobandi ideology of Islam.

HuA was reported to have several thousand armed supporters who are believed to be located in Azad Kashmir, Pakistan, and in the southern area of the Kashmir and Doda regions of India.

Hezb-E Islami Gulbuddin (HIG)

The primary aim of Hezb-E Islami Gulbuddin (HIG) is to seek the creation of a fundamentalist Islamic state in Afghanistan. HIG was originally founded in 1977 by Gulbuddin Hekmatyar. During the invasion of Afghanistan by Soviet forces, HIG operated near the Pakistani border where they had a strong presence in areas such as Kumar, Laghman, Jalabad, and Pakita. Gulbuddin Hekmatyar opposed the 2001 attack by the US on the Taliban in Afghanistan and as a result continues to launch attacks not only on US forces but also the US-supported Karzai Government.

Hizballah Military Wing

Hizballah is committed to the armed resistance for the State of Israel and aims to seize all Palestinian territories and Jerusalem from Israel. Hizballah, translated as the 'Party of God', is one of the most infamous terrorist organizations operating in the world today. Hizballah was established in 1982 in Lebanon and was originally the militant wing of a religious group, the Shi'a, designed to provide a proactive arm in the protest against social and political deprivation. Hizballah has expressed its objectives as wishing to remove foreign influences from Lebanon to create an independent and Islamic Lebanon.

International Sikh Youth Federation (ISYF)

The International Sikh Youth Federation (ISYF) is an organization committed to the creation of an independent state of Khalistan for Sikhs within India. ISYF was founded in 1984 following the events of Operation Blue Star. On 3 June 1984, the then Prime Minister of India, Indira Ghandi, ordered the military to conduct Operation Blue Star, which provided a military response to remove the Sikh militants from the Golden Temple in Amristar, India. It was believed that Sikh militia had gained a stronghold within the Golden Temple complex resulting in a deterioration of law and order in the Punjab. Operation Blue Star is considered to be a political disaster as official Indian military figures reveal that 83 soldiers were killed with a further 248 being injured. These figures also indicate that 492 militants were killed together with innocent civilians including women and children.

Irish National Liberation Army (INLA)

The primary aim of the Irish National Liberation Army during 'The Troubles' was to protect members of the Irish Republican Socialist Movement from attacks by the Official Irish Republican Army. The Irish National Liberation Army, which is also referred to as the 'INLA', is translated into Irish as 'Arm Saoirse Naisiunta na hEirehame'. The INLA emerged in 1974 and was founded as the army of the Irish Republican Socialist Party, primarily established to defend attacks from Official Irish Republican Army activists.

Irish People's Liberation Organisation (IPLO)

The primary objective of the Irish People's Liberation Organisation is to destroy the Irish Republican Socialist Movement. The Irish People's Liberation Organisation is a small Irish republican paramilitary organization which is also referred to as 'IPLO'. IPLO emerged from a violent split with the Irish National Liberation Army (INLA) whose aim during 'The Troubles' was to protect members of the Irish Republican Socialist Movement from attacks by the Official Irish Republican Army.

Irish Republican Army (IRA)

The Irish Republican Army (IRA) has two key aims, first, it is devoted to removing British forces from Northern Ireland, and secondly, to unifying Ireland. The IRA is translated from Irish as 'Oglaigh na hEireann', and is the leading Republican paramilitary group in Ireland which has existed in one form or another since 1919. The IRA is a military organization descended from the Irish Volunteers. The original IRA, more commonly referred to as the 'Old IRA', was operational from 1922 until a split in 1970. The split brought about two main groups, the Provisional IRA (PIRA) and the Official IRA. The title 'IRA' which appears on the list of proscribed organizations is considered sufficient to cover the numerous splinter groups and breakaway factions of the IRA which include; Provisional Irish Republican Army (PIRA), Official Irish Republican Army (OIRA), Real Irish Republican Army, and the Continuity Irish Republican Army (CIRA).

Islamic Army of Aden (IAA)

The primary aim of the Islamic Army of Aden (IAA) is to overthrow the current Yemeni Government thereby establishing an Islamic state following Sharia law.

IAA emerged during 1998 following the release of a series of communications stating that it supported the ideology of al Qa'ida and former leader, Usama bin Laden. IAA also expressed its intention to overthrow the Yemeni Government calling for operations to be conducted against US and other Western interests in Yemen. IAA has been engaged in a series of bomb attacks and kidnappings to progress its cause but its most notorious terrorist attack is the suicide boat bombing of the US Navy destroyer, USS Cole, on 12 October 2002 in Yemen which killed 17 US sailors.

Islamic Jihad Union (IJU)

The primary aim of the Islamic Jihad Union (IJU) is the elimination of the current Uzbek regime creating an Islamic-democratic state in Uzbekistan. On 13 October 2005, Hazel Blears MP, testified before the House of Commons that IJU should be banned because it posed a threat to British interests overseas. Evidence to support the proscription of IJU was provided during the arrest of two men suspected of being members of IJU in Frankfurt, Germany, on 18 September 2008. German prosecutors revealed that two men had been arrested on suspicion of links with the Pakistan-based IJU which they described as a modern successor to al Qa'ida.

Islamic Movement of Uzbekistan (IMU)

The primary aim of the Islamic Movement of Uzbekistan (IMU) is to establish an Islamic state in Uzbekistan. It is also reported to have expressed an intention to establish a broader state over the entire Turkestan area. IMU, which is also referred to as the Islamic Party of Turkestan, originally focused upon overthrowing the government of Uzbek President, Islam Karimov, planning to replace it with an Islamic state of Uzbekistan. The group is now believed to have expanded its aims intending to create an Islamic state in all Central Asia, including all of Kazakhstan, Tajikistan, Turkmenistan, Uzbekistan, and China's Xinxiang province.

Jaish e Mohammed (JeM)

The primary aim of Jaish e Mohammed (JeM) is to liberate Kashmir from Indian control. JeM has also expressed an intention to destroy the US and India wishing to unify the various Kashmiri militant groups to achieve these objectives. JeM is an Islamist group based in Pakistan which focuses its terrorist activities within Kashmir. Jaish e Mohammed is translated into Arabic as the 'Army of Mohammed' whose leader is Maulana Masood Azhar. Azhar was a member of Harkat-Ul-Mujahideen (HuM) who received support and guidance from the former leader of al Qa'ida, Usama bin Laden.

Jammat-ul Mujahideen Bangladesh (JMB)

The primary aim of Jammat-ul Mujahideen Bangladesh (JMB) is to establish the rule of Islam in Bangladesh, opposing the creation of democracy. Jammat-ul Mujahideen Bangladesh, which is also referred to as 'JMB', and translated from Arabic as the 'Party of the Mujahideen', is an Islamist terrorist organization operating within Bangladesh. JMB first came to prominence on 20 May 2002 when eight of its members were arrested in the Parbatiput and Dinajpur districts of Bangladesh being found in possession of 25 petrol bombs. The group has claimed responsibility for numerous fatal bomb attacks across Bangladesh, including a series of coordinated bomb attacks on 17 August 2005 at 300 separate locations in 30 cities.

Jeemah Islamiyah (JI)

The primary aim of Jeemah Islamiyah (JI) is the creation of a unified Islamic state in Singapore, Malaysia, Indonesia, and the Southern Philippines. JI is a militant Islamic separatist movement suspected of killing hundreds of civilians and is dedicated to the establishment of a fundamentalist Islamic state. JI is believed to have been established as a network of several Islamic groups by Abu Bakar Bashir and Abdullah Sungkar who propagated the belief of Darukl Islam, a conservative strain of Islam. JI formed as a network of terrorist cells which provided financial support to al Qa'ida.

Khuddam Ul-Islam (KuI) and Jamaat Ul-Furquan (JuF)

The aim of both Khuddam Ul-Islam (KuI) and Jamaat Ul-Furquan (JuF) is to unite Indian-administered Kashmir with Pakistan. It also aims to establish a radical Islamic state in Pakistan seeking to destroy India and the US. KuI and JuF have stated that they will achieve their objectives by the recruitment of new jihadis, and through securing the release of imprisoned Kashmiri militants.

Kongra Gele Kurdistan (PKK)

PKK/KADEK/KG is primarily a separatist movement that seeks an independent Kurdish state in southeast Turkey. The PKK changed its name to KADEK and then to Kongra Gele Kurdistan, although the PKK acronym is still used by parts of the movement.

Lashkar e Tayyaba (LT)

The primary aim of Lashkar e Tayyaba (LT), is to seek independence for Kashmir creating an Islamic state. LT is believed to be the largest and most active militant group located in the Lahore region of Pakistan. LT is translated in Arabic as the 'Army of the Right-eous' or the 'Army of the Pure'. LT was formed in 1991 to support the military activities of other terrorist groups in Pakistan and Afghanistan. LT are an active terrorist group having conducted a series of attacks on Indian armed forces in Jammu and Kashmir. LT can be distinguished from other terrorist groups operating to liberate Kashmir for its operations conducted against security forces which are well planned and executed. They also are believed to have been involved in numerous massacres of innocent and unarmed non-Muslim villagers.

Liberation Tigers of Tamil Eelam (LTTE)

The aim of the Liberation Tigers of Tamil Eelam (LTTE) is to seek a separate Tamil state in the north and east of Sri Lanka. LTTE are more commonly known as the 'Tamil Tigers' and were founded in 1972 becoming the most powerful group in Sri Lanka fighting for a distinct Tamil state. LTTE is a militant Tamil nationalist organization that has waged a war of violence since the 1970s against the Government of Sri Lanka in order to create a separate Tamil state. LTTE is an outlawed terrorist organization in 32 countries.

Libyan Islamic Fighting Group (LIFG)

The Libyan Islamic Fighting Group (LIFG) sought to replace the former Libyan regime with a hard-line Islamic state. It is also believed to be part of the wider global Islamist extremist movement as inspired by al Qa'ida. LIFG was formed in the early 1990s in Afghanistan. The group relocated to Libya where it sought to overthrow Colonel Mu'ammar Kaddaffi. LIFG mounted several operations inside Libya in pursuit of its cause which included a failed attempt to assassinate Colonel Mu'ammar Kaddafi during 1996.

Loyalist Volunteer Force (LVF)

The Loyalist Volunteer Force (LVF) seeks to prevent a political settlement with Irish nationalists in Northern Ireland by attacking Catholic politicians, civilians, and Protestant politicians who endorse the Northern Ireland Peace Process. The LVF is a loyalist paramilitary group in Northern Ireland. LVF broke away from the Ulster Volunteer Force being led by Billy Wright, a former lay preacher who was arrested and charged with menacing behaviour receiving an eight-year prison term. Whilst serving his sentence in the LVF wing of HMP Maze Prison, members of INLA shot him dead on 27 December 1997.

Orange Volunteers (OV)

The primary aim of the Orange Volunteers is to ensure that Ulster remains British, defending the loyalist community from republican violence. The Orange Volunteers, who are also referred to as 'OV', are an Ulster loyalist paramilitary group in Northern Ireland. The OV motto 'addaces fortuna juvat' translates from Irish as 'Fortune Favours the Bold'. OV was established in 1998 following the Drumcree conflict which is an ongoing dispute over parades in the town of Portadown in Northern Ireland. The route of the parade taken by the Protestant Orange Order is between Portadown town centre and the Dumcree parish church to the north which is predominantly Catholic.

Palestinian Islamic Jihad – Shaqaqi (PIJ)

The primary aim of Palestinian Islamic Jihad—Shaqaqi (PIJ) is to end the Israeli occupation of Palestine and to create an Islamic state. PIJ is an outlawed terrorist group in the US, Israel, across Europe, Japan, Australia, and Canada. PIJ opposes the existence of the state of Israel, the Middle East Peace Process, and the Palestinian Authority and has carried out suicide bombings against Israeli targets.

Red Hand Commandos (RHC)

The aim of the Red Hand Commandos is to fight to ensure that Ulster remains British and to defend the loyalist community from republican violence. The Red Hand Commandos, which is also referred to as 'RHC' is a Northern Irish loyalist paramilitary group having close links with the Ulster Volunteer Force (UVF). RHC was founded in 1970 in response to a series of violent attacks on a loyalist parade as they marched on Newtownards Road in Ulster. RHC supported the conditions and signing of the Good Friday Agreement of 1998.

Red Hand Defenders (RHD)

The Red Hand Defenders (RHD) seek to prevent a political settlement with Irish nationalists opposing the peace process and maintaining the status of Northern Ireland as part of the UK. The RHD are a loyalist paramilitary group which emerged following the series of violent clashes that occurred between loyalists and republicans as a result of the Dumcree crisis in July 1998. The violence began when the Protestant Orange Order was not allowed to march along its annual route in Portadown, Northern Ireland. The RHD opposes the Irish Republican Army (IRA) and its supporters. It has conducted a number of violent attacks which have included arson, bombings, and murders.

Revolutionary Peoples' Liberation Party—Front (DHKP-C)

The aim of the Revolutionary Peoples' Liberation Party—Front (DHKP-C) is to establish a Marxist-Leninist regime in Turkey. The Revolutionary Peoples' Liberation Party—Front, is also known as Devrimci Halk Kurtulus Partisi—Cephesi, more commonly referred to as 'DHKP-C'. DHKP-C is an outlawed terrorist organization in Turkey, the European Union, the US, and the UK under the provisions of the Terrorism Act 2000. DHKP-C is a Turkish group whose origins can be traced back to the 1970s.

Salafist Group for Call and Combat (GSPC)

The aim of the Salafist Group for Call and Combat (GSPC) is to create an Islamic state in Algeria. The Salafist Group for Call and Combat, translated in French as 'Groupe Salafiste pour la Predication et le Combat', is also known as the 'Hassan Hattab Faction' and was founded by Hassan Hattab who was born in Rouiba, Algeria. Having trained as a paratrooper during his national service, Hattab joined the radical Islamist guerrilla movement, the Armed Islamic Group (GIA). He became a regional commander for GIA but broke away from GIA following disagreements over the killing of innocent civilians resulting in the creation of GSPC.

Saor Eire (Free Ireland)

The primary aim of Saor Eire is to achieve an independent revolutionary leadership for the working class and working farmers seeking to overthrow British imperialism and its ally, Irish capitalism. Saor Eire, translated in Irish as 'Free Ireland', is a left-wing political organization established in September 1931 by members of the Irish Republican Army. Saor Eire is an organization of workers and working farmers which has been referred to as the 'Revolutionary Workers' Party'. The name 'Saor Eire' has been used occasionally since its foundation by various Republican factions.

Saved Sect or Saviour Sect

The primary aim of the Saved Sect is to encourage violent extremism through the dissemination of materials that glorify acts of terrorism. The Saved Sect, which is also known as the Saviour Sect is a splinter group of Al-Muajiroun which disseminates materials that glorify acts of terrorism. The Saved Sect was established in November 2005 and believes that Muslims living in the Western world do not follow traditional Islamic values and seeks to remind Muslims of true Islamic values. The name of the group is taken from a tradition or 'hadith' ascribed to the Prophet Mohammed which states that: 'My nation will be divided into 73 sects; all of them will be in the Fire except for one (the saved sect).'

Note: the Government laid Orders, in January 2010 and November 2011, which provide that Al Muhajiroun, Islam4UK, Call to Submission, Islamic Path, London School of Sharia, and Muslims Against Crusades should be treated as alternative names for the organization which is already proscribed under the names Al Ghurabaa and the Saved Sect.

Sipah-E Sahaba Pakistan (SSP) and Lashkar-E Jhangvi (LeJ)

The aim of both Sipah-E Sahaba Pakistan (SSP) and Lashkar-E Jhangvi (LeJ) are to transform Pakistan into a Sunni state under Sharia law. Sipah-E Sahaba Pakistan, which is also referred to as 'SSP', is also known as Millat-E Islami Pakistan (MIP). SSP was renamed MIP in April 2003 but may also be referred to as SSP. A splinter group of SSP is Lashkar-E Jhangvi (LeJ). All of these groups are proscribed organizations under the provisions of the Terrorism Act 2000. SSP is also believed to seek all Shia Muslims to be declared as K-afirs or non-believers expressing an intention to participate in the destruction of other religions including Judaism, Christianity, and Hinduism. SSP strongly opposes the US and Pakistani relationship following the 9/11 terrorist attacks and subsequent 'war on terror'.

Tehrik Nefaz-e Shari'at Muhammadi (TNSM)

The primary aim of Tehrik Nefaz-e Shari'at Muhammadi (TNSM) is to seek the enforcement of Islamic law in Pakistan. TNSM is translated from Arabic as the 'Movement for the Enforcement of Islamic Laws'. TNSM are dedicated to enforcing the rule of Islamic law in Pakistan and is widely regarded as one of the most dangerous terrorist groups operating within the North-West Frontier Province (NWFP). TNSM has conducted regular attacks against coalition and Afghan government forces in Afghanistan and is believed to provide direct support to al Qa'ida and the Taliban.

Tehrik-e Taliban Pakistan (TTP)

Tehrik-e Taliban Pakistan (TTP) has carried out a large number of mass casualty attacks in Pakistan and Afghanistan since 2007. The group have announced various objectives and demands, such as the enforcement of Sharia law, resistance against the Pakistani army, and the removal of NATO forces from Afghanistan. TTP have also been involved in attacks in the West, including the attempted New York Times Square car bomb during May 2010.

Teyre Azadiye Kurdistan (TAK)

The primary aim of Teyre Azadiye Kurdistan (TAK) is to secure Kurdish secession from Turkey. Teyre Azadiye Kurdistan is translated as the 'Kurdistan Freedom Falcons', more commonly known as TAK which is a militant paramilitary organization operating in southern Turkey and northern Iraq. It is widely acknowledged that TAK is a splinter faction of Partiya Karkerern Kurdistan, commonly referred to as 'PKK'. PKK has Marxist-Leninist roots and was formed in the late 1970s launching an armed conflict against the Turkish Government in 1984 where it called for an independent Kurdish state within Turkey.

Ulster Defence Association (UDA)

The aim of the Ulster Defence Association (UDA) is to defend the loyalist community from republican violence rejecting the unification of Ireland while seeking independence for Ulster. The UDA is a loyalist paramilitary organization in Northern Ireland. The UDA was created in 1971 and operated as an umbrella organization for a number of militant loyalist groups. Until 10 August 1992, the UDA was a legal organization until it was outlawed following links to paramilitary attacks.

Ulster Freedom Fighters (UFF)

The primary aim of the Ulster Freedom Fighters is to support the activities of the Ulster Defence Association which aims to defend the loyalist community from republican violence. The Ulster Freedom Fighters, who are also referred to as 'UFF', is a loyalist paramilitary organization in Northern Ireland which emerged from the Ulster Defence Association (UDA) in the early 1970s being used to conduct their military tasks. The activities of UFF have included attacks against civilians as well as members of the Irish Republican Army. As the military wing of the UDA, the UFF was originally intended to react and respond to acts of republican violence against Protestants in Northern Ireland.

Ulster Volunteer Force (UVF)

The aim of the Ulster Volunteer Force is to fight to ensure that Ulster remains British and to defend the loyalist community from republican violence. The Ulster Volunteer Force, which is also referred to as the 'UVF', is a loyalist paramilitary organization based in Northern Ireland which was formed in May 1966. The UVF has focused its activities around East Antrim, County Armagh, and the Shankhill district of Belfast. The UVF is recognized as being one of the most active and violent loyalist groups that operated during 'The Troubles'. Statistics compiled by the University of Ulster reveal that the UVF is believed to be responsible for 426 killings between 1969 and 2001 of which 350 were civilians and 12 were republican paramilitaries.

Appendix 3

Delivering CONTEST: Government Departmental Roles and Responsibilities

Department	Roles and Responsibilities
Cabinet Office (CO)	Supports the National Security Council and the Cabinet Office Briefing Room (COBR), oversees the Single Intelligence Account and also services the Joint Intelligence Committee, which sets strategic intelligence-gathering priorities and delivers strategic intelligence assessments. The Civil Contingencies Secretariat of the Cabinet Office leads cross-government work on many aspects of Prepare.
Centre for the Protection of the National Infrastructure (CPNI)	Provides integrated protective security advice (covering physical, personnel, and cyber security) to businesses and organizations across the national infrastructure aimed at reducing vulnerability to terrorism and other threats.
Crown Prosecution Service (CPS)	The government department responsible for prosecuting criminal cases investigated by the police in England and Wales.
Department for Business, Innovation and Skills (BIS)	In connection with CONTEST, provides guidance and support to higher and further education sectors on tackling violent extremism.
Department for Communities and Local Government (DCLG)	Sets policy on supporting local government, communities, and neighbourhoods; regeneration; housing; planning, building, and the environment; and fire. As part of its work on the Big Society, DCLG is developing a new approach to integration.
Department for Education (DfE)	Has responsibility for ensuring that young people are protected from exposure to extremism and extremist views in or outside schools.

Appendix 3: Delivering CONTEST

Department	Roles and Responsibilities
The Department of Energy & Climate Change (DECC)	Contributes to the Protect and Prepare strands of CONTEST as lead government department for energy. DECC is responsible for ensuring the security of the nation's energy supplies (electricity, gas, and oil) and civil nuclear sites from all risks, including malicious attack. The Department's work also includes contributing to the UK's policy on nuclear safeguards and non-proliferation issues; sponsoring the Civil Nuclear Police Authority and Civil Nuclear Constabulary; and managing the nuclear and radiological elements of the UK's Global Threat Reduction Programme.
Department for Environment, Food and Rural Affairs (DEFRA)	Responsible for dealing with the impact of a terrorist incident on the natural environment, plant and animal health, food and drinking water supplies, waste management (excluding radioactive waste), farming, fisheries, and rural communities. DEFRA has lead government department responsibility for the recovery phase of a chemical, biological, radiological, and nuclear (CBRN) incident.
Department for International Development (DFID)	Manages Britain's aid to developing countries. DFID uses its resources for the purpose of poverty reduction overseas. Its activities can contribute to CONTEST by addressing underlying social and economic issues, helping governments in key countries to improve governance and security, economic stability and employment opportunities, and access to basic services.
Department for Transport (DfT)	The security regulator of most of the transport sector including aviation, maritime, and rail. It aims, to protect the travelling public, transport facilities, and those employed in the transport industry from acts of terrorism.
Department of Health (DH)	Oversees the health sector's commitment and contribution to CONTEST. The sector's key priorities include improving, protecting, and maintaining the health of the population by ensuring the country's ability to respond to and cope with threat-derived mass casualty

emergencies, including catastrophic acts of terrorism (CBRN). Its activities contribute to the crowded places and hazardous substances work; and with health designated as one of the nine national infrastructure sectors, it also contributes to the UK's critical national infrastructure programme.

Devolved Administrations

Responsible in Northern Ireland, Scotland, and Wales for the functions which have been devolved to them according to their different devolution settlements. All three Devolved Administrations are responsible for health, education, and local government. Policing and justice are devolved in Scotland and Northern Ireland.

Foreign and Commonwealth Office (FCO)

Has overall responsibility for coordinating the delivery of CONTEST overseas, and chairs the cross-government Overseas CONTEST Group (OCG).

Government Communications Headquarters (GCHQ)

Has two important missions: Signals Intelligence (known as SIGINT) and Information Assurance (IA). SIGINT work provides vital information to support government policymaking and operations in the fields of national security, military operations, law enforcement, and economic well-being. Information Assurance is about protecting government data—communications and information systems—from hackers and other threats.

Government Office for Science (GO-Science)

Headed by the Government Chief Scientific Adviser, is responsible for ensuring that all levels of government, including the Prime Minister and Cabinet, receive the best scientific advice possible. GO-Science is engaged across CONTEST to ensure it is underpinned by robust science, including peer review.

HM Treasury

Leads on asset freezing and is the joint lead with OSCT on terrorist financing. In 2007, HM Treasury set up a dedicated Asset Freezing Unit to handle counter-terrorist and other asset-freezing work. HM Treasury's Financial Crime Team, with OSCT, coordinates the delivery of our strategy for tackling terrorist finance.

Appendix 3: Delivering CONTEST

Department	Roles and Responsibilities
Home Office: the Office for Security and Counter Terrorism (OSCT)	Has overall responsibility for coordinating the CONTEST strategy. OSCT's primary responsibilities are to: support the Home Secretary and other ministers in developing, directing, and implementing CONTEST across government; deliver aspects of the counter-terrorism strategy directly, for example legislation, policing (in England and Wales), UK border, protective security policy; facilitate oversight of the Security Service, its operations, and police counter-terrorism operations and coordinate counter-terrorism crisis management.
Joint Terrorism Analysis Centre (JTAC)	The UK's centre for the all-source analysis and assessment of international terrorism. JTAC sets threat levels and issues analytical reporting to government departments and agencies.
Ministry of Defence (MOD)	Contributes to CONTEST using its military capability and supports Pursue through its capability to disrupt terrorist groups overseas, as well as through intelligence collection, counter-terrorism capacity-building for partner nations, and support to overseas law enforcement and security agencies. Its support to conflict-prevention work also contributes to CONTEST objectives. In the event of a terrorist attack that exceeds the capability or immediate capacity of the UK civilian response, the MOD can provide support to Prepare through military aid to the civil authorities.
Ministry of Justice (MoJ)	Responsible for ensuring that there is sufficient capacity in the criminal justice system to deal with terrorism cases, and that they are dealt with efficiently, effectively, and securely. The National Offender Management Service (an agency of the MoJ) manages the risks posed by terrorist offenders, in partnership with the police and security and intelligence agencies. The Youth Justice Board is a Non-Departmental Public Body (NDPB) which is sponsored by the MoJ and is responsible for delivering a range of prevention programmes designed to support individuals who are vulnerable to recruitment by violent extremists.

National Counter Terrorism Security Office (NaCTSO)	A police unit co-located with CPNI. NaCTSO's work is divided into three areas: protection of crowded places; protection of hazardous sites and dangerous substances; and assisting the CPNI to protect the critical national infrastructure.
National Crime Agency (NCA)	The new National Crime Agency (NCA), established in 2013, serves to strengthen the operational response to organized crime and better secure the border through more effective national tasking and enforcement action. The NCA will build effective two-way relationships with police forces, law enforcement agencies, and other partners.
National Security Council (NSC)	Brings together key ministers, and military and intelligence chiefs, under the chairmanship of the Prime Minister. The NSC ensures a strategic and coordinated approach across the whole of government to national security issues.
Northern Ireland Office (NIO	The government department that supports the Secretary of State for Northern Ireland.
Police, Police National Counter Terrorism network (PNCTN) and Special Branch (SB)	The police service is responsible for disrupting or responding to terrorist incidents in the UK.
Scotland Office	The government department that supports the Secretary of State for Scotland
Secret Intelligence Service (SIS)	Collects intelligence overseas to promote and defend the national security and the economic well-being of the UK. It supports Security Service work in the UK.
Security Service (MI5)	Responsible for protecting the UK against threats to national security. Notably terrorism (where it leads the investigation of terrorism in the UK), espionage and sabotage, the activities of agents of foreign powers, and actions intended to overthrow or undermine parliamentary democracy by political, industrial, or violent means.
UK Border Agency (UKBA)	An agency of the Home Office. The UK Border Agency is responsible for securing the UK border and controlling migration in the UK.
Wales Office	The government department that supports the Secretary of State for Wales.

Police and Criminal Evidence Act 1984, Code H Revised Code of Practice in Connection with:

The Detention, Treatment and Questioning by Police Officers of Persons in Police Detention under Section 41 of, and Schedule 8 to, the Terrorism Act 2000

The Treatment and Questioning by Police Officers of Detained Persons in respect of whom an Authorisation to Question after Charge has been given under Section 22 of the Counter-Terrorism Act 2008

1 General

1.0 The powers and procedures in this Code must be used fairly, responsibly, with respect for the people to whom they apply and without unlawful discrimination. The Equality Act 2010 makes it unlawful for police officers to discriminate against, harass or victimise any person on the grounds of the 'protected characteristics' of age, disability, gender reassignment, race, religion or belief, sex and sexual orientation, marriage and civil partnership, pregnancy and maternity when using their powers. When police forces are carrying out their functions, they also have a duty to have regard to the need to eliminate unlawful discrimination, harassment and victimisation and to take steps to foster good relations.

1.1 This Code of Practice applies to, and *only* to:

(a) persons in police detention after being arrested under section 41 of the Terrorism Act 2000 (TACT) and detained under section 41 of, or Schedule 8 to that Act and *not charged*, and

(b) detained persons in respect of whom an authorisation has been given under section 22 of the Counter-Terrorism Act 2008 (post-charge questioning of terrorist suspects) to interview them in which case, section 15 of this Code will apply.

1.2 The provisions in PACE Code C apply when a person:

(a) is in custody *otherwise* than as a result of being arrested [under] section 41 of TACT or detained for examination under Schedule 7 to TACT (see *paragraph 1.4*);

(b) is charged with an offence, or

(c) is being questioned about any offence after being charged with that offence *without* an authorisation being given under section 22 of the Counter-Terrorism Act 2008.

See *Note 1N*.

1.3 In this Code references to an offence and to a person's involvement or suspected involvement in an offence where the person has not been charged with an offence, include being concerned, or suspected of being concerned, in the commission, preparation or instigation of acts of terrorism.

1.4 The Code of Practice issued under paragraph 6 of Schedule 14 to TACT applies to persons detained for examination under Schedule 7 to TACT. See *Note 1N*.

1.5 All persons in custody must be dealt with expeditiously, and released as soon as the need for detention no longer applies.

1.6 There is no provision for bail under TACT before or after charge. See *Note 1N*.

1.7 An officer must perform the assigned duties in this Code as soon as practicable. An officer will not be in breach of this Code if delay is justifiable and reasonable steps are taken to prevent unnecessary delay. The custody record shall show when a delay has occurred and the reason. See *Note 1H*.

1.8 This Code of Practice must be readily available at all police stations for consultation by:
- police officers;
- police staff;
- detained persons;
- members of the public.

1.9 The provisions of this Code:
- include the *Annexes*;
- do not include the *Notes for Guidance*.

1.10 If an officer has any suspicion, or is told in good faith, that a person of any age may be mentally disordered or otherwise mentally vulnerable, in the absence of clear evidence to dispel that suspicion, the person shall be treated as such for the purposes of this Code. See *Note 1G*.

1.11 For the purposes of this Code, a juvenile is any person under the age of 17. If anyone appears to be under 17, and there is no clear evidence that they are 17 or over, they shall be treated as a juvenile for the purposes of this Code.

1.12 If a person appears to be blind, seriously visually impaired, deaf, unable to read or speak or has difficulty orally because of a speech impediment, they shall be treated as such for the purposes of this Code in the absence of clear evidence to the contrary.

1.13 'The appropriate adult' means, in the case of a:
(a) juvenile:
    (i) the parent, guardian or, if the juvenile is in the care of a local authority or voluntary organisation, a person representing that authority or organisation;
    (ii) a social worker of a local authority;
    (iii) failing these, some other responsible adult aged 18 or over who is not a police officer or employed by the police.
(b) person who is mentally disordered or mentally vulnerable: See *Note 1D*.
    (i) a relative, guardian or other person responsible for their care or custody;
    (ii) someone experienced in dealing with mentally disordered or mentally vulnerable people but who is not a police officer or employed by the police;
    (iii) failing these, some other responsible adult aged 18 or over who is not a police officer or employed by the police.

1.14 If this Code requires a person be given certain information, they do not have to be given it if at the time they are incapable of understanding what is said, are violent or may become violent or in urgent need of medical attention, but they must be given it as soon as practicable.

1.15 References to a custody officer include any police officer who for the time being, is performing the functions of a custody officer.

1.16 When this Code requires the prior authority or agreement of an officer of at least inspector or superintendent rank, that authority may be given by a sergeant or chief inspector authorised by section 107 of PACE to perform the functions of the higher rank under TACT.

1.17 In this Code:
(a) 'designated person' means a person other than a police officer, designated under the Police Reform Act 2002, Part 4 who has specified powers and duties of police officers conferred or imposed on them;
(b) reference to a police officer includes a designated person acting in the exercise or performance of the powers and duties conferred or imposed on them by their designation.
(c) where a search or other procedure to which this Code applies may only be carried out or observed by a person of the same sex as the detainee, the gender of the detainee and other parties present should be established and recorded in line with Annex I of this Code.

1.18 Designated persons are entitled to use reasonable force as follows:
(a) when exercising a power conferred on them which allows a police officer exercising that power to use reasonable force, a designated person has the same entitlement to use force; and
(b) at other times when carrying out duties conferred or imposed on them that also entitle them to use reasonable force, for example:
  • when at a police station carrying out the duty to keep detainees for whom they are responsible under control and to assist any other police officer or designated person to keep any detainee under control and to prevent their escape.
  • when securing, or assisting any other police officer or designated person in securing, the detention of a person at a police station.
  • when escorting, or assisting any other police officer or designated person in escorting, a detainee within a police station.

- for the purpose of saving life or limb; or
- preventing serious damage to property.

1.19 Nothing in this Code prevents the custody officer, or other officer given custody of the detainee, from allowing police staff who are not designated persons to carry out individual procedures or tasks at the police station if the law allows. However, the officer remains responsible for making sure the procedures and tasks are carried out correctly in accordance with the Codes of Practice (see *Note 3F*). Any such person must be:

(a) a person employed by a police force and under the direction and control of the Chief Officer of that force;

(b) employed by a person with whom a police force has a contract for the provision of services relating to persons arrested or otherwise in custody.

1.20 Designated persons and other police staff must have regard to any relevant provisions of this Code.

1.21 References to pocket books include any official report book issued to police officers or other police staff.

Notes for Guidance

1A Although certain sections of this Code apply specifically to people in custody at police stations, those there voluntarily to assist with an investigation should be treated with no less consideration, e.g. offered refreshments at appropriate times, and enjoy an absolute right to obtain legal advice or communicate with anyone outside the police station.

1B A person, including a parent or guardian, should not be an appropriate adult if they:
- *are:*
  - *~ suspected of involvement in the offence or involvement in the commission, preparation or instigation of acts of terrorism;*
  - *~ the victim;*
  - *~ a witness;*
  - *~ involved in the investigation.*
- *received admissions prior to attending to act as the appropriate adult.*

Note: If a juvenile's parent is estranged from the juvenile, they should not be asked to act as the appropriate adult if the juvenile expressly and specifically objects to their presence.

1C If a juvenile admits an offence to, or in the presence of, a social worker or member of a youth offending team other than during the time that person is acting as the juvenile's appropriate adult, another appropriate adult should be appointed in the interest of fairness.

1D In the case of people who are mentally disordered or otherwise mentally vulnerable, it may be more satisfactory if the appropriate adult is someone experienced or trained in their care rather than a relative lacking such qualifications. But if the detainee prefers a relative to a better qualified stranger or objects to a particular person their wishes should, if practicable, be respected.

1E A detainee should always be given an opportunity, when an appropriate adult is called to the police station, to consult privately with a solicitor in the appropriate adult's absence if they want. An appropriate adult is not subject to legal privilege.

1F A solicitor or independent custody visitor (formerly a lay visitor) present at the police station in that capacity may not be the appropriate adult.

1G 'Mentally vulnerable' applies to any detainee who, because of their mental state or capacity, may not understand the significance of what is said, of questions or of their replies. 'Mental disorder' is defined in the Mental Health Act 1983, section 1(2) as 'any disorder or disability of mind'. When the custody officer has any doubt about the mental state or capacity of a detainee, that detainee should be treated as mentally vulnerable and an appropriate adult called.

1H Paragraph 1.7 is intended to cover delays which may occur in processing detainees e.g. if:
- *a large number of suspects are brought into the station simultaneously to be placed in custody;*
- *interview rooms are all being used;*
- *there are difficulties contacting an appropriate adult, solicitor or interpreter.*

1I The custody officer must remind the appropriate adult and detainee about the right to legal advice and record any reasons for waiving it in accordance with section 6.

1J Not used

1K This Code does not affect the principle that all citizens have a duty to help police officers to prevent crime and discover offenders. This is a civic rather than a legal duty; but when police officers are trying to discover whether, or by whom, offences have been committed, they are entitled to question any person from whom they think useful information can be obtained, subject to the restrictions imposed by this Code. A person's declaration that they are unwilling to reply does not alter this entitlement.

1L If a person is moved from a police station to receive medical treatment, or for any other reason, the period of detention is still calculated from the time of arrest under section 41 of TACT (or, if a person was being detained under TACT Schedule 7 when arrested, from the time at which the examination under Schedule 7 began).

1M Under Paragraph 1 of Schedule 8 to TACT, all police stations are designated for detention of persons arrested under section 41 of TACT. Paragraph 4 of Schedule 8 requires that the constable who arrests a person under section 41 takes them as soon as practicable to the police station which the officer considers is 'most appropriate'.

1N The powers under Part IV of PACE to detain and release on bail (before or after charge) a person arrested under section 24 of PACE for any offence (see PACE Code G (Arrest)) do not apply to persons whilst they are detained under the terrorism powers following their arrest/detention under section 41 of, or Schedule 7 to, TACT. If when the grounds for detention under these powers cease the person is arrested under section 24 of PACE for a specific offence, the detention and bail provisions of PACE will apply and must be considered from the time of that arrest.

2 Custody records

2.1 When a person is:

- brought to a police station following arrest under TACT section 41,
- arrested under TACT section 41 at a police station having attended there voluntarily,
- brought to a police station and there detained to be questioned in accordance with an authorisation under section 22 of the Counter-Terrorism Act 2008 (post-charge questioning) (see *Notes 15A* and *15B*), or
- at a police station and there detained when authority for post-charge questioning is given under section 22 of the Counter-Terrorism Act 2008 (see *Notes 15A* and *15B*),

they should be brought before the custody officer as soon as practicable after their arrival at the station or, if appropriate, following the authorisation of post-charge questioning or following arrest after attending the police station voluntarily see *Note 3H*. A person is deemed to be 'at a police station' for these purposes if they are within the boundary of any building or enclosed yard which forms part of that police station.

2.2 A separate custody record must be opened as soon as practicable for each person described in paragraph 2.1. All information recorded under this Code must be recorded as soon as practicable in the custody record unless otherwise specified. Any audio or video recording made in the custody area is not part of the custody record.

2.3 If any action requires the authority of an officer of a specified rank, this must be noted in the custody record, subject to paragraph 2.8.

2.3A If a person is arrested under TACT, section 41 and taken to a police station as a result of a search in the exercise of any stop and search power to which PACE Code A (Stop and search) or the 'search powers code' issued under TACT applies, the officer carrying out the search is responsible for ensuring that the record of that stop and search is made as part of the person's custody record. The custody officer must then ensure that the person is asked if they want a copy of the search record and if they do, that they are given a copy as soon as practicable. The person's entitlement to a copy of the search record which is made as part of their custody record is in addition to, and does not affect, their entitlement to a copy of their custody record or any other provisions of section 2 (Custody records) of this Code. See Code A *paragraph 4.2B* and the TACT search powers code *paragraph 5.3.5*).

2.4 The custody officer is responsible for the custody record's accuracy and completeness and for making sure the record or copy of the record accompanies a detainee if they are transferred to another police station. The record shall show the:
• time and reason for transfer;
• time a person is released from detention.

2.5 A solicitor or appropriate adult must be permitted to inspect a detainee's custody record as soon as practicable after their arrival at the station and at any other time whilst the person is detained. Arrangements for this access must be agreed with the custody officer and may not unreasonably interfere with the custody officer's duties or the justifiable needs of the investigation.

2.6 When a detainee leaves police detention or is taken before a court they, their legal representative or appropriate adult shall be given, on request, a copy of the custody record as soon as practicable. This entitlement lasts for 12 months after release.

2.7 The detainee, appropriate adult or legal representative shall be permitted to inspect the original custody record once the detained person is no longer being held under the provisions of TACT section 41 and Schedule 8 or being questioned after charge as authorised under section 22 of the Counter-Terrorism Act 2008 (see *section 15*), provided they give reasonable notice of their request. Any such inspection shall be noted in the custody record.

2.8 All entries in custody records must be timed and identified by the maker. Nothing in this Code requires the identity of officers or other police staff to be recorded or disclosed in the case of enquiries linked to the investigation of terrorism. In these cases, they shall use their warrant or other identification numbers and the name of their police station, see *Note 2A*. If records are entered on computer [these] shall also be timed and contain the operator's identification.

2.9 The fact and time of any detainee's refusal to sign a custody record, when asked in accordance with this Code, must be recorded.

Note for Guidance

2A   The purpose of paragraph 2.8 is to protect those involved in terrorist investigations or arrests of terrorist suspects from the possibility that those arrested, their associates or other individuals or groups may threaten or cause harm to those involved.

3 Initial action

(a) Detained persons—normal procedure

3.1 When a person to whom paragraph 2.1 applies is at a police station, the custody officer must make sure the person is told clearly about the following continuing rights which may be exercised at any stage during the period in custody:
(i)   the right to have someone informed of their arrest as in *section 5*;
(ii) the right to consult privately with a solicitor and that free independent legal advice is available;
(iii) the right to consult this Code of Practice. See *Note 3D*.

3.2 The detainee must also be given:
- a written notice setting out:
  ~ the above three rights;
  ~ the arrangements for obtaining legal advice;
  ~ the right to a copy of the custody record as in *paragraph 2.6*;
  ~ the caution in the terms prescribed in *section 10*.
- an additional written notice briefly setting out their entitlements while in custody, see *Notes 3A* and *3B*.

Note: The detainee shall be asked to sign the custody record to acknowledge receipt of these notices. Any refusal must be recorded on the custody record.

3.3 A citizen of an independent Commonwealth country or a national of a foreign country, including the Republic of Ireland, must be informed as soon as practicable about their rights of communication with their High Commission, Embassy or Consulate. See *section 7*.

3.4 The custody officer shall:
- record that the person was arrested under section 41 of TACT and the reason(s) for the arrest on the custody record. See *paragraph 10.2* and *Note 3G*.
- note on the custody record any comment the detainee makes in relation to the arresting officer's account but shall not invite comment. If the arresting officer is not physically present when the detainee is brought to a police station, the arresting officer's account must be made available to the custody officer remotely or by a third party on the arresting officer's behalf;
- note any comment the detainee makes in respect of the decision to detain them but shall not invite comment;
- not put specific questions to the detainee regarding their involvement in any offence, nor in respect of any comments they may make in response to the arresting officer's account or the decision to place them in detention. *See paragraphs 14.1* and *14.2* and *Notes 3H, 14A* and *14B*. Such an exchange is likely to constitute an interview as in *paragraph 11.1* and require the associated safeguards in section 11.

See *paragraph 11.8A* in respect of unsolicited comments.

If the first review of detention is carried out at this time, see paragraphs 14.1 and 14.2, and Part II of Schedule 8 to the Terrorism Act 2000 in respect of action by the review officer.

3.5 The custody officer or other custody staff as directed by the custody officer shall:
(a) ask the detainee, whether at this time, they:
  (i) would like legal advice, see *paragraph 6.4*;
  (ii) want someone informed of their detention, see *section 5*;
(b) ask the detainee to sign the custody record to confirm their decisions in respect of (*a*);
(c) determine whether the detainee:
  (i) is, or might be, in need of medical treatment or attention, see *section 9*;
  (ii) requires:
    • an appropriate adult;
    • help to check documentation;
    • an interpreter.
(d) record the decision in respect of (*c*).

Where any duties under this paragraph have been carried out by custody staff at the direction of the custody officer, the outcomes shall, as soon as practicable, be reported to the custody officer who retains overall responsibility for the detainee's care and safe custody and ensuring it complies with this Code. See *Note 3I*.

3.6 When these needs are determined, the custody officer is responsible for initiating an assessment to consider whether the detainee is likely to present specific risks to custody staff, any individual who may have contact with detainee (e.g. legal advisers, medical staff), or themselves. Such assessments should always include a check on the Police National Computer, to be carried out as soon as practicable, to identify any risks highlighted in relation to the detainee. Although such assessments are primarily the custody officer's responsibility, it will be necessary to obtain information from other sources, especially the investigation team, *see Note 3E*, the arresting officer or an appropriate healthcare professional, see *paragraph 9.15*. Reasons for delaying the initiation or completion of the assessment must be recorded.

3.7 Chief Officers should ensure that arrangements for proper and effective risk assessments required by *paragraph 3.6* are implemented in respect of all detainees at police stations in their area.

3.8 Risk assessments must follow a structured process which clearly defines the categories of risk to be considered and the results must be incorporated in the detainee's custody record. The custody officer is responsible for making sure those responsible for the detainee's custody are appropriately briefed about the risks. The content of any risk assessment and any analysis of the level of risk relating to the person's detention is not required to be shown or provided to the detainee or any person acting on behalf of the detainee. If no specific risks are identified by the assessment, that should be noted in the custody record. See *Note 3F* and *paragraph 9.15*.

3.8A The content of any risk assessment and any analysis of the level of risk relating to the person's detention is not required to be shown or provided to the detainee or any person acting on behalf of the detainee. But information should not be withheld from any person acting on the detainee's behalf, for example, an appropriate adult, solicitor or interpreter, if to do so might put that person at risk.

3.9 Custody officers are responsible for implementing the response to any specific risk assessment, which should include for example:
- reducing opportunities for self harm;
- calling an appropriate healthcare professional;

- increasing levels of monitoring or observation;
- reducing the risk to those who come into contact with the detainee.

See *Note 3F*

3.10 Risk assessment is an ongoing process and assessments must always be subject to review if circumstances change.

3.11 If video cameras are installed in the custody area, notices shall be prominently displayed showing cameras are in use. Any request to have video cameras switched off shall be refused.

3.12 A constable, prison officer or other person authorised by the Secretary of State may take any steps which are reasonably necessary for:

(a) photographing the detained person;

(b) measuring the person, or

(c) identifying the person.

3.13 Paragraph 3.12 concerns the power in TACT Schedule 8 Paragraph 2. The power in TACT Schedule 8 Paragraph 2 does not cover the taking of fingerprints, intimate samples or non- intimate samples, which is covered in TACT Schedule 8 paragraphs 10 to 15.

(b) Detained persons—special groups

3.14 If the detainee appears deaf or there is doubt about their hearing or speaking ability or ability to understand English, and the custody officer cannot establish effective communication, the custody officer must, as soon as practicable, call an interpreter for assistance in the action under *paragraphs 3.1 to 3.5*. See *section 13*.

3.15 If the detainee is a juvenile, the custody officer must, if it is practicable, ascertain the identity of a person responsible for their welfare. That person:

- may be:
  ~ the parent or guardian;
  ~ if the juvenile is in local authority or voluntary organisation care, or is otherwise being looked after under the Children Act 1989, a person appointed by that authority or organisation to have responsibility for the juvenile's welfare;
  ~ any other person who has, for the time being, assumed responsibility for the juvenile's welfare.
- must be informed as soon as practicable that the juvenile has been arrested, why they have been arrested and where they are detained. This right is in addition to the juvenile's right in *section 5* not to be held incommunicado. See *Note 3C*.

3.16 If a juvenile is known to be subject to a court order under which a person or organisation is given any degree of statutory responsibility to supervise or otherwise monitor them, reasonable steps must also be taken to notify that person or organisation (the 'responsible officer'). The responsible officer will normally be a member of a Youth Offending Team, except for a curfew order which involves electronic monitoring when the contractor providing the monitoring will normally be the responsible officer.

3.17 If the detainee is a juvenile, mentally disordered or otherwise mentally vulnerable, the custody officer must, as soon as practicable:
• inform the appropriate adult, who in the case of a juvenile may or may not be a person responsible for their welfare, as in *paragraph 3.15*, of:
  ~ the grounds for their detention;
  ~ their whereabouts.
• ask the adult to come to the police station to see the detainee.

3.18 If the appropriate adult is:
• already at the police station, the provisions of *paragraphs 3.1* to *3.5* must be complied with in the appropriate adult's presence;
• not at the station when these provisions are complied with, they must be complied with again in the presence of the appropriate adult when they arrive.

3.19 The detainee shall be advised that:
• the duties of the appropriate adult include giving advice and assistance;
• they can consult privately with the appropriate adult at any time.

3.20 If the detainee, or appropriate adult on the detainee's behalf, asks for a solicitor to be called to give legal advice, the provisions of *section 6* apply.

3.21 If the detainee is blind, seriously visually impaired or unable to read, the custody officer shall make sure their solicitor, relative, appropriate adult or some other person likely to take an interest in them and not involved in the investigation is available to help check any documentation. When this Code requires written consent or signing the person assisting may be asked to sign instead, if the detainee prefers. This paragraph does not require an appropriate adult to be called solely to assist in checking and signing documentation for a person who is not a juvenile, or mentally disordered or otherwise mentally vulnerable (see *paragraph 3.17*).

(d) Documentation

3.22 The grounds for a person's detention shall be recorded, in the person's presence if practicable.

3.23 Action taken under *paragraphs 3.14* to *3.22* shall be recorded.

Notes for Guidance

3A The notice of entitlements should:
- list the entitlements in this Code, including:
  - ~ *visits and contact with outside parties where practicable, including special provisions for Commonwealth citizens and foreign nationals;*
  - ~ *reasonable standards of physical comfort;*
  - ~ *adequate food and drink;*
  - ~ *access to toilets and washing facilities, clothing, medical attention, and exercise when practicable.*
- mention the:
  - ~ *provisions relating to the conduct of interviews;*
  - ~ *circumstances in which an appropriate adult should be available to assist the detainee and their statutory rights to make representation whenever the period of their detention is reviewed.*

3B In addition to notices in English, translations should be available in Welsh, the main minority ethnic languages and the principal European languages whenever they are likely to be helpful. Audio versions of the notice should also be made available. Access to 'easy read' illustrated versions should also be provided if they are available.

3C If the juvenile is in local authority or voluntary organisation care but living with their parents or other adults responsible for their welfare, although there is no legal obligation to inform them, they should normally be contacted, as well as the authority or organisation unless suspected of involvement in the offence concerned. Even if the juvenile is not living with their parents, consideration should be given to informing them.

3D The right to consult this or other relevant Codes of Practice does not entitle the person concerned to delay unreasonably any necessary investigative or administrative action whilst they do so. Examples of action which need not be delayed unreasonably include:
- *searching detainees at the police station;*
- *taking fingerprints or non-intimate samples without consent for evidential purposes.*

3E The investigation team will include any officer involved in questioning a suspect, gathering or analysing evidence in relation to the offences of which the detainee is suspected of having committed. Should a custody officer require information from the investigation team, the first point of contact should be the officer in charge of the investigation.

3F Home Office Circular 32/2000 provides more detailed guidance on risk assessments and identifies key risk areas which should always be considered.

3G Arrests under TACT section 41 can only be made where an officer has reasonable grounds to suspect that the individual concerned is a 'terrorist'. This differs from the PACE power of arrest in that it need not be linked to a specific offence. There may also be circumstances where an arrest under TACT is made on the grounds of sensitive information which can not be disclosed. In such circumstances, the grounds for arrest may be given in terms of the interpretation of a 'terrorist' set out in TACT section 40(1)(a) or (b).

3H For the purpose of arrests under TACT section 41, the review officer is responsible for authorising detention (see paragraphs 14.1 and 14.2, and Notes 14A and 14B). The review officer's role is explained in TACT Schedule 8 Part II. A person may be detained after arrest pending the first review, which must take place as soon as practicable after the person's arrest.

3I A custody officer or other officer who, in accordance with this Code, allows or directs the carrying out of any task or action relating to a detainee's care, treatment, rights and entitlements by another officer or any police staff must be satisfied that the officer or police staff concerned are suitable, trained and competent to carry out the task or action in question.

4 Detainee's property

(a) Action

4.1 The custody officer is responsible for:
(a) ascertaining what property a detainee:
   (i) has with them when they come to the police station, either on first arrival at the police station or any subsequent arrivals at a police station in connection with that detention;
   (ii) might have acquired for an unlawful or harmful purpose while in custody.
(b) the safekeeping of any property taken from a detainee which remains at the police station.
The custody officer may search the detainee or authorise their being searched to the extent they consider necessary, provided a search of intimate parts of the body or involving the removal of more than outer clothing is only made as in *Annex A*. A search may only be

carried out by an officer of the same sex as the detainee. See *Note 4A* and *Annex I*.

4.2 Detainees may retain clothing and personal effects at their own risk unless the custody officer considers they may use them to cause harm to themselves or others, interfere with evidence, damage property, effect an escape or they are needed as evidence. In this event the custody officer may withhold such articles as they consider necessary and must tell the detainee why.

4.3 Personal effects are those items a detainee may lawfully need, use or refer to while in detention but do not include cash and other items of value.

(b) Documentation

4.4 It is a matter for the custody officer to determine whether a record should be made of the property a detained person has with him or had taken from him on arrest (*see Note 4D*). Any record made is not required to be kept as part of the custody record but the custody record should be noted as to where such a record exists. Whenever a record is made the detainee shall be allowed to check and sign the record of property as correct. Any refusal to sign shall be recorded.

4.5 If a detainee is not allowed to keep any article of clothing or personal effects, the reason must be recorded.

Notes for Guidance

4A PACE, Section 54(1) and paragraph 4.1 require a detainee to be searched when it is clear the custody officer will have continuing duties in relation to that detainee or when that detainee's behaviour or offence makes an inventory appropriate. They do not require every detainee to be searched, e.g. if it is clear a person will only be detained for a short period and is not to be placed in a cell, the custody officer may decide not to search them. In such a case the custody record will be endorsed 'not searched', paragraph 4.4 will not apply, and the detainee will be invited to sign the entry. If the detainee refuses, the custody officer will be obliged to ascertain what property they have in accordance with paragraph 4.1.

4B Paragraph 4.4 does not require the custody officer to record on the custody record property in the detainee's possession on arrest if, by virtue of its nature, quantity or size, it is not practicable to remove it to the police station.

4C Paragraph 4.4 does not require items of clothing worn by the person be recorded unless withheld by the custody officer as in paragraph 4.2.

4D Section 43(2) of TACT allows a constable to search a person who has been arrested under section 41 to discover whether they have anything in their possession that may constitute evidence that they are a terrorist.

5 Right not to be held incommunicado

(a) Action

5.1 Any person to whom this Code applies who is held in custody at a police station or other premises may, on request, have one named person who is a friend, relative or a person known to them who is likely to take an interest in their welfare informed at public expense of their whereabouts as soon as practicable. If the person cannot be contacted the detainee may choose up to two alternatives. If they cannot be contacted, the person in charge of detention or the investigation has discretion to allow further attempts until the information has been conveyed. See *Notes 5D* and *5E*.

5.2 The exercise of the above right in respect of each person nominated may be delayed only in accordance with *Annex B*.

5.3 The above right may be exercised each time a detainee is taken to another police station or returned to a police station having been previously transferred to prison. This Code does not afford such a right to a person on transfer to a prison, where a detainee's rights will be governed by Prison Rules see *Annex J paragraph 4*.

5.4 If the detainee agrees, they may at the custody officer's discretion, receive visits from friends, family or others likely to take an interest in their welfare, or in whose welfare the detainee has an interest. Custody Officers should liaise closely with the investigation team (*see Note 3E*) to allow risk assessments to be made where particular visitors have been requested by the detainee or identified themselves to police. In circumstances where the nature of the investigation means that such requests can not be met, consideration should be given, in conjunction with a representative of the relevant scheme, to increasing the frequency of visits from independent visitor schemes. See *Notes 5B* and *5C*.

5.5 If a friend, relative or person with an interest in the detainee's welfare enquires about their whereabouts, this information shall be given if the suspect agrees and *Annex B* does not apply. See *Note 5E*.

5.6 The detainee shall be given writing materials, on request, and allowed to telephone one person for a reasonable time, see *Notes 5A* and *5F*. Either or both these privileges may be denied or delayed if an officer of inspector rank or above considers sending a letter or making a telephone call may result in any of the consequences in *Annex B paragraphs 1* and *2*, particularly in relation to the making of a telephone call in a language which an officer listening to the call (see *paragraph 5.7*) does not understand. See *Note 5G*.

Nothing in this paragraph permits the restriction or denial of the rights in *paragraphs 5.1* and *6.1*.

5.7 Before any letter or message is sent, or telephone call made, the detainee shall be informed that what they say in any letter, call or message (other than in a communication to a solicitor) may be read or listened to and may be given in evidence. A telephone call may be terminated if it is being abused *see Note 5G*. The costs can be at public expense at the custody officer's discretion.

5.8 Any delay or denial of the rights in this section should be proportionate and should last no longer than necessary.

(b) Documentation

5.9 A record must be kept of any:
(a) request made under this section and the action taken;
(b) letters, messages or telephone calls made or received or visit received;
(c) refusal by the detainee to have information about them given to an outside enquirer, or any refusal to see a visitor. The detainee must be asked to countersign the record accordingly and any refusal recorded.

Notes for Guidance

5A A person may request an interpreter to interpret a telephone call or translate a letter.

5B At the custody officer's discretion and subject to the detainee's consent, visits should be allowed when possible, subject to sufficient personnel being available to supervise a visit and any possible hindrance to the investigation. Custody Officers should bear in mind the exceptional nature of prolonged TACT detention and consider the potential benefits that visits may bring to the health and welfare of detainees who are held for extended periods.

5C Official visitors should be given access following consultation with the officer who has overall responsibility for the investigation provided the detainee consents, and they do not compromise safety or security or unduly delay or interfere with the progress of an investigation. *Official visitors should still be required to provide appropriate identification and subject to any screening process in place at the place of detention. Official visitors may include:*

- *An accredited faith representative;*
- *Members of either House of Parliament;*
- *Public officials needing to interview the prisoner in the course of their duties;*
- *Other persons visiting with the approval of the officer who has overall responsibility for the investigation;*
- *Consular officials visiting a detainee who is a national of the country they represent subject to section 7 of this Code.*

Visits from appropriate members of the Independent Custody Visitors Scheme should be dealt with in accordance with the separate Code of Practice on Independent Custody Visiting.

5D *If the detainee does not know anyone to contact for advice or support or cannot contact a friend or relative, the custody officer should bear in mind any local voluntary bodies or other organisations that might be able to help. Paragraph 6.1 applies if legal advice is required.*

5E *In some circumstances it may not be appropriate to use the telephone to disclose information under paragraphs 5.1 and 5.5.*

5F *The telephone call at paragraph 5.6 is in addition to any communication under paragraphs 5.1 and 6.1. Further calls may be made at the custody officer's discretion.*

5G *The nature of terrorism investigations means that officers should have particular regard to the possibility of suspects attempting to pass information which may be detrimental to public safety, or to an investigation.*

6 Right to legal advice

(a) Action

6.1 Unless *Annex B* applies, all detainees must be informed that they may at any time consult and communicate privately with a solicitor, whether in person, in writing or by telephone, and that free independent legal advice is available from the duty solicitor. Where an appropriate adult is in attendance, they must also be informed of this right. See *paragraph 3.1, Note 1I, Notes 6B and 6J*

6.2 A poster advertising the right to legal advice must be prominently displayed in the charging area of every police station. See *Note 6G.*

6.3 No police officer should, at any time, do or say anything with the intention of dissuading any person who is entitled to legal advice in accordance with this Code, from obtaining legal advice. See *Note 6ZA*.

6.4 The exercise of the right of access to legal advice may be delayed exceptionally only as in *Annex B*. Whenever legal advice is requested, and unless *Annex B* applies, the custody officer must act without delay to secure the provision of such advice. If, on being informed or reminded of this right, the detainee declines to speak to a solicitor in person, the officer should point out that the right includes the right to speak with a solicitor on the telephone (see *paragraph 5.6*). If the detainee continues to waive this right the officer should ask them why and any reasons should be recorded on the custody record or the interview record as appropriate. Reminders of the right to legal advice must be given as in *paragraphs 3.5, 11.3* of this Code and PACE Code D on the Identification of Persons by Police Officers, *paragraphs 3.17(ii)* and *6.3*. Once it is clear a detainee does not want to speak to a solicitor in person or by telephone they should cease to be asked their reasons. See *Note 6J*.

6.5 An officer of the rank of Commander or Assistant Chief Constable may give a direction under TACT Schedule 8 paragraph 9 that a detainee may only consult a solicitor within the sight and hearing of a qualified officer. Such a direction may only be given if the officer has reasonable grounds to believe that if it were not, it may result in one of the consequences set out in TACT Schedule 8 paragraph 8(4) or (5)(c). See *Annex B paragraph 3* and *Note 6I*. A 'qualified officer' means a police officer who:

(a) is at least the rank of inspector;
(b) is of the uniformed branch of the force of which the officer giving the direction is a member, and
(c) in the opinion of the officer giving the direction, has no connection with the detained person's case.

Officers considering the use of this power should first refer to *Home Office Circular 40/2003*.

6.6 In the case of a person who is a juvenile or is mentally disordered or otherwise mentally vulnerable, an appropriate adult should consider whether legal advice from a solicitor is required. If the person indicates that they do not want legal advice, the appropriate adult has the right to ask for a solicitor to attend if this would be in the best interests of the person. However, the person cannot be forced to see the solicitor if they are adamant that they do not wish to do so.

6.7 A detainee who wants legal advice may not be interviewed or continue to be interviewed until they have received such advice unless:

(a) *Annex B* applies, when the restriction on drawing adverse inferences from silence in *Annex C* will apply because the detainee is not allowed an opportunity to consult a solicitor; or

(b) an officer of superintendent rank or above has reasonable grounds for believing that:

   (i) the consequent delay might:

- lead to interference with, or harm to, evidence connected with an offence;
- lead to interference with, or physical harm to, other people;
- lead to serious loss of, or damage to, property;
- lead to alerting other people suspected of having committed an offence but not yet arrested for it;
- hinder the recovery of property obtained in consequence of the commission of an offence.

See *Note 6A*

   (ii) when a solicitor, including a duty solicitor, has been contacted and has agreed to attend, awaiting their arrival would cause unreasonable delay to the process of investigation.

Note: In these cases the restriction on drawing adverse inferences from silence in *Annex C* will apply because the detainee is not allowed an opportunity to consult a solicitor.

(c) the solicitor the detainee has nominated or selected from a list:

   (i) cannot be contacted;

   (ii) has previously indicated they do not wish to be contacted; or

   (iii) having been contacted, has declined to attend; and

- the detainee has been advised of the Duty Solicitor Scheme but has declined to ask for the duty solicitor;
- in these circumstances the interview may be started or continued without further delay provided an officer of inspector rank or above has agreed to the interview proceeding.

Note: The restriction on drawing adverse inferences from silence in *Annex C* will not apply because the detainee is allowed an opportunity to consult the duty solicitor;

(d) the detainee changes their mind, about wanting legal advice or (as the case may be) about wanting a solicitor present at the interview, and states that they no longer wish to speak to a solicitor. In these circumstances the interview may be started or continued without delay provided that:

   (i) an officer of inspector rank or above:

- speaks to the detainee to enquire about the reasons for their change of mind (see *Note 6J*), and
- makes, or directs the making of, reasonable efforts to ascertain the solicitor's expected time of arrival and to inform the solicitor that the suspect has stated that they wish to change their mind and the reason (if given);
    - (ii) the detainee's reason for their change of mind (if given) and the outcome of the action in (i) are recorded in the custody record;
    - (iii) the detainee, after being informed of the outcome of the action in (i) above, confirms in writing that they want the interview to proceed without speaking or further speaking to a solicitor or (as the case may be) without a solicitor being present and do not wish to wait for a solicitor by signing an entry to this effect in the custody record;
    - (iv) an officer of inspector rank or above is satisfied that it is proper for the interview to proceed in these circumstances and:
- gives authority in writing for the interview to proceed and if the authority is not recorded in the custody record, the officer must ensure that the custody record shows the date and time of the authority and where it is recorded; and
- takes or directs the taking of, reasonable steps to inform the solicitor that the authority has been given and the time when the interview is expected to commence and records or causes to be recorded, the outcome of this action in the custody record.
    - (v) When the interview starts and the interviewer reminds the suspect of their right to legal advice (see *paragraph 11.3*) and the Code of Practice issued under paragraph 3 of Schedule 8 to the Terrorism Act 2000 for the video recording with sound of interviews, the interviewer shall then ensure that the following is recorded in the interview record made in accordance with that Code:
        - confirmation that the detainee has changed their mind about wanting legal advice or (as the case may be) about wanting a solicitor present and the reasons for it if given;
        - the fact that authority for the interview to proceed has been given and, subject to *paragraph 2.8*, the name of the authorising officer;
        - that if the solicitor arrives at the station before the interview is completed, the detainee will be so informed without delay and a break will be taken to allow them to speak to the solicitor if they wish, unless *paragraph 6.7(a)* applies, and
        - that at any time during the interview, the detainee may again ask for legal advice and that if they do, a break will

be taken to allow them to speak to the solicitor, unless
paragraph 6.7(a), (b), or *(c)* applies.

Note: In these circumstances the restriction on drawing adverse
inferences from silence in *Annex C* will not apply because the
detainee is allowed an opportunity to consult a solicitor if they
wish.

6.8 If *paragraph 6.7(a)* applies, where the reason for authorising the
delay ceases to apply, there may be no further delay in permitting
the exercise of the right in the absence of a further authorisation
unless *paragraph 6.7(b), (c)* or *(d)* applies. If *paragraph 6.7(b)(i)* applies,
once sufficient information has been obtained to avert the risk,
questioning must cease until the detainee has received legal advice
unless *paragraph 6.7(a), (b)(ii), (c)* or *(d)* applies.

6.9 A detainee who has been permitted to consult a solicitor shall
be entitled on request to have the solicitor present when they are
interviewed unless one of the exceptions in *paragraph 6.7* applies.

6.10 The solicitor may only be required to leave the interview if
their conduct is such that the interviewer is unable properly to put
questions to the suspect. See *Notes 6C* and *6D*.

6.11 If the interviewer considers a solicitor is acting in such a way,
they will stop the interview and consult an officer not below superintendent rank, if one is readily available, and otherwise an officer
not below inspector rank not connected with the investigation.
After speaking to the solicitor, the officer consulted will decide if the
interview should continue in the presence of that solicitor. If they
decide it should not, the suspect will be given the opportunity to
consult another solicitor before the interview continues and that
solicitor given an opportunity to be present at the interview. See
Note 6D.

6.12 The removal of a solicitor from an interview is a serious step
and, if it occurs, the officer of superintendent rank or above who
took the decision will consider if the incident should be reported to
the Solicitors Regulatory Authority. If the decision to remove the
solicitor has been taken by an officer below superintendent rank,
the facts must be reported to an officer of superintendent rank or
above who will similarly consider whether a report to the Solicitors
Regulatory Authority would be appropriate. When the solicitor concerned is a duty solicitor, the report should be both to the Solicitors
Regulatory Authority and to the Legal Services Commission.

6.13 'Solicitor' in this Code means:
- a solicitor who holds a current practising certificate;
- an accredited or probationary representative included on the register of representatives maintained by the Legal Services Commission.

6.14 An accredited or probationary representative sent to provide advice by, and on behalf of, a solicitor shall be admitted to the police station for this purpose unless an officer of inspector rank or above considers such a visit will hinder the investigation and directs otherwise. Hindering the investigation does not include giving proper legal advice to a detainee as in *Note 6C*. Once admitted to the police station, *paragraphs 6.7* to *6.11* apply.

6.15 In exercising their discretion under *paragraph 6.14*, the officer should take into account in particular:
- whether:
  ~ the identity and status of an accredited or probationary representative have been satisfactorily established;
  ~ they are of suitable character to provide legal advice,
- any other matters in any written letter of authorisation provided by the solicitor on whose behalf the person is attending the police station. See *Note 6E*.

6.16 If the inspector refuses access to an accredited or probationary representative or a decision is taken that such a person should not be permitted to remain at an interview, the inspector must notify the solicitor on whose behalf the representative was acting and give them an opportunity to make alternative arrangements. The detainee must be informed and the custody record noted.

6.17 If a solicitor arrives at the station to see a particular person, that person must, unless *Annex B* applies, be so informed whether or not they are being interviewed and asked if they would like to see the solicitor. This applies even if the detainee has declined legal advice or, having requested it, subsequently agreed to be interviewed without receiving advice. The solicitor's attendance and the detainee's decision must be noted in the custody record.

(b) Documentation

6.18 Any request for legal advice and the action taken shall be recorded.

6.19 A record shall be made in the interview record if a detainee asks for legal advice and an interview is begun either in the absence of a solicitor or their representative, or they have been required to leave an interview.

Notes for Guidance

6ZA No police officer or police staff shall indicate to any suspect, except to answer a direct question, that the period for which they are liable to be detained, or the time taken to complete the interview, might be reduced:
- *if they do not ask for legal advice or do not want a solicitor present when they are interviewed; or*
- *if after asking for legal advice, they change their mind about wanting it or (as the case may be) wanting a solicitor present when they are interviewed and agree to be interviewed without waiting for a solicitor.*

6A In considering if paragraph 6.7(b) applies, the officer should, if practicable, ask the solicitor for an estimate of how long it will take to come to the station and relate this to the time detention is permitted, the time of day (i.e. whether the rest period under paragraph 12.2 is imminent) and the requirements of other investigations. If the solicitor is on their way or is to set off immediately, it will not normally be appropriate to begin an interview before they arrive. If it appears necessary to begin an interview before the solicitor's arrival, they should be given an indication of how long the police would be able to wait so there is an opportunity to make arrangements for someone else to provide legal advice. Nothing within this section is intended to prevent police from ascertaining immediately after the arrest of an individual whether a threat to public safety exists (see paragraph 11.2).

6B A detainee has a right to free legal advice and to be represented by a solicitor. This Note for Guidance explains the arrangements which enable detainees to whom this Code applies to obtain legal advice. An outline of these arrangements is also included in the Notice of Rights and Entitlements given to detainees in accordance with paragraph 3.2.

The detainee can ask for free advice from a solicitor they know or if they do not know a solicitor or the solicitor they know cannot be contacted, from the duty solicitor.

To arrange free legal advice, the police should telephone the Defence Solicitor Call Centre (DSCC). The call centre will contact either the duty solicitor or the solicitor requested by the detainee as appropriate.

When a detainee wants to pay for legal advice themselves:
- *the DSCC will contact a solicitor of their choice on their behalf;*
- *they should be given an opportunity to consult a specific solicitor or another solicitor from that solicitor's firm. If this solicitor is not available, they may choose up to two alternatives. If these alternatives*

are not available, the custody officer has discretion to allow further attempts until a solicitor has been contacted and agreed to provide advice;

- *they are entitled to a private consultation with their chosen solicitor on the telephone or the solicitor may decide to come to the police station;*
- *if their chosen solicitor cannot be contacted, the DSCC may still be called to arrange free legal advice.*

Apart from carrying out duties necessary to implement these arrangements, an officer must not advise the suspect about any particular firm of solicitors.

6C *The solicitor's only role in the police station is to protect and advance the legal rights of their client. On occasions this may require the solicitor to give advice which has the effect of the client avoiding giving evidence which strengthens a prosecution case. The solicitor may intervene in order to seek clarification, challenge an improper question to their client or the manner in which it is put, advise their client not to reply to particular questions, or if they wish to give their client further legal advice. Paragraph 6.9 only applies if the solicitor's approach or conduct prevents or unreasonably obstructs proper questions being put to the suspect or the suspect's response being recorded. Examples of unacceptable conduct include answering questions on a suspect's behalf or providing written replies for the suspect to quote.*

6D *An officer who takes the decision to exclude a solicitor must be in a position to satisfy the court the decision was properly made. In order to do this they may need to witness what is happening.*

6E *If an officer of at least inspector rank considers a particular solicitor or firm of solicitors is persistently sending probationary representatives who are unsuited to provide legal advice, they should inform an officer of at least superintendent rank, who may wish to take the matter up with the Solicitors Regulatory Authority.*

6F *Subject to the constraints of Annex B, a solicitor may advise more than one client in an investigation if they wish. Any question of a conflict of interest is for the solicitor under their professional code of conduct. If, however, waiting for a solicitor to give advice to one client may lead to unreasonable delay to the interview with another, the provisions of paragraph 6.7(b) may apply.*

6G *In addition to a poster in English, a poster or posters containing translations into Welsh, the main minority ethnic languages and the principal European languages should be displayed wherever they are likely to be helpful and it is practicable to do so.*

6H Not used

6I Whenever a detainee exercises their right to legal advice by consulting or communicating with a solicitor, they must be allowed to do so in private. This right to consult or communicate in private is fundamental. Except as allowed by the Terrorism Act 2000, Schedule 8, paragraph 9, if the requirement for privacy is compromised because what is said or written by the detainee or solicitor for the purpose of giving and receiving legal advice is overheard, listened to, or read by others without the informed consent of the detainee, the right will effectively have been denied. When a detainee speaks to a solicitor on the telephone, they should be allowed to do so in private unless a direction under Schedule 8, paragraph 9 of the Terrorism Act 2000 has been given or this is impractical because of the design and layout of the custody area, or the location of telephones. However, the normal expectation should be that facilities will be available, unless they are being used, at all police stations to enable detainees to speak in private to a solicitor either face to face or over the telephone.

6J A detainee is not obliged to give reasons for declining legal advice and should not be pressed to do so.

7 Citizens of independent Commonwealth countries or foreign nationals

(a) Action

7.1 A detainee who is a citizen of an independent Commonwealth country or a national of a foreign country, including the Republic of Ireland, has the right, upon request, to communicate at any time with the appropriate High Commission, Embassy or Consulate. That detainee must be informed as soon as practicable of this right and asked if they want to have their High Commission, Embassy or Consulate told of their whereabouts and the grounds for their detention. Such a request should be acted upon as soon as practicable. See *Note 7A*.

7.2 A detainee who is a citizen of a country with which a bilateral consular convention or agreement is in force requiring notification of arrest, must also be informed that subject to *paragraph 7.4*, notification of their arrest will be sent to the appropriate High Commission, Embassy or Consulate as soon as practicable, whether or not they request it. Details of the countries to which this requirement currently applies are available from

http://www.fco.gov.uk/en/publications-and-documents/treaties/treaty-texts/prisoner- transfer-agreements.

7.3 Consular officers may, if the detainee agrees, visit one of their nationals in police detention to talk to them and, if required, to arrange for legal advice. Such visits shall take place out of the hearing of a police officer.

7.4 Notwithstanding the provisions of consular conventions, if the detainee claims that they are a refugee or have applied or intend to apply for asylum the custody officer must ensure that the United Kingdom Borders Agency (UKBA) are informed as soon as practicable of the claim. UKBA will then determine whether compliance with relevant international obligations requires notification of arrest to be sent and will inform the custody officer as to what action police need to take.

(b) Documentation

7.5 A record shall be made:
- when a detainee is informed of their rights under this section and of any requirement in paragraph 7.2;
- of any communications with a High Commission, Embassy or Consulate, and
- of any communications with UKBA about a detainee's claim to be a refugee or to be seeking asylum and the resulting action taken by police.

Note for Guidance

7A The exercise of the rights in this section may not be interfered with even though Annex B applies.

8 Conditions of detention

(a) Action

8.1 So far as it is practicable, not more than one detainee should be detained in each cell.

8.2 Cells in use must be adequately heated, cleaned and ventilated. They must be adequately lit, subject to such dimming as is compatible with safety and security to allow people detained overnight to sleep. No additional restraints shall be used within a locked cell unless absolutely necessary and then only restraint equipment, approved for use in that force by the Chief Officer, which is reasonable and necessary in the circumstances having regard to the detainee's demeanour and with a view to ensuring their safety and the safety of others. If a detainee is deaf, mentally disordered or otherwise mentally vulnerable, particular care must be taken when deciding whether to use any form of approved restraints.

8.3 Blankets, mattresses, pillows and other bedding supplied shall be of a reasonable standard and in a clean and sanitary condition.

8.4 Access to toilet and washing facilities must be provided.

8.5 If it is necessary to remove a detainee's clothes for the purposes of investigation, for hygiene, health reasons or cleaning, replacement clothing of a reasonable standard of comfort and cleanliness shall be provided. A detainee may not be interviewed unless adequate clothing has been offered.

8.6 At least two light meals and one main meal should be offered in any 24 hour period. See *Note 8B*. Drinks should be provided at meal times and upon reasonable request between meals. Whenever necessary, advice shall be sought from the appropriate healthcare professional, see *Note 9A*, on medical and dietary matters. As far as practicable, meals provided shall offer a varied diet and meet any specific dietary needs or religious beliefs the detainee may have. Detainees should also be made aware that the meals offered meet such needs. The detainee may, at the custody officer's discretion, have meals supplied by their family or friends at their expense. See *Note 8A*.

8.7 Brief outdoor exercise shall be offered daily if practicable. Where facilities exist, indoor exercise shall be offered as an alternative if outside conditions are such that a detainee can not be reasonably expected to take outdoor exercise (e.g., in cold or wet weather) or if requested by the detainee or for reasons of security. See *Note 8C*.

8.8 Where practicable, provision should be made for detainees to practice religious observance. Consideration should be given to providing a separate room which can be used as a prayer room. The supply of appropriate food and clothing, and suitable provision for prayer facilities, such as uncontaminated copies of religious books, should also be considered. See *Note 8D*.

8.9 A juvenile shall not be placed in a cell unless no other secure accommodation is available and the custody officer considers it is not practicable to supervise them if they are not placed in a cell or that a cell provides more comfortable accommodation than other secure accommodation in the station. A juvenile may not be placed in a cell with a detained adult.

8.10 Police stations should keep a reasonable supply of reading material available for detainees, including but not limited to, the main religious texts. See *Note 8D*. Detainees should be made aware that such material is available and reasonable requests for such material should be met as soon as practicable unless to do so would:

(i) interfere with the investigation; or

(ii) prevent or delay an officer from discharging his statutory duties, or those in this Code.

If such a request is refused on the grounds of (i) or (ii) above, this should be noted in the custody record and met as soon as possible after those grounds cease to apply.

(b) Documentation

8.11 A record must be kept of replacement clothing and meals offered.

8.12 The use of any restraints on a detainee whilst in a cell, the reasons for it and, if appropriate, the arrangements for enhanced supervision of the detainee whilst so restrained, shall be recorded. See *paragraph 3.9*

Notes for Guidance

8A In deciding whether to allow meals to be supplied by family or friends, the custody officer is entitled to take account of the risk of items being concealed in any food or package and the officer's duties and responsibilities under food handling legislation. If an officer needs to examine food or other items supplied by family and friends before deciding whether they can be given to the detainee, he should inform the person who has brought the item to the police station of this and the reasons for doing so.

8B Meals should, so far as practicable, be offered at recognised meal times, or at other times that take account of when the detainee last had a meal.

8C In light of the potential for detaining individuals for extended periods of time, the overriding principle should be to accommodate a period of exercise, except where to do so would hinder the investigation, delay the detainee's release or charge, or it is declined by the detainee.

8D Police forces should consult with representatives of the main religious communities to ensure the provision for religious observance is adequate, and to seek advice on the appropriate storage and handling of religious texts or other religious items.

9 Care and treatment of detained persons

(a) General

9.1 Notwithstanding other requirements for medical attention as set out in this section, detainees who are held for more than 96 hours must be visited by an appropriate healthcare professional at least once every 24 hours.

9.2 Nothing in this section prevents the police from calling an appropriate healthcare professional, to examine a detainee for the purposes of obtaining evidence relating to any offence in which the detainee is suspected of being involved. See *Note 9A*.

9.3 If a complaint is made by, or on behalf of, a detainee about their treatment since their arrest, or it comes to notice that a detainee may have been treated improperly, a report must be made as soon as practicable to an officer of inspector rank or above not connected with the investigation. If the matter concerns a possible assault or the possibility of the unnecessary or unreasonable use of force, an appropriate healthcare professional must also be called as soon as practicable.

9.4 Detainees should be visited at least every hour. If no reasonably foreseeable risk was identified in a risk assessment, see *paragraphs 3.6 to 3.10*, there is no need to wake a sleeping detainee. Those suspected of being under the influence of drink or drugs or both or of having swallowed drugs, see *Note 9C*, or whose level of consciousness causes concern must, subject to any clinical directions given by the appropriate healthcare professional, see *paragraph 9.15*:
- be visited and roused at least every half hour;
- have their condition assessed as in *Annex H*;
- and clinical treatment arranged if appropriate.

See *Notes 9B, 9C* and *9G*

9.5 When arrangements are made to secure clinical attention for a detainee, the custody officer must make sure all relevant information which might assist in the treatment of the detainee's condition is made available to the responsible healthcare professional. This applies whether or not the healthcare professional asks for such information. Any officer or police staff with relevant information must inform the custody officer as soon as practicable.

(b) Clinical treatment and attention

9.6 The custody officer must make sure a detainee receives appropriate clinical attention as soon as reasonably practicable if the person:

(a) appears to be suffering from physical illness; or

(b) is injured; or

(c) appears to be suffering from a mental disorder; or

(d) appears to need clinical attention.

9.7 This applies even if the detainee makes no request for clinical attention and whether or not they have already received clinical attention elsewhere. If the need for attention appears urgent, e.g. when indicated as in *Annex H*, the nearest available healthcare professional or an ambulance must be called immediately.

9.8 The custody officer must also consider the need for clinical attention as set out in *Note 9C* in relation to those suffering the effects of alcohol or drugs.

9.9 If it appears to the custody officer, or they are told, that a person brought to a station under arrest may be suffering from an infectious disease or condition, the custody officer must take reasonable steps to safeguard the health of the detainee and others at the station. In deciding what action to take, advice must be sought from an appropriate healthcare professional. See *Note 9D*. The custody officer has discretion to isolate the person and their property until clinical directions have been obtained.

9.10 If a detainee requests a clinical examination, an appropriate healthcare professional must be called as soon as practicable to assess the detainee's clinical needs. If a safe and appropriate care plan cannot be provided, the appropriate healthcare professional's advice must be sought. The detainee may also be examined by a medical practitioner of their choice at their expense.

9.11 If a detainee is required to take or apply any medication in compliance with clinical directions prescribed before their detention, the custody officer must consult the appropriate healthcare professional before the use of the medication. Subject to the restrictions in *paragraph 9.12*, the custody officer is responsible for the safekeeping of any medication and for making sure the detainee is given the opportunity to take or apply prescribed or approved medication. Any such consultation and its outcome shall be noted in the custody record.

9.12 No police officer may administer or supervise the self-administration of medically prescribed controlled drugs of the types and forms listed in the Misuse of Drugs Regulations 2001, Schedule 2 or 3. A detainee may only self-administer such drugs under the personal supervision of the registered medical practitioner authorising their use or other appropriate healthcare professional. The custody officer may supervise the self-administration of, or authorise other custody staff to supervise the self-administration of, drugs listed in Schedule 4 or 5 if the officer has consulted the appropriate healthcare professional authorising their use and both are satisfied self-administration will not expose the detainee, police officers or anyone else to the risk of harm or injury.

9.13 When appropriate healthcare professionals administer drugs or authorise the use of other medications, or consult with the custody officer about allowing self administration of drugs listed in Schedule 4 or 5, it must be within current medicines legislation and the scope of practice as determined by their relevant regulatory body.

9.14 If a detainee has in their possession, or claims to need, medication relating to a heart condition, diabetes, epilepsy or a condition of comparable potential seriousness then, even though *paragraph 9.6* may not apply, the advice of the appropriate healthcare professional must be obtained.

9.15 Whenever the appropriate healthcare professional is called in accordance with this section to examine or treat a detainee, the custody officer shall ask for their opinion about:
- any risks or problems which police need to take into account when making decisions about the detainee's continued detention;
- when to carry out an interview if applicable; and
- the need for safeguards.

9.16 When clinical directions are given by the appropriate healthcare professional, whether orally or in writing, and the custody officer has any doubts or is in any way uncertain about any aspect of the directions, the custody officer shall ask for clarification. It is particularly important that directions concerning the frequency of visits are clear, precise and capable of being implemented. See *Note 9E*.

(c) Documentation

9.17 A record must be made in the custody record of:
(a) the arrangements made for an examination by an appropriate healthcare professional under *paragraph 9.3* and of any complaint reported under that paragraph together with any relevant remarks by the custody officer;

(b) any arrangements made in accordance with *paragraph 9.6*;

(c) any request for a clinical examination under *paragraph 9.10* and any arrangements made in response;

(d) the injury, ailment, condition or other reason which made it necessary to make the arrangements in (*a*) to (*c*); See *Note 9F*

(e) any clinical directions and advice, including any further clarifications, given to police by a healthcare professional concerning the care and treatment of the detainee in connection with any of the arrangements made in (*a*) to (*c*); See *Notes 9D* and *9E*

(f) if applicable, the responses received when attempting to rouse a person using the procedure in *Annex H*. See *Note 9G*.

9.18 If a healthcare professional does not record their clinical findings in the custody record, the record must show where they are recorded. See *Note 9F*. However, information which is necessary to custody staff to ensure the effective ongoing care and well being of the detainee must be recorded openly in the custody record, see *paragraph 3.8* and *Annex G, paragraph 7*.

9.19 Subject to the requirements of *Section 4*, the custody record shall include:

• a record of all medication a detainee has in their possession on arrival at the police station;

• a note of any such medication they claim to need but do not have with them.

Notes for Guidance

9A A 'healthcare professional' means a clinically qualified person working within the scope of practice as determined by their relevant statutory regulatory body. Whether a healthcare professional is 'appropriate' depends on the circumstances of the duties they carry out at the time.

9B Whenever possible juveniles and mentally vulnerable detainees should be visited more frequently.

9C A detainee who appears drunk or behaves abnormally may be suffering from illness, the effects of drugs or may have sustained injury, particularly a head injury which is not apparent. A detainee needing or dependent on certain drugs, including alcohol, may experience harmful effects within a short time of being deprived of their supply. In these circumstances, when there is any doubt, police should always act urgently to call an appropriate healthcare professional or an ambulance. Paragraph 9.6 does not apply to minor ailments or injuries which do not need attention. However, all such *ailments or injuries must be recorded in the custody record and any doubt must be resolved in favour of calling the appropriate healthcare professional.*

9D *It is important to respect a person's right to privacy and information about their health must be kept confidential and only disclosed with their consent or in accordance with clinical advice when it is necessary to protect the detainee's health or that of others who come into contact with them.*

9E *The custody officer should always seek to clarify directions that the detainee requires constant observation or supervision and should ask the appropriate healthcare professional to explain precisely what action needs to be taken to implement such directions.*

9F *Paragraphs 9.17 and 9.18 do not require any information about the cause of any injury, ailment or condition to be recorded on the custody record if it appears capable of providing evidence of an offence.*

9G *The purpose of recording a person's responses when attempting to rouse them using the procedure in Annex H is to enable any change in the individual's consciousness level to be noted and clinical treatment arranged if appropriate.*

10 Cautions

(a) When a caution must be given

10.1 A person whom there are grounds to suspect of an offence, see *Note 10A*, must be cautioned before any questions about an offence, or further questions if the answers provide the grounds for suspicion, are put to them if either the suspect's answers or silence, (i.e. failure or refusal to answer or answer satisfactorily) may be given in evidence to a court in a prosecution.

10.2 A person who is arrested, or further arrested, must be informed at the time if practicable, or if not, as soon as it becomes practicable thereafter, that they are under arrest and of the grounds and reasons for their arrest, see *paragraph 3.4*, *Note 3G* and *Note 10B*.

10.3 As required by *section 3* of PACE Code G, a person who is arrested, or further arrested, must also be cautioned unless:
(a) it is impracticable to do so by reason of their condition or behaviour at the time;
(b) they have already been cautioned immediately prior to arrest as in *paragraph 10.1*.

(b) Terms of the cautions

10.4 The caution which must be given:

(a) on arrest;

(b) on all other occasions before a person is charged or informed they may be prosecuted; see *PACE Code C, section 16*, and

(c) before post-charge questioning under section 22 of the Counter-Terrorism Act 2008 (see *section 15.9*),

should, unless the restriction on drawing adverse inferences from silence applies, see *Annex C*, be in the following terms:

'You do not have to say anything. But it may harm your defence if you do not mention when questioned something which you later rely on in Court. Anything you do say may be given in evidence.'

Where the use of the Welsh Language is appropriate, a constable may provide the caution directly in Welsh in the following terms:

'Does dim rhaid i chi ddweud dim byd. Ond gall niweidio eich amddiffyniad os na fyddwch chi'n sôn, wrth gael eich holi, am rywbeth y byddwch chi'n dibynnu arno nes ymlaen yn y Llys. Gall unrhyw beth yr ydych yn ei ddweud gael ei roi fel tystiolaeth.'

See *Note 10F*

10.5 *Annex C, paragraph 2* sets out the alternative terms of the caution to be used when the restriction on drawing adverse inferences from silence applies.

10.6 Minor deviations from the words of any caution given in accordance with this Code do not constitute a breach of this Code, provided the sense of the relevant caution is preserved. See *Note 10C*.

10.7 After any break in questioning under caution, the person being questioned must be made aware they remain under caution. If there is any doubt the relevant caution should be given again in full when the interview resumes. See *Note 10D*.

10.8 When, despite being cautioned, a person fails to co-operate or to answer particular questions which may affect their immediate treatment, the person should be informed of any relevant consequences and that those consequences are not affected by the caution. Examples are when a person's refusal to provide:

- their name and address when charged may make them liable to detention;
- particulars and information in accordance with a statutory requirement.

(c) Special warnings under the Criminal Justice and Public Order Act 1994, sections 36 and 37

10.9 When a suspect interviewed at a police station or authorised place of detention after arrest fails or refuses to answer certain questions, or to answer satisfactorily, after due warning, see *Note 10E*, a court or jury may draw such inferences as appear proper under the Criminal Justice and Public Order Act 1994, sections 36 and 37. Such inferences may only be drawn when:

(a) the restriction on drawing adverse inferences from silence, see *Annex C*, does not apply; and

(b) the suspect is arrested by a constable and fails or refuses to account for any objects, marks or substances, or marks on such objects found:
  • on their person;
  • in or on their clothing or footwear;
  • otherwise in their possession; or
  • in the place they were arrested;

(c) the arrested suspect was found by a constable at a place at or about the time the offence for which that officer has arrested them is alleged to have been committed, and the suspect fails or refuses to account for their presence there.

When the restriction on drawing adverse inferences from silence applies, the suspect may still be asked to account for any of the matters in (*b*) or (*c*) but the special warning described in *paragraph 10.10* will not apply and must not be given.

10.10 For an inference to be drawn when a suspect fails or refuses to answer a question about one of these matters or to answer it satisfactorily, the suspect must first be told in ordinary language:

(a) what offence is being investigated;
(b) what fact they are being asked to account for;
(c) this fact may be due to them taking part in the commission of the offence;
(d) a court may draw a proper inference if they fail or refuse to account for this fact;
(e) a record is being made of the interview and it may be given in evidence if they are brought to trial.

(d) Juveniles and persons who are mentally disordered or otherwise mentally vulnerable

10.10A The information required in *paragraph 10.10* must not be given to a suspect who is a juvenile or who is mentally disordered or otherwise mentally vulnerable unless the appropriate adult is present.

10.11 If a juvenile or a person who is mentally disordered or otherwise mentally vulnerable is cautioned in the absence of the appropriate adult, the caution must be repeated in the adult's presence.

(e) Documentation

10.12 A record shall be made when a caution is given under this section, either in the interviewer's pocket book or in the interview record.

Notes for Guidance

10A There must be some reasonable, objective grounds for the suspicion, based on known facts or information which are relevant to the likelihood the offence has been committed and the person to be questioned committed it.

10B An arrested person must be given sufficient information to enable them to understand that they have been deprived of their liberty and the reason they have been arrested, e.g. when a person is arrested on suspicion of committing an offence they must be informed of the suspected offence's nature, when and where it was committed, see Note 3G. The suspect must also be informed of the reason or reasons why the arrest is considered necessary. Vague or technical language should be avoided.

10C If it appears a person does not understand the caution, the person giving it should explain it in their own words.

10D It may be necessary to show to the court that nothing occurred during an interview break or between interviews which influenced the suspect's recorded evidence. After a break in an interview or at the beginning of a subsequent interview, the interviewing officer should summarise the reason for the break and confirm this with the suspect.

10E The Criminal Justice and Public Order Act 1994, sections 36 and 37 apply only to suspects who have been arrested by a constable or an officer of Revenue and Customs and are given the relevant warning by the police or Revenue and Customs officer who made the arrest or who is investigating the offence. They do not apply to any interviews with suspects who have not been arrested.

10F Nothing in this Code requires a caution to be given or repeated when informing a person not under arrest they may be prosecuted for an offence. However, a court will not be able to draw any inferences under the Criminal Justice and Public Order Act 1994, section 34, if the person was not cautioned.

11 Interviews—general

(a) Action

11.1 An interview in this Code is the questioning of a person arrested on suspicion of being a terrorist which, under *paragraph 10.1*, must be carried out under caution. Whenever a person is interviewed they must be informed of the grounds for arrest, see *Note 3G*.

11.2 Following the arrest of a person under section 41 TACT, that person must not be interviewed about the relevant offence except at a place designated for detention under Schedule 8 paragraph 1 of the Terrorism Act 2000, unless the consequent delay would be likely to:

(a) lead to:
- interference with, or harm to, evidence connected with an offence;
- interference with, or physical harm to, other people; or
- serious loss of, or damage to, property;

(b) lead to alerting other people suspected of committing an offence but not yet arrested for it; or

(c) hinder the recovery of property obtained in consequence of the commission of an offence.

Interviewing in any of these circumstances shall cease once the relevant risk has been averted or the necessary questions have been put in order to attempt to avert that risk.

11.3 Immediately prior to the commencement or re-commencement of any interview at a designated place of detention, the interviewer should remind the suspect of their entitlement to free legal advice and that the interview can be delayed for legal advice to be obtained, unless one of the exceptions in *paragraph 6.7* applies. It is the interviewer's responsibility to make sure all reminders are recorded in the interview record.

11.4 At the beginning of an interview the interviewer, after cautioning the suspect, see *section 10*, shall put to them any significant statement or silence which occurred in the presence and hearing of a police officer or other police staff before the start of the interview and which have not been put to the suspect in the course of a previous interview. See *Note 11A*. The interviewer shall ask the suspect whether they confirm or deny that earlier statement or silence and if they want to add anything.

11.5 A significant statement is one which appears capable of being used in evidence against the suspect, in particular a direct admission of guilt. A significant silence is a failure or refusal to answer a question or answer satisfactorily when under caution, which might, allowing for the restriction on drawing adverse inferences from silence, see *Annex C*, give rise to an inference under the Criminal Justice and Public Order Act 1994, Part III.

11.6 No interviewer may try to obtain answers or elicit a statement by the use of oppression. Except as in *paragraph 10.8*, no interviewer shall indicate, except to answer a direct question, what action will be taken by the police if the person being questioned answers questions, makes a statement or refuses to do either. If the person asks directly what action will be taken if they answer questions, make a statement or refuse to do either, the interviewer may inform them what action the police propose to take provided that action is itself proper and warranted.

11.7 The interview or further interview of a person about an offence with which that person has not been charged or for which they have not been informed they may be prosecuted, must cease when:
(a) the officer in charge of the investigation is satisfied all the questions they consider relevant to obtaining accurate and reliable information about the offence have been put to the suspect, this includes allowing the suspect an opportunity to give an innocent explanation and asking questions to test if the explanation is accurate and reliable, e.g. to clear up ambiguities or clarify what the suspect said;
(b) the officer in charge of the investigation has taken account of any other available evidence; and
(c) the officer in charge of the investigation, or in the case of a detained suspect, the custody officer, see *PACE Code C paragraph 16.1*, reasonably believes there is sufficient evidence to provide a realistic prospect of conviction for that offence. See *Note 11B*.

(b) Interview records

11.8 Interviews of a person detained under section 41 of, or Schedule 8 to, TACT must be video recorded with sound in accordance with the Code of Practice issued under paragraph 3 of Schedule 8 to the Terrorism Act 2000, or in the case of post-charge questioning authorised under section 22 of the Counter-Terrorism Act 2008, the Code of Practice issued under section 25 of that Act.

11.8A A written record shall be made of any comments made by a suspect, including unsolicited comments, which are outside the context of an interview but which might be relevant to the offence. Any such record must be timed and signed by the maker. When practicable the suspect shall be given the opportunity to read that record and to sign it as correct or to indicate how they consider it inaccurate. See *Note 11E*.

(c) Juveniles and mentally disordered or otherwise mentally vulnerable people

11.9 A juvenile or person who is mentally disordered or otherwise mentally vulnerable must not be interviewed regarding their involvement or suspected involvement in a criminal offence or offences, or asked to provide or sign a written statement under caution or record of interview, in the absence of the appropriate adult unless *paragraphs 11.2, 11.11 to 11.13* apply. See *Note 11C*.

11.10 If an appropriate adult is present at an interview, they shall be informed:

- they are not expected to act simply as an observer; and
- the purpose of their presence is to:
  - ~ advise the person being interviewed;
  - ~ observe whether the interview is being conducted properly and fairly;
  - ~ facilitate communication with the person being interviewed.

The appropriate adult may be required to leave the interview if their conduct is such that the interviewer is unable properly to put questions to the suspect. This will include situations where the appropriate adult's approach or conduct prevents or unreasonably obstructs proper questions being put to the suspect or the suspect's responses being recorded. If the interviewer considers an appropriate adult is acting in such a way, they will stop the interview and consult an officer not below superintendent rank, if one is readily available, and otherwise an officer not below inspector rank not connected with the investigation. After speaking to the appropriate adult, the officer consulted will decide if the interview should continue without the attendance of that appropriate adult. If they decide it should not, another appropriate adult should be obtained before the interview continues, unless the provisions of *paragraph 11.11* below apply.

(d) Vulnerable suspects—urgent interviews at police stations

11.11 The following persons may not be interviewed unless an officer of superintendent rank or above considers delay will lead to the consequences in *paragraph 11.2(a)* to *(c)*, and is satisfied the interview would not significantly harm the person's physical or mental state (see *Annex G*):

(a) a juvenile or person who is mentally disordered or otherwise mentally vulnerable if at the time of the interview the appropriate adult is not present;

(b) anyone other than in *(a)* who at the time of the interview appears unable to:
   • appreciate the significance of questions and their answers; or
   • understand what is happening because of the effects of drink, drugs or any illness, ailment or condition;

(c) a person who has difficulty understanding English or has a hearing disability, if at the time of the interview an interpreter is not present.

11.12 These interviews may not continue once sufficient information has been obtained to avert the consequences in *paragraph 11.2(a)* to *(c)*.

11.13 A record shall be made of the grounds for any decision to interview a person under *paragraph 11.11*.

Notes for Guidance

11A Paragraph 11.4 does not prevent the interviewer from putting significant statements and silences to a suspect again at a later stage or a further interview.

11B The Criminal Procedure and Investigations Act 1996 Code of Practice, paragraph 3.5 states 'In conducting an investigation, the investigator should pursue all reasonable lines of enquiry, whether these point towards or away from the suspect. What is reasonable will depend on the particular circumstances.' Interviewers should keep this in mind when deciding what questions to ask in an interview.

11C Although juveniles or people who are mentally disordered or otherwise mentally vulnerable are often capable of providing reliable evidence, they may, without knowing or wishing to do so, be particularly prone in certain circumstances to provide information that may be unreliable, misleading or self-incriminating. Special care should always be taken when questioning such a person, and the appropriate adult should be involved if there is any doubt about a person's age, mental state or capacity. Because of the risk of unreliable evidence it is also important to obtain corroboration of any facts admitted whenever possible.

11D *Consideration should be given to the effect of extended detention on a detainee and any subsequent information they provide, especially if it relates to information on matters that they have failed to provide previously in response to similar questioning see Annex G.*

11E *Significant statements described in paragraph 11.4 will always be relevant to the offence and must be recorded. When a suspect agrees to read records of interviews and other comments and sign them as correct, they should be asked to endorse the record with, e.g. 'I agree that this is a correct record of what was said' and add their signature. If the suspect does not agree with the record, the interviewer should record the details of any disagreement and ask the suspect to read these details and sign them to the effect that they accurately reflect their disagreement. Any refusal to sign should be recorded.*

12 Interviews in police stations

(a) Action

12.1 If a police officer wants to interview or conduct enquiries which require the presence of a detainee, the custody officer is responsible for deciding whether to deliver the detainee into the officer's custody. An investigating officer who is given custody of a detainee takes over responsibility for the detainee's care and treatment for the purposes of this Code until they return the detainee to the custody officer when they must report the manner in which they complied with the Code whilst having custody of the detainee.

12.2 Except as below, in any period of 24 hours a detainee must be allowed a continuous period of at least 8 hours for rest, free from questioning, travel or any interruption in connection with the investigation concerned. This period should normally be at night or other appropriate time which takes account of when the detainee last slept or rested. If a detainee is arrested at a police station after going there voluntarily, the period of 24 hours runs from the time of their arrest (or, if a person was being detained under TACT Schedule 7 when arrested, from the time at which the examination under Schedule 7 began) and not the time of arrival at the police station. The period may not be interrupted or delayed, except:
(a) when there are reasonable grounds for believing not delaying or interrupting the period would:
   (i) involve a risk of harm to people or serious loss of, or damage to, property;
   (ii) delay unnecessarily the person's release from custody;
   (iii) otherwise prejudice the outcome of the investigation;

(b) at the request of the detainee, their appropriate adult or legal representative;

(c) when a delay or interruption is necessary in order to:
   (i) comply with the legal obligations and duties arising under *section 14*;
   (ii) to take action required under *section 9* or in accordance with medical advice.

If the period is interrupted in accordance with (*a*), a fresh period must be allowed. Interruptions under (*b*) and (*c*), do not require a fresh period to be allowed.

12.3 Before a detainee is interviewed the custody officer, in consultation with the officer in charge of the investigation and appropriate healthcare professionals as necessary, shall assess whether the detainee is fit enough to be interviewed. This means determining and considering the risks to the detainee's physical and mental state if the interview took place and determining what safeguards are needed to allow the interview to take place. The custody officer shall not allow a detainee to be interviewed if the custody officer considers it would cause significant harm to the detainee's physical or mental state. Vulnerable suspects listed at *paragraph 11.11* shall be treated as always being at some risk during an interview and these persons may not be interviewed except in accordance with *paragraphs 11.11 to 11.13*.

12.4 As far as practicable interviews shall take place in interview rooms which are adequately heated, lit and ventilated.

12.5 A suspect whose detention without charge has been authorised under TACT Schedule 8, because the detention is necessary for an interview to obtain evidence of the offence for which they have been arrested, may choose not to answer questions but police do not require the suspect's consent or agreement to interview them for this purpose. If a suspect takes steps to prevent themselves being questioned or further questioned, e.g. by refusing to leave their cell to go to a suitable interview room or by trying to leave the interview room, they shall be advised their consent or agreement to interview is not required. The suspect shall be cautioned as in *section 10*, and informed if they fail or refuse to co-operate, the interview may take place in the cell and that their failure or refusal to co-operate may be given in evidence. The suspect shall then be invited to co-operate and go into the interview room.

12.6 People being questioned or making statements shall not be required to stand.

12.7 Before the interview commences each interviewer shall, subject to the qualification at *paragraph 2.8*, identify themselves and any other persons present to the interviewee.

12.8 Breaks from interviewing should be made at recognised meal times or at other times that take account of when an interviewee last had a meal. Short refreshment breaks shall be provided at approximately two hour intervals, subject to the interviewer's discretion to delay a break if there are reasonable grounds for believing it would:

(i)   involve a:
  • risk of harm to people;
  • serious loss of, or damage to, property;
(ii) unnecessarily delay the detainee's release;
(iii) otherwise prejudice the outcome of the investigation.
   See *Note 12B*

12.9 During extended periods where no interviews take place, because of the need to gather further evidence or analyse existing evidence, detainees and their legal representative shall be informed that the investigation into the relevant offence remains ongoing. If practicable, the detainee and legal representative should also be made aware in general terms of any reasons for long gaps between interviews. Consideration should be given to allowing visits, more frequent exercise, or for reading or writing materials to be offered see *paragraph 5.4, section 8* and *Note 12C*.

12.10 If during the interview a complaint is made by or on behalf of the interviewee concerning the provisions of any of the Codes, or it comes to the interviewer's notice that the interviewee may have been treated improperly, the interviewer should:

(i) record the matter in the interview record;
(ii) inform the custody officer, who is then responsible for dealing with it as in *section 9*.

(b) Documentation

12.11 A record must be made of the:
• time a detainee is not in the custody of the custody officer, and why;
• reason for any refusal to deliver the detainee out of that custody.

12.12 A record shall be made of:
• the reasons it was not practicable to use an interview room; and
• any action taken as in *paragraph 12.5*.

The record shall be made on the custody record or in the interview record for action taken whilst an interview record is being kept, with a brief reference to this effect in the custody record.

12.13 Any decision to delay a break in an interview must be recorded, with reasons, in the interview record.

12.14 All written statements made at police stations under caution shall be written on forms provided for the purpose.

12.15 All written statements made under caution shall be taken in accordance with *Annex D*. Before a person makes a written statement under caution at a police station they shall be reminded about the right to legal advice. See *Note 12A*.

Notes for Guidance

12A It is not normally necessary to ask for a written statement if the interview was recorded in accordance with the Code of Practice issued under TACT Schedule 8 Paragraph 3. Statements under caution should normally be taken in these circumstances only at the person's express wish. A person may however be asked if they want to make such a statement.

12B Meal breaks should normally last at least 45 minutes and shorter breaks after two hours should last at least 15 minutes. If the interviewer delays a break in accordance with paragraph 12.8 and prolongs the interview, a longer break should be provided. If there is a short interview, and another short interview is contemplated, the length of the break may be reduced if there are reasonable grounds to believe this is necessary to avoid any of the consequences in paragraph 12.8(i) to (iii).

12C Consideration should be given to the matters referred to in paragraph 12.9 after a period of over 24 hours without questioning. This is to ensure that extended periods of detention without an indication that the investigation remains ongoing do not contribute to a deterioration of the detainee's well-being.

13 Interpreters

(a) General

13.1 Chief officers are responsible for making sure appropriate arrangements are in place for provision of suitably qualified interpreters for people who:

- are deaf;
- do not understand English.

See *Note 13A*

(b) Foreign languages

13.2 Unless *paragraphs 11.2, 11.11* to *11.13* apply, a person must not be interviewed in the absence of a person capable of interpreting if:

(a) they have difficulty understanding English;
(b) the interviewer cannot speak the person's own language;
(c) the person wants an interpreter present.

13.3 Not used

13.4 In the case of a person making a statement to a police officer or other police staff other than in English:

(a) the interpreter shall record the statement in the language it is made;
(b) the person shall be invited to sign it;
(c) an official English translation shall be made in due course.

(c) Deaf people and people with speech difficulties

13.5 If a person appears to be deaf or there is doubt about their hearing or speaking ability, they must not be interviewed in the absence of an interpreter unless they agree in writing to being interviewed without one or *paragraphs 11.2, 11.11* to *11.13* apply.

13.6 An interpreter should also be called if a juvenile is interviewed and the parent or guardian present as the appropriate adult appears to be deaf or there is doubt about their hearing or speaking ability, unless they agree in writing to the interview proceeding without one or *paragraphs 11.2, 11.11* to *11.13* apply.

13.7 Not used

(d) Additional rules for detained persons

13.8 All reasonable attempts should be made to make the detainee understand that interpreters will be provided at public expense.

13.9 If *paragraph 6.1* applies and the detainee cannot communicate with the solicitor because of language, hearing or speech difficulties, an interpreter must be called. The interpreter may not be a police officer or any other police staff when interpretation is needed for the purposes of obtaining legal advice. In all other cases a police officer or other police staff may only interpret if the detainee and the appropriate adult, if applicable, give their agreement in writing or if the interview is audibly recorded or visually recorded as in the Code of Practice issued under TACT Schedule 8 Paragraph 3.

13.10 When the custody officer cannot establish effective communication with a person charged with an offence who appears deaf or there is doubt about their ability to hear, speak or to understand English, arrangements must be made as soon as practicable for an interpreter to explain the offence and any other information given by the custody officer.

(e) Documentation

13.11 Action taken to call an interpreter under this section and any agreement to be interviewed in the absence of an interpreter must be recorded.

Note for Guidance

13A Whenever possible, interpreters should be provided in accordance with national arrangements approved or prescribed by the Secretary of State.

14 Reviews and Extensions of Detention under the Terrorism Act 2000

(a) General

14.1 The powers and duties of the review officer are in the Terrorism Act 2000, Schedule 8, Part II. See *Notes 14A* and *14B*. A review officer should carry out their duties at the police station where the detainee is held and be allowed such access to the detainee as is necessary to exercise those duties.

14.2 For the purposes of reviewing a person's detention, no officer shall put specific questions to the detainee:
- regarding their involvement in any offence; or
- in respect of any comments they may make:
  - ~ when given the opportunity to make representations; or
  - ~ in response to a decision to keep them in detention or extend the maximum period of detention.

Such an exchange could constitute an interview as in *paragraph 11.1* and would be subject to the associated safeguards in *section 11*.

14.3 If detention is necessary for longer than 48 hours from the time of arrest (or if a person was being detained under TACT Schedule 7, from the time at which the examination under Schedule 7 began, a police officer of at least superintendent rank, or a Crown Prosecutor may apply for a warrant of further detention or for an extension or further extension of such a warrant under paragraph 29 or (as the case may be) 36 of Part III of Schedule 8 to the Terrorism Act 2000. See *Note 14C*.

14.4 When an application is made for a warrant as described in *paragraph 14.3*, the detained person and their representative must be informed of their rights in respect of the application. These include:

(i)   the right to a written notice of the application; See *Note 14G*.
(ii) the right to make oral or written representations to the judicial authority/High Court judge about the application;
(iii) the right to be present and legally represented at the hearing of the application, unless specifically excluded by the judicial authority/High Court judge;
(iv) their right to free legal advice (see *section 6* of this Code).

(b) Transfer of persons detained for more than 14 days to prison

14.5 If the Detention of Terrorists Suspects (Temporary Extension) Bill is enacted and in force, a High Court judge may extend or further extend a warrant of further detention to authorise a person to be detained beyond a period of 14 days from the time of their arrest (or if they were being detained under TACT Schedule 7, from the time at which their examination under Schedule 7 began). The provisions of *Annex J* will apply when a warrant of further detention is so extended or further extended.

14.6 Not used

14.7 Not used

14.8 Not used

14.9 Not used

14.10 Not used

(c) Documentation

14.11 It is the responsibility of the officer who gives any reminders as at *paragraph 14.4*, to ensure that these are noted in the custody record, as well any comments made by the detained person upon being told of those rights.

14.12 The grounds for, and extent of, any delay in conducting a review shall be recorded.

14.13 Any written representations shall be retained.

14.14 A record shall be made as soon as practicable about the outcome of each review and, if applicable, the grounds on which the review officer authorises continued detention. A record shall also be made as soon as practicable about the outcome of an application for a warrant of further detention or its extension.

14.15 Not used

Notes for Guidance

14A TACT Schedule 8 Part II sets out the procedures for review of detention up to 48 hours from the time of arrest under TACT section 41 (or if a person was being detained under TACT Schedule 7, from the time at which the examination under Schedule 7 began). These include provisions for the requirement to review detention, postponing a review, grounds for continued detention, designating a review officer, representations, rights of the detained person and keeping a record. The review officer's role ends after a warrant has been issued for extension of detention under Part III of Schedule 8.

14B A review officer may authorise a person's continued detention if satisfied that detention is necessary:
(a) to obtain relevant evidence whether by questioning the person or otherwise;
(b) to preserve relevant evidence;
(c) while awaiting the result of an examination or analysis of relevant evidence;
(d) for the examination or analysis of anything with a view to obtaining relevant evidence;
(e) pending a decision to apply to the Secretary of State for a deportation notice to be served on the detainee, the making of any such application, or the consideration of any such application by the Secretary of State;
(f) pending a decision to charge the detainee with an offence.

14C Applications for warrants to extend detention beyond 48 hours, may be made for periods of 7 days at a time (initially under TACT Schedule 8 paragraph 29, and extensions thereafter under TACT Schedule 8, paragraph 36), up to a maximum period of 14 days (or 28 days if the Detention of Terrorists Suspects (Temporary Extension) Bill) is enacted and in force) from the time of their arrest (or if they were being detained under TACT Schedule 7, from the time at which their examination under Schedule 7 began). Applications may be made for shorter periods than 7 days, which must be specified. The judicial authority or High Court judge may also substitute a shorter period if they feel a period of 7 days is inappropriate.

14D *Unless Note 14F applies, applications for warrants that would take the total period of detention up to 14 days or less should be made to a judicial authority, meaning a District Judge (Magistrates' Court) designated by the Lord Chief Justice to hear such applications.*

14E *If by virtue of the relevant provisions described in Note 14C being enacted the maximum period of detention is extended to 28 days, any application for a warrant which would take the period of detention beyond 14 days from the time of arrest (or if a person was being detained under TACT Schedule 7, from the time at which the examination under Schedule 7 began), must be made to a High Court Judge.*

14F *If, when the Detention of Terrorists Suspects (Temporary Extension) Bill is enacted and in force, an application is made to a High Court judge for a warrant which would take detention beyond 14 days and the High Court judge instead issues a warrant for a period of time which would not take detention beyond 14 days, further applications for extension of detention must also be made to a High Court judge, regardless of the period of time to which they refer.*

14G *TACT Schedule 8 Paragraph 31 requires a notice to be given to the detained person if a warrant is sought for further detention. This must be provided before the judicial hearing of the application for that warrant and must include:*
(a) notification that the application for a warrant has been made;
(b) the time at which the application was made;
(c) the time at which the application is to be heard;
(d) the grounds on which further detention is sought.
A notice must also be provided each time an application is made to extend or further extend an existing warrant.

14H *An officer applying for an order under TACT Schedule 8 Paragraph 34 to withhold specified information on which they intend to rely when applying for a warrant of further detention or the extension or further extension of such a warrant, may make the application for the order orally or in writing. The most appropriate method of application will depend on the circumstances of the case and the need to ensure fairness to the detainee.*

14I *After hearing any representations by or on behalf of the detainee and the applicant, the judicial authority or High Court judge may direct that the hearing relating to the extension of detention under Part III of Schedule 8 is to take place using video conferencing facilities. However, if the judicial authority requires the detained person to be physically present at any hearing, this should be complied with as soon as practicable. Paragraph 33(4) to (9) of TACT Schedule 8 govern the hearing of applications via video-link or other means.*

14J *Not used*

14K *Not used*

15 Charging and post-charge questioning in terrorism cases

(a) Charging

15.1 Charging of detained persons is covered by PACE and guidance issued under PACE by the Director of Public Prosecutions. Decisions to charge persons to whom this Code (H) applies, the charging process and related matters are subject to section 16 of PACE Code C.

(b) Post-charge questioning

15.2 Under section 22 of the Counter-Terrorism Act 2008, a judge of the Crown Court may authorise the questioning of a person about an offence for which they have been charged, informed that they may be prosecuted or sent for trial, if the offence:
- is a terrorism offence as set out in section 27 of the Counter-Terrorism Act 2008; or
- is an offence which appears to the judge to have a terrorist connection. See *Note 15C*.

The decision on whether to apply for such questioning will be based on the needs of the investigation. There is no power to detain a person solely for the purposes of post-charge questioning. A person can only be detained whilst being so questioned (whether at a police station or in prison) if they are already there in lawful custody under some existing power. If at a police station the contents of *sections 8* and *9* of this Code must be considered the minimum standards of treatment for such detainees.

15.3 The Crown Court judge may authorise the questioning if they are satisfied that:
- further questioning is necessary in the interests of justice;

- the investigation for the purposes of which the further questioning is being proposed is being conducted diligently and expeditiously; and
- the questioning would not interfere unduly with the preparation of the person's defence to the charge or any other criminal charge that they may be facing.

See *Note 15E*

15.4 The judge authorising questioning may specify the location of the questioning.

15.5 The judge may only authorise a period up to a maximum of 48 hours before further authorisation must be sought. The 48 hour period would run continuously from the commencement of questioning. This period must include breaks in questioning in accordance with *paragraphs 8.6* and *12.2* of this Code (see *Note 15B*).

15.6 Nothing in this Code shall be taken to prevent a suspect seeking a voluntary interview with the police at any time.

15.7 For the purposes of this section, any reference in *sections 6, 10, 11, 12* and *13* of this Code to:
- 'suspect' means the person in respect of whom an authorisation has been given under section 22 of the Counter-Terrorism Act 2008 (post-charge questioning of terrorist suspects) to interview them;
- 'interview' means post-charge questioning authorised under section 22 of the Counter-Terrorism Act 2008;
- 'offence' means an offence for which the person has been charged, informed that they may be prosecuted or sent for trial and about which the person is being questioned; and
- 'place of detention' means the location of the questioning specified by the judge (see *paragraph 15.4*),

and the provisions of those sections apply (as appropriate), to such questioning (whether at a police station or in prison) subject to the further modifications in the following paragraphs:

Right to legal advice

15.8 In *section 6* of this Code, for the purposes of post-charge questioning:
- access to a solicitor may not be delayed under *Annex B*; and
- *paragraph 6.5* (direction that a detainee may only consult a solicitor within the sight and hearing of a qualified officer) does not apply.

Cautions

15.9 In *section 10* of this Code, unless the restriction on drawing adverse inferences from silence applies (see *paragraph 15.10*), for the purposes of post-charge questioning, the caution must be given in the following terms before any such questions are asked:

'You do not have to say anything. But it may harm your defence if you do not mention when questioned something which you later rely on in Court. Anything you do say may be given in evidence.'

Where the use of the Welsh Language is appropriate, a constable may provide the caution directly in Welsh in the following terms:

'Does dim rhaid i chi ddweud dim byd. Ond gall niweidio eich amddiffyniad os na fyddwch chi'n sôn, wrth gael eich holi, am rywbeth y byddwch chi'n dibynnu arno nes ymlaen yn y Llys. Gall unrhyw beth yr ydych yn ei ddweud gael ei roi fel tystiolaeth.'

15.10 The only restriction on drawing adverse inferences from silence, see *Annex C*, applies in those situations where a person has asked for legal advice and is questioned before receiving such advice in accordance with *paragraph 6.7(b)*.

Interviews

15.11 In *section 11*, for the purposes of post-charge questioning, whenever a person is questioned, they must be informed of the offence for which they have been charged or informed that they may be prosecuted, or that they have been sent for trial and about which they are being questioned.

15.12 *Paragraph 11.2* (place where questioning may take place) does not apply to post-charge questioning.

Recording post-charge questioning

15.13 All interviews must be video recorded with sound in accordance with the separate Code of Practice issued under section 25 of the Counter-Terrorism Act 2008 for the video recording with sound of post-charge questioning authorised under section 22 of the Counter-Terrorism Act 2008 (see *paragraph 11.8*).

Notes for Guidance

15A If a person is detained at a police station for the purposes of post-charge questioning, a custody record must be opened in accordance with section 2 of this Code. The custody record must note the power under which the person is being detained, the time at which the person was transferred into police custody, their time of arrival at the police station and their time of being presented to the custody officer.

15B *The custody record must note the time at which the interview process commences. This shall be regarded as the relevant time for any period of questioning in accordance with paragraph 15.5 of this Code.*

15C *Where reference is made to 'terrorist connection' in paragraph 15.2, this is determined in accordance with section 30 of the Counter-Terrorism Act 2008. Under section 30 of that Act a court must in certain circumstances determine whether an offence has a terrorist connection. These are offences under general criminal law which may be prosecuted in terrorism cases (for example explosives-related offences and conspiracy to murder). An offence has a terrorist connection if the offence is, or takes place in the course of, an act of terrorism or is committed for the purposes of terrorism (section 98 of the Act). Normally the court will make the determination during the sentencing process, however for the purposes of post-charge questioning, a Crown Court Judge must determine whether the offence could have a terrorist connection.*

15D *The powers under section 22 of the Counter-Terrorism Act 2008 are separate from and additional to the normal questioning procedures within this code. Their overall purpose is to enable the further questioning of a terrorist suspect after charge. They should not therefore be used to replace or circumvent the normal powers for dealing with routine questioning.*

15E *Post-charge questioning has been created because it is acknowledged that terrorist investigations can be large and complex and that a great deal of evidence can come to light following the charge of a terrorism suspect. This can occur, for instance, from the translation of material or as the result of additional investigation. When considering an application for post-charge questioning, the police must 'satisfy' the judge on all three points under paragraph 15.3. This means that the judge will either authorise or refuse an application on the balance of whether the conditions in paragraph 15.3 are all met. It is important therefore, that when making the application, to consider the following questions:*
- *What further evidence is the questioning expected to provide?*
- *Why was it not possible to obtain this evidence before charge?*
- *How and why was the need to question after charge first recognised?*
- *How is the questioning expected to contribute further to the case?*
- *To what extent could the time and place for further questioning interfere with the preparation of the person's defence (for example if authorisation is sought close to the time of a trial)?*
- *What steps will be taken to minimise any risk that questioning might interfere with the preparation of the person's defence?*

This list is not exhaustive but outlines the type of questions that could be relevant to any asked by a judge in considering an application.

16 Testing persons for the presence of specified Class A drugs

16.1 The provisions for drug testing under section 63B of PACE (as amended by section 5 of the Criminal Justice Act 2003 and section 7 of the Drugs Act 2005), do not apply to persons to whom this Code applies. Guidance on these provisions can be found in section 17 of PACE Code C.

ANNEX A—INTIMATE AND STRIP SEARCHES

A Intimate search

1. An intimate search consists of the physical examination of a person's body orifices other than the mouth. The intrusive nature of such searches means the actual and potential risks associated with intimate searches must never be underestimated.

(a) Action

2. Body orifices other than the mouth may be searched if authorised by an officer of inspector rank or above who has reasonable grounds for believing that the person may have concealed on themselves anything which they could and might use to cause physical injury to themselves or others at the station and the officer has reasonable grounds for believing that an intimate search is the only means of removing those items.

3. Before the search begins, a police officer or designated detention officer, must tell the detainee:
(a) that the authority to carry out the search has been given;
(b) the grounds for giving the authorisation and for believing that the article cannot be removed without an intimate search.

4. An intimate search may only be carried out by a registered medical practitioner or registered nurse, unless an officer of at least inspector rank considers this is not practicable, in which case a police officer may carry out the search. See *Notes A1 to A5*.

5. Any proposal for a search under *paragraph 2* to be carried out by someone other than a registered medical practitioner or registered nurse must only be considered as a last resort and when the authorising officer is satisfied the risks associated with allowing the item to remain with the detainee outweigh the risks associated with removing it. See *Notes A1 to A5*.

6. An intimate search at a police station of a juvenile or mentally disordered or otherwise mentally vulnerable person may take place only in the presence of an appropriate adult of the same sex (see *Annex I*), unless the detainee specifically requests a particular adult of the opposite sex who is readily available. In the case of a juvenile the search may take place in the absence of the appropriate adult only if the juvenile signifies in the presence of the appropriate adult they do not want the adult present during the search and the adult agrees. A record shall be made of the juvenile's decision and signed by the appropriate adult.

7. When an intimate search under *paragraph 2* is carried out by a police officer, the officer must be of the same sex as the detainee (see *Annex I*). A minimum of two people, other than the detainee, must be present during the search. Subject to *paragraph 6*, no person of the opposite sex who is not a medical practitioner or nurse shall be present, nor shall anyone whose presence is unnecessary. The search shall be conducted with proper regard to the sensitivity and vulnerability of the detainee.

(b) Documentation

8. In the case of an intimate search under *paragraph 2*, the following shall be recorded as soon as practicable, in the detainee's custody record:
- the authorisation to carry out the search;
- the grounds for giving the authorisation;
- the grounds for believing the article could not be removed without an intimate search;
- which parts of the detainee's body were searched;
- who carried out the search;
- who was present;
- the result.

9. If an intimate search is carried out by a police officer, the reason why it was impracticable for a registered medical practitioner or registered nurse to conduct it must be recorded.

B Strip search

10. A strip search is a search involving the removal of more than outer clothing. In this Code, outer clothing includes shoes and socks.

(a) Action

11. A strip search may take place only if it is considered necessary to remove an article which a detainee would not be allowed to keep, and the officer reasonably considers the detainee might have concealed such an article. Strip searches shall not be routinely carried out if there is no reason to consider that articles are concealed.

The conduct of strip searches

12. When strip searches are conducted:

(a) a police officer carrying out a strip search must be the same sex as the detainee (see *Annex I*);

(b) the search shall take place in an area where the detainee cannot be seen by anyone who does not need to be present, nor by a member of the opposite sex (see *Annex I*) except an appropriate adult who has been specifically requested by the detainee;

(c) except in cases of urgency, where there is risk of serious harm to the detainee or to others, whenever a strip search involves exposure of intimate body parts, there must be at least two people present other than the detainee, and if the search is of a juvenile or mentally disordered or otherwise mentally vulnerable person, one of the people must be the appropriate adult. Except in urgent cases as above, a search of a juvenile may take place in the absence of the appropriate adult only if the juvenile signifies in the presence of the appropriate adult that they do not want the adult to be present during the search and the adult agrees. A record shall be made of the juvenile's decision and signed by the appropriate adult. The presence of more than two people, other than an appropriate adult, shall be permitted only in the most exceptional circumstances;

(d) the search shall be conducted with proper regard to the sensitivity and vulnerability of the detainee in these circumstances and every reasonable effort shall be made to secure the detainee's co-operation and minimise embarrassment. Detainees who are searched shall not normally be required to remove all their clothes at the same time, e.g. a person should be allowed to remove clothing above the waist and redress before removing further clothing;

(e) if necessary to assist the search, the detainee may be required to hold their arms in the air or to stand with their legs apart and bend forward so a visual examination may be made of the genital and anal areas provided no physical contact is made with any body orifice;

(f) if articles are found, the detainee shall be asked to hand them over. If articles are found within any body orifice other than the mouth, and the detainee refuses to hand them over, their removal would constitute an intimate search, which must be carried out as in *Part A*;

(g) a strip search shall be conducted as quickly as possible, and the detainee allowed to dress as soon as the procedure is complete.

(b) Documentation

13. A record shall be made on the custody record of a strip search including the reason it was considered necessary, those present and any result.

Notes for Guidance

A1 *Before authorising any intimate search, the authorising officer must make every reasonable effort to persuade the detainee to hand the article over without a search. If the detainee agrees, a registered medical practitioner or registered nurse should whenever possible be asked to assess the risks involved and, if necessary, attend to assist the detainee.*

A2 *If the detainee does not agree to hand the article over without a search, the authorising officer must carefully review all the relevant factors before authorising an intimate search. In particular, the officer must consider whether the grounds for believing an article may be concealed are reasonable.*

A3 *If authority is given for a search under paragraph 2, a registered medical practitioner or registered nurse shall be consulted whenever possible. The presumption should be that the search will be conducted by the registered medical practitioner or registered nurse and the authorising officer must make every reasonable effort to persuade the detainee to allow the medical practitioner or nurse to conduct the search.*

A4 *A constable should only be authorised to carry out a search as a last resort and when all other approaches have failed. In these circumstances, the authorising officer must be satisfied the detainee might use the article for one or more of the purposes in paragraph 2 and the physical injury likely to be caused is sufficiently severe to justify authorising a constable to carry out the search.*

A5 *If an officer has any doubts whether to authorise an intimate search by a constable, the officer should seek advice from an officer of superintendent rank or above.*

ANNEX B—DELAY IN NOTIFYING ARREST OR ALLOWING ACCESS TO LEGAL ADVICE FOR PERSONS DETAINED UNDER THE TERRORISM ACT 2000

A Delays under TACT Schedule 8

1. The rights as in *sections 5* or *6*, may be delayed if the person is detained under the Terrorism Act 2000, section 41, has not yet been charged with an offence and an officer of superintendent rank or above has reasonable grounds for believing the exercise of either right will have one of the following consequences:

(a) interference with or harm to evidence of a serious offence,

(b) interference with or physical injury to any person,

(c) the alerting of persons who are suspected of having committed a serious offence but who have not been arrested for it,

(d) the hindering of the recovery of property obtained as a result of a serious offence or in respect of which a forfeiture order could be made under section 23,

(e) interference with the gathering of information about the commission, preparation or instigation of acts of terrorism,

(f) the alerting of a person and thereby making it more difficult to prevent an act of terrorism, or

(g) the alerting of a person and thereby making it more difficult to secure a person's apprehension, prosecution or conviction in connection with the commission, preparation or instigation of an act of terrorism.

2. These rights may also be delayed if the officer has reasonable grounds for believing that:

(a) the detained person has benefited from his criminal conduct (to be decided in accordance with Part 2 of the Proceeds of Crime Act 2002), and

(b) the recovery of the value of the property constituting the benefit will be hindered by—

    (i) informing the named person of the detained person's detention (in the case of an authorisation under paragraph 8(1)(a) of Schedule 8 to TACT), or

    (ii) the exercise of the right under paragraph 7 (in the case of an authorisation under paragraph 8(1)(b) of Schedule 8 to TACT).

3. Authority to delay a detainee's right to consult privately with a solicitor may be given only if the authorising officer has reasonable grounds to believe the solicitor the detainee wants to consult will, inadvertently or otherwise, pass on a message from the detainee or act in some other way which will have any of the consequences specified under paragraph 8 of Schedule 8 to the Terrorism Act 2000. In these circumstances the detainee must be allowed to choose another solicitor. See *Note B3*.

4. If the detainee wishes to see a solicitor, access to that solicitor may not be delayed on the grounds they might advise the detainee not to answer questions or the solicitor was initially asked to attend the police station by someone else. In the latter case the detainee must be told the solicitor has come to the police station at another person's request, and must be asked to sign the custody record to signify whether they want to see the solicitor.

5. The fact the grounds for delaying notification of arrest may be satisfied does not automatically mean the grounds for delaying access to legal advice will also be satisfied.

6. These rights may be delayed only for as long as is necessary but not beyond 48 hours from the time of arrest (or if a person was being detained under TACT Schedule 7, from the time at which the examination under Schedule 7 began). If the above grounds cease to apply within this time the detainee must as soon as practicable be asked if they wish to exercise either right, the custody record noted accordingly, and action taken in accordance with the relevant section of this Code.

7. A person must be allowed to consult a solicitor for a reasonable time before any court hearing.

B Documentation

8. The grounds for action under this Annex shall be recorded and the detainee informed of them as soon as practicable.

9. Any reply given by a detainee under *paragraph 6* must be recorded and the detainee asked to endorse the record in relation to whether they want to receive legal advice at this point.

C Cautions and special warnings

10. When a suspect detained at a police station is interviewed during any period for which access to legal advice has been delayed under this Annex, the court or jury may not draw adverse inferences from their silence.

Notes for Guidance

B1 Even if Annex B applies in the case of a juvenile, or a person who is mentally disordered or otherwise mentally vulnerable, action to inform the appropriate adult and the person responsible for a juvenile's welfare if that is a different person, must nevertheless be taken as in paragraph 3.15 and 3.17.

B2 In the case of Commonwealth citizens and foreign nationals, see Note 7A.

B3 *A decision to delay access to a specific solicitor is likely to be a rare occurrence and only when it can be shown the suspect is capable of misleading that particular solicitor and there is more than a substantial risk that the suspect will succeed in causing information to be conveyed which will lead to one or more of the specified consequences.*

ANNEX C - RESTRICTION ON DRAWING ADVERSE INFERENCES FROM SILENCE AND TERMS OF THE CAUTION WHEN THE RESTRICTION APPLIES

(a) The restriction on drawing adverse inferences from silence

1. The Criminal Justice and Public Order Act 1994, sections 34, 36 and 37 as amended by the Youth Justice and Criminal Evidence Act 1999, section 58 describe the conditions under which adverse inferences may be drawn from a person's failure or refusal to say anything about their involvement in the offence when interviewed, after being charged or informed they may be prosecuted. These provisions are subject to an overriding restriction on the ability of a court or jury to draw adverse inferences from a person's silence. This restriction applies:

(a) to any detainee at a police station who, before being interviewed, see *section 11* or being charged or informed they may be prosecuted, see *section 15*, has:
    (i) asked for legal advice, see *section 6, paragraph 6.1*;
    (ii) not been allowed an opportunity to consult a solicitor, including the duty solicitor, as in this Code; and
    (iii) not changed their mind about wanting legal advice, see *section 6, paragraph 6.7(d)*.

Note the condition in (ii) will:
~ apply when a detainee who has asked for legal advice is interviewed before speaking to a solicitor as in *section 6, paragraph 6.6(a)* or *(b)*;
~ not apply if the detained person declines to ask for the duty solicitor, see *section 6, paragraphs 6.7(b)* and *(c)*.

(b) to any person who has been charged with, or informed they may be prosecuted for, an offence who:
    (i) has had brought to their notice a written statement made by another person or the content of an interview with another person which relates to that offence, see PACE Code C *section 16, paragraph 16.4*;
    (ii) is interviewed about that offence, see PACE Code C *section 16, paragraph 16.5*; or
    (iii) makes a written statement about that offence, see *Annex D paragraphs 4 and 9*,

unless post-charge questioning has been authorised in accordance with section 22 of the Counter-Terrorism Act 2008, in which case the restriction will apply only if the person has asked for legal advice, see *section 6, paragraph 6.1*, and is questioned before receiving such advice in accordance with *paragraph 6.7(b)*. See *paragraph 15.11*.

(b) Terms of the caution when the restriction applies

2. When a requirement to caution arises at a time when the restriction on drawing adverse inferences from silence applies, the caution shall be:

'You do not have to say anything, but anything you do say may be given in evidence.'

Where the use of the Welsh Language is appropriate, the caution may be used directly in Welsh in the following terms:

'Does dim rhaid i chi ddweud dim byd, ond gall unrhyw beth yr ydych chi'n ei ddweud gael ei roi fel tystiolaeth.'

3. Whenever the restriction either begins to apply or ceases to apply after a caution has already been given, the person shall be re-cautioned in the appropriate terms. The changed position on drawing inferences and that the previous caution no longer applies shall also be explained to the detainee in ordinary language. See *Note C1*.

Notes for Guidance

C1 The following is suggested as a framework to help explain changes in the position on drawing adverse inferences if the restriction on drawing adverse inferences from silence:
(a) begins to apply:
'The caution you were previously given no longer applies. This is because after that caution:
(i) you asked to speak to a solicitor but have not yet been allowed an opportunity to speak to a solicitor. See paragraph 1(a); or
(ii) you have been charged with/informed you may be prosecuted. See paragraph 1(b).
'This means that from now on, adverse inferences cannot be drawn at court and your defence will not be harmed just because you choose to say nothing. Please listen carefully to the caution I am about to give you because it will apply from now on. You will see that it does not say anything about your defence being harmed.'
(b) ceases to apply before or at the time the person is charged or informed they may be prosecuted, see paragraph 1(a);
'The caution you were previously given no longer applies. This is because after that caution you have been allowed an opportunity to speak to a solicitor. Please listen carefully to the caution I am about to give you because it will apply from now on. It explains how your defence at court may be affected if you choose to say nothing.'

ANNEX D—WRITTEN STATEMENTS UNDER CAUTION

(a) Written by a person under caution

1. A person shall always be invited to write down what they want to say.

2. A person who has not been charged with, or informed they may be prosecuted for, any offence to which the statement they want to write relates, shall:

(a) unless the statement is made at a time when the restriction on drawing adverse inferences from silence applies, see *Annex C*, be asked to write out and sign the following before writing what they want to say:

'I make this statement of my own free will. I understand that I do not have to say anything but that it may harm my defence if I do not mention when questioned something which I later rely on in court. This statement may be given in evidence.';

(b) if the statement is made at a time when the restriction on drawing adverse inferences from silence applies, be asked to write out and sign the following before writing what they want to say;

'I make this statement of my own free will. I understand that I do not have to say anything. This statement may be given in evidence.'

3. When a person, on the occasion of being charged with or informed they may be prosecuted for any offence, asks to make a statement which relates to any such offence and wants to write it they shall:

(a) unless the restriction on drawing adverse inferences from silence, see *Annex C*, applied when they were so charged or informed they may be prosecuted, be asked to write out and sign the following before writing what they want to say:

'I make this statement of my own free will. I understand that I do not have to say anything but that it may harm my defence if I do not mention when questioned something which I later rely on in court. This statement may be given in evidence.';

(b) if the restriction on drawing adverse inferences from silence applied when they were so charged or informed they may be prosecuted, be asked to write out and sign the following before writing what they want to say:

'I make this statement of my own free will. I understand that I do not have to say anything. This statement may be given in evidence.'

4. When a person, who has already been charged with or informed they may be prosecuted for any offence, asks to make a statement which relates to any such offence and wants to write it they shall be asked to write out and sign the following before writing what they want to say:

'I make this statement of my own free will. I understand that I do not have to say anything. This statement may be given in evidence.'

5. Any person writing their own statement shall be allowed to do so without any prompting except a police officer or other police staff may indicate to them which matters are material or question any ambiguity in the statement.

(b) Written by a police officer or other police staff

6. If a person says they would like someone to write the statement for them, a police officer, or other police staff shall write the statement.

7. If the person has not been charged with, or informed they may be prosecuted for, any offence to which the statement they want to make relates they shall, before starting, be asked to sign, or make their mark, to the following:
(a) unless the statement is made at a time when the restriction on drawing adverse inferences from silence applies, see *Annex C*:

'I, ..., wish to make a statement. I want someone to write down what I say. I understand that I do not have to say anything but that it may harm my defence if I do not mention when questioned something which I later rely on in court. This statement may be given in evidence.';

(b) if the statement is made at a time when the restriction on drawing adverse inferences from silence applies:

'I, ..., wish to make a statement. I want someone to write down what I say. I understand that I do not have to say anything. This statement may be given in evidence.'

8. If, on the occasion of being charged with or informed they may be prosecuted for any offence, the person asks to make a statement which relates to any such offence they shall before starting be asked to sign, or make their mark to, the following:
(a) unless the restriction on drawing adverse inferences from silence applied, see *Annex C*, when they were so charged or informed they may be prosecuted:

'I, ..., wish to make a statement. I want someone to write down what I say. I understand that I do not have to say any-

thing but that it may harm my defence if I do not mention when questioned something which I later rely on in court. This statement may be given in evidence.';

(b) if the restriction on drawing adverse inferences from silence applied when they were so charged or informed they may be prosecuted:

'I, ..., wish to make a statement. I want someone to write down what I say. I understand that I do not have to say anything. This statement may be given in evidence.'

9. If, having already been charged with or informed they may be prosecuted for any offence, a person asks to make a statement which relates to any such offence they shall before starting, be asked to sign, or make their mark to:

'I, ..., wish to make a statement. I want someone to write down what I say. I understand that I do not have to say anything. This statement may be given in evidence.'

10. The person writing the statement must take down the exact words spoken by the person making it and must not edit or paraphrase it. Any questions that are necessary, e.g. to make it more intelligible, and the answers given must be recorded at the same time on the statement form.

11. When the writing of a statement is finished the person making it shall be asked to read it and to make any corrections, alterations or additions they want. When they have finished reading they shall be asked to write and sign or make their mark on the following certificate at the end of the statement:

'I have read the above statement, and I have been able to correct, alter or add anything I wish. This statement is true. I have made it of my own free will.'

12. If the person making the statement cannot read, or refuses to read it, or to write the above mentioned certificate at the end of it or to sign it, the person taking the statement shall read it to them and ask them if they would like to correct, alter or add anything and to put their signature or make their mark at the end. The person taking the statement shall certify on the statement itself what has occurred.

ANNEX E—SUMMARY OF PROVISIONS RELATING TO MENTALLY DISORDERED AND OTHERWISE MENTALLY VULNERABLE PEOPLE

1. If an officer has any suspicion, or is told in good faith, that a person of any age may be mentally disordered or otherwise mentally

vulnerable, or mentally incapable of understanding the significance of questions or their replies that person shall be treated as mentally disordered or otherwise mentally vulnerable for the purposes of this Code. See *paragraph 1.10*

2. In the case of a person who is mentally disordered or otherwise mentally vulnerable, 'the appropriate adult' means:

(a) a relative, guardian or other person responsible for their care or custody;

(b) someone experienced in dealing with mentally disordered or mentally vulnerable people but who is not a police officer or employed by the police;

(c) failing these, some other responsible adult aged 18 or over who is not a police officer or employed by the police.

See *paragraph 1.13(b)* and *Note 1D*

3. If the detention of a person who is mentally vulnerable or appears to be suffering from a mental disorder is authorised by the review officer (see *paragraphs 14.1* and *14.2* and *Notes 14A* and *14B*), the custody officer must as soon as practicable inform the appropriate adult of the grounds for detention and the person's whereabouts, and ask the adult to come to the police station to see them. If the appropriate adult:

• is already at the station when information is given as in *paragraphs 3.1* to *3.5* the information must be given in their presence;

• is not at the station when the provisions of *paragraph 3.1* to *3.5* are complied with these provisions must be complied with again in their presence once they arrive.

See *paragraphs 3.15* to *3.16*

4. If the appropriate adult, having been informed of the right to legal advice, considers legal advice should be taken, the provisions of *section 6* apply as if the mentally disordered or otherwise mentally vulnerable person had requested access to legal advice. See *paragraph 3.20* and *Note E1*.

5. The custody officer must make sure a person receives appropriate clinical attention as soon as reasonably practicable if the person appears to be suffering from a mental disorder or in urgent cases immediately call the nearest appropriate healthcare professional or an ambulance. It is not intended these provisions delay the transfer of a detainee to a place of safety under the Mental Health Act 1983, section 136 if that is applicable. If an assessment under that Act is to take place at a police station, the custody officer must consider whether an appropriate healthcare professional should be called to conduct an initial clinical check on the detainee. See *paragraph 9.6* and *9.8*

6. If a mentally disordered or otherwise mentally vulnerable person is cautioned in the absence of the appropriate adult, the caution must be repeated in the appropriate adult's presence. See *paragraph 10.11*

7. A mentally disordered or otherwise mentally vulnerable person must not be interviewed or asked to provide or sign a written statement in the absence of the appropriate adult unless the provisions of *paragraphs 11.2* or *11.11* to *11.13* apply. Questioning in these circumstances may not continue in the absence of the appropriate adult once sufficient information to avert the risk has been obtained. A record shall be made of the grounds for any decision to begin an interview in these circumstances. See *paragraphs 11.2, 11.9* and *11.11* to *11.13*

8. If the appropriate adult is present at an interview, they shall be informed they are not expected to act simply as an observer and the purposes of their presence are to:
• advise the interviewee
• observe whether or not the interview is being conducted properly and fairly
• facilitate communication with the interviewee
See *paragraph 11.10*

9. If the custody officer charges a mentally disordered or otherwise mentally vulnerable person with an offence or takes such other action as is appropriate when there is sufficient evidence for a prosecution this must be carried out in the presence of the appropriate adult if they are at the police station. A copy of the written notice embodying any charge must be given to the appropriate adult. See *PACE Code C Section 16*

10. An intimate or strip search of a mentally disordered or otherwise mentally vulnerable person may take place only in the presence of the appropriate adult of the same sex, unless the detainee specifically requests the presence of a particular adult of the opposite sex. A strip search may take place in the absence of an appropriate adult only in cases of urgency when there is a risk of serious harm to the detainee or others. See *Annex A, paragraphs 6* and *12(c)*

11. Particular care must be taken when deciding whether to use any form of approved restraints on a mentally disordered or otherwise mentally vulnerable person in a locked cell. See *paragraph 8.2*

Notes for Guidance

E1 *The purpose of the provision at paragraph 3.20 is to protect the rights of a mentally disordered or otherwise mentally vulnerable detained person who does not understand the significance of what is said to them. If the detained person wants to exercise the right to legal advice, the appropriate action should be taken and not delayed until the appropriate adult arrives. A mentally disordered or otherwise mentally vulnerable detained person should always be given an opportunity, when an appropriate adult is called to the police station, to consult privately with a solicitor in the absence of the appropriate adult if they want.*

E2 *Although people who are mentally disordered or otherwise mentally vulnerable are often capable of providing reliable evidence, they may, without knowing or wanting to do so, be particularly prone in certain circumstances to provide information that may be unreliable, misleading or self-incriminating. Special care should always be taken when questioning such a person, and the appropriate adult should be involved if there is any doubt about a person's mental state or capacity. Because of the risk of unreliable evidence, it is important to obtain corroboration of any facts admitted whenever possible.*

E3 *Because of the risks referred to in Note E2, which the presence of the appropriate adult is intended to minimise, officers of superintendent rank or above should exercise their discretion to authorise the commencement of an interview in the appropriate adult's absence only in exceptional cases, if it is necessary to avert an immediate risk of serious harm. See paragraphs 11.2, 11.11 to 11.13*

ANNEX F—Not used

ANNEX G—FITNESS TO BE INTERVIEWED

1. This Annex contains general guidance to help police officers and healthcare professionals assess whether a detainee might be at risk in an interview.

2. A detainee may be at risk in an interview if it is considered that:
(a) conducting the interview could significantly harm the detainee's physical or mental state;
(b) anything the detainee says in the interview about their involvement or suspected involvement in the offence about which they are being interviewed might be considered unreliable in subsequent court proceedings because of their physical or mental state.

3. In assessing whether the detainee should be interviewed, the following must be considered:

(a) how the detainee's physical or mental state might affect their ability to understand the nature and purpose of the interview, to comprehend what is being asked and to appreciate the significance of any answers given and make rational decisions about whether they want to say anything;

(b) the extent to which the detainee's replies may be affected by their physical or mental condition rather than representing a rational and accurate explanation of their involvement in the offence;

(c) how the nature of the interview, which could include particularly probing questions, might affect the detainee.

4. It is essential healthcare professionals who are consulted consider the functional ability of the detainee rather than simply relying on a medical diagnosis, e.g. it is possible for a person with severe mental illness to be fit for interview.

5. Healthcare professionals should advise on the need for an appropriate adult to be present, whether reassessment of the person's fitness for interview may be necessary if the interview lasts beyond a specified time, and whether a further specialist opinion may be required.

6. When healthcare professionals identify risks they should be asked to quantify the risks. They should inform the custody officer:
- whether the person's condition:
  - ~ is likely to improve;
  - ~ will require or be amenable to treatment; and
- indicate how long it may take for such improvement to take effect.

7. The role of the healthcare professional is to consider the risks and advise the custody officer of the outcome of that consideration. The healthcare professional's determination and any advice or recommendations should be made in writing and form part of the custody record.

8. Once the healthcare professional has provided that information, it is a matter for the custody officer to decide whether or not to allow the interview to go ahead and if the interview is to proceed, to determine what safeguards are needed. Nothing prevents safeguards being provided in addition to those required under the Code. An example might be to have an appropriate healthcare professional present during the interview, in addition to an appropriate adult, in order constantly to monitor the person's condition and how it is being affected by the interview.

ANNEX H—DETAINED PERSON: OBSERVATION LIST

1. If any detainee fails to meet any of the following criteria, an appropriate healthcare professional or an ambulance must be called.

2. When assessing the level of rousability, consider:

Rousability—can they be woken?
- go into the cell
- call their name
- shake gently

Response to questions—can they give appropriate answers to questions such as:
- What's your name?
- Where do you live?
- Where do you think you are?

Response to commands—can they respond appropriately to commands such as:
- Open your eyes!
- Lift one arm, now the other arm!

3. Remember to take into account the possibility or presence of other illnesses, injury, or mental condition, a person who is drowsy and smells of alcohol may also have the following:
- Diabetes
- Epilepsy
- Head injury
- Drug intoxication or overdose
- Stroke

ANNEX I—ESTABLISHING GENDER OF PERSONS FOR THE PURPOSE OF SEARCHING

1. Certain provisions of this and other PACE Codes explicitly state that searches and other procedures may only be carried out by, or in the presence of, persons of the same sex as the person subject to the search or other procedure. See *Note I1*.

2. All searches and procedures must be carried out with courtesy, consideration and respect for the person concerned. Police officers

should show particular sensitivity when dealing with transgender individuals (including transsexual persons) and transvestite persons (see *Notes I2, I3* and *I4*).

(a) Consideration

3. In law, the gender (and accordingly the sex) of an individual is their gender as registered at birth unless they have been issued with a Gender Recognition Certificate (GRC) under the Gender Recognition Act 2004 (GRA), in which case the person's gender is their acquired gender. This means that if the acquired gender is the male gender, the person's sex becomes that of a man and, if it is the female gender, the person's sex becomes that of a woman) and they must be treated as their acquired gender.

4. When establishing whether the person concerned should be treated as being male or female for the purposes of these searches and procedures, the following approach which is designed to minimise embarrassment and secure the person's co-operation should be followed:

(a) The person must not be asked whether they have a GRC (see *paragraph 8*);

(b) If there is no doubt as to as to whether the person concerned should be treated as being male or female, they should be dealt with as being of that sex.

(c) If at any time (including during the search or carrying out the procedure) there is doubt as to whether the person should be treated, or continue to be treated, as being male or female:

   (i)   the person should be asked what gender they consider themselves to be. If they express a preference to be dealt with as a particular gender, they should be asked to indicate and confirm their preference by signing the custody record or, if a custody record has not been opened, the search record or the officer's notebook. Subject to (ii) below, the person should be treated according to their preference;

   (ii) if there are grounds to doubt that the preference in (i) accurately reflects the person's predominant lifestyle, for example, if they ask to be treated as woman but documents and other information make it clear that they live predominantly as a man, or vice versa, they should be treated according to what appears to be their predominant lifestyle and not their stated preference;

   (iii) If the person is unwilling to express a preference as in (i) above, efforts should be made to determine their predominant lifestyle and they should be treated as such. For example, if they appear to live predominantly as a woman, they should be treated as being female; or

(iv) if none of the above apply, the person should be dealt with according to what reasonably appears to have been their sex as registered at birth.

5. Once a decision has been made about which gender an individual is to be treated as, each officer responsible for the search or procedure should where possible be advised before the search or procedure starts of any doubts as to the person's gender and the person informed that the doubts have been disclosed. This is important so as to maintain the dignity of the person and any officers concerned.

(b) Documentation

6. The person's gender as established under *paragraph 4(c)(i)* to *(iv)* above must be recorded in the person's custody record, or if a custody record has not been opened, on the search record or in the officer's notebook.

7. Where the person elects which gender they consider themselves to be under *paragraph 4(b)(i)* but following *4(b)(ii)* is not treated in accordance with their preference, the reason must be recorded in the search record, in the officer's notebook or, if applicable, in the person's custody record.

(c) Disclosure of information

8. Section 22 of the GRA defines any information relating to a person's application for a GRC or to a successful applicant's gender before it became their acquired gender as 'protected information'. Nothing in this Annex is to be read as authorising or permitting any police officer or any police staff who has acquired such information when acting in their official capacity to disclose that information to any other person in contravention of the GRA. Disclosure includes making a record of 'protected information' which is read by others.

Note for Guidance

I1 Provisions to which paragraph 1 applies include:
- *In Code C; paragraph 4.1 and Annex A paragraphs 5, 6, 11 and 12 (searches, strip and intimate searches of detainees under sections 54 and 55 of PACE);*
- *In Code A; paragraphs 2.8 and 3.6 and Note 4;*

- *In Code D; paragraph 5.5 and Note 5F (searches, examinations and photographing of detainees under section 54A of PACE) and paragraph 6.9 (taking samples);*
- *In Code H; paragraph 4.1 and Annex A paragraphs 6, 7 and 12 (searches, strip and intimate searches under sections 54 and 55 of PACE of persons arrested under section 41 of the Terrorism Act 2000).*

I2 While there is no agreed definition of transgender (or trans), it is generally used as an umbrella term to describe people whose gender identity (self-identification as being a woman, man, neither or both) differs from the sex they were registered as at birth. The term includes, but is not limited to, transsexual people.

I3 Transsexual means a person who is proposing to undergo, is undergoing or has undergone a process (or part of a process) for the purpose of gender reassignment which is a protected characteristic under the Equality Act 2010 (see paragraph 1.0) by changing physiological or other attributes of their sex. This includes aspects of gender such as dress and title. It would apply to a woman making the transition to being a man and a man making the transition to being a woman as well as to a person who has only just started out on the process of gender reassignment and to a person who has completed the process. Both would share the characteristic of gender reassignment with each having the characteristics of one sex, but with certain characteristics of the other sex.

I4 Transvestite means a person of one gender who dresses in the clothes of a person of the opposite gender. However, a transvestite does not live permanently in the gender opposite to their birth sex.

I5 Chief officers are responsible for providing corresponding operational guidance and instructions for the deployment of transgender officers and staff under their direction and control to duties which involve carrying out, or being present at, any of the searches and procedures described in paragraph 1. The guidance and instructions must comply with the Equality Act 2010 and should therefore complement the approach in this Annex.

ANNEX J—TRANSFER OF PERSONS DETAINED FOR MORE THAN 14 DAYS TO PRISON

1. When a warrant of further detention is extended or further extended by a High Court judge to authorise a person's detention beyond a period of 14 days from the time of their arrest (or if they were being detained under TACT Schedule 7, from the time at which their examination under Schedule 7 began), the person must be transferred from detention in a police station to detention in a des-

ignated prison as soon as is practicable after the warrant is issued,
unless:

(a) the detainee specifically requests to remain in detention at a
police station and that request can be accommodated, or

(b) there are reasonable grounds to believe that transferring the
detainee to a prison would:
   (i) significantly hinder a terrorism investigation;
   (ii) delay charging of the detainee or their release from custody, or
   (iii) otherwise prevent the investigation from being conducted
diligently and expeditiously.

Any grounds in (b)(i) to (iii) above which are relied upon for not
transferring the detainee to prison must be presented to the senior
judge as part of the application for the extension or further
extension of the warrant. See *Note J1.*

2. If at any time during which a person remains in detention at a
police station under the warrant, the grounds at (b)(i) to (iii) cease to
apply, the person must be transferred to a prison as soon as
practicable.

3. Police should maintain an agreement with the National Offender
Management Service (NOMS) that stipulates named prisons to
which individuals may be transferred under this paragraph. This
should be made with regard to ensuring detainees are moved to the
most suitable prison for the purposes of the investigation and their
welfare, and should include provision for the transfer of male,
female and juvenile detainees. Police should ensure that the Governor of a prison to which they intend to transfer a detainee is given
reasonable notice of this. Where practicable, this should be no later
than the point at which a warrant is applied for that would take the
period of detention beyond 14 days.

4. Following a detainee's transfer to a designated prison, their
detention will be governed by the terms of Schedule 8 to TACT 2000
and the Prison Rules and this Code of Practice will not apply during
any period that the person remains in prison detention. The Code
will once more apply if the person is transferred back from prison
detention to police detention. In order to enable the Governor to
arrange for the production of the detainee back into police custody,
police should give notice to the Governor of the relevant prison as
soon as possible of any decision to transfer a detainee from prison
back to a police station. Any transfer between a prison and a police
station should be conducted by police and this Code will be applicable during the period of transit. See *Note 2J*. A detainee should
only remain in police custody having been transferred back from a

prison, for as long as is necessary for the purpose of the investigation.

5. The investigating team and custody officer should provide as much information as necessary to enable the relevant prison authorities to provide appropriate facilities to detain an individual. This should include, but not be limited to:

(i)   medical assessments

(ii)   security and risk assessments

(iii)   details of the detained person's legal representatives

(iv)   details of any individuals from whom the detained person has requested visits, or who have requested to visit the detained person.

6. Where a detainee is to be transferred to prison, the custody officer should inform the detainee's legal adviser beforehand that the transfer is to take place (including the name of the prison). The custody officer should also make all reasonable attempts to inform:

• family or friends who have been informed previously of the detainee's detention; and

• the person who was initially informed of the detainee's detention in accordance with *paragraph 5.1*.

7. Any decision not to transfer a detained person to a designated prison under *paragraph 1*, must be recorded, along with the reasons for this decision. If a request under *paragraph 1(a)* is not accommodated, the reasons for this should also be recorded.

Notes for Guidance

J1 Transfer to prison is intended to ensure that individuals who are detained for extended periods of time are held in a place designed for longer periods of detention than police stations. Prison will provide detainees with a greater range of facilities more appropriate to longer detention periods.

J2 This Code will only apply as is appropriate to the conditions of detention during the period of transit. There is obviously no requirement to provide such things as bed linen or reading materials for the journey between prison and police station.

Code of Practice for Authorised Officers Acting under Schedule 1 to the Anti-terrorism, Crime and Security Act 2001

1. General

1. This code of practice applies to the exercise by an authorised officer of functions of Schedule 1 to the Anti-terrorism, Crime and Security Act 2001 (the Act). The code is issued under paragraph 6(1) of Schedule 14 to the Terrorism Act 2000 (and amended by the Anti-terrorism, Crime and Security Act 2001 (Commencement) Order 2001).

2. 'Authorised officer' for the purpose of this code has the same meaning as in paragraph 19(1) of Schedule 1 to the Act. It therefore applies to an immigration officer and a customs officer when exercising functions under Schedule 1 to the Act as well as to a constable exercising these functions. The code does not apply in other circumstances in which seizure, detention or forfeiture powers are exercised. Nor does the code apply where a customs officer or constable exercises powers of seizure and detention of cash under Part 2 of the Drug Trafficking Act 1994 (DTA).

3. 'Cash' has the same meaning as in paragraph 1 of Schedule 1 to the Act. Reference to an officer's rank includes an officer acting temporarily in that rank.

4. The code should be available at all police stations for consultation by the police and members of the public. It should also be available at police offices at ports (within the meaning of Schedule 7 to the Terrorism Act 2000) where the powers are, or are likely to be used. The code should also form part of the published instructions or guidance for immigration officers and customs officers.

Authority to seize cash

5. Any decision to seize cash under the Act must be authorised:

- where seizure is undertaken by a police constable, by a police officer of the rank of Inspector or above;
- where seizure is undertaken by an immigration officer, by a Chief Immigration Officer;
- where seizure is undertaken by a customs officer, by a Customs Officer Pay Band 7 or above.

Authorisation to seize cash should be obtained prior to actual seizure of the cash itself. Verbal authorisation should be supported by written authorisation as soon as is reasonably practicable.

Use of the powers by immigration and customs officers

6. The powers to seize and detain cash under the Act should only be exercised by an immigration officer or customs officer exceptionally. If such an officer develops a suspicion in the course of exercising his/her powers under the Immigration Act 1971, the Customs and Excise Management Act 1979 or the Police and Criminal Evidence Act 1984 that cash found is liable to be seized under the Act he/she should alert a police officer at the earliest opportunity in order to continue any investigation. The person or persons carrying the cash should be informed of the suspicion and of the action taken (or proposed) to inform the police.

Scope

7. There is no minimum or maximum limit on the amount of cash which may be seized.

8. Under Schedule 1 to the Act an authorised officer may seize and detain cash (for up to 48 hours) where he/she has reasonable grounds for suspecting that the cash:-
(a)
- is intended to be used for the purposes of terrorism;
- consists of resources of a proscribed organisation; or
- is or represents property obtained by or in return for acts of terrorism or acts carried out for the purposes of terrorism (although this is subject to the exceptions set out at paragraph 16 of Schedule 1 to the Act);
  and
(b) is found at any place in the United Kingdom.

Seizure of cash

9. 'Reasonable grounds for suspecting' are likely to depend upon particular circumstances and the authorised officer should take into account such factors as how the cash was discovered, the amount

involved, its origins, intended movement, destination, reasons given for a cash as opposed to normal banking transaction, whether the courier(s) and/or the owners of the cash (if different) have any links with terrorists, terrorist groups or sympathisers, whether here or overseas. Where the authorised officer has suspicions about the cash he/she should give the person who has possession of it a reasonable opportunity to provide an explanation on the details of its ownership, origins, purpose, destination and reasons for moving the amount in this way and to provide the authorised officer with supporting documentation. The authorised officer should make clear to the person that anything said will be noted and used in the event that the cash is seized and an application made to the court for its detention or forfeiture.

10. If the authorised officer believes the person has committed an offence and/or is to be arrested he or she should be cautioned and questioned in the normal way. A customs or immigration officer acting in the capacity of an authorised officer may wish or need to refer the matter to a police officer in such instances.

11. The cash should be counted in the presence of the person and another officer. Cash should not be taken out of sight of the person carrying it unless and until it is seized.

12. Where cash is seized, the authorised officer should inform the person carrying it that he suspects that it is cash within one or more of the provision(s) of paragraph 1(1) of Schedule 1 to the Act and the reasons for suspecting this.

13. The authorised officer should physically seize the cash and give a written notification (see Annex) to the person from whom the cash is seized. (This includes the sender and intended recipient of unattended parcels and other containers.) This notification explains that an application may be made for detention of the cash within 48 hours of seizure and provides details of the court to which the application will be made. It also advises the person that he or she is entitled to appear at the court hearing either in person or represented by a solicitor. It advises finally that cash will be released no later than the end of the period of 48 hours from the time of seizure unless an order for its further detention is granted.

14. Where the cash is not in sterling, the figure should be entered in the relevant currency. The examining officers should not attempt to convert the currency into sterling. Similarly, where the cash is in different forms (for example, postal orders, ordinary cheques, travellers' cheques, bankers' drafts, bearer bonds or bearer shares) a description and their value should be recorded on the written notification and receipt.

15. The authorised officer should explain the contents of the notification to the person from whom the cash has been taken and what he or she has to do in order to try to get it back. The authorised officer should make every reasonable effort to ensure that the person concerned understands. The person should be asked to sign the statement in the written notification that the content of the notice has been read and understood and the authorised officer should give a copy of the notification to him. If the person refuses to sign the authorised officer should endorse the form "refused to sign" and initial the endorsement.

16. If the person does not appear to understand what is being said or the authorised officer has doubts as to the person's ability to speak English the officer should make every reasonable effort to communicate so as to be satisfied that the person understands what is required of him or her, where necessary, using someone who can act as an interpreter.

Detention of cash seized

17. The authorised officer should record in the written notification the time and date when the cash is first seized. He must release the cash and return it to the person unless a court order is obtained no later than 48 hours after the cash has been first seized.

18. The authorised officer or the Commissioners for Customs and Excise should apply in writing without delay to the relevant court for an order to detain the cash. In Scotland, the authorised officer should report the matter without delay to the procurator fiscal who is responsible for making the application to the sheriff. A copy of the written application should be given to the person from whom the cash has been seized, wherever practicable at the time of the seizure in order to give him/her the maximum time in which to make an application to the court to contest seizure and secure the release of the cash. An application for the detention of cash should be authorised by a police officer of the rank of Inspector or above.

19. Where cash is deposited in an interest bearing account in accordance with paragraph 4 of Schedule 1 to the Act, the authorised officer should ensure a central record is kept of the details of the account and when the cash was deposited. To ensure interest accrued is accurately accounted, separate records for each cash seizure deposit should be kept.

20. When an order to detain cash has been granted the authorised officer should keep under review whether continued detention of the cash is justified. But this does not apply where an application for forfeiture has been made and not concluded, where an application has been made under paragraph 9 of Schedule 1 to the Act by a person who claims to be a victim and not concluded or where criminal proceedings have been commenced in connection with the cash and not concluded, whether in the United Kingdom or elsewhere. If for any reason the authorised officer considers he is no longer justified in detaining the cash he/she should release it and return it to the person from whom it was seized Where detained cash is to be released, the authorised officer should inform the court without delay (in Scotland, the procurator fiscal is responsible for notifying the sheriff that detained cash is to be released). A decision to release the cash should be authorised by a police officer of the rank of Inspector or above.

21. An application to renew an order to detain cash beyond 6 months and up to the maximum limit of 2 years (beginning with the date when the first order was made), should be authorised by a police officer of the rank of superintendent or above. In Scotland, the procurator fiscal is responsible for making further applications.

Forfeiture

22. Any application under paragraph 6 of Schedule 1 to the Act by or on behalf of the authorised officer for the forfeiture of cash must be authorised by a police officer of the rank of superintendent or above who, prior to any application being made, should review the facts in order to be satisfied on the balance of probabilities that the cash is cash to which Schedule 1 to the Act applies. In Scotland, applications for the forfeiture of detained cash are made to the sheriff by the Scottish Ministers.

Security of cash seized

23. Any cash seized or received by a constable under the Act should be handled in accordance with any standing instructions or orders in force. Without prejudice to any such instructions or orders the authorised officer who seizes cash should ensure that it is held in a safe, secure place until either released or lodged in an interest accruing account under paragraph 4 of Schedule 1 to the Act following a detention order under paragraph 3(2) of Schedule 1 to the Act.

24. Cash seized by an immigration officer or a customs officer must be handed at the earliest opportunity to the police officer with responsibility for investigating whether an application for its continued detention is to be made. The amount delivered to the police officer should be agreed and a receipt given for it by the police officer receiving it.

Annex

NOTIFICATION OF CASH SEIZURE UNDER PARAGRAPH 2 OF SCHEDULE 1 TO THE ANTI-TERRORISM, CRIME AND SECURITY ACT 2001

Under paragraph 2 of Schedule 1 to the Anti-terrorism, Crime and Security Act 2001, cash to the value of..........in..........(currency) */postal orders */ cheques*/ travellers' cheques*/ bankers' drafts*/ bearer bonds*/ bearer shares* was seized on..........(date) at..........(place).

Any application for continued detention of the cash under paragraph 3 of Schedule 1 to the Anti-terrorism, Crime and Security Act 2001 must be made not later than the period of 48 hours from the period beginning with the time when it was seized.

An application will be made by a constable*/ customs officer*/ immigration officer*/ the Commissioners for Customs and Excise* to the magistrates' court at.........../*by the procurator fiscal to the sheriff's court at..........

You will receive a copy of the written application to the court with notification of the hearing. You are entitled to appear in court at the hearing, either in person or represented by a solicitor.

If no application for continued detention of the cash is made within the period of 48 hours mentioned above, the cash seized must be released.

Signed..

Time..

Date..

I................acknowledge that cash to the value of...............
in (currency)*/postal orders*/cheques*/travellers' cheques*/bankers' drafts*/bearer bonds*/bearer shares* has been seized from me and that I have read and understood this notification.

Signed..

Time..

Date..

* Delete as necessary.

Code of Practice for Examining Officers under the Terrorism Act 2000

General

1 This code of practice applies to the exercise by examining officers of their functions under the Terrorism Act 2000 ("the Act").

2 The notes for guidance are not provisions of the code but are guidance to examining officers on its application and interpretation.

3 The term "examining officer" for the purpose of this code has the same meaning as in paragraph 1(1) of Schedule 7 to the Act ("the Schedule"), i.e. a constable, immigration officer or customs officer designated for the purpose of the Schedule by the Secretary of State and the Commissioners of Her Majesty's Revenue and Customs. The code only applies to immigration or designated customs officers when they are exercising their functions as examining officers under the Act and not in any other circumstances, for example where someone is examined under the Immigration Act 1971 or the Customs and Excise Management Act 1979.

4 For the purposes of this code:
- "port" and "border area" have the same meaning as in the Schedule;
- Common Travel Area ("CTA") has the same meaning as in section 1(3) of the Immigration Act 1971;
- a child means anyone who appears to be under the age of 17 in the absence of clear evidence that he/she is older. In Scotland, a child means anyone under the age of 16 except where that person is between 16 and 18 and is the subject of a supervision requirement imposed by a Children's hearing; or a person whose case has been referred to a children's hearing in relation to a corresponding order made by a court in England, Wales or Northern Ireland.

5 The code should be available at all police stations for consultation by the police and members of the public. It must also be available at police offices at ports or in the border area where the powers are, or are likely to be used. The code should also form part of the published

departmental instructions/guidance for immigration officers and customs officers.

Immigration and customs officers

6 Only exceptionally should an immigration officer or customs officer exercise functions under the Act and then only when
- a police officer is not readily available; or
- if specifically requested to do so by a police officer of the rank of sergeant or above.

In all cases where it is reasonably practicable the authority of a Chief Immigration Officer in the case of an immigration officer, or in the case of a customs officer, a Higher Officer or above, should be obtained for any action taken under the Act. Where it has not been practicable to achieve prior authorisation, the Chief Immigration Officer or the Customs Higher Officer or above should be notified of the action taken as soon as possible after the exercise of functions has begun.

Scope of the Examination

7 The power to examine someone under the Schedule applies:
- to a person on a ship, aircraft or international train which has arrived at any place in Great Britain or Northern Ireland (whether from within or outside Great Britain or Northern Ireland) (see paragraph 2(3) of the Schedule);[1]
- where the examining officer believes that a person's presence at the port or in the border area (in Northern Ireland) is connected with his entering or leaving Great Britain or Northern Ireland or his travelling by air within Great Britain or within Northern Ireland (see paragraph 2(2) of the Schedule);

"Belief" should be justifiable and much will depend on the individual circumstances. For example:
- the presence of a member of the public in a controlled, international or Common Travel Area arrivals or departure area or common departure lounge at a port;
- where someone is waiting to be, is being, or has been checked in for a flight or ferry to or from Great Britain or Northern Ireland:

[1] The Channel Tunnel (International Arrangements) (Amendment) Order 2001 provides that examining officers can exercise Schedule 7 powers: (a) under paragraph 2(3) on an international train; and (b) under paragraph 2(2) at a railway station or other place where persons embark or disembark, or where goods are loaded on or from an international train service.

may be indicators that a person can be examined under the Schedule.

8 The examples given above are not intended as an exhaustive list. Presence alone however may not be sufficient without other indicators of travel.

Examination powers

9 The purpose of questioning and associated powers is to determine whether a person appears to be someone who is or has been concerned in the commission, preparation or instigation of acts of terrorism. The powers, which are additional to the powers of arrest under the Act, should not be used for any other purpose.

10 An examining officer may question a person whether or not he suspects that the person is or has been concerned in the commission, preparation or instigation of an act of terrorism and may stop that person for the purposes of determining whether this appears to be the case. Examining officers should therefore make every reasonable effort to exercise the power in such a way as to minimise causing embarrassment or offence to a person who is being questioned.

Notes for guidance on paragraphs 9 and 10

The powers to stop, question, detain and search persons under Schedule 7 do not require an examining officer to have any grounds for suspicion against any individual prior to the exercise of the powers. Therefore examining officers must take into account that many people selected for examination using Schedule 7 powers will be entirely innocent of any unlawful activity.

The powers must be used proportionately, reasonably, with respect and without unlawful discrimination. All persons being stopped and questioned by examining officers must be treated in a respectful and courteous manner.

Examining officers must take particular care to ensure that the selection of persons for examination is not solely based on their perceived ethnic background or religion. The powers must be exercised in a manner that does not unfairly discriminate against anyone on the grounds of age, race, colour, religion, creed, gender or sexual orientation. To do so would be unlawful. It is the case that it will not always be possible for an examining officer working at a port to know the identity, provenance or destination of a passenger until they have stopped and questioned them.

Although the exercise of Schedule 7 powers is not based on an examining officer having any suspicion against any individual, the powers should not be used arbitrarily. An examining officer's decision to exercise their Schedule 7 powers at ports must be based on the threat posed by the various terrorist groups active in and outside the United Kingdom. When deciding whether to exercise their Schedule 7 powers, examining officers should base their decisions on a number of considerations, including factors such as;

- *known and suspected sources of terrorism;*
- *Individuals or groups whose current or past involvement in acts or threats of terrorism is known or suspected and supporters or sponsors of such activity who are known or suspected;*
- *Any information on the origins and/or location of terrorist groups;*
- *Possible current, emerging and future terrorist activity;*
- *The means of travel (and documentation) that a group or individuals involved in terrorist activity could use;*
- *Emerging local trends or patterns of travel through specific ports or in the wider vicinity that may be linked to terrorist activity.*

Selections for examination should be based on informed considerations such as those outlined above and must be in connection with the threat posed by the various terrorist groups active in and outside the United Kingdom. A person's perceived ethnic background or religion must not be used alone or in combination with each other as the sole reason for selecting the person for examination.

Schedule 7 powers are to be used solely for the purpose of ascertaining if the person examined is or has been concerned in the commission, preparation or instigation of acts of terrorism. The powers must not be used to stop and question persons for any other purpose. An examination must cease and the examinee must be informed that it has ended once it has been ascertained that the person examined does not appear to be or to have been concerned in the commission, preparation or instigation of acts of terrorism.

Unless the examining officer arrests the person using powers under the Act, a person being examined under Schedule 7 need not be cautioned.

11 The examining officer should explain to the person concerned either verbally or in writing, that they are being examined under Schedule 7 of the Terrorism Act 2000 and that the officer has the power to detain that person should they refuse to co-operate and insist on leaving. The examining officer should keep the length of examination to the minimum that is practicable. An examination begins after a person has been stopped and screening questions have been asked (see note). Once an examination lasts for one hour, an explanatory notice of examination, a TACT 1 form which is set out at annex A to this code, must be served by the examining officer on the person. The contents of the TACT 1 form should be explained to the person by the examining officer. Where a person's examination is protracted or where it is thought likely to be protracted, the examining officer should make arrangements to ensure that the person has the opportunity to have refreshments at regular intervals.

Note for guidance on paragraph 11

The examination begins at the point at which any of the following occurs:
- *After screening questions are asked and/or*
- *The person or vehicle is directed to another place for examination.*

A person who is being examined/detained cannot be examined/detained for a period exceeding nine hours.

12 Where a person is being asked screening questions by an examining officer who is not a police officer and it appears necessary to begin an examination of that person, the examining officer should refer him/her to a police officer at the port or, in the border area, or a police station at the earliest opportunity. The examining officer should agree the time and date of the commencement of the examination with the police officer receiving the person and both should keep a record of that time and date.

13 If the person concerned does not appear to understand what is being said to them, or if the examining officer doubts the person's ability to understand English, every reasonable effort should be made to communicate with him/her so as to ensure that the person comprehends what is required of him/her, where practicable using someone who can act as an interpreter.

Records of Examinations

14 Records of all examinations should be kept locally at a port, border area or police station in the event of a complaint or query but in addition a record of all exams over an hour should be held centrally for statistical purposes. The record should include the name of the person examined; the total duration of the examination from the start until completion; whether the person was detained and if so when detention began and ended.

15 Records of examination that last under an hour or in the case of a child of any duration should be kept at the port, border area or at a police station for reference purposes in the event of a complaint or query. Records of examination that last over an hour, however, should be kept centrally for statistical purposes.

16 The examining officer should keep a record of any examination of someone believed to be an unaccompanied child. The record should include the name and age (if known) of the child. If any of these records are kept by an examining officer who is not also a police officer, the details including the time examination began should be passed to a police officer who has been, is or is to be involved in the examination of the person, as soon as practicable.

Children and other vulnerable people

17 Special care should be taken when considering whether to question someone, where it is evident that the person is a child. A child travelling with a parent or guardian or responsible person over 18 (for example a teacher, social worker, or group leader where the child is part of an organised party) should be examined in their presence.

18 A child aged under 16 travelling alone should not normally be examined in detail unless an adult is present. Where such a child is travelling with a friend or relative who is 18 or over, the examining officer should consider allowing that person to be present during any routine examinations unless that person is thought to be exerting influence or pressure which could be detrimental or is otherwise obstructive to the child's interest. If a more detailed examination is considered necessary it should only take place in the presence of a parent, a guardian, or (if the child is in care) a representative of the care authority or voluntary organisation, a social worker, or an adult who is not a police officer or employed by the police and who has been appointed to represent the child's interests. The term 'in care' is used in this code to cover all cases in which a child is 'looked after' by a local authority under the terms of the Children Act 1989, the Children (Northern Ireland) Order 1995 or is subject to a supervision order under the Children (Scotland) Act 1995.

19 Examining officers should bear in mind that children can be easily intimidated when examined especially if they are travelling alone but, equally, that they can be vulnerable to exploitation by adults wishing to further terrorist aims. Examining officers are not therefore precluded from examining children but should do so only where absolutely necessary, for example where it is believed that the child may be caught up in some way, wittingly or otherwise, in the commission, preparation or instigation of any act of terrorism and the examining officer believes it is necessary in the child's best interests or in the interests of the public to speak to him/her.

20 These principles apply to other vulnerable people such as those who have a mental disorder or are mentally handicapped. 'Mental disorder' is a generic term which has the meaning given to it in Section 1(2) of the Mental Health Act 1983 as amended by the Mental Health Act 2007, that is, any disorder or disability of mind, which includes reference to 'mental disorder' as defined in Article 3(1) of the Mental Health (NI) Order 1986 as 'a state of arrested or incomplete development of mind which includes significant impairment and social functioning'.

Detention

21 An examining officer may detain a person in order to examine him/her for the purpose set out in paragraph 9 above. A Notice of Detention (TACT 2 form as set out at annex B) should be served by the examining officer on the person. No combination of examination/detention can exceed nine hours. The examining officer should exercise the power to detain a person and arrange for that person to be taken to a police station for further examination as soon as is practicable if the examination cannot, for any reason, proceed or continue at the port or, in the case of the border area, that location.

22 Where a person is detained under Schedule 7 at a place other than a police station, the examining officer should inform the detained person that he/she is not under arrest or caution but that he/she is being detained under the provisions of Schedule 7 to the Act. The examining officer should explain that this in itself does not necessarily mean that the examining officer suspects the detained person to be concerned in the commission, preparation or instigation of acts of terrorism, and that the purpose of the questioning is to enable the examining officer to determine whether the detained person appears to be such a person. The examining officer should advise the detained person that, under paragraph 5 of Schedule 7 to the Act he/she has a duty to give the officer all the information in his/her possession which the officer requests in connection with his determining whether the person appears to be, or has been, concerned in the commission preparation or instigation of acts of terrorism. The detained person should also be reminded that not complying with this duty is a criminal offence under paragraph 18(1) of Schedule 7 to the Act.

Note for guidance on paragraph 21 and 22

Examination and detention under Schedule 7 are not the same. A person being examined will not necessarily need to be detained and it is envisaged that most examinations will be conducted without the need to detain the person. Detention will be required usually where a person refuses to co-operate and insists on leaving. In such circumstances, it may not always be necessary to take the person to a police station: detention may be short lived, for example to complete an examination.

Fingerprints

23 Once a person has been detained an examining officer can take steps which are reasonably necessary to identify them (this does not include a power to take fingerprints or samples (see paragraph 2 of Schedule 8 to the Act)). However, under paragraphs 10 to 15 of Schedule 8 (in England and Wales) and 20 in Scotland a **constable** has the power to take a detained person's fingerprints and this can be for identification purposes.

24 Fingerprints may be taken at a port where the individual has been detained and written consent has been obtained from the individual. However, where consent has been refused a person **must** be taken to **a police station and a police officer of at least the rank of superintendent must authorise the taking of the individual's fingerprints**. A person should not be detained for the purpose of only taking their fingerprints.

Production of information

25 The examining officer should specify, in accordance with paragraph 5 of Schedule 7, the kind of information which he expects the person concerned to produce for examination/inspection.

Note for guidance on paragraph 25

Information requested by an examining officer includes electronic devices and data and passwords to those electronic devices and data. Where the information is located elsewhere, for example on another server, and is accessed via a mobile phone or internet connection, further warrantry or other authority would be required.

26 The examining officer should give the person concerned a reasonable opportunity to produce information, documents or evidence of identity before conducting a search (see paras 28 to 35 below); and should bear in mind that people travelling to and from

Northern Ireland, any place in Great Britain or Northern Ireland (whether from within or outside Great Britain or Northern Ireland) and within the Common Travel Area may not be carrying a passport. An examining officer may nonetheless inspect a passport if one is carried by the person concerned. An examining officer may use electronic equipment in order to identify persons and property.

Property

27 Under Paragraph 11 of Schedule 7 an examining officer may seize and detain for the purpose of examination anything produced during an examination or found during a search for a period of up to seven days beginning with the day on which the detention commences. If anything is found which in the opinion of the examining officer may be needed for use in criminal proceedings or which he believes may be needed in connection with a decision by the Secretary of State whether to make a deportation order under the Immigration Act 1971, it may be detained for as long as is necessary.

Searches

28 An examining officer may search a person who is being questioned for the purpose set out in paragraph 9 above, and their belongings, including baggage. He may also under paragraph 10 authorise another person to carry out a search on his behalf (see note). As under paragraph 10 above every reasonable effort should be made to reduce to a minimum the potential embarrassment or offence that may be caused to a person being searched. A baggage search does not have to be carried out by someone of the same sex, but whenever reasonably possible should be if an objection is raised. If it is not practicable to do so, the examining officer should note the objection in the officer's official notebook but may proceed with the search (See note).

Note for guidance on paragraph 28

Section 115 gives effect to Schedule 14 (which makes provision for the use of reasonable force by an "examining officer" for the purpose of exercising a power conferred on him by Schedule 7 apart from the power to question someone under paragraphs 2 and 3 of the Schedule). Where an examining officer exercises powers of search in a port or border area under Schedule 7 of this Act there is no requirement for any notice of search to be provided regarding the search of that person, their vehicle or belongings or any boat, aircraft or train. Only examining officers who have been trained to exercise search functions should carry out searches under Schedule 7.

29 A personal search should only be carried out by someone of the same sex. This is a requirement under paragraph 8(3) of the Schedule.

30 The examining officer should bear in mind that the power must not be used for any purpose other than to determine whether the person appears to be someone who is, or has been, concerned in the commission, preparation or instigation of acts of terrorism. This does not, however, necessarily preclude a search being carried out under other powers (for example where the examining officer is a constable and has other powers by virtue of common law or other statute).

31 When a search of a person is carried out the examining officer should, if not uniformed, show a warrant card or similar evidence of his/her authority but need not give his/her name.

32 If requested, the examining officer should nonetheless provide sufficient information to the person (or his/her representative), such as an identification number and location which would enable the officer to be identified in the event of any query or complaint.

Strip Search

33 A strip search is a search involving the removal of more than outer clothing. This search power does not extend to requiring a person to undergo an intimate search (searching a person's body orifice other than the mouth). Strip searches should not be undertaken routinely and can only be conducted when a person has been detained. A strip search at a port may take place where an examining officer has reasonable grounds to suspect that a person has concealed something which may be evidence that he is a person who appears to be, or to have been, concerned in the commission, preparation or instigation of acts of terrorism, or where it is suspected the article itself may have been used for such purposes. Strip searches should not be undertaken routinely.

34 The following procedures should be observed when strip searches are conducted:
(a) an officer carrying out a strip search must be of the same sex as the person searched;
(b) the search should take place in an area where the person being searched cannot be seen by anyone who does not need to be present, nor by a member of the opposite sex (except an

appropriate adult whose presence has been specifically requested by the person being searched);

(c) except in cases of urgency, where there is a risk of serious harm to the person being searched or to others or whenever a strip search involves exposure of intimate parts of the body, there should be at least two people present other than the person being searched, and if the search is of a child or a mentally disordered or mentally handicapped person, one of the people should be an appropriate adult. Except in urgent cases as above, a search of a child may take place in the absence of the appropriate adult only if the child signifies, in the presence of the appropriate adult, that he/she prefers the search to be done in the appropriate adult's absence and the appropriate adult agrees. A record should be made of the child's decision and signed by the appropriate adult. The presence of more than two people, other than an appropriate adult, should be permitted only in the most exceptional circumstances;

(d) The search should be conducted with the proper regard to the sensitivity and vulnerability of the person concerned in these circumstances and, every reasonable effort should be made to secure the person's co-operation and minimise embarrassment. Persons who are searched should not normally be required to have all their clothes removed at the same time, for example, a man should be allowed to put on his shirt before removing his trousers and a woman should be allowed to put on her blouse and upper garments before further clothing is removed;

(e) Where necessary to assist the search, the person may be required to hold his/her arms in the air or to stand with his/her legs apart and to bend forward so that a visual examination may be made of the genital and anal areas, provided that no physical contact is made with any body orifice;

(f) If, during the search, articles are found, the person should be asked to hand them over;

(g) A strip search should be conducted as quickly as possible and the person allowed to dress as soon as the procedure is complete.

35 A record should be made of a strip search, including the reason why it was considered necessary to undertake it, those present and the outcome of the search.

36 The above provisions also apply to any person authorised under paragraph 10 of the Schedule by an examining officer to carry out a search on the officer's behalf.

Landing/Embarkation Cards

37 The examining officer may require a person to complete a landing/embarkation card whether or not the officer suspects the person is or has been concerned in the commission, preparation or instigation of acts of terrorism. The examining officer should bear in mind that, as with questioning, embarrassment or offence can easily be caused to people who have no terrorist connections and who may feel victimised. The principles referred to in paragraph 10 above therefore also apply when an examining officer requires the completion and handing over of a card.

38 Paragraph 37 applies only if an order under paragraph 16 of the Schedule is in force requiring a person (on request by an examining officer) to complete or hand to the officer a landing or embarkation card.

Note for guidance on paragraph 37

The cards referred to under paragraph 16 of Schedule 7 requires persons, if so required by an examining officer, to provide such information, and in such form as set out in The Terrorism Act 2000 (Carding) Order 2001 (Statutory Instrument 2001 No. 426). The cards shall be produced and paid for by the police, not the aviation/maritime industry. Landing cards issued under the Immigration Act 1971 are not acceptable substitutes and should not be used.

Duties and Rights

39 The duties and rights of a person subject to examination/detention must be displayed prominently in a place where the person will be able to read them. If the examining officer doubts the person's ability to understand English, every reasonable effort shall be made to communicate the relevant information, where practicable using someone who can act as an interpreter.

Complaints

40 Complaints about the conduct of examining officers or treatment of an individual during an examination should be directed to:

Police officers: the Chief Constable of the force responsible for the port/airport where the person has been examined/detained.

Complaints about the conduct of immigration and customs officers or treatment of an individual by an immigration and customs officer during examination/detention should be directed to:

United Kingdom Border Agency
Border Force Complaints Team
Building 25
Priory Court
St Johns Road
Dover
Kent
CT17 9SH

Annex A

TACT 1: Notice of Examination

(Schedule 7 to the Terrorism Act 2000)

General

This notice is to inform you that you are being questioned under the provisions of Schedule 7 to the Terrorism Act 2000 as someone whose presence at a port or in the border area (in Northern Ireland) is connected with entering or leaving any place in Great Britain or Northern Ireland. This applies to a person travelling by air, ship, aircraft or international train which has arrived at any place in Great Britain or Northern Ireland (whether from within or outside Great Britain or Northern Ireland). This also applies to someone whose presence is connected with entering or leaving a port where juxtaposed controls operate such as Coquelles, France.

This in itself does not necessarily mean that the examining officer who is questioning you suspects that you are a person who is, or has been, concerned in the commission, preparation or instigation of acts of terrorism. The purpose of the questioning is to enable him to determine whether you appear to be such a person.

At this stage you are not under caution, arrest or detention. However should the circumstances change you will be notified.

Your duties

Whilst being questioned you must:

(a) Give the examining officer all the information in your possession which the officer requests;

(b) Give the examining officer, if he so requests, a valid passport or another document with a photograph which establishes your identity;

(c) Declare whether you have with you any documents of a kind specified by the examining officer and, if he so requests, give them to him.

(d) Give the examining officer on request any document which he has with him and which is of a kind specified by the officer.

You may be asked, or have been asked to complete and hand to the officer an arrival or embarkation card. If so, you have a duty to comply with that request.

Appendix 6: **Code of Practice for Examining Officers**

If you deliberately fail to comply with any of these duties, you could be prosecuted under paragraph 18(1) of Schedule 7 to the Terrorism Act 2000.

Powers

An examining officer may:

(a) search you or anything which you have with you, or belongs to you including your luggage and vehicle. This includes anything an examining officer reasonably believes has been, or is about to be on a ship or aircraft.

(b) for a period not exceeding 7 days, detain anything which is given to him during questioning, or is found during a search, for the purposes of an examination.

(c) detain without a time limit anything which he believes may be needed for use as evidence in criminal proceedings.

(d) detain without a time limit anything which may be needed in connection with a decision by the Secretary of State whether to make a deportation order under the Immigration Act 1971.

Detention

The examining officer also has the authority to detain you, if necessary, for up to 9 hours from the time your examination began.

Other Information

You can request that a friend, a relative or a person who is known to you, or is likely to take an interest in your welfare is informed that you are being questioned and your location.

You can request to consult either in person, in writing or on the telephone, privately with a solicitor. *Examination will not be delayed pending the arrival of a solicitor*. If you do not wish to do so now, you may do so later and at any time while you are being questioned.

Consultation with a solicitor **will not** be at public expense. You do not have a right to have someone informed or to contact a solicitor whilst being examined. Informing someone or contacting a solicitor will be at the discretion of an examining officer.

Complaints

Complaints about the conduct of officers or your treatment during your examination/detention should be directed to the Chief

Constable of the force responsible for the port/airport where you have been examined/detained.

Complaints about the conduct of immigration and customs officers or treatment of an individual by an immigration and customs officer during examination/detention should be directed to:

United Kingdom Border Agency

Border Force Complaints Team

Building 25

Priory Court

St Johns Road

Dover

Kent

CT17 9SH

Notice of Examination

Served on Day:..........................date:..........................
at:........................hours

By (Warrant No): Witnessed by (Warrant No.) (Interpreter/App. Adult/Solicitor):

....

Signature of person examined:

....

Content verbally explained to subject by:

....

Annex B

TACT 2: Notice of Detention (INTERIM 2011)

(Schedule 7 to the Terrorism Act 2000)

Detention

To...

You have been detained under paragraph 6 of Schedule 7 to the Terrorism Act 2000, so that an Examining Officer may exercise his power under paragraph 2 of that Schedule to determine whether you appear to be a person who is or has been concerned in the commission, preparation or instigation of acts of terrorism.

At this stage you are not under caution or arrest, however should the circumstances change you will be notified.

Your duties

Whilst being questioned you must:

(a) Give the examining officer all the information in your possession which the officer requests;

(b) Give the examining officer if he so requests, a valid passport or another document with a photograph which establishes your identity;

(c) Declare whether you have with you any documents of a kind specified by the examining officer and, if he so requests, give them to him.

(d) Give the examining officer on request any document which you have with you and which is of a kind specified by the officer.

You may be asked, or have been asked to complete and hand to the officer an arrival or embarkation card. If so, you have a duty to comply with that request. If you deliberately fail to comply with any of these duties, you could be prosecuted under paragraph 18(1) of Schedule 7 to the Terrorism Act 2000.

Do you want someone informed?

You may, if you wish, at public expense, have a friend, a relative or a person who is known to you, or is likely to take an interest in your welfare, informed that you are being detained here. *NB. Under paragraph 8 of Schedule 8 to the Terrorism Act 2000, or paragraph 16 of Schedule 8 in Scotland, an officer of at least the rank of Superintendent may delay this right.*

Do you want to contact a solicitor?

You may consult either in person, in writing or on the telephone, privately with a solicitor. If you do not wish to do so now, you may do so later and at any time while you are detained. *NB. Under paragraph 8 of Schedule 8 to the Terrorism Act 2000, or paragraph 16 of Schedule 8 in Scotland, an officer of at least the rank of Superintendent may delay this right.*

If you do not have details of a solicitor details of an independent solicitor can be supplied to you. Consultation with a solicitor may be at Public Expense, your entitlement to which will be assessed by the solicitor you contact.

Notice of Detention

Served on Day:....................date:....................at:.....
..............hours

By (Warrant No):...

Witnesses by (Warrant No):

....

Signature of detained person:

....

Witnessed by: (interpreter/App.Adult/Solicitor):

....

Code of Practice for the video recording with sound of interviews of persons detained under section 41 of, or Schedule 7 to, the Terrorism Act 2000 and post-charge questioning of persons authorised under sections 22 or 23 of the Counter-Terrorism Act 2008

Foreword

This Code of Practice is issued by the Secretary of State (and in so far as it applies in Scotland, with the concurrence of the Lord Advocate) in accordance with paragraph 3(4)(a) of Schedule 8 to the Terrorism Act 2000 and section 25(3) of the Counter-Terrorism Act 2008.

The following must be recorded in accordance with this Code:

- any interview by a constable of a person detained under section 41 of the Terrorism Act 2000 which takes place in a police station in England, Wales or Scotland;
- any questioning by a constable of a person detained for examination under Schedule 7 to the Terrorism Act 2000 which takes place in a police station in England, Wales or Scotland;
- any interview by a constable of a person which takes place in accordance with an authorisation under section 22 of the Counter-Terrorism Act 2008 (post-charge questioning) anywhere in England and Wales; and
- any interview by a constable of a person which takes place in accordance with an authorisation under section 23 of the Counter-Terrorism Act 2008 (post-charge questioning) anywhere in Scotland.

Under paragraph 4(7) of Schedule 8 to the 2000 Act and section 26(8) of the 2008 Act, this Code is admissible in evidence in criminal and civil proceedings and shall be taken into account by any court or tribunal in any case in which it appears to the court or tribunal to be relevant.

1 General

1.1 This Code of Practice applies to the video recording with sound of:

(a) any interview of a person detained under section 41 of the Terrorism Act 2000 (TACT) which takes place at a police station in England, Wales or Scotland.

(b) any questioning of a person detained for examination under Schedule 7 to TACT which takes place at a police station in England, Wales or Scotland;

(c) any interview of a person which takes place in accordance with an authorisation under section 22 of the Counter-Terrorism Act 2008 at any place (including a police station) in England or Wales or under section 23 of that Act at any place (including a police station) in Scotland.

1.2 The notes for guidance included are not provisions of this Code. They are guidance to police officers and others about its application and interpretation.

1.3 This Code of Practice must be readily available at the place where any interview or post-charge questioning to which this Code applies takes place for consultation by police officers and other police staff, the persons mentioned in *paragraph 1.1* above, prosecutors, members of the public, appropriate adults and solicitors.

1.4 In this Code, references to 'police station' include any place which has been designated by the Secretary of State under paragraph 1(1) of Schedule 8 to TACT as a place at which persons may be detained under section 41 of that Act.

1.5 The video recording of interviews shall be carried out openly to instil confidence in its reliability as an impartial and accurate record of the interview.

1.6 Nothing in this Code shall detract from:

• the requirements of the Code of Practice H issued under section 66 of the Police and Criminal Evidence Act 1984 (PACE[1]) as it applies in England and Wales to the detention, treatment and questioning of persons detained under section 41 of TACT and to

---

[1] PACE does not apply in Scotland.

persons in respect of whom an authorisation for post-charge questioning has been given under section 22 of the Counter Terrorism Act 2008 (post-charge questioning of terrorist suspects).
- The requirements of the Code of Practice for Examining Officers issued under paragraph 6(1) of Schedule 14 to TACT as it applies to the detention, questioning and treatment of persons detained for examination under Schedule 7.

1.7 In this Code:
(a) if an interview mentioned in paragraph 1.1(a) or (c) takes place:
- in England or Wales, the term 'appropriate adult' has the same meaning as in Code H, *paragraph 1.13*; and the term 'solicitor' has the same meaning as in Code H, *paragraph 6.13*.
- in Scotland, the term 'solicitor' means an enrolled solicitor which means a member of the Law Society of Scotland who is entitled to practice in Scotland.
(b) In the case of a person mentioned in *paragraph 1.1(b)*, the term 'appropriate adult' means an adult whose status and role are as described in paragraphs 17 and 18 of the Code of Practice for Examining Officers issued under paragraph 6(1) of Schedule 14 to TACT.

1.8 Any reference in this Code to video recording shall be taken to mean video recording with sound and in this Code:
(a) 'recording medium' means any removable, physical video recording medium (such as magnetic tape, optical disc or solid state memory) which can be played and copied; and
(b) 'secure digital network' is a computer network system which enables an original interview video recording to be stored as a digital multi media file or a series of such files, on a secure file server which is accredited by the National Accreditor for Police Information Systems in accordance with the UK Government Protective Marking Scheme. See *section 7* of this Code.

1.9 *Sections 2* to *6* of this Code set out the procedures and requirements which apply to all interviews together with the provisions which apply only to interviews recorded using removable media. *Section 7* sets out the provisions which apply to interviews recorded using a secure digital network and specifies the provisions in *sections 2* to *6* which do not apply to secure digital network recording.

2 Interviews to be video recorded with sound

2.1 Subject to *paragraph 2.7*, the interviews described in *paragraph 1.1* must be video recorded with sound in accordance with this Code.

2.2 The whole of each interview shall be recorded, including the taking and reading back of any statement.

2.3 On occasions it may be necessary to delay an interview to make arrangements to overcome any difficulties or problems that might otherwise prevent the record being made, for example, non-availability of suitable recording equipment and interview facilities. If a person refuses to go into or remain in a suitable interview room, see Code H *paragraph 12.5*, and the custody officer considers, on reasonable grounds, that the interview should not be delayed, the interview may, at the custody officer's discretion, be conducted in a cell using portable recording equipment. The reasons for this shall be recorded.

2.4 Before any interview to which this Code applies starts, the person concerned and any appropriate adult and interpreter shall be given a written notice which explains the requirement that under this Code the interview must be video recorded with sound. At the same time, the person, the appropriate adult and interpreter shall be informed verbally of the content of the notice.

2.5 If the person to be interviewed or the appropriate adult raises objections to the interview being recorded, either at the outset or during the interview or during the break in the interview, the interviewing officer shall explain that the interview is being recorded in order to protect both the person being interviewed and the interviewing officer and that there is no opt out facility.

2.6 A sign or indicator which is visible to the suspect must show when the recording equipment is recording.

2.7 In the case of an interview mentioned in *paragraph 1.1(b)* with a Schedule 7 TACT detainee, but not in any other case, a uniformed officer not below the rank of inspector who is not involved with the investigation (the authorising officer) may, if the conditions in *paragraph 2.8* are satisfied, give authority in writing for the interviewing officer not to video record or, as the case may be, continue to video record, that interview. In this case:

(a) the interview or its continuation, shall, without exception, be audio recorded and *paragraph 2.3* shall apply accordingly;

(b) references in this Code to such an interview being video recorded shall be replaced by references to the interview being audio recorded, and

(c) the authorising officer shall make a note in specific terms of the reasons for not video recording the interview. See *Note 2G*.

2.8 The conditions referred to in *paragraph 2.7* are:

(a) if it is not reasonably practicable to video record or, as the case may be, continue to video record, the interview because of failure of the recording equipment or the non-availability of a suitable interview room or recording equipment; and

(b) the authorising officer considers on reasonable grounds that the interview, or continuation of the interview, should not be delayed until the failure has been rectified or until a suitable room or recording equipment becomes available.

Notes for guidance

2A Guidance on assessing a juvenile or individuals' fitness and mental wellbeing prior to interviewing is provided at paragraphs 11.9 to 11.13 of PACE Code H or for Schedule 7 interviews at paragraphs 17 to 20 of the Code of Practice for Examining Officers under the Terrorism Act 2000.

2B If the person to be interviewed is deaf or does not understand English and is detained under section 41 of TACT or their questioning after charge has been authorised under the Counter-Terrorism Act 2008, the provisions in section 13 of PACE Code H (Interpreters) should be applied. If the person is detained under Schedule 7, then paragraph 39 of the Code of Practice for Examining Officers should be observed.

2C The person must be reminded of their right to free legal advice in accordance with;

- *section 6 and paragraph 11.3 of PACE Code H if detained under section 41 for interview;*
- *'Form TACT 2: Notice of Detention' (as revised by Home Office Circular 7 of 2011) in the Code of Practice for Examining Officers under Schedule 7 if detained under Schedule 7; or*
- *paragraph 15.8 of PACE Code H in the case of post-charge questioning authorised under section 22 of the Counter-Terrorism Act 2008.*

2D Delaying or denying a person access to legal advice before interview is subject to the following provisions;

- *Annex B or paragraphs 6.7 to 6.9 of PACE Code H if the person is detained for interview under section 41*

- 'Form TACT 2: Notice of Detention' (as revised by Home Office Circular 7 of 2011) in the Code of Practice for Examining Officers under Schedule 7 if the person is detained under Schedule 7; or
- paragraph 15.8 of PACE Code H in the case of post-charge questioning authorised under section 22.

2E Qualified access to legal advice when interviewing a person detained under section 41, is subject to paragraph 6.5 of PACE Code H.

2F In Scotland a person should be reminded of their right to legal advice and the terms of the ACPOS Manual of Guidance on Solicitor Access should be followed. Any delay in access to a solicitor should be carried out in line with the provisions contained within the "Guidelines on the Detention, Treatment and Questioning by Police Officers of Persons Arrested Under Section 41 and Schedule 8 of the Terrorism Act 2000."

2G A decision not to video record an interview mentioned in paragraph 1.1(b) with a Schedule 7 detainee for any reason may be the subject of comment if a case comes to court. The authorising officer should therefore be prepared to justify their decision in each case.

3 Recording and sealing of master recordings

3.1 The camera(s) shall be placed in the interview room so as to ensure coverage of as much of the room as is practically possible whilst the interviews are taking place. See *Note 3A*

3.2 One recording, the master recording, will be sealed in the suspect's presence. A second recording will be used as a working copy. The master recording is either of the two recordings used in a twin deck/drive machine or the only recording in a single deck/drive machine. The working copy is either the second/third recording used in a twin/triple deck/drive machine or a copy of the master recording made by a single deck/drive machine. See *Notes 3B* and *3C*.

[This paragraph does not apply to interviews recorded using a secure digital network, see paragraphs 7.3 to 7.5]

3.3 For the purpose of any interview to which this Code applies, no interviewing officer or other officer is required to record or disclose their identity. To protect the identity of officers, the officer may keep their backs to the camera and may use their warrant or other identification number and the name of the police station to which they are attached.

Notes for Guidance

3A Interviewing officers will wish to arrange that, as far as possible, video recording arrangements are unobtrusive. It must be clear to the person being interviewed, however, that there is no opportunity to interfere with the recording equipment or the recording media.

3B The purpose of sealing the master copy before it leaves the presence of the person being interviewed is to establish their confidence that the integrity of the recording is preserved. If a single deck/drive machine is used the working copy of the master recording must be made in the presence of the person being interviewed without the master recording leaving their sight. The working copy shall be used for making further copies if required.

3C The recording of the interview may be used for identification procedures in accordance with paragraph 3.21 or Annex E of Code D. When a known person is not available or has ceased to be available the identification officer may make arrangements for a video identification. Any suitable moving or still image may be used and these may be obtained covertly if necessary.

4. The Interview

(a) General

4.1 Attention is drawn to the provisions of PACE Code H which describe the restrictions on drawing adverse inferences from a person's failure or refusal to say anything about their involvement in an offence when interviewed before or after being charged or informed they may be prosecuted and how those restrictions affect the terms of the caution and determine whether a special warning under Sections 36 and 37 of the Criminal Justice and Public Order Act 1994 can be given.

4.2 The provisions described in *paragraph 4.1* are:
- section 10 (cautions) and Annex C which apply to interviews of persons detained in England or Wales under section 41 of TACT; and
- paragraphs 15.9 to 15.10 which apply to post-charge questioning authorised under section 22 of the Counter-Terrorism Act which takes place in England or Wales.

Note: The requirement to caution does not apply to interviews of persons detained for examination under Schedule 7.

(b) Commencement of Interviews

4.3 When the person to be interviewed is brought into the interview room the interviewing officer shall without delay, but in sight of the person, load the recording equipment and set it to record. The recording media must be unwrapped or otherwise opened in the presence of the suspect. See *Note 4A [This paragraph does not apply to interviews recorded using a secure digital network, see paragraphs 7.3 and 7.4].*

4.4 The interviewing officer shall then tell the person formally about the video recording with sound and point out the sign or indicator which shows that the recording equipment is activated and recording. See *paragraph 2.6*. The interviewing officer shall:

(a) say the interview is being video recorded with sound (see *paragraph 2.4*);

(b) give their warrant or other identification number and state the police station they are attached to, and provide these details in relation to any other police officer present (see *paragraph 3.5*);

(c) ask the person to be interviewed and any other party present (e.g. a solicitor) to identify themselves;

(d) state the date, time of commencement and place of the interview; and

(e) state that the person to be interviewed will be given a notice about what will happen to the copies of the recording. *[This sub-paragraph does not apply to interviews recorded using a secure digital network, see paragraphs 7.3 and 7.5 to 7.6]*

See *Note 4A*

4.5 Any person entering the interview room after the interview has commenced shall be invited by the interviewing officer to identify themselves for the purpose of the video recording and state the reason why they have entered the interview room.

4.6 The interviewing officer shall then caution the person and remind the person of their entitlement to free and independent legal advice and their right to consult a solicitor. See *Notes 2C and 2F*

Note: The requirement to caution does not apply to interviews of persons detained for examination under Schedule 7.

4.7 If the interview takes place in England and Wales, in accordance with *paragraph 11.4* of Code H, the interviewing officer shall then put to the person being interviewed any significant statement or silence (i.e. failure or refusal to answer a question or to answer it satisfactorily) which occurred in the presence and hearing of a police officer or other police staff before the start of the interview and which have not been put to the person in the course of a previous interview. The interviewer shall then ask the suspect whether they wish to confirm or deny that earlier statement or silence and if they want to add anything. The terms 'significant statement' and 'significant silence' have the same meaning as in *paragraph 11.5* of PACE Code H.

4.8 If the interview takes place in Scotland the interviewing officer shall then put to the person being interviewed any statement which appears capable of being used in evidence against the person, in particular a direct admission of guilt, which occurred before the start of the interview and which have not been put to the person in the course of a previous interview and shall ask the person whether they wish to confirm or deny that earlier statement and whether they wish to add anything.

(c) Interviews with the deaf or with those who do not understand English

4.9 If the person appears to be deaf or there is doubt about their hearing or speaking ability, they must not be interviewed in the absence of an interpreter unless a relevant exemption applies. See *Note 2B*

(d) Objections and complaints by the person

4.10 If the detained person or an appropriate adult raises objections to the interview being video recorded, either at the outset or during the interview or during a break in the interview the provisions outlined in *paragraph 2.7* should be followed.

4.11 If in the course of an interview at a police station a complaint is made by the person being questioned, or on their behalf, about their detention, treatment or questioning or if the complaint is that the provisions of this Code have not been observed, or it comes to notice or it comes to the interviewer's notice that the interviewee may have been treated improperly, then the interviewing officer shall record the matter in the interview record (see *Note 4G*) and inform the custody officer, who is responsible for dealing with the complaint in accordance with *paragraph 9.3* of Code H (if in England or Wales) or recognised procedure if in Scotland. If the person is being interviewed in accordance with an authorisation under section 22 or 23 of the Counter-Terrorism Act 2008 (post-charge questioning) elsewhere than at a police station, then the interviewing officer shall record the matter in the interview record (see *Note 4G*) and inform the appropriate detention manager at the place where the person is being detained, of that complaint.

4.12 If the person being interviewed indicates that they wish to tell the interviewer about matters not directly connected with the matter about which they are being interviewed and that they are unwilling for these matters to be recorded, the suspect shall be given the opportunity to tell the interviewer about these matters after the conclusion of the formal interview.

(e) Changing the recording media

4.13 When the recording equipment indicates that the recording media has only a short time left to run, the interviewer shall so inform the person being interviewed and round off that part of the interview. If the interviewer leaves the room for a second set of recording media, the suspect shall not be left unattended. The interviewer will remove the recording media from the recording equipment and insert the new recording media which shall be unwrapped or opened in the person's presence. The recording equipment shall then be set to record on the new media. To avoid confusion between the recording media, the interviewer shall mark the media with an identification number immediately after they are removed from the recorder.

[This paragraph does not apply to interviews recorded using a secure digital network as this does not use removable media, see paragraphs 1.8(b), 7.3 and 7.13 to 7.14.]

(f) Taking a break during the interview

4.14 When a break is taken, the fact that a break is to be taken, the reason for it and the time shall be recorded on the video record.

4.15 When the break is taken and the interview room vacated by the suspect, the recording media shall be removed from the recorder and the procedures for the conclusion of an interview followed. See *paragraph 4.21*

4.16 When a break is to be a short one, and both the person being interviewed and a police officer remain in the interview room, the recording may be stopped. There is no need to remove the recording media and when the interview recommences the recording should continue on the same recording media. The time the interview recommences shall be recorded on the video record.

4.17 After any break in an interview under caution, the interviewing officer must, before resuming the interview remind the person of their right to legal advice if they have not exercised it (see *Notes 2C* and *2F*); and

- in England or Wales, remind the person that they remain under caution (see *paragraphs 4.1* and *4.2*) or if there is any doubt, give the caution in full again; and
- in Scotland, give the caution again in full.

See *Notes 4D* and *4E*

[Paragraphs 4.14 to 4.17 do not apply to interviews recorded using a secure digital network, see paragraphs 7.3 and 7.7 to 7.9]

(g) Failure of recording equipment

4.18 If there is a failure of equipment which can be rectified quickly, e.g. by inserting new recording media, the appropriate procedures set out in paragraph 4.13 shall be followed. When the recording is resumed the interviewer shall explain what has happened and video record the time the interview recommences. If, however, it is not possible to continue video recording on that particular recorder and no alternative equipment is readily available, the interview must cease until suitable equipment is available. See *Note 4F*

[This paragraph does not apply to interviews recorded using a secure digital network, see paragraphs 7.3 and 7.10]

(h) Removing used recording media from recording equipment

4.19 Recording media which is removed from the recording equipment during the course of an interview shall be retained and the procedures set out in *paragraph 4.21* followed.

[This paragraph does not apply to interviews recorded using a secure digital network as this does not use removable media, see 1.8(b), 7.3 and 7.13 to 7.14.]

(i) Conclusion of interview

4.20 At the conclusion of the interview, the person being interviewed shall be offered the opportunity to clarify anything he or she has said and asked if there is anything that they wish to add.

4.21 At the conclusion of the interview, including the taking and reading back of any written statement, the time shall be recorded in the video record and the recording shall be stopped. The interviewer shall seal the master recording with a master recording label and treat it as an exhibit in accordance with force standing orders. The interviewer shall (subject to *paragraph 3.5*) sign the label and also ask the person, their solicitor and any appropriate adult or other third party present during the interview to sign it. If the person or third party refuses to sign the label, an officer of at least the rank of inspector, or if one is not available, the custody officer, shall be called into the interview room and asked (subject to *paragraph 3.5*) to sign it.

4.22 The suspect shall be handed a notice which explains

- how the video recording will be used;
- the arrangements for access to it;
- that if they are charged or informed they will be prosecuted, a copy of the video recording will be supplied as soon as practicable or as otherwise agreed between the suspect and police or on the order of a court.

[Paragraphs 4.20 to 4.22 do not apply to interviews recorded using a secure digital network, see paragraphs 7.3 and 7.11 to 7.12]

Notes for Guidance

4A For the purposes of voice identification, the interviewer should ask the suspect and any other people present to identify themselves.

4B Where the custody officer is called immediately to deal with the complaint, the recorder should, if possible, be left to run until the custody officer has entered the room and spoken to the person being interviewed. Continuation or termination of the interview should be at the interviewer's discretion pending action by an inspector under Code H, paragraph 9.3. In the case of those being questioned under section 22 in a designated place other than a police station, the appropriate detention manager should be informed.

4C If the complaint is about a matter not connected with this Code or the person's detention, treatment or questioning, the decision to continue is at the interviewer's discretion. When the interviewer decides to continue the interview, they shall tell the person the complaint will be brought to the custody officer's attention at the conclusion of the interview. When the interview is concluded the interviewer must, as soon as practicable, inform the custody officer about the existence and nature of the complaint made. In the case of those being questioned under section 22 or 23 in a designated place other than a police station, the appropriate detention manager/custody officer should be informed.

4D In England and Wales, when considering whether to caution again after a break, the officer should bear in mind that he or she may have to satisfy a court that the person understood that they were still under caution when the interview resumed. In Scotland, the officer should always caution in full after a break.

4E The interviewer should bear in mind that it may be necessary to satisfy the court that nothing occurred during a break in an interview or between interviews which influenced the person's recorded evidence. On the re-commencement of an interview, the officer should consider summarising on the recording the reason for the break and confirming this with the person.

4F If any part of the recording media breaks or is otherwise damaged during the interview, the recording should be sealed as a master copy in the presence of the suspect. The undamaged part, if any, should be copied in the person's presence before the master copy is sealed. If the recording is irretrievable the interview should be started again with new recording media.

4G Where reference is made to the 'interview record' this means the actual video recording of the interview.

5 After the interview

5.1 The interviewing officer shall make a note in their pocket book that the interview has taken place and that it has been video recorded. They shall also make a note of the date of the interview, the time it commenced, its duration, any breaks that were taken and the date and the identification number of the master recording.

5.2 Where no proceedings follow in respect of the person whose interview was recorded, the recording media must be kept securely in accordance with *paragraph 6.1* and *Note 6A*.

[This section (paragraphs 5.1, 5.2 and Note 5A) does not apply to interviews recorded using a secure digital network, see paragraphs 7.3 and 7.13 to 7.14].

Note for guidance

5A Any written record of a video recorded interview should be made in accordance with national guidelines approved by the Secretary of State, and with regard to the advice contained in the Manual of Guidance for the preparation, processing and submission of prosecution files.

---

6. Media Security

(a) General

6.1 The officer in charge of the police station at which interviews are video recorded in accordance with this Code shall make arrangements for the master recordings to be kept securely and their movements accounted for on the same basis as other material which may be used for evidential purposes, in accordance with force standing orders. See *Note 6A*

(b) Breaking master recording seal for criminal proceedings

6.2 A police officer may only break the seal on a master copy, which is required for criminal trial or appeal proceedings, with the appropriate authority. If in England and Wales it is necessary to gain access to the master copy, the police officer shall arrange for its seal to be broken in the presence of a representative of the Crown Prosecution Service. The person who has been interviewed or their legal adviser shall be informed and given a reasonable opportunity to be present. If they or their legal representative are present they shall be invited to reseal and sign the master copy. If neither accepts or neither is present, this shall be done by the representative of the Crown Prosecution Service. See *Notes 6B* and *6C*

(c) Breaking master recording seal: other cases

6.3 In England and Wales the chief officer of police is responsible for establishing arrangements for breaking the seal of the master copy where no criminal proceedings result, or the criminal proceedings to which the interview relates, have been concluded and it becomes necessary to break the seal. These arrangements should be those which the chief officer considers are reasonably necessary to demonstrate to the person interviewed and any other party who may wish to use or refer to the video recording that the master recording has not been tampered with and that the video recording remains accurate. See *Note 6D*

6.4 Subject to *paragraph 6.6*, a representative of each party must be given a reasonable opportunity to be present when the seal is broken and the master copy is copied and re-sealed.

6.5 If one or more of the parties is not present when the master recording seal is broken because they cannot be contacted or refuse to attend or *paragraph 6.6* applies, arrangements should be made for an independent person such as a custody visitor, to be present.

Alternatively, or as an additional safeguard, arrangements should be made for a film or photographs to be taken of the procedure.

6.6 *Paragraph 6.5* does not require a person to be given an opportunity to be present when:
(a) it is necessary to break the master copy seal for the proper and effective further investigation of the original offence or the investigation of some other offence; and
(b) the officer in charge of the investigation has reasonable grounds to suspect that allowing such an opportunity might prejudice any such an investigation or criminal proceedings which may be brought as a result or endanger any person. See *Note 6E*

(d) Documentation

6.7 When a master copy seal is broken, copied and re-sealed, a record must be made of the procedure followed, including the date; time; place and persons present.

[This section (paragraphs 6.1 to 6.7 and Notes 6A to 6C) does not apply to interviews recorded using a secure digital network, see paragraphs 7.3 and 7.13 to 7.14]

Notes for Guidance

6A This section is concerned with the security of the master copies sealed at the conclusion of the interview. Care must be taken of working copies of recordings since their loss or destruction may lead unnecessarily to the need to have access to master copies.

6B In England and Wales if the master recording has been delivered to the Crown Court for their keeping after committal for trial the Crown Prosecutor will apply to the Chief Clerk of the Crown Court for its release for unsealing by the Crown Prosecutor.

6C Reference to the Crown Prosecution Service or to the Crown Prosecutor in this part of the Code shall be taken to include any other body or person with a statutory responsibility for prosecution for which the police recorded interview is required.

6D The most common reasons for needing access to master copies that are not required for criminal proceedings arise from civil actions and complaints against police and civil actions between individuals arising out of allegations of crime investigated by police.

6E Paragraph 6.6 could apply, for example, when one or more of the outcomes or likely outcomes of the investigation might be; (i) the prosecution of one or more of the original suspects, (ii) the prosecution of someone previously not suspected, including someone who was originally a witness; and (iii) any original suspect being treated as a prosecution witness and when premature disclosure of any police action, particularly through contact with any parties involved, could lead to a real risk of compromising the investigation and endangering witnesses.

7. Recording of Interviews by Secure Digital Network

7.1 A secure digital network does not use removable media and this section specifies the provisions which will apply when a secure digital network is used.

7.2 The following requirements are solely applicable to the use of a secure digital network for the recording of interviews.

(a) Application of sections 1 to 6 of Code

7.3 Sections 1 to 6 of this Code apply to recordings made on a secure digital network except for the following paragraphs:
- *Paragraph 3.2* under "Recording and sealing of master recordings";
- *Paragraph 4.3* under "(b) Commencement of interviews";
- *Paragraph 4.4(e)* under "(b) Commencement of interviews";
- *Paragraphs 4.13 to 4.22* under "(e) Changing recording media", "(f) Taking a break during interview", "(g) Failure of recording equipment", "(h) Removing recording media from the recorder" and "(i) Conclusion of interview";
- *Paragraphs 6.1 to 6.7* under "Media security".

(b) Commencement of Interview

7.4 When the suspect is brought into the interview room, the interviewer shall without delay and in the sight of the suspect, switch on the recording equipment and enter the information necessary to log on to the secure network and start recording.

7.5 The interviewer must then inform the suspect that the interview is being recorded using a secure digital network and that recording has commenced.

7.6 In addition to the requirements of *paragraph 4.4 (a)* to *(d)* above, the interviewer must inform the person that:
- they will be given access to the recording of the interview in the event that they are charged or informed that they will be prosecuted

but if they are not charged or informed that they will be prosecuted they will only be given access as agreed with the police or on the order of a court; and

- they will be given a written notice at the end of the interview setting out their rights to access the recording and what will happen to the recording.

(c) Taking a break during interview

7.7 When a break is taken, the fact that a break is to be taken, the reason for it and the time shall be recorded on the audio recording. The recording shall be stopped and the procedures in *paragraphs 7.11* and *7.12* for the conclusion of an interview followed.

7.8 When the interview recommences the procedures in *paragraphs 7.4* to *7.6* for commencing an interview shall be followed to create a new file to record the continuation of the interview. The time the interview recommences shall be recorded on the audio recording.

7.9 After any break in the interview the interviewer must, before resuming the interview, remind the person being questioned that they remain under caution or, if there is any doubt, give the caution in full again. See *Note 4G*

(d) Failure of recording equipment

7.10 If there is an equipment failure which can be rectified quickly, e.g. by commencing a new secure digital network recording, the interviewer shall follow the appropriate procedures as in *paragraphs 7.7* to *7.9*. When the recording is resumed the interviewer shall explain what happened and record the time the interview recommences. If, however, it is not possible to continue recording on the secure digital network the interview should be recorded on removable media as in *paragraph 4.3*. See *Note 4F*

(e) Conclusion of interview

7.11 At the conclusion of the interview, the suspect shall be offered the opportunity to clarify anything he or she has said and asked if there is anything they want to add.

7.12 At the conclusion of the interview, including the taking and reading back of any written statement:
(a) the time shall be recorded.
(b) the suspect shall be handed a notice (see *Note 7A*) which explains:

- how the video recording will be used;
- the arrangements for access to it;
- that if they are charged or informed that they will be prosecuted, they will be given access to the recording of the interview either electronically or by being given a copy on removable recording media, but if they are not charged or informed that they will prosecuted, they will only be given access as agreed with the police or on the order of a court.

(c) the suspect must be asked to confirm that they have received a copy of the notice at *sub-paragraph (b)* above. If the suspect fails to accept or to acknowledge receipt of the notice, the interviewer will state for the recording that a copy of the notice has been provided to the suspect and that they have refused to take a copy of the notice or have refused to acknowledge receipt.

(d) the time shall be recorded and the interviewer shall notify the suspect that the recording is being saved to the secure network. The interviewer must save the recording in the presence of the suspect. The suspect should then be informed that the interview is terminated.

(f) After the interview

7.13 The interviewer shall make a note in their pocket book that the interview has taken place, was audibly recorded, its time, duration and date and the original recording's identification number.

7.14 If no proceedings follow in respect of the person whose interview was recorded, the recordings must be kept securely as in *paragraphs 7.15* and *7.16*.

(g) Security of secure digital network interview records

7.15 Interview record files are stored in read only format on nonremovable storage devices, for example, hard disk drives, to ensure their integrity. The recordings are first saved locally to a secure nonremovable device before being transferred to the remote network device. If for any reason the network connection fails, the recording remains on the local device and will be transferred when the network connections are restored.

7.16 Access to interview recordings, including copying to removable media, must be strictly controlled and monitored to ensure that access is restricted to those who have been given specific permission to access for specified purposes when this is necessary. For example, police officers and CPS lawyers involved in the preparation of any prosecution case, persons interviewed if they have been charged or informed they may be prosecuted and their legal representatives.

Note for Guidance

7A The notice at paragraph 7.12 above should provide a brief explanation of the secure digital network and how access to the recording is strictly limited. The notice should also explain the access rights of the suspect, his or her legal representative, the police and the prosecutor to the recording of the interview. Space should be provided on the form to insert the date and the file reference number for the interview.

Terrorism Act 2000 (Issued Under S47AB as Amended by the Protection of Freedoms Act 2012) Code of Practice (England, Wales and Scotland) for the Exercise of Stop and Search Powers Under Sections 43 and 43A of the Terrorism Act 2000, and the Authorisation and Exercise of Stop and Search Powers Relating to Section 47A of, and Schedule 6B to, the Terrorism Act 2000

1. Introduction

1.1. The Purpose of this Code is:

1.1.1. To set out the basic principles for the use of powers by police officers under sections 43 and 43A of the Terrorism Act 2000 and the authorisation and use of powers by police officers under section 47A of, and Schedule 6B to, the Terrorism Act 2000.

1.1.2. To reflect that the powers under section 47A and Schedule 6B entirely replace those previously found in sections 44–47 of the 2000 Act and are not simply a modification of those provisions. As such they carry different criteria for both authorisation and use.

1.1.3. In respect of the powers under section 47A and Schedule 6B, to provide clarity that the threshold for making an authorisation is higher under these powers and the way in which the powers may be exercised is also different from under the provisions of sections 44–47. There is far greater circumscription in the use of these powers and the manner in which these powers are to be implemented by the police. Section 47A powers should only be authorised where other powers or measures are insufficient to deal with the threat and, even where authorised, officers should still consider whether section 47A powers are the most appropriate to use.

1.1.4. To promote the fundamental principles to be observed by the police and to preserve the effectiveness of, and public confidence in, the use of police powers to stop and search. If these fundamental principles are not observed, public confidence in the use of these powers to stop and search may be affected. Failure to use the powers in the proper manner also reduces their effectiveness.

1.1.5. To ensure that the intrusion on the liberty of the person stopped and searched is as limited as possible and to clarify that detention for the purposes of a search should take place at or near the location of the stop and last only as long as necessary.

1.1.6. To set out that those using the powers may be required to justify the use of such powers, in relation both to individual searches and the overall pattern of their activity in this regard, to their supervisory officers or in court. Any misuse of the powers is likely to be harmful to counter-terrorism policing and lead to mistrust of the police. Officers must also be able to explain their actions to the member of the public searched. The misuse of these powers can lead to disciplinary action. Proportionate use of the powers can contribute towards the primary purpose of counter-terrorism work: ensuring the safety of the public.

1.1.7. To reiterate guidance found in the Police and Criminal Evidence Act 1984 (PACE)[1] Code A that officers must not search a person, even with his or her consent, where no power to search is applicable.[2] Even where a person is prepared to submit to a search voluntarily, the person must not be searched unless the necessary legal power exists, and the search must be in accordance with the relevant power and the provisions of this code. The only exception, where an officer does not require a specific power, applies to searches of persons entering sports grounds or other premises carried out with their consent given as a condition of entry.

---

[1] PACE does not apply in Scotland.
[2] This does not affect the position in Scotland where there can be voluntary compliance with a search in terms of Scottish common law.

1.2. Basic Application of this Code:

1.2.1. This code applies to any authorisation or exercise of relevant stop and search powers by a police officer, which commences after midnight on the day The Terrorism Act 2000 (Codes of Practice for the Exercise of Stop and Search Powers) Order 2012 comes into force.

1.2.2. This code of practice is issued under section 47AB of the Terrorism Act 2000.

1.2.3. The effect of this code is set out in section 47AE of the Terrorism Act 2000: constables must have regard to the code and the code is admissible in criminal or civil proceedings (although a breach of the code itself does not make a person liable to any such proceedings).

1.2.4. Powers to stop and search must be used fairly, responsibly, and in accordance with the Equality Act 2010.

1.2.5. Chief Constables, police authorities and the Mayor's Office for Policing and Crime have a duty to have regard to this code of practice when discharging a function to which this code relates. This code must be followed unless there is good reason not to do so, in which case the decision not to follow this code should be recorded in writing.

1.2.6. This code of practice must be readily available at all police stations for consultation by police officers, police staff, detained persons and members of the public.

1.2.7. This code of practice applies to all police forces in England, Wales and Scotland, including the British Transport Police, the Ministry of Defence Police and the Civil Nuclear Constabulary. It does not apply to police forces in Northern Ireland—a separate code governs those police forces.

1.2.8. References to police authorities refer only to police authorities in England and Wales, the Mayor's Office for Policing and Crime, the British Transport Police Authority, Civil Nuclear Police Authority and Ministry of Defence Police Committee.

1.2.9. References in this code to the information required in an authorisation refer to a written authorisation or written confirmation of an oral authorisation.

2. Scope of this Code:

2.1. Powers of Stop and Search:

2.1.1. This code concerns the

a) exercise of stop and search powers conferred by section 43 and 43A of the Terrorism Act 2000, and

b) authorisation and exercise of powers to stop and search in specified areas or places at specified times contained in section 47A of, and Schedule 6B to, the Terrorism Act 2000.

2.1.2. Sections 43, 43A and 47A of the Terrorism Act 2000 as amended by the Protection of Freedoms Act 2012.

2.2. Definition of Terrorism:

2.2.1. Terrorism is defined by section 1 of the Terrorism Act 2000. In summary the term 'terrorism' in the 2000 Act means the use or threat of action where:

• the action used or threatened:
  - involves serious violence against a person or serious damage to property;
  - endangers a person's life, other than that of the person committing the action;
  - creates a serious risk to the health or safety of the public or a section of the public; or
  - is designed seriously to interfere with or seriously to disrupt an electronic system.

• the use or threat is designed to influence the government or an international governmental organisation, or intimidate the public or a section of the public; and

• the use or threat is made for the purpose of advancing a political, religious, racial or ideological cause.

3. Section 43 of the Terrorism Act 2000

3.1. Legal Background

3.1.1. Section 43(1) of the Terrorism Act 2000 provides a power for a constable to stop and search a person whom he or she reasonably suspects is a terrorist, to discover whether that person has anything in their possession which may constitute evidence they are a terrorist.

3.1.2. Section 43(2) of the Terrorism Act 2000 provides a power for a constable to search a person arrested under section 41 of that Act to discover whether that person has anything in their possession which may constitute evidence they are a terrorist. It does not require prior reasonable suspicion that such evidence may be found.

3.1.3. There are two powers to stop and search a vehicle with reasonable suspicion, introduced by amendments to the Terrorism Act 2000. The first is under section 43(1), where the officer reasonably suspects a person in a vehicle to be a terrorist and stops the vehicle in order to carry out a search. Under section 43(4B), the officer may also search the vehicle and anything in it or on it during the course of a search. The second is under section 43A, which provides a power for a constable to stop and search a vehicle which he or she reasonably suspects is being used for the purposes of terrorism, to search the vehicle and its occupants for evidence that it is being used for those purposes.

3.1.4. Given they require reasonable suspicion in order to be exercised, the use of powers under sections 43(1) and 43A should be prioritised for the purposes of stopping and searching individuals for the purposes of preventing or detecting terrorism. The authorisation of the no suspicion powers under section 47A should only be considered as a last resort, where reasonable suspicion powers are considered inadequate to respond to the threat. Use of the search powers under section 47A should only be made (in an authorised area) when the powers in sections 43 and 43A are not appropriate.

3.2. Stopping and Searching Persons and Vehicles under section 43(1)

3.2.1. A police officer may stop and search a person under section 43(1) of the Terrorism Act 2000 if they reasonably suspect that the person is a terrorist, to discover whether or not they have in their possession anything which may constitute evidence that they are a terrorist. This power may be used at any time or in any place when the threshold of reasonable suspicion is met. No authorisation is required.

3.2.2. If, when exercising the power to stop a person under section 43(1), a constable stops a vehicle, he or she may search the vehicle, and anything in or on it, under section 43(4B).

3.2.3. A person who is in the same vehicle as someone an officer reasonably suspects to be a terrorist may not be searched by virtue of this power, solely on the basis that they are with a person whom an officer reasonably suspects is a terrorist. However, anything otherwise in or on the vehicle may be searched to discover whether there is anything that may constitute evidence that the person the officer suspects to be a terrorist is a terrorist. The person may only be searched (under section 43(1)) if the officer reasonably suspects that they too are a terrorist.

3.2.4. The powers under section 43 to search a person includes the power to search anything that person is carrying with them, such as a bag, container or other object.

3.2.5. For searches of persons under section 43, the statutory requirement for the officer to be of the same sex as the persons to be searched has been repealed but where an officer of the same sex as the person to be searched is readily available, they should carry out the search. However, if an officer of the same sex is not available, searches may be carried out by an officer of the opposite sex (*see paragraph 3.2.8.*). Officers should have particular regard to the sensitivities of some religious communities in respect of being searched by a member of the opposite sex.

3.2.6. An officer need not be in uniform to carry out a stop and search of a person under section 43(1). However, in accordance with section 2(9)(b) of PACE, a constable stopping a vehicle under section 43(4A) or section 43A, must be in uniform.

3.2.7. A person can only be required to remove more than an outer coat, jacket or gloves if the search takes place out of public view and is near the place where that person was stopped. Unlike searches authorised under section 47A, a person cannot be required to remove their headgear and footwear in public. This does not, however, prevent an officer from placing his or her hand inside the pockets of the outer clothing, or feeling round the inside of collars, socks and shoes if this is considered reasonably necessary in the circumstances to look for the object of the search or to remove and examine any item reasonably suspected to be the object of the search. For the same reasons, subject to the restrictions on the removal of headgear, a person's hair may also be searched in public.

3.2.8. Where on reasonable grounds it is considered necessary to conduct a more thorough search (e.g. by requiring a person to take off a T-shirt), this must be done out of public view, for example, in a police van or police station if there is one nearby. Any search involving the removal of more than an outer coat, jacket, gloves, headgear or footwear, or any other item concealing identity, should only be conducted by an officer of the same sex as the person searched and may not be made in the presence of anyone of the opposite sex unless the person being searched specifically requests it. If a search involves exposure of intimate parts of the body and a police station is not nearby, particular care must be taken to ensure that the location is suitable in that it enables the search to be conducted in accordance with the requirements of paragraph 11 of Annex A to PACE Code C.

3.3. Stopping and Searching Vehicles under section 43A

3.3.1. Section 43A of the Terrorism Act 2000 allows a constable to stop and search a vehicle which he or she reasonably suspects is being used for the purposes of terrorism, for evidence that the vehicle is being used for such purposes. The constable may search anything in or on the vehicle or any person (including drivers, crew and passengers) in the vehicle to discover whether there is anything which may constitute evidence that the vehicle is being used for the purposes of terrorism. Section 43A may be used to search unattended vehicles where an officer reasonably suspects the vehicle is being used for the purposes of terrorism.

3.3.2. If the officer reasonably suspects a person in a vehicle of being a terrorist, but does not suspect the vehicle is being used at that time for the purposes of terrorism, the power under section 43(1) should be used.

3.3.3. The power in section 43A may be used on the basis of information or intelligence about (for example) ownership or user(s) of the vehicle, previous involvement of the vehicle in terrorist or suspected terrorist activity or observation of how the vehicle is being used (for instance, if a vehicle is parked outside a potential target for long periods, or if a vehicle appears to be following a suspicious or repetitive route) or the nature of the vehicle or its contents (for example, if a non-commercial vehicle appears to be carrying gas canisters).

3.3.4. Searches may be undertaken of anything in or on the vehicle, but care should be taken not to damage a vehicle as part of a search, or in the case of an unattended vehicle, in order to gain entry into it.

3.3.5. Vehicles stopped under section 43A and persons in those vehicles may be detained only for as long as is necessary to carry out the searches—at or near the place the vehicle was stopped.

3.4. Reasonable Grounds for Suspicion

3.4.1. Reasonable grounds for suspicion depend on the circumstances in each case. There must be an objective basis for the suspicion (that the person is a terrorist or that the vehicle is being used for the purposes of terrorism) based on relevant facts, information, and/or intelligence. Reasonable suspicion must rely on intelligence or information about, or behaviour by, the person or vehicle concerned. Unless the police have a description of a suspect, a person's physical appearance (including any of the 'protected characteristics' set out in the Equality Act 2010), cannot be used alone or in combination with each other or with any other factor, as the reason for searching that person. Reasonable suspicion cannot be based upon generalisations or stereotypical images of certain groups or categories of people as more likely to be involved in terrorist activity.

3.4.2. Reasonable suspicion may exist without specific information or intelligence but on the basis of the behaviour of a person. For example, reasonable suspicion that a person is a terrorist may arise from the person's behaviour at or near a location which has been identified as a potential target for terrorists.

3.4.3. However, reasonable suspicion should normally be linked to credible and current intelligence or information, such as information describing an article being carried, a suspected terrorist, or intelligence about a particular or general threat insofar as it relates to a specific target or type of potential target. Searches based on credible and current intelligence or information are more likely to be effective.

3.4.4. Searches are more likely to be effective, legitimate, and secure public confidence when reasonable suspicion is based on a range of factors. The overall use of these powers is more likely to be effective when up to date and accurate intelligence or information is communicated to officers and they are well-informed about the nature of the terrorist threat, potential targets and ways in which terrorists are known to operate.

3.4.5. An officer who has reasonable grounds for suspicion may detain the person concerned in order to carry out a search. Before carrying out a search the officer may ask questions: for example about the person's behaviour or presence in circumstances which gave rise to the suspicion. As a result of this conversation with the person, the reasonable grounds for suspicion necessary to search may remain or, because of a satisfactory explanation, may be eliminated—in which case no search should be conducted. The conversation may also reveal reasonable grounds to suspect the possession of unlawful articles such as drugs or non-terrorist related articles, in which case a search may be continued using a different, appropriate search power. Reasonable grounds for suspicion however cannot be provided retrospectively by a conversation with the individual or by their refusal to answer any questions asked (see paragraph 3.4.10.).

3.4.6. Where the powers under section 43(1) or 43(4A) and 43(4B) are exercised in Scotland, the officer should administer a formal caution at common law prior to conducting the search. Failure to do so may affect the admissibility of statements made in response to anything found as a result of a search.

3.4.7. In some circumstances preparatory questioning may be unnecessary, but in general a brief conversation or exchange will be desirable not only as a means of avoiding unsuccessful searches, but by providing an opportunity to explain the grounds for the stop/search (*see paragraph 5.2.1.*), to gain co-operation and reduce any tension there might be surrounding the stop/search.

3.4.8. Where a person is lawfully detained for the purpose of a search, but no search in the event takes place, the detention will not thereby have been rendered unlawful.

3.4.9. If, as a result of questioning before a search, or because of other circumstances which come to the attention of the officer, there cease to be reasonable grounds for suspecting that the person is a terrorist or the vehicle is being used for the purposes of terrorism, the officer may not conduct a search under section 43 or 43A. In the absence of any other lawful power to search or detain, the person is free to leave at will at that stage and must be so informed.

3.4.10. There is no power to stop or detain a person in order to find grounds for a search. Police officers have many encounters with members of the public which do not involve detaining people. If reasonable grounds for suspicion emerge during such an encounter, the officer may search the person, even though no grounds existed when the encounter began. If an officer is detaining someone for the purpose of a search, he or she should inform the person as soon as detention begins.

3.4.11. The grounds for stopping and searching a person under section 43A are the same as the grounds for arrest under section 41 of the Terrorism Act 2000: reasonable suspicion that the person is a terrorist. Stop and search is a less intrusive power than arrest and will be more appropriate in many situations e.g. in encounters with individuals where a stop and search may help to allay suspicions. Stop and search should not be used in any situation where it is more appropriate to arrest or where an officer believes it may put him, or members of the public, in danger.

4. Authorisations under section 47A

4.1. Meeting the Test for Making an Authorisation:

4.1.1. The powers to stop and search under section 47A represent a significant divergence from the usual requirement to have reasonable suspicion when exercising stop and search powers. The powers are therefore only exercisable by a constable in uniform in an area where and during a period when an authorisation given by a senior officer is in force. The test for authorising section 47A powers is that the person giving it: must reasonably suspect that an act of terrorism will take place and considers that the powers are necessary to prevent such an act and that the area(s) or place(s) specified in the authorisation are no greater than is necessary and the duration of the authorisation is no longer than is necessary to prevent such an act.

4.1.2. An authorisation under section 47A may only be made by an officer of ACPO or ACPOS rank (i.e. at least the rank of assistant chief constable or, in the case of the Metropolitan and City of London Police, a commander). Authorising officers must be either substantive or on temporary promotion to the qualifying rank. Officers who are acting in the rank may not give authorisations.

4.1.3. The Secretary of State must be notified of any authorisation and must confirm any authorisation specified to exceed 48 hours, if it is to remain in force beyond 48 hours.

4.1.4. An authorisation may only be given where there is intelligence or circumstances which lead the authorising officer to reasonably suspect that an act of terrorism will take place. The authorising officer must also be satisfied that the powers are 'necessary' to prevent such an act of terrorism. This will involve an assessment that other powers are not sufficient to deal with the situation. Authorising officers should always consider whether it is appropriate to authorise the powers in the particular circumstances, with regard to:
• The safety of the public;
• The safety of officers; and
• The necessity of the powers in relation to the threat.

4.1.5. The following may be taken into account when deciding whether to give an authorisation, but should not form the sole basis of such a decision:

a) There is a general high threat from terrorism;

b) A particular site or event is deemed to be 'high risk' or vulnerable.

4.1.6. An authorisation may not be given on the basis that:

a) The use of the powers provides public reassurance;

b) The powers are a useful deterrent or intelligence-gathering tool.

4.1.7. An authorisation should not provide for the powers to be used other than where they are considered necessary to prevent the suspected act of terrorism. Authorisations must be as limited as possible and linked to addressing the suspected act of terrorism. In determining the area(s) or place(s) it is necessary to specify in the authorisation, an authorising officer may need to consider the possibility that terrorists may change their method or target of attack, or that there are a number of potential targets. It will be necessary to consider what the appropriate operational response to the intelligence is (e.g. whether to conduct stop and search around suspected target sites or areas or routes which could allow the police to intercept a terrorist or vehicle). However, any authorisations must be as limited as possible and based on an assessment of the existing intelligence.

4.1.8. One authorisation may be given which encompasses a number of different places or areas within a police force area (whether those are included in response to the same or different threats). The authorisation must set out the necessity for including each of these areas or places and the necessity for the length of time for which the authorisation lasts in respect of each area or place.

4.1.9. A new authorisation should be given if there is a significant change in the nature of the particular threat (or the authorising officer's understanding of it) which formed the basis of an existing authorisation. In such circumstances it will be appropriate to cancel the earlier authorisation.

4.1.10. The authorisation should also include details of how the exercise of the powers is necessary to prevent the act of terrorism. This means an explanation of how the authorisation will counter the threat i.e. why the stopping and searching of individuals and/or vehicles without suspicion is necessary to prevent the suspected act of terrorism. The consideration of necessity will also involve an assessment of why other measures (in particular the stop and search powers in section 43 of the 2000 Act) are not sufficient to address the threat.

4.1.11. If during the currency of an authorisation, the authorising officer no longer reasonably suspects that an act of terrorism of the description given in the authorisation will take place or no longer considers that the powers are necessary to prevent such an act, the authorising officer must cancel the authorisation immediately and inform the Secretary of State.

4.1.12. If, during the currency of an authorisation, the authorising officer believes that the duration or geographical extent of the authorisation is no longer necessary for the prevention of such an act of terrorism, he or she must substitute a shorter period, or more restricted geographical area. In that instance, the officer must inform the Secretary of State but the Secretary of State need not confirm such changes.

4.2. Information in Support of an Authorisation

4.2.1. Authorisations should where practicable, be given in writing. Where an authorisation is given orally, it should be confirmed in writing as soon as possible after it is given. Written authorisations and written confirmation of oral authorisations should include the information set out in this section and be provided on the form in Annex C.

4.2.2. Intelligence Picture: The authorising officer should provide a detailed account of the intelligence which has given rise to their reasonable suspicion that an act of terrorism will take place. This should include classified material where it exists, which should be provided to the Secretary of State, with the authorisation, by a secure means of communication. References to classified reporting may be used instead of verbatim reports or quotes, but the reporting referenced must have been considered by the authorising officer in making the authorisation, and must be available to the Secretary of State when considering whether to confirm an authorisation.

4.2.3. Geographical Extent: Detailed information should be provided to identify the geographical area(s) or place(s) covered by the authorisation. Where possible, maps of the authorised area should be included. The area authorised should be no wider than necessary. Authorisations which cover entire force areas are not justifiable under section 47A and Schedule 6B, unless there are exceptional circumstances which support such an authorisation.[3]

4.2.4. If an authorisation is one which covers a similar geographical area to one which immediately preceded it, information should be provided as to how the intelligence has changed since the previous authorisation was given, or if it has not changed, that it has been reassessed in the process of deciding on giving the new authorisation, and that it remains pertinent, and why.

4.2.5. Duration: The **maximum** period for an authorisation is 14 days. An authorisation should be given for no longer than necessary and should not be made for the maximum period unless it is necessary based on intelligence about the specified threat. Justification should be provided for the length of an authorisation, setting out why the intelligence supports the amount of time authorised. If an authorisation is one which is similar to another immediately preceding it, information should be provided as to why a new authorisation is justified and why the period of the initial authorisation was not sufficient. Where different areas or places are specified within one authorisation, different time periods may be specified in relation to each of these areas or places—indeed the time period necessary for each will need to be considered and justified.

4.2.6. Briefing Provided: Information should be provided which demonstrates that all officers involved in exercising section 47A powers receive appropriate briefing in the use of the powers, including the provisions of this code, and the reason for the use of the powers on each relevant occasion.

4.2.7. Tactical Deployment: The authorising officer should provide information about how the powers will be used and why. The extent to which there are objective factors (*see paragraph 4.9.3. for examples*) that can be used as a basis for the powers tactical deployment will depend on the intelligence available and will, therefore, vary. Where the intelligence is very limited, officers may not be able to use behavioral indicators or information contained in the intelligence and may have to conduct stop and searches in a less targeted way. Constables must not, however, stop and search an individual

---

[3] Force wide authorisations may be justifiable in respect of City of London Police, purely because of the size of the force area. However, the geographical area should still be no greater than necessary.

or vehicle where they consider that there is no possibility of the individual being a terrorist or the vehicle being used for terrorism.

4.2.8. Given the powers are generally being used on the basis of objective factors, constables should consider whether powers requiring reasonable suspicion are more appropriate and should only use the powers conferred by a section 47A authorisation, if they are satisfied that they cannot meet a threshold of reasonable suspicion sufficient to use other police powers.

4.3. Successive or Replacement Authorisations

4.3.1. Once an authorisation is coming to an end, a new authorisation may be given. However, authorising officers should remember that the powers under sections 44 to 46 of the Terrorism Act 2000, under which authorisations were made by some forces on a virtually indefinite basis, have been repealed. 'Rolling' authorisations are not permitted under the powers in section 47A of, and Schedule 6B to, the Terrorism Act 2000.

4.3.2. A new authorisation covering the same or substantially the same areas or places as a previous authorisation may be given if the intelligence which informed the initial authorisation has been subject to fresh assessment and the officer giving the authorisation is satisfied that the test for authorisation is still met on the basis of that assessment. Where a successive authorisation is given, it may be given before the expiry of the existing authorisation, but that existing authorisation should be cancelled.

4.3.3. In the exceptional circumstances where a new authorisation is given in respect of a different threat during the currency of an existing authorisation in that force area, that existing authorisation need not be cancelled if it continues to be necessary.

4.4. Information for Authorising Officers

4.4.1. Authorising officers should always consider whether giving an authorisation under section 47A is the most appropriate power to use in the circumstances.

4.4.2. An authorisation may be given orally or in writing. If given orally, the authorisation must be confirmed in writing as soon as possible. All authorisations must include the time and date they were given and the time or date of expiry (or, times or dates where more than one area is authorised and where applicable). This must be no later than 14 days from the date on which the authorisation was given (although the maximum 14 days may only be authorised where necessary to address the particular threat (see paragraph 4.2.5). The maximum 14 day period should not be seen as the 'norm'—it is a maximum. An authorisation must specify an end time no later than 23.59hrs on the 14th day after it was given (or if only the date is given, that date must be the 14th day—and the time will be taken as 23:59hrs on that date):

- For example, if an authorisation is made at 08.00hrs on 1st November, the specified end time must be no later than 23.59hrs on 14th November, rather than 07.59 on 15th November.

4.4.3. Authorisations begin at the point at which they are signed, or when they are given orally by the authorising officer before being confirmed in writing. The written authorisation, or written confirmation of an oral authorisation, must state the time at which the authorising officer gave it. A new authorisation covering a similar area as an existing authorisation may be given before the expiry of the previous one if necessary, to avoid the need to give the subsequent authorisation at the exact time the existing one expires (*see paragraphs 4.3.1.– 4.3.3.*).

4.4.4. When a section 47A authorisation has been given, the authorising officer should ensure that officers who will take part in any subsequent stop and search operations are briefed on the fact of the authorisation, its intended use and on the provisions on section 47A of, and Schedule 6B to, the Terrorism Act 2000 and the provisions of this code. Officers should also be briefed on the availability of other powers and the circumstances in which these may be more appropriate (*see paragraph 4.9.1*).

4.4.5. In terms of the requirement to inform the Secretary of State of each authorisation and the requirement for an authorisation to be confirmed by the Secretary of State if it is to last beyond 48 hours, the relevant Secretary of State is the Home Secretary.

4.5. Confirmation within the Home Office

4.5.1. Where practicable, an authorising officer should inform the Home Office that he or she intends to give an authorisation and provide a draft of that authorisation before it is given.

4.5.2. The authorising officer must inform the Secretary of State as soon as reasonably practicable once an authorisation under section 47A of the Terrorism Act 2000 has been given. In practice, the police force should aim to have provided the written authorisation to the Home Office within 2 hours of an authorisation being given.

4.5.3. Authorisations remain lawful for up to 48 hours without Secretary of State approval. If the authorisation is not confirmed within a 48 hour period, it ceases to have effect at the end of the 48 hours. If confirmed, the authorisation remains in effect until the expiry time specified in the authorisation by the authorising officer (or an earlier time subsequently substituted by the Secretary of State or a senior officer) or until it is cancelled by a senior officer or by the Secretary of State.

4.6. Notification of Other Police Forces and the Police Authority

4.6.1. Home Office and Scottish forces should notify any non-Home Office force when an authorisation covers areas for which both forces have a responsibility (i.e. British Transport Police, Ministry of Defence Police or Civil Nuclear Constabulary). Similarly, where an authorisation is given by a senior officer in the British Transport Police, the Ministry of Defence Police or the Civil Nuclear Constabulary, the authorising officer should notify the Home Office police force(s) which has responsibility for the police area where the authorisation is given. The authorising officer should also notify their police authority.[4] The authorisation provided to the Home Secretary should include confirmation that both such notifications (to other police forces and to the relevant police authority) have taken place.

4.7. Short-Term Authorisation—Under Forty-Eight Hours

4.7.1. In the event an authorisation for the use of section 47A powers is given for a period of less than 48 hours the authorising officer must inform the Secretary of State of the authorisation as soon as reasonably practicable. Where it is reasonably practicable to do so, the Secretary of State may confirm or cancel the authorisation prior to its expiry.

4.7.2. Where practicable, the authorising officer should inform the Secretary of State that he or she intends to make a short term authorisation in advance of doing so.

---

[4] Authorising officers within the Metropolitan Police Service should notify the Mayor's Office for Policing and Crime. Authorising officers within the Ministry of Defence Police should notify the MoD Police Committee.

4.7.3. The test for a short term authorisation is the same as an authorisation of longer duration. 'Rolling' short term authorisations are not permitted.

4.8. Internal Waters

4.8.1. For the purposes of the Terrorism Act 2000, the term 'vehicle' includes any vessel or hovercraft. And the term 'driver' includes the captain or any person in control of the vehicle, or any member of its crew.[5]

4.8.2. Section 47A authorisations can specify any place or area within a police force area. Police force areas cover inland waters such as lakes, reservoirs and rivers and extend to the low water line at the coast. Police force areas do not cover the sea below the low water line.

4.8.3. Internal waters are defined in detail by the United Nations Convention on the Law of the Sea (UNCLOS); but are typically bays, the estuaries of large rivers and the sea near larger islands. Further information on the extent of internal waters can be obtained by contacting police marine units or the Law of the Sea Division of the United Kingdom Hydrographic Office (UKHO), by email at los@ukho.gov.uk or telephone: 01823 337 900. A map indicating the extent of internal waters can be found on their website by following the links to UK Territorial Sea Limits at http://www.ukho.gov.uk.

4.8.4. A section 47A authorisation can cover any internal waters adjacent to the area specified in the authorisation.

4.8.5. Section 47A powers cannot be authorised in territorial seas that are not internal waters. If officers need to stop and search a vessel in UK territorial waters then other powers should be used.

4.9. Exercising Stop and Search Powers under section 47A

<u>General Use</u>

4.9.1. When exercising section 47A powers, officers should have a basis for selecting individuals or vehicles to be stopped and searched. This basis will be set by the tactical briefing on the use of powers described in paragraph 4.2.7. Constables should still consider whether powers requiring reasonable suspicion are more appropriate

---

[5] The term 'vehicle' also includes an aircraft and a train, and the term 'driver' includes a pilot or any person in control of the aircraft or any member of the crew and any member of the train's crew.

and should only use the powers conferred by a section 47A authorisation, if they are satisfied that they cannot meet a threshold of reasonable suspicion.

4.9.2. Searches conducted under section 47A may be carried out only for the purpose of discovering whether there is anything that may constitute evidence that the vehicle being searched is being used for the purposes of terrorism, or the individual being searched is a terrorist.[6] The search can therefore only be carried out to look for anything that would link the vehicle or the person to terrorism.

4.9.3. When selecting individuals to be stopped and searched, officers should consider the following:
- Deciding which power to use—If a section 47A authorisation is in place, the powers conferred by that authorisation may be used as set out in paragraph 4.9.1. above. However, if there is a reasonable suspicion that a person is a terrorist or a vehicle is being used for the purposes of terrorism, then powers requiring reasonable suspicion in section 43 or 43A of the Terrorism Act 2000 should be used as appropriate instead.
- Selecting an individual or vehicle using indicators:
  a) Geographical extent—What are the geographical limits of the authorisation and what are the parameters within which the briefing allows stops and searches to be conducted?
  b) Behaviour—is the person to be stopped and searched acting in a manner that gives cause for concern, or is a vehicle being used in such a manner?
  c) Clothing—could the clothing conceal an article of concern, which may constitute evidence that a person is a terrorist?
  d) Carried items—could an item being carried conceal an article that could constitute evidence that a person is a terrorist or a vehicle is being used for the purposes of terrorism?
- Explanation—officers should be reminded of the need to explain to people why they or their vehicles are being searched.

4.9.4. A constable exercising the power conferred by an authorisation under section 47A may not require a person to remove any clothing in public except for headgear, footwear, an outer coat, a jacket or gloves. Officers should be aware of the cultural sensitivities that may be involved in the removal of headgear.

---

[6] A 'terrorist' in the context of these powers means a person within the meaning of section 40(1)(b) of the Terrorism Act 2000 (i.e. a person who is or has been concerned in the commission, preparation or instigation of acts of terrorism).

4.10. Briefing and Tasking

4.10.1. Officers should use the information provided in a briefing to influence their decision to stop and search an individual. Officers should also be fully briefed on and aware of the differences between searches under sections 43, 43A and 47A of the Terrorism Act 2000, and the circumstances in which it is appropriate to use these powers.

4.10.2. The stop and search powers under section 47A of the Terrorism Act 2000 should only be used by officers who have been briefed about their use.

4.10.3. Officers should be reminded that other powers of stop and search may be more appropriate to use.

4.10.4. Officers should be reminded of the need to record information and provide anyone who is stopped and searched, or whose vehicle is stopped and searched, with written confirmation that the stop and search took place and details of the power used. Accurate recording of information is essential in order to monitor the use of the powers, safeguard against misuse and provide individuals with information about the powers which have been used.

4.10.5. The briefing should make officers aware of relevant current information and intelligence including potential threats to locations. Briefings should be as comprehensive as possible in order to ensure officers understand the nature and justification of the operation (which will in turn help officers to understand what evidence they are looking for in the course of a search), while recognising that it may not be possible or appropriate to communicate highly sensitive intelligence to all officers.

4.10.6. Officers should be reminded of the grounds for exercising the powers i.e. only for the purpose of discovering whether there is anything that may constitute evidence that the vehicle being searched is being used for the purposes of terrorism, or the individual being searched is a terrorist. The purpose of the search must therefore be to look for items which connect the vehicle or individual being searched to terrorism, rather than generally for items which could be used (e.g. by another individual in different circumstances) in connection with terrorism.[7]

---

[7] Section 45 of the Terrorism Act 2000 (which is no longer applicable) specified that the purpose of the search under the repealed powers was to search for articles of a kind which could be used in connection with terrorism. Officers should note the different purpose of the search under section 47A.

4.10.7. Briefings should also provide officers with a form of words that they can use when explaining the use of stop and search powers under section 47A of the Terrorism Act 2000. Officers should be reminded at the briefing of the importance of providing the public with as much information as possible about why the stop and search is being undertaken. The following list can help officers to explain the use of the powers when dealing with the public:

- The power that is being used and the fact that an authorisation is in place;
- That the powers conferred by section 47A can be exercised without reasonable suspicion;
- What the operation is seeking to do, e.g. to prevent terrorist activity in response to a specific threat;
- Why the person or vehicle was selected to be searched; and
- What entitlements the person has.

4.10.8. It may also be useful to issue officers with an aide-memoire of search powers in relation to terrorism.

4.10.9. In order to demonstrate that the powers are used appropriately and proportionately, the briefing process must be robust and auditable. All officers involved in the process should be reminded that they are fully accountable in law for their own actions. For further information on briefing, see ACPO (2006) Guidance on the National Briefing Model.

4.10.10. Officers should be given clear instructions about where, when and how they should use their powers. If a section 47A authorisation is in place, officers should be clearly tasked so that the power is used appropriately and proportionately. For further information see ACPO (2006) Practice Advice on Tasking and Co-ordination.

4.10.11. There may be exceptional circumstances where it is impractical to brief officers before they are deployed. Where this occurs, supervisors should provide officers with a briefing as soon as possible after deployment.

4.11. Avoiding Discrimination

4.11.1. The Equality Act 2010 makes it unlawful for police officers to discriminate against, harass or victimise any person on the grounds of age, disability, gender reassignment, race, religion or belief, sex, sexual orientation, marriage or civil partnership, pregnancy or maternity in the discharge of their powers. When police forces are carrying out their functions they also have a duty to have due regard to the need to eliminate unlawful discrimination, harassment and victimisation, to advance equality of opportunity and to foster good relations.

4.11.2. Racial or religious profiling is the use of racial, ethnic, religious or other stereotypes, rather than individual behaviour or specific intelligence, as a basis for making operational or investigative decisions about who may be involved in criminal activity.

4.11.3. Officers should take care to avoid any form of racial or religious profiling when selecting people to search under section 47A powers. Profiling in this way may amount to an act of unlawful discrimination, as would selecting individuals for a search on the grounds of any of the other protected characteristics listed in paragraph 4.11.1. Profiling people from certain ethnicities or religious backgrounds may also lose the confidence of communities.

4.11.4. Great care should be taken to ensure that the selection of people is not based solely on ethnic background, perceived religion or other protected characteristic. A person's appearance or ethnic background will sometimes form part of a potential suspect's description, but a decision to search a person should be made only if such a description is available.

4.11.5. Following the failed attacks on the London Underground on 21 July 2005, the approximate age and visible ethnicity of the suspects were quickly identified but little else was immediately known about them. In similar circumstances it may be appropriate to focus searches on people matching the descriptions of the suspects.

4.11.6. Terrorists can come from any background; there is no profile for what a terrorist looks like. In recent years, criminal acts motivated by international terrorism and aimed against people in the United Kingdom have been carried out or attempted by White, Black and Asian British citizens.

4.12. Health and Safety

4.12.1. When undertaking any search, officers should always consider their own safety and the health and safety of others. Officers should have an appropriate level of personal safety training and be in possession of personal protective equipment. Officers carrying out searches should use approved tactics to keep themselves and the public safe. For further information on personal safety training, see ACPO Guidance on Personal Safety Training.

4.12.2. If, during the course of a stop and search, there is a suspicion that a person is in possession of a hazardous device or substance, an officer should immediately request the assistance of officers appropriately trained and equipped to deal with the situation. For further information, refer to local force policy and the ACPO 2009 Manual of Guidance on the Management, Command and Deployment of Armed Officers.

4.13. Photography/Film

4.13.1. There has been widespread concern amongst photographers and journalists about the use of stop and search powers in relation to photography. It is important that police officers are aware, in exercising their counter-terrorism powers, that:

a) members of the public and media do not need a permit to film or photograph in public places;

b) it is not an offence for a member of the public or journalist to take photographs/film of a public building; and

c) the police have no power to stop the filming or photographing of incidents or police personnel.

4.13.2. Police officers can under section 47A stop and search someone taking photographs/film within an authorised area just as they can stop and search any other member of the public in the proper exercise of their discretion in accordance with the legislation and provisions of this code (*see paragraph 4.9.3.*). But an authorisation itself does not prohibit the taking of photographs or digital images.

4.13.3. Further guidance on the use of counter-terrorism powers and photography can be found on the Home Office and police websites.

4.13.4. On the rare occasion that an officer reasonably suspects that photographs/film are being taken as part of hostile terrorist reconnaissance, a search under section 43(1) of the Terrorism Act 2000 or an arrest should be considered. Whilst terrorists may undertake hostile reconnaissance as part of their planning and this could entail the use of a camera or video equipment, it is important that police officers do not automatically consider photography/filming as suspicious behaviour. The size of the camera/video equipment should not be considered as a risk indicator.

4.13.5. Film and memory cards may be seized as part of the search if the officer reasonably suspects they are evidence that the person is a terrorist, or a vehicle is being used for the purposes of terrorism, but officers do not have a legal power to delete images or destroy film. Cameras and other devices should be left in the state they were found and forwarded to appropriately trained staff for forensic examination. The person being searched should never be asked or allowed to turn the device on or off because of the danger of evidence being lost or damaged.

4.13.6. Seizures of cameras etc. may only be made, following a stop and search, where the officer reasonably suspects that they constitute evidence that the person is a terrorist or that the vehicle is being used for the purposes of terrorism as the case may be.

4.14. Seizure of Items

4.14.1. An officer may seize and retain anything which he or she discovers in the course of a search and reasonably suspects may constitute evidence that the person concerned is a terrorist within the meaning of section 40(1)(b) of the Terrorism Act 2000 or the vehicle concerned is being used for the purposes of terrorism.

4.14.2. Anything seized may be retained for as long as necessary in all the circumstances. This includes retention for use as evidence at a trial for an offence.

4.14.3. A record should be made of any item seized or retained and made available with a copy of the record of the stop and search (*see sections 5.3. and 5.4.*). If reasonable suspicion ceases to apply, the item should be returned to the individual from whom it was seized, or the person in charge of the vehicle from which it was seized unless there are other grounds for retaining it (e.g. in respect of the investigation of a separate offence). If there appears to be a dispute over the ownership of the article, it may be retained for as long as necessary to determine the lawful owner.

5. General

5.1. Conduct of Stops and Searches

5.1.1. All stops and searches must be carried out with courtesy, consideration and respect for the person concerned. Individuals who understand the reason for being stopped and searched are more likely to have a positive experience of an encounter. This has a significant impact on public confidence in the police. Every reasonable effort must be made to minimise the embarrassment that a person being searched may experience. The co-operation of the person to be searched must be sought in every case, even if the person initially objects to the search. A forcible search may be made only if it has been established that the person is unwilling to co-operate or resists. Reasonable force may be used as a last resort if necessary to conduct a search or to detain a person or vehicle for the purposes of a search.

5.1.2. The length of time for which a person or vehicle may be detained must be reasonable and kept to a minimum. The search must be carried out at or near the place where the person or vehicle was first stopped. A person or vehicle may be detained under the stop and search powers at a place other than where the person or vehicle was first stopped, only if that place, be it a police station or elsewhere, is nearby. Such a place should be located within a reasonable travelling distance using whatever mode of travel (on foot or by vehicle) is appropriate.

5.2. Steps to be Taken Prior to a Search

5.2.1. Before any search of a detained person or attended vehicle takes place the officer must take reasonable steps to give their identification number and name of police station (*see paragraph 5.3.1.*) to the person to be searched or to the person in charge of the vehicle to be searched and to give that person the following information:

a) that they are being detained for the purposes of a search;

b) the legal search power which is being exercised; and

c) a clear explanation of:

    (i) the object of the search (i.e. to search for evidence that the person is a terrorist or that a vehicle is being used for the purposes of terrorism);

    (ii) in the case section 47A of the Terrorism Act 2000, the nature of the power, the fact an authorisation has been given and a brief explanation of why individuals are being stopped and searched, or

    (iii) in the case of section 43 or 43A, the grounds for suspicion.

d) that they are entitled to a copy of the record of the search if one is made if they ask within 3 months from the date of the search[8] and that:

    (i) if they are not arrested and taken to a police station as a result of the search and it is practicable to make the record on the spot, then immediately after the search is completed they will be given (subject to being called to an incident of higher priority (*see paragraphs 5.3.1.–5.3.3.*)) if they request, either:

---

[8] Not applicable in Scotland.

- a copy of the record, or
- a receipt which explains how they can obtain a copy of the full record or access to an electronic copy of the record.[9]

(ii) if they are arrested and taken to a police station as a result of the search, that the record will be made at the station as part of their custody record and they will be given, if they request, a copy of their custody record which includes a record of the search as soon as practicable whilst they are at the station.

5.2.2. A person who is not provided with an immediate copy of a stop and search record may request a copy within 3 months of being stopped and searched. In addition a person is also entitled, on application, to a written statement that they were stopped by virtue of the powers conferred by section 47A(2) or (3), if requested within 12 months of the stop taking place.

5.2.3. If the person to be searched, or person in charge of a vehicle to be searched, does not appear to understand what is being said, or there is any doubt about the person's ability to understand English, the officer must take reasonable steps to bring information regarding the person's rights to his or her attention. If the person is deaf or cannot understand English and is accompanied by someone, then the officer may try to establish whether that person can interpret or otherwise help the officer to give the required information.[10] This does not preclude an officer from conducting a search once he or she has taken reasonable steps to explain the person's rights. In some situations forces should consider having information leaflets produced in languages other than English.

5.3. Recording Requirements

<u>Searches which do not result in an arrest</u>

5.3.1. When an officer carries out a search under sections 43(1), 43A or in the exercise of powers conferred by an authorisation under section 47A and the search does not result in the person searched or person in charge of the vehicle searched, being arrested and taken to a police station, a record must be made of it at the time, electronically or on paper, unless there are circumstances which make this wholly impracticable (*see paragraph 5.2.1.d) and section 5.3.3.*). If a

---

[9] A receipt may take the form of a simple business card which includes sufficient information to locate the record should the person ask for copy, for example, the date and place of the search or a reference number.

[10] The officer may consider a language line service more appropriate.

record is not made at the time of the stop and search, the officer must make the record as soon as practicable after the search is completed. There may be situations in which it is not practicable to obtain the information necessary to complete a record, but the officer should make every reasonable effort to do so. If it is not possible to complete a record in full, an officer must make every reasonable effort to at least record details of the date, time and place where the stop and search took place, the power under which it was carried out and the officer's identification number.

5.3.2. If the record is made at the time, the person who has been searched or who is in charge of the vehicle that has been searched must be asked if they want a copy of the record and if they do, they must (*subject to paragraph 5.3.3.*) be given immediately, either:

(i) a copy of the record, or

(ii) a receipt which explains how they can obtain a copy of the full record or access to an electronic copy of the record.

5.3.3. An officer is not required to provide a copy of the full record or a receipt at the time if they are called to an incident of higher priority.

5.3.4. In situations where it is not practicable to provide a written copy of the record or immediate access to an electronic copy of the record or a receipt at the time, the officer should give the person details of the police station at which they may request a copy of the record.

<u>Searches which result in an arrest</u>

5.3.5. If a search in the exercise of any power to which this Code applies results in a person being arrested and taken to a police station, the officer carrying out the search is responsible for ensuring that a record of the search is made as part of their custody record. The custody officer must then ensure that the person is asked if they want a copy of the record and if they do, that they are given a copy as soon as practicable.

5.4. Record of Search

5.4.1. The record of a search must always include the following information:

a) A note of the self defined ethnicity, and, if different, the ethnicity as perceived by the officer making the search, of the person searched or of the person in charge of the vehicle searched (as the case may be) (*see paragraph 5.4.2.*);

b) The date, time and place the person or vehicle was searched;

c) The object of the search;

d) In the case of:

    (i)   the powers under section 47A of the Terrorism Act 2000, the nature of the power, the fact an authorisation has been given and the reason the person or vehicle was selected for the search;

    (ii) the powers under section 43 or 43A, the grounds for suspicion.

e) the officer's warrant number or other identification number (*see paragraph 5.4.4.*).

5.4.2. Officers should record the self-defined ethnicity of every person stopped according to the categories used in the 2001 census question listed at Annex B. The person should be asked to select one of the five main categories representing broad ethnic groups and then a more specific cultural background from within this group. An additional 'Not stated' box is available but should not be offered to respondents explicitly. Officers should be aware and explain to members of the public, especially where concerns are raised, that this information is required to obtain a true picture of stop and search activity and to help improve ethnic monitoring, eliminate any discriminatory practice, and promote effective use of the powers. If the person gives what appears to the officer to be an 'incorrect' answer (e.g. a person who appears to be white states that they are black), the officer should record the response that has been given and then record their own perception of the person's ethnic background by using the PNC classification system.

5.4.3. For the purposes of completing the search record, there is no requirement to record the name, address and date of birth of the person searched or the person in charge of a vehicle which is searched and the person is under no obligation to provide this information.[11] An officer may remind a person that providing these details will ensure that the police force is able to provide information about the stop and search in future should the person request that information (*see paragraphs 5.2.1.d) and 5.2.2.*) or if it is otherwise required.

5.4.4. The names of police officers are not required to be shown on the search record in the case of operations linked to the

---

[11] This does not apply in Scotland for a search carried out with reasonable grounds for suspicion where section 13 of the Criminal Procedure (Scotland) Act 1995 applies.

investigation of terrorism or otherwise where an officer reasonably believes that recording names might endanger the officers. In such cases (including in relation to section 47A searches) the record must show the officers' warrant or other identification number and duty station.

5.4.5. A record is required for each person and each vehicle searched. However, if a person is in a vehicle and both are searched, and the object and grounds of the search are the same, only one record need be completed. If more than one person in a vehicle is searched, separate records for each search of a person must be made. If only a vehicle is searched, the self-defined ethnic background of the person in charge of the vehicle must be recorded, unless the vehicle is unattended.

5.4.6. The record of the grounds for making a search must, briefly but informatively, explain the reason for suspecting the person concerned, by reference to the person's behaviour and/or other circumstances, or, in the case of searches under section 47A, the reason why a particular person or vehicle was selected.

5.4.7. After searching an unattended vehicle, or anything in or on it, an officer must leave a notice in it (or on it, if things on it have been searched without opening it) recording the fact that it has been searched.

5.4.8. The notice must include the name of the police station to which the officer concerned is attached and state where a copy of the record of the search may be obtained and how (if applicable) an electronic copy may be accessed and where any application for compensation should be directed.

5.4.9. The vehicle must, if practicable, be left secure.

5.5. Monitoring and Supervising the Use of Stop and Search Powers

5.5.1. Supervising officers must monitor the use of stop and search powers. They should consider in particular whether there is any evidence that they are being exercised on the basis of stereotyped images or inappropriate generalisations. Supervising officers should satisfy themselves that the practice of officers under their supervision in stopping, searching and recording is fully in accordance with this code. Supervisors must also examine whether the records reveal any trends or patterns which give cause for concern, and if so take appropriate action to address this.

5.5.2. Supervision and monitoring must be supported by the compilation of comprehensive statistical records of stops and searches at force, area and local level. Any apparently disproportionate use of the powers by particular officers or groups of officers or in relation to specific sections of the community should be identified and investigated. Statistical data on the use of the powers should be provided quarterly (in arrears) to the Home Office.

5.5.3. In order to promote public confidence in the use of the powers, forces in consultation with police authorities must make arrangements for the records to be scrutinised by representatives of the community, and to explain the use of the powers at a local level. Arrangements for public scrutiny of records should take account of the right to confidentiality of those stopped and searched.

5.6. Use of Powers by PCSOs (England & Wales only)

5.6.1. Under the Police Reform Act 2002, Police Community Support Officers (PCSOs) may (where an authorisation is in place) search vehicles and anything carried by individuals under section 47A, provided they have been designated under the 2002 Act by their chief constable, and that they are in the company of a constable who is supervising them. PCSOs may not, however, search people or people's clothing under the section 47A powers. PCSOs can stop:
- Any pedestrian; and
- Any vehicle;

and search
- Anything carried by a pedestrian;
- Any vehicle;
- Anything carried by a driver or passenger; and
- Anything on or in a vehicle.

5.6.2. Authorising officers may consider whether to include PCSOs within a stop and search operation authorised by section 47A. If PCSOs are to use the powers available, they should be properly briefed on the limitations set out in this section, as well as being briefed on the appropriate use of the powers.

6. Community Engagement

6.1. Community Engagement

6.1.1. Stop and search is one of the ways in which the police can protect communities from terrorism. Ongoing community engagement is essential in improving relationships with the community and can help to:

a) Increase confidence in the Police Service through a greater understanding of why the powers of stop and search are needed and the reasons for their use;
b) Improve public reassurance;
c) Increase the flow of information and intelligence from the community to the Police Service, which can help to assist with investigations and, ultimately, the prevention of terrorist activity; and
d) Minimise any possible negative impact of police activities within communities.

6.1.2. Police forces may, for example, use existing community engagement arrangements. However, where stop and search powers affect sections of the community with whom channels of communication are difficult or non existent, these should be identified and put in place. For example, if section 47A authorisations have primarily been made around transport hubs, effort should be made to engage with people using those hubs.

6.1.3. When planning a counter-terrorism search operation, police authorities and the local CONTEST prevent strategic partnership should be involved at the earliest opportunity to provide advice and assistance in identifying mechanisms for engaging with communities. For further information on the government's counter-terrorism strategy, see http://www.homeoffice.gov.uk/counter-terrorism/uk-counter-terrorism-strat/

6.1.4. If a force has a 'PREVENT' lead officer they should be engaged with the planning process. Police forces may also consider using the media to inform and reassure the community. Note: Use of the media is not an alternative to community consultation.

6.1.5. Other stakeholders that the Police Service should consider engagement with include:
(i)   Community Safety Partnerships (CSPs);
(ii)   Local Criminal Justice Boards (LCJBs);
(iii) Local Strategic Partnerships (LSPs); and
(iv)   Neighbourhood Panels.

6.2 Retrospective and Ongoing Engagement

6.2.1. The stop and search powers under section 47A of the Terrorism Act 2000 are only for use in circumstances where the authorising officer reasonably suspects an act of terrorism will take place and it will not always be possible to carry out community engagement prior to authorisation. In these circumstances, police forces should carry out a retrospective review of the use of the powers, including the stakeholders above.

6.2.2. Police forces should continue to monitor the use of section 47A powers for the duration of an authorisation, both in discussion with community representatives and by explaining how and why the powers are being used to individuals who are stopped and searched.

6.2.3. Officers should be ready to explain to individuals why the powers are in place, insofar as this can be communicated without disclosing sensitive intelligence or causing undue alarm. Stop and search operations should form part of wider counter-terrorism policing, and public awareness of the powers should be considered as part of any wider communications strategy associated with an operation.

6.3 The Role of Police Authorities

6.3.1. Police authorities continue to have a role in working with their local force to build community confidence in the appropriate use of stop and search.

6.3.2. The Association of Police Authorities (APA) has developed guidance for police authorities which offers both practical advice and examples of good practice to help raise awareness of stop and search.

6.3.3. Where section 47A searches under the Terrorism Act 2000 have been carried out in a particular police force area, the police authority may review the use of these powers by that force. For searches carried out within the metropolitan police district, the Mayor's Office for Policing and Crime may review the use of these powers. Such a review may focus on supervision, briefing and analysis of the statistics recorded. This review may also involve members of the community.

For details of the annexes to this Code of Practice, please go to http://www.homeoffice.gov.uk/publications/counter-terrorism/stop-search-code-of-practice or PNLD reference D30105

Appendix 9
Officers' Powers and Duties

Inspectors' powers and duties

5.3.4 Recording of interviews and Codes of Practice (power to require appropriate adult to leave interview in absence of superintendent under Code H para 11.10)

5.3.5 Detained person status and rights (qualified officer under para 9(1) of Sch 8 to the Terrorism Act 2000)

5.3.10 Detention—review officer, representations and record of review (review of detention under paras 24–28 of Sch 8 to the Terrorism Act 2000)

5.5.11 Information about security of dangerous substances and about persons with access to such substances (power to give notice to occupier re dangerous substances under section 61(1) and (7) of the Anti-terrorism Crime and Security Act 2001)

Superintendents' powers

4.3.3 Use of internet for encouragement of terrorism (power to serve notice under section 3 of the Terrorism Act 2006)

4.4.15 Financial information (power to investigate terrorist finance/to apply for disclosure order that requires financial institution to provide customer information)

5.1.1 Obtaining information (overview of powers under Schedule 5)

5.1.2 Search warrants (urgent cases, see notes (m) and (n))

5.1.3 Application for search warrants—non-residential premises

5.1.5 Search warrants—excluded and special procedure material (urgent cases, see notes (k) and (l))

5.2.3 Designation of cordons

5.2.4 Police power to enter and search premises, search persons, seize and retain relevant material in cordoned area (note (f))

5.3.4 Recording of interviews (Superintendent to be consulted where appropriate adult required to leave interview (see note (c)))

5.3.5 Detained person—status and rights (delay right to have someone informed/right to legal advice)

5.3.6 Taking of fingerprints and samples (without consent and intimate samples)

5.3.10 Detention—review officer, representations and record of review

5.3.11 Warrant of further detention (application for such warrant and extension)

5.4.11 Passenger and crew information: police powers (request such information)

5.6.4 Arrest and detention pending control order (delay right to have someone informed/right to legal advice)

5.8.1.1 Cause explosion likely to endanger life or property (authorise entry/search/seizure in urgent cases)

Assistant Chief Constables'/Commanders' powers

5.2.2 Authorisation to invoke powers to stop and search in specified locations (s47A of the Terrorism Act 2000)

5.2.6 Power to restrict parking (power under section 48 of the Terrorism Act 2000)

5.3.5 Detained person status and rights (power to give direction that detained person can consult solicitor within hearing of qualified officer under para 9(2) of Sch 8 to the Terrorism Act 2000)

Bibliography and References

Books and Reports

ACPO *Interim Practice Advice on Stop and Search in Relation to the Terrorism Act 2000* (ACPO and NCPE, 2005).

—— *Neighbourhood Policing Performance Guide* (ACPO, 2007).

—— and National Counter Terrorism Security Office *Counter Terrorism Protective Security Advice for Cinemas and Theatres* (ACPO, 2008).

—— *National Counter-Terrorism Policing Structure—Building Capacity* (ACPO, 2008).

Baylis, J and Smith, S *The Globalization of World Politics: An Introduction to International Relations* 2nd edn (Oxford: Oxford University Press, 2007).

Beuter, LE, Bongor, B, Brown, LM, Breckenridge, JN, and Zimbardo, PG *Psychology of Terrorism* (Oxford: Oxford University Press, 2007).

Bowers, R, Jones, A, and Lodge, HD *Blackstone's Guide to the Terrorism Act 2006* (Oxford: Oxford University Press, 2006).

Brown, D *Combating International Crime: The Longer Arm of the Law* (Oxon: Routledge-Cavendish, 2008).

Bruce, S *The Red Hand: Protestant Paramilitaries in Northern Ireland* (Oxford: Oxford University Press, 1992).

Carlile, Lord *Operation Pathway: Report Following Review* (2009).

Chandler, M and Gunaratna, R *Countering Terrorism: Can We Meet The Threat of Global Violence?* (London: Reakton Books, 2007).

Combs, CC *Terrorism in the 21st Century* 3rd edn (Upper Saddle River, NJ: Prentice Hall, 2003).

Coogan, P *The IRA* (London: HarperCollins, 1995).

Davies, B *Terrorism: Inside A World Phenomenon* (London: Virgin Books, 2003).

Davies, L *Educating Against Extremism* (Stoke-on-Trent: Trentham Books, 2008).

European Union *The European Union Counter-Terrorism Strategy* (Council of the European Union, 14469/4/05 REV 4, 2005).

European Union *EU Action Plan on Combating Terrorism* (Council of the European Union, 15358/1/05/Rev1, 2005).

Flanagan, Sir R *The Review of Policing—Final Report* (2008).

Harfield, C and Harfield, K *Covert Investigation* (Oxford: Oxford University Press, 2005).

Bibliography and References

HM Government *Countering International Terrorism; The United Kingdom's Strategy* (2006a).

—— *Report into the London Terrorist Attacks on 7 July 2005* (2006b).

—— *Threat Levels—The System to Assess the Threat from International Terrorism* (2006c).

—— *The Definition of Terrorism—A Report by Lord Carlile of Berriew Q.C. Independent Reviewer of Terrorism Legislation* (2007).

—— *Preventing Violent Extremism—A Strategy for Delivery* (2008a).

—— *Report on the Operation in 2007 of the Terrorism Act 2000 and of the Terrorism Act 2006* (2008b).

—— *The National Security Strategy of the United Kingdom—Security in an Interdependent World* (2008c).

—— *The Prevent Strategy—A Guide for Local Partners in England and Wales* (2008d).

—— *The United Kingdom's Cyber Security Strategy* (2009).

—— *The United Kingdom's Strategy for Countering International Terrorism—CONTEST* (2009).

—— *London 2012 Olympic and Paralympic Safety and Security Strategy* (2009).

HM Revenue & Customs *Protecting Society against Crime and Terrorism* (2006).

Home Office *Extremism: Protecting People and Property* (2001).

—— *Borders, Immigration and Identity Action Plan: Using the National Identity Scheme to Strengthen our Borders and Enforce Compliance within the UK* (2006).

—— '*Our Shared Values—A Shared Responsibility*', First International Conference on Radicalisation and Political Violence (2007).

—— *From The Neighbourhood To The National: Policing Our Communities Together*, Green Paper (Cm 7448, 2008a).

—— *Working Together To Protect The Public: The Home Office Strategy 2008–11* (2008b).

—— and UK Border Agency *A Strong New Force at the Border* (2008c).

—— and UK Border Agency *Enforcing the Deal—Our Plans for Enforcing the Immigration Laws in the United Kingdom's Communities* (2008d).

Houck, M *Forensic Science: Modern Methods of Solving Crime* (London: Preager, 2007).

Kilcommins, S and Vaughan, B *Terrorism, Rights and the Rule of Law: Negotiating Justice in Ireland* (Cullompton: Willan Publishing, 2008).

Moloney, E *A Secret History of the IRA* 2nd edn (London: Pearson Penguin Books, 2007).

Niksch, L *Abu Sayyaf: Target of Philippine—US Anti-Terrorism Co-operation* (Washington DC: Library of Congress, 2002).

Patterson, H *Ireland Since 1939: The Persistence of Conflict* (London: Pearson Penguin Books, 2007).

Rapoport, DC *Inside Terrorist Organisations* 2nd edn (London: Frank Cass, 2001).

Ratcliffe, J *Intelligence-Led Policing* (Cullompton: Willan Publishing, 2008).

Silke, A *Terrorists, Victims and Society: Psychological Perspectives on Terrorism and its Consequences* (Chichester: Wiley, 2003).

Sinclair, A *An Anatomy of Terror: A History of Terrorism* (London: Macmillan, 2003).

Sterba, JP *Terrorism and International Justice* (Oxford: Oxford University Press, 2003).

Sutherland, Lord *Opinion of the High Court of Justiciary at Camp Zeist, Netherlands* (1998).

Walker, C *Blackstone's Guide to Anti-Terrorism Legislation* (Oxford: Oxford University Press, 2002).

Whittaker, DJ *The Terrorism Reader* (London: Routledge, 2001).

—— *Terrorism: Understanding the Global Threat* (London: Longman, 2002).

Wright, Lawrence *The Looming Tower: Al-Qaeda's Road to 9/11* (New York: Penguin Books, 2006).

Online articles

BBC (1988) 'On This Day—Harrods Bomb Blast Kills Six' <http://news.bbc.co.uk/onthisday/hi/dates/stories/december/17/newsid_2538000/2538147.stm> accessed December 2012.

BBC (1997) 'IRA Prisoners Taste Freedom' <http://news.bbc.co.uk/1/hi/uk/40874.stm> accessed November 2008.

BBC (2001a) 'Republican Fugitives Freed on Licence' <http://news.bbc.co.uk/1/hi/northern_ireland/1244975.stm> accessed November 2008.

BBC (2001b) 'Y2K Bomb Plot Man Convicted' <http://news.bbc.co.uk/1/hi/world/americas/1265159.stm> accessed September 2008.

BBC (2003a), 'Flashbacks—Golden Temple Attack' <http://news.bbc.co.uk/go/pr/fr/-/1/hi/world/south_asia/3774035.stm> accessed September 2008.

BBC (2003b) 'Profile: Gulbuddin Hekmatyar' <http://news.bbc.co.uk/1/hi/world/middle_east/2701547.stm> accessed October 2008.

BBC (2005a) 'Call for Police to Solve Sikh Murder' <http://news.bbc.co.uk/1/hi/uk/4354435.stm> accessed September 2008.

Bibliography and References

BBC (2005b) '"Millennium Bomber" Gets 22 Years' <http://news.
bbc.co.uk/go/pr/fr/-/1/hi/world/americas/4722409.stm>
accessed September 2008.

BBC (2006a) 'Groups Banned by New Terror Law' <http://news.
bbc.co.uk/1/hi/uk_politics/5188136.stm> accessed October
2008.

BBC (2006b) 'Militants Jailed for Bali Attacks' <http://news.bbc.co.
uk/1/hi/world/asia-pacific/5322498.stm> accessed October
2008.

BBC (2006c) 'Video of 7 July Bomber Released' <http://news.bbc.
co.uk/2/hi/uk_news/5154714.stm> accessed November 2008.

BBC (2007a) 'Glasgow Airport Attack Man Dies' <http://news.bbc.
co.uk/2/hi/uk_news/scotland/glasgow_and_west/6928854.stm>
accessed October 2008.

BBC (2007b) 'Police Avert Car Bomb "Carnage"' <http://news.bbc.
co.uk/2/hi/uk_news/6252276.stm> accessed October 2008.

BBC (2008) 'Profile: Ayman al-Zawahiri' <http://news.bbc.co.uk/1/
hi/world/middle_east/1560834.stm> accessed December 2012.

BBC (2009a) 'Three Arrested over Constable Stephen Carroll
Murder' <http://news.bbc.co.uk/1/hi/northern_ireland/
8505672.stm> accessed December 2012.

BBC (2009b) 'Murder Police Examine Base CCTV' <http://news.
bbc.co.uk/1/hi/northern_ireland/7931774.stm> accessed
December 2012.

CBC News (2005) 'Air India: Key Characters' <http://www.cbc.ca/
news/background/airindia/key_characters.html> accessed
September 2008.

Guardian (2009) 'Real IRA claims murder of soldiers in Northern
Ireland' <http://www.guardian.co.uk/uk/2009/mar/08/
northern-ireland-soldiers-killed-antrim> accessed December 2012.

History Commons (2008a) 'Profile: Jaish-e-Mohammed (JeM)'
<http://www.historycommons.org/entity.jsp?entity=jaish-e-
mohammed> accessed September 2008.

—— (2008b) 'Profile: Al-Gama'a al-Islamiyya' <http://www.
historycommons.org/entity.jsp?entity=al-gama_a_al-islamiyya_1>
accessed December 2012.

India Defence (2006) 'Balochistan Liberation Army Targets Quetta'
<http://www.india-defence.com/reports-1546> accessed October
2008.

Jenkins, R and McGory, D (2007) 'How Al-Qaeda tried to bring
Baghdad to Birmingham' <http://www.timesonline.co.uk/tol/
news/uk/crime/article1308572.ece> accessed October 2008.

National Commission on Terrorisrt Attacks upon the United States
(2002) '9/11 Commission Report' <http://www.9-11commission.
gov/report/index.htm> accessed December 2012.

National Counter-Terrorism Security Office (2008) 'Who we are, what we do and how we do it' <http://www.nactso.gov.uk> accessed October 2008.

Pike, J and Aftergood, S (2003) 'Moroccan Islamic Combatant Group (GICM)' <http://www.fas.org/irp/world/para/gicm.htm> accessed October 2008.

Police Service of Northern Ireland (2010) 'The murder of Constable Stephen Carroll—first anniversary appeal' <http://www.psni. police.uk/index/updates/appeals_for_information_2010/pr_ stephen_carroll_first_anniversary_appeal.htm> accessed December 2012.

Protherto, M (2008) 'Hizbollah builds up covert army for a new assault against Israel' *The Guardian*, <http://www.guardian. co.uk/world/2008/apr/27/israelandthepalestinians.lebanon> accessed April 2008.

Telegraph (2009) 'Bob Quick Resigns Over Terror Blunder' <http:// www.telegraph.co.uk/news/uknews/5129561/Bob-Quick-resigns-over-terror-blunder.html> accessed December 2012.

Upadhyay, R (2007) 'Harkat-ul-Jihad-al-Islami Bangladesh—A Cocktail of ISI, Al-Qaeda and Taliban' <http://intellibriefs. blogspot.com/2007/08/harkat-ul-jihad-al-islami-bangladesh. html> accessed October 2008.

Zaidi, M, and Watson, P (2004) 'Militant Flourishes in Plain Sight' <http://articles.latimes.com/2004/jan/25/world/fg-jihadis25> accessed September 2008.

Newspaper and Journal articles

Beech, G 'Anti-Terrorism Training—9/11 Report: Flight Training' *Jane's Police Review*, 2008.

——'Anti-Terrorism Training—Ports/Border' *Jane's Police Review*, 18 July 2008.

——'Anti-Terrorism Training—Schedule 7' *Jane's Police Review*, 25 July 2008.

——'Anti-Terrorism Training—Stop & Search Section 43' *Jane's Police Review*, 3 October 2008.

——'Anti-Terrorism Training—Stop & Search Section 44' *Jane's Police Review*, 10 October 2008.

Clarke, P 'Learning from Experience—Counter-Terrorism in the UK since 9/11' The Inaugural Colin Cramphorn Memorial Lecture, Policy Exchange (London, 2007).

Fresco, A, McGory, D, and Norfolk, A 'Video of Suicide Bomber Released' *The Times*, 6 July 2006.

Gardham, D and Rayner, G 'British suicide bombers planned to blow airliners out of the sky' *Daily Telegraph*, 4 April 2008.

Bibliography and References

Manningham-Buller, Dame E 'Partnership and Continuous Improvement in Countering Twenty-First Century Terrorism' *Policing: A Journal of Policy and Practice*, Vol. I, No. 1.

Spencer, P 'Anti-Terrorism Training—Control Orders' *Jane's Police Review*, 20 June 2008.

—— 'Anti-Terrorism Training—Camp Culture' *Jane's Police Review*, 15 August 2008.

Staniforth, A 'Tackling Terrorism—Know Your Enemy' *Jane's Police Review*, 22 February 2008.

—— 'Tackling Terrorism—Action Plan' *Jane's Police Review*, 29 February 2008.

—— 'Tackling Terrorism—Team Effort' *Jane's Police Review*, 7 March 2008.

—— 'Tackling Terrorism—Changing Tactics' *Jane's Police Review*, 14 March 2008.

—— 'Tackling Terrorism—Mind Games' *Jane's Police Review*, 21 March 2008.

—— 'Tackling Terrorism—Chain of Command' *Jane's Police Review*, 28 March 2008.

—— 'Tackling Terrorism—Methods of Mayhem' *Jane's Police Review*, 4 April 2008.

—— 'Tackling Terrorism—Right Balance' *Jane's Police Review*, 11 April 2008.

—— 'Tackling Terrorism—Legal Challenge' *Jane's Police Review*, 18 April 2008.

—— 'Tackling Terrorism—First Line Response' *Jane's Police Review*, 25 April 2008.

—— 'Anti-Terrorism Training—Security' *Jane's Police Review*, 2nd May 2008.

—— 'Anti-Terrorism Training—Terrorism Bill 2008' *Jane's Police Review*, 9 May 2008.

—— 'Anti-Terrorism Training—Terrorism & the Media' *Jane's Police Review*, 16 May 2008.

—— 'Anti-Terrorism Training—Membership' *Jane's Police Review*, 30 May 2008.

—— 'Anti-Terrorism Training—Forensic Awareness' *Jane's Police Review*, 6 June 2008.

—— 'Anti-Terrorism Training—Prevent' *Jane's Police Review*, 13 June 2008.

—— 'Anti-Terrorism Training—Pursue' *Jane's Police Review*, 27 June 2008.

—— 'Anti-Terrorism Training—Protect' *Jane's Police Review*, 11 July 2008.

—— 'Anti-Terrorism Training—Al-Qaeda' *Jane's Police Review*, 1 August 2008.

—— 'Terrorism and the Olympics—Hitler's Hijack' *Jane's Police Review*, 8 August 2008.

—— 'Terrorism and the Olympics—Munich Massacre' *Jane's Police Review*, 15 August 2008.

—— 'Anti-terrorism Training—Nationalism' *Jane's Police Review*, 22 August 2008.

—— 'Terrorism and the Olympics—The Olympic Bomber' *Jane's Police Review*, 22 August 2008.

—— 'Anti-Terrorism Training—Suicide Attack' *Jane's Police Review*, 29 August 2008.

—— 'Terrorism and the Olympics—Olympic Spirit' *Jane's Police Review*, 29 August 2008.

—— 'Anti-Terrorism Training—9/11 Report' *Jane's Police Review*, 5 September 2008.

—— 'Anti-Terrorism Training—9/11 Report: Impact' *Jane's Police Review*, 26 September 2008.

—— 'Anti-Terrorism Training—Police Reform' *Jane's Police Review*, 17 October 2008.

—— 'Anti-Terrorism Training—UK Security' *Jane's Police Review*, 24 October 2008.

—— 'Anti-Terrorism Training—42 Days' *Jane's Police Review*, 31 October 2008.

—— 'Anti-Terrorism Training—Hotline' *Jane's Police Review*, 14 November 2008.

—— 'Anti-Terrorism Training—Defining Terrorism' *Jane's Police Review*, 21 November 2008.

—— 'Anti-Terrorism Training—Prepare' *Jane's Police Review*, 12 June 2009.

—— 'Anti-Terrorism Training—Contest' *Jane's Police Review*, 26 June 2009.

—— 'Anti-Terrorism Training—Beslan Siege' *Jane's Police Review*, 4 September 2009.

—— 'Anti-Terrorism Training—New Strategy' *Jane's Police Review*, 25 September 2009.

—— 'Anti-Terrorism Training—Pain, no gain' *Jane's Police Review*, 13 November 2009.

—— 'Anti-Terrorism Training—Co-operation' *Jane's Police Review*, 20 November 2009.

—— 'Anti-Terrorism Training—Airey Neave' *Jane's Police Review*, 4 December 2009.

—— 'Anti-Terrorism Training—Cyber strategy' *Jane's Police Review*, 22 January 2010.

—— 'Anti-Terrorism Training—Sensitive data' *Jane's Police Review*, 5 February 2010.

Bibliography and References

——'Anti-Terrorism Training—Al-Qaeda' *Jane's Police Review*, 12 March 2010.

——'Anti-Terrorism Training—Financing' *Jane's Police Review*, 2 April 2010.

——'Anti-Terrorism Training—Afghanistan' *Jane's Police Review*, 27 November 2010.

Szabo, R 'Anti-Terrorism Training—Hostile Reconnaissance' *Jane's Police Review*, 4 July 2008.

——'Anti-Terrorism Training—Inciting' *Jane's Police Review*, 15 August 2008.

Index

Index

Index

Index

Index

Index

Index